Revenue Statistics in Africa 2024

FACILITATION AND TRUST AS DRIVERS OF VOLUNTARY TAX COMPLIANCE IN SELECTED AFRICAN TAX ADMINISTRATIONS

1990-2022

This work is published under the responsibility of the Secretary-General of the OECD, the Executive Secretary of ATAF and the Chairperson of the AUC. The opinions expressed and arguments employed herein do not necessarily reflect the official views of the Member countries of the OECD or its Development Centre, or of the member countries of the African Union or of ATAF.

This document was produced with the financial assistance of the European Union. The views expressed herein can in no way be taken to reflect the official opinion of the European Union.

This document, as well as any data and map included herein, are without prejudice to the status of or sovereignty over any territory, to the delimitation of international frontiers and boundaries and to the name of any territory, city or area.

The names of countries, maps and territories and territorial disclaimers used in this joint publication follow the practice of the OECD.

Please cite this publication as:
OECD/AUC/ATAF (2024), *Revenue Statistics in Africa 2024: Facilitation and Trust as Drivers of Voluntary Tax Compliance in Selected African Tax Administrations*, OECD Publishing, Paris, https://doi.org/10.1787/78e9af3a-en.

ISBN 978-92-64-80476-0 (print)
ISBN 978-92-64-87229-5 (PDF)
ISBN 978-92-64-54809-1 (HTML)
ISBN 978-92-64-43429-5 (epub)

Revenue Statistics in Africa
ISSN 2617-653X (online)

Photo credits: Cover © some of the graphic elements in the main cover illustration were adapted from Freepik.com.

Corrigenda to OECD publications may be found at: https://www.oecd.org/en/publications/support/corrigenda.html.

Foreword

Revenue Statistics in Africa 2024 is a joint publication by the OECD Centre for Tax Policy and Administration, the OECD Development Centre, the African Union Commission and the African Tax Administration Forum (ATAF) , with technical support from the African Development Bank and the Cercle de réflexion et d'échange des dirigeants des administrations fiscales and with financial support from the governments of Ireland, Japan, Luxembourg, the Netherlands, Norway, Spain, Sweden, Switzerland, the United Kingdom and from the European Union.

The report presents detailed, internationally comparable data on tax and non-tax revenues for 36 African countries. Its approach is based on the well-established methodology of the OECD Interpretative Guide, which has become an essential reference for OECD members and many non-member countries, and which is contained in this report as Annex A. Comparisons are also made with the average for OECD economies and for the economies featured in *Revenue Statistics in Latin America and the Caribbean* and *Revenue Statistics in Asia and the Pacific*.

The term "taxes" in this publication is confined to "compulsory, unrequited payments to general government". Taxes are "unrequited" in the sense that benefits provided by government to taxpayers are not normally in proportion to their payments. The OECD methodology classifies a tax according to its base: income, profits and capital gains (classified under heading 1000), payroll (heading 3000), property (heading 4000), goods and services (heading 5000), and other taxes (heading 6000). Compulsory social security contributions paid to general government are treated as taxes and classified under heading 2000. The concept and classification of taxes are set out in greater detail in Annex A.

The term "non-tax revenues" includes all general government revenues that do not meet the OECD definition of taxation. Revenues that do not constitute taxation include grants (e.g. foreign aid), returns on government market investments, rents on the extraction of resources from public lands, sales of government-produced goods and services, and the collection of fines and forfeits. More details on these types of revenues are provided in Annex B.

Chapter 1 and Chapter 2 of this report provide an overview of the main trends in tax and non-tax revenues respectively in the 36 participating countries from 2013 to 2022. Chapter 3 is a special feature on facilitation and trust as drivers of voluntary tax compliance in selected African tax administrations based on a study by ATAF. Chapter 4 explores the level of tax revenues by main tax category and how the respective tax structures of the 36 countries have evolved since 1990. Chapters 5 and 6 provide detailed information on tax and non-tax revenues on a country-by-country basis as well as a comparison of the non-tax revenue mix over time in the 36 countries.

Acknowledgements

Revenue Statistics in Africa 2024 has been jointly produced by the Organisation for Economic Co-operation and Development (OECD) Centre for Tax Policy and Administration (CTP), the OECD Development Centre (DEV), the African Union Commission (AUC) and the African Tax Administration Forum (ATAF), with the technical support of the African Development Bank (AfDB) and the Cercle de réflexion et d'échange des dirigeants des administrations fiscales (CREDAF). It has also received financial support from the governments of Ireland, Japan, Luxembourg, the Netherlands, Norway, Spain, Sweden, Switzerland and the United Kingdom as well as from the European Union.

The staff from these organisations with responsibility for producing the publication were: Emmanuelle Modica, Leonie Cedano, Talita Yamashiro Fordelone, Jingjjng Xia, Michael Sharratt and Alexander Pick of CTP under the supervision of the Director Manal Corwin, Deputy Directors Ben Dickinson and Achim Pross, the Head of the Tax Policy and Statistics Division, Kurt Van Dender; Sébastien Markley and Arthur Minsat of DEV under the supervision of the Director Ragnheiður Elín Árnadóttir, Deputy Director Federico Bonaglia and the Senior Communications Manager Henri-Bernard Solignac-Lecomte; Patrick Ndzana Olomo, Head of Economic Policy and Sustainable Development, AUC-Economic Development, Tourism, Trade, Industry, Mining (ETTIM), Rumbidzai Treddah Manhando, Programme Coordinator, ETTIM, Luckystar Miyandazi, Tax and Domestic Revenue Mobilisation Adviser, ETTIM, Ronnel Sisamu, Legal Advisor, ETTIM, Paul Sikazwe, Debt Advisor, ETTIM Adoum Gagoloum, Head of Economics Statistics Division-African Union Institute for Statistics (STATAFRIC) and Jose Awong Alene, Ag. Head, Statistics System Coordination & Innovation-STATAFRIC under the supervision of Djamel Ghrib, Director Economic Development, Integration and Trade of ETTIM and Botho Kebabonye Bayendi, Ag. Executive Director STATAFRIC, at the AUC; Frankie Mbuyamba, Manager, Regional Coordination and Senior Specialist, Applied Research and Statistics at ATAF, Ezera Madzivanyika, Research Manager at ATAF, Ronald Waiswa, Specialist, Applied Research and Statistics at ATAF and Nthabiseng Debeila, Specialist, Applied Research and Statistics at ATAF. Elizabeth Nash and Delphine Grandrieux (DEV) and Rebekka Hviid Kanstrup, Hazel Healy and Antonia Vanzini (CTP) assisted with the production and publication of this report. Stephanie Coic produced the cover.

The special feature (Chapter 3) is based on "An analysis of facilitation and trust as the key drivers of voluntary tax compliance in selected African tax administrations", a study by Ezera Madzivanyika, Ronald Waiswa, Nthabiseng Debeila (ATAF) and Dr Ismail Kintu (Makerere University) under the overall direction of Anthony Munanda, the Head of ATAF's Domestic Resource Mobilisation division.

The authors would like to thank the officials at the finance ministries, national tax agencies and national statistical institutes of the countries participating in this initiative who gathered and compiled the national data and provided their invaluable knowledge and expertise on their country's revenue collection systems and data. In particular, the authors would like to thank the focal points appointed for each country and their colleagues who facilitated the technical work: Joseph Edward Williams and Seitebaleng Fologang for Botswana; Mariame Dabo and Michel Yaméogo for Burkina Faso; Carlos José Oliveira Bentub and Gilson Gomes Pina for Cabo Verde; Edouard Kalawa and Erith Nghogue for Cameroon; Rogangoum Kodindouma Hervé for Chad; Yacouba Fofana and Alex Koula Pouhe for Côte d'Ivoire; Jean Gaston Manya Onakudu

Aletshu, Freddy Milambo Mbombo, Rémy Mbondo, Bembe Bodiko, Elisabeth Dikisha Dietu, Floribert Masuku Mambambu, Jean-Fidèle Yakala Mboma, Liliane Bilonda Mukuta and Patricia Mbombo Bikila-Webe for the Democratic Republic of the Congo; Frédéric Ngolele for the Republic of the Congo ; Alaa Abdel-Rahman and Nariman Zahran for Egypt; Teodoro Mbá, Benita Ebang Nzang and Juan Pedro Akieme for Equatorial Guinea; Dlamini Eric Thembinkosi, Phiri Vincent, Dlamini Nomalungelo and Mamba Lwemvelo for Eswatini; Wilfried Igor Pouba, Egère Mamadou Guibinga and Doris Nseng Nseng and Ghislain Nzoumbangoye for Gabon; Edward Asuo Afram and Francis Bright Mensah for Ghana; Mamadouba Babara Camara and Damou Moussa Conde for Guinea; George Kebaya, Alex Muhanji and Alex Mwangi for Kenya; Bokang Thetsane and T'sele Mokhathali for Lesotho; Donah for Madagascar; Mussa Bonomali, Natasha Kandoje, Chimvano Thawani and Alick Wella for Malawi; Siaka Samaké and Boubacar Diakité for Mali; Mohamed Falilou Gueye for Mauritania; Jimmy Stephen Badjonat, Meeshrani Balgobin, Dharmarajen Changeya, Roshan Oree and Meethoo Jawahir for Mauritius; Naima Akboul, El Mostafa Bennani, Rabah Chemlal, Abderrahim Mezroui, Anass Nahil and for Morocco; Filipe Uamba for Mozambique; Mahnaem Haidula and Nelago Ekandjo for Namibia; Mahamadou Djibrilla for Niger; Cephas B. Tiye and Benjamin Pever for Nigeria; Roy Valence Gasangwa and Denis Mukama for Rwanda; Papa Malick Diallo for Senegal; Franca Sicobo and Rudy Sinon for Seychelles; Mohamed Alie Bah and Philip Michael Kargbo for Sierra Leone; Mampho Baholo, Mohamed Somane for Somalia; Paul Dreyer, Lawrence Gqesha, Mamiky Leolo, Tshepo Makgoro, Denis Marais, Nontokozo Mnqayi, Dr. Sisa Shiba, Vivienne Smithdorf, Mmaphuti Thlaku and Darlington Zhou for South Africa; Ouro-Adoï Abdelganiou and Imrane Moussa for Togo; Saoussen Boumaiza for Tunisia; Ronald Nyenje Makumbi, Jova Mayega and Allen Nassanga for Uganda; Ezekiel Phiri, Eliya Lungu and Jonathan Msoni for Zambia.

This document was produced with the financial support from the governments of Ireland, Japan, Luxembourg, the Netherlands, Norway, Spain, Sweden, Switzerland, the United Kingdom and from the European Union. The views expressed herein can in no way be taken to reflect the official opinion of the governments of donor countries or of the European Union.

Table of contents

Tables

Figures

Boxes

Executive summary

Revenue Statistics in Africa 2024 presents internationally comparable indicators on tax and non-tax revenues up to 2022 for 36 African countries, including Mozambique, Somalia and Zambia for the first time. The *Revenue Statistics in Africa* initiative is a unique tool for tracking progress in domestic resource mobilisation and for informing the design and analysis of tax policy across Africa. As such, it contributes to the United Nations' Sustainable Development Goals (SDGs), the Addis Ababa Action Agenda and the African Union's Agenda 2063. It also contributes to the implementation of the second phase of the Pan-African Statistics Programme, a joint initiative between the African Union and the European Union that aims to improve measurement of progress in the process of African Integration by promoting the use of statistical data of quality in the Africa Integration decision making process and policy monitoring. This edition of *Revenue Statistics in Africa* includes a special feature on *Facilitation and Trust as Drivers of Voluntary Tax Compliance in Selected African Tax Administrations*.

Tax revenues

In 2022, the average tax-to-GDP ratio (total tax revenues including social security contributions as a percentage of GDP) for the 36 countries in this publication was 16.0%, an increase of 0.5 percentage points (p.p.) relative to 2021. This was the second consecutive annual increase, following a rise of 0.3 p.p. in 2021; as a result, Africa's average tax-to-GDP ratio was 0.5 p.p. above its level prior to the COVID-19 pandemic (15.5% in 2019). However, average tax revenues in Africa remained below the levels in Asia and the Pacific (19.3%), Latin America and the Caribbean (LAC, 21.5%), and OECD countries (34.0%) in 2022. Tax-to-GDP ratios varied widely across African countries in 2022, from 2.6% in Somalia to 33.5% in Tunisia; 19 of the 36 countries recorded a ratio below 15%.

Tax revenues as a percentage of GDP increased in 23 countries, decreased in 11 and remained unchanged in two between 2021 and 2022. Chad and the Democratic Republic of the Congo recorded the largest increases in their tax-to-GDP ratio, of 3.3 p.p. and 3.6 p.p. respectively, driven by significant increases in corporate income tax (CIT) revenues on the back of higher profits from the extractive sector. By contrast, the largest declines occurred in Mali and Sierra Leone (1.9 p.p. in both cases), due to declines in revenues from taxes on goods and services caused by trade disruption in both countries.

Despite a challenging macroeconomic context characterised by high inflation and a slowdown in growth, all 36 countries except Mali recorded increases in nominal GDP and in nominal tax revenues in 2022. Higher CIT revenues drove the increase in tax revenues, rising by 0.4 p.p. on average across the 36 countries due primarily to growth in profits from the oil and gas sector attributable to higher commodity prices. Meanwhile, revenues from taxes on goods and services increased by 0.1% of GDP in 2022. Within this category, revenues from VAT and import duties both increased by 0.1% of GDP on average while excises decreased by 0.1% of GDP. Revenues from personal income tax (PIT) and social security contributions remained unchanged.

Higher tax-to-GDP ratios in many African countries over the last ten years reflect ongoing efforts to enhance fiscal systems. Between 2013 and 2022, the Africa average tax-to-GDP ratio rose by 1.1 p.p.

while the averages for the LAC region and OECD countries increased by 0.8 p.p. and 1.4 p.p. respectively. Tax-to-GDP ratios rose in 25 of the 36 African countries between 2013 and 2022 and declined in 11.

All main revenue categories increased between 2013 and 2022 at approximately the same pace as a share of GDP. Income tax revenues increased by 0.4 p.p. while revenues from taxes and goods and services grew by 0.5 p.p. Taxes on goods and services remained the main source of tax revenues in Africa in 2022, accounting for an average of 51.3% of total tax revenues, with VAT accounting for 27.0%. Within this category, trade taxes declined as a percentage of total tax revenues but increased by 0.1% of GDP. Meanwhile, taxes on income and profits accounted for 39.3% of total tax revenues on average in 2022: 16.2% from PIT, 21.2% from CIT and 1.9% that was unallocable between them.

Non-tax revenues

Non-tax revenues in Africa in 2022 amounted to 6.2% of GDP on average among the 35 countries reporting data on these revenues for that year. Non-tax revenues ranged from 0.7% of GDP in South Africa to 23.7% in the Republic of the Congo. Non-tax revenues exceeded 10% of GDP in five countries, three of which (Botswana, Lesotho and Namibia) received most of their non-tax revenues from the Southern African Customs Union (SACU) Common Revenue Pool. Non-tax revenues were higher than tax revenues in Botswana, Equatorial Guinea, Lesotho and the Republic of the Congo.

In 2022, average non-tax revenues in Africa increased by 0.4 p.p. of GDP from the previous year. This increase was driven by increases of 0.4 p.p. in both revenues from rents and royalties and from other property income (e.g. interest and dividends) amid rising commodity prices, though it was partially offset by a decline in SACU revenues. In contrast, grants remained unchanged between 2021 and 2022.

Higher oil and gas royalties, interest and dividends drove the largest increases in non-tax revenues as a share of GDP, which were found in the Republic of the Congo and Equatorial Guinea (8.7 p.p. and 13.3 p.p. respectively). For the first time, this edition of *Revenue Statistics in Africa* analyses the highly detailed information on extractive-related revenues provided by participating countries.

Sources of non-tax revenues varied by country in 2022. Most non-tax revenue came from grants for nine countries whereas the majority was derived from rents and royalties in eight countries. The remaining 14 countries, excluding the four net recipient SACU countries, relied more on other sources of non-tax revenues, such as interest and dividends and fees for goods and services.

Between 2013 and 2022, average non-tax revenues decreased by 1.1 p.p. of GDP mostly due to declines of 0.5 p.p. in grant revenues and of 0.8 p.p. in other non-tax revenues (mostly SACU revenues). This decline offset the increase in tax revenues over the same period, underscoring the financing challenges African countries face as they look to achieve the SDGs against a backdrop of rising debt levels and higher spending needs in the wake of the COVID-19 pandemic.

Facilitation and trust as drivers of voluntary tax compliance in selected African tax administrations

The special feature chapter written by ATAF examines the role of facilitation and public trust in driving voluntary tax compliance as a means of increasing revenue levels across African countries. The chapter identifies good practices by tax administrations in selected African countries, including innovations in the digitalisation of tax systems and taxpayer education programmes. However, increased funding is needed to enable greater automation of tax systems and seamless exchange of information across government agencies. In order to enhance trust in African tax systems and thus drive voluntary tax compliance, African tax administrations and other government agencies also need to work together to demonstrate that tax revenues are put to good use.

Abbreviations and acronyms

AIGE	Aéroport International Gnassingbé Eyadéma (Gnassingbé Eyadéma International Airport - Togo)
AIT	Advance Income Tax (Malawi)
ANICT	Agence Nationale d'Investissement des Collectivités Territoriales (National Investment Agency for Territorial Communities - Mali)
APU	Administrations publiques (Public administrations - Cameroon)
AR	Autorités Régionales (Regional Authorities - Mali)
ARC	African Risk Capacity (Niger)
ATAF	African Tax Administration Forum
AU	African Union
AUC	African Union Commission
BCEAO	Banque centrale des États de l'Afrique de l'Ouest (Central Bank of West African States - Niger, Togo)
BELN	Botswana, Eswatini, Lesotho and Namibia
BIC	Bénéfices industriels et commerciaux (Industrial and commercial profits tax - Congo, Guinea, Mali, Mauritania, Togo)
BN	Budget national (National budget - Mali)
BNC	Bénéfices non commerciaux (Non-commercial profits - Congo, Guinea, Mauritania, Niger)
CANAM	Caisse Nationale d'Assurance Maladie (National Health Insurance Fund - Mali)
CBE	Central Bank of Egypt (Egypt)
CEDEAO	Communauté économique des États de l'Afrique de l'Ouest (Economic Community of West African States - Cabo Verde, Niger)
CFA	Communauté Financière Africaine (African Financial Community)
CGRAE	Caisse générale de retraite des agents de l'État (General pension fund for state employees - Côte d'Ivoire)
CGT	Capital Gains Tax (South Africa)
CIT	Corporate income tax
CMSS	Caisse Malienne de Sécurité Sociale (Malian Social Security Fund - Mali)
CNAM	Caisse Nationale d'Assurance Maladie (National Health Insurance Fund - Mauritania)
CNPS	Caisse nationale de prévoyance sociale (National Social Security Fund - Côte d'Ivoire)
CNSS	Caisse Nationale de Sécurité Sociale (National Social Security Fund - Congo, Mauritania)
CODEC	Contribution au développement économique ((Contribution to economic development (- Senegal)
COHO	Commissariat à l'Organisation du Hadj et de la Oumra (Office of the Hajj and Umrah Organization - Niger)
CPS	Contribution pour prestation de service (Contribution for service provision - Mali)
CRF	Caisse de Retraite des Fonctionnaires (Civil Servants Retirement Fund - Congo)
CRN	Contribution à la reconstruction nationale (Contribution to national reconstruction - Côte d'Ivoire)
CSG	Contribution Sociale Généralisée (Generalized Social Contribution - Mauritius)
CSR	Corporate Social Responsibility Tax (Seychelles)
CSS	Caisse de Sécurité Sociale (Social Security Fund - Senegal)
DCPF	Droits de conservation de la propriété foncière (Rights to conservation of land ownership - Togo)
DDF	Domestic Development Fund (Botswana)
DFS	Droit fiscal de sortie (Exit tax right - Mauritania)
DGA	Direção Geral das Alfândegas (Directorate-General of Customs - Cabo Verde)
DGCI	Direcção Geral de Contribução e Impostos (General Directorate of Contribution and Taxes - Cabo Verde)
DGD	Direction générale des Douanes (Directorate General of Customs)
DGDA	Direction générale des douanes et accises (General Directorate of Customs and Excise - Congo, Dem. Rep.)
DGI	Direction générale des Impôts (General Directorate of Taxes)
DGRAD	Direction générale des Recettes Administratives, Judiciaires, Domaniales et de Participation (General Directorate of Administrative, Judicial, State and Participation Revenue - Congo, Dem. Rep.)
DGTCP	Direction générale du Trésor et de la Comptabilité Publique (General Directorate of the Treasury and Public Accounting - Niger)
DND	Direction Nationale des Douanes (National Customs Directorate - Guinea, Mali)
DNDC	Direction Nationale du Domaine et des Cadastres (National Directorate of Land and Cadastres - Mali)
DNI	Direction Nationale des Impôts (National Tax Directorate - Guinea)

DST	Digital Services Tax (Kenya)
DT	Dividends Tax (South Africa)
ECOWAS	Economic Community of West African States
EDRL	Energy Debt Recovery Levy (Ghana)
EEZ	Exclusive Economic Zone (Seychelles)
EFL	Energy Fund Levy (Ghana)
EGPC	Egyptian General Petroleum Corporation (Egypt)
EMTL	Electronic Money Transfer Levy (Nigeria)
ETI	Employment Tax Incentive (South Africa)
FA	Finance Act (Nigeria)
FDD	Fonds pour le développement durable (Sustainable Development Fund - Mali)
FER	Fonds d'Entretien Routier (Road Maintenance Fund - Guinea)
FGS	Federal Government of Somalia (Somalia)
FMS	Federal Member States (Somalia)
FMV	Foreign Motor Vehicles Levy (Kenya)
FSA	Financial Services Authority (Seychelles)
FSH	Fonds de soutien à l'habitat (Housing support fund - Côte d'Ivoire)
GEOGAM	Guinea Equatorial Oil and Gas Marketing, Ltd. (Equatorial Guinea)
GSM	Global System for Mobile Communications (Guinea)
HIPC	Heavily indebted poor countries (Madagascar)
IATA	International Air Transport Association (Somalia)
IGL	Impôt Général Libératoire (General tax - Chad)
IGR	Impôt Général sur le Revenu (General Income Tax - Niger)
IMF	International Monetary Fund
IMF	Impôt Minimum Forfaitaire (Minimum Flat Tax - Mauritania)
IMF	Impôt Minimum Fiscal (Minimum Tax - Chad)
IMP	Impôt sur marché public (Tax on public market - Madagascar)
INPS	L'Institut National de Prévoyance Sociale (The National Institute of Social Welfare - Mali)
INSESO	Instituto Nacional de Seguridad Social de Guinea Ecuatorial (National Institute of Social Security of Guinea Ecuatorial - Equatorial Guinea)
IPRES	L'Institution de prévoyance retraite du Sénégal (The Senegal Retirement Insurance Institution - Senegal)
IPVCI	Impôt spécial sur la plus-value de cessions immobilières (Special tax on capital gains on real estate transfers - Niger)
IPVI	Impôts sur les plus-values immobilières (Taxes on real estate capital gains - Madagascar)
IR	Impôt sur le revenu (Income tax - Madagascar, Togo)
IRCM	Impôt sur les Revenus des Capitaux Mobiliers (Tax on Income from Movable Capital - Madagascar)
IRNS	Impôt sur les revenus non salariaux (Tax on non-wage income - Madagascar)
IRPC	Imposto sobre o Rendimento das Pessoas Colectivas (Imposto sobre o Rendimento das Pessoas Colectivas - Mozambique)
IRPS	Imposto Rendimento de Pessoas Singulares (Imposto Rendimento de Pessoas Singulares - Mozambique)
IRSA	Impôt sur les Revenus Salariaux et Assimilés (Tax on Wage and Similar Income - Madagascar)
IRVM	Impôt sur le revenu des valeurs mobilières (Securities income tax - Niger)
IRVN	Revenu des valeurs mobilières (Income from securities - Congo)
IS	Impôt synthétique (Synthetic tax - Madagascar)
IS	Impôt sur les societés (Corporate tax - Mali)
ISB	Impôt sur les bénéfices (Profit tax - Niger)
ITS	Impôt sur les traitement et salaires (Tax on salaries and wages)
KAA	Kenya Airports Authority (Kenya)
KEBS	Kenya Bureau of Standards (Kenya)
KRA	Kenya Revenue Authority (Kenya)
LGA	Local Government Areas (Nigeria)
MDAs	Municipalities, Departments and Agencies (Ghana)
MID	Maurice Île Durable (Mauritius Sustainable Island - Mauritius)
MMDA	Metropolitan, Municipal and District Assemblies (Ghana)
NASENI	National Agency for Science and Engineering Infrastructure (Nigeria)
NESL	National Electrification Scheme Levy (Ghana)
NFSL	National Fiscal Stabilisation Levy (Ghana)
NHIL	National Health Insurance Levy (Ghana)
NHIS	National Health Insurance Scheme (Ghana)
NPF	National Pension Fund (Mauritius)
NPRA	National Pensions Regulatory Authority (Ghana)
NRL	National Reconstruction Levy (Ghana)
NSF	National Savings Fund (Mauritius)
NTIC	Nouvelles technologies de l'information et de la communication (New information and communication technologies - Côte d'Ivoire)

OCC	Office du Classement du Coton (Cotton Grading Office - Mali)
OCIPEF	Oficina de control, Información y Promoción de las Especies Forestales (Control Office, Information and Promotion of Forest Species - Equatorial Guinea)
OECD	Organisation for Economic Co-operation and Development
OML	Oil Mining Leases (Nigeria)
ONEM	Office National de l'Emploi (National Employment Office - Congo, Dem. Rep.)
OPL	Oil Prospecting Licenses (Nigeria)
PADSP	Prélèvement pour l'apurement de la dette du secteur pétrolier (Levy for the settlement of the oil sector debt - Togo)
PAYE	Pay-as-you-earn tax
PC	Prélèvement communautaire Cedeao (ECOWAS community levy - Mauritania)
PGT	Paierie Générale du Trésor (General Payroll of the Treasury - Madagascar, Mali)
PIT	Personal income tax
PLL	Public Lighting Levy (Ghana)
PMU	Société du pari mutuel urbain (Urban Pari-Mutuel Society - Mali)
PNT	Ingresos petroleros no tributarios (Non-tax oil revenue revenues - Equatorial Guinea)
PPTE	Pays pauvres très endettés (Highly indebted poor countries - Mali)
PTF	Police Trust Fund (Nigeria)
RAF	Road Accident Fund (South Africa)
RDP	Reconstruction and Development Fund Programme (South Africa)
RER	Redevance entretien routier (Road maintenance fee - Guinea)
RER	Redevance d'Exploitation (Operating Fee - Mauritania)
RFL	Road Fund Levy (Ghana)
RM	Redevance minière (Mining royalty - Niger)
RSE	Taxe de responsabilité sociale des entreprises (Corporate social responsibility tax - Seychelles)
RTI	Radiodiffusion télévision ivoirienne (Ivorian television broadcasting - Côte d'Ivoire)
RUC	Road User Charge (Sierra Leone)
RUTEL	Redevance sur l'accès ou l'utilisation du réseau des télécommunications publiques (Fee for access to or use of the public telecommunications network - Senegal)
SACU	Southern African Customs Union
SARL	Société à responsabilité limitée (Limited liability company - Congo, Dem. Rep.)
SARS	South African Revenue Service (South Africa)
SCA	Suez Canal Authority (Egypt)
SNIM	Société Nationale Industrielle et Minière de Mauritanie (National Industrial and Mining Company of Mauritania - Mauritania)
SPF	Seychelles Pensions Fund (Seychelles)
SPP	Soutien à la politique pétrolière (Support for oil policy - Togo)
SSF	Social Security Fund (Seychelles)
SSNIT	Social Security and National Insurance Trust (Ghana)
STC	Secondary Tax on Companies (South Africa)
TAF	Taxe sur les armes à feu (Gun tax - Niger)
TAF	Taxe sur les activités financières (Financial activities tax - Senegal)
TAFI	Taxe sur les activités financières (Financial activities tax - Niger)
TAP	Taxe d'apprentissage (Apprenticeship tax - Niger)
TART	Taxe d'acces au reseau de télécommunications (Telecommunications network access tax - Guinea)
TARTOP	Taxe sur l'accès au réseau des télécommunications ouvert au public (Tax on access to the telecommunications network open to the public - Mali)
TATTIE	Taxe sur la terminaison du Trafic International Entrant (Tax on termination of Inbound International Traffic - Niger)
TBA	Taxe sur les boissons alcoolisés (Tax on alcoholic beverages - Niger)
TBVC	Transkei, Bophuthatswana, Venda and Ciskei (South Africa)
TCA	Taxe sur la chiffre d'affaires (Turnover tax - Cameroon)
TCFGE	Taxe sur certains frais généraux des entreprises (Tax on certain general business expenses - Niger)
TCG	Taxe de Consommation sur la carte à Gratter (Consumption tax on the scratch card - Mauritania)
TCI	Taxe conjoncturelle à l'importation (temporary import tax) (Temporary import tax - Niger)
TCT	Taxe sur la Consommation Téléphonique (Tax on Telephone Consumption - Guinea)
TDP	Taxe degréssive de protection (Gradual protection tax - Mali)
TEA	Taxe d'exploitation artisanale (Artisanal exploitation tax - Niger)
TEBA	Taxe à l'émission des billets d'avion (Air ticket issuance tax - Togo)
TEE	Taxe d'État de l'Entreprenant (State Entrepreneur Tax - Côte d'Ivoire)
TF	Titre foncière (Land title - Mali)
TFEAR	Taxe forfaitaire sur la réexportation (Flat tax on re-export - Niger)
TFPNB	Taxes foncières sur les propriétés non bâties (Property taxes on undeveloped properties - Togo)
TIC	Information and communication technology
TIPP	Taxe intérieure sur les produits pétroliers (Internal tax on petroleum products - Mali, Niger)
TJH	Taxe sur les jeux de hasard (Tax on games of chance - Niger)
TME	Taxe Minière à l'Extraction (Mining Tax on Extraction - Guinea)

TMT	Tourism Marketing Tax (Seychelles)
TOFE	Tableau des opérations financières de l'Etat (Table of State financial operations - Congo)
TPCE	Taxe sur la publicité commerciale extérieure (Tax on outdoor commercial advertising - Niger)
TPV	Taxe sur les plus-values de cession (Tax on capital gains on sale - Togo)
TSB	Taxe spécifique sur les boissons (Specific tax on drinks - Congo)
TSPDF	Taxe spéciale pour la préseration et développement forestier (Special tax for forestry preservation and development - Côte d'Ivoire)
TSS	Taxe spéciale sur les societés (Special corporate tax - Congo)
TST	Taxe spécifique sur le tabac (Specific tax on tobacco - Congo)
TUA	Taxe Unique sur les assurances (Single tax on insurance - Niger)
TURTEL	Taxe sur l'utilisation du réseau de télécommunication (Tax on the use of the telecommunications network - Niger)
TVM	Taxe sur les véhicules à moteur (Motor vehicle tax - Togo)
UEMOA	Union économique et monétaire ouest-africaine (West African Economic and Monetary Union - Niger)
UIF	Unemployment Insurance Fund (South Africa)
VAT	Value added tax
WAEMU	West African Economic and Monetary Union

1 Tax revenue trends, 2013-22

Chapter 1 discusses the latest tax revenue trends as well as the evolution of tax revenues over the past decade across 36 African countries. The analysis focuses primarily on the level and structure of tax revenues for individual countries and on average across the African continent. Average tax revenue indicators for African countries are compared with averages for other regions.

Introduction

Achieving the African Union's Agenda 2063, the United Nations' Sustainable Development Goals (SDGs) and implementing the Addis Ababa Action Agenda require mobilising additional finance in general, and domestic resources in particular, to fund public goods and services. Taxation provides a predictable and sustainable source of government revenue, in contrast with the volatility of other important sources of public revenues, such as grants and royalties. For African countries, where external debt and dependency on volatile resource revenues present notable economic challenges, enhancing domestic resource mobilisation is not just a fiscal strategy; it's also a critical pathway to achieving self-reliance, economic resilience and sustainable development, aligning specifically with the aspirations set out in the African Union's Agenda 2063 for a self-sufficient, integrated and prosperous Africa.

Revenue Statistics in Africa presents an internationally comparable set of indicators on tax and non-tax revenues that can be used to track progress on domestic resource mobilisation and to inform tax policy and reform. The report and its data also contribute to the *Pan-African Statistics Programme*, a joint effort between the African Union and the European Union to strengthen statistical capacity in Africa by providing quality revenue statistics data that can inform decision-making processes and policy monitoring towards African integration. The progress of the *Pan-African Statistics Programme* demonstrates a commitment towards data-driven and context-sensitive policymaking in Africa. Accurate and relevant data is foundational for formulating policies that resonate with Africa's distinctive economic and political landscapes and societal nuances, thereby propelling more effective and impactful initiatives on the ground.

This edition of *Revenue Statistics in Africa* includes data on tax revenues up to and including 2022. This first chapter analyses the evolution of the tax-to-GDP ratio, tax structure and share of tax revenue by level of government in 36 African countries: Botswana, Burkina Faso, Cabo Verde, Cameroon, Chad, the Republic of the Congo, the Democratic Republic of the Congo, Côte d'Ivoire, Equatorial Guinea, Egypt, Eswatini, Gabon, Ghana, Guinea, Lesotho, Kenya, Madagascar, Malawi, Mali, Mauritania, Mauritius, Morocco, Mozambique, Namibia, Niger, Nigeria, Rwanda, Senegal, the Seychelles, Sierra Leone, Somalia, South Africa, Togo, Tunisia, Uganda and Zambia. Mozambique, Somalia and Zambia are included for the first time in this edition.

This chapter also compares the averages of the 36 African countries with the averages of 36 Asian and Pacific economies (OECD, 2024[1]), 26 Latin American and Caribbean (LAC) countries (OECD et al., 2024[2]), and 38 OECD countries (OECD, 2024[3]). The discussion supplements the detailed country information on tax revenues in Chapter 5.

Tax-to-GDP ratios in Africa

Tax revenue trends across African countries in 2022

Exploring tax-to-GDP ratios in the 36 African countries in this publication reveals a multitude of economic realities. The wide-ranging ratios underscore the economic diversity within the continent, each telling a story of fiscal potential and challenges unique to each country. Understanding and navigating these differences is crucial for designing effective tax policies that bolster economic stability and drive development in Africa.

The unweighted average tax-to-GDP ratio of the 36 countries in this report was 16.0% in 2022 (Figure 1.1) and increased by 0.5 percentage points (p.p.) from its level in 2021. The tax-to-GDP ratio is measured as tax revenues (including compulsory social security contributions paid to general government) as a proportion of gross domestic product (GDP).[1] In comparison, the average tax-to-GDP ratios in Asia and the Pacific, Latin America and the Caribbean, and OECD countries were 19.3%, 21.5% and 34.0% respectively in 2022.

Africa's low average tax-to-GDP ratio relative to the level in other regions demonstrates the constrained fiscal space within which African countries operate. This limits their ability to channel substantial investments into sectors like healthcare, education and infrastructure, which are central to sustainable development and societal well-being in Africa. Addressing these gaps is imperative for unleashing Africa's developmental potential, ensuring inclusive and sustainable growth across the continent.

Figure 1.1. Total tax revenues, including and excluding social security contributions, as a percentage of GDP, 2022

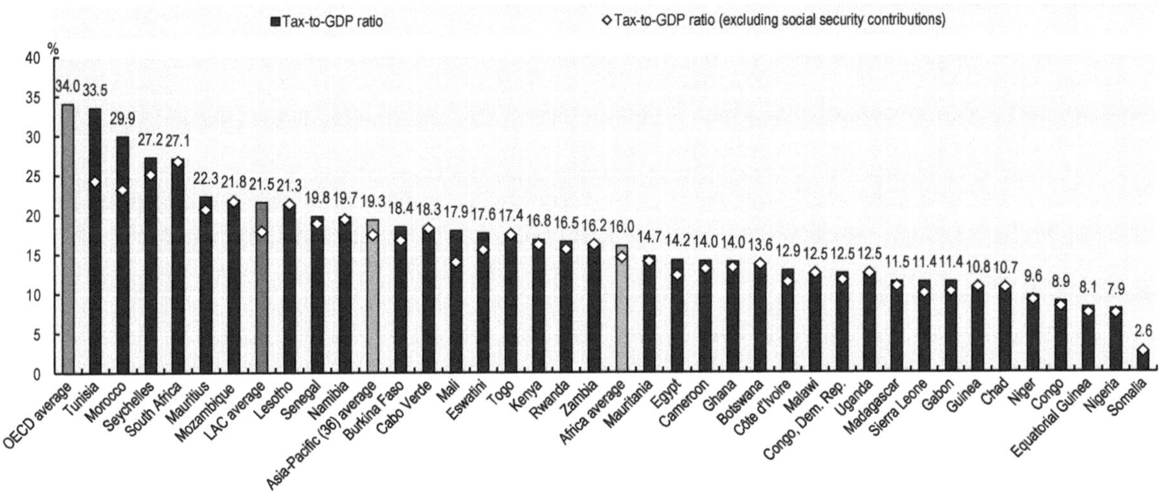

Note: Data include sub-national government tax revenues for Eswatini, Mauritius, Morocco, Nigeria (state revenues only), Somalia and South Africa for 2022. The Africa average and the averages for Asia-Pacific (36 economies), LAC (26 countries) and the OECD (38 countries) are unweighted.

The Africa average should be interpreted with caution as data on social security contributions are not available for Chad, Guinea, Togo, Uganda and Zambia and are only partially available for Cameroon and Senegal. Social security contributions for Botswana, Lesotho and Malawi are deemed to be zero as they do not meet the criteria to be classified as social security contributions set out in the OECD classification of taxes in the Interpretative Guide.

The tax-to-GDP ratio for South Africa includes payments made by South Africa to the Southern African Customs Union pool.

Source: Tables 4.1 and 4.2 in Chapter 4 and (OECD/ATAF/AUC, 2024[4]), *"Revenue Statistics in Africa: Comparative tables"*, http://data-explorer.oecd.org/s/dx:

StatLink https://stat.link/ts7aof

Tax-to-GDP ratios varied widely across the countries included in this publication in 2022, ranging from 2.6% in Somalia to 33.5% in Tunisia. Morocco, Tunisia, the Seychelles and South Africa had tax-to-GDP ratios above 25%; 13 countries recorded tax-to-GDP ratios between 15% and 25%, while 19 countries had tax-to-GDP ratios below 15%.

Changes in tax revenues and in GDP in nominal terms

This section analyses changes in nominal tax revenues and nominal GDP in 2022 and the resulting changes in tax-to-GDP ratios, which it compares to changes in 2021. The value of the tax-to-GDP ratio depends on two components; its numerator (tax revenue) and its denominator (GDP) (see Box 1.1). This means that the changes in tax-to-GDP ratios reflect changes in nominal tax revenues as well as changes in nominal GDP.

Box 1.1. Methodology: the tax-to-GDP ratio

The tax ratios shown in this publication express aggregate tax revenues as a percentage of GDP. Both the numerator and the denominator may be subject to historical revision. The tax-to-GDP ratio needs to be interpreted with caution: nominal tax revenues and nominal GDP may change in the same direction (both increasing or both decreasing) but the tax-to-GDP ratio will go in the opposite direction if the relative change in nominal tax revenues is smaller than the relative change in nominal GDP.

The numerator (tax revenues)

This publication uses revenue figures that are submitted annually by focal points from national Ministries of Finance, tax administrations or statistics offices. Historical tax revenue data are subject to revisions each year, with more important revisions in latest years. Past figures may also change from one edition to the next when new data are obtained by focal points to improve the publication.

In 28 African countries covered in this report, the reporting year coincides with the calendar year. The remaining eight countries report on the basis of a July-June fiscal year or an April-March fiscal year.[1]

The denominator (GDP)

The GDP figures used in this publication are sourced from the *World Economic Outlook* (*WEO*) published by the IMF. Using these GDP figures ensures a maximum of consistency across countries, as well as international comparability. GDP figures are also revised and updated to reflect better data sources and improved estimation procedures, or to move towards new internationally agreed guidelines for measuring the value of GDP. It is nonetheless important to acknowledge and account for the distinctive economic, sociopolitical and historical factors within African countries that profoundly influence GDP metrics.

The most recent available figures from the *WEO* were published in April 2024 (IMF, 2024[5]) and include GDP revisions made by some countries to align with the most recent System of National Accounts (SNA 2008). There are notable revisions of GDP figures in this report relative to last year's edition for Cabo Verde, Chad, Congo, Lesotho, Mauritania (the GDP figures for 2021 for these countries were revised by +/- 3% or more).

The difference between the 2021 tax-to-GDP ratios in the 2023 and 2024 editions following revisions to tax revenues and GDP ranged from -2.6 p.p. in Chad to 1.6 p.p. in Malawi and Sierra Leone.

Note: 1. The fiscal year in Eswatini, Lesotho, Namibia and Botswana runs from April to March. This means that reporting year 2022 is Q2/2022–Q1/2023. The fiscal year for Egypt, Kenya, Malawi and Mauritius (years prior to 2010 and for 2016 onwards) ends on 30 June. The reporting year 2022 includes Q2/2021–Q2/2022. Some countries report certain components of tax revenues on a different basis depending on the nature of the revenues. For example, revenues in Rwanda are reported on a calendar year except for social security contributions, which are reported on a fiscal year basis ending 30 June since 2008. Another example is South Africa, whose data is on a calendar year except for social security contributions and taxes at provincial and local levels (reported on a fiscal year basis ending 31 March).

In 2022, the countries covered by this report recorded median growth of 13.9% in nominal tax revenues relative to the previous year, while nominal GDP grew by 11.7% over the same period. Figure 1.2 shows year-on-year changes in nominal tax revenues and nominal GDP between 2021 and 2022 by country. All countries except Mali recorded increases in nominal tax revenues in 2022. The Democratic Republic of the Congo and Chad recorded increases of more than 60%. All countries recorded increases in nominal GDP in 2022; in 24 countries, this increase was less than the increase in tax revenues, leading to higher tax-to-GDP-ratios relative to 2021. In eleven countries, nominal GDP rose by more than nominal tax revenues, causing the tax-to-GDP ratio to decline.

Figure 1.2. Year-on-year change in nominal tax revenues and nominal GDP, 2022

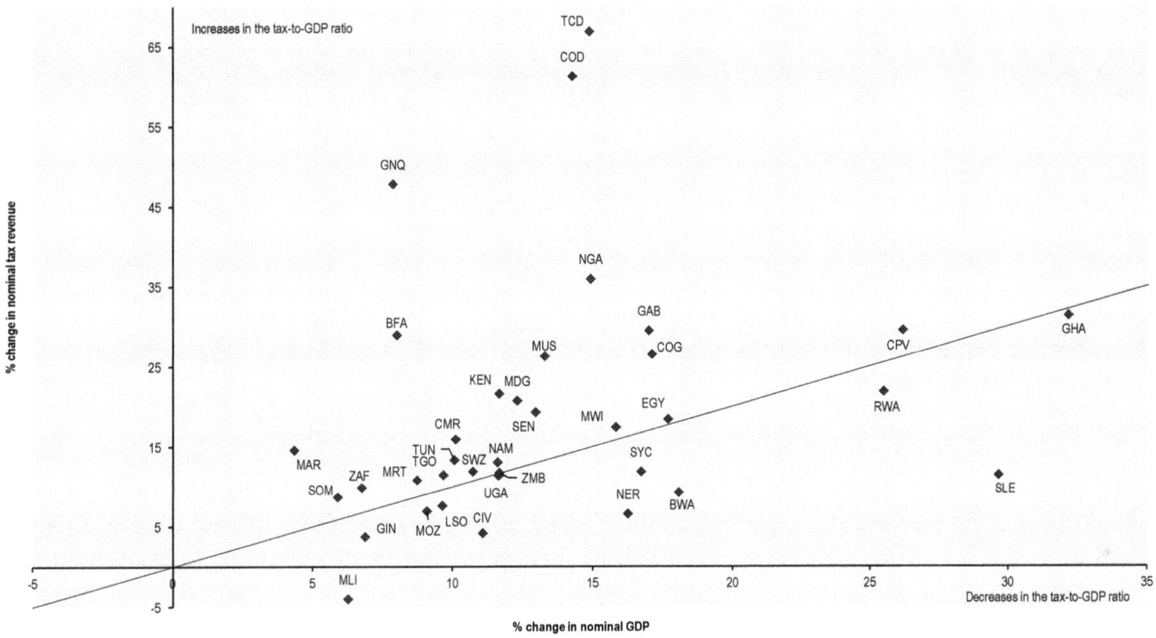

Note: Data include sub-national government tax revenues for Eswatini, Mauritius, Morocco, Nigeria (state revenues only), Somalia and South Africa for 2022. Total tax revenues for Chad, Togo, Uganda and Zambia do not include social security contributions as the data are not available.
Source: Authors' calculations based on data in (OECD/ATAF/AUC, 2024[4]), *"Revenue Statistics in Africa: Comparative tables"*, http://data-explorer.oecd.org/s/dx and in (IMF, 2024[5]) for figures of nominal GDP.

StatLink https://stat.link/s9c1n8

The average tax-to-GDP ratio of the African countries covered in this report increased by 0.5 p.p. between 2021 and 2022, following a rise of 0.3 p.p. between 2020 and 2021. As a share of GDP, tax revenues increased in 23 countries, decreased in 11 and remained unchanged in two (Figure 1.3). Although tax revenues also increased in 23 countries and decreased in 12 countries in 2021, increases were of a greater magnitude in 2022 than in 2021 (1.2 p.p. on average in 2022 compared to 1.0 p.p. in 2021) whereas decreases were smaller (-0.9 p.p. on average in 2022 compared to -1.1 p.p. in 2021).

In 2022, Chad and the Democratic Republic of Congo registered the largest increases in their tax-to-GDP ratio, of 3.3 p.p. and 3.6 p.p. respectively. In contrast, the tax-to-GDP ratios of both Sierra Leone and Mali decreased by 1.9 p.p. between 2021 and 2022, the largest decline among the countries in the report.

Figure 1.3. Year-on-year changes in tax-to-GDP ratios in African countries in 2021 and 2022

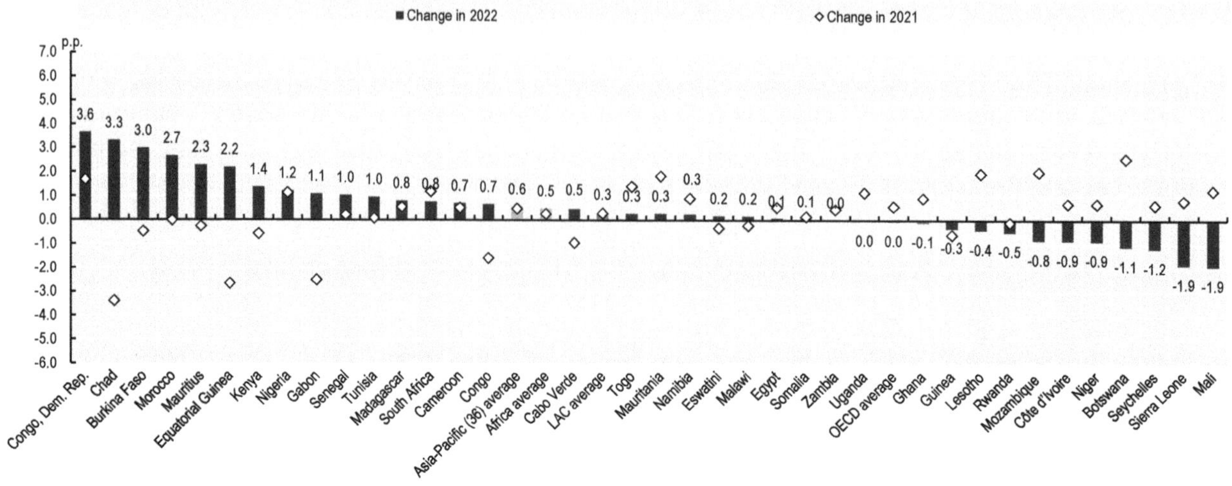

Note: The figures include sub-national government tax revenues for Eswatini, Mauritius, Morocco, Nigeria (state revenues only), Somalia and South Africa.

The Africa average and the averages for Asia-Pacific (36 countries), LAC (26 countries) and the OECD (38 countries) are unweighted.

The change in the Africa average should be interpreted with caution as data for social security contributions are not available or are partial in certain countries.[2]

Source: Authors' calculations based on data in Table 4.1 in Chapter 4 and (OECD/ATAF/AUC, 2024[4])*"Revenue Statistics in Africa: Comparative tables"*, http://data-explorer.oecd.org/s/dx.

StatLink https://stat.link/sblv3u

In 2022, Africa faced a challenging macroeconomic backdrop, as regional GDP growth slowed to 4.0% in real terms from 4.9% in 2021 (AUC/OECD, 2024[6]), This slowdown was attributed to tightening global financial conditions, trade disruptions and supply bottlenecks. Growth was also impaired by the increasing impact of climate change and extreme weather events (AfDB, 2023[7]). As in the rest of the world, inflation rose strongly in Africa in 2022, leading to higher food and energy prices. In response, some governments in the region adopted measures to reduce the impact of higher international prices on consumers, including reductions or exemptions of taxes on goods and services, such as VAT and excises[3] that reduced tax revenues. Meanwhile, higher prices in the oil and mineral sector led to higher profits and hence to higher revenues from corporate taxes in 2022 in countries that produce these resources (ATAF, 2023[8]).

Although tax-to-GDP ratios have rebounded from the COVID-19 shock in many African countries, the recovery has been uneven across the continent. In 2022, the tax-to-GDP ratio was above the level in 2019 (prior to the pandemic) in 21 of the 36 countries, while it was below this level in 15 countries.

In 2022, the Africa average tax-to-GDP ratio was 0.5 p.p. above its 2019 level (15.5%). This was also the case for the Asia-Pacific region, whose average tax-to-GDP ratio increased in 2021 and 2022, by 0.5 p.p. and 0.6 p.p. respectively after a contraction of 1.0 p.p. in 2020 (see Figure 1.4). By contrast, the average tax-to-GDP ratio in the LAC region had not regained its pre-pandemic level by 2022 despite increases of 0.3 p.p. in both 2021 and 2022. The OECD average has exceeded its 2019 level since 2020.

Figure 1.4. Year-on-year change in regional average tax-to-GDP ratios by region, 2020-22

Percentage points of GDP

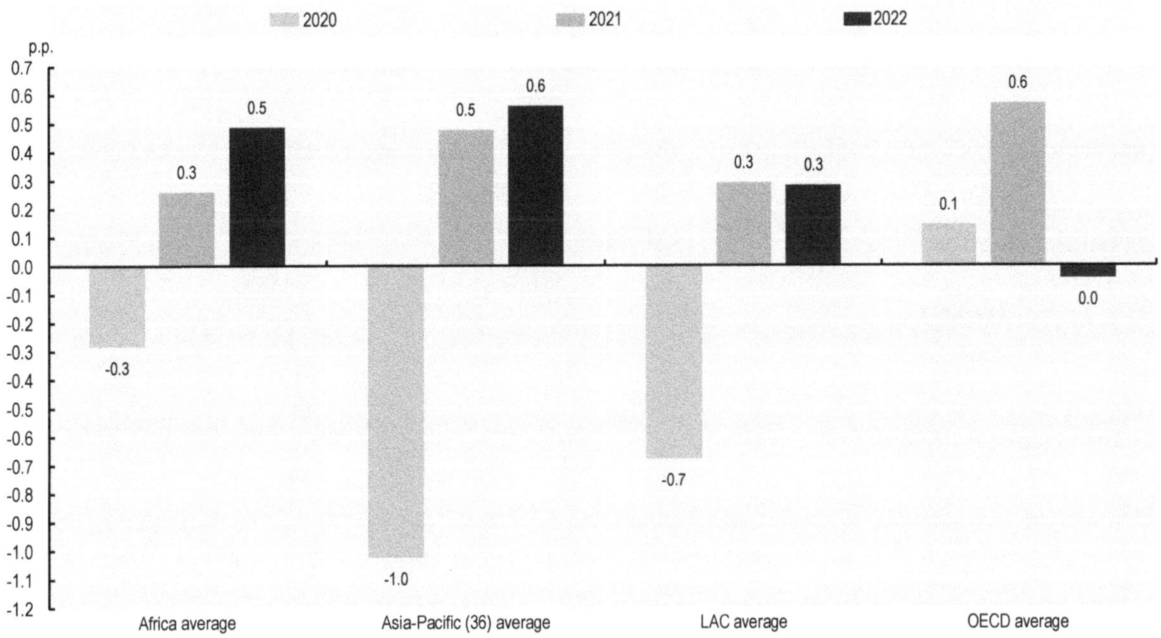

Note: Changes in tax revenues as percentage of GDP between periods are rounded to one decimal place in this chapter.
The Africa average and the averages for Asia-Pacific (36 countries), LAC (26 countries) and the OECD (38 countries) are unweighted.
The change in the Africa average should be interpreted with caution as data for social security contributions are not available or are partial in certain countries[2].
Source: Authors' calculations based on data in Table 4.1 in Chapter 4 and (OECD/ATAF/AUC, 2024[4]), *"Revenue Statistics in Africa: Comparative tables"*, http://data-explorer.oecd.org/s/dx.

StatLink https://stat.link/d8fsag

Changes in revenues by tax type

Between 2021 and 2022, revenues from corporate income tax (CIT) increased by 0.4% of GDP on average across the 36 countries in this publication, driving the overall increase in tax revenues in the region. Revenues from taxes on goods and services increased by 0.1% of GDP over the period. Within taxes on goods and services, revenues from value added taxes (VAT) and import duties both increased by 0.1% of GDP on average whereas excises decreased by 0.1% of GDP over the period.

Table 1.1 shows year-on-year changes in tax revenues as a share of GDP by main tax category for the average of African countries in this report since 2020.

- Revenues from taxes on goods and services were most adversely affected by the impact of the COVID-19 pandemic in 2020, decreasing by 0.4% of GDP.
- Revenues rebounded strongly in 2021 boosted by VAT revenue collections, which recorded the largest fall in 2020.
- Revenues from income taxes as a percentage of GDP remained unchanged in 2020 and 2021 and showed a strong increase in 2022 driven by growth in CIT revenues.

- Revenues from PIT remained unchanged as a percentage of GDP since 2020. Social security contributions fell by 0.1% of GDP in 2020 and were unchanged thereafter.

Table 1.1. Annual changes in tax revenues as a share of GDP by category, 2020-22

Year-on-year change, p.p.

	2020	2021	2022
Income taxes	**0.0**	**0.0**	**0.4**
Personal income tax (PIT)	0.0	0.0	0.0
Corporate income tax (CIT)	0.0	0.0	0.4
Social security contributions	**0.1**	**0.0**	**0.0**
Property taxes	**0.0**	**0.0**	**0.0**
Taxes on goods and services	**-0.4**	**0.3**	**0.1**
VAT	-0.4	0.2	0.1
Excises	0.0	0.0	-0.1
Customs	-0.1	0.1	0.1
Other taxes on goods and services	0.0	0.0	0.0
Residual	**0.0**	**0.0**	**0.0**
Total tax	**-0.3**	**0.3**	**0.5**

Note: "Other taxes on goods and services" includes all taxes on goods and services (heading 5000) excluding VAT (heading 5111) excises (heading 5121) and customs duties (heading 5123). "Residual" refers to includes all taxes not elsewhere reported in the table, which includes payroll taxes (heading 3000) and other taxes (heading 6000).
Source: Source: Authors' calculations based on data in (OECD/ATAF/AUC, 2024[4]), *"Revenue Statistics in Africa: Comparative tables"*, http://data-explorer.oecd.org/s/dx.

Major changes in tax-to-GDP ratios in African countries in 2022

Figure 1.5 presents changes in tax-to-GDP ratios between 2021 and 2022 by main tax heading across the 36 countries and on average for Africa. The largest increases (in Chad and the Democratic Republic of the Congo) were mainly driven by increases in income tax revenues while the largest decreases (in Mali and Sierra Leone) were mainly due to decreases in revenues from taxes on goods and services.

The tax-to-GDP ratio of the Democratic Republic of Congo increased 3.6 p.p. between 2021 and 2022. Favourable economic conditions led to a 3.0 p.p. rise in income tax revenue in 2022. The largest increases were in the mineral sector, where corporate profits increased due to higher global prices. The digitalisation of tax declarations and payments also contributed to improved mobilisation of tax revenues in 2022 (Ministère des Finances de al République Démocratique du Congo, 2023[9]).

The 3.3 p.p. increase in Chad's tax-to-GDP ratio was mainly driven by an increase of 3.8 p.p. in CIT revenues over the period. The oil sector was the principal factor behind the increase: CIT revenues from oil companies increased by 3.6 p.p. in 2022 due to higher oil prices (African Development Bank, 2023[10]).

Figure 1.5. Change in tax-to-GDP ratios by main tax heading and country, between 2021 and 2022

Percentage points (p.p.)

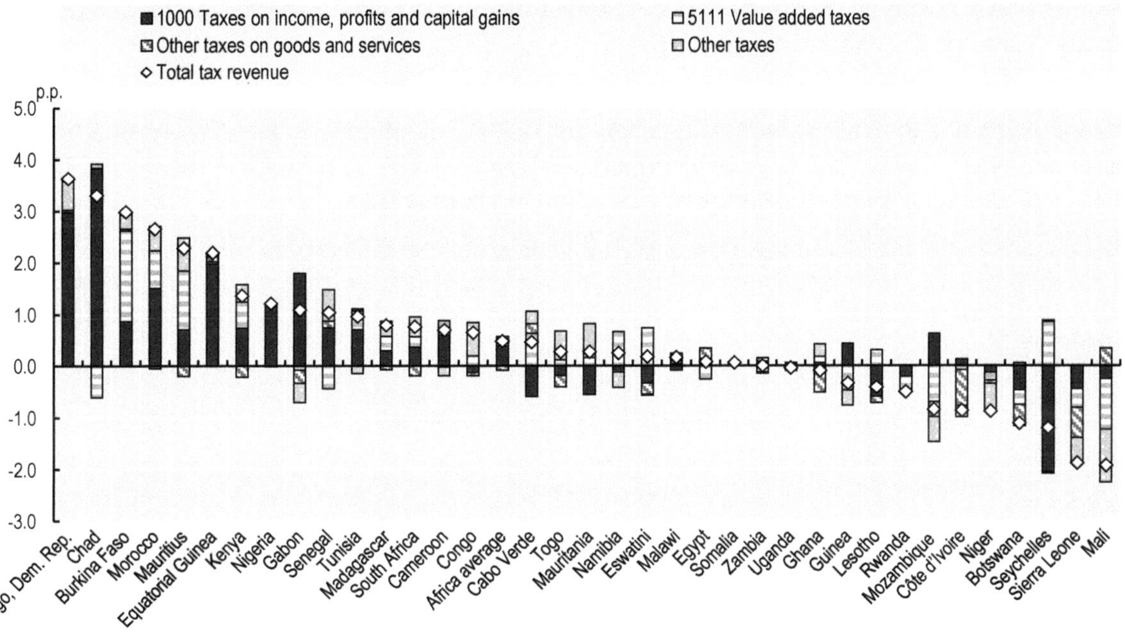

Note: The Africa average should be interpreted with caution as data for social security contributions are not available or are partial in certain countries[2]. See the country tables in Chapter 4 for further information.
Source: Authors' calculations based on data in (OECD/ATAF/AUC, 2024[4]), *"Revenue Statistics in Africa: Comparative tables"*, http://data-explorer.oecd.org/s/dx.

StatLink https://stat.link/qo3re8

In Sierra Leone, the tax-to-GDP ratio decreased by 1.9 p.p. in 2022, primarily due to a drop of 1.3 p.p. in revenues from taxes on goods and services. Sierra Leone is highly dependent on imports, notably of basic commodities such as rice and fuel, making it highly vulnerable to external economic shocks and fluctuations in global commodity prices (Danladi, 2020[11]). It was significantly impacted by a doubling of inflation in 2022 compared with 2021. As a result, Sierra Leone depreciated its exchange rate, trade was disrupted, and household consumption fell in 2022. This contributed to the reduction in tax revenues between 2021 and 2022 (African Development Bank, 2023[12]).

Tax revenues declined in nominal terms in Mali while the economy grew in 2022. As a percentage of GDP, tax revenues in Mali fell by 1.9 p.p. between 2021 and 2022, driven by declines in VAT revenues (of 1.0 p.p.) and non-VAT revenues from taxes on goods and services (of 0.8 p.p.). These occurred in a context of ECOWAS economic and financial sanctions against Mali in 2022, which affected Mali's imports. As a result, revenues from VAT on imports and customs duties fell significantly in 2022 compared to 2021 (by 23% and 10% in nominal terms) (IMF, 2023[13]) (Direction générale du Trésor de La France, 2024[14]).

The Seychelles' tax-to-GDP ratio declined by 1.2 p.p. due to a fall in CIT revenues of 1.7 p.p. A reduction of the standard CIT rate from 25% to 15% from January 2022 onwards contributed to the decline in the tax-to-GDP ratio over the period (ATAF, 2023[8]).

Evolution of tax-to-GDP ratios since 2013

In 2022, Africa's average tax-to-GDP ratio was 1.1 p.p. higher than in 2013. In comparison, the averages for the LAC region and OECD countries increased by 0.8 p.p. and 1.4 p.p. respectively between 2013 and 2022. The overall growth in tax revenues in Africa since 2013 was disrupted by falls in oil and gas prices in 2015 and the COVID-19 shock in 2020.

Africa's average tax-to-GDP ratio increased from 14.9% of GDP in 2013 to 15.3% in 2015 but decreased the following years due to a fall in commodity revenues. In 2017, it returned to the 2013 level. The average then increased until 2019 to 15.5% of GDP (Figure 1.6), followed by a contraction due to the COVID-19 pandemic. The years 2021 and 2022 marked a rebound in tax revenues.

Figure 1.6. Average tax-to-GDP ratios for Africa, Asia-Pacific, LAC and OECD, 2000-22

Percentage of GDP

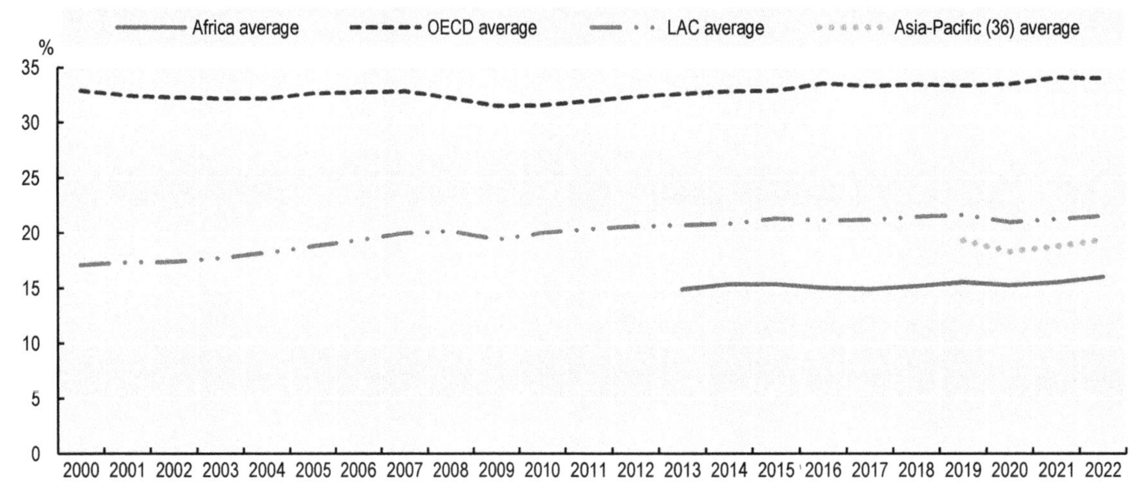

Note: The Africa average should be interpreted with caution as data for social security contributions are not available or are partial in certain countries[2]. The figures include sub-national government tax revenues for Cabo Verde (2008-2020), Eswatini, Mauritania (2009-2018), Mauritius, Morocco, Nigeria (only state revenues), Somalia (from 2019) and South Africa (from 2003).
The Africa average and the averages for Asia-Pacific (36 countries), LAC (26 countries) and the OECD (38 countries) are unweighted.
Source: Table 4.1 in Chapter 4 and (OECD/ATAF/AUC, 2024[4]), *"Revenue Statistics in Africa: Comparative tables"*, http://data-explorer.oecd.org/s/dx.

StatLink https://stat.link/97qvex

All main revenue categories increased between 2013 and 2022 at approximately the same pace. Revenues from taxes and goods and services increased by 0.5 p.p. between 2013 and 2022: VAT accounted for 0.2 p.p. of that increase to reach 4.5 % of GDP in 2022.

PIT also contributed to the increase in the African average tax-to-GDP ratio, rising from 2.6% of GDP in 2013 to 2.8% in 2022. CIT revenues increased by 0.2 p.p. over this period mainly due to the increase of 0.4 p.p. between 2021 and 2022. CIT revenues declined as a share of GDP between 2014 and 2016, in part due to falls in oil and mineral prices and decreases in CIT rates across the continent.

Figure 1.7. Revenue from taxes on income and profits, VAT and other tax headings, 2013-22

Percentage of GDP

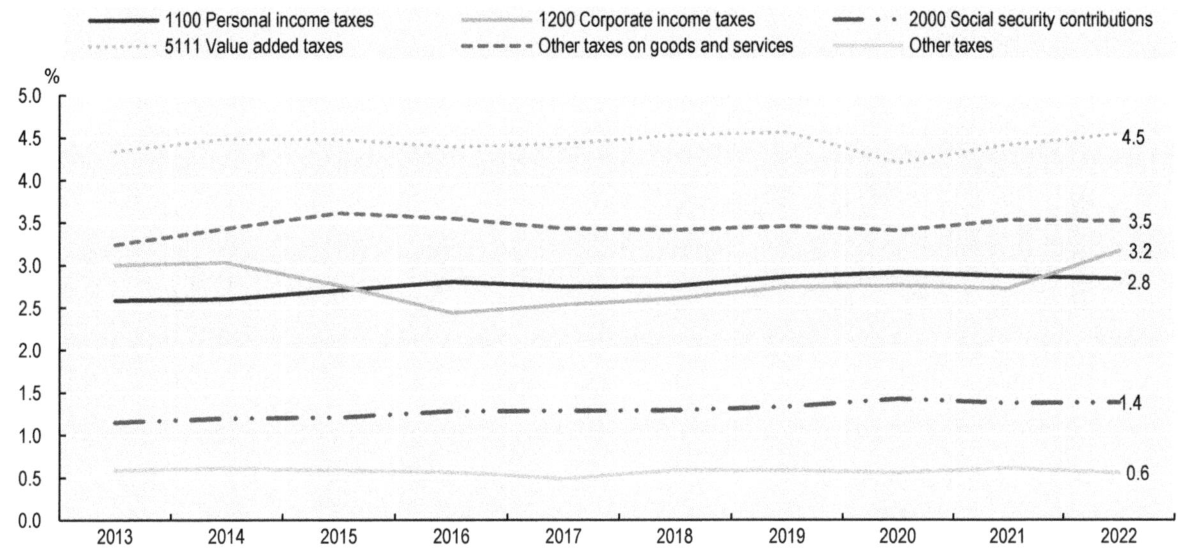

Note: The Africa averages should be interpreted with caution as data for social security contributions are not available or are partial in a few countries[2]. The figures include sub-national government tax revenues for Cabo Verde (2008-2020), Eswatini, Mauritania (2009-2018), Mauritius, Morocco, Nigeria (only state revenues), Somalia (from 2019) and South Africa (from 2003).

Source: Authors' calculations based on (OECD/ATAF/AUC, 2024[4]) *"Revenue Statistics in Africa: Comparative tables"*, http://data-explorer.oecd.org/s/dx.

StatLink https://stat.link/uy1758

Figure 1.8 presents changes in tax revenues as a share of GDP across the 36 countries and for the Africa, LAC and OECD averages between 2013 and 2022 by tax type and overall. Tax-to-GDP ratios rose in 25 African countries between 2013 and 2022 and declined in 11 countries. Tunisia recorded the largest increase over the period (of 5.4 p.p.), which was mainly attributable to higher revenues from PIT (2.6 p.p.), VAT (1.4 p.p.) and social security contributions (1 p.p.). During this period, Tunisia undertook extensive reforms to its tax policy and administration to mobilise tax revenues. In addition, increases in PIT revenues and social security contributions arose partly from 147% increase in payroll brought about by successive wage gains under post-revolutionary trade union pressure (OECD/ATAF/AUC, 2021[15]).

Figure 1.8. Change in tax-to-GDP ratios by country and main tax heading, between 2013 and 2022

Percentage points

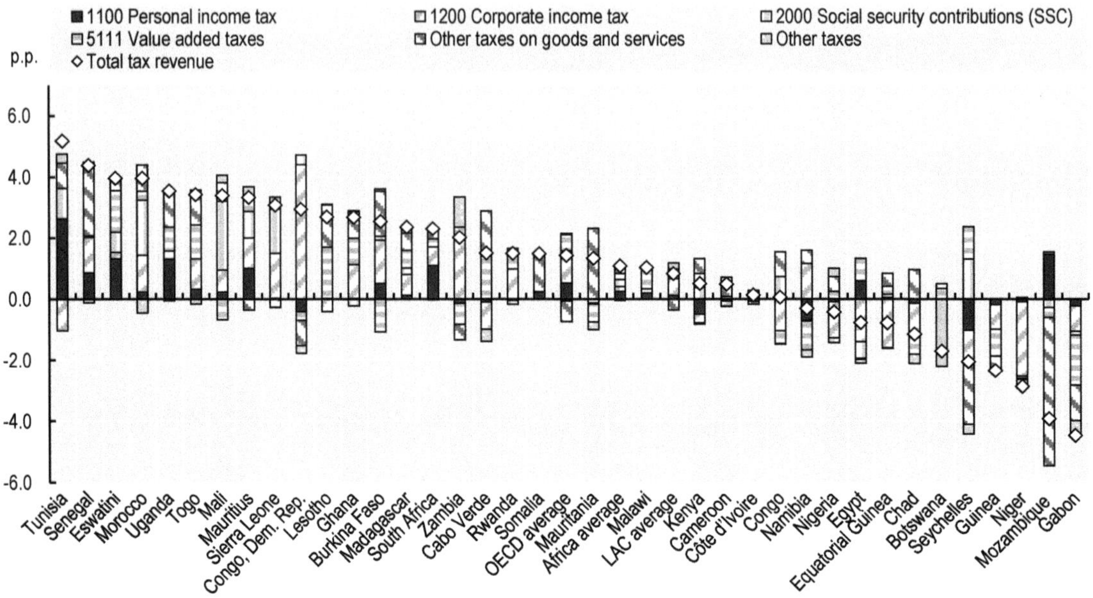

Note: The Africa average should be interpreted with caution as data for social security contributions are not available or are partial in a few countries[2]. The figures include sub-national government tax revenues for Cabo Verde (2008-2020), Eswatini, Mauritania (2009-2018), Mauritius, Morocco, Nigeria (only state revenues), Somalia (from 2019) and South Africa (from 2003).

Source: Authors' calculations based on (OECD/ATAF/AUC, 2024[4]), *"Revenue Statistics in Africa: Comparative tables"*, http://data-explorer.oecd.org/s/dx.

StatLink https://stat.link/jptrd9

As Figure 1.8 shows, recent progress in domestic resource mobilisation has varied significantly across African countries. This is further demonstrated by Figure 1.9, which shows that tax revenues in Togo and Chad followed very different trajectories since 2010.

Togo's tax-to-GDP ratio showed strong and steady growth over this period, increasing by 6.8 p.p. between 2010 and 2022 and exceeding the African average from 2014 (except in 2018). Over the period, Togo made significant efforts to improve revenue collection procedures in its three revenue administrations and undertook several reforms to mobilise tax revenues. Measures implemented by Togo between 2010 and 2012 included the monitoring and modernisation of revenue collection and information systems, as well as measures to tackle fraud and tax evasion. Another reform was the establishment of the OTR (*Office Togolais des recettes*), which unified customs and tax services into a single administration in 2014. More recently, Togo introduced tax identification numbers, reduced tax exemptions and established controls to combat corruption (IMF, 2019[16]).

Figure 1.9. Tax-to-GDP ratios in Chad, Togo and for the Africa average, 2000-22

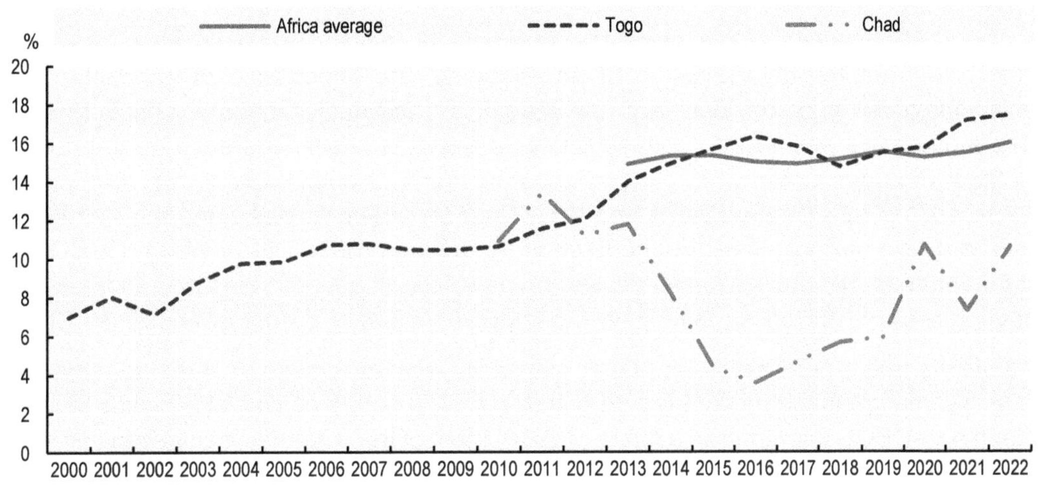

Note: The Africa average should be interpreted with caution as data for social security contributions are not available or are partial in a few countries[2]. See the country tables in Chapter 4 for further information.
Source: Authors' calculations based on (OECD/ATAF/AUC, 2024[4]), *"Revenue Statistics in Africa: Comparative tables"*, http://data-explorer.oecd.org/s/dx .

StatLink https://stat.link/bvimfh

Tax levels in Chad, on the other hand, were highly volatile between 2010 and 2022. Resource endowments significantly influence tax-to-GDP ratios (see Box 1.2), and this is particularly true for Chad, an oil-dependent economy whose tax revenues have been highly affected by oil prices. Chad recorded a significant decrease in tax revenues as a percentage of GDP between 2011 and 2016, from 13.4% (its highest level) to 3.6% (its lowest level). This was mainly caused by a decrease in revenues from CIT, which predominantly comes from oil companies. Oil prices fell between mid-2014 and early 2016, after which they were volatile (especially during and after the COVID-19 pandemic); tax revenues as a share of GDP fluctuated accordingly.

Box 1.2. Factors influencing tax levels

Countries' tax-to-GDP ratios are influenced by a variety of factors. These include macroeconomic characteristics such as the diversification of an economy, the importance of agriculture, resource endowments, openness to trade, debt and the size of the informal economy. Location is relevant: landlocked countries are less able to impose taxes on goods and services entering the country than island countries. Changes in countries' political situation, such as social unrest, can also influence tax levels. The capacity of tax administrations and tax morale (or willingness of companies and individuals to pay taxes) are also strongly linked to the level of tax revenues (OECD, 2014[17]) (OECD, 2019[18]). The Special Feature of this publication is focused on how African governments can address one of the factors affecting tax-to-GDP ratios, namely how to improve voluntary tax compliance (see Chapter 3).

Figure 1.10 shows tax-to-GDP ratios and GDP per capita across regions. It illustrates that tax levels tend to be higher in high-income countries. In general, OECD countries collect a higher amount of tax revenues than non-OECD countries as a share of GDP. Most of the countries included in this publication have lower income per capita and lower tax-to-GDP ratios than OECD and LAC countries. Levels of GDP per capita vary more among African countries than among LAC and OECD countries.

Figure 1.10. Tax-to-GDP ratios and GDP per capita (in PPP) in African, LAC, OECD and selected Asian and Pacific economies, 2022

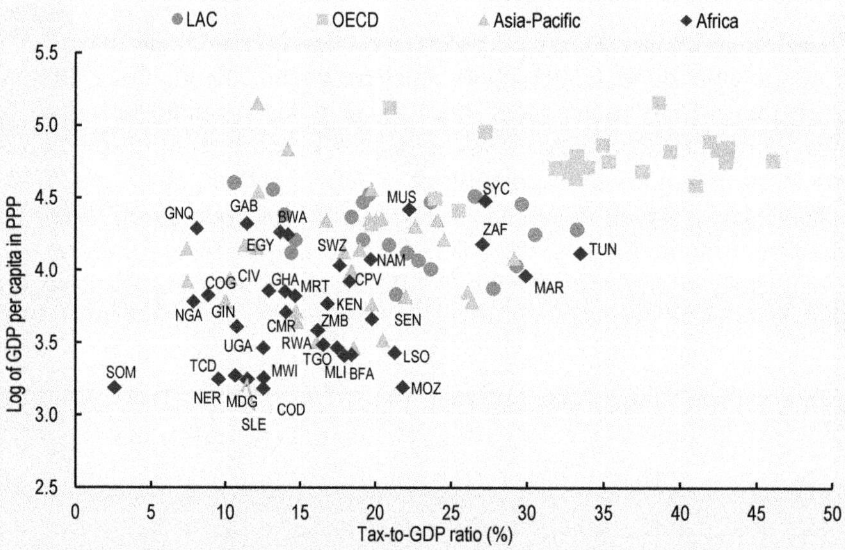

Note: The y-axis is on a logarithmic scale. The purchasing-power-parity (PPP) between two countries is the rate at which the currency of one country needs to be converted into that of a second country to ensure that a given amount of the first country's currency will purchase the same volume of goods and services in the second country as it does in the first. The implied PPP conversion rate is expressed as national currency per current international dollar. An international dollar has the same purchasing power as the US dollar has in the United States. An international dollar is a hypothetical currency that is used as a means of translating and comparing costs from one country to the other using a common reference point, the US dollar (definitions derived from (IMF, 2019[19]) and (World Bank, 2024[20]))
Source: (IMF, 2024[5]) for GDP per capita. Tax-to-GDP ratios are sourced from (OECD/ATAF/AUC, 2024[4]), *"Revenue Statistics in Africa: Comparative tables"*, http://data-explorer.oecd.org/s/dx, Global Revenue Statistics (database), (OECD, 2024[21]), https://www.oecd.org/en/data/datasets/global-revenue-statistics-database.html.

StatLink https://stat.link/9nld17

Countries' financing needs depend in part on their income level, which is an important consideration in understanding tax levels in different countries. The gap between public revenues and development financing tends to be larger in countries with lower per-capita incomes, making mobilisation of additional public revenues particularly critical (Gaspar et al., 2019[22]). The COVID-19 crisis reduced tax revenues in most countries while resulting in significant increases in spending needs and public debt. Renewed efforts to reform tax policy and administrations with a view to increasing revenues have become even more of a priority in the aftermath of the COVID-19 crisis.

Tax structures in African countries

The composition of a country's tax revenues across different tax types is known as its tax structure or tax mix. This is an important indicator since different taxes have different economic and social effects. The tax structures in the 36 countries in this publication reflect different policy choices, economic structures and conditions, tax administration capabilities and historical factors.

Tax structures in 2022

The 36 countries covered in this report can be divided into three broad groups according to their principal source of revenue: (i) VAT; (ii) other taxes on goods and services; and (iii) income taxes. Figure 1.11 shows the decomposition of tax revenues across all countries included in this publication, differentiating between income taxes (both personal and corporate), social security contributions, and taxes on goods and services (including VAT and other goods and services taxes).

Taxes on goods and services was the principal source of tax revenues for 22 countries (the first two groups of countries in Figure 1.11). Among these countries, taxes on goods and services generated between 37.4% of tax revenues in Tunisia and 87.1% of tax revenues in Somalia. VAT accounted for the largest share of revenues from taxes on goods and services in most of the countries in this group whereas other taxes on goods and services were the leading source of revenues for eight countries.

For 14 countries, taxes on income and profits accounted for the principal share of total tax revenues. Within this group, income tax revenues ranged from 43.1% of total tax revenues in Egypt to 74.9% in Equatorial Guinea. Twenty-one of the 36 countries received a higher share of tax revenues from CIT than from PIT in 2022. The share of CIT revenue was particularly large in Chad and Equatorial Guinea, where they accounted for more than 60% of total taxes.

Figure 1.11. Tax structure by country, 2022

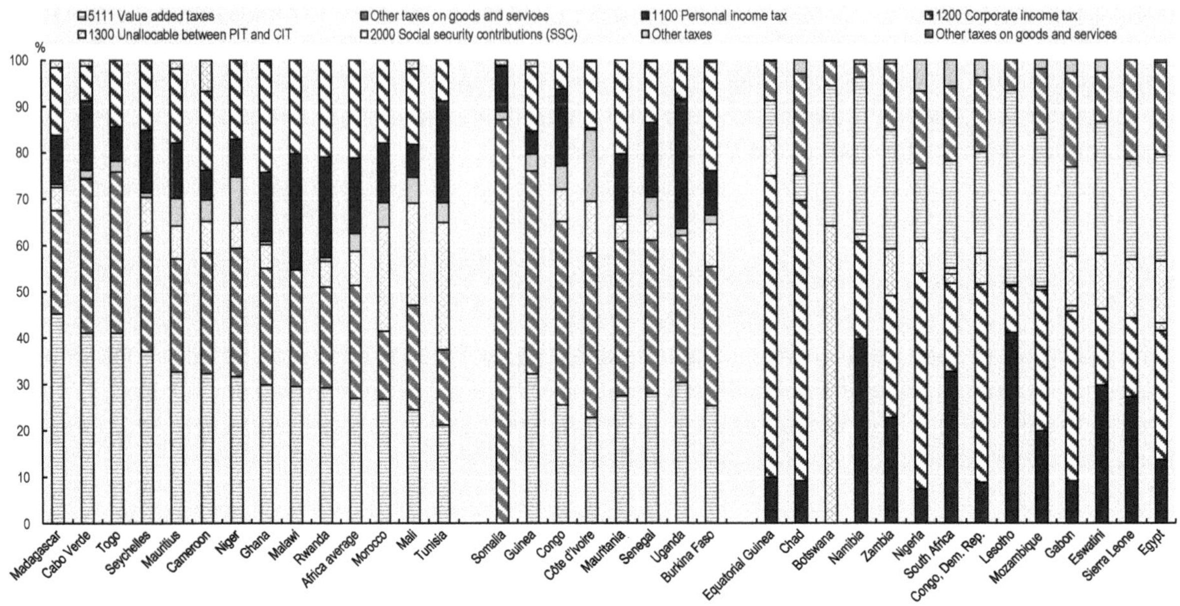

Note: Figures include sub-national government tax revenues for Eswatini, Mauritius, Morocco, Nigeria (state revenues only), Somalia and South Africa.

The breakdown of revenue from income tax by personal income tax and corporate income tax is not available in Botswana.

Source: Authors' calculations based on data from (OECD/ATAF/AUC, 2024[4]), *"Revenue Statistics in Africa: Comparative tables"*, http://data-explorer.oecd.org/s/dx.

StatLink https://stat.link/1ohn70

The importance of social security contributions in total tax revenues varies greatly across the 31 countries for which data is available in this publication. In 2022, the share was highest in Mali, Morocco and Tunisia, exceeding 20% of total tax; in the remaining countries social security contributions generated less than 0.2% of total tax revenues in Cabo Verde to around 13.5% in Egypt (Figure 1.11).

The variation in social security contributions reflects a diversity of social security programmes and contribution rates, with many countries using a variety of systems to fund social benefits. For example, social security contributions in South Africa finance the Unemployment Insurance Fund while other benefits, such as social assistance programmes covering old age, sickness and maternity, are financed by general revenues. In contrast, social security schemes in Morocco and Tunisia are modelled on the French system and provide a wide range of benefits on a contributory basis, including old age, disability, sickness and maternity, work injury (Tunisia), unemployment (Morocco) and family benefits (SSA, 2015[23]).

Figure 1.12. Tax structures for Africa, LAC, Asia-Pacific and the OECD, 2022

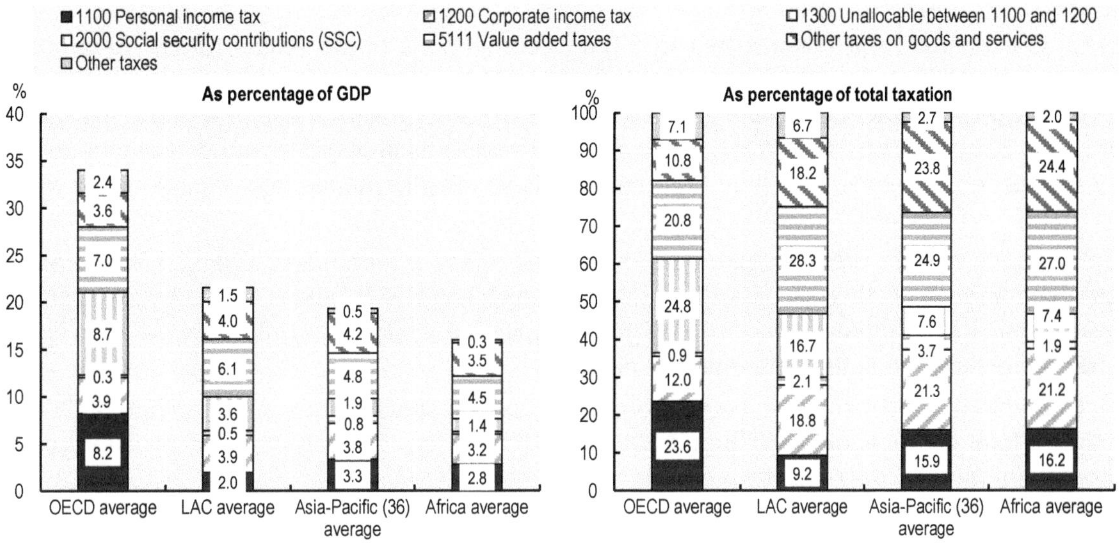

Note: The Africa average, the averages for Asia-Pacific (36 economies), LAC (26 countries) and the OECD (38 countries) are unweighted. The Africa average should be interpreted with caution as data for social security contributions are not available or are partial in certain countries.[2]
Source: Authors' calculations based on data on (OECD/ATAF/AUC, 2024[4]), *"Revenue Statistics in Africa: Comparative tables"*, http://data-explorer.oecd.org/s/dx.

StatLink https://stat.link/ge9ftk

In 2022, VAT generated the largest share of tax revenues on average for the countries included in this publication (Figure 1.12). VAT revenues accounted for 27.0% of total tax revenues on average, higher than the Asia-Pacific (36) average of 24.9% but lower than the LAC average of 28.3%. All three regions had a significantly larger share of tax revenues collected from VAT compared to the average for OECD countries, for which VAT revenues accounted for 20.8% of total tax revenues. VAT revenues for the Africa average were lower than all the other regions when measured as a share of GDP (4.5% of GDP in Africa, compared to 4.8% in Asia-Pacific, 6.1% in the LAC region and 7.0% in the OECD).

Relative to the other regions, Africa recorded the highest share of non-VAT taxes on goods and services (other taxes on goods and services in the graphs) at 24.4% of total tax revenues. Trade taxes represent an important source of revenue for Africa amounting to about half of non-VAT taxes on goods and services revenues in 2022. This share is likely to evolve with the ongoing implementation of the African Continental Free Trade Area (AfCFTA) (see Box 1.3).

CIT revenues as a share of total tax revenues in Africa averaged 21.2% in 2022, a similar level to the Asia-Pacific (36) average but higher than the LAC and OECD average shares (18.8% and 12.0%, respectively). Reported as a percentage of GDP, the average share of CIT revenues for Africa (3.3%) was lower than the other regional averages in 2022 (around 3.8% in Asia-Pacific and 3.9%, for the OECD and LAC averages) (Figure 1.12). By contrast, the African average share of PIT revenues (16.2% of total tax revenues) was lower than the OECD average of 23.7% but higher than the LAC and Asia-Pacific (36) averages (9.2% and 15.9%, respectively). As a percentage of GDP, the average level of PIT revenues across the OECD was nearly triple the Africa average.

Box 1.3. Trade tax revenues in Africa in the context of AfCFTA

The African Continental Free Trade Area (AfCFTA), a cornerstone of the African Union's Agenda 2063, will progressively eliminate taxes on goods traded within Africa and boost intra-Africa trade. The AfTCA aims to encourage investment and job creation to enhance the competitiveness of Africa in the medium to long term (AU, 2024[24]). The AfCFTA is expected to offset declines in public revenues from the removal of tariffs by stimulating economic growth in the region, thus yielding revenues from income taxes and other taxes on goods and services.

Revenue Statistics in Africa provides harmonised data on trade tax revenues according to three categories: 5123 (customs and import duties), 5124 (taxes on exports), and 5127 (other taxes on international trade and transactions). It is important to bear in mind that a significant proportion of intra-African trade is informal and therefore not included in the data reported here.

Figure 1.13 and Figure 1.14 show revenues from trade taxes respectively as a percentage of GDP and a percentage of total tax revenue in 2013 and 2022 for 31 countries covered in this publication (excluding SACU countries)[1] and for the regional averages.

Figure 1.13. Trade taxes by country, 2013 and 2022, percentage of GDP

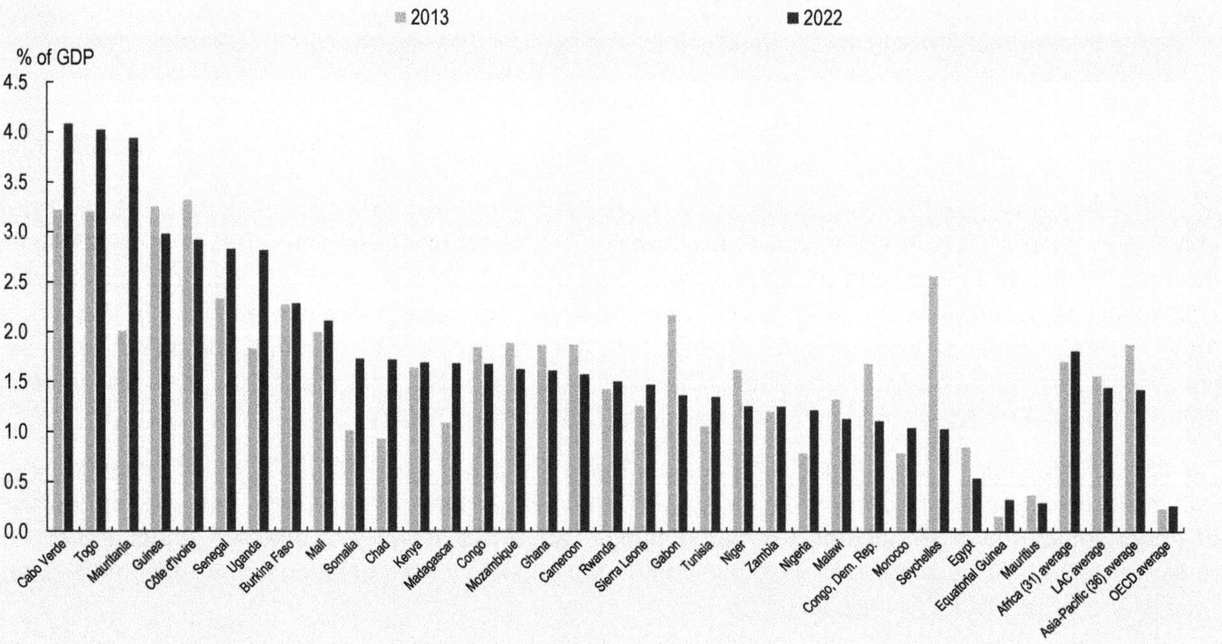

Note: Figure does not include the five SACU countries: Botswana, Eswatini, Lesotho, Namibia, and South Africa.
Source: Authors' calculations based on data from (OECD/ATAF/AUC, 2024[4]) *"Revenue Statistics in Africa: Comparative tables"*, http://data-explorer.oecd.org/s/dx.

StatLink https://stat.link/bxo13r

On average in African countries, revenues from trade taxes amounted to a larger proportion of GDP (1.8%) than in the LAC region (1.4%) and the Asia-Pacific region (1.4%) in 2022, while trade tax revenues in OECD countries averaged 0.3% of GDP in 2022. Revenue from trade taxes amounted to more than 3% of GDP in four African countries and less than 1% of GDP in three in 2022.

Revenues from trade taxes declined as a proportion of GDP between 2013 and 2022 in 18 of the non-SACU countries and increased in 13. On average, trade tax revenues as a percentage of GDP increased by 0.1 p.p. in Africa between 2013 and 2022 while they remained unchanged or declined in the other regions over the same period.

Revenues from trade taxes as a share of total tax revenues stood at 14.5% on average for the non-SACU African countries in 2022. In other regions, this share was lower than 8% of total tax revenues. Trade tax revenues accounted for more than 20% of total tax revenues in seven of the 31 countries and less than 5% in six countries. Somalia recorded the largest share (66.9% of total tax revenues), although it was in 10th place in terms of revenues from trade taxes as a percentage of GDP.

Revenues from trade taxes remain an especially important source of income among countries at lower-income levels. On average, trade taxes generated 17.6% of total tax revenues for low-income African countries covered in the report and 13.7% for lower-middle income countries, indicating that these countries may be particularly vulnerable to the elimination of tariffs under AfCFTA (OECD/ATAF/AUC, 2019[25]). In contrast, trade taxes accounted for 5.7% of total tax revenues in upper middle-income countries.

Between 2013 and 2022, revenue from trade taxes declined as a proportion of total tax revenues on average and in 17 non-SACU countries, while it increased in 14. A decline in trade taxes as a share of total tax revenues on average across Africa was also observed in other regions.

Figure 1.14. Trade taxes by country, 2013 and 2022, percentage of total tax revenues

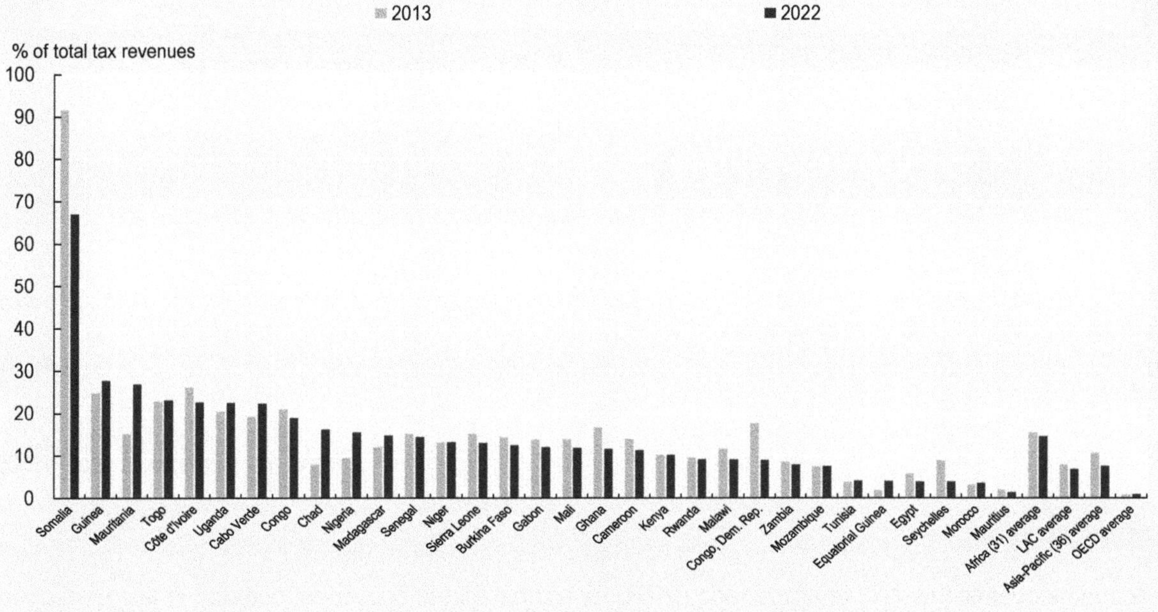

Note: Figure does not include the five SACU countries: Botswana, Eswatini, Lesotho, Namibia, and South Africa.
Source: Authors' calculations based on data from *"Revenue Statistics in Africa: Comparative tables"*, http://data-explorer.oecd.org/s/dx.

StatLink https://stat.link/8du1yw

Note: 1. These trade tax statistics do not cover revenues from the five member states of the Southern African Customs Union (South Africa, Botswana, Eswatini, Lesotho and Namibia) as these countries have a revenue sharing agreement in which their customs duties and excise taxes are entered into a Common Revenue Pool before being redistributed among their members. The income these countries receive from the revenue-sharing formula is reported as non-tax revenue (please see Chapter 2).

Evolution of tax structures, 2013-22

Between 2013 and 2022, the Africa average tax structure hardly changed. It only shifted very slightly towards a greater share for social security contributions and a marginally smaller share for consumption-related taxes.

The shares of PIT and VAT revenues in the average tax structure for the African countries in this publication have slightly declined although revenues from both sources increased as a percentage of GDP, to 2.8% and 4.5% of GDP, respectively, in 2022 (Figure 1.15). In contrast, the share of CIT and social security contributions in total tax revenues between 2013 and 2022 increased by 0.3 p.p. and 0.8 p.p. respectively.

Figure 1.15. Africa average tax structure as a percentage of GDP and total tax revenues, 2013-22

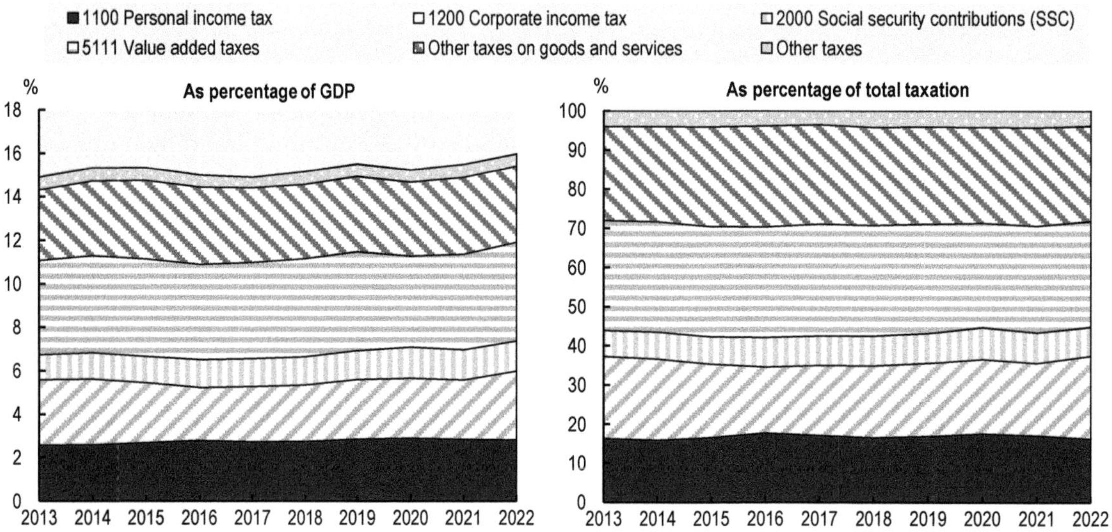

Note: The Africa average is unweighted. The Africa average should be interpreted with caution as data for social security contributions are not available or are only partially available in certain countries.[2]
Source: Authors' calculations based on data on (OECD/ATAF/AUC, 2024[4]), *"Revenue Statistics in Africa: Comparative tables"*, http://data-explorer.oecd.org/s/dx.

StatLink https://stat.link/2i05ka

VAT revenue ratio

This section discusses the VAT revenue ratio (VRR) for almost all the countries included in this publication. The VRR "measures the difference between the VAT revenue actually collected and what would theoretically be raised if VAT was applied at the standard rate to the entire potential tax base in a "pure" VAT regime and all revenue was collected" (OECD, 2024[26]).

The VRR is the ratio of actual VAT revenues to the product of final consumption (net of VAT revenues) and the standard VAT rate. The calculation is shown below:

$$\frac{\text{VAT revenues}}{(\text{final consumption expenditure} - \text{VAT revenues})\ x \text{ standard VAT rate}}$$

This indicator provides insights into VAT revenue loss related to exemptions and reduced rates, fraud, evasion and tax planning as well as weaknesses in tax administrations. However, the indicator needs to be interpreted with caution and with reference to the underlying characteristics of the VAT system in each country, as a high VRR could result from cascading effects[4] or failure to refund VAT input credits. Other factors may increase the ratio, for example when place-of-taxation rules for international trade diverge from the destination principle (OECD, 2024[26]).

Informality can also have an impact on VRRs. In many African countries, a high proportion of the workforce operates in the informal sector. Not being registered for tax purposes, they do not benefit from VAT refunds for their inputs (AfDB/OECD/UNDP, 2016[27]). The interpretation of the VRR is also more difficult for countries relying significantly on tourism: these countries may record a high VRR because purchases by non-residents are not included in final consumption expenditure (the denominator) but in exports whereas the VAT on these purchases is included in the overall VAT revenues (the numerator) (Keen, 2013[28]). Another factor that may be linked to the previous point relates to the level of trade: countries with relatively a high ratio of trade to GDP tend to show high VRRs, probably because collecting VAT at the point of entry of a country is easier than collecting in the domestic market (Ebrill, L. P., Keen, M., & Perry, V. J., 2001[29]).

Figure 1.16. VAT revenue ratio by country, 2022

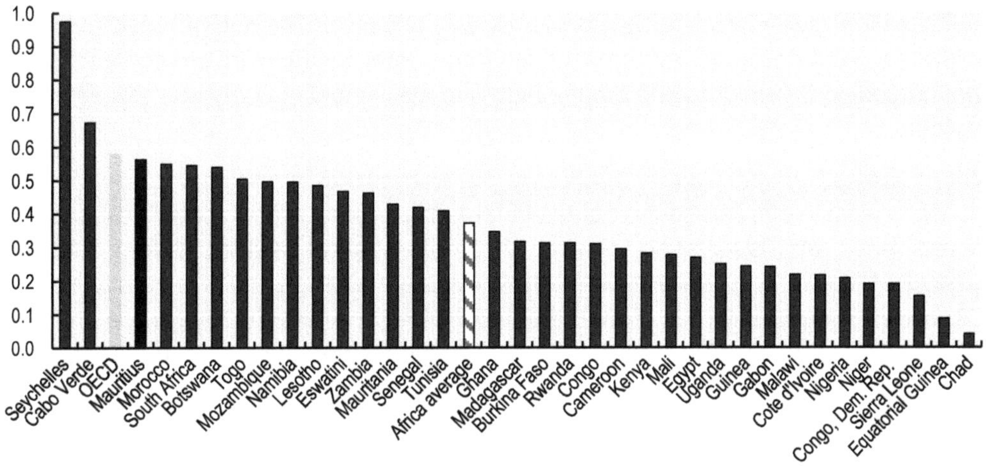

Source: The figure does not include Somalia as it does not operate a VAT system. VAT rates and the OECD VRR are sourced from Consumption Tax Trends (OECD, 2024[26]), the final expenditure consumption figures from the World Economic Outlook (IMF, 2024[5]) and VAT revenues from the country tables in Chapter 5.

StatLink https://stat.link/hc690f

Figure 1.16 shows the VRR for the 35 countries in this publication that operate a VAT system (which excludes Somalia). In 2022, the average VRR for these countries stood at 0.37, which was below the OECD average of 0.58. The VRRs ranged widely: the Seychelles, Cabo Verde and Mauritius had the highest VRRs (0.97, 0.67 and 0.56, respectively) while Equatorial Guinea and Chad had the lowest (0.09 and 0.04 respectively).

The Seychelles has a relatively broad-based VAT system and there are no reduced VAT rates, although there are a few VAT exemptions for basic necessities such as agricultural and pharmaceutical products and for fuels (OECD, 2020[30]). In addition, the high VRR could be partly due to the importance of tourism: revenue from VAT is primarily generated through the Seychelles' tourism sector, which is taxed at the standard rate and contributes about half of total VAT receipts (OECD, 2020[30]).

The tourism sector also plays an important role in the economies of both Cabo Verde and Mauritius (World Bank, 2024[31]) (Ministry of Tourism, 2023[32]) and could partly explain their higher VRR. Although the VRR of Mauritius is relatively high, (IMF, 2024[33]) argues that VAT collection in the country could be improved by removing exemptions, addressing compliance issues and lowering VAT thresholds to widen the tax net.

Chad's low VRR is linked to low levels of VAT revenue collection (amounting to 0.6% of GDP in 2022 and about 1% of non-oil GDP) as a result of weak VAT administration, VAT exemptions, deficiencies in the VAT refund mechanism, and the large informal sector (IMF, 2019[34]).

Trade (mostly imports) is more than 40% of GDP in Seychelles, Cabo Verde and Mauritius, whereas it is less than 15% in Chad and Equatorial Guinea. This finding supports previous findings that a high level of trade generally tends a higher VRR (Ebrill, L. P., Keen, M., & Perry, V. J., 2001[29]). Countries with high imports as a percentage of GDP such Cabo Verde and the Seychelles also recorded a high share of VAT on imports as a percentage of VAT revenues (62% and 37% respectively in 2022) whereas this proportion was low for Equatorial Guinea and Chad (12% and 4% respectively in 2022).

Environmentally related tax revenues

Through the Paris Agreement of 2016, countries have committed to decarbonising their economies by the middle of this century, implying a shift away from fossil fuels as a source of energy. To reduce emissions and drive decarbonisation, more and more countries are deploying environmentally-related taxes and price-based policy instruments. By incorporating a price signal into consumer decisions, systems of environmental taxation give effect to the polluter-pays principle to favour greener over more polluting economic activities. Well-designed systems of environmental taxation in effect can thereby influence environmental outcomes by encouraging businesses and households to consider the environmental costs of their behaviour.

The 2023 Africa Climate Summit, Nairobi Declaration takes note that in addressing environmentally-related tax revenues, it is crucial to emphasise the acute vulnerabilities many African countries grapple with, arising from the unpredictable and devastating impacts of climate change (African Union, 2023[35]). Prolonged droughts, unyielding floods and wildfires brought by climate change inflict a heavy humanitarian and economic toll, undermining livelihoods, health and education, and threatening peace and security across the continent. Despite not being historical contributors to global warming, African countries bear its harsh consequences, underscoring the urgent need for global collaborative efforts.

An environmentally-related tax is a tax whose base is a physical unit (or a proxy of a physical unit) of something that has a proven, specific harmful impact on the environment regardless of whether the tax is intended to change behaviours or is levied for another purpose (OECD, 2005[36]). Revenues from taxes on energy can increase in the medium term if countries increase effective tax rates on the carbon content of fuels (Marten and van Dender, 2019[37]). A joint ITF and OECD study shows how revenues from road transport can be stabilised in the long term through a mix of taxing distance driven, vehicles and fuel (OECD/ITF, 2019[38]).

Although environmentally-related taxes are not a category in the standard OECD classification of tax revenues, they can be identified through the detailed list of specific taxes included for most countries within this overarching classification. It is on this basis that they are included in the OECD Policy Instruments for the Environment (PINE) database (OECD, 2024[39]).[5] In 2020, the OECD started collecting Environmentally Related Tax Revenue (ERTR) accounts in line with the System of Environmental and Economic Accounting; ERTRs are disaggregated by industries and households.

A detailed examination of country-specific taxes for 34 of the 36 African countries[6] in this report with ERTR data demonstrates that, on average, revenues from environmentally related taxes amounted to 1.0% of GDP in 2022, a higher level than the LAC and Asia-Pacific unweighted averages of 0.8% and 0.7% of GDP, respectively but lower than the OECD (1.8% of GDP). Across Africa, ERTRs ranged from less than 0.1% of GDP in the Republic of the Congo, Nigeria and Somalia to 3.5% in the Seychelles (Figure 1.17). These figures should be treated with caution as it is not possible to identify the precise level of ERTRs for each country; the level of revenues shown in Figure 1.17 depends in part on the granularity of tax revenue data available.

Figure 1.17. Environmentally related tax revenues by country and main tax base, 2022

Percentage of GDP

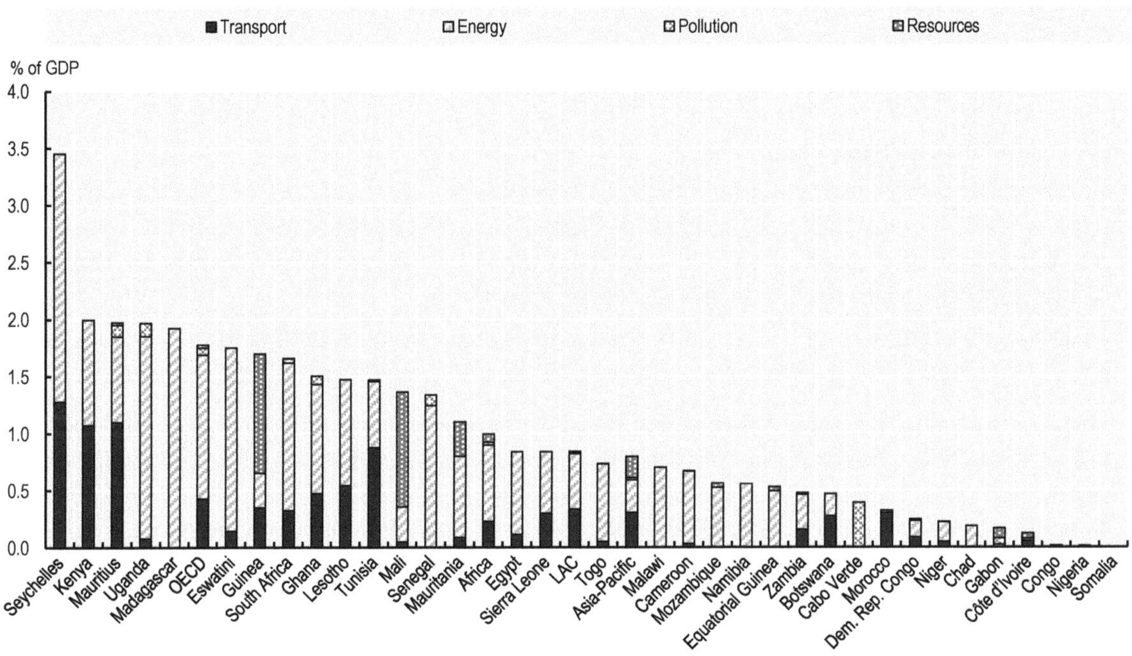

Note: The figures of environmentally related tax revenues depend on the granularity of tax revenue data provided by participating countries. Burkina Faso and Rwanda are excluded as it has not been possible to identify environmentally related tax revenue data in 2022.

Source: Authors' calculations based on data on (OECD/ATAF/AUC, 2024[4]), PINE database for the OECD, LAC and Asia-Pacific averages (OECD, 2024[39])

StatLink https://stat.link/vsgzjb

ERTRs can be split into different categories of tax base, notably energy (e.g., fossil fuels and electricity), transport, pollution and resources (e.g., mining and fossil fuel extraction).

- In 2022, revenues from energy taxes generated the majority of ERTRs among the countries in this publication (0.7% of GDP on average). Taxes on energy products accounted for the largest share of ERTRs in 20 of the 34 countries.
- Revenues from motor vehicles and transport services accounted for most of the remainder (approximately one-third of ERTRs and 0.2% of GDP on average). They were the main source of ERTRs for four countries.
- Revenues from other environmentally related bases are smaller, at 0.1% of GDP on average for natural resources and pollution combined. Taxes on natural resource extraction were most prominent in Gabon, Guinea and Mali. A pollution tax in the form of a levy on non-biodegradable packaging was the main source of ERTRs in Cabo Verde.
- On average, the structure of ERTRs in Africa is very similar to the OECD and the LAC region. By contrast, Asia-Pacific economies rely equally on taxes on energy, resources and transport.

Analysis of environmental taxes in the Africa region needs to be understood in the context of the extensive use of fossil fuel subsidies. Latest figures from the IEA indicate that fossil fuel consumption subsidies rose to an unprecedented USD 1 trillion globally in 2022. Rising fuel prices pushed many countries to increase fossil fuel subsidies to keep prices at an affordable level for households and companies (IEA, 2023[40]). Among the countries in this publication, Egypt, Gabon, Ghana and Nigeria provided fossil fuel consumption subsidies amounting to about USD 66.2.5 billion, USD 385.4 million, USD 2.6 billion and USD 18.7 billion, respectively, in 2022 (IEA, 2023[41]). These amounts represented a significant increase compared to 2021 for all four countries, with increases ranging from 136% in Egypt to 350% in Gabon. These subsidies may add significantly to countries' borrowing needs, forcing some African countries (such as Ghana, Kenya and Nigeria) to remove some subsidies in 2022 or 2023 (Africa Business Insider, 2023[42]).

Tax revenues by Regional Economic Community and by income group

Regional Economic Communities

The 36 countries included in this publication belong to one or more Regional Economic Communities (RECs) on the continent, which facilitate economic integration between their members (African Union, 2024[43]). This section describes tax revenue trends and tax structures in five RECs, namely the East African Community (EAC), the Economic Community of Central African States (ECCAS), the Economic Community of West African States (ECOWAS), the Arab Maghreb Union (AMU) and the Southern African Development Community (SADC)[7].

Revenue Statistics in Africa includes many members of these RECs but not all; coverage ranges from 57% for EAC to 80% for SADC. The indicators showing average tax revenue levels and tax structures among the five RECs only include the member states participating in *Revenue Statistics in Africa*.

The average tax-to-GDP ratios for SADC and AMU exceeded the Africa average of 16.0% in 2022 (at 18.6% and 26.0%, respectively), while the average tax-to-GDP ratios for ECCAS, ECOWAS and EAC were below the Africa average (11.7%, 14.4% and 14,6%, respectively). Between 2013 and 2022, average tax-to-GDP ratios rose in all five RECs, with increases ranging from 0.8 p.p. in ECCAS to 2.3 p.p. in EAC and 3.2 p.p. in AMU. Tax-to-GDP ratios increased by 1.2 p.p. in SADC and by 1.4 p.p. in ECOWAS on average (Figure 1.18).

Figure 1.18. Tax revenue trends in RECs and the Africa average, 2000-22

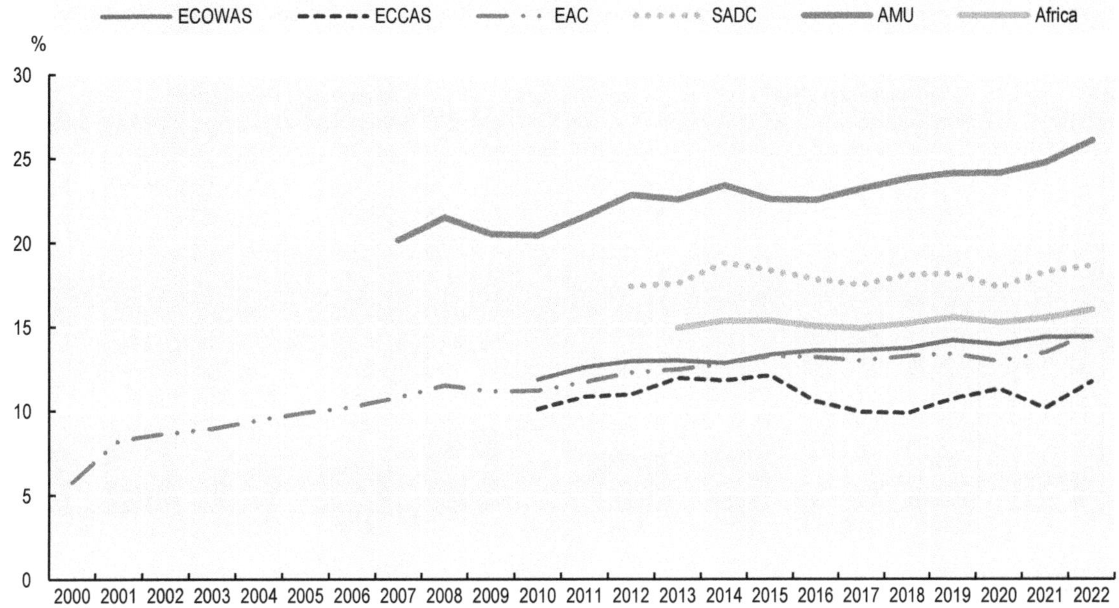

Note: The Africa and the RECs average should be interpreted with caution as data for social security contributions are not available or are partial in certain countries[2]. The average for each REC is calculated with reference to the member countries participating in *Revenue Statistics in Africa*. Please see Endnote 10 for more details.
Source: Authors' calculations based on data on (OECD/ATAF/AUC, 2024[4]), *"Revenue Statistics in Africa: Comparative tables"*, http://data-explorer.oecd.org/s/dx

StatLink https://stat.link/zn68br

Tax structures varied across the RECs in 2022, albeit with some commonalities between them.

- Income taxes were the principal source of revenues for ECCAS countries on average, with CIT representing the highest share of total tax revenues (35.6%). CIT revenues contributed a larger share of tax revenues in ECCAS than in any of the other RECs.
- Taxes on goods and services was the main source of revenues for EAC, ECOWAS and AMU. Within taxes on goods and services, EAC and AMU levied a slightly larger share of VAT revenues than revenues from non-VAT taxes on goods and services ("other taxes on goods and services" in Figure 1.19). Although ECOWAS has the largest share of VAT revenues among the three RECs, non-VAT taxes on goods and services accounted for the largest share of tax revenues at 29.4%.VAT revenues in these three RECs ranged from 25.2% in AMU to 28.5% in ECOWAS.
- Income taxes and taxes on goods and services were equally important as a percentage of total tax revenues for SADC countries on average. VAT was the principal source of SADC tax revenues, amounting to 31.9%, and represented the largest share compared to the other RECs. VAT revenues accounted for twice as much in SADC countries on average than revenues from other taxes on goods and services (15.3%). PIT was the second-largest source of tax revenues in SADC; at 21.3% of tax revenues, the share of PIT was also the largest among all RECs analysed here.
- Revenue from social security contributions accounted for less than 10% of total tax revenues in all the RECs except AMU, where they contributed to 18.1% of total taxation in 2022.

Figure 1.19. Tax structure in RECs, 2022

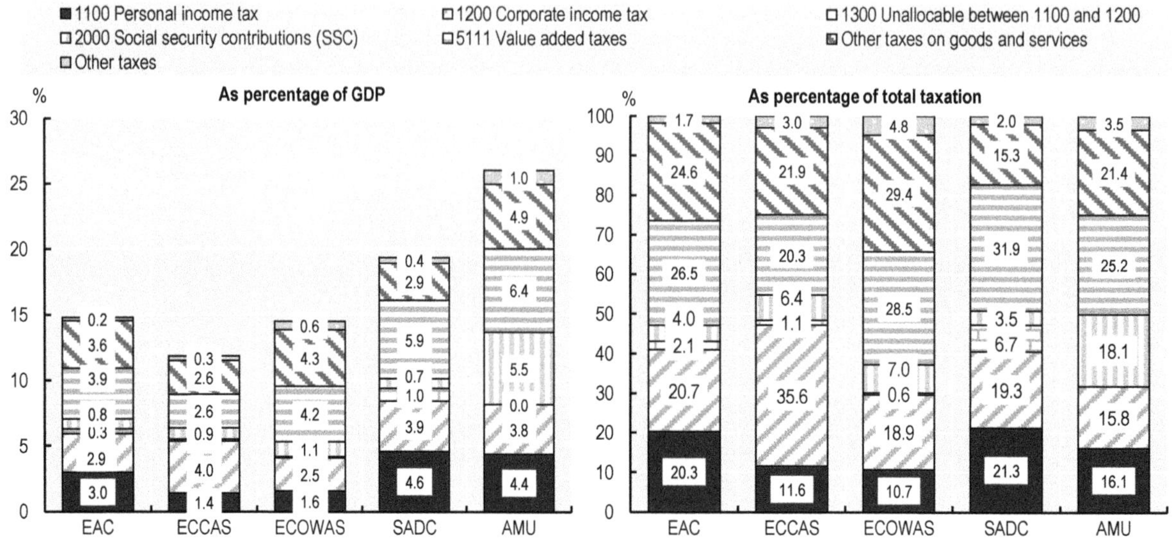

Note: The REC averages only take into account data from the member countries participating in *Revenue Statistics in Africa*. Please see endnote 10 for more details.

Source: Authors' calculations based on data on (OECD/ATAF/AUC, 2024[4]), *"Revenue Statistics in Africa: Comparative tables"*, http://data-explorer.oecd.org/s/dx

StatLink https://stat.link/qmgd0a

As a percentage of GDP, revenues from the main tax categories varied greatly across the RECs:

- Average PIT revenues ranged from 1.4% of GDP in ECCAS to 4.6% in SADC while CIT revenues ranged from 2.5% of GDP in ECOWAS to 4% in ECCAS. PIT and CIT revenues were of similar magnitude in SADC and AMU on average.
- VAT revenues and revenues from non-VAT taxes on goods and services were lowest in ECCAS (both 2.6% of GDP) and highest in AMU on average (6.4% and 4.9% of GDP respectively).
- Social security contributions ranged from 0.7% of GDP in SADC to 5.5% in AMU on average.

Tax revenues and tax structures by income group

Countries participating in *Revenue Statistics in Africa* are categorised according to one of four income groups as defined by the World Bank (World Bank, 2024[44]): low income (13 countries), lower middle-income (16 countries), upper middle-income (6 countries) and high income (1 country, the Seychelles). This section presents trends in tax-to-GDP ratios and the tax structure in 2022 by income group, excluding the high-income group because of the limited coverage (the Seychelles is thus not included in the analysis).

The average tax-to-GDP ratio for each income group shown in Figure 1.20 confirms the tendency for more-developed countries to have higher tax-to-GDP ratios (discussed in Box 1.2). In 2022, the average tax-to-GDP ratios of the lower middle-income countries and upper middle-income countries were higher than the Africa average, at 16.9% and 17.8% respectively. In contrast, the average tax-to-GDP ratio of low-income countries was 13.5%, which was below the Africa average and below the threshold of 15% considered as a tipping point to accelerate growth and development (Gaspar, Mansour and Vellutini, 2023[45]).

Figure 1.20. Tax revenue trends by income group and for the Africa average, 2000-22

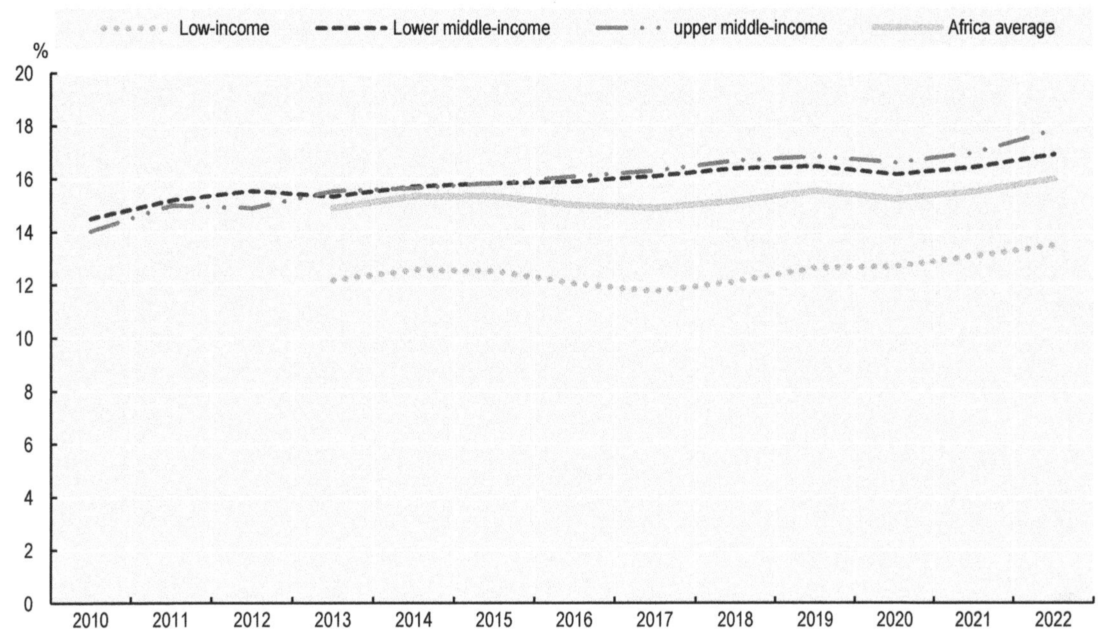

Note: The Africa average should be interpreted with caution as data on social security contributions are not available or are partial in certain countries.[2] Income groupings follow the World Bank classification (World Bank, 2024[44]).
Source: Authors' calculations based on data on (OECD/ATAF/AUC, 2024[4]), *"Revenue Statistics in Africa: Comparative tables"*, http://data-explorer.oecd.org/s/dx.

StatLink https://stat.link/ndlzqw

A combination of a large informal sector and a high reliance on foreign aid often pushes low-income countries towards a lower level of tax collections and a narrower tax base (Besley and Persson, 2014[46]) (Bachas, Jensen and Gadenne, 2024[47]). It is especially crucial for low-income countries to increase tax revenues as they often lack steady sources of funding and confront the greatest spending needs.

On average, tax revenues as a share of GDP increased for all income groups. between 2013 and 2022. Tax revenues in low-income countries increased by 1.3 p.p. over the period while they rose by 1.6 p.p. in lower middle-income countries and by 2.3 p.p. in upper middle-income countries.

The tax categories contributing most to the increase in tax revenues between 2013 and 2022 vary across income groups. The rise in tax revenues in low-income countries was primarily due to higher income tax revenues, mainly from CIT. Revenues from non-VAT taxes on goods and services were the main factor behind the growth in tax revenues in lower middle-income and upper middle-income countries.

Figure 1.21 presents the tax structure as a percentage of GDP and as a share of total tax revenues for the Africa average and the three income groups. The tax structure in the low-income countries and in lower middle-income countries is characterised by a high reliance on taxes on goods and services (respectively 55.0% and 52.8% of tax revenues in 2022). In contrast, the average tax mix of upper middle-income countries has a greater share of income taxes (55.1%).

Within taxes on goods and services, VAT ranged between 24.6% to 27.9% of total tax revenues across the three income groups on average. As concerns non-VAT taxes on goods and services, upper middle-income countries showed the lowest share as a percentage of total tax revenues on average whereas low-income countries recorded the largest share (respectively 12.9% and 28.9% of total tax revenues).

Conversely, the share of PIT in 2022 was highest in the upper middle-income countries (17.2% of total tax revenues) and lowest in low-income countries (14.8%).

(Bachas, Jensen and Gadenne, 2024[47]) explain that taxes on goods and services as a share of total taxes tend to decrease with economic development, while the share of PIT tends to increase. They contend that the PIT base expands as countries develop and the workforce transitions from self-employment to dependant employment (contributing to a transition from the informal sector to the formal sector). This transition is supported by the increasing market share of larger firms, which leads to a higher share of employees in the workforce. These trends tend to result in higher PIT revenues as well as a smaller informal sector in countries with higher incomes. Low-income countries find it difficult to enforce taxes on self-employed and low-earning workers and tend to exempt this sector of the workforce even though it tends to represent most workers.

Figure 1.21. Tax structures of African countries by income group, 2022

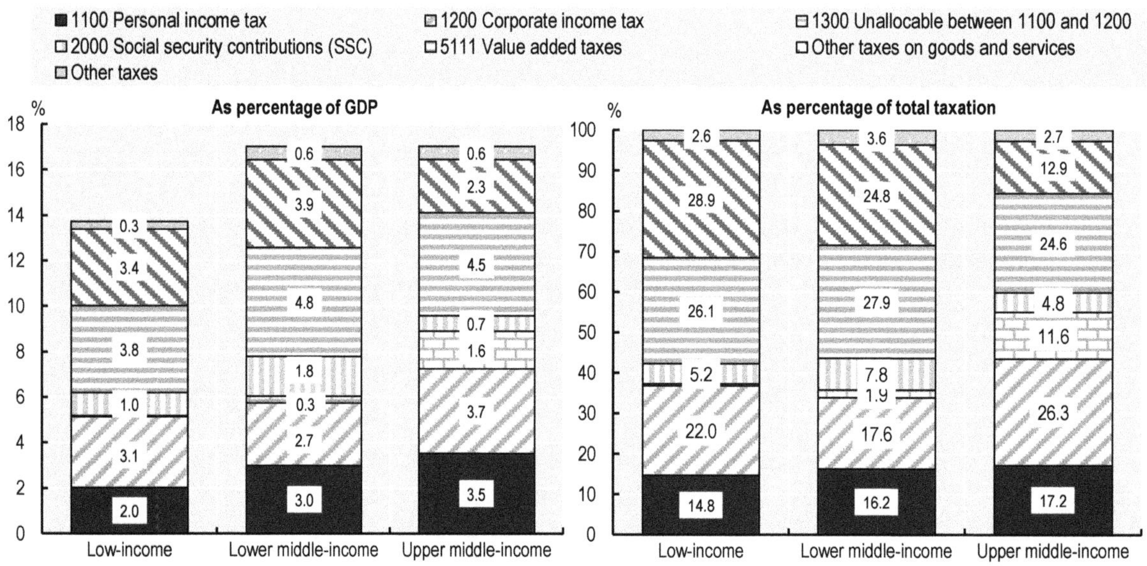

Note: Income groupings follow World Bank classification (World Bank, 2024[44]).
Source: Authors' calculations based on data on (OECD/ATAF/AUC, 2024[4]), *"Revenue Statistics in Africa: Comparative tables"*, http://data-explorer.oecd.org/s/dx.

StatLink https://stat.link/z5y2lv

Taxes by level of government

Analysis of taxation by level of government for the countries participating in this publication is limited by the fact that data on sub-national tax revenues are only available for six countries: Eswatini, Mauritius, Morocco, Nigeria[8], Somalia and South Africa. In 2022, sub-national government revenues accounted for 0.3% of total tax revenues in Mauritius, 2.1% in Eswatini, 2.8% in Morocco, 4.2% in South Africa, 12.0% in Nigeria and 35.1% in Somalia

Revenues from property taxes are the most important source of reported tax revenue for sub-national governments in Eswatini, Mauritius, Morocco and South Africa. They accounted for all the reported tax revenue collected locally in Eswatini, Mauritius and South Africa and for more than 80% in Morocco. In contrast, sub-national government tax revenues in Nigeria are mostly sourced from income taxes and in Somalia from taxes on goods and services.

References

AfDB (2023), *Africa economic outlook; Mobilizing Private Sector financing for Climate and Green Growth in Africa*, https://www.afdb.org/en/documents/african-economic-outlook-2023-highlights. [7]

AfDB/OECD/UNDP (2016), *African Economic Outlook 2016: Sustainable Cities and Structural Transformation*, OECD Publishing, Paris, https://doi.org/10.1787/aeo-2016-en. [27]

Africa Business Insider (2023), *African countries that removed fuel subsidies between 2022 and 2023*, https://africa.businessinsider.com/local/markets/african-countries-that-removed-fuel-subsidies-between-2022-and-2023/ms3t33v. [42]

African Development Bank (2023), *Country Focus Report 2023 - Chad- Mobilizing Private Sector Financing for Climate and Green Growth*, https://www.afdb.org/en/documents/rapport-pays-2023-tchad-mobiliser-les-financements-du-secteur-prive-en-faveur-du-climat-et-de-la-croissance-verte. [10]

African Development Bank (2023), *Country Focus Report 2023 - Sierra Leone - Mobilizing Private Sector Financing for Climate and Green Growth*, https://www.afdb.org/en/documents/country-focus-report-2023-sierra-leone-mobilizing-private-sector-financing-climate-and-green-growth. [12]

African Union (2024), *Regional Economic Communities | African Union*, https://au.int/en/recs (accessed on 9 October 2024). [43]

African Union (2023), *The african leaders Nairobi declaration on climate*, https://www.afdb.org/sites/default/files/2023/09/08/the_african_leaders_nairobi_declaration_on_climate_change-rev-eng.pdf. [35]

ATAF (2023), *African Tax Outlook (ATO)*. [8]

AU (2024), *About The AfCFTA*, https://au-afcfta.org/about/. [24]

AUC/OECD (2024), *Africa's Development Dynamics 2024: Skills, Jobs and Productivity*, OECD Publishing, Paris/African Union Commission, Addis Ababa, https://doi.org/10.1787/df06c7a4-en. [6]

Bachas, P., A. Jensen and L. Gadenne (2024), *Tax Equity in Low- and Middle-Income Countries*, https://pubs.aeaweb.org/doi/pdfplus/10.1257/jep.38.1.55. [47]

Besley, T. and T. Persson (2014), *Why Do Developing Countries Tax So little?*, https://pubs.aeaweb.org/doi/pdfplus/10.1257/jep.28.4.99. [46]

Danladi, J. (2020), "International Commodity prices and inflation dynamics in Sierra Leone", *African Economic Research Consortium, Research paper 382*, https://aercafrica.org/wp-content/uploads/2020/07/Research-Paper-382.pdf. [11]

Direction générale du Trésor de La France (2024), *Mali: situation économique et financière*, https://www.tresor.economie.gouv.fr/Pays/ML/mali-situation-economique-et-financiere (accessed on 10 October 2024). [14]

Ebrill, L. P., Keen, M., & Perry, V. J. (2001), *4 Understanding the Revenue Performance of VATs". In The Modern VAT*, https://doi.org/10.5089/9781589060265.071.ch004. [29]

Gaspar, V. et al. (2019), *Fiscal Policy and Development : Human, Social, and Physical Investments for the SDGs*, https://www.imf.org/en/Publications/Staff-Discussion-Notes/Issues/2019/01/18/Fiscal-Policy-and-Development-Human-Social-and-Physical-Investments-for-the-SDGs-46444 (accessed on 20 September 2021). [22]

Gaspar, V., M. Mansour and C. Vellutini (2023), *Countries Can Tap Tax Potential to Finance Development Goals*, https://meetings.imf.org/en/IMF/Home/Blogs/Articles/2023/09/19/countries-can-tap-tax-potential-to-finance-development-goals. [45]

IEA (2023), *Fossil fuels database*, https://www.iea.org/data-and-statistics/data-product/fossil-fuel-subsidies-database (accessed on 18 October 2024). [41]

IEA (2023), *Tracking the impact of government support*, https://www.iea.org/topics/fossil-fuel-subsidies. [40]

IMF (2024), *Mauritius: Selected Issues. IMF Staff Country Reports, 2024(140), A001*, https://doi.org/10.5089/9798400276965.002.A001. [33]

IMF (2024), *World Economic Outlook Database, April 2024*, https://www.imf.org/en/Publications/WEO/weo-database/2024/April (accessed on 20 April 2023). [5]

IMF (2023), "Mali: 2023 Article IV Consultation-Press Release; Staff Report; Staff Supplement; and Statement by the Executive Director for Mali", *Country Report No. 2023/209*, https://www.imf.org/en/Publications/CR/Issues/2023/06/14/Mali-2023-Article-IV-Consultation-Press-Release-Staff-Report-Staff-Supplement-and-Statement-534760. [13]

IMF (2019), "L'équipe du FMI achève une mission de revue au Togo", *Communiqué de presse N° 19/473*, https://www.imf.org/fr/News/Articles/2019/12/18/pr19473-togo-imf-staff-completes-review-mission. [16]

IMF (2019), *Selected Issues. IMF Staff Country Reports, 2019(259)*, https://doi.org/10.5089/9781513509648.002.A002. [34]

IMF (2019), *World Economic Outlook - Frequently Asked Questions*, https://www.imf.org/external/pubs/ft/weo/faq.htm#q4d (accessed on 6 September 2019). [19]

Keen, M. (2013), *The anatomy of VAT, WP/13/111*, IMF, https://www.imf.org/en/Publications/WP/Issues/2016/12/31/The-Anatomy-of-the-VAT-40543. [28]

Marten, M. and K. van Dender (2019), "The use of revenues from carbon pricing", *OECD Taxation Working Papers*, No. 43, OECD Publishing, Paris, https://doi.org/10.1787/3cb265e4-en. [37]

Ministère des Finances de al République Démocratique du Congo (2023), *Blog : La Direction Générale des impôts a realisé des exploits en 2022*, https://dgi.gouv.cd/la-direction-generale-des-impots-dgi-a-realise-des-exploits-en-2022/ (accessed on 2024 October 10). [9]

Ministry of Tourism (2023), *Annual report on performance for financial year 2022/23*. [32]

OECD (2024), *Consumption Tax Trends 2024: VAT/GST and Excise, Core Design Features and Trends*, OECD Publishing, https://doi.org/10.1787/dcd4dd36-en. [26]

OECD (2024), *Global Revenue Statistics Database*, OECD, https://www.oecd.org/en/data/datasets/global-revenue-statistics-database.html. [21]

OECD (2024), *PINE database*, http://www.oecd.org/environment/tools-evaluation/environmentaltaxation.htm. [39]

OECD (2024), *Revenue Statistics 2024*, OECD Publishing, Paris, https://doi.org/10.1787/c87a3da5-en. [3]

OECD (2024), *Revenue Statistics in Asia and the Pacific 2024: Tax Revenue Buoyancy in Asia*, OECD Publishing, Paris, https://doi.org/10.1787/e4681bfa-en. [1]

OECD (2020), *OECD Tax Policy Reviews: Seychelles 2020*, OECD Tax Policy Reviews, OECD Publishing, Paris, https://doi.org/10.1787/cba38d19-en. [30]

OECD (2019), *Tax Morale: What Drives People and Businesses to Pay Tax?*, OECD Publishing, https://doi.org/10.1787/f3d8ea10-en. [18]

OECD (2014), *Development Co-operation Report 2014: Mobilising Resources for Sustainable Development*, OECD Publishing, Paris, https://doi.org/10.1787/dcr-2014-en. [17]

OECD (2005), *Glossary of statistical terms*, https://stats.oecd.org/glossary/detail.asp?ID=6437. [36]

OECD/ATAF/AUC (2024), *Revenue Statistics in Africa: Comparative tables*, OECD Publishing, Paris. [4]

OECD/ATAF/AUC (2021), *Revenue Statistics in Africa 2021: 1990-2019*, OECD Publishing, Paris, https://doi.org/10.1787/14e1edb1-en-fr. [15]

OECD/ATAF/AUC (2019), *Revenue Statistics in Africa 2019: 1990-2017*, OECD Publishing, Paris, https://doi.org/10.1787/5daa24c1-en-fr. [25]

OECD et al. (2024), *Revenue Statistics in Latin America and the Caribbean 2024*, OECD Publishing, Paris, https://doi.org/10.1787/33e226ae-en. [2]

OECD/ITF (2019), *Tax revenue implications from the decarbonisation of road transport: scenarios for Slovenia*, OECD, https://doi.org/10.1787/87b39a2f-en. [38]

SSA (2015), *Social Security Through the World: Africa*, SSA Publication Social Security Administration, Washington, DC, http://www.ssa.gov/policy/docs/progdesc/ssptw/2014-2015/africa/ssptw15africa.pdf. [23]

World Bank (2024), *Cabo Verde Economic Update - Blue Economy : The Latent Potential of Fisheries and Aquaculture in Cabo Verde*, https://documents.worldbank.org/en/publication/documents-reports/documentdetail/099060624085036575/p5004821bf54600a41b38315f0d172005a1 (accessed on 9 October 2024). [31]

World Bank (2024), *International Comparison Program*, https://www.worldbank.org/en/programs/icp. [20]

World Bank (2024), *World Bank Country and Lending Groups*, https://datahelpdesk.worldbank.org/knowledgebase/articles/906519. [44]

Notes

[1] The Africa average should be interpreted with caution as data on social security contributions are not available for Chad, the Democratic Republic of the Congo (prior to 2012), Equatorial Guinea (prior to 2013), Guinea, Madagascar (prior to 2011), Namibia (prior to 2009), the Republic of the Congo (prior to 2018), Sierra Leone (prior to 2018), Togo and Uganda and Zambia and are only partially available for Cameroon and Senegal. Social security contributions for Botswana, Lesotho and Malawi are deemed to be zero as they do not meet the criteria to be classified as social security contributions set out in the OECD classification of taxes in the OECD Interpretative Guide.

2 Data on social security contributions are not available for Chad, the Democratic Republic of the Congo (prior to 2012), Equatorial Guinea (prior to 2013), Guinea, Madagascar (prior to 2011), Namibia (prior to 2009), the Republic of the Congo (prior to 2018), Sierra Leone (prior to 2018), Togo, and Uganda and Zambia and are only partially available in Cameroon and Senegal. Social security contributions for Botswana, Lesotho and Malawi are deemed to be zero as they do not meet the criteria to be classified as social security contributions set out in the OECD classification of taxes in the OECD Interpretative Guide.

3 Based on participating countries' responses (e.g. Botswana, the Democratic Republic of the Congo).

4 'Cascading' refers to a situation where tax is levied on a product at every stage of its production and distribution without allowing for a deduction of the tax paid at previous stages. For example, a wholesaler cannot claim a VAT credit for the raw materials he bought for its own production because no VAT was paid on them initially.

5 The PINE database classifies environmentally related taxes under four bases:

- Energy: This covers taxation of energy products such as fossil fuels and electricity also including fuels for transportation such as petrol and diesel. All CO2-related taxes are in this category.
- Motor vehicles and transport services: This category includes imports or sales taxes on transport equipment, recurrent taxes on ownership, registration or road use of motor vehicles, and other transport-related taxes.

- Resources: This category includes taxes on mining and quarrying, forestry, wildlife and fisheries.
- Pollution: This category includes taxes on ozone-depleting substances, water and wastewater, waste management.

6 Burkina Faso and Rwanda are excluded as it has not been possible to identify environmentally related tax revenue data in 2022.

7 The composition of these RECs is as follows:

- East African Community (EAC): Burundi, DRC, Kenya, Rwanda, Somalia, South Sudan, Uganda and Tanzania. All EAC countries except Burundi, South Sudan and Tanzania are covered in this publication.
- Economic Community of Central African States (ECCAS): Angola, Burundi, Cameroon, the Central African Republic, Congo, Gabon, Equatorial Guinea, DRC, Rwanda, Sao Tome and Principe and Chad. All countries in ECCAS except Angola, Burundi, the Central African Republic and Sao Tome and Principe are covered in this publication.
- Economic Community of West African States (ECOWAS): Benin, Burkina Faso, Cabo Verde, Cote d'Ivoire, Gambia, Ghana, Guinea, Guinea-Bissau, Liberia, Mali, Niger, Nigeria, Senegal, Sierra Leone and Togo. All ECOWAS countries except Benin, Gambia, Guinea-Bissau and Liberia are covered in this publication.
- Southern African Development Community (SADC): Angola, Botswana, DRC, Eswatini, Lesotho, Madagascar, Malawi, Mauritius, Mozambique, Namibia, Seychelles, South Africa, Tanzania, Zambia and Zimbabwe. All countries in SADC except Angola, Tanzania and Zimbabwe are covered in this publication.
- Arab Maghreb Union (AMU): Algeria, Libya, Mauritania, Morocco and Tunisia. Algeria and Libya are not covered in this publication.

8 Sub-national tax revenues for Nigeria include state revenues but exclude local government revenues.

2 Non-tax revenue trends, 2013-22

Chapter 2 discusses the latest trends in non-tax revenues as well as the evolution of non-tax revenues over the past decade across 35 African countries. The chapter examines the level and structure of non-tax revenues for individual countries and on average across the continent. It includes in-depth analysis of revenues from extractive industries.

Introduction

A complete picture of public finances requires statistics that go beyond taxation, especially for many African countries that obtain substantial revenues in the form of grants or royalties from oil and minerals. *Revenue Statistics in Africa* collects statistics on both tax and non-tax revenues, non-tax revenues being government revenues that do not meet the OECD definition of taxation.[1] Although there are some important methodological differences between tax and non-tax revenues, they need to be included in any accounting of a country's total financial resources.[2] This chapter provides cross-country comparisons of non-tax revenues for the countries in this publication.[3]

The main categories of non-tax revenues reported here are:[4]

- grants from foreign governments or international organisations (budget aid, food aid, capital transfers, current transfers, project grants, programme grants, international debt relief, etc.);
- rents and royalties (such as oil or mining royalties);
- other property income (interest, dividends and other returns on government investment);
- sales of goods and services (which include some administrative fees);
- fines and penalties (including fines and penalties due to tax violations);
- miscellaneous and unidentified revenues (non-tax revenues that cannot be classified according to the other categories).

Non-tax revenues as a percentage of GDP

Non-tax revenues in Africa in 2022 amounted to 6.2% of GDP on average among the 35 countries reporting this data for this edition of *Revenue Statistics in Africa*.[5] On average, the amount of non-tax revenues collected in each country was 52% of the amount of tax revenues. Non-tax revenues ranged from 0.7% of GDP in South Africa to 23.7% of GDP in the Republic of the Congo. Botswana, Lesotho, Equatorial Guinea, the Republic of the Congo and Somalia were the only countries for which non-tax revenues were higher than tax revenues in 2022 (Figure 2.1).

Botswana, Lesotho, Eswatini and Namibia are net recipients of funds from the Southern African Customs Union (SACU) Common Revenue Pool (see Box 2.1), which leads to non-tax revenues being higher and tax revenues being lower than otherwise would be the case. Equatorial Guinea and the Republic of the Congo, meanwhile, collect twice as much extractive-related revenues as a percentage of GDP than any other country in the report. Somalia has relied mostly on grants to fund its government expenditures, as it has built its fiscal capacity since the end of a civil war in 2012 and has faced many economic challenges (Khan and Khan, 2022[1]). As a result, its non-tax revenues were twice as high as its tax revenues at 5.2% of GDP (mostly grants) in 2022.

Figure 2.1. Total tax and non-tax revenues by country, 2022

Percentage of GDP

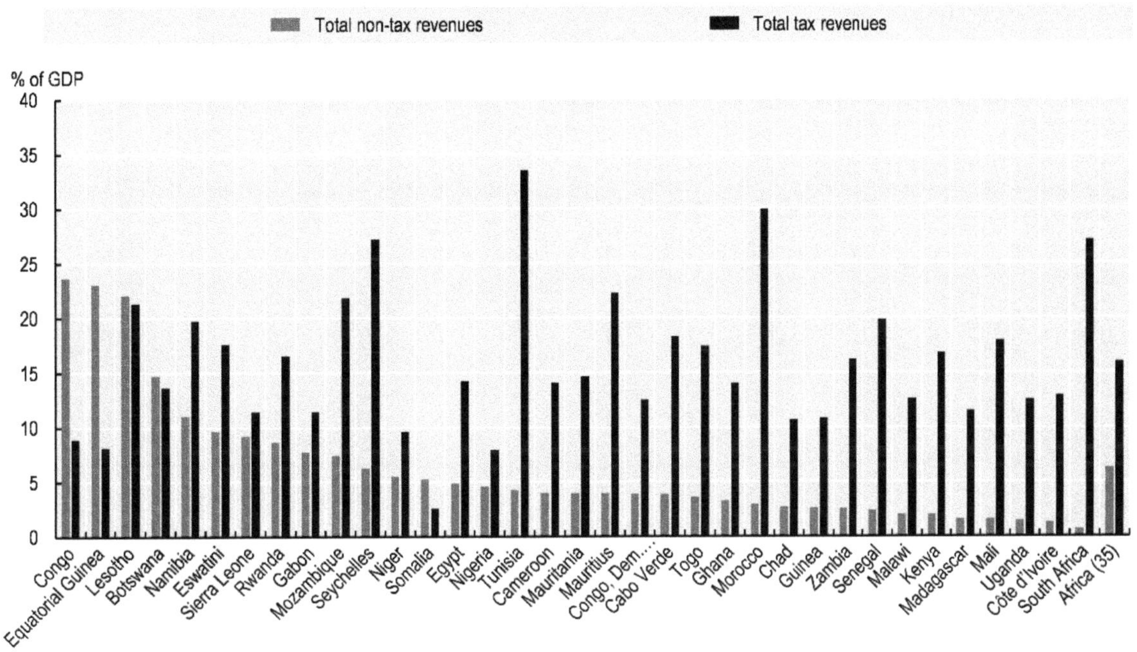

Note: Non-tax revenue includes sub-national non-tax government revenues for Eswatini, Kenya, Mauritius, Morocco, Nigeria, and Somalia, the only countries for which such revenues are reported. In 2022, these represented, respectively, 1%, 14%, 4%, 42%, 6% and 4% of all non-tax revenue collected for each country. South Africa reported some local and regional taxes, but no local and regional non-tax revenues. The tax-to-GDP ratios and non-tax-to-GDP ratios need to be interpreted with caution for some countries due to incomplete data. Burkina Faso provided data on tax revenues in 2024 but data on non-tax revenues were not available for this edition. See the country tables in Chapters 5 and 6 for further information. "Africa (35)" refers to the average for the 35 African countries reporting non-tax revenues in this report.

Source: Table 4.1 in Chapter 4 and Table 6.1 in Chapter 6 and (OECD/ATAF/AUC, 2024[2]), "Revenue Statistics in Africa: Comparative tables", http://data-explorer.oecd.org/s/dx.

StatLink https://stat.link/a1ryo5

Non-tax revenues in 2022 were 0.4 percentage points (p.p.) higher as a share of GDP than in 2021 (Figure 2.2). This increase was driven by an increase of 0.4 p.p. in revenues from rents and royalties and from other property income, though it was partially offset by a decline in "other revenues" (mostly SACU revenues in Botswana, Lesotho, Eswatini and Namibia). Combined with the increase of 0.5 p.p. in tax revenues, this equated to a 0.8 p.p. increase in public revenues (tax and non-tax) on average across the 35 countries in 2022.

The uptick in non-tax revenues for the Africa average between 2021 and 2022 followed five years in which non-tax revenues remained around 5.8% of GDP. Before that, the average ratio of non-tax revenues to GDP declined from a high of 7.3% of GDP in 2013 to a low of 5.1% in 2016.

Over the period 2013-22, non-tax revenues declined by 1.1 p.p., mostly due to declines of 0.5 p.p. in grant revenues and of 0.8 p.p. in other non-tax revenues (mostly SACU revenues). This decrease in non-tax revenues offset the increase in tax revenues over this period: the average sum of tax and non-tax revenues over this period declined by 0.1 p.p., despite African countries' progress in tax revenue mobilisation.

Figure 2.2. Africa average non-tax revenues, 2013-22

Percentage of GDP

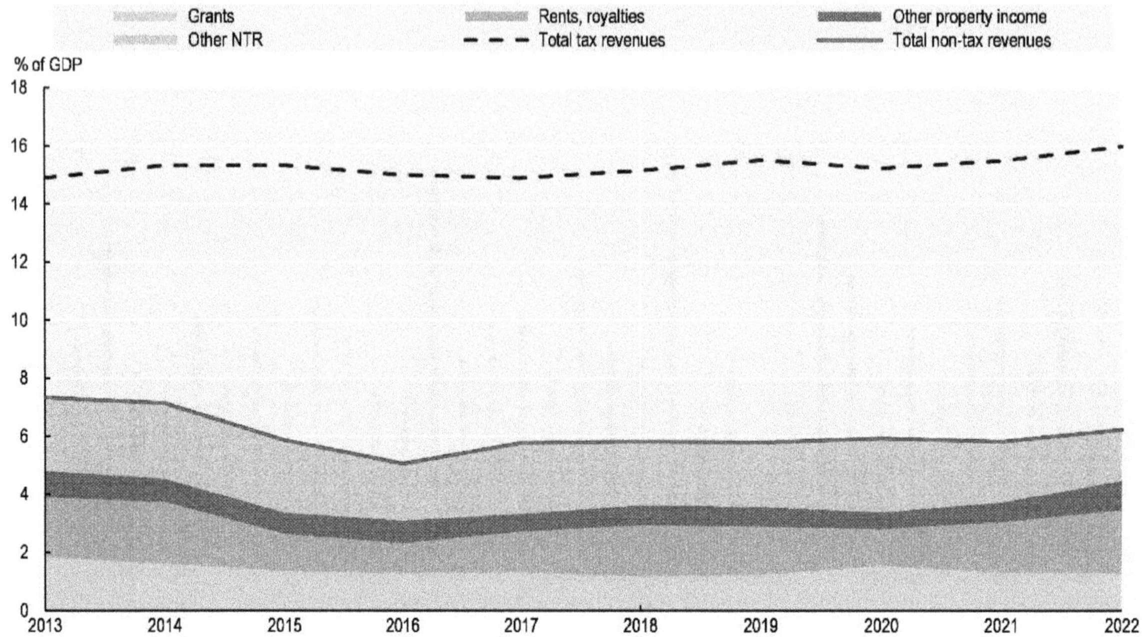

Note: Africa average is calculated over 35 African countries excluding Burkina Faso, for which data on tax revenues was available, but not non-tax revenues. "Other NTR" in this figure includes all non-tax revenues aside from grants and property income. This includes sales of goods and services, fines and penalties, and miscellaneous and unidentified revenues (including SACU revenues).
Source: Authors' calculations based on data from (OECD/ATAF/AUC, 2024[2]), "Revenue Statistics in Africa: Comparative tables", http://data-explorer.oecd.org/s/dx.

StatLink https://stat.link/fds95v

Country groupings by main source of non-tax revenues

Figure 2.3 shows the contribution of each major sub-category of non-tax revenues to total non-tax revenues for each country in 2022. In this figure, “other NTR” can include sales of goods and services, fines and penalties, or miscellaneous and unidentified revenues, but mostly consists of SACU revenues. In Panel A, revenues are shown as a percentage of GDP while in Panel B, they are shown as a percentage of total non-tax revenues. Four distinct groups are apparent in the data:

- Nine countries received a majority of their non-tax revenues in the form of grants. On average, these countries received grant revenue equivalent to 3.5% of GDP in 2022.
- Eight countries received most of their non-tax revenues from rents and royalties. For all these countries aside from Zambia and South Africa, the two countries with the lowest non-tax revenues as a percentage of GDP, oil and gas royalties provided the majority of non-tax revenues. On average, rents and royalties for these countries were equivalent to 5.4% of GDP.
- Botswana, Eswatini, Lesotho and Namibia, the four countries neighbouring South Africa that belong to SACU, received substantial non-tax revenues via transfers from the SACU Common Revenue Pool. On average, these countries collected non-tax revenues outside of grants and rents and royalties equivalent to 11.4% of GDP.
- For the remaining 14 countries, neither grants nor rents and royalties constituted a majority of non-tax revenues. Grants were the largest source of non-tax revenues for Côte d’Ivoire, Senegal and the Democratic Republic of the Congo but were less than 50% of total non-tax revenues. Similarly, rents and royalties were the largest source of non-tax revenues for Guinea and Tunisia but were less than half of non-tax revenues. For the other countries, the main sources of non-tax revenues included: interest and dividends for Botswana, Equatorial Guinea, Mali, and Seychelles; other property income aside from rents, royalties, interest and dividends for Mauritius; fees for goods and services for Cabo Verde, Egypt, Ghana, and Morocco; and miscellaneous and unallocated revenues for Kenya.

Figure 2.3. Structure of non-tax revenues by African country, 2022

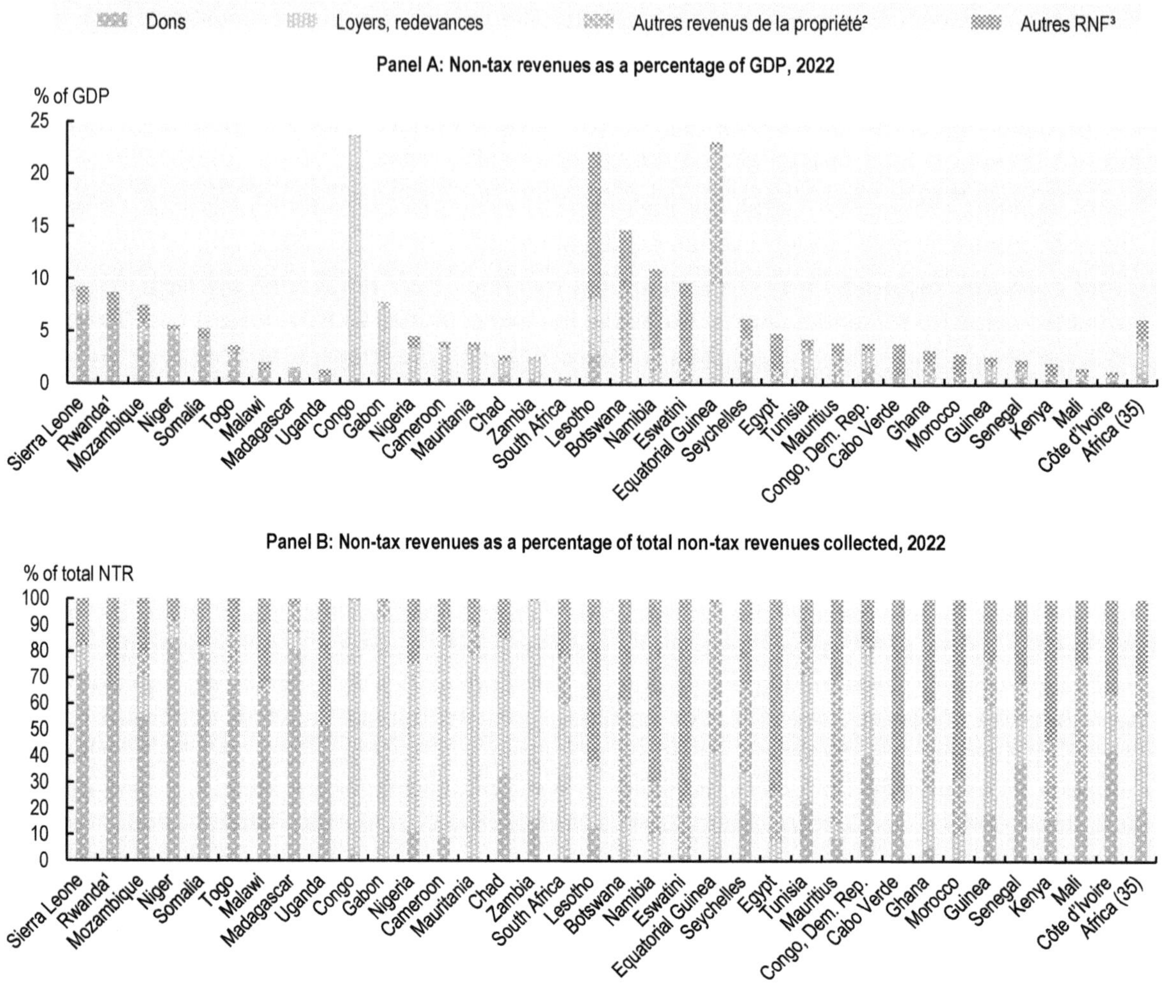

Note: Data include sub-national government non-tax revenues for Eswatini, Kenya, Mauritius, Morocco and Nigeria. "Africa (35)" refers to the average for the 35 African countries reporting non-tax revenues in this report. NTR = "non-tax revenues".

1. For Rwanda, non-tax revenues aside from grants were not disaggregated in the data and are therefore classified as miscellaneous and unidentified revenues.

2. Interest, dividends, and other property income aside from rents and royalties.

3. All other non-tax revenues not elsewhere specified, including sales of goods and services, fines, penalties and forfeits, SACU revenues, and unidentified revenues.

See the country tables in Chapters 5 and 6 for further information.

Source: Table 6.2 in Chapter 6 and (OECD/ATAF/AUC, 2024[2]), "Revenue Statistics in Africa: Comparative tables", http://data-explorer.oecd.org/s/dx.

StatLink https://stat.link/8abi0l

Price and volume changes between 2019 and 2022

The post-COVID period has been characterised by major disruptions in price levels in Africa. These price changes had different impacts on different tax and revenue bases. As Figure 2.4 shows, for African countries reporting non-tax revenues in this publication, double-digit increases in both average non-tax revenues and average GDP occurred in 2022. Nominal non-tax revenues increased by 27.4%

between 2021 and 2022 on average but much of this increase was driven by accelerating inflation rather than real growth in non-tax revenues. Consumer price inflation increased between 2021 and 2022, from 5.6% to 9.2%, while the GDP deflator, a measure of the degree to which price changes drive increases in nominal GDP, also rose, from 7.1% in 2021 to 8.3% in 2022.

The base for tax revenues is generally contained within the national economy, which means that in the absence of changes in tax policy or administration, and in the case of a broad-based system of taxation, changes in nominal tax revenues would generally be correlated with changes in nominal GDP. In the case of non-tax revenues as a percentage of GDP, however, the numerator and the denominator may be affected by different sets of prices. Resource revenues, for example, are affected by a combination of internationally determined commodity prices and exchange rates, as will be explained in the section on revenues from the extractive sector at the end of this chapter.

Figure 2.4. Africa average percentage change in nominal GDP and price levels, 2019-2022

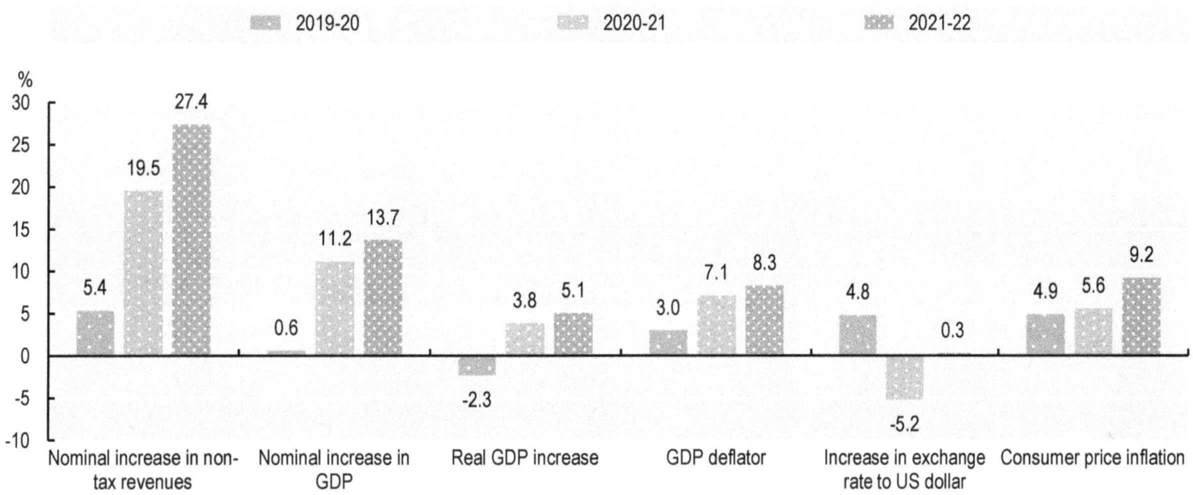

Note: Africa average is calculated over 35 African countries excluding Burkina Faso, for which data on tax revenues was available, but not non-tax revenues. All figures are year-over-year percentage changes in the unweighted average between 2021 and 2022 after adjustments were made to the annual statistics to align them to the fiscal year according to which tax and non-tax revenues were reported.
Source: Authors' calculations based on data from (OECD/ATAF/AUC, 2024[2]), *"Revenue Statistics in Africa: Comparative tables"*, http://data-explorer.oecd.org/s/dx, from the April 2024 edition of the *World Economic Outlook* (IMF, 2024[3]) and from the IMF *International Financial Statistics* (IFS) dataset (IMF, 2023[4]).

StatLink https://stat.link/pmbg9k

Grants, meanwhile, are determined by foreign economies and will therefore be sensitive to both exchange rates and inflation in the receiver country. The amount of local currency for a given amount of grants denominated in USD will change from year to year, while at the same time, the purchasing power of the local currency will also change.

Between 2019 and 2020, the increase in the average exchange rate (+4.8%) offset the average rate of inflation in African countries (+4.9%). Grants denominated in USD therefore had roughly the same value in local economies in 2020 as they did in 2019. Between 2021 and 2022, on the other hand, USD exchange rates declined on average for African countries, which meant that the value of grants denominated in USD was eroded both by inflation and by declining USD exchange rates. The sensitivity of grants to exchange rate fluctuations highlights the vulnerability of some African economies to external financial support and underscores the need for enhanced domestic revenue mobilisation in those countries.

Changes in non-tax revenues by category, 2021-22

This section analyses changes in non-tax revenues between 2021 and 2022 by category. Certain countries saw unusually large changes in non-tax revenues in 2022 (Figure 2.5): five countries recorded the largest increase in non-tax revenues as a share of GDP in the last ten years, while five countries recorded the largest decrease in the same indicator. Non-tax revenues increased as a share of GDP by 8.7 p.p. and 13.3 p.p. in the Republic of the Congo and Equatorial Guinea, respectively, due to increases in oil and gas revenues that drove up rents and royalties and interest and dividends. The largest decrease occurred in Lesotho, which saw a drop of 9.3 p.p. due to a fall in revenue from the SACU Common Revenue Pool.

Figure 2.5. Changes in non-tax revenues by country and revenue type, 2021-22

Percentage of GDP

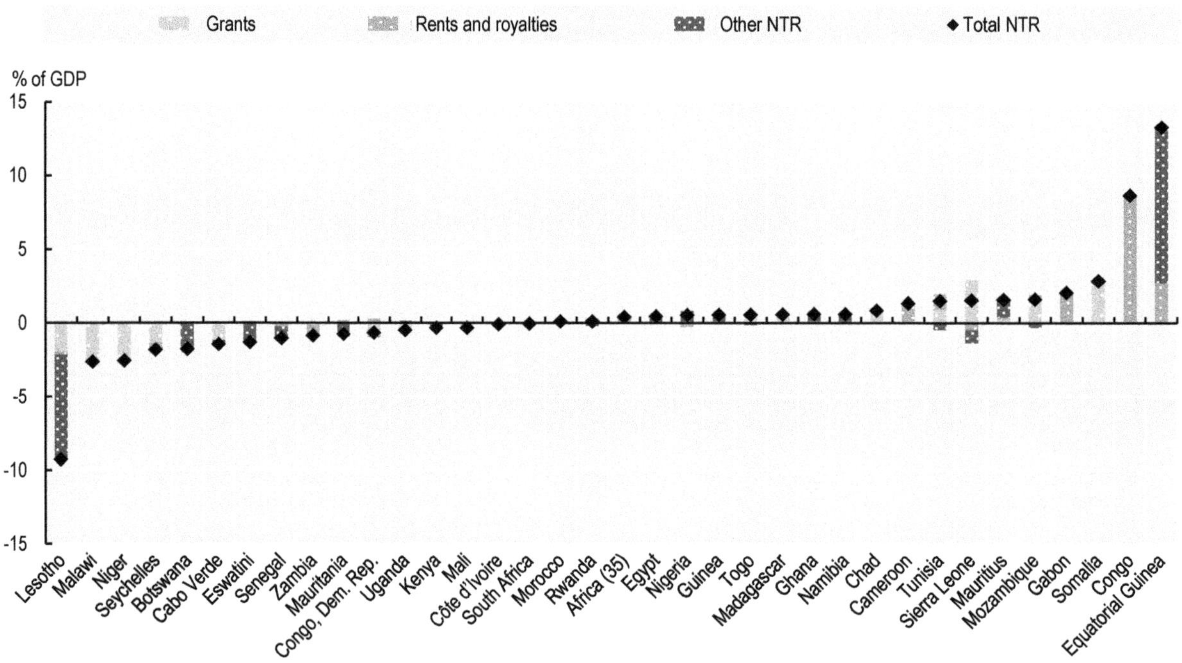

Note: The black diamonds correspond to the sum of the percentage point changes in grants, rents and royalties and other non-tax revenues between 2021 and 2022. "Africa (35)" refers to the average for the 35 African countries reporting non-tax revenues in this report. NTR = "non-tax revenues".

Source: Authors' calculations based on data from (OECD/ATAF/AUC, 2024[2]), *"Revenue Statistics in Africa: Comparative tables"*, http://data-explorer.oecd.org/s/dx.

StatLink https://stat.link/7lk1p6

Between 2021 and 2022, grant revenues as a percentage of GDP were unchanged on average across the 35 countries. However, changes in grant revenues were the largest driver of change in non-tax revenues for 14 countries, although increases in some countries offset decreases in others. Grants increased in seven of these countries and declined in the other seven. The same was also true of non-tax revenues aside from grants or rents and royalties. The average change in other non-tax revenues as a percentage of GDP was zero, but it was still the largest driver of change in non-tax revenues for 15 countries; seven countries observed increases in this indicator and eight saw decreases.

Grants

Some countries in *Revenue Statistics in Africa* receive substantial grant revenues while for others grants are negligible. On average, grant revenues for the 35 African countries in this publication amounted to 1.3% of GDP in 2022. Sixteen countries received grant revenues amounting to less than 0.5% of GDP in 2022, the same number as in 2021 (Figure 2.6). Most countries receiving grants amounting to less than 0.5% of GDP in 2022 are middle-income according to the World Bank's classification based on gross national income (GNI) per capita (World Bank, 2024[5]), with the exceptions of Guinea and Mali, which are low-income countries. Most of the countries receiving grants equivalent to more than 1% of GDP in 2022 were low income, with the exception of Lesotho (lower middle-income) and the Seychelles (high income).

Figure 2.6. Grants by country, 2021 and 2022

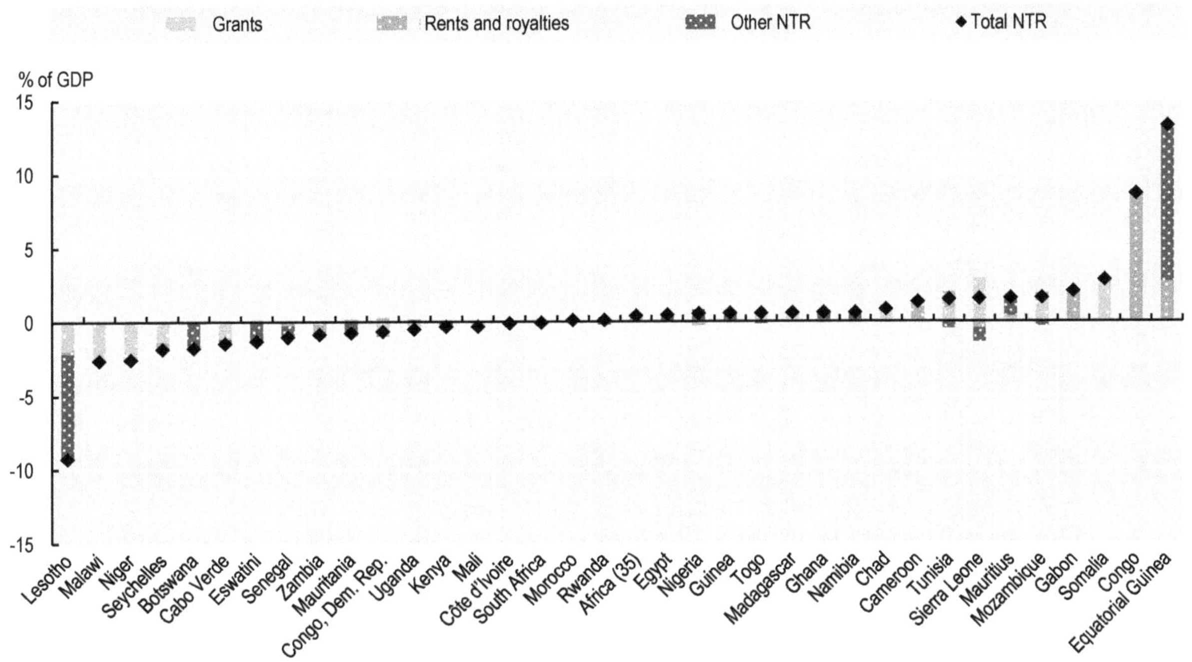

Source: Tables 6.2 and 6.3 in Chapter 6 and (OECD/ATAF/AUC, 2024[2]), "Revenue Statistics in Africa: Comparative tables", http://data-explorer.oecd.org/s/dx. "Africa (35)" refers to the average for the 35 African countries reporting non-tax revenues in this report.

StatLink https://stat.link/ghmylf

Figure 2.7 presents grants as a percentage of GDP received by countries and their GNI per capita. The empty upper right-hand quadrant indicates that higher-income African countries receive proportionately lower grant revenues. However, many countries occupy the bottom left quadrant, indicating that they receive relatively low levels of grant income despite having lower incomes. For example, while Guinea, Lesotho and Zambia all had GNI per capita around 1 200 US dollars in 2022, Lesotho's grants as a percentage of GDP were 2.9%, over six times higher than the level in Guinea and Zambia.

Grant revenues reported by national authorities do not necessarily represent the full breadth of foreign aid received by countries. Countries may receive aid in the form of concessional loans or in a way that is not directed towards the central government (e.g., support to non-governmental organisations, scholarships, in-donor refugee costs). Loans are not considered revenue and are therefore not included among the tax and non-tax revenues reported here.

Figure 2.7. Grants as a percentage of GDP and GNI per capita by country, 2022

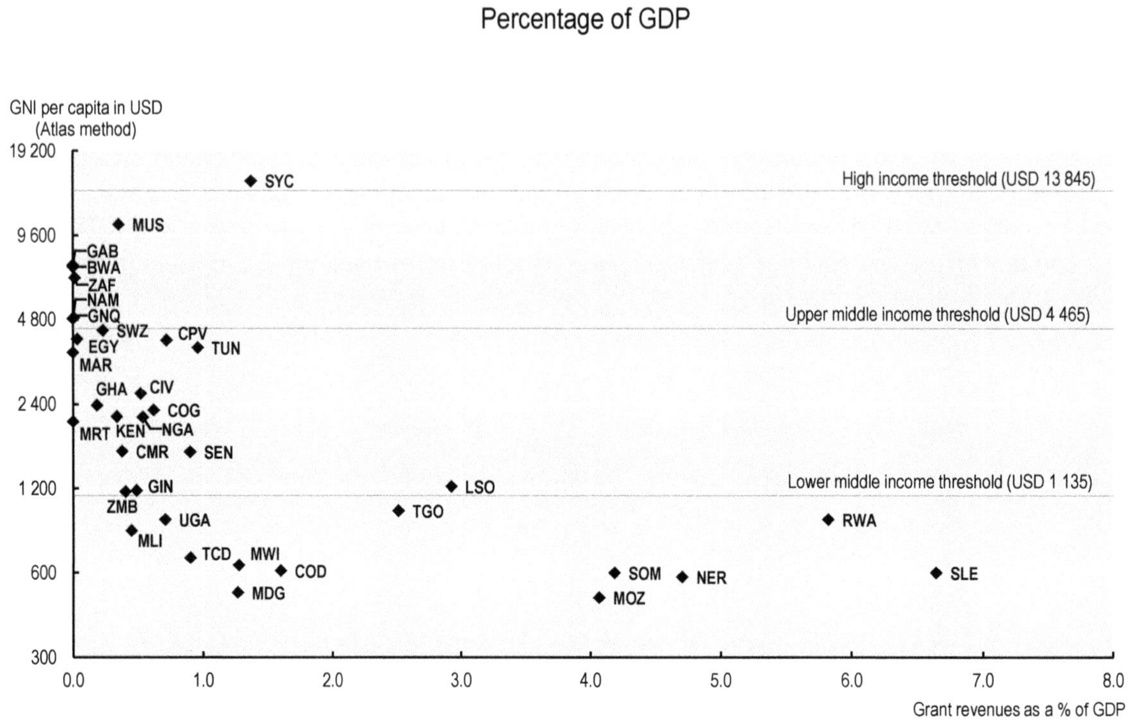

Note: GNI figures are converted to USD using the World Bank Atlas Method (World Bank, 2024[6]). BWA = "Botswana"; CIV = "Côte d'Ivoire"; CMR = "Cameroon"; COD = "Congo, Dem. Rep."; COG = "Congo"; CPV = "Cabo Verde"; EGY = "Egypt"; GAB = "Gabon"; GHA = "Ghana"; GIN = "Guinea"; GNQ = "Equatorial Guinea"; KEN = "Kenya"; LSO = "Lesotho"; MAR = "Morocco"; MDG = "Madagascar"; MLI = "Mali"; MOZ = "Mozambique"; MRT = "Mauritania"; MUS = "Mauritius"; MWI = "Malawi"; NAM = "Namibia"; NER = "Niger"; NGA = "Nigeria"; RWA = "Rwanda"; SEN = "Senegal"; SLE = "Sierra Leone"; SOM = "Somalia"; SWZ = "Eswatini"; SYC = "Seychelles"; TCD = "Chad"; TGO = "Togo"; TUN = "Tunisia"; UGA = "Uganda"; ZAF = "South Africa"; ZMB = "Zambia".

Source: Table 6.2 in Chapter 6, and World Bank *World Development Indicators* (database) (World Bank, 2024[7]) and (OECD/ATAF/AUC, 2024[2]), "*Revenue Statistics in Africa: Comparative tables*", http://data-explorer.oecd.org/s/dx.

StatLink https://stat.link/4f0krx

This difference can be illustrated by looking at statistics on foreign aid to African countries as reported by donor countries. Figure 2.8 shows that Official Development Assistance (ODA) payments made to African countries greatly exceed the amount paid directly to African governments, due to concessional loans or grants that are not directly received by African governments. Although the countries receiving the most net ODA tend to receive the most grant revenues, the relationship is not linear. Sierra Leone and Malawi both receive net ODA between 11% and 13% of GDP, while the level of grants as a percentage of GDP in Sierra Leone was five times higher than that of Malawi.

Grant revenues and foreign aid are overlapping concepts. It may be difficult however to align aid statistics as reported by donor countries with the grant revenues reported by recipient countries due to data, methodological and conceptual issues.

- Grant revenues have some overlap with ODA, as defined by the OECD Development Assistance Committee (DAC).[6] Grants covered by this publication focus on revenues received by countries from foreign governments and international organisations. ODA is a measure of donor countries' efforts to support development in low- and middle-income countries. ODA not only covers flows captured under "grants" in this publication (budget aid, food aid, capital transfers, current transfers, project grants, programme grants, international debt relief, etc.), but also encompasses concessional loans, in-kind technical assistance, in-donor administrative costs and in-donor refugee costs, as well as other activities that do not generate a (net) revenue flow to the country. The volume of ODA provided by a donor to a given country will thus be different from – and often higher than – the volume of grants reported by that country in *Revenue Statistics*.

- Statistics collected by the DAC on ODA flows to African countries include public flows from all members of the DAC and some countries outside the DAC, as well as multilateral organisations such as the World Bank, the IMF and the UN. Statistics on development co-operation provided by some large non-OECD economies, such as Brazil, the People's Republic of China, India and Indonesia, are not included (OECD, 2023[8]).

Countries relying on grant revenues often face sudden drops in grants from one year to the next. Eight countries in this publication reported a single-year drop in grant revenues of at least 2% of GDP in at least one year between 2012 and 2022.

Figure 2.8. Grants and net official development assistance received by country, 2022

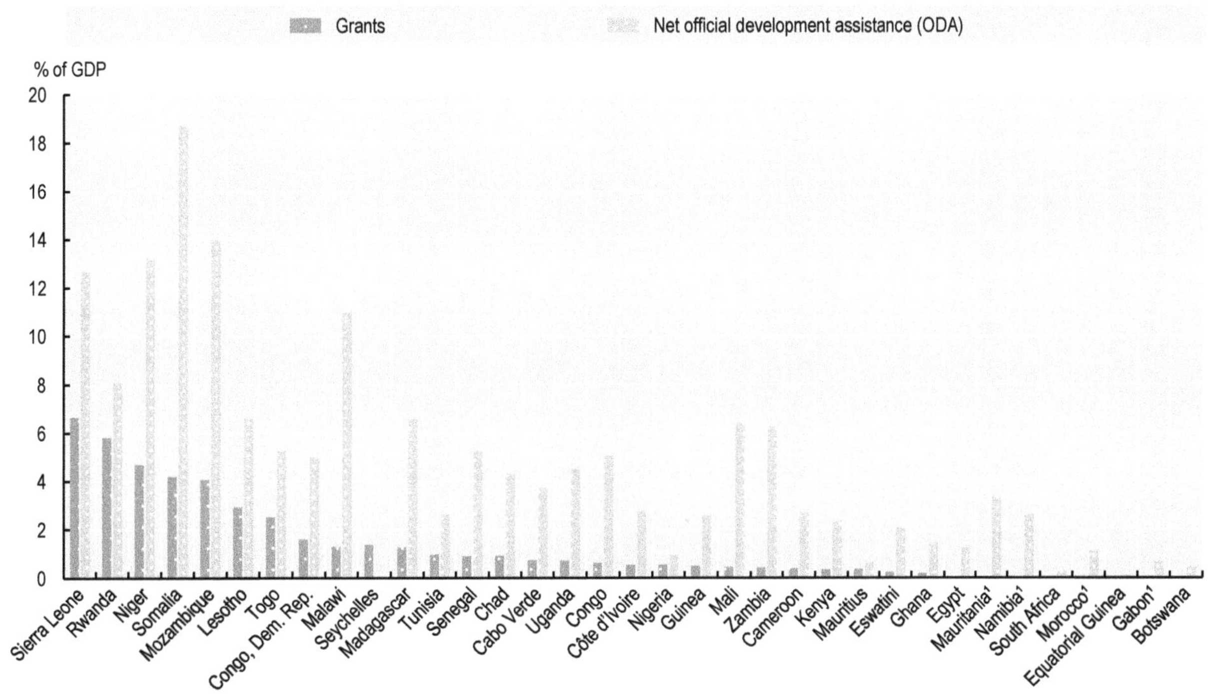

Note: Figures for net ODA include donations from the 32 member countries of the OECD Development Assistance Committee (DAC), 20 non-DAC economies, as well as multilateral institutions, and private donations. Some major donor countries, such as Brazil, the People's Republic of China, India, Indonesia, and Russia and are not yet accounted for in these data.
1. No grant revenues were reported for Gabon, Morocco, Mauritania and Namibia in 2022.
Source: Table 6.2 in Chapter 6 and OECD Development Assistance Committee (OECD-DAC, 2024[9]) for the ODA data and (OECD/ATAF/AUC, 2024[2]), "*Revenue Statistics in Africa: Comparative tables*", http://data-explorer.oecd.org/s/dx.

StatLink https://stat.link/n38d5v

Property income

Property income, or the revenues countries obtain through their status as owner of property, amounted to 3.2% of GDP for African countries on average in 2022 (Figure 2.9). This was an increase of 0.8 p.p. from 2021. Three-quarters of this increase, or 0.6 p.p., can be attributed to two countries: Equatorial

Guinea, which saw an increase of 13.5 p.p., and the Republic of the Congo, which saw an increase of 8.6 p.p. In 2022, Equatorial Guinea began collecting gas monetisation revenues (Lupachik, 2023[10]). This revenue, classified as interest and dividends, amounted to 567 billion CFA francs (USD 909 million) or 7.7% of GDP in 2022, which was close to the total tax revenue Equatorial Guinea collected that year.

Figure 2.9. Rents and royalties and other property income by country, 2021 and 2022

Percentage of GDP

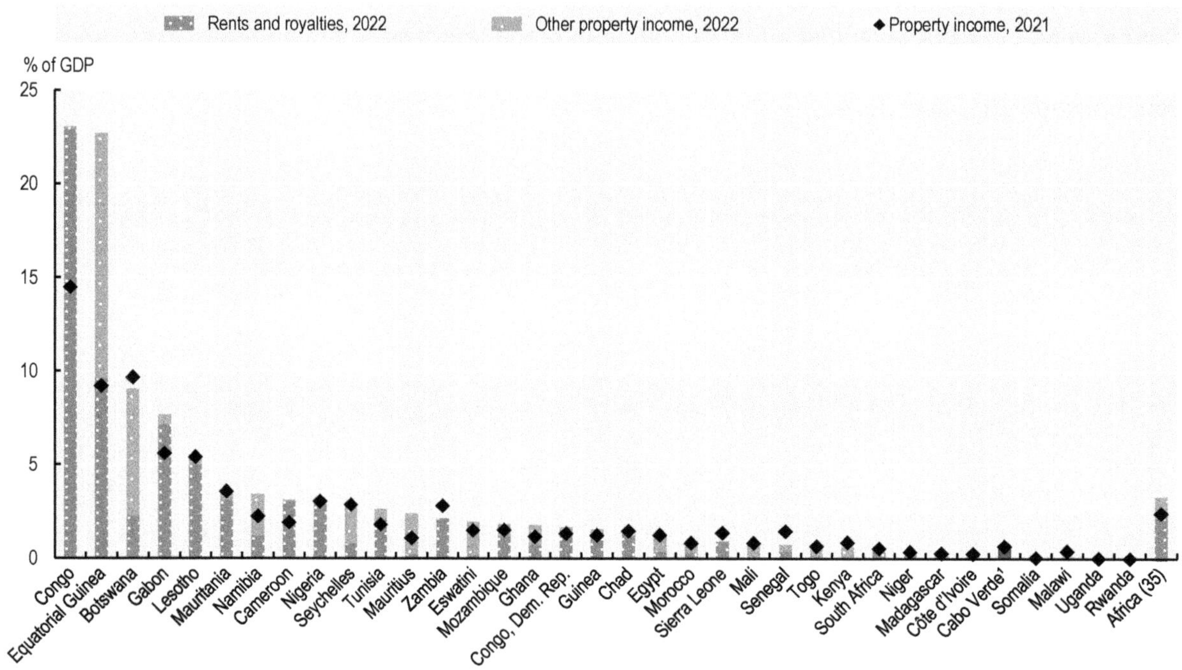

Note: Burkina Faso and Rwanda are excluded as the data are not available. "Africa (35)" refers to the average for the 35 African countries reporting non-tax revenues in this report.

1. Cabo Verde property income is not disaggregated.

Source: Authors' calculations based on Tables 6.5-6.39 and Table 4.17 and (OECD/ATAF/AUC, 2024[2]), "*Revenue Statistics in Africa: Comparative tables*", "*Revenue Statistics in Africa: Comparative tables*", http://data-explorer.oecd.org/s/dx.

StatLink https://stat.link/2zk3wj

Rents and royalties are revenues generated from property the government owns, usually by prospecting and extracting non-renewable resources from government land or from harvesting government-owned farms and forests. Interest and dividends are returns on government-owned investments in corporations. Most property income for African countries came in the form of rents and royalties in 2022, which were on average 59% of all property income among the 33 countries reporting. For countries collecting property income equivalent to at least 1% of GDP, this was 64%.

Most property income in African countries comes from resource extraction. Eighty percent of the total rents and royalties collected by African countries, expressed in US dollars, came from rents on extractive industries, and 38% of interest and dividends came from government stakes in corporations involved in resource extraction. These revenues will be discussed in more detail in the section on revenues from extractive industries.

Rents and royalties from sources other than resource extraction in 2022 included water royalties in Lesotho, which amounted to 3.6% of GDP, royalties from the Suez Canal in Egypt (USD 348 million, or 0.07% of GDP) and telecom licences in Guinea, Mauritania and Somalia. Most interest and dividends come from various kinds of corporations, including public and private companies or public monopolies, or they are unspecified investment income collected by other institutions, such as the interest and dividends collected by social security funds in the Seychelles. Central bank investment income is also reported here, such as the revenue collected by the Bank of Botswana and central bank profits in Tunisia.

Other non-tax revenues

Certain countries generate substantial non-tax revenues from the normal operations of government. These can be divided into sales of goods and services, fines and penalties, and miscellaneous and unidentified non-tax revenues. The challenges in compiling non-tax revenues in general are often encountered with these kinds of revenues, since they are typically not collected by tax administrations and are often not defined by legislation. They might not even be captured by government budgets. This can therefore lead to underestimates of revenues for institutions and governments that have less taxing authority and are therefore more reliant on non-tax revenues, such as, for example, municipal governments.

For all these categories of revenues, there can be arguments about the degree to which they are unrequited or compulsory, and therefore whether they are more properly classified as taxes. The question of which administrative fees are taxes and which are not is discussed in Annexes A and B. Fines and penalties on tax violations are sometimes reported as part of tax revenues, which could lead to an under-reporting of total revenues for fines and penalties. Finally, miscellaneous and unidentified revenues are by definition revenues for which little information is available that can be used in order to determine whether or not these constitute taxes or non-tax revenues.

Sales of goods and services and administrative fees

Governments produce goods and services both as a market- and as a non-market participant. As a market participant, governments sometimes provide goods and services that can also be obtained from private companies (such as food or transportation). At the same time, they also provide services in the course of administering programmes and executing laws that are unique to the function of government. Fees charged for these non-market services are generally classified as administrative fees.

Administrative fees are often difficult to classify since they occupy a grey area between payments for services (which are non-tax revenues) and compulsory unrequited payments collected during government operations (which are taxes).[7] Court fees and fees for driver's licences, passports, patent registrations and marriage certificates tend to be classified as non-tax revenues. When administrative fees are classified as taxes, they are typically assigned to one of the following categories:

- 4400 Taxes on financial and capital transactions (for example, taxes on sales of land);
- 5200 Taxes on use of goods and performing activities (for example hunting licences, vehicle registrations);
- 6000 Other taxes (for example, sales of fiscal stamps, where stamps are used to pay for taxes and administrative fees).

Seven countries generated non-tax revenues from sales of goods and services and administrative fees equivalent to at least 1% of GDP in 2022 (Figure 2.10): Egypt (2.3% of GDP), Cabo Verde (2.2%), the Seychelles (1.8%), Mozambique (1.4%), Ghana (1.3%), Morocco (1.1%) and Sierra Leone (1.1%).

Figure 2.10. Sales of goods and services and administrative fees, 2022

Percentage of GDP

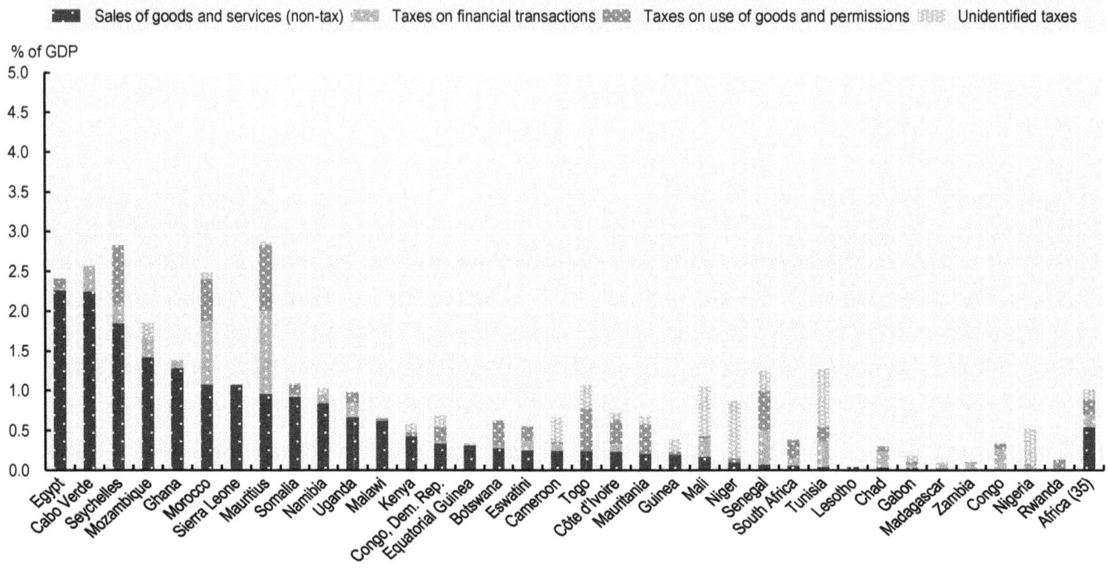

Note: Figures reported here include sub-national tax revenues for Mauritius, Morocco, Nigeria, Somalia, and South Africa and sub-national non-tax revenues for Eswatini, Kenya, Mauritius, Morocco, and Somalia, the only countries for which such revenues were reported for 2022. "Africa (35)" refers to the average for the 35 African countries reporting non-tax revenues in this report.

Source: Authors' calculations based on Tables 5.1-5.36 and 6.5-6.39 and Table 4.17 and (OECD/ATAF/AUC, 2024[2]), "*Revenue Statistics in Africa: Comparative tables*", http://data-explorer.oecd.org/s/dx.

StatLink https://stat.link/j2hi9q

The composition of revenues from sales of goods and services and administrative fees varied by country. In Cabo Verde, 97% of revenues listed under sales of goods and services were fees. In Ghana, most of these revenues were sub-national revenues reported as either "Municipalities, Departments and Agencies", or "Metropolitan, Municipal and District Assemblies". In Morocco, 48% of revenue from government sales of goods and services were collected at the local level.

Miscellaneous or unidentified revenue

Some notable categories of non-tax revenue do not fit within any of the categories listed above, including:

- capital transfers not included elsewhere;
- voluntary donations to government agencies from individuals or private corporations (not including donations from international organisations, which are classified as grants);
- private payments to government made as a result of major court settlements or insurance claims (such as the EUR 100 million payment Arcelor Mittal agreed to pay to the government of Senegal after a court case following the cancelation of an iron mine (RFI, 2014[11]));
- payments covering different categories in the classification where a breakdown is not available;
- payments whose proper classification is unknown due to a lack of data. Rwanda did not disaggregate non-tax revenue outside of grants, so these were included in this category;
- SACU revenues to Botswana, Eswatini, Lesotho and Namibia (see Box 2.1).

Box 2.1. SACU revenues

The Southern African Customs Union (SACU) incorporates Botswana, Eswatini, Lesotho, Namibia and South Africa. Its vision is "an economic community with equitable and sustainable development, dedicated to the welfare of its people for a common future".

Headquartered in Windhoek, Namibia, SACU is the oldest customs union in the world, having been founded in 1899 between the British colony of Cape of Good Hope and the Orange Free State Boer Republic. Subsequent agreements in 1910 and 1969 included Botswana, Eswatini and Lesotho. Following Namibia's independence in 1990 and the end of apartheid in South Africa in 1994, new negotiations led to the current SACU agreement, which was signed in 2002.

The SACU agreement provides for free movement of SACU manufactured products within the union, without application of tariffs or duties. It also provides for common external tariffs and for the payment of customs and excise duties into a common pool to be shared between the SACU countries under the revenue-sharing formula set out in the Annex to the agreement. SACU is the only one of the five customs unions in Africa for which revenues from such arrangements were reported in *Revenue Statistics in Africa*[1].

The revenue-sharing agreement includes three components:

- A customs component, which divides the gross amount of customs duties according to the value of goods each country imports from other SACU countries in a given year (as a percentage of intra-SACU imports).
- An excise component, which divides the gross amount of excise duties according to each country's GDP as a percentage of SACU's combined GDP.
- A development component, which is funded from 15% of the excise component and is weighted towards less developed SACU countries using a formula based on GDP per capita.

In this publication, revenue from excises, tariffs and customs duties are included as tax revenues in the SACU country that collected the revenue. They are included under headings 5121 (Excises) and 5123 (Customs and import duties) in the tax revenue tables. Revenues received from the SACU Common Revenue Pool are included as miscellaneous revenue in the non-tax revenue tables, as seen in Table 6.13 for Eswatini. In the case of South Africa, where payments exceed the revenue share received from the Pool, the payments net of the share received are recorded as a memorandum item in the non-tax revenue table (Table 6.23).

1: Two of the eight regional economic communities (RECs) recognised by the African Union are customs unions: the East African Community (EAC) and Economic Community of West African States (ECOWAS). The other customs unions are the Central African Economic and Monetary Community (CEMAC), the West African Economic and Monetary Union (WAEMU) and SACU.
Source: (SACU, 2017[12]), (SACU, 2014[13]).

Miscellaneous and unidentified revenues can be a significant component of non-tax revenues in certain countries. These include exceptional voluntary contributions to the government in Tunisia, capital transfers from special statutory funds in Mauritius and, in Morocco, payments made to government in exchange for the right to compete with state institutions in the provision of services.

The volatility of miscellaneous and unidentified revenues may be due to large capital transfers, revenue streams that are short-lived or funds that are reclassified as unidentified due to lack of information. The higher values for this category could reflect uncertainty as to the true amount of revenue within other non-tax revenue classifications.

Southern African Customs Union revenues

All five members of SACU collect customs and excise taxes under a unified tax regime and then transfer those funds to the SACU Common Revenue Pool. The SACU Common Revenue Pool in turn redistributes the tax moneys collected according to a revenue-sharing formula. South Africa possesses the main ports of entry into Southern Africa and ends up collecting almost all the customs duties and excises allocated to the SACU Common Revenue Pool. South Africa therefore makes net payments into the SACU Revenue Pool while the other SACU countries are net recipients.

SACU revenues to South Africa are negligible but they have a strong impact on the finances of the other members of the customs union (Figure 2.11). In 2022, these revenues amounted to 5.4%, 7.2%, 13.7% and 6.7% of GDP, respectively, in Botswana, Eswatini, Lesotho and Namibia.

Besides exogenous economic shocks, member countries also see their SACU revenues rise and fall due to changes in the parameters used in the revenue-sharing formula. The economic shock of the global financial crisis rendered many economic forecasts of the time inaccurate; because SACU payments were calculated based on these forecasts, major adjustments to SACU payments were required in 2010 and 2011 to compensate for years of overpayments into the SACU pool (Mongardini et al., 2011[14]).

A similar situation occurred in 2014, when a slowdown in South Africa's economy caused forecasts to be revised downward; Eswatini, Lesotho and Namibia's SACU revenues declined as a percentage of GDP in 2015 and 2016, although this trend was reversed in 2017.

In 2020, customs and excise tax revenues collected in the SACU countries were lower than was forecast in the previous year due to the COVID-19 pandemic. This meant that the SACU Common Revenue Pool made overpayments in 2020 that needed to be repaid the following year, making SACU revenues higher than the long-term trend in 2020 and lower than the long-term trend in 2021.

Figure 2.11. Total SACU and other non-tax revenues by country

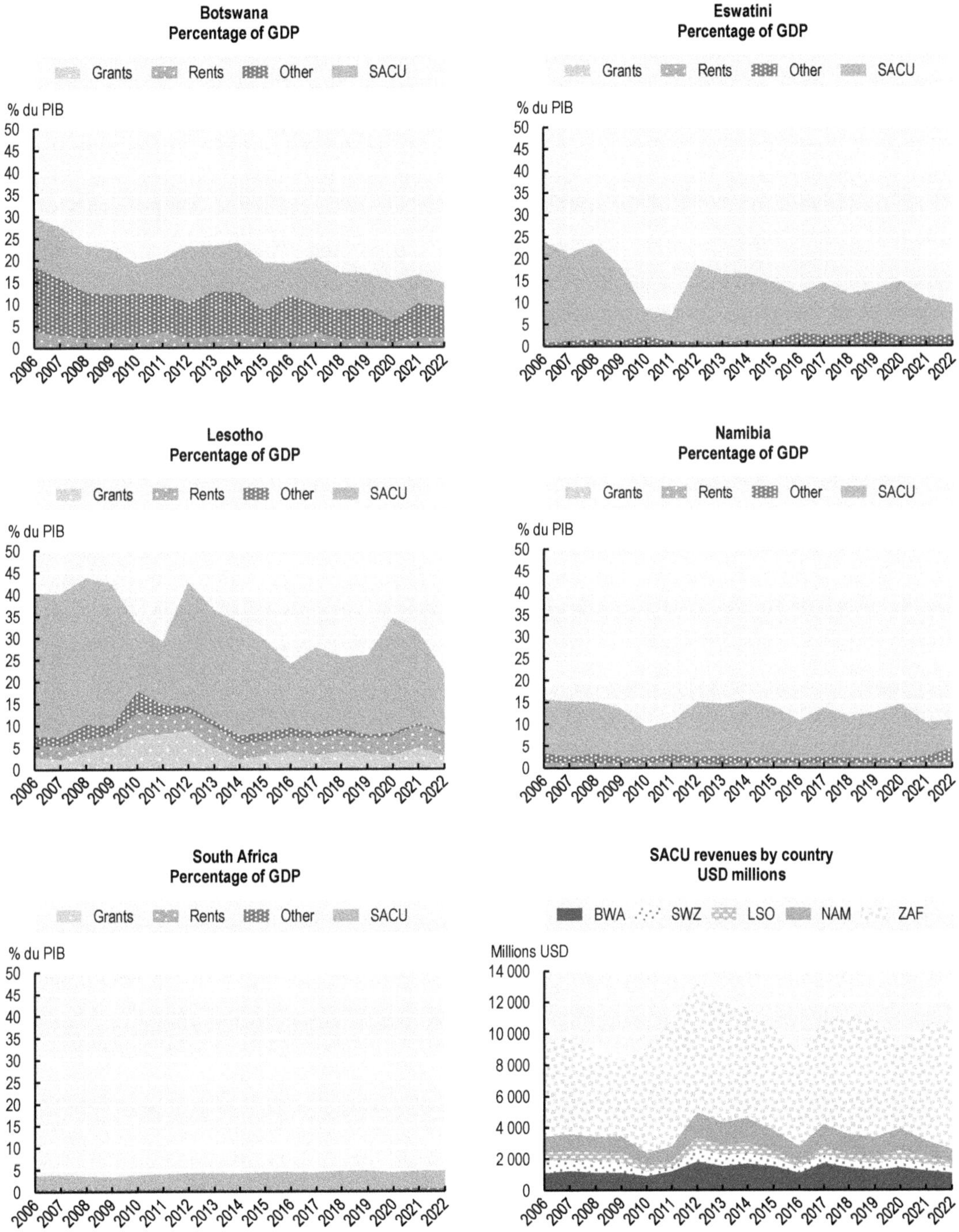

Note: SACU revenues reported here are classified as non-tax revenues for all countries presented here except for South Africa. For South Africa, SACU revenues received by the government of South Africa are classified under customs duties and excise taxes, and not non-tax revenues. These correspond to the annual disbursements by country from the SACU Common Revenue Pool.

Source: Authors' calculations based on data from and (OECD/ATAF/AUC, 2024[2]), "*Revenue Statistics in Africa: Comparative tables*", http://data-explorer.oecd.org/s/dx.

StatLink https://stat.link/r4thls

Revenues from extractive industries

Revenue Statistics in Africa seeks to distinguish between national revenues coming from the extraction of natural resources, which are referred to in this report as extractive-related revenues, and other forms of revenue. Revenues from extractive industries, which include oil, gas, minerals, forestry and fishing, are highly dependent on commodity prices which are set globally, and highly volatile, exposing government budgets to risks that are difficult to foresee. Additionally, assessments of tax and revenue policy should account for the fact that natural resource endowments, especially mineral resources, are independent of a country's human resources and level of development, and resource revenues are generally not sensitive to economic and social policy.

The exploitation of non-renewable natural resources like oil, gas, and minerals represents a depletion of national wealth, and therefore brings up the issue of opportunity costs when it comes to under-selling, or under-monetising these resources by national governments. For these reasons, an analysis of resource-related revenues, and if possible, a distinction between renewable and non-renewable resource-related revenues, is important to the analysis of revenue policy in African countries.

The detailed country-specific revenue categories provided in *Revenue Statistics in Africa* permits an identification of many of the national revenues that can be attributed to extractive industries in certain countries, depending on the level of detail in the data submitted by participating countries. For example, Ghana's "Income/profit tax on oil companies" can be identified as an extractive-related revenue (see Table 5.13. in Chapter 5), as can "Revenue from oil" reported under "rents and royalties" for Nigeria (Table 6.29. in Chapter 6). Using this methodology, for each category of revenue, the total amount of revenue that is explicitly reported as extractive-related can be estimated.

This methodology may undercount revenues from the extractive industry since the distinction between extractive and non-extractive revenues is not always made in *Revenue Statistics in Africa* data. For this reason, efforts to introduce this distinction in more revenue categories and for more countries are ongoing. For example, for the first time in this report, the revenue data for the Democratic Republic of the Congo, Niger and Sierra Leone distinguishes between revenues from oil and minerals and other forms of revenue (see Tables 5.6, 5.25 and 5.30 in Chapter 5, and Tables 6.9, 6.28 and 6.33 in Chapter 6).

Potentially compounding the risk of undercounting, this methodology does not factor in the indirect impacts of extractive industries on public revenues. In some countries, extractive industries such as petroleum and minerals have a significant impact on growth across the economy and could have a significant multiplier effect. This industry could therefore have an impact on all forms of tax and non-tax revenues, including, for example, VAT revenues that can be boosted by macro-economic spillovers from the mining sector, or higher corporate taxes on hotels that have seen increased business from mining corporations.

Box 2.2. Public financing with natural resource wealth

There are various mechanisms by which natural resources generate revenues or savings for government.[1] Rents and royalties are the most direct means of deriving revenue from natural resource wealth. The government charges fees to companies and individuals in exchange for the right to access government lands. It does this in its capacity as landowner and these fees are generally decided through negotiation. These are recorded under property income.

Payment for services provided by the government is another source of non-tax revenue paid for by businesses in the primary sector. This can include, for example, payments for environmental inspections or for the construction of infrastructure, or, in the case of Mauritius, payment for weather data and maps. These are recorded under sales of goods and services.

Public ownership (full or partial) of a corporation that exploits natural resources on the government's behalf results in government revenues in the form of profits and dividends. These are recorded under property income. For example, the revenues collected by the government of Botswana from dividends it receives from its 50% stake in Debswana, the company that operates the main diamond mines in Botswana, are recorded under property income (MiningTechnology, 2020[15]).

Taxes targeting natural resource exploitation could be introduced, such as an excise tax on the sale of materials extracted from public lands or a tax on mining that targets the activity, rather than the individual or company exploiting natural resources. These, too, will be recorded as taxes. Such taxes on mining exist in Niger and Senegal, which impose taxes on mining activities that are classified in *Revenue Statistics* under other taxes on goods and services.

Companies and individuals exploiting natural resources are generally subject to the same taxes (such as income taxes and value-added taxes) as other economic entities. Revenues from these general taxes will be included in government financial statements but not necessarily attributed to sectors exploiting natural resources.

Companies and individuals may use some of the wealth they obtain from natural resource extraction to build infrastructure or provide services, sometimes as a condition for accessing publicly-owned natural resources. Where this satisfies demand for public investment or services, it could result in savings on government expenditure, but it would not be recorded as revenue. For example, in Guinea, a railway line connecting the Simandou iron ore mine to the port of Morebaya is being built by Rio Tinto, the Winning Consortium Group and la Compagnie du TransGuinéen (a public corporation) (Klein, 2024[16]).

Note: 1. Taxes on oil extraction can include corporate income tax, excise taxes on energy products, un-refunded sales taxes such as VATs and non-tax revenue can include royalties, profit sharing, dividends received from state enterprises, and other investment income received from government direct participation in extractive enterprises (Mansour and Rota-Graziosi, 2013[17]).

Figure 2.12 shows the reported extractive-related revenues identified using the methodology above for different revenue streams. Panel A shows for each type of revenue, the percentage of revenue collected by each African country reported as coming from extractive industries. Panel B shows for each revenue category, the total extractive-related revenues collected as a percentage of GDP. As explained in Box 2.2, African governments have different strategies for capturing natural resource wealth, and this is shown here in the number of different kinds of revenue that are reported as extractive-related.

Most of the revenues explicitly identified as extractive-related in the *Revenue Statistics in Africa* data are concentrated in a few revenue categories. The categories for which more than 10% of revenues come from extractive industries are corporate income taxes, recurrent property taxes, mining taxes (classified as other taxes on specific goods and services), export taxes, rents and royalties, and interest and dividends.

On average, 63% of rents and royalties were extractive-related, the only revenue category for which this was a majority. On average, extractive-related revenues for the 35 African countries amounted to 3.3% of GDP in 2022. Extractive-related revenues reported under corporate income tax, rents and royalties, and interest and dividends added up to 3.1% of GDP on average among African countries in 2022, which corresponds to 96% of the total extractive-related revenues. It is possible, however, that more extractive-related revenues in other revenue categories are less likely to be identified as such.

Figure 2.12. Extractive-related revenues, by type of revenue, 2022

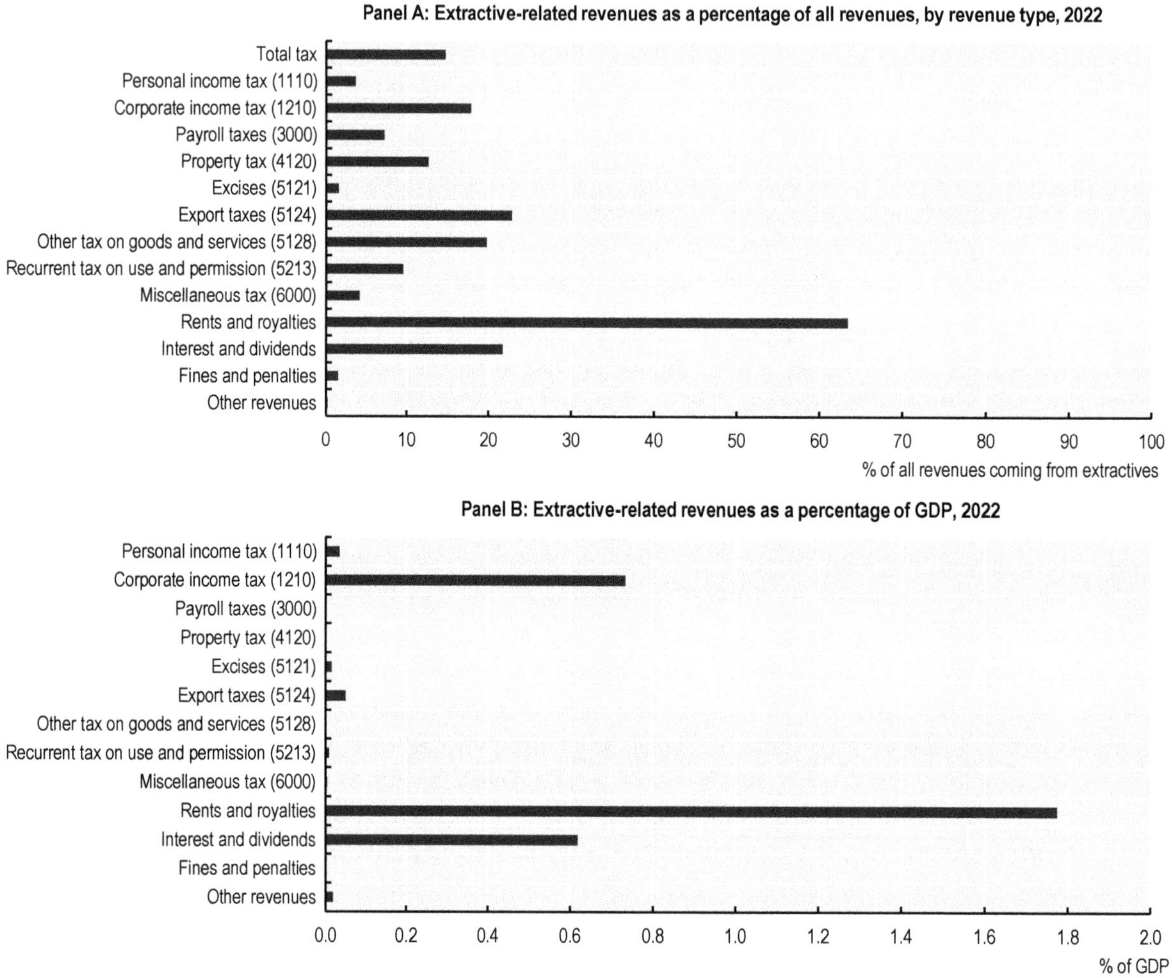

Note: These revenues include only tax and non-tax revenues that are clearly labelled as coming from minerals, fishing, forestry or oil and gas extraction within the *Revenue Statistics in Africa* datasets. This does not cover all tax and non-tax coming from resource extractions. Burkina Faso, Cabo Verde, Eswatini, Madagascar, Malawi, Rwanda, and Senegal reported no revenues that could be identified as coming from companies involved in resource extraction.
Source: Authors' calculations based on Tables 5.1-5.36 and 6.5-6.39 and Table 4.17 and (OECD/ATAF/AUC, 2024[2]), "*Revenue Statistics in Africa: Comparative tables*", http://data-explorer.oecd.org/s/dx.

StatLink https://stat.link/n2r04k

Most extractive-related tax revenues come from corporate taxes on oil companies. Extractive-related revenues were far more likely to be identified within income taxes than consumption taxes. It is more administratively straightforward to distinguish between extractive and non-extractive companies within corporate taxation since these taxes are collected at the level of corporations. Identifying extractive-related VAT or other consumption revenues requires linking each transaction to the entity making the purchase. However, some consumption taxes could be identified as extractive-related if they target the products of resource extraction. Some countries levy taxes on exports of extracted commodities, for example, to recapture some of the natural resource value at the point where it leaves the country. For example, South Africa and Guinea both tax diamond exports.

In Figure 2.13, tax and non-tax revenues that have been explicitly identified as being extractive-related within the *Revenue Statistics in Africa* datasets are shown for each country. The oil-rich countries of Equatorial Guinea and the Republic of the Congo stand out, with total extractive-related revenues as a percentage of GDP of 28.1% and 22.9%. No other African country had extractive-related revenues above 10% of GDP aside from Gabon, for which this figure was 10.2% of GDP. Thirteen countries – Cabo Verde, Eswatini, Kenya, Madagascar, Malawi, Mauritius, Morocco, Rwanda, Senegal, Somalia, South Africa, Togo and Uganda – reported either no or negligible extractive-related revenues. On average, the 35 African countries reported extractive revenues amounting to 3.3% of GDP, with extractive-related tax revenues amounting to 0.9% of GDP and extractive-related non-tax revenues amounting to 2.4% of GDP.

Figure 2.13. Resource-related tax and non-tax revenues by country, 2022

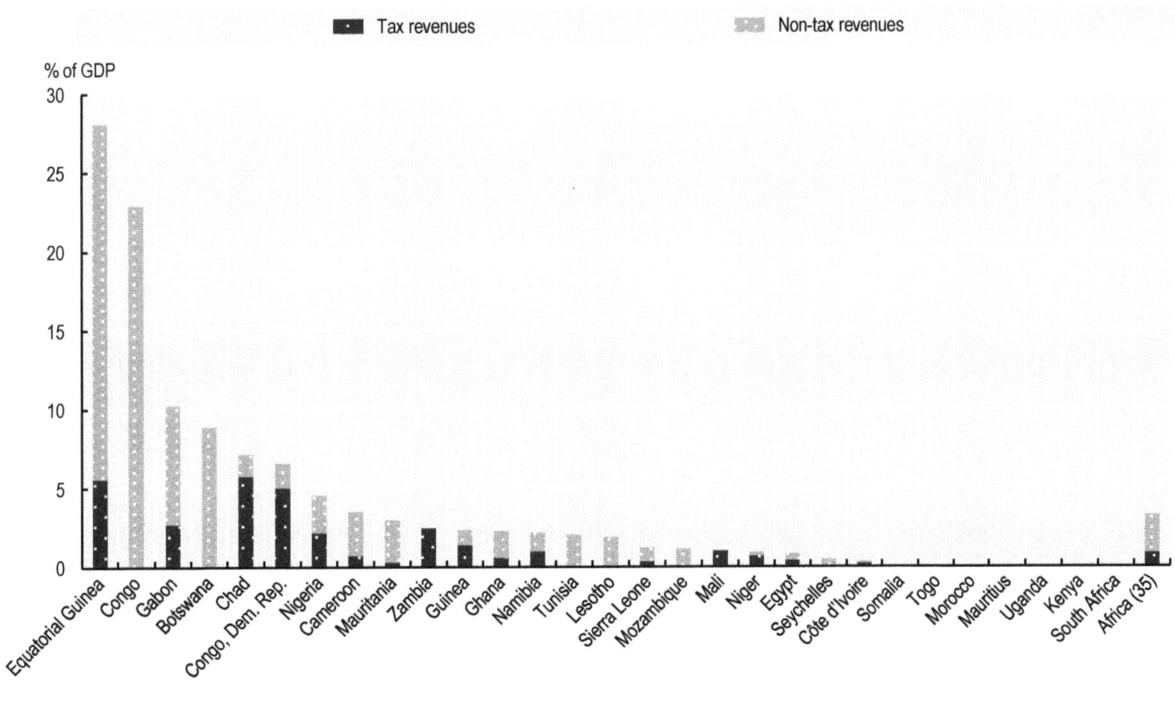

Note: The Africa average is calculated over 35 African countries excluding Burkina Faso, for which data on tax revenues was available, but not non-tax revenues. These revenues include only tax and non-tax revenues that are clearly labelled as coming from mining, fishing, forestry or oil and gas extraction within the Revenue Statistics in Africa datasets. This does not cover all tax and non-tax coming from resource extractions. Cabo Verde, Eswatini, Madagascar, Malawi, Rwanda and Senegal reported no revenues that could be identified as coming from companies involved in resource extraction. "Africa (35)" refers to the average for the 35 African countries reporting non-tax revenues in this report.
Source: Authors' calculations based on Tables 5.1-5.36 and 6.5-6.39 and Table 4.17 and (OECD/ATAF/AUC, 2024[2]), "*Revenue Statistics in Africa: Comparative tables*", http://data-explorer.oecd.org/s/dx.

StatLink https://stat.link/f1x2de

Figure 2.14 shows the same extractive-related revenues broken down by the associated resources. Oil and gas are shown to have the largest impact on public revenues, accounting for almost the entirety of the revenues for four of the top five countries in terms of extractive revenues, the exception being Botswana, which collects mineral revenues amounting to 8.9% of GDP, one quarter of which is in the form of royalties, and three quarters in the form of dividends from mining companies. Only Mozambique and Equatorial Guinea explicitly reported gas revenues.

Equatorial Guinea's oil and gas revenues in 2022 came in the form of petroleum royalties (34%), corporate taxes (18%), oil dividends (11%), shareholder participation in oil revenues (7%) and personal income tax (2%). Extractive revenues for the Republic of the Congo come mostly from revenues from the *Société nationale des pétroles du Congo* (SNPC, a national oil company). SNPC is a part-shareholder in all private oil and gas ventures in the country, as well as having full ownership of some oil projects (EY/CNC, 2022[18]). The revenues associated with the SNPC are classified as rents and royalties in this publication, but actually constitute a mix of different revenue streams and occupy the conceptual boundaries between resource rents and investment income.

Figure 2.14. Tax and non-tax extractive-related revenues, by associated resource

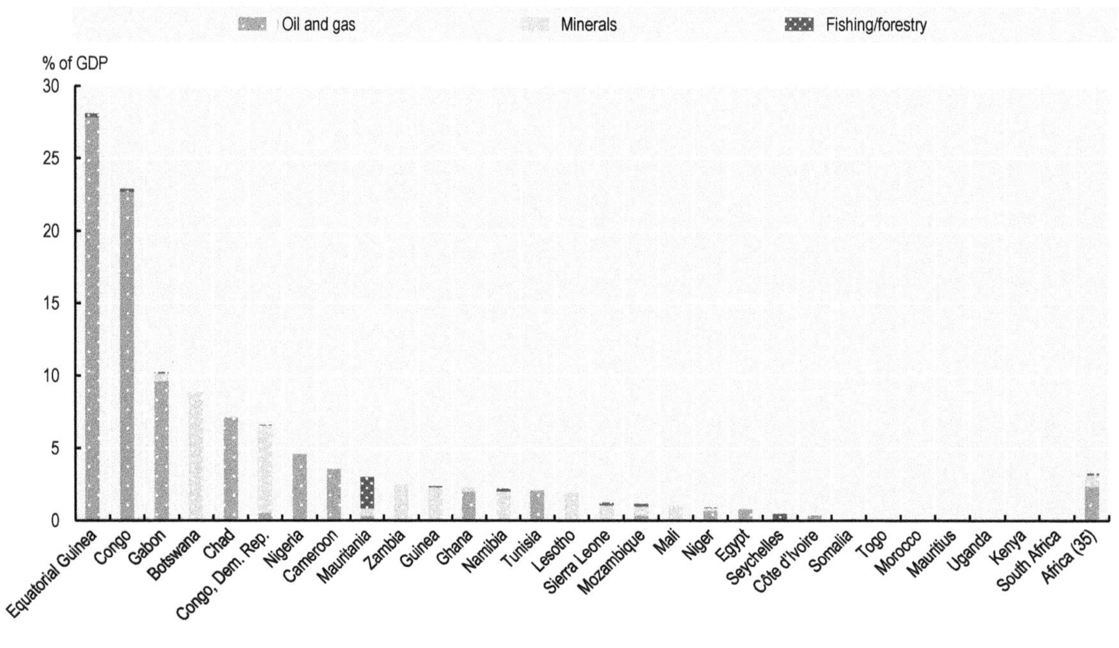

Note: These revenues include only tax and non-tax revenues that are clearly labelled as coming from mining, fishing, forestry or oil and gas extraction within the Revenue Statistics in Africa datasets. This does not cover all tax and non-tax coming from resource extractions. Burkina Faso, Cabo Verde, Eswatini, Madagascar, Malawi, Rwanda and Senegal reported no revenues that could be identified as coming from companies involved in resource extraction. "Africa (35)" refers to the average for the 35 African countries reporting non-tax revenues in this report.

Source: Authors' calculations based on Tables 5.1-5.36 and 6.5-6.39 and Table 4.17 and (OECD/ATAF/AUC, 2024[2]), "*Revenue Statistics in Africa: Comparative tables*", http://data-explorer.oecd.org/s/dx.

StatLink https://stat.link/jw4svm

For many African countries, the bulk of non-tax revenues come from extractive-related revenues (Figure 2.15). For nine African countries, they constitute the majority of non-tax revenues, and for three African countries, Equatorial Guinea, Gabon, and the Republic of the Congo, they represent over 95%.

Extractive-related non-tax revenues take the form of rents and royalties, or interest and dividends, with all other forms of non-tax revenues generally negligible, aside from some fines and penalties on mining companies reported in the Democratic Republic of the Congo and some fishing fines in Mauritania. For all but three African countries, the main form of extractive-related revenues was rents and royalties, with Equatorial Guinea, Botswana, Ghana collecting more extractive-related revenues in the form of interest and dividends.

Figure 2.15. Extractive-related non-tax revenues as percentage of total non-tax revenue, by revenue type

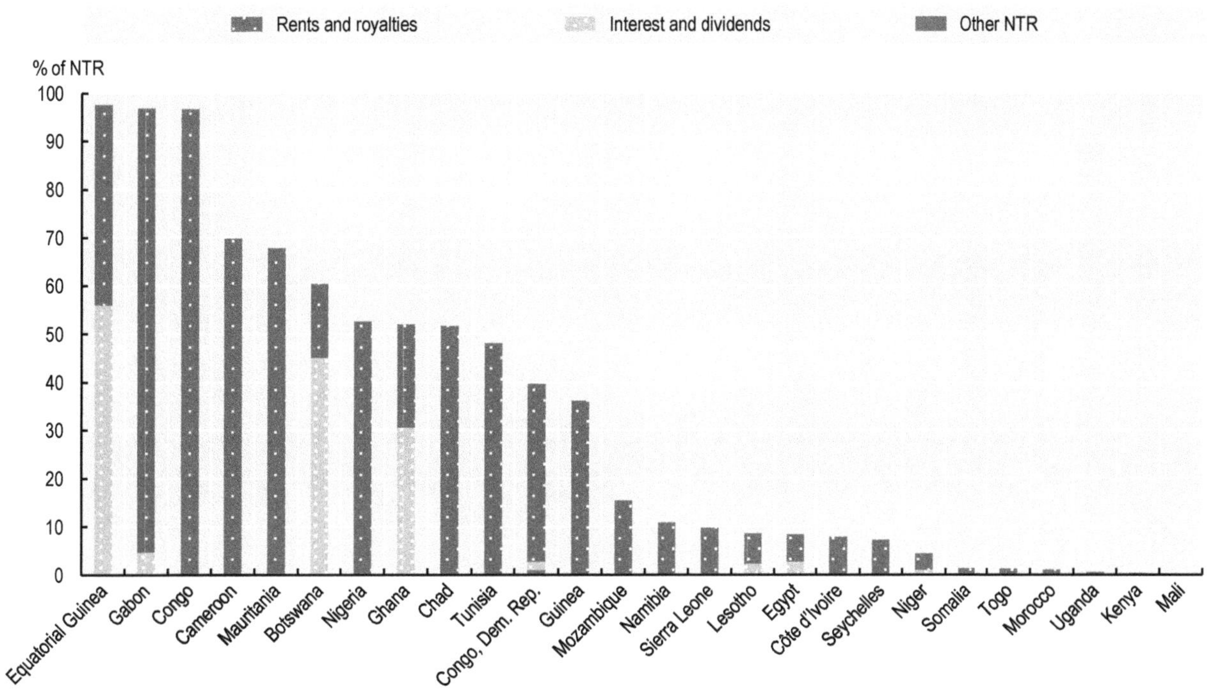

Note: These revenues include only non-tax revenues that are clearly labelled as coming from minerals, fishing, forestry or oil and gas extraction within the *Revenue Statistics in Africa* datasets. This does not cover all non tax revenue coming from resource extractions. Burkina Faso, Cabo Verde, Eswatini, Madagascar, Malawi, Mauritius, Rwanda, Senegal, South Africa and Zambia reported no revenues that could be identified as coming from companies involved in resource extraction. NTR = "non-tax revenues".
Source: Authors' calculations based on Tables 5.1-5.36 and 6.5-6.39 and Table 4.17 and (OECD/ATAF/AUC, 2024[2]), "*Revenue Statistics in Africa: Comparative tables*", http://data-explorer.oecd.org/s/dx.

StatLink https://stat.link/0z532m

Rents and royalties in 2022 were the main form of resource-related revenues for 16 African countries and accounted for 49% of the USD 48 billion collected in extractive-related revenues among all the African countries reporting, followed by total taxes, at 41% and other non-tax revenues such as interest and dividends at 9%.

Figure 2.16 shows extractive revenues identified among tax revenues. Nineteen countries reported some revenues, of which 16 of these reported more than 1% of their tax revenues as coming from companies involved in extraction.

Figure 2.16. Extractive-related tax revenues as a percentage of total tax revenue, by tax type

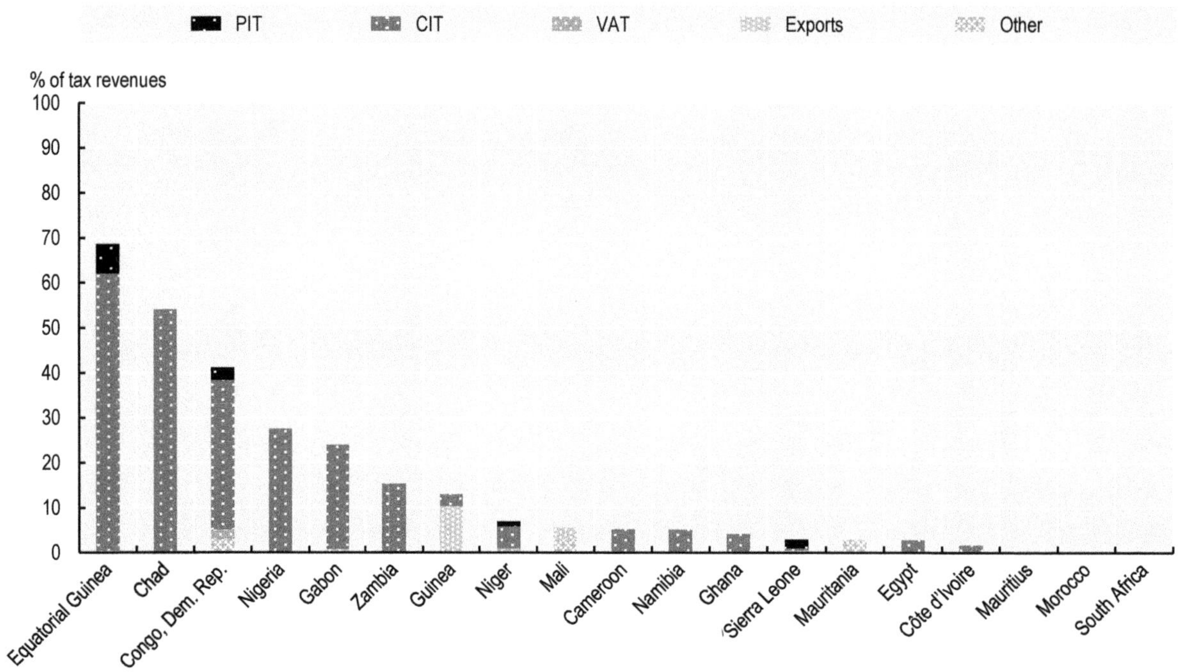

Note: These revenues include only tax revenues that are clearly labelled as coming from minerals, fishing, forestry or oil and gas extraction within the *Revenue Statistics in Africa* datasets. This does not cover all tax revenue coming from resource extractions. Botswana, Burkina Faso, Cabo Verde, the Republic of the Congo, Eswatini, Kenya, Lesotho, Madagascar, Malawi, Mozambique, Rwanda, Senegal, Seychelles, Somalia, Togo, Tunisia and Uganda reported no revenues that could be identified as coming from companies involved in resource extraction. PIT = "personal income tax"; CIT = "corporate income tax"; VAT = "value-added tax".

StatLink https://stat.link/je5yzi

The impact of commodity prices

Economies across the African continent are strongly affected by global commodity markets. However African governments collect extractive-related revenues, these tend to be a highly volatile source of finance. Six countries (the Republic of the Congo, Equatorial Guinea, Gabon, Lesotho, Mauritania and Nigeria) collected rents and royalties equivalent to 5% of GDP or more in at least one of the last ten years and they all registered at least one year-on-year increase in rents and royalties of over 35% and one year-on-year decrease of over 27% as a percentage of GDP.

Raw commodities are a major component of the exports of most of the countries included within this publication. These include:

- aluminium (over 25% of exports in Guinea):
- cobalt (over 20% of exports in the Democratic Republic of the Congo)
- copper (over 25% of exports in the Democratic Republic of the Congo, The Republic of the Congo and Zambia)
- diamonds (over 25% of exports in Botswana and Lesotho)
- gold (over 25% of exports in Burkina Faso, Ghana, Guinea, Mali, Mauritania, Niger, Rwanda, Somalia, Togo and Uganda)
- iron (over 25% of exports in Mauritania and Sierra Leone)
- natural gas (over 25% of exports in Equatorial Guinea)
- oil (over 25% of exports in Cameroon, Chad, the Republic of the Congo, Gabon, Ghana, Equatorial Guinea and Nigeria)
- fish (over 25% of exports in Cabo Verde and the Seychelles).

The COVID-19 pandemic introduced both supply and demand shocks, which impacted the prices of basic commodities (Figure 2.17). Despite double-digit drops in natural gas, petroleum and phosphate prices in 2020, these commodities bounced back in 2021 and 2022: in 2022, the price of petroleum was 50% higher than it was in 2019, while coal, phosphate and potassium chloride were triple their price in 2019. The price of natural gas in the United States and Europe was, respectively, two and half times and seven and a half times higher than in 2019.

Figure 2.17. Price changes of key commodities, 2019-22

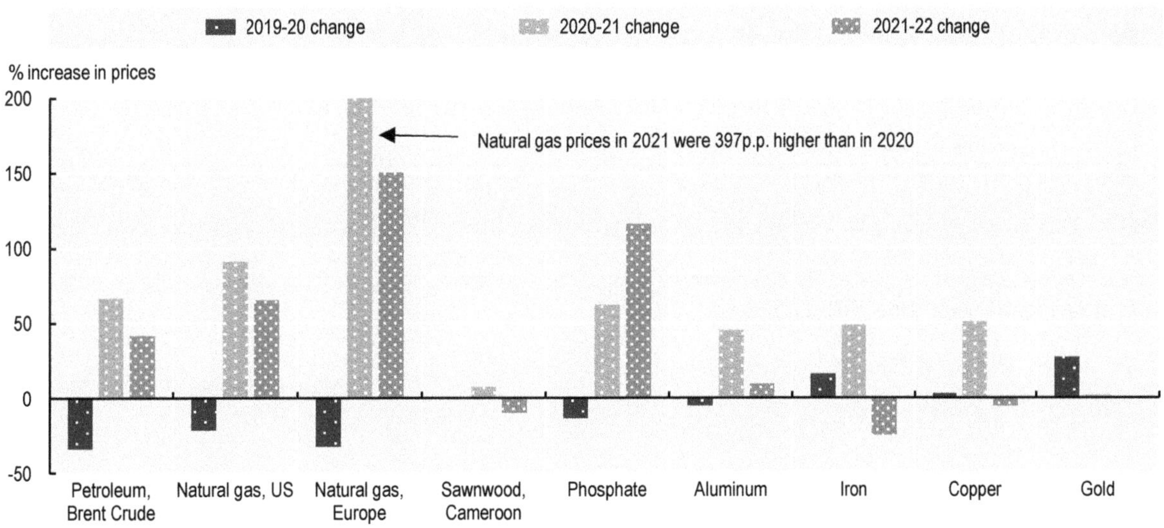

Source: World Bank Commodity Price Data (The Pink Sheet) (World Bank, 2024[19]).

StatLink https://stat.link/brwtx9

The largest changes in the value of commodity exports from *Revenue Statistics in Africa* have tended to coincide with price shocks (Figure 2.18). This underlines the vulnerability of African economies to global oil and gas price shifts and underscores the critical need for economic diversification to mitigate the risks associated with heavy reliance on oil revenues (Usman and Landry, 2021[20]) and (World Bank, 2023[21]).

While African countries are gradually amplifying their mineral exports, generating significant revenues from these remains a challenge (World Bank, 2023[22]). This situation emphasises the imperative for African countries to fortify their strategies for tapping into the revenue potential of diverse mineral resources.

Figure 2.18. Rents and royalties and commodity exports, Africa average, 2010-22

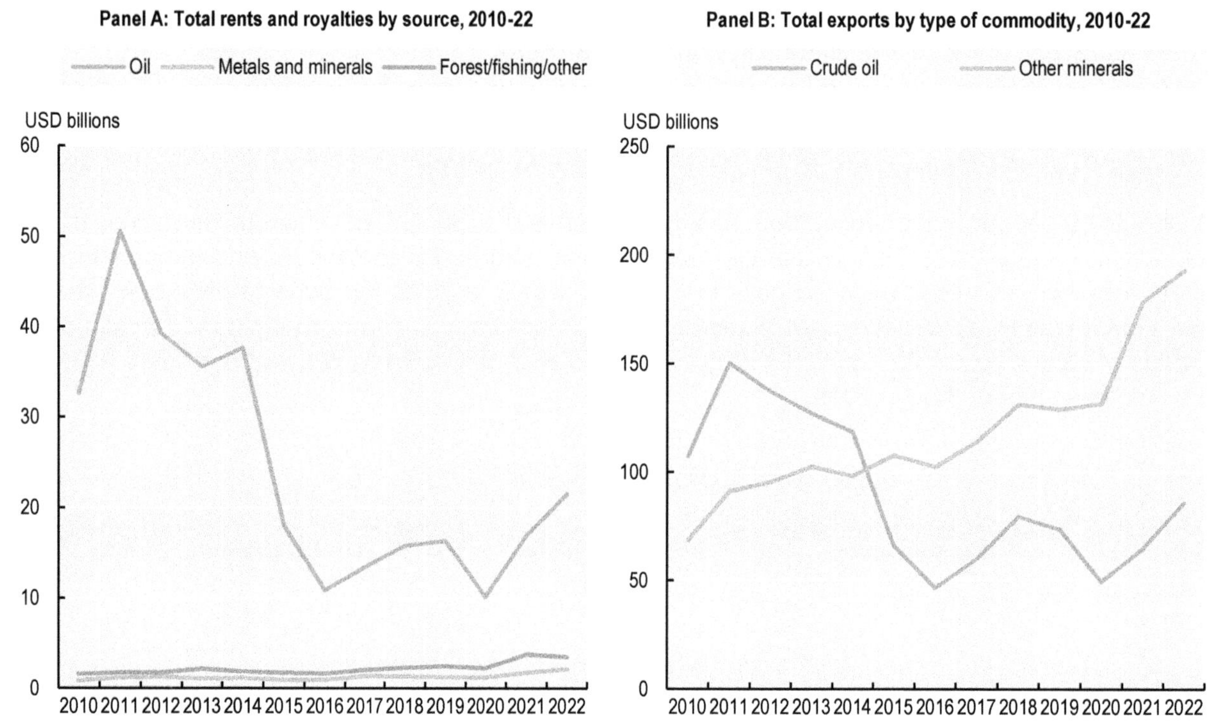

Source: Authors' calculations from detailed Revenue Statistics in Africa data for Panel A, and for panel B, data from BACI International Trade Database at the Product-Level from (CEPII, 2023[23]).

StatLink https://stat.link/xhop6f

References

CEPII (2023), *BACI International Trade Database at the Product-Level*, http://www.cepii.fr/CEPII/en/bdd_modele/bdd_modele_item.asp?id=37 (accessed on 1 February 2023). [23]

EY/CNC (2022), *Société Nationale des Pétroles du Congo - Rapports des Commissaires aux comptes sur les états financiers annuels et Spécial sur les conventions réglementées, Exercie clos le 31 décembre 2022*, https://www.finances.gouv.cg/sites/default/files/documents/SNPC_2022_RGRS%20SOCIAUX.pdf. [18]

Group, W. (ed.) (2024), *The World Bank Atlas method - detailed methodology*, https://datahelpdesk.worldbank.org/knowledgebase/articles/378832-what-is-the-world-bank-atlas-method (accessed on 2024). [6]

IMF (2024), *World Economic Outlook, April 2024 Edition (database)*, https://www.imf.org/en/Publications/WEO/weo-database/2024/April. [3]

IMF (2023), *IMF International Financial Statistics (IFS) database*, https://data.imf.org/?sk=4c514d48-b6ba-49ed-8ab9-52b0c1a0179b (accessed on 11 September). [4]

Khan, O. and S. Khan (2022), *Customs reforms help Somalia increase tax revenue despite COVID-19 and fragility*, https://blogs.worldbank.org/en/governance/customs-reforms-help-somalia-increase-tax-revenue-despite-covid-19-and-fragility. [1]

Klein, A. (2024), *4 Railway Projects to Watch in West Africa*, https://energycapitalpower.com/4-railway-projects-to-watch-in-west-africa/. [16]

Lupachik, M. (2023), *Equatorial Guinea's Gas Mega Hub Ignites West Africa's LNG Potential*, http://www.spglobal.com/commodityinsights/en/ci/research-analysis/equatorial-guineas-gas-mega-hub-ignites-west-africas-lng-poten.html. [10]

Mansour, M. and G. Rota-Graziosi (2013), "Tax Coordination, Tax Competition, and Revenue Mobilization in the West African Economic and Monetary Union", *IMF Working Paper*, Vol. 13/163, https://www.imf.org/en/Publications/WP/Issues/2016/12/31/Tax-Coordination-Tax-Competition-and-Revenue-Mobilization-in-the-West-African-Economic-and-40756. [17]

MiningTechnology (2020), *Debswana diamond mines*, https://www.mining-technology.com/projects/debswana/ (accessed on 20 September 2020). [15]

Mongardini, J. et al. (2011), *In the wake of the global economic crisis: adjusting to lower revenue of the Southern African Customs*, International Monetary Fund, https://www.imf.org/external/pubs/ft/dp/2011/afr1101.pdf. [14]

OECD (2023), *DAC Data submitters*, http://www.oecd.org/dac/financing-sustainable-development/development-finance-standards/dacdatasubmitters.htm (accessed on 29 August 2023). [8]

OECD (2023), *Revenue Statistics 2023*, OECD Publishing, Paris, https://doi.org/10.1787/6e87f932-en. [25]

OECD/ATAF/AUC (2024), *Revenue Statistics in Africa: Comparative tables*, OECD Publishing, Paris, http://data-explorer.oecd.org/s/pn. [2]

OECD et al. (2024), *Revenue Statistics in Latin America and the Caribbean 2024*, OECD Publishing, Paris, https://doi.org/10.1787/58a2dc35-en-es. [24]

OECD-DAC (2024), *International Development Statistics (IDS) online databases*, http://www.oecd.org/dac/stats/idsonline (accessed on 4 September 2024). [9]

RFI (2014), *Le gros chèque d'Arcelor Mittal au Sénégal*, http://www.rfi.fr/economie/20140605-le-gros-cheque-arcelor-mittal-senegal. [11]

SACU (2017), *Southern African Customs Union Agreement 2002 (As amended on 12 April 2013)*, http://www.sacu.int/list.php?type=Agreements. [12]

SACU (2014), *Implementing a Common Agenda Towards Regional Integration: 2014 Annual Report*, http://www.sacu.int/docs/reports_annual/2014/annual_report.pdf. [13]

Usman, Z. and D. Landry (2021), *Economic Diversification in Africa: How and Why It Matters*, Carnegie Endowment for International Peace., https://carnegieendowment.org/research/2021/04/economic-diversification-in-africa-how-and-why-it-matters?lang=en. [20]

World Bank (2024), *World Bank Commodity Price Data (The Pink Sheet)*, https://www.worldbank.org/en/research/commodity-markets. [19]

World Bank (2024), *World Bank Country and Lending Groups*, https://datahelpdesk.worldbank.org/knowledgebase/articles/906519. [5]

World Bank (2024), *World Development Indicators*, https://data.worldbank.org/ (accessed on 28 June 2024). [7]

World Bank (2023), *Economic Diversification Away from Oil is Crucial for the Republic of Congo's Long-Term Growth and Prosperity: World Bank Report*, https://www.worldbank.org/en/news/press-release/2023/03/15/economic-diversification-away-from-oil-is-crucial-for-the-republic-of-congo-long-term-growth-and-prosperity. [21]

World Bank (2023), *Maximizing Revenues from Natural Resource Wealth Could Yield Big Fiscal and Environmental Dividends for African Countries*, https://www.worldbank.org/en/news/press-release/2023/05/09/maximizing-revenues-from-natural-resource-wealth-could-yield-big-fiscal-and-environmental-dividends-for-african-countrie. [22]

Notes

1 Please see the *Interpretative Guide* to non-tax revenue in Annex B of this report for the definitions of these revenue categories.

2 Several methodological issues are present in non-tax revenues which do not necessarily arise in tax statistics. Some revenues, such as administrative fees, might be used as cost-recovery mechanisms and subtracted from cost figures rather than reported as revenues. This could be the case for local governments or other public institutions for which data only exists on net transfers of funds to the central government. If sales of goods and services are reported without deduction of costs, this could overstate a government's revenues. Grants, legal settlements and mining and oil contracts involve large payments by external entities such as multinational corporations and foreign governments who may be subject to different national oversight mechanisms. Some resource-rich countries may negotiate large payments from resource extraction payments as a lump sum that bundles together many categories of both tax and non-tax revenue, making detailed breakdowns less feasible. Finally, non-tax revenues are often under the responsibility of different authorities than tax revenues, and sometimes there is not necessarily a separation made between revenues and expenses, so these revenues might not necessarily follow the same reporting standard. Please see Annex B for more details on the methodology used for non-tax revenues.

3 There is no comparison with the averages of the 27 Latin American and Caribbean (LAC) countries [see (OECD et al., 2024[24])] or the 38 OECD countries [see (OECD, 2023[25])], as these publications do not cover non-tax revenues.

4 Please see also Annex B.

5 Burkina Faso provided data on tax revenues for this edition of *Revenue Statistics in Africa* but data on non-tax revenues were not available for this edition.

6 The official definition of ODA is: "flows to countries and territories on the Development Assistance Committee List of ODA Recipients and to multilateral institutions which are provided by official agencies, including state and local governments, or by their executive agencies. In addition, each transaction must be administered with the promotion of the economic development and welfare of developing countries as its main objective; and be concessional in character and conveys a grant element of at least 25% (calculated at a rate of discount of 10%)". Further information is available at: www.oecd.org/dac/financing-sustainable-development/index-terms.htm#ODA.

7 See paragraphs 9-13 of the OECD Interpretative Guide in Annex A for an explanation of how administrative fees are classified in this publication.

3 Facilitation and trust as drivers of voluntary tax compliance in selected African tax administrations

Chapter 3, the Special Feature of this report, examines how facilitation and trust can enhance voluntary tax compliance in African countries. Based on a study carried out by the African Tax Administration Forum, the chapter analyses initiatives undertaken by African tax administrations to enhance voluntary compliance as an essential means of enhancing tax revenues.

Introduction

This Special Feature is based on a study by the African Tax Administration Forum (ATAF) on voluntary tax compliance in African countries.[1] The study aims to (i) examine the role of facilitation and public trust in both the tax administration and government generally in driving voluntary tax compliance and (ii) identify good practices around voluntary tax compliance initiatives from selected countries that can be used for peer-to-peer learning. It is based on qualitative interviews that were held with officials from eight African Tax Administrations (ATAs) and analysis of published literature on initiatives to improve voluntary tax compliance by different ATAs.

This topic is fundamental to enhancing domestic resource mobilisation in African countries. As noted in Chapter 1 of this report, tax-to-GDP ratios across African countries are, on average, lower than those in other regions, weakening the continent's ability to achieve the Sustainable Development Goals and the African Union's Agenda 2063. At the same time, the proportion of tax revenues that African countries use to finance debt service costs has increased sharply, especially since the COVID-19 pandemic, thereby reducing the resources available for social spending and public investment.

The success of policies to increase revenues and improve the effectiveness of Africa's tax systems will in part depend on the extent to which citizens and businesses are willing to comply with their tax obligations. More broadly, analysis of voluntary tax compliance provides valuable insights into the social contract between citizens and governments. The first section of this chapter discusses the concept of voluntary tax compliance and identifies facilitation and trust as key drivers thereof. The second section presents key findings stemming from policies implemented by African countries to enhance voluntary tax compliance. A third section summarises possible avenues by which ATAs might enhance voluntary tax compliance based on the innovations that are currently being undertaken by African countries.

Voluntary tax compliance and the role of facilitation and trust

Voluntary tax compliance can be defined as the willingness of taxpayers to adhere to diverse laws and regulations related to taxation. There are four main pillars of voluntary tax compliance: registration, on time filing, on time payment and on time reporting (Betts, 2022[1]) (OECD, 2004[2]). An analysis of voluntary tax compliance is crucial because the tax system should be understood as a formal institution in the social contract between citizens and governments. Taxation brings in vital funds for public services and initiatives. In this context, the responsibility of the government is hinged on openness, fairness, and accountability, while citizens are obliged to comply. A just and equitable tax system that appeals to taxpayers everywhere is necessary for a sustainable taxpaying culture.

Measuring voluntary tax compliance is not straightforward: it is not an event where one can easily separate those taxpayers that willingly comply from those that do not. Rather, it is a process whereby taxpayers are required to adhere to different business processes, including registration with the tax administration, declaring timely and accurate tax returns, and making accurate and timely tax payments (Betts, 2022[1]) (OECD, 2004[2]).

In the context of tax compliance, 'voluntary' means that the taxpayer complies without any push or pull factors such as (i) fear of enforcement by the tax administration, (ii) the need to acquire certain services (such as acquiring a tax clearance certificate in the case of bidders for public tenders) or (iii) the use of a withholding tax regime where the taxpayer has no choice whether to comply or not.

Voluntary compliance denotes a state by which both taxpayers and their advisors are willing to truthfully abide by their tax obligations based on the tax regulations without coercion (Chindengwike and Kira, 2022[3]). Underlining the value of promoting the voluntary tax compliance, efforts undertaken by tax administrations to ensure taxpayers meet their obligations weigh on public finances. Revenue collection costs stood at 2.12% of total revenues in 2022 in countries included in the *African Tax Outlook*, above the benchmark of 1% for developing countries. A higher cost of collection indicates that ATAs are using significant resources to mobilise revenues (ATAF, 2023[4]).

This study focuses on two main drivers of voluntary tax compliance that stood out from the in-depth interviews carried out with ATAs: facilitation and trust. The main objectives of the study are two-fold:

- To carry out an in-depth evaluation of the facilitation and trust measures in selected ATAs for enhancing voluntary tax compliance.
- To identify good practices around voluntary tax compliance initiatives from selected countries that can be used for peer-to-peer learning.

The study findings were obtained through three different methods, including textual/document analysis, where several publications were referred to in order to understand the status, initiatives and good practices in different tax administrations; an online survey, which was followed up by in-depth interviews with eight selected ATAs; and a survey administered to taxpayers through a few tax administrations. The survey to taxpayers was not well-responded to although a few key lessons could still be gleaned from it.

Facilitation

The role of facilitation in voluntary compliance is to create a favourable environment which will enable a taxpayer to comply. This means that tax administrations aim to simplify taxpayers' experience with the tax administration to ensure that they meet their obligations seamlessly. In its essence, facilitation assumes taxpayers' default position is to comply and reserves enforcement for those who refuse; it also articulates the need for a service-oriented approach (Waiswa, Akol and Nalukwago, 2020[5]), (Kirchler, 2021[6]).

The Tax Administration Diagnostic Assessment Tool (TADAT) provides guidelines to tax administrators to improve voluntary tax compliance (TADAT, 2019[7]). These guidelines include:

1. Providing taxpayers with information through a variety of user-friendly channels for instance, frequently asked questions, brochures, publishing practice notes etc.
2. Customise tax related information to suit different categories of taxpayers.
3. Convenient and cost-effective service delivery to taxpayers.
4. Regular update of tax information to reflect the changes in the tax regime.
5. Introducing measures that can reduce compliance costs.

Seamless and efficient services for taxpayers can be achieved through the use of technology to automate business processes and attain efficiencies to ensure higher levels of compliance (ATAF, 2021[8]). To gain legitimacy, the automation and digitalisation of tax systems must adapt to the local environment. It is therefore important for tax administrators to craft user-friendly systems that consider the uniqueness of the taxpayer.

In the past two decades, ATAs have embraced the use of technology in simplifying key tax administration processes such as registration of taxpayers, filing of tax returns and tax payments as well as customs business processes. Today, over 70% of ATAs have digital tax registers, while over 80% use electronic filing of tax returns and tax payments (ATAF, 2024[9]).

However, there is sub-optimal usage of technology. There remain some ATAs where key processes are not fully automated, and there is a lack of communication between the implementation of the digital platforms and the users, meaning some ATAs still find it difficult to orient and train users on the new systems (ATAF, 2023[4]). As such, some ATAs do not make sufficient use of data from declarations to trace non-filers.

While information technology is well appreciated in transforming tax administration and facilitating tax compliance, informal sector businesses may not be captured, a situation worsened by inadequate information technology infrastructure that not all firms can embrace. According to (ATAF, 2021[8]), countries included in the *African Tax Outlook* that have invested in information and communication technology solutions have not yet achieved the results they expected.

Taxpayer education also plays an important role in facilitating tax compliance. Placing taxpayers or clients at the centre of the design of taxpayer education and services is one of the findings of the continental guidelines on taxpayer education in Africa (African Tax Administration Forum, 2021[10]). The positive impact on tax compliance of firms knowing their tax obligations was reinforced by the findings of (African Tax Administration Forum, 2021[10]), which also emphasised the importance of ATAs understanding the context of taxpayers to anticipate how to tailor their offerings.

In Africa, a lack of sufficient tax knowledge remains a key obstacle to voluntary tax compliance (Kira, 2017[11]) (Tanui, 2016[12]) (Nalishebo and Halwampa, 2014[13]); (OECD, 2019[14])). Many taxpayers do not know what taxes they owe to the government, what their obligations are, or when and how to meet those obligations (Isbell, 2017[15]) (Aiko and Logan, 2014[16]). In a study conducted in Rwanda, less than a quarter of respondents knew in which month was the deadline for filing taxes (Mascagini, Santoro and Mukama, 2019[17]). Similarly, a survey in Uganda revealed that almost half of taxpayers (45%) were not able to submit a tax return on their own and 56% were unable to claim a tax refund that they may be entitled to (Waiswa, Akol and Nalukwago, 2020[5]).

Educating taxpayers empowers them to navigate tax systems and therefore makes them more likely to comply (Waiswa, Akol and Nalukwago, 2020[5]). (Olaniyi et al., 2023[18]) established in a study in Nigeria that tax education has a significant positive relationship with personal income tax compliance. A study by (Amaning et al., 2021[19]) showed a positive relationship between the use of various media for taxpayer education and tax compliance among small and medium-sized enterprises in Ghana; since these enterprises are mainly operating in the informal sector, it was important that targeted training be established to foster voluntary compliance.

Aside from improving the likelihood of tax compliance, tax training reduces taxpayers' vulnerability to exploitation by expensive tax agents and corrupt tax officials. Similarly, informed taxpayers are better able to take advantage of the tax benefits available to them, such as allowable deductions, hence protecting them from paying more than they should (Benzarti, 2015[20]).

Trust

The legitimacy of a government and the ability of the state to accomplish its economic development goals depend in large part on the trust of citizens. Trust is also at the core of the behaviour of individuals towards their tax obligations (Gebrihet, Gebresilassie and Woldu, 2024[21]) (OECD, 2019[22]). Given the role of tax in state building and economic development relevant to achieve Agenda 2063, it is important from an African perspective to determine the interplay between trust and voluntary tax compliance and, in particular, to identify how tax administrations on the continent have crafted means of increasing taxpayers' trust in the state.

In Uganda, the effectiveness of government, as well as its level of transparency and accountability, have an impact on tax compliance (Nkundabanyanga et al., 2017[23]). A study by (Kumi et al., 2023[24]) found that trust was one of the determinants that positively affect voluntary compliance in Ghana and that trustworthiness was negatively related with tax enforcement. This implies that voluntary tax compliance is a result of taxpayers' intrinsic motivation caused by trustworthiness and that authorities that regularly enforce face trust challenges with taxpayers.

A study by (Kogler et al., 2023[25]) in 44 countries (including Egypt, Ghana, Morocco and South Africa) using the shadow economy as proxy for tax compliance established that trust in the tax authority has a positive association with tax compliance. In addition, (Nwokoye et al., 2023[26]) established a significant positive relationship between tax reductions, capital allowances, simplifying communication, deterrence messages, tax morale messages, tax audit, enforcement penalties, ease of tax filing, basic government services, political legitimacy and tax compliance. On the other hand, they established that tax rates, tax holidays, collusive evasion, perceptions of corruption and infrastructure deficiency have a significant negative relationship with tax compliance.

Results in a study from Togo showed that citizens' negative attitudes towards bribes, the severity of penalties and the legitimacy of customs duties are positively correlated with tax compliance (Soglo and Amedanou, 2023[27]). Voluntary tax compliance may not only be predicted by behavioural and deterrence factors alone but political will may also play a part.

In the area of trust, most ATAs still operate below international good practice around dispute resolution mechanisms (ATAF & IMF, 2022[28]). Concerns about poor use of taxpayer money, corruption in government generally and tax administrations generate mistrust, thereby affecting voluntary tax compliance. Higher non-compliance results in frequent tax audits and investigations that cost tax administrations time and financial resources.

Key findings on voluntary tax compliance from African countries

The World Bank's framework for improving tax compliance consists of three broad channels: (i) facilitation; (ii) enforcement; and (iii) creating public trust in government and its spending practices (Prichard et al., 2019[29]). This section discusses what ATAs have done to promote facilitation and public trust, the gaps that remain as well as success stories from selected countries.

Facilitation

Facilitation can be achieved in various ways, including taxpayer education, simplifying tax administration systems and processes, offering support services and simplifying digital systems.

Taxpayer education

ATAs have dedicated considerable effort and resources to educating taxpayers and the population at large. Almost all ATAs that submitted data and statistics for the 2023 edition of the *African Tax Outlook* (29 out of 30) have specific divisions to educate taxpayers, although seven of them reported that they do not allocate a budget to these functions (ATAF, 2023[4]). Only Zimbabwe Revenue Authority (ZIMRA) indicated that it does not have a dedicated office in charge of taxpayer education, although it allocates a budget to taxpayer education. Overall, it is reported that tax education is generally underfunded in African countries (ATAF, 2023[4]), (ATAF, 2024[9]).

There are various initiatives to educate taxpayers[2] and most of these are common in many tax administrations. Some of the initiatives include:

- **Tax seminars and workshops.** This is one of the most common ways to educate taxpayers in Africa. ATAs invite taxpayers for training sessions organised in a class-room environment. The sessions are sometimes targeted at specific groups of taxpayers (usually small taxpayers).
- **Mobile tax units.** Since seminars are organised in central places (mostly urban centres), many traders find it hard to attend. Some TAs now use vehicles fitted with speakers to move around sensitising the population on tax issues. Kenya Revenue Authority (KRA) and South Africa Revenue Service (SARS) have been operating mobile tax units (MTUs) for some time (Mascagini and Santoro, 2018[30])). The Uganda Revenue Authority (URA) also recently started using its own branded buses as MTUs.

- **Radio and television talk shows and adverts**. These are also common in many ATAs. Officials from a tax administration book sessions on radio and television programmes to address specific topics. Some ATAs have organised content that is run as adverts on radio and TV.
- **Tax television channels**. A few tax administrations have established television channels. One example is KRATV, which the KRA uses to disseminate tax information. The KRA records videos on how to complete different tax obligations such as how to file a tax return, how to apply for a tax identification number and how to make a tax payment. It then uploads these recordings on the KRATV network which taxpayers can access at any time. The URA has a similar initiative known as URATV. This, however, is internal to URA staff. The URA also records videos on how to complete different tax obligations and uploads them on its YouTube channel.
- **Tax education in schools and universities.** ATAs are also targeting future taxpayers by taking tax education to schools and universities. The KRA empowers young school children and advises them to sensitise their guardians about tax matters. A similar approach was implemented by the URA, which formed tax clubs in schools that hold debates on taxation topics. Similar tax clubs in schools are reported to have been implemented in Mauritius, Rwanda and Tanzania (OECD, 2021[31]).
- **A customised programme for newly registered taxpayers**. The Rwanda Revenue Authority has a special programme that targets newly registered taxpayers, teaching them about the basics of taxation such as what taxes they are liable to pay, when and how to pay, and how to amend their registration details. An impact evaluation reveals that this programme improved tax compliance among those who received training relative to those that did not, increasing the probability of declaring tax returns by 27 percentage points as well as increasing the amounts declared (Mascagini, Santoro and Mukama, 2019[17]).

Service centres and one stop shops

ATAs are working to take services as close to taxpayers as possible. Many ATAs have done this through opening branches in most busy places across the country. Some countries have opened one stop shops (OSS). In an OSS, different government agencies such as those responsible for licensing or registering businesses and the tax authority are brought together under one roof so that individuals can use the services of different authorities in the same visit. An evaluation of administrative interventions aimed at improving tax compliance among small and medium enterprises in Uganda revealed that the OSS had a relatively large impact on both the number of newly registered taxpayers and the revenue collected (Jouste, Nalukwago and Waiswa, 2021[32]).

In Kenya, the government established an OSS commonly known as Huduma centres in almost all major towns. These include a counter for KRA services that is used to receive feedback from taxpayers as well as conveying tax information. The aim of the government was to bring services closer to communities that are commonly interrupted by Internet breakdown.

In Rwanda, the government merged eight government institutions in 2008 to create an OSS known as the Rwanda Development Board (RDB). The RDB is under the supervision of the office of the president and its main goal is to promote business and investment growth in the country. In the RDB, several government services such as business and investment registration, tax incentives management and visa facilitation are offered under one roof.

Call / contact centres

ATAF has found that call centre services encourage voluntary tax compliance (2022[33]). ATAs such as Nigeria's Federal Inland Revenue Services (FIRS), URA and KRA have established call centres that operate like those of telecom companies and banks. A taxpayer can reach out to the tax administration by phone or by email 24 hours a day. Taxpayer requests are recorded and tracked on how they have been responded to and how long it took to respond.

The head of the URA contact centre reported that they no longer receive complaints from taxpayers about delayed or non-response from the URA regarding their complaints and/or support requests. Calls, emails and social media are all managed in the contact centre and the head of the contact centre monitors how many calls or emails are received, how many have been responded to, and the time taken to respond on a real-time basis.

In Mauritius, taxpayers and revenue officers from the Mauritius Revenue Authority (MRA) engage in tax-related conversations by video call. This visualisation simplifies explanations and illustrations made by the revenue officers.

The Eswatini Revenue Services established the Electronic Tarif Tool (ETT), which is used by taxpayers to lodge complaints and appeals related to customs classifications. The ETT is structured to easily capture taxpayer information.

Digitalisation of tax administration

African countries have embraced the digitalisation of tax systems due to its capacity to simplify tax compliance, reduce opportunities for collusion and corruption among tax officials through the reduction of face-to-face interactions, and generally improve the efficiency of tax administrations. Thanks to digitalisation, ATAs also increasingly possess platforms for disseminating information, for example through their online portals (websites). Digital systems also enhance the evidence base for decisions related to tax policy and administration (OECD, 2006[34]), (OECD, 2017[35]), (Mayega et al., 2021[36]).

Today, key tax administration systems and processes such as taxpayer registration, filing of tax returns and making tax payments are now digitalised in most ATAs. In the 2023 edition of the *African Tax Outlook*, 29 out of 31 member countries reported that they have implemented online filing and 97% reported that they have online payment systems (ATAF, 2023[4]). ATAs have also progressively integrated their systems and processes across government agencies. Box 3.1 provides some examples of the different ways in which ATAs are using technology to enhance compliance.

Empirical studies reveal that increased use of technology in tax administration in Africa is associated with higher revenue collections. For instance, a study on the impact of system automation on revenue collection in Kenya showed that the number of transactions and the revenue amount collected increased significantly after the introduction of the SIMBA system (Gitaru, 2017[37]).

In Uganda, a study by (Jouste, Milly and Waiswa, 2021[38]) shows that the number of presumptive taxpayers increased rapidly after the introduction of a new e-filing system. Similarly, a recent taxpayer registration reform that involves issuing an instant Tax Identification Number has resulted in a dramatic rise in new taxpayer registrations, with registrations in the new instant channel accounting for more than a third of total registrations in the last four years (Scarpini et al., 2024[39]).

In South Africa, SARS reports that advanced technologies such as machine learning and Artificial Intelligence have improved tax compliance. For instance, SARS processed 4.3 million VAT returns in 2022, over 90% of which were processed by an automated tax processor and machine learning algorithms without human intervention.

Box 3.1. Using technology to facilitate tax compliance

The uptake of digital solutions by tax administrations has increased in the past decade. These cover a wide range of processes, including return filing and registration, and can be enhanced through integration with other government systems.

In terms of **simplifying return filing**, recent reforms have focused on the introduction of electronic fiscal receipting and invoicing systems for value added tax (VAT). With these systems, transaction information on sales and purchases is automatically shared with the tax administration on a real time basis. At the end of a given period, a VAT return for the period is automatically populated; the taxpayer checks the information and, if they agree with what is generated by the system, they click the 'Submit' button to complete the filing process. In financial year 2023/24, KRA and URA introduced an auto-populated VAT return.

Meanwhile, MRA now auto-populates the income tax return form by inter-linking its systems with those of private sector players and government institutions, departments and agencies. Respondents from the MRA reported that the return can now be completed in less than five minutes because most of the fields are auto-populated.

The personal income tax return is also auto-populated in South Africa based on third-party data such as returns submitted by the employers. Individuals are notified about their populated returns via email and requested to log into their accounts to validate the information on the return; if this information is correct, they submit the return in less than five minutes. If they do not agree with what is prepopulated in the returns, they can amend but are required to upload supporting evidence.

To simplify the **payment process**, ATAs have diversified payment options to enhance taxpayer convenience. Today, very few tax administrations still handle cash; this only happens in a few remote locations that are far from banking facilities. A few ATAs have blended banking and mobile digital payment platforms which may include mobile banking. For instance, 'MPESA' in KRA, 'airtel' and 'MTN mobile money' in URA, and 'Econet' in ZIMRA. Morocco uses the 'Daribati' mobile application while in Madagascar they make use of 'e'Hetra' to make tax payments.

The MRA has implemented a unique online payments system through direct debits. The taxpayer's bank account is automatically debited with an amount equivalent to the validated tax liability immediately after the taxpayer files an income tax return.

Besides automating key tax administration processes, governments in African countries are increasingly **integrating their tax administration systems with other government systems**, thereby simplifying compliance processes.

- In South Africa, SARS integrated its systems with that of the Companies and Intellectual Property Commission (CIPC) so that if a company is registered with the CIPC, it is automatically registered with SARS.
- In Mauritius, the 'I Network system' used by MRA auto-registers taxpayers immediately after their registration information is captured by the registration bureau or with Local Government.
- In Uganda, the URA introduced Instant TIN (Tax Identification Number) technology. With this, a TIN that used to take between 1-3 days to be issued is now issued in less than five minutes. The URA integrated its systems with the National Identification and Registration Authority (NIRA) so that if one applies on the URA system the details are automatically checked against those in the NIRA system; if valid, a TIN is issued.

While the benefits of introducing digital systems and their continuous improvements are many, three main challenges remain. These include (i) intermittent Internet functionality, (ii) exorbitant costs of system acquisition and/or development, and (iii) low computer literacy rates. Initiatives to improve Internet connectivity and lower Internet costs, as well as training for the population on how to navigate systems, should be continuously implemented. Similarly, leveraging available IT skills within tax administrations to develop customised IT systems should be prioritised by ATAs that are in the early stages of developing their systems.

In the medium to long term, the ATAF should speed up its idea of developing a continental IT system that can easily be customised to specific country needs similar to UNCTAD's ASYCUDA world system that is now used by 102 countries in the management of international trade data and processes (UNCTAD, 2023[40]).

Voluntary tax disclosure programmes / amnesty

A voluntary disclosure programme (VDP) is a tool widely used by both developed and developing countries as a means of encouraging voluntary tax compliance among taxpayers and boosting revenue collections. VDPs require taxpayers who were hiding from tax authorities either within the country or in the diaspora to declare incomes or assets and only be assessed on the principal tax obligation. The incentive to taxpayers is the waiver of any penalties and interest on evaded taxes, while tax authorities benefit from collecting revenue with minimum costs. It is reported that VDPs have resulted in EUR 90 billion of additional tax assessments since 2009 around the world and that developing countries specifically have identified at least EUR 30 billion in additional tax assessments (ATAF, 2024[41]).

If not managed properly, there is a risk that a VDP can undermine tax morale amongst compliant taxpayers. This is because those granted access to a VDP will obtain a benefit even though they have been non-compliant with their tax obligations. If implemented well, the public benefits from the increased revenues and improvements in tax morale (ATAF, 2024[41]).

Several African countries have implemented VDPs, and they report collecting significant revenue from these programmes. For instance, South Africa held a VDP for 11 months between 2016 and 2017 and it is reported that the programme resulted in the disclosure of USD 1.8 billion of foreign assets and the recovery of approximately USD 296 million in tax revenues. Nigeria ran a two-year VDP between 2017 and 2019 that raised an additional USD 162 million in tax revenues and resulted in an increase in the number of registered taxpayers from 14 million in 2016 to 19 million in 2018. A tax amnesty programme in Zambia resulted in an increase in the recovery of tax arrears from 10% in 2021 to 16% in 2022. Countries such as Kenya and Uganda are also implementing VDPs but the results from these programmes have yet to be ascertained (ATAF, 2024[9]) (ATAF, 2024[41]).

Creating trust in government and the tax administration agency

Creating trust is crucial to building taxpayer morale as a driver of voluntary compliance. Building trust addresses the role of fairness, ethics, equity, reciprocity and accountability of tax systems and government as a whole, as well as its spending practices. According to (Prichard et al., 2019[29]), taxpayers are more likely to voluntarily comply if:

- Tax systems are administered in a just manner whereby all taxpayers are treated and/or penalised fairly and, in case of abuse of their rights, there are remedies available.
- The tax burden is equitably distributed such that everyone is seen to be paying their fair share. In this case, there is need for (i) horizontal equity, whereby taxpayers with similar economic circumstances pay a similar level of taxes and (ii) vertical equity, whereby the better-off pay more as a share of their income than the less wealthy and, in the case of firms, there is relative balance of effective tax burdens across differently sized firms.

- Tax revenues are translated into public goods and services that taxpayers are satisfied with. This calls for the government to be more accountable to taxpayers for the taxes collected.

There is scope for both the government and tax authorities to gain more trust from the taxpayers. Afrobarometer surveys conducted in 34 African countries reveal that on average more than half (52%) of Africans do not trust their government and that 54% believe that corruption has increased within the government (Figure 3.1). Such negative perceptions undermine tax morale and consequently tax compliance. On average, more than half (56%) of respondents in the 34 countries where the Afrobarometer survey was conducted thought it very likely that the rich pay bribes to avoid taxes. On the other hand, 57% stated that it is less likely for ordinary people to avoid taxes by paying bribes (Table 3.1).

Figure 3.1. Public opinions on trust and level of corruption in government (average for 34 African countries)

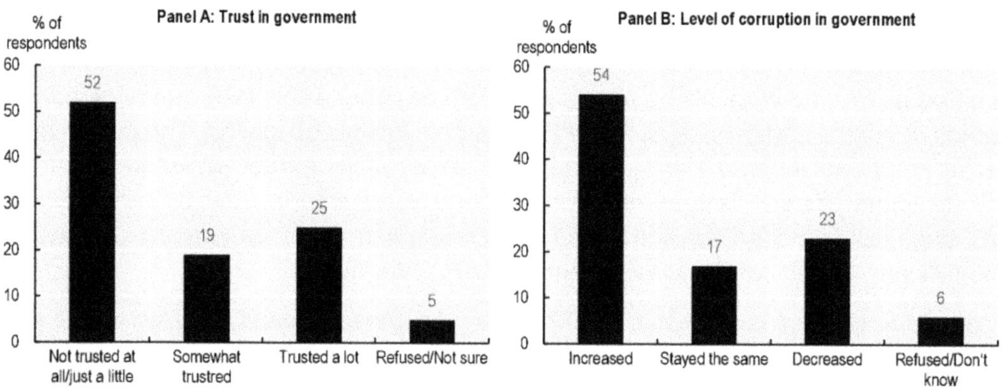

Source: Authors' computations from Afrobarometer Survey Round 7.

StatLink https://stat.link/vyk5dh

Table 3.1. Public opinions on paying bribes to avoid taxes (average for 34 African countries)

Opinions on paying bribes to tax officials	Less likely	Somewhat likely	Very likely	Refused/ don't know
Ordinary people pay bribe to avoid taxes	57%	23%	15%	4%
Rich people pay bribe to avoid taxes	20%	20%	56%	4%

Source: Authors' computations from Afrobarometer Survey Round 7.

The public often task ATAs with explaining how the tax revenues have been utilised. ATAs have thus taken on the role that would otherwise be done by another arm of government such as the Ministry of Finance of trying to provide evidence of what government revenues have been used for. Some initiatives include:

- **National taxpayer appreciation and accountability days.** These are national days meant to (i) appreciate compliant taxpayers; (ii) provide some level of accountability of what government has been able to do during the year using tax revenues; (iii) to educate taxpayers on tax issues; and (iv) to offer tax services (mostly registration of taxpayers). Countries such as Kenya, Rwanda, Tanzania, Burundi, Mozambique and Senegal have been implementing this initiative for years. ATAs organise these events in collaboration with other government agencies that are invited to showcase what they have done using tax revenues.

- **Publicising government works on televisions and billboards.** ATAs have designed adverts that are run on TV and billboards displayed in town and city centres showing government works. In Uganda, the URA runs a "Because of You Campaign" that informs the public that it is because of their contribution through taxes that government has been able to offer the different services.
- **Open minds forums.** These are intended to seek public opinions on new tax measures that the government intends to introduce. In Madagascar, the tax administration conducts working meetings with local business operators and accountants at the beginning of the financial year to brainstorm on how the tax policies and administrative procedures can be amicably handled.

Besides trying to improve trust in government, ATAs also implement initiatives that seek to improve public trust in themselves, including:

- **Press briefs.** These are done to inform the public about how much the TA tax administration been able to collect in each period. Usually, the media are invited to attend this event with the objective of informing the rest of public about how much has been collected by the TA.
- **Specialised divisions to improve both staff and process integrity.** Almost all tax administrations have a dedicated team to address integrity concerns for staff and business processes. These are tasked to conduct compliance checks on staff and take appropriate disciplinary action when required. These divisions also audit systems and business processes to verify if these perform as per the service level agreements.

Conclusions and recommendations

Facilitation and trust are key drivers of voluntary compliance among ATAs. While traditional approaches have favoured the 'stick' approach to increasing compliance through enforcement, the modern approach is to build a rapport between government and citizens, so that each party fulfils their obligations regarding the social contract. While many ATAs have fared well around facilitation, several are still lagging on the issue of building public trust.

This study demonstrates the wealth of information that is available for peer-to-peer exchanges and benchmarking among ATAs on innovative ways of enhancing voluntary tax compliance across the different tax administrations.

Specific innovations for facilitation have been implemented across a number of areas:

- In terms of tax education, innovations that could be considered by ATAs include (i) a dedicated tax education programme targeted at newly registered taxpayers; (ii) MTUs to take tax education to rural areas, (iii) tax television channels; and (iv) targeted tax education programmes for the youth in schools.
- Tax education programmes should not only focus on maximising tax compliance but also on dissemination of information about public services, budget transparency and government accountability.
- One stop shops where several government services are offered under a single roof.
- To improve the registration process, ATAs should encourage integration with other government services.
- To simplify return filing, ATAs should consider auto-populating tax returns. This calls for automation of key tax administration systems, access to third-party data and system integration within a given country.
- ATAs should diversify payment platforms by blending banking services with those of telecom companies using mobile money services.

It can be concluded through interviews responses that many ATAs have developed digital platforms with the assistance of costly foreign expertise. Maintaining these platforms and implementing recommended corrections also comes with a high cost. It is noteworthy that several ATAs are revamping their tax administration systems. For example, ZIMRA has taken steps to revamp their cumbersome and expensive tax systems by developing a new one using local expertise. IT procurement needs to be accompanied by a wider digitalisation process that clearly identifies what is needed and is accompanied by the necessary human resources (OECD, 2021[42]).

To harness the benefits of digitalisation, it is recommended that, in the long run, ATAs, with support from their respective governments, should focus on developing affordable, user-friendly and customised tax administration systems that are automated, digitalised and integrated. Additionally, there is a need to build local capacity to maintain systems through hands-on training and system upgrades. Another option is for ATAF to champion this initiative by developing a continental IT system that can easily be customised to specific country needs.

To promote integration of services, African governments should focus on enhancing infrastructure to enable seamless exchange of information among different government agencies. Ministries of Finance should collaborate with Ministries responsible for Communication and Information Technology to ensure the provision of adequate infrastructure across their respective jurisdictions. Moreover, effective coordination among the Ministry of Finance, Ministry of Information Technology, Ministry of Commerce/Trade, the National Business Registration Bureau, and the private sector is essential for enabling the linkage of the private sector to ATA systems.

Voluntary tax compliance has been hindered by the budget constraints faced by many ATAs. In particular, many ATAs lack adequate funds to build or upgrade tax systems. In some cases, they rely on expensive external expertise that is procured through cumbersome and lengthy procurement processes. Increased budgetary support for communication and Information Technology services is also needed to enable government agencies to operate in an automated environment and to seamlessly exchange information.

Facilitation of taxpayers and creating public trust in government and its spending practices as well as creating trust in the tax administration itself, are two critical channels of encouraging taxpayers to voluntarily comply. Although tax administrations are mostly responsible for facilitation and have limited control over increasing public trust in government, tax administrations should create a good image before the public through shunning corruption. ATAs should strive to address integrity issues as a means of enhancing trust in African tax systems in order to drive voluntary tax compliance.

On the other hand, trust in government remains a major issue of concern in Africa. Legislators should be cognisant of the significance of initiatives aimed at fostering trust. Trust is fostered by open communication, justice and accountability. Individuals are more inclined to voluntarily comply with their responsibilities when they have faith in government. Building more trust in government can promote voluntary compliance and improve tax morale.

In general, improving voluntary compliance specifically - and revenue mobilisation generally - requires a whole-of-government approach. The tax administration and other government agencies need to work together to demonstrate that tax revenues are properly utilised and that the government is determined to fight corruption and poor usage of taxpayer money. High-ranking government officials, politicians and influential citizens in society should set good examples by demonstrating that they are compliant with their tax obligations.

References

African Tax Administration Forum (2021), *Continental Taxpayer Education Practical Guidelines*, ATAF, Pretoria. [10]

Aiko, R. and C. Logan (2014), *Africa's willing taxpayers thwarted by opaque tax systems, corruption*, https://www.afrobarometer.org/wp-content/uploads/2022/02/ab_r5_policypaperno7.pdf. [16]

Amaning, N. et al. (2021), "Tax Compliance among Ghanaian SMEs: How impactful is Taxpayer Education?", *International Journal of Academic Research in Business and Social Science*, Vol. 10(4), pp. 40-58, https://doi.org/10.6007/IJARAFMS/v10-i4/8332. [19]

ATAF (2024), *African Tax Outlook*, African Tax Administration Forum, Pretoria, https://www.ataftax.org/african-tax-outlook. [9]

ATAF (2024), *ATAF Guide on Implementation of the Voluntary Disclosure Programme*, African Tax Administration Forum, Pretoria. [41]

ATAF (2023), *African Tax Outlook*, African Tax Administration Forum, Pretoria, https://www.ataftax.org/african-tax-outlook. [4]

ATAF (2022), *African Tax Outlook*, African Tax Administration Forum, Pretoria. [33]

ATAF (2021), *African Tax Outlook*, African Tax Administration Forum, Pretoria, https://www.ataftax.org/african-tax-outlook. [8]

ATAF & IMF (2022), *Tax Administration Challenges in Africa: A Comparative Analysis from Findings of the Tax Administration Diagnostic Assessment Tool (TADAT) Assessments*, https://www.tadat.org/assets/files/ATAF_TADAT_Joint_Paper_AnalysisofTax_Administration_in_Africa_2022_ENGLISH.pdf. [28]

Benzarti, Y. (2015), *How Taxing Is Tax Filing? Leaving Money on the Table Because of Hassle Costs*, https://doi.org/10.2139/ssrn.2412703. [20]

Betts, S. (2022), *Revenue Administration Compliance Risk Management Framework to Drive Revenue Performance*, Internation Monetary Fund, https://www.imf.org/en/Publications/TNM/Issues/2022/08/26/Revenue-Administration-Compliance-Risk-Management-Overarching-Framework-to-Drive-Revenue-520479. [1]

Chindengwike, J. and A. Kira (2022), "The Effect of Tax Rate on Taxpayers' Voluntary Compliance in Tanzania", *Journal of Accounting and Finance*, Vol. 10(5), pp. 889-896, https://doi.org/10.13189/ujaf.2022.100501. [3]

Gebrihet, H., Y. Gebresilassie and G. Woldu (2024), "Trust, Corruption, and Tax Compliance in Fragile States: On a Quest for Transforming Africa into Future Global Powerhouse", *Social Sciences*, Vol. 13(1)/3, https://doi.org/10.3390/socsci13010003. [21]

Gitaru, K. (2017), *The Impact Of System Automation On Revenue Collection in Kenya Revenue Authority (A Case Study of SIMBA)*, University Library of Munich, Germany, https://mpra.ub.uni-muenchen.de/80343/1/MPRA_paper_80343.pdf. [37]

Isbell, T. (2017), *Tax compliance Africans affirm civic duty but lack trust in tax department*, https://www.afrobarometer.org/publication/pp43-tax-compliance-africans-affirm-civic-duty-lack-trust-tax-department/. [15]

Jouste, M., N. Milly and R. Waiswa (2021), *Do tax administrative interventions targeted at small businesses improve tax compliance and revenue collection? Evidence from Ugandan administrative tax data.*, Helsinki, UNUWIDER, https://doi.org/10.35188/UNU-WIDER/2021/951-8. [38]

Jouste, M., M. Nalukwago and R. Waiswa (2021), *Do tax administrative interventions targeted at small businesses improve tax compliance and revenue collection?: Evidence from Ugandan administrative tax data*, Helsinki: UNU-WIDER, https://doi.org/10.35188/UNU-WIDER/2021/951-8. [32]

Kira, A. (2017), "An Evaluation of Governments' Initiatives in Enhancing Small Taxpayers' Voluntary Tax Compliance in Developing Countries", *International Journal of Academic Research in Accounting, Finance and Management Sciences*, Vol. 7(1)/January, pp. 253-267. [11]

Kirchler, E. (2021), *Strengthening Tax Compliance by Balancing Authorities' Power and Trustworthiness*, Cambridge University Press, https://doi.org/10.1017/9781108759458.055. [6]

Kogler, C. et al. (2023), "Perceptions of trust and power are associated with tax compliance: A cross-cultural study", *Economic and Political Studies*, Vol. 11/3, pp. 365-381, https://doi.org/10.1080/20954816.2022.2130501. [25]

Kumi, R. et al. (2023), "Voluntary and enforced tax compliance determinants and impact among agrochemical businesses in Ghana", *Arab Gulf Journal of Scientific Research*, https://doi.org/10.1108/AGJSR-03-2023-0133. [24]

Mascagini, G. and F. Santoro (2018), *What is the Role of Taxpayer Education in Africa?*, Brighton: IDS: ICTD Tax Administration Paper 1. [30]

Mascagini, G., F. Santoro and D. Mukama (2019), *Teach to Comply? Evidence from a Taxpayer Education Programme in Rwanda*, Brighton, IDS: ICTD. [17]

Mayega, J. et al. (2021), *How Clean Are Our Taxpayer Returns? Data Management in Uganda Revenue Authority*, Brighton: IDS. [36]

Nalishebo, S. and A. Halwampa (2014), *Uncovering the Unknown: An Analysis of Tax Evasion in Zambia.* [13]

Nkundabanyanga, S. et al. (2017), "Tax compliance in a developing country", *Journal of Economic Studies*, Vol. 44(6), pp. 937-957, https://doi.org/10.1108/JES-03-2016-0061. [23]

Nwokoye, E. et al. (2023), "Fiscal Incentives and Tax Compliance Behaviour in Industrial Clusters: A Survey of Clusters in South-East Nigeria", *Journal of African business*, Vol. 24/1, https://doi.org/10.1080/15228916.2022.2031827. [26]

OECD (2021), *Building Tax Culture, Compliance and Citizenship: A Global Source Book on Taxpayer Education, Second Edition*, OECD Publishing, Paris, https://doi.org/10.1787/18585eb1-en. [31]

OECD (2021), *Building Tax Culture, Compliance and Citizenship: A Global Source Book on Taxpayer Education, Second Edition*, OECD Publishing, Paris, https://doi.org/10.1787/18585eb1-en. [43]

OECD (2021), *Supporting the Digitalisation of Developing Country Tax Administrations*, OECD, Paris, http://www.oecd.org/tax/forum-on-tax-administration/publications-and-products/supporting-the-digitalisation-of-developing-country-taxadministrations.htm. [42]

OECD (2019), *Tax Morale: What Drives People and Businesses to Pay Tax?*, OECD Publishing, Paris, https://www.oecd-ilibrary.org/taxation/tax-morale_f3d8ea10-en. [22]

OECD (2019), *Tax Morale: What Drives People and Businesses to Pay Tax?*, OECD Publishing, Paris, https://doi.org/10.1787/f3d8ea10-en. [14]

OECD (2017), *Revenue Statistics in Asian Countries: Trends in Indonesia, Japan, Kazakhstan, Korea, Malaysia, the Philippines and Singapore*, OECD Publishing, Paris, https://doi.org/10.1787/9789264278943-en. [35]

OECD (2006), *Using Third Party Information Reports to Assist Taxpayers Meet their Return Filing Obligations – Country Experiences with the Use of Pre-Populated Personal Tax Returns*, OECD Publishing, Paris. [34]

OECD (2004), *Compliance Risk Management: Managing and Improving Tax Compliance*, OECD Publishing, Paris, http://www.oecd.org/tax/forum-on-tax-administration/publications-and-products/compliance/33818656.pdf. [2]

Olaniyi, O. et al. (2023), "Tax administration and personal income tax compliance in Nigeria: A PLS-SEM approach", *International Journal of Applied Economics, Finance and Accounting*, Vol. 17/1, pp. 117-126, https://doi.org/10.33094/ijaefa.v17i1.1088. [18]

Prichard, W. et al. (2019), *Innovations in Tax Compliance: Conceptual Framework*, World Bank, https://documents1.worldbank.org/curated/en/816431569957130111/pdf/Innovations-in-Tax-Compliance-Conceptual-Framework.pdf. [29]

Scarpini, C. et al. (2024), *Enhancing Taxpayer Registration with Inter-Institutional Data Sharing – Evidence from Uganda*, Brighton: Institute of Development Studies, https://doi.org/10.19088/ICTD.2024.047. [39]

Soglo, K. and I. Amedanou (2023), "Determinants of business tax compliance: A case study of Togo", *Journal of Accounting and Taxation*, Vol. 15(2), pp. 39-63, https://doi.org/10.5897/JAT2023.0559. [27]

TADAT (2019), *Tax Administration Diagnostic Assessment Tool Field Guide*, TADAT, https://www.tadat.org/assets/files/TADAT%20Field%20Guide%202019%20-%20English.pdf. [7]

Tanui, P. (2016), "Demystifying the key taxation concepts to improve compliance by small and medium enterprises in Kenya", *European Journal of Accounting, Auditing and Finance*, Vol. 4/6, pp. 47-60. [12]

UNCTAD (2023), *ASYCUDA Report 2022/23. Accelerating Climate Smart Trade Facilitation*, Geneva: United Nations Conference on Trade and Development, https://unctad.org/publication/asycuda-report-20222023. [40]

Waiswa, R., D. Akol and M. Nalukwago (2020), *Who can make Ugandan Taxpayers more Compliant?*, Brighton, Institute of Development Studies, https://www.ictd.ac/publication/make-uganda-taxpayers-more-compliant-ura/. [5]

Notes

[1] The study was prepared by staff in the Applied Research and Statistics Unit (Dr Ezera Madzivanyika, Mr Ronald Waiswa and Dr Nthabiseng Debeila) and Dr Ismail Kintu from Makerere University under the management of Dr Ezera Madzivanyika and overall direction of M. Anthony Munanda, the Head of ATAF's Domestic Resource Mobilisation (DRM) division.

[2] For additional information on taxpayer education, please consult (OECD, 2021[43]).

4 Tax levels and tax structures, 1990-2022

Comparative tables, 1990-2022

In all of the following tables, a ("..") indicates not available. The main series in this volume covers the years 1990 to 2022.Figures referring to 1991-99 and 2011 in Tables 4.1 and 4.2 and figures relating to 1990-94, 1996-99, 2001-04, 2006-09, 2011-14 and 2016-17 in Tables 4.5 to 4.19 have been omitted because of lack of space. Complete series are, however, available online at the OECD Data Explorer and can be accessed at https://data-explorer.oecd.org/ within the theme Taxation/Global tax revenue or by searching for African tax revenues.

Table 4.1. Total tax revenue as percentage of GDP, 1990-2022

	1990	2000	2005	2006	2007	2008	2009	2010	2011	2012
Botswana	..	..	15.4	15.6	14.1	17.4	16.0	15.8	16.0	14.3
Burkina Faso	..	10.2	11.7	12.1	12.6	11.9	12.6	14.0	13.4	14.9
Cabo Verde	10.5	15.6	20.4	23.8	25.6	26.3	19.3	17.3	18.4	16.6
Cameroon	..	10.8	11.0	11.5	12.0	12.0	12.3	11.5	12.5	13.0
Chad	..	..	..	..	..	..	..	10.9	13.4	11.2
Congo	..	3.8	5.9	5.6	5.9	6.0	8.0	7.1	7.6	7.0
Congo, Dem. Rep.[1]	..	0.6	4.9	5.5	6.3	7.6	8.0	8.3	8.7	10.6
Côte d'Ivoire	15.6	11.1	11.3	11.7	12.4	12.2	12.2	11.9	11.1	12.8
Egypt[2]	..	..	15.7	17.4	17.1	16.8	17.0	15.5	15.5	13.9
Equatorial Guinea	..	..	8.2	9.7	7.5	7.8	12.8	7.6	7.0	8.8
Eswatini	..	10.7	11.6	11.7	11.8	12.9	12.9	13.9	13.9	12.8
Gabon[3,4]	..	..	..	..	..	..	..	..	..	..
Ghana	..	7.8	10.5	9.9	10.0	10.5	10.4	10.8	11.8	12.0
Guinea	..	7.5	8.4	8.5	8.8	9.5	10.2	10.0	10.4	14.3
Kenya	..	..	14.7	14.7	16.0	16.7	16.0	15.9	16.7	16.2
Lesotho	..	..	14.3	13.9	16.5	17.3	18.6	19.3	19.7	21.2
Madagascar[2]	..	9.4	8.7	9.2	9.8	11.4	9.4	8.5	9.0	8.7
Malawi	..	..	9.0	9.0	9.7	10.3	10.9	11.3	11.6	10.3
Mali[2]	..	11.4	14.5	14.1	14.3	13.3	14.4	14.1	14.0	14.2
Mauritania[3]	..	..	..	..	10.0	10.2	10.4	9.8	10.6	13.5
Mauritius[5]	22.0	18.1	17.7	17.6	16.8	18.5	18.9	18.7	18.7	19.3
Morocco[2,3]	..	20.3	23.0	24.2	26.4	28.7	25.6	25.5	26.2	27.3
Mozambique										
Namibia	..	0.0	0.0	16.6	17.2	17.7	17.9	18.6	21.5	19.9
Niger	..	7.0	8.0	8.4	8.8	8.8	10.1	9.4	13.1	10.4
Nigeria	..	..	..	..	..	..	..	7.3	9.7	9.4
Rwanda[2]	..	8.5	10.7	11.3	11.5	12.5	12.1	12.3	13.0	13.7
Senegal[6]	..	13.1	15.3	15.7	16.2	15.2	15.0	15.9	16.0	16.1
Seychelles	..	..	..	..	..	27.9	28.8	30.7	32.8	31.2
Sierra Leone	..	..	7.8	8.2	7.6	8.1	8.2	9.1	9.1	9.7
Somalia										
South Africa[7]	21.9	20.1	22.8	24.0	25.3	25.3	23.2	23.1	24.0	24.4
Togo	..	7.0	9.9	10.7	10.8	10.5	10.5	10.7	11.6	12.0
Tunisia[2,3]	..	23.3	23.1	23.2	24.0	25.6	25.5	25.9	27.7	27.7
Uganda	..	8.3	9.3	9.4	9.5	9.3	8.5	8.3	8.4	8.5
Zambia	..	..	..	..	..	..	..	..	..	..
Africa average[8]	**..**	**..**	**..**	**..**	**..**	**..**	**..**	**..**	**..**	**..**
Asia-Pacific (36) average[9]	**..**	**..**	**..**	**..**	**..**	**..**	**..**	**17.9**	**18.2**	**18.8**
LAC average[10]	**14.6**	**17.1**	**18.8**	**19.3**	**20.0**	**20.2**	**19.4**	**20.0**	**20.4**	**20.6**
OECD average[11]	**30.9**	**32.9**	**32.6**	**32.8**	**32.9**	**32.2**	**31.5**	**31.5**	**31.9**	**32.3**

	2013	2014	2015	2016	2017	2018	2019	2020	2021	2022
Botswana	15.3	16.0	13.4	14.6	13.3	13.3	13.7	12.2	14.7	13.6
Burkina Faso	15.9	14.3	14.6	15.3	16.2	16.8	17.3	15.9	15.4	18.4
Cabo Verde	16.8	15.9	17.6	17.5	18.2	19.6	18.7	18.7	17.8	18.3
Cameroon	13.6	13.8	14.1	13.7	14.0	14.2	13.9	12.8	13.3	14.0
Chad	11.8	8.2	4.4	3.6	4.7	5.7	5.9	10.7	7.3	10.7
Congo	8.8	9.8	13.2	12.5	10.3	7.6	8.2	9.8	8.2	8.9
Congo, Dem. Rep.[1]	9.6	9.1	9.4	8.3	6.7	7.6	7.6	7.2	8.9	12.5
Côte d'Ivoire	12.7	12.2	12.6	13.0	13.1	12.9	12.8	13.1	13.7	12.9
Egypt[2]	15.0	14.0	13.9	15.0	14.9	15.5	15.2	13.6	14.1	14.2
Equatorial Guinea	8.9	9.8	12.0	7.1	6.6	6.6	9.8	8.6	5.9	8.1
Eswatini	13.6	14.9	15.0	16.1	17.0	17.4	18.3	17.8	17.4	17.6
Gabon[3,4]	15.9	16.5	15.3	12.3	10.9	10.4	12.1	12.8	10.3	11.4
Ghana	11.3	11.9	12.9	13.1	13.4	13.7	13.2	13.1	14.0	14.0
Guinea	13.1	13.1	13.0	14.0	12.8	12.0	12.2	11.7	11.1	10.8
Kenya	16.3	17.4	17.0	17.2	17.5	16.8	16.5	16.0	15.4	16.8
Lesotho	18.6	18.9	19.3	19.3	19.3	21.4	21.1	19.8	21.7	21.3
Madagascar[2]	9.1	8.8	9.3	9.6	10.4	10.9	11.1	10.1	10.7	11.5
Malawi	11.5	12.7	12.0	12.0	13.2	12.8	12.5	12.6	12.4	12.5
Mali[2]	14.5	14.2	15.6	16.9	17.3	13.8	18.1	18.6	19.8	17.9
Mauritania[3]	13.3	15.1	14.5	14.2	14.4	15.1	13.8	12.6	14.4	14.7
Mauritius[5]	18.9	18.9	18.8	19.0	19.2	19.7	20.4	20.2	20.0	22.3

Table 4.1. Total tax revenue as percentage of GDP, 1990 2022 (continued)

	2013	2014	2015	2016	2017	2018	2019	2020	2021	2022
Morocco[2,3]	26.0	25.7	24.6	25.4	25.9	26.2	26.4	27.3	27.3	29.9
Mozambique	25.8	34.3	31.7	25.0	19.4	21.2	21.0	20.7	22.7	21.8
Namibia	20.0	21.1	21.5	21.1	20.4	19.4	20.2	18.5	19.5	19.7
Niger	12.4	12.1	12.3	10.2	9.5	11.2	10.4	9.8	10.5	9.6
Nigeria	8.3	7.7	6.1	5.3	5.7	6.4	6.0	5.5	6.7	7.9
Rwanda[2]	15.0	15.4	16.2	16.3	16.2	16.9	17.3	17.1	17.0	16.5
Senegal[6]	15.4	16.2	16.4	17.0	16.7	17.3	18.7	18.5	18.7	19.8
Seychelles	29.3	29.6	28.7	29.3	29.4	30.1	29.0	27.8	28.4	27.2
Sierra Leone	8.3	8.7	9.9	10.6	10.8	12.5	13.3	12.5	13.3	11.4
Somalia	1.1	1.1	1.2	1.2	1.4	1.7	2.0	2.4	2.5	2.6
South Africa[7]	24.8	25.4	26.4	26.0	26.0	26.5	26.1	25.1	26.3	27.1
Togo	14.0	14.9	15.7	16.3	15.8	14.8	15.5	15.7	17.2	17.4
Tunisia[2,3]	28.3	29.3	28.5	27.9	29.2	29.9	32.1	32.5	32.5	33.5
Uganda	9.0	9.3	10.4	11.0	11.4	11.7	12.1	11.4	12.5	12.5
Zambia	14.1	15.3	14.3	13.0	14.9	16.2	16.2	15.7	16.1	16.2
Africa average[8]	**14.9**	**15.3**	**15.3**	**15.0**	**14.9**	**15.2**	**15.5**	**15.2**	**15.5**	**16.0**
Asia-Pacific (36) average[9]	**18.8**	**18.2**	**18.4**	**17.8**	**18.6**	**19.1**	**19.3**	**18.3**	**18.8**	**19.3**
LAC average[10]	**20.7**	**20.9**	**21.3**	**21.2**	**21.2**	**21.5**	**21.6**	**21.0**	**21.3**	**21.5**
OECD average[11]	**32.6**	**32.8**	**32.9**	**33.5**	**33.3**	**33.5**	**33.4**	**33.5**	**34.1**	**34.0**

.. Not available

Note: The figures include sub-national government tax revenues for Cabo Verde (2008-2020), Eswatini, Mauritania (2009-2018), Mauritius, Morocco, Nigeria (only state revenues), Somalia (from 2019) and South Africa (from 2003). Sub-national government tax revenues are not available in other countries.

Data on social security contributions are not available for Chad, the Democratic Republic of the Congo (prior to 2012), Equatorial Guinea (prior to 2013), Guinea, Madagascar (prior to 2011), Namibia (prior to 2009), the Republic of the Congo (prior to 2018), Sierra Leone (prior to 2018), Togo, Uganda and Zambia and are only partially available in Cameroon and Senegal. Social security contributions for Botswana, Lesotho and Malawi are deemed to be zero as they do not meet the criteria to be classified as social security contributions set out in the OECD classification of taxes in the *OECD Interpretative Guide*.

In Ghana, Lesotho, Malawi, Nigeria, Sierra Leone and Uganda, revenues from property taxes are mainly levied by local governments for which data on revenue are not available. In the Democratic Republic of the Congo, only data for property taxes levied by the Direction Générale des Recettes Administratives, Judiciaires, Domaniales et de Participation (DGRAD) are available since 2010.

See the country tables in Chapter 5 for further information on data issues for individual countries.

1. The figures should be interpreted with caution as they are affected by macroeconomic instability in the early 2000s. For the years prior to 2010, the figures exclude some revenues collected by the Direction Générale des Recettes Administratives, Judiciaires, Domaniales et de Participation (DGRAD), which are estimated to be less than 1% of total tax revenue. See Table 5.7 in Chapter 5 for further information.
2. Egypt, Madagascar, Mali, Morocco, Rwanda and Tunisia do not include social security contributions in the tax-to-GDP ratio in their official publications as these countries do not consider them to be taxes. They are included as tax revenue in this publication, following the classification set out in the OECD Interpretative Guide.
3. Social security contributions are estimated in Gabon (years prior to 2015), Mauritania (2021 and 2022), Morocco (years prior to 2002), and Tunisia (2022).
4. The figures should be interpreted with caution for years prior to 2014 as customs revenues (representing roughly 50% of tax revenues) are estimated for these years.
5. The fiscal year for Mauritius changed in 2010 and in 2015. Figures for 2015 needed to be estimated as a result.
6. These figures include contributions to the Senegalese Pension Institute (IPRES) (estimated prior to 2006) and contributions to the social security fund (CSS) (from 2012 as data for previous years are not available).
7. Includes payments made by South Africa to the Southern African Customs Union (SACU) Common Revenue Pool.
8. Represents an unweighted average of the 36 African countries in this publication. The Africa average should be interpreted with caution as data for social security contributions (category 2000) and property taxes (category 4000) are not available or are partial in a few countries. See the country tables in Chapter 5 for further information.
9. Represents an unweighted average for 36 Asian and Pacific economies included in the publication *Revenue Statistics in Asia and the Pacific 2024*.
10. Represents an unweighted average for 26 Latin American and Caribbean (LAC) countries included in the publication *Revenue Statistics in Latin America and the Caribbean 2024*.
11. Represents an unweighted average for 38 OECD countries in the OECD publication *Revenue Statistics 2024*.

Table 4.2. Total tax revenue (excluding social security) as percentage of GDP

	1990	2000	2005	2006	2007	2008	2009	2010	2011	2012
Botswana	..	..	15.4	15.6	14.1	17.4	16.0	15.8	16.0	14.3
Burkina Faso	..	8.6	10.2	10.5	11.0	10.4	11.1	12.4	12.0	13.5
Cabo Verde	10.5	14.8	19.8	23.3	25.5	26.2	19.2	17.3	18.4	16.6
Cameroon	..	9.9	10.2	10.7	11.2	11.2	11.4	10.6	11.5	12.0
Chad	..	..	..	..	..	..	..	10.9	13.4	11.2
Congo	..	3.8	5.9	5.6	5.9	6.0	8.0	7.1	7.6	7.0
Congo, Dem. Rep.[1]	..	0.6	4.9	5.5	6.3	7.6	8.0	8.3	8.7	10.1
Côte d'Ivoire	14.6	10.1	10.4	10.8	11.4	11.3	11.2	11.0	10.3	11.6
Egypt	..	..	12.8	14.6	14.0	14.0	14.5	13.0	13.0	11.4
Equatorial Guinea	..	..	8.2	9.7	7.5	7.8	12.8	7.6	7.0	8.8
Eswatini	..	9.5	10.2	10.2	10.2	11.4	11.1	12.0	12.2	11.3
Gabon[2]	..	..	..	..	..	..	..	..	..	..
Ghana	..	7.1	9.7	8.8	8.9	9.5	9.1	9.9	10.8	11.1
Guinea	..	7.5	8.4	8.5	8.8	9.5	10.2	10.0	10.4	14.3
Kenya	..	..	14.5	14.5	15.8	16.5	15.9	15.7	16.5	16.0
Lesotho	..	..	14.3	13.9	16.5	17.3	18.6	19.3	19.7	21.2
Madagascar	..	9.4	8.7	9.2	9.8	11.4	9.4	8.5	8.7	8.3
Malawi	..	..	9.0	9.0	9.7	10.3	10.9	11.3	11.6	10.3
Mali	..	10.5	13.1	12.7	12.8	11.8	12.8	12.8	12.3	12.5
Mauritania	..	..	..	..	9.4	9.5	9.8	9.1	10.0	12.8
Mauritius[3]	21.1	17.3	17.0	16.9	16.2	17.8	18.3	18.0	18.0	18.6
Morocco	..	18.1	19.1	19.8	22.0	24.5	21.2	21.1	21.4	22.3
Mozambique	..	..	..	26.5	30.7	20.6	28.7	25.8	29.0	20.9
Namibia	..	0.0	0.0	16.6	17.2	17.7	17.6	18.3	21.1	19.5
Niger	..	6.6	7.7	8.1	8.4	8.4	9.7	8.9	12.5	9.9
Nigeria	..	..	..	..	..	..	..	6.7	9.1	8.7
Rwanda	..	8.1	9.9	10.6	10.7	11.6	11.3	11.6	12.1	12.8
Senegal	..	12.6	14.7	15.1	15.5	14.5	14.3	15.0	15.3	15.1
Seychelles	..	..	..	..	..	22.6	23.9	27.9	32.2	30.6
Sierra Leone	..	..	7.8	8.2	7.6	8.1	8.2	9.1	9.1	9.7
Somalia	..	..	..	..	..	..	..	..	..	..
South Africa[4]	21.9	20.1	22.4	23.6	24.9	24.9	22.8	22.8	23.6	24.0
Togo	..	7.0	9.9	10.7	10.8	10.5	10.5	10.7	11.6	12.0
Tunisia	..	18.3	17.8	17.5	18.1	19.4	18.9	18.9	20.1	19.8
Uganda	..	8.3	9.3	9.4	9.5	9.3	8.5	8.3	8.4	8.5
Zambia	..	..	..	..	..	..	..	..	..	14.7
Africa average[5]	**..**	**..**	**..**	**..**	**..**	**..**	**..**	**..**	**..**	**..**
Asia-Pacific (36) average[6]	**..**	**..**	**..**	**..**	**..**	**..**	**..**	**16.4**	**16.7**	**17.3**
LAC average[7]	**12.4**	**14.3**	**16.1**	**16.6**	**17.2**	**17.3**	**16.3**	**16.8**	**17.1**	**17.2**
OECD average[8]	**23.8**	**24.5**	**24.3**	**24.5**	**24.6**	**23.9**	**22.8**	**22.9**	**23.3**	**23.6**

	2013	2014	2015	2016	2017	2018	2019	2020	2021	2022
Botswana	15.3	16.0	13.4	14.6	13.3	13.3	13.7	12.2	14.7	13.6
Burkina Faso	14.3	12.7	12.8	13.5	14.4	14.9	15.4	14.4	13.7	16.7
Cabo Verde	16.7	15.9	17.6	17.4	18.2	19.5	18.7	18.7	17.7	18.2
Cameroon	12.6	13.0	13.3	12.7	13.0	13.2	12.8	11.8	12.3	13.1
Chad	11.8	8.2	4.4	3.6	4.7	5.7	5.9	10.7	7.3	10.7
Congo	8.8	9.8	13.2	12.5	10.3	7.0	7.5	9.0	7.5	8.3
Congo, Dem. Rep.[1]	9.0	8.5	8.8	7.8	6.2	7.1	6.8	6.4	8.1	11.7
Côte d'Ivoire	11.3	10.8	11.2	11.5	11.6	11.4	11.4	11.5	12.2	11.4
Egypt	12.5	11.3	11.6	12.0	12.3	13.1	12.8	11.7	12.2	12.3
Equatorial Guinea	8.4	9.2	11.3	6.3	5.9	5.9	9.0	7.7	5.3	7.5
Eswatini	12.2	13.1	13.0	14.1	14.7	14.9	15.9	15.4	15.1	15.5
Gabon[2]	..	15.1	14.3	10.6	9.2	8.8	10.6	11.2	9.0	10.2
Ghana	10.3	10.8	11.7	12.3	12.5	13.0	12.5	12.1	13.3	13.2
Guinea	13.1	13.1	13.0	14.0	12.8	12.0	12.2	11.7	11.1	10.8
Kenya	16.0	17.2	16.8	16.7	17.1	16.2	15.9	15.4	14.9	16.2
Lesotho	18.6	18.9	19.3	19.3	19.3	21.4	21.1	19.8	21.7	21.3
Madagascar	8.8	8.5	8.9	9.2	10.0	10.3	10.6	9.5	10.2	10.9
Malawi	11.5	12.7	12.0	12.0	13.2	12.8	12.5	12.6	12.4	12.5
Mali	12.8	12.4	13.7	14.7	15.0	11.7	15.2	15.3	16.2	14.0
Mauritania	12.7	14.2	13.6	13.4	13.7	14.4	13.1	11.9	13.7	14.1

Table 4.2. Total tax revenue (excluding social security) as percentage of GDP (continued)

	2013	2014	2015	2016	2017	2018	2019	2020	2021	2022
Mauritius[3]	18.2	18.2	18.0	18.2	18.5	18.9	19.6	19.3	18.7	20.7
Morocco	21.0	20.7	19.7	20.3	20.6	20.8	20.5	20.5	20.8	23.2
Mozambique	25.3	33.8	31.1	24.7	19.4	21.1	21.0	20.5	22.6	21.7
Namibia	19.7	20.8	21.1	20.8	20.0	19.1	19.9	18.2	19.1	19.4
Niger	11.9	11.5	11.7	9.7	8.9	10.7	9.8	9.2	9.9	9.1
Nigeria	7.6	7.0	5.5	4.8	5.1	5.8	5.3	4.9	6.1	7.4
Rwanda	14.0	14.4	15.2	15.2	15.2	15.9	16.3	16.1	16.0	15.6
Senegal	14.4	15.2	15.3	15.9	15.6	16.1	17.5	17.4	17.8	18.9
Seychelles	28.5	28.5	27.6	28.3	28.3	27.9	27.5	26.0	26.7	25.1
Sierra Leone	8.3	8.7	9.9	10.6	10.8	10.9	11.8	11.0	11.7	10.0
Somalia	1.1	1.1	1.2	1.2	1.4	1.7	2.0	2.4	2.5	2.6
South Africa[4]	24.4	25.0	26.0	25.6	25.7	26.1	25.8	24.8	26.0	26.7
Togo	14.0	14.9	15.7	16.3	15.8	14.8	15.5	15.7	17.2	17.4
Tunisia	20.1	21.2	20.1	19.1	20.1	21.2	23.0	22.4	22.9	24.3
Uganda	9.0	9.3	10.4	11.0	11.4	11.7	12.1	11.4	12.5	12.5
Zambia	14.1	15.3	14.3	13.0	14.9	16.2	16.2	15.7	16.1	16.2
Africa average[5]	**13.8**	**14.1**	**14.1**	**13.7**	**13.6**	**13.9**	**14.2**	**13.8**	**14.1**	**14.6**
Asia-Pacific (36) average[6]	**17.4**	**16.8**	**17.0**	**16.4**	**17.1**	**17.5**	**17.6**	**16.5**	**16.9**	**17.5**
LAC average[7]	**17.2**	**17.3**	**17.6**	**17.5**	**17.4**	**17.7**	**17.9**	**17.1**	**17.5**	**17.9**
OECD average[8]	**23.8**	**24.1**	**24.1**	**24.7**	**24.5**	**24.5**	**24.5**	**24.4**	**25.1**	**25.3**

.. Not available

Note: The figures include sub-national government tax revenues for Cabo Verde (2008-2020), Eswatini, Mauritania (2009-2018), Mauritius, Morocco, Nigeria (only state revenues), Somalia (from 2019) and South Africa (from 2003). Sub-national government tax revenues are not available in other countries. In Ghana, Lesotho, Malawi, Nigeria, Sierra Leone and Uganda, revenues from property taxes are mainly levied by local governments for which data on revenue are not available. In the Democratic Republic of the Congo, only data for property taxes levied by the Direction Générale des Recettes Administratives, Judiciaires, Domaniales et de Participation (DGRAD) are available since 2010.

See the country tables in Chapter 5 for further information on data issues for individual countries.

1. The figures should be interpreted with caution as they are affected by macroeconomic instability in the early 2000s. For the years prior to 2010, the figures exclude some revenues collected by the *Direction Générale des Recettes Administratives, Judiciaires, Domaniales* et de Participation (DGRAD), which are estimated to be less than 1% of total tax revenue. See Table 5.7 in Chapter 5 for further information.
2. The figures should be interpreted with caution for years prior to 2014 as customs revenues (representing roughly 50% of tax revenues) are estimated for these years.
3. The fiscal year for Mauritius changed in 2010 and in 2015. Figures for 2015 needed to be estimated as a result.
4. Includes payments made by South Africa to the Southern African Customs Union (SACU) Common Revenue Pool.
5. Represents an unweighted average of the 36 African countries in this publication.
6. Represents an unweighted average for 36 Asian and Pacific economies included in the publication *Revenue Statistics in Asia and the Pacific 2024*.
7. Represents an unweighted average for 26 Latin American and Caribbean (LAC) countries included in the publication *Revenue Statistics in Latin America and the Caribbean 2024*.
8. Represents an unweighted average for 38 OECD countries in the OECD publication *Revenue Statistics 2024*.

Table 4.3. Tax revenue of the main headings as percentage of GDP, 2022

	1000 Income & profits	2000 Social security	3000 Payroll	4000 Property	5000 Goods and services	6000 Other taxes
Botswana	8.8	0.0	0.0	0.0	4.8	0.0
Burkina Faso	6.2	1.7	0.2	0.1	10.2	0.1
Cabo Verde	4.3	0.0	0.0	0.3	13.6	0.0
Cameroon	4.2	1.0	0.2	0.1	8.2	0.3
Chad	7.4	..	0.1	0.2	2.9	0.0
Congo	2.0	0.6	0.2	0.3	5.8	0.0
Congo, Dem. Rep.	6.4	0.8	0.3	0.1	4.7	0.1
Côte d'Ivoire	1.9	1.4	1.5	0.4	7.5	0.1
Egypt[1]	6.1	1.9	0.0	0.1	6.1	0.0
Equatorial Guinea	6.1	0.7	0.0	0.0	1.4	0.0
Eswatini	8.1	2.1	0.0	0.5	6.9	0.0
Gabon	5.4	1.2	0.1	0.2	4.5	0.1
Ghana	5.5	0.7	0.0	0.1	7.7	0.0
Guinea	2.2	..	0.2	0.0	8.2	0.2
Kenya	7.1	0.6	0.0	0.0	9.0	0.1
Lesotho	11.0	0.0	0.0	..	10.4	0.0
Madagascar[1]	3.1	0.6	0.0	0.1	7.8	0.0
Malawi	5.7	0.0	0.0	..	6.8	0.0
Mali[1]	4.5	4.0	0.1	0.3	8.4	0.6
Mauritania[2]	5.0	0.6	0.0	0.0	8.9	0.1
Mauritius	6.7	1.6	0.2	1.1	12.7	0.0
Morocco[1]	9.2	6.7	0.0	1.5	12.4	0.1
Mozambique	11.0	0.2	0.0	0.3	10.3	0.2
Namibia	12.0	0.3	0.0	0.1	7.2	0.1
Niger	2.4	0.5	0.1	0.2	5.7	0.7
Nigeria	4.3	0.6	0.0	0.1	2.6	0.4
Rwanda[1]	7.0	0.9	0.0	0.1	8.4	0.0
Senegal	5.9	0.9	0.2	0.5	12.1	0.3
Seychelles	7.8	2.1	0.0	0.2	17.1	0.0
Sierra Leone	5.0	1.4	0.0	..	4.9	0.0
Somalia	0.3	0.0	0.0	0.0	2.3	0.0
South Africa[3]	14.5	0.3	0.3	1.2	10.6	0.0
Togo	3.8	..	0.0	0.1	13.2	0.3
Tunisia[1,2]	10.3	9.2	0.4	0.3	12.5	0.7
Uganda	4.6	..	0.0	0.2	7.8	0.0
Zambia	9.6	..	0.0	0.1	6.5	0.0
Africa average[4]	**6.3**	**1.4**	**0.1**	**0.3**	**8.1**	**0.1**
Asia-Pacific (36) average[5]	**7.7**	**1.9**	**0.1**	**0.6**	**9.0**	**0.2**
LAC average[6]	**6.3**	**3.6**	**0.2**	**0.9**	**10.1**	**0.4**
OECD average[7]	**11.3**	**9.2**	**0.5**	**1.9**	**10.6**	**0.2**

.. Not available

Note: The figures include sub-national government tax revenues for Cabo Verde (2008-2020), Eswatini, Mauritania (2009-2018), Mauritius, Morocco, Nigeria (only state revenues), Somalia (from 2019) and South Africa (from 2003). Sub-national government tax revenues are not available in other countries.

Data on social security contributions are not available for Chad, the Democratic Republic of the Congo (prior to 2012), Equatorial Guinea (prior to 2013), Guinea, Madagascar (prior to 2011), Namibia (prior to 2009), the Republic of the Congo (prior to 2018), Sierra Leone (prior to 2018), Togo, Uganda and Zambia and are only partially available in Cameroon and Senegal. Social security contributions for Botswana, Lesotho and Malawi are deemed to be zero as they do not meet the criteria to be classified as social security contributions set out in the OECD classification of taxes in the OECD Interpretative Guide.

In Ghana, Lesotho, Malawi, Nigeria, Sierra Leone and Uganda, revenues from property taxes are mainly levied by local governments for which data on revenue are not available. In the Democratic Republic of the Congo only data for property taxes levied by the Direction Générale des Recettes Administratives, Judiciaires, Domaniales et de Participation (DGRAD) are available since 2010. The figures for heading 4000 for Ghana in 2022 represent only the introduction of new taxes on money transfers and are still missing data on local property taxes for those years.

1. Egypt, Madagascar, Mali, Morocco, Rwanda and Tunisia do not include social security contributions in the tax-to-GDP ratio in their official publications as these countries do not consider them to be taxes. They are included as tax revenue in this publication, following the classification set out in the OECD Interpretative Guide.
2. Social security contributions are estimated in Mauritania and Tunisia.
3. The figures for heading 5000 taxes on goods and services should be interpreted with caution as they include payments made by South Africa to the Southern African Customs Union (SACU) Common Revenue Pool.
4. Represents an unweighted average of the 36 African countries in this publication. The Africa average should be interpreted with caution as data for social security contributions (category 2000) and property taxes (category 4000) are not available or are partial in a few countries. See the country tables in Chapter 5 for further information.
5. Represents an unweighted average for 36 Asian and Pacific economies included in the publication *Revenue Statistics in Asia and the Pacific 2024.*

6. Represents an unweighted average for 26 Latin American and Caribbean (LAC) countries included in the publication *Revenue Statistics in Latin America and the Caribbean 2024*.
7. Represents an unweighted average for 38 OECD countries in the OECD publication *Revenue Statistics 2024*.

Table 4.4. Tax revenue of the main headings as percentage of total taxes, 2022

	1000 Income and profits	2000 Social security	3000 Payroll	4000 Property	5000 Goods and services	6000 Other taxes
Botswana	64.2	0.0	0.0	0.3	35.5	0.0
Burkina Faso	33.5	9.1	0.8	0.7	55.4	0.5
Cabo Verde	23.8	0.2	0.0	1.8	74.2	0.0
Cameroon	30.2	6.8	1.7	0.7	58.3	2.2
Chad	69.6	..	0.9	2.1	27.4	0.0
Congo	22.9	6.9	1.9	3.0	65.1	0.1
Congo, Dem. Rep.	51.5	6.7	2.2	0.5	37.9	1.2
Côte d'Ivoire	15.1	11.2	11.5	3.3	58.3	0.7
Egypt[1]	43.1	13.5	0.0	0.6	42.8	0.0
Equatorial Guinea	74.9	8.1	0.0	0.0	16.7	0.3
Eswatini	46.2	12.0	0.0	2.8	39.0	0.0
Gabon	46.9	10.7	0.7	1.6	39.5	0.6
Ghana	39.2	5.1	0.0	0.7	55.0	0.0
Guinea	20.4	..	2.0	0.2	76.0	1.4
Kenya	42.0	3.7	0.0	0.0	53.6	0.6
Lesotho	51.4	0.0	0.0	..	48.6	0.0
Madagascar[1]	26.8	5.0	0.0	0.6	67.6	0.1
Malawi	45.3	0.0	0.0	..	54.6	0.1
Mali[1]	25.3	22.1	0.7	1.4	47.0	3.5
Mauritania[2]	34.0	4.2	0.1	0.1	60.9	0.7
Mauritius	29.9	7.1	0.7	5.0	57.1	0.2
Morocco[1]	30.8	22.5	0.0	5.0	41.4	0.3
Mozambique	50.3	0.7	0.0	1.2	47.1	0.8
Namibia	60.8	1.4	0.0	0.6	36.8	0.3
Niger	25.3	5.4	0.6	1.9	59.3	7.5
Nigeria	53.9	7.0	0.3	0.8	32.4	5.7
Rwanda[1]	42.6	5.5	0.0	0.9	51.0	0.0
Senegal	29.6	4.7	1.1	2.3	61.0	1.3
Seychelles	28.7	7.8	0.0	0.9	62.6	0.0
Sierra Leone	44.2	12.7	0.0	..	43.1	0.0
Somalia	11.1	0.0	0.0	0.8	87.1	0.9
South Africa[3]	53.8	1.3	1.1	4.6	39.2	0.0
Togo	21.8	..	0.1	0.6	75.8	1.7
Tunisia[1,2]	30.8	27.5	1.1	1.0	37.4	2.2
Uganda	36.4	..	0.0	1.5	62.1	0.1
Zambia	59.2	..	0.3	0.6	40.0	0.0
Africa average[4]	**39.3**	**7.4**	**0.8**	**1.5**	**51.3**	**0.9**
Asia-Pacific (36) average[5]	**39.9**	**7.6**	**0.3**	**2.9**	**48.8**	**1.1**
LAC average[6]	**29.8**	**16.7**	**1.0**	**3.8**	**46.5**	**2.2**
OECD average[7]	**36.5**	**24.8**	**1.3**	**5.3**	**31.5**	**0.6**

.. Not available

Note: The figures include sub-national government tax revenues for Cabo Verde (2008-2020), Eswatini, Mauritania (2009-2018), Mauritius, Morocco, Nigeria (only state revenues), Somalia (from 2019) and South Africa (from 2003). Sub-national government tax revenues are not available in other countries.

Data on social security contributions are not available for Chad, the Democratic Republic of the Congo (prior to 2012), Equatorial Guinea (prior to 2013), Guinea, Madagascar (prior to 2011), Namibia (prior to 2009), the Republic of the Congo (prior to 2018), Sierra Leone (prior to 2018), Togo, Uganda and Zambia and are only partially available in Cameroon and Senegal. Social security contributions for Botswana, Lesotho and Malawi are deemed to be zero as they do not meet the criteria to be classified as social security contributions set out in the OECD classification of taxes in the OECD Interpretative Guide.

In Ghana, Lesotho, Malawi, Nigeria, Sierra Leone and Uganda, revenues from property taxes are mainly levied by local governments for which data on revenue are not available.. The figures for heading 4000 for Ghana in 2022 represent only the introduction of new taxes on money transfers and are still missing data on local property taxes for those years.

1. Egypt, Madagascar, Mali, Morocco, Rwanda and Tunisia do not include social security contributions in the tax-to-GDP ratio in their official publications as these countries do not consider them to be taxes. They are included as tax revenue in this publication, following the classification set out in the OECD Interpretative Guide.
2. Social security contributions are estimated in Mauritania and Tunisia.
3. The figures for heading 5000 taxes on goods and services should be interpreted with caution as they include payments made by South Africa to the Southern African Customs Union (SACU) Common Revenue Pool.
4. Represents an unweighted average of the 36 African countries in this publication. The Africa average should be interpreted with caution as data for social security contributions (category 2000) and property taxes (category 4000) are not available or are partial in a few countries. See the country tables in Chapter 5 for further information.
5. Represents an unweighted average for 36 Asian and Pacific economies included in the publication *Revenue Statistics in Asia and the Pacific 2024*.

6. Represents an unweighted average for 26 Latin American and Caribbean (LAC) countries included in the publication *Revenue Statistics in Latin America and the Caribbean 2024.*
7. Represents an unweighted average for 38 OECD countries in the OECD publication *Revenue Statistics 2024*.

Table 4.5. Taxes on income and profits (1000) as percentage of GDP

	1995	2000	2005	2010	2015	2018	2019	2020	2021	2022
Botswana	..	..	11.3	10.4	9.1	8.6	8.6	7.4	9.2	8.8
Burkina Faso	..	2.5	2.4	2.7	3.4	4.3	4.8	4.5	5.3	6.2
Cabo Verde	5.1	5.5	6.3	5.2	5.6	6.0	5.8	5.6	4.9	4.3
Cameroon	2.2	3.0	3.2	3.1	4.6	3.8	3.8	3.7	3.6	4.2
Chad	..	..	..	8.2	2.4	2.9	2.7	6.7	3.6	7.4
Congo	..	1.8	1.8	2.3	4.9	1.7	2.2	2.7	2.2	2.0
Congo, Dem. Rep.	..	0.2	0.9	2.2	3.3	3.3	3.2	2.4	3.5	6.4
Côte d'Ivoire	1.8	1.8	1.5	1.5	1.5	1.8	1.6	1.6	1.8	1.9
Egypt	..	..	6.3	6.8	6.1	6.2	5.9	6.0	6.0	6.1
Equatorial Guinea	..	..	7.5	6.8	9.9	4.4	7.5	6.2	4.1	6.1
Eswatini	5.4	5.5	6.2	7.2	7.3	8.4	8.8	8.4	8.5	8.1
Gabon	..	..	..	4.0	6.0	4.0	5.7	5.8	3.6	5.4
Ghana	..	2.3	2.9	3.9	4.1	5.3	5.6	5.4	5.4	5.5
Guinea	..	0.7	1.0	2.3	2.8	2.3	1.9	1.9	1.8	2.2
Kenya	..	..	5.3	6.4	7.8	7.3	7.0	7.2	6.3	7.1
Lesotho	..	..	8.4	11.8	12.0	12.1	11.8	10.9	11.5	11.0
Madagascar	1.0	1.5	1.9	2.4	2.1	2.6	2.8	2.6	2.8	3.1
Malawi	..	..	3.8	5.0	5.8	6.1	6.0	5.9	5.7	5.7
Mali	1.6	1.6	2.4	3.5	3.8	3.3	4.0	4.9	4.8	4.5
Mauritania	..	..	..	3.4	4.9	4.4	4.3	4.9	5.5	5.0
Mauritius[1]	2.5	2.3	3.0	4.8	4.7	5.0	5.5	5.8	5.9	6.7
Morocco	..	5.3	7.1	7.4	7.3	8.0	7.9	8.3	7.7	9.2
Mozambique	..	..	..	4.8	8.9	10.0	9.3	10.1	10.3	11.0
Namibia	..	..	..	11.7	12.8	12.1	12.6	12.6	12.1	12.0
Niger	..	1.3	1.5	2.4	3.1	2.4	2.3	2.3	2.5	2.4
Nigeria	..	..	..	4.6	3.7	3.8	3.4	2.8	3.1	4.3
Rwanda	..	2.2	3.1	4.5	6.2	6.8	6.9	7.1	7.3	7.0
Senegal	..	2.9	3.5	4.1	4.1	4.7	5.2	5.1	5.1	5.9
Seychelles	..	..	..	9.1	8.9	9.4	9.0	9.1	9.9	7.8
Sierra Leone	..	..	2.3	2.8	4.1	4.9	5.1	5.0	5.5	5.0
Somalia	..	..	..	..	0.0	0.1	0.2	0.3	0.2	0.3
South Africa	10.5	11.4	12.0	12.0	13.7	13.7	13.6	12.8	14.2	14.5
Togo	..	1.5	2.3	1.8	2.6	3.0	3.3	3.1	4.0	3.8
Tunisia	..	5.3	6.7	7.7	8.5	7.9	10.2	10.0	9.6	10.3
Uganda	1.2	1.5	2.7	2.6	3.6	4.0	4.3	4.3	4.6	4.6
Zambia	..	..	..	..	**6.8**	**7.2**	**7.9**	**8.6**	**9.5**	**9.6**
Africa average[2]	..	..	..	..	**5.7**	**5.6**	**5.9**	**5.9**	**5.9**	**6.3**
Asia-Pacific (36) average[3]	..	..	..	**6.6**	**6.9**	**7.2**	**7.5**	**7.2**	**7.4**	**7.7**
LAC average[4]	**3.7**	**4.0**	**5.0**	**5.5**	**5.7**	**5.7**	**5.7**	**5.7**	**5.7**	**6.3**
OECD average[5]	**10.8**	**11.4**	**11.2**	**10.2**	**10.9**	**11.3**	**11.3**	**11.3**	**11.9**	**12.3**

.. Not available

Note: The figures include sub-national government tax revenues for Somalia from 2019. Sub-national government tax revenues are not available in other countries.

1. The fiscal year for Mauritius changed in 2010 and in 2015. Figures for 2015 needed to be estimated as a result.
2. Represents an unweighted average of the 36 African countries in this publication.
3. Represents an unweighted average for 36 Asian and Pacific economies included in the publication *Revenue Statistics in Asia and the Pacific 2024.*
4. Represents an unweighted average for 26 Latin American and Caribbean (LAC) countries included in the publication *Revenue Statistics in Latin America and the Caribbean 2024.*
5. Represents an unweighted average for 38 OECD countries in the OECD publication *Revenue Statistics 2024.*

Table 4.6. Taxes on income and profits (1000) as percentage of total taxation

	1995	2000	2005	2010	2015	2018	2019	2020	2021	2022
Botswana	..	..	73.3	65.3	67.9	64.7	63.0	61.1	62.6	64.2
Burkina Faso	..	24.7	20.9	19.3	23.2	25.4	27.8	28.1	34.3	33.5
Cabo Verde	33.5	35.7	30.9	30.0	31.5	30.5	30.9	30.2	27.8	23.8
Cameroon	24.0	28.1	28.7	27.1	32.3	27.0	27.4	28.7	27.3	30.2
Chad	..	..	..	75.1	54.2	51.7	45.2	62.1	48.8	69.6
Congo	..	48.2	30.3	32.6	36.8	22.3	27.3	27.7	26.2	22.9
Congo, Dem. Rep.	..	34.0	18.5	26.5	35.1	43.3	42.3	33.0	39.1	51.5
Côte d'Ivoire	15.0	16.4	13.7	12.8	12.0	13.7	12.3	12.3	13.2	15.1
Egypt	..	..	40.0	43.6	43.8	40.0	39.1	43.9	42.4	43.1
Equatorial Guinea	..	..	91.3	89.1	82.5	66.8	76.3	71.6	69.3	74.9
Eswatini	52.6	51.0	53.6	51.7	48.7	48.3	48.2	47.2	48.6	46.2
Gabon	..	..	..	31.3	39.5	38.9	47.1	45.0	34.5	46.9
Ghana	..	28.9	27.4	36.1	32.1	38.7	42.2	40.9	38.5	39.2
Guinea	..	9.1	11.9	23.4	21.4	19.0	15.7	16.2	15.8	20.4
Kenya	..	..	35.9	40.2	46.0	43.8	42.5	45.0	40.9	42.0
Lesotho	..	..	58.5	60.9	62.2	56.3	56.0	55.3	53.2	51.4
Madagascar	15.4	15.7	21.6	27.6	22.8	23.5	25.5	26.0	26.0	26.8
Malawi	..	..	42.7	44.2	48.7	48.0	47.5	47.3	46.5	45.3
Mali	21.3	14.5	16.6	24.7	24.5	23.9	22.4	26.3	24.2	25.3
Mauritania	..	..	..	34.8	33.4	29.4	31.5	38.6	38.5	34.0
Mauritius[1]	14.7	13.0	16.7	25.7	25.0	25.4	26.9	28.7	29.7	29.9
Morocco	..	26.0	31.0	28.9	29.8	30.7	30.0	30.4	28.3	30.8
Mozambique	..	..	..	18.2	28.2	47.4	44.4	48.9	45.6	50.3
Namibia	..	..	..	63.0	59.4	62.1	62.4	68.1	62.3	60.8
Niger	..	18.8	18.8	26.0	25.2	21.1	21.9	23.5	24.3	25.3
Nigeria	..	..	..	63.5	60.3	60.5	57.0	49.8	46.3	53.9
Rwanda	..	26.0	28.6	36.2	38.1	40.3	39.8	41.3	42.6	42.6
Senegal	..	22.1	23.1	25.9	25.3	27.2	27.7	27.5	27.3	29.6
Seychelles	..	..	..	29.5	31.0	31.1	31.0	32.7	34.7	28.7
Sierra Leone	..	..	29.4	31.4	41.9	39.5	38.3	39.9	41.3	44.2
Somalia	..	..	..	..	2.1	6.3	7.6	10.6	9.8	11.1
South Africa	53.8	56.7	52.6	52.1	51.8	51.6	52.0	50.8	53.9	53.8
Togo	..	20.9	23.6	16.5	16.6	20.3	21.4	19.8	23.2	21.8
Tunisia	..	22.6	28.9	29.7	30.0	26.5	31.7	30.9	29.5	30.8
Uganda	14.8	18.2	29.0	31.5	34.7	34.3	35.2	37.6	36.8	36.4
Zambia	..	..	..	..	47.4	44.7	48.6	55.0	58.7	59.2
Africa average[2]	**..**	**..**	**..**	**..**	**37.4**	**36.8**	**37.4**	**38.4**	**37.6**	**39.3**
Asia-Pacific (36) average[3]	**..**	**..**	**..**	**35.9**	**37.9**	**37.6**	**37.9**	**38.5**	**38.4**	**39.9**
LAC average[4]	**21.5**	**22.4**	**25.1**	**26.4**	**26.5**	**26.6**	**26.6**	**27.0**	**27.3**	**29.8**
OECD average[5]	**33.0**	**33.9**	**33.8**	**32.2**	**33.1**	**34.0**	**33.9**	**33.8**	**35.1**	**36.5**

.. Not available

Note: The figures include sub-national government tax revenues for Somalia (from 2019). Sub-national government tax revenues are not available in other countries.

1. The fiscal year for Mauritius changed in 2010 and in 2015. Figures for 2015 needed to be estimated as a result.
2. Represents an unweighted average of the 36 African countries in this publication.
3. Represents an unweighted average for 36 Asian and Pacific economies included in the publication *Revenue Statistics in Asia and the Pacific 2024*.
4. Represents an unweighted average for 26 Latin American and Caribbean (LAC) countries included in the publication *Revenue Statistics in Latin America and the Caribbean 2024*.
5. Represents an unweighted average for 38 OECD countries in the OECD publication *Revenue Statistics 2024*.

Table 4.7. Social security contributions (2000) as percentage of GDP

	1995	2000	2005	2010	2015	2018	2019	2020	2021	2022
Botswana	..	..	0.0	0.0	0.0	0.0	0.0	0.0	0.0	0.0
Burkina Faso	..	1.6	1.5	1.5	1.7	1.9	1.9	1.5	1.7	1.7
Cabo Verde	0.0	0.8	0.6	0.0	0.0	0.0	0.0	0.0	0.0	0.0
Cameroon	0.8	0.9	0.8	1.0	0.8	1.0	1.0	1.0	1.0	1.0
Chad	..	..	..	..	..	..	..	..	..	..
Congo	..	..	..	..	..	0.6	0.7	0.8	0.7	0.6
Congo, Dem. Rep.	..	..	..	..	0.5	0.5	0.8	0.8	0.8	0.8
Côte d'Ivoire	0.7	1.0	0.9	1.0	1.4	1.5	1.4	1.5	1.5	1.4
Egypt[1]	..	..	2.9	2.5	2.3	2.4	2.4	1.8	1.9	1.9
Equatorial Guinea	..	..	0.0	0.0	0.8	0.7	0.7	0.9	0.7	0.7
Eswatini	1.6	1.2	1.4	1.9	1.9	2.5	2.4	2.4	2.3	2.1
Gabon[2]	..	..	..	1.5	1.0	1.5	1.5	1.7	1.4	1.2
Ghana	..	0.7	0.9	0.9	1.2	0.7	0.7	1.0	0.7	0.7
Guinea	..	..	..	..	..	..	..	..	..	..
Kenya	..	..	0.2	0.2	0.2	0.5	0.6	0.6	0.5	0.6
Lesotho	..	..	0.0	0.0	0.0	0.0	0.0	0.0	0.0	0.0
Madagascar[1]	..	..	..	..	0.4	0.6	0.5	0.6	0.4	0.6
Malawi	..	..	0.0	0.0	0.0	0.0	0.0	0.0	0.0	0.0
Mali[1]	0.8	0.9	1.4	1.4	1.9	2.2	2.9	3.3	3.7	4.0
Mauritania[2]	..	..	..	0.7	0.9	0.8	0.7	0.7	0.6	0.6
Mauritius[3]	0.9	0.8	0.7	0.7	0.8	0.7	0.8	0.9	1.3	1.6
Morocco[1,2]	..	2.2	3.8	4.5	4.9	5.5	5.9	6.8	6.4	6.7
Mozambique	..	..	..	..	..	..	..	..	..	..
Namibia	..	..	..	0.4	0.4	0.3	0.3	0.4	0.3	0.3
Niger	..	0.4	0.3	0.5	0.6	0.5	0.6	0.5	0.6	0.5
Nigeria	..	..	..	0.6	0.6	0.5	0.6	0.6	0.5	0.6
Rwanda[1]	..	0.4	0.7	0.8	1.0	1.0	1.0	1.1	1.0	0.9
Senegal[4]	..	0.5	0.6	0.9	1.1	1.2	1.2	1.1	1.0	0.9
Seychelles	..	..	..	2.8	1.1	2.2	1.5	1.8	1.7	2.1
Sierra Leone	..	..	..	..	..	1.5	1.5	1.5	1.6	1.4
Somalia	..	..	..	..	..	..	..	..	..	..
South Africa	0.0	0.0	0.4	0.4	0.4	0.4	0.4	0.3	0.3	0.3
Togo	..	..	..	..	..	..	..	..	..	..
Tunisia[1,2]	..	5.0	5.3	7.0	8.4	8.7	9.1	10.0	9.7	9.2
Uganda	..	..	..	..	..	..	..	..	..	..
Zambia	..	..	..	..	..	..	..	..	..	..
Africa average[5]	**..**	**..**	**..**	**..**	**1.2**	**1.3**	**1.3**	**1.4**	**1.4**	**1.4**
Asia-Pacific (36) average[6]	**..**	**..**	**..**	**1.5**	**1.4**	**1.5**	**1.7**	**1.8**	**1.8**	**1.9**
LAC average[7]	**2.5**	**2.7**	**2.7**	**3.2**	**3.7**	**3.7**	**3.8**	**3.9**	**3.7**	**3.6**
OECD average[8]	**8.5**	**8.4**	**8.3**	**8.6**	**8.8**	**8.9**	**8.9**	**9.2**	**9.0**	**8.7**

.. Not available

Note: Data on social security contributions are not available for Chad, the Democratic Republic of the Congo (prior to 2012), Equatorial Guinea (prior to 2013), Guinea, Madagascar (prior to 2011), Namibia (prior to 2009), the Republic of the Congo (prior to 2018), Sierra Leone (prior to 2018), Togo, Uganda and Zambia; and are only partially available in Cameroon and Senegal. Social security contributions for Botswana, Lesotho and Malawi are deemed to be zero as they do not meet the criteria to be classified as social security contributions set out in the OECD classification of taxes in the *OECD Interpretative Guide*.

1. Egypt, Madagascar, Mali, Morocco, Rwanda and Tunisia do not include social security contributions in the tax-to-GDP ratio in their official publications as these countries do not consider them to be taxes. They are included as tax revenue in this publication, following the classification set out in the OECD Interpretative Guide.
2. Social security contributions are estimated in Gabon (years prior to 2015), Mauritania (2021 and 2022), Morocco (years prior to 2002), and Tunisia (2022).
3. The fiscal year for Mauritius changed in 2010 and in 2015. Figures for 2015 needed to be estimated as a result.
4. These figures include contributions to the Senegalese Pension Institute (IPRES, estimated prior to 2006) and contributions to the social security fund (CSS, from 2012 as data for previous years are not available).
5. Represents an unweighted average of the 36 African countries in this publication. The Africa average should be interpreted with caution as data for social security contributions (category 2000) are not available or are partial in a few countries.
6. Represents an unweighted average for 36 Asian and Pacific economies included in the publication *Revenue Statistics in Asia and the Pacific 2024*.
7. Represents an unweighted average for 26 Latin American and Caribbean (LAC) countries included in the publication *Revenue Statistics in Latin America and the Caribbean 2024*.
8. Represents an unweighted average for 38 OECD countries in the OECD publication *Revenue Statistics 2024*.

Table 4.8. Social security contributions (2000) as percentage of total taxation

	1995	2000	2005	2010	2015	2018	2019	2020	2021	2022
Botswana	..	..	0.0	0.0	0.0	0.0	0.0	0.0	0.0	0.0
Burkina Faso	..	15.9	13.2	11.0	11.8	11.1	10.9	9.7	10.9	9.1
Cabo Verde	0.0	5.2	2.8	0.2	0.1	0.2	0.2	0.2	0.2	0.2
Cameroon	8.3	8.1	7.4	8.6	6.0	7.2	7.3	8.1	7.6	6.8
Chad	..	..	..	..	..	..	..	..	..	..
Congo	..	..	..	..	..	8.0	8.2	8.5	8.6	6.9
Congo, Dem. Rep.	..	..	..	..	5.8	6.3	10.2	11.5	8.7	6.7
Côte d'Ivoire	5.6	8.8	8.3	8.0	11.2	11.4	11.3	11.6	11.1	11.2
Egypt[1]	..	..	18.3	16.0	16.8	15.4	15.8	13.6	13.7	13.5
Equatorial Guinea	..	..	0.0	0.0	6.3	9.9	7.5	10.2	11.1	8.1
Eswatini	15.5	11.6	11.9	13.6	13.0	14.1	13.0	13.3	13.3	12.0
Gabon[2]	..	..	..	11.4	6.7	14.8	12.5	12.9	13.2	10.7
Ghana	..	9.4	8.1	8.6	9.0	5.2	5.2	8.0	5.2	5.1
Guinea	..	..	..	..	..	..	..	..	..	..
Kenya	..	..	1.3	1.1	1.4	3.2	3.4	3.6	3.5	3.7
Lesotho	..	..	0.0	0.0	0.0	0.0	0.0	0.0	0.0	0.0
Madagascar[1]	..	..	..	..	4.3	5.9	4.6	6.1	4.1	5.0
Malawi	..	..	0.0	0.0	0.0	0.0	0.0	0.0	0.0	0.0
Mali[1]	10.6	7.7	9.5	9.8	12.3	15.7	16.2	17.7	18.5	22.1
Mauritania[2]	..	..	..	6.8	6.2	5.1	5.0	5.4	4.5	4.2
Mauritius[3]	5.6	4.5	3.8	3.6	4.1	3.8	4.1	4.7	6.5	7.1
Morocco[1,2]	..	11.0	16.7	17.5	19.8	20.8	22.5	24.8	23.7	22.5
Mozambique	..	..	..	1.1	1.7	0.3	0.3	0.8	0.4	0.7
Namibia	..	..	..	1.9	1.7	1.8	1.7	2.0	1.6	1.4
Niger	..	5.6	3.9	5.5	4.8	4.7	5.4	5.6	5.3	5.4
Nigeria	..	..	..	7.5	9.9	8.4	10.7	11.5	8.2	7.0
Rwanda[1]	..	5.0	6.9	6.4	6.0	5.9	5.9	6.2	5.7	5.5
Senegal[4]	..	4.0	4.1	5.8	6.7	6.8	6.4	5.9	5.2	4.7
Seychelles	..	..	..	9.1	3.9	7.2	5.2	6.4	6.1	7.8
Sierra Leone	..	..	..	..	..	12.2	11.2	12.3	11.9	12.7
Somalia	..	..	..	..	0.0	0.0	0.0	0.0	0.0	0.0
South Africa	0.0	0.0	1.5	1.6	1.5	1.3	1.3	1.4	1.3	1.3
Togo	..	..	..	..	..	..	..	..	..	..
Tunisia[1,2]	..	21.6	22.7	27.0	29.5	29.1	28.3	30.9	29.7	27.5
Uganda	..	..	..	..	..	..	..	..	..	..
Zambia	..	..	..	..	..	..	..	..	..	..
Africa average[5]	**..**	**..**	**..**	**..**	**6.9**	**7.6**	**7.6**	**8.2**	**7.7**	**7.4**
Asia-Pacific (36) average[6]	**..**	**..**	**..**	**6.5**	**6.3**	**6.5**	**7.3**	**7.7**	**7.7**	**7.6**
LAC average[7]	**15.4**	**15.5**	**14.5**	**15.8**	**16.9**	**17.2**	**17.4**	**18.4**	**17.5**	**16.7**
OECD average[8]	**25.5**	**24.9**	**25.0**	**26.6**	**25.9**	**25.9**	**25.9**	**26.5**	**25.6**	**24.8**

.. Not available

Note: Data on social security contributions are not available for Chad, the Democratic Republic of the Congo (prior to 2012), Equatorial Guinea (prior to 2013), Guinea, Madagascar (prior to 2011), Namibia (prior to 2009), the Republic of the Congo (prior to 2018), Sierra Leone (prior to 2018), Togo, Uganda and Zambia; and are only partially available in Cameroon and Senegal. Social security contributions for Botswana, Lesotho and Malawi are deemed to be zero as they do not meet the criteria to be classified as social security contributions set out in the OECD classification of taxes in the OECD Interpretative Guide.

1. Egypt, Madagascar, Mali, Morocco, Rwanda and Tunisia do not include social security contributions in the tax-to-GDP ratio in their official publications as these countries do not consider them to be taxes. They are included as tax revenue in this publication, following the classification set out in the OECD Interpretative Guide.
2. Social security contributions are estimated in Gabon (years prior to 2015), Mauritania (2021 and 2022), Morocco (years prior to 2002), and Tunisia (2022).
3. The fiscal year for Mauritius changed in 2010 and in 2015. Figures for 2015 needed to be estimated as a result.
4. These figures include contributions to the Senegalese Pension Institute (IPRES, estimated prior to 2006) and contributions to the social security fund (CSS, from 2012 as data for previous years are not available).
5. Represents an unweighted average of the 36 African countries in this publication. The Africa average should be interpreted with caution as data for social security contributions (category 2000) are not available or are partial in a few countries.
6. Represents an unweighted average for 36 Asian and Pacific economies included in the publication *Revenue Statistics in Asia and the Pacific 2024*.
7. Represents an unweighted average for 26 Latin American and Caribbean (LAC) countries included in the publication *Revenue Statistics in Latin America and the Caribbean 2024*.
8. Represents an unweighted average for 38 OECD countries in the OECD publication *Revenue Statistics 2024*.

Table 4.9. Taxes on property (4000) as percentage of GDP

	1995	2000	2005	2010	2015	2018	2019	2020	2021	2022
Botswana	..	..	0.0	0.1	0.0	0.0	0.0	0.0	0.0	0.0
Burkina Faso	..	0.0	0.1	0.1	0.1	0.1	0.1	0.1	0.2	0.1
Cabo Verde	0.8	0.8	0.9	0.9	0.9	0.9	0.8	0.9	0.3	0.3
Cameroon	0.2	0.2	0.1	0.1	0.1	0.1	0.1	0.1	0.1	0.1
Chad	..	..	..	0.3	0.1	0.1	0.3	0.4	0.3	0.2
Congo	..	0.1	0.0	0.2	0.7	0.2	0.3	0.3	0.3	0.3
Congo, Dem. Rep.	..	..	..	0.0	0.0	0.0	0.1	0.1	0.1	0.1
Côte d'Ivoire	0.2	0.3	0.4	0.3	0.3	0.4	0.4	0.4	0.4	0.4
Egypt	..	..	0.1	0.1	0.1	0.1	0.1	0.1	0.1	0.1
Equatorial Guinea	..	..	0.0	0.0	0.0	0.0	0.0	0.0	0.0	0.0
Eswatini	0.2	0.3	0.3	0.3	0.3	0.5	0.5	0.3	0.3	0.5
Gabon	..	..	..	0.0	0.2	0.2	0.1	0.2	0.2	0.2
Ghana	..	..	..	..	..	..	..	..	..	0.1
Guinea	..	0.0	0.0	0.0	0.0	0.1	0.0	0.0	0.0	0.0
Kenya	..	..	0.0	0.0	0.0	0.0	0.0	0.0	0.0	0.0
Lesotho	..	..	..	..	..	..	..	..	..	..
Madagascar	0.1	0.1	0.1	0.1	0.1	0.1	0.1	0.1	0.1	0.1
Malawi	..	..	..	..	..	..	..	..	..	..
Mali	0.2	0.1	0.2	0.2	0.2	0.3	0.3	0.3	0.3	0.3
Mauritania[1]	..	..	..	0.4	0.7	0.4	0.0	0.0	0.0	0.0
Mauritius[2]	1.3	1.2	1.0	1.1	1.0	1.0	0.9	0.9	1.0	1.1
Morocco	..	1.2	1.4	1.5	1.8	1.4	1.3	1.2	1.5	1.5
Mozambique	..	..	..	0.2	0.2	0.3	0.3	0.4	0.6	0.3
Namibia	..	..	..	0.2	0.2	0.1	0.1	0.1	0.1	0.1
Niger	..	0.1	0.1	0.1	0.0	0.1	0.1	0.2	0.2	0.2
Nigeria	..	..	..	..	..	..	..	..	0.1	0.1
Rwanda	..	0.0	0.0	0.0	0.0	0.0	0.0	0.2	0.1	0.1
Senegal	..	0.3	0.4	0.5	0.4	0.4	0.4	0.4	0.6	0.5
Seychelles	..	..	..	1.1	0.7	0.5	0.6	0.5	0.4	0.2
Sierra Leone	..	..	..	..	..	..	..	..	..	..
Somalia	..	..	..	..	0.0	0.0	0.0	0.0	0.0	0.0
South Africa	0.3	0.4	1.3	1.3	1.3	1.6	1.6	1.7	1.1	1.2
Togo	..	0.0	0.0	0.1	0.1	0.1	0.1	0.1	0.1	0.1
Tunisia	..	0.3	0.2	0.3	0.3	0.3	0.3	0.3	0.3	0.3
Uganda	..	..	..	..	0.1	0.0	0.2	0.1	0.2	0.2
Zambia	..	..	..	..	0.2	0.1	0.1	0.1	0.1	0.1
Africa average[3]	**..**	**..**	**..**	**..**	**0.3**	**0.3**	**0.3**	**0.3**	**0.3**	**0.3**
Asia-Pacific (36) average[4]	**..**	**..**	**..**	**0.7**	**0.7**	**0.7**	**0.6**	**0.7**	**0.7**	**0.6**
LAC average[5]	**0.8**	**0.7**	**1.0**	**0.8**	**0.9**	**0.9**	**0.9**	**0.8**	**0.9**	**0.9**
OECD average[6]	**1.5**	**1.7**	**1.7**	**1.6**	**1.8**	**1.8**	**1.8**	**1.9**	**1.9**	**1.8**

.. Not available

Note: The figures include sub-national government tax revenues for Cabo Verde (2008-2020), Eswatini, Mauritania (2009-2018), Mauritius and Somalia (from 2019). Sub-national government tax revenues are not available in other countries.

In Ghana, Lesotho, Malawi, Nigeria, Sierra Leone and Uganda, revenues from property taxes are mainly levied by local governments, for which data are not available. In the Democratic Republic of the Congo, only data for property tax revenues levied by the Direction Générale des Recettes Administratives, Judiciaires, Domaniales et de Participation (DGRAD) are available since 2010. The figures for heading 4000 for Uganda starting in 2014, Nigeria starting in 2021 and Ghana starting in 2022 represent only the introduction of new taxes on money transfers in these countries and are still missing data on local property taxes for those years. See the country tables in Chapter 5 for further information.

1. Sub-national government tax revenues are missing from 2019.
2. The fiscal year for Mauritius changed in 2010 and in 2015. Figures for 2015 needed to be estimated as a result.
3. Represents an unweighted average of the 36 African countries in this publication. The Africa average should be interpreted with caution as data for property taxes (category 4000) are not available or are partial in a few countries.
4. Represents an unweighted average for 36 Asian and Pacific economies included in the publication *Revenue Statistics in Asia and the Pacific 2024.*
5. Represents an unweighted average for 26 Latin American and Caribbean (LAC) countries included in the publication *Revenue Statistics in Latin America and the Caribbean 2024.*
6. Represents an unweighted average for 38 OECD countries in the OECD publication *Revenue Statistics 2024.*

Table 4.10. Taxes on property (4000) as percentage of total taxation

	1995	2000	2005	2010	2015	2018	2019	2020	2021	2022
Botswana	..	..	0.2	0.4	0.3	0.3	0.3	0.3	0.3	0.3
Burkina Faso	..	0.4	0.5	0.7	0.8	0.7	0.7	0.8	1.5	0.7
Cabo Verde	5.3	5.3	4.3	5.5	5.2	4.7	4.5	4.7	1.9	1.8
Cameroon	1.6	1.6	1.2	1.1	0.9	0.8	0.8	0.9	0.9	0.7
Chad	..	..	..	3.1	3.2	1.6	4.6	3.5	4.1	2.1
Congo	..	1.3	0.8	2.6	5.1	2.7	3.4	3.0	3.9	3.0
Congo, Dem. Rep.	..	..	..	0.6	0.4	0.7	0.7	0.8	0.6	0.5
Côte d'Ivoire	1.7	2.8	3.1	2.4	2.6	2.9	3.1	2.9	3.1	3.3
Egypt	..	..	0.7	0.6	0.6	0.6	0.7	0.6	0.7	0.6
Equatorial Guinea	..	..	0.0	0.0	0.0	0.1	0.0	0.0	0.0	0.0
Eswatini	2.0	2.6	2.3	2.0	1.7	2.6	2.6	1.5	1.8	2.8
Gabon	..	..	..	0.4	1.5	1.5	1.1	1.7	1.5	1.6
Ghana	..	..	..	..	..	..	..	..	..	0.7
Guinea	..	0.4	0.1	0.2	0.2	0.4	0.2	0.2	0.1	0.2
Kenya	..	..	0.1	0.2	0.1	0.0	0.0	0.0	0.0	0.0
Lesotho	..	..	..	..	..	..	..	..	..	..
Madagascar	1.1	0.7	0.8	0.6	0.8	0.8	0.6	0.6	0.6	0.6
Malawi	..	..	..	..	..	..	..	..	..	..
Mali	2.2	1.3	1.7	1.6	1.5	2.0	1.7	1.5	1.4	1.4
Mauritania[1]	..	..	..	4.3	4.8	2.9	0.1	0.2	0.2	0.1
Mauritius[2]	7.7	6.4	5.5	5.7	5.2	4.9	4.6	4.2	4.9	5.0
Morocco	..	5.9	6.1	5.9	7.4	5.3	5.1	4.3	5.4	5.0
Mozambique	..	..	..	0.6	0.7	1.6	1.3	2.0	2.8	1.2
Namibia	..	..	..	0.9	1.0	0.6	0.5	0.5	0.7	0.6
Niger	..	1.1	0.9	0.8	0.4	0.7	1.2	1.8	1.7	1.9
Nigeria	..	..	..	..	..	..	..	..	0.9	0.8
Rwanda	..	0.2	0.0	0.0	0.1	0.1	0.1	0.9	0.8	0.9
Senegal	..	2.0	2.6	3.1	2.4	2.5	2.4	2.4	3.2	2.3
Seychelles	..	..	..	3.5	2.6	1.7	2.2	1.8	1.4	0.9
Sierra Leone	..	..	..	..	..	..	..	..	..	..
Somalia	..	..	..	..	0.0	1.9	0.8	0.7	1.4	0.8
South Africa	1.7	1.8	5.6	5.7	5.1	5.9	6.3	6.8	4.1	4.6
Togo	..	0.4	0.4	0.8	0.8	0.8	0.8	0.8	0.5	0.6
Tunisia	..	1.1	1.0	1.0	1.1	0.9	0.9	0.8	1.0	1.0
Uganda	..	..	..	..	0.5	0.4	1.4	1.1	1.4	1.5
Zambia	..	..	..	..	1.2	0.5	0.8	0.6	0.5	0.6
Africa average[3]	**..**	**..**	**..**	**..**	**1.9**	**1.7**	**1.7**	**1.7**	**1.7**	**1.5**
Asia-Pacific (36) average[4]	**..**	**..**	**..**	**3.6**	**3.2**	**3.2**	**3.2**	**3.4**	**3.3**	**2.9**
LAC average[5]	**4.7**	**3.9**	**5.4**	**4.2**	**4.2**	**3.9**	**4.0**	**3.7**	**4.0**	**3.8**
OECD average[6]	**5.1**	**5.3**	**5.4**	**5.4**	**5.7**	**5.5**	**5.5**	**5.7**	**5.6**	**5.3**

.. Not available

Note: The figures include sub-national government tax revenues for Eswatini, Mauritania (2009-2018), Mauritius, Morocco, Nigeria (only state revenues) and South Africa (from 2002). Sub-national government tax revenues are not available in other countries.

In Ghana, Lesotho, Malawi, Nigeria, Sierra Leone and Uganda, revenues from property taxes are mainly levied by local governments, for which data are not available. In the Democratic Republic of the Congo, only data for property tax revenues levied by the Direction Générale des Recettes Administratives, Judiciaires, Domaniales et de Participation (DGRAD) are available since 2010. The figures for heading 4000 for Uganda starting in 2014, Nigeria starting in 2021 and Ghana starting in 2022 represent only the introduction of new taxes on money transfers in these countries and are still missing data on local property taxes for those years. See the country tables in Chapter 5 for further information.

1. Sub-national government tax revenues are missing from 2019.
2. The fiscal year for Mauritius changed in 2010 and in 2015. Figures for 2015 needed to be estimated as a result.
3. Represents an unweighted average of the 36 African countries in this publication. The Africa average should be interpreted with caution as data for property taxes (category 4000) are not available or are partial in a few countries.
4. Represents an unweighted average for 36 Asian and Pacific economies included in the publication *Revenue Statistics in Asia and the Pacific 2024*.
5. Represents an unweighted average for 26 Latin American and Caribbean (LAC) countries included in the publication *Revenue Statistics in Latin America and the Caribbean 2024*.
6. Represents an unweighted average for 38 OECD countries in the OECD publication *Revenue Statistics 2024*.

Table 4.11. Taxes on goods and services (5000) as percentage of GDP

	1995	2000	2005	2010	2015	2018	2019	2020	2021	2022
Botswana	..	..	4.1	5.4	4.3	4.6	5.0	4.7	5.5	4.8
Burkina Faso	..	5.8	7.5	9.4	9.1	10.3	10.2	9.5	8.0	10.2
Cabo Verde	9.3	8.4	12.6	11.1	11.1	12.7	12.0	12.2	12.5	13.6
Cameroon	6.1	6.7	6.7	6.9	8.0	8.8	8.4	7.5	8.0	8.2
Chad	..	..	..	2.3	1.7	2.6	2.9	3.5	3.3	2.9
Congo	..	1.7	4.0	4.3	7.3	4.8	4.8	5.7	4.8	5.8
Congo, Dem. Rep.	..	0.4	3.3	5.4	5.1	3.3	3.2	3.7	4.2	4.7
Côte d'Ivoire	8.4	6.6	7.2	7.9	7.9	7.7	7.8	8.0	8.4	7.5
Egypt	..	..	6.5	6.2	5.4	6.8	6.7	5.7	6.1	6.1
Equatorial Guinea	..	..	0.7	0.7	1.2	1.3	1.5	1.4	1.1	1.4
Eswatini	3.1	3.7	3.7	4.5	5.5	6.1	6.6	6.7	6.3	6.9
Gabon[1]	..	..	..	7.1	7.9	4.5	4.6	5.1	4.8	4.5
Ghana	..	4.8	6.8	6.0	7.6	7.7	6.9	6.7	7.9	7.7
Guinea	..	6.7	7.3	7.5	9.9	9.3	9.8	9.4	9.0	8.2
Kenya	..	..	9.2	9.1	8.8	8.7	8.8	8.1	8.5	9.0
Lesotho	..	..	5.9	7.6	7.3	9.4	9.3	8.8	10.2	10.4
Madagascar	5.4	7.8	6.6	6.1	6.7	7.6	7.6	6.8	7.4	7.8
Malawi	..	..	5.1	6.3	6.1	6.6	6.6	6.6	6.6	6.8
Mali	4.5	8.2	10.0	8.5	8.9	7.7	9.8	9.1	10.2	8.4
Mauritania	..	..	..	5.3	8.0	9.5	8.7	7.0	8.2	8.9
Mauritius[2]	11.7	13.5	12.8	12.1	12.2	12.8	13.0	12.4	11.6	12.7
Morocco	..	11.3	10.4	11.9	10.4	11.2	11.1	11.0	11.6	12.4
Mozambique	..	..	..	20.8	21.8	10.7	11.3	9.6	11.4	10.3
Namibia	..	..	..	6.1	8.0	6.8	7.1	5.4	6.8	7.2
Niger	..	5.0	5.8	5.9	7.3	7.4	6.6	5.8	6.2	5.7
Nigeria	..	..	..	1.9	1.6	1.6	1.6	1.8	2.6	2.6
Rwanda	..	5.9	6.9	7.1	9.1	9.1	9.4	8.8	8.7	8.4
Senegal	..	9.1	10.4	10.1	10.3	10.2	11.3	10.7	11.5	12.1
Seychelles	..	..	..	17.8	17.9	18.1	17.9	16.4	16.4	17.1
Sierra Leone	..	..	5.5	6.2	5.7	6.0	6.7	6.0	6.2	4.9
Somalia	..	..	..	..	1.2	1.5	1.9	2.1	2.2	2.3
South Africa	8.5	8.0	8.9	9.1	10.7	10.6	10.2	10.1	10.4	10.6
Togo	..	5.2	7.2	8.4	12.6	11.3	11.8	12.1	12.8	13.2
Tunisia	..	12.1	10.4	10.2	10.2	11.9	11.4	11.2	11.9	12.5
Uganda	6.4	6.8	6.6	5.6	6.7	7.6	7.7	6.9	7.7	7.8
Zambia	..	..	..	..	7.3	8.8	8.1	6.9	6.5	6.5
Africa average[3]	**..**	**..**	**..**	**..**	**8.1**	**7.9**	**8.0**	**7.6**	**7.9**	**8.1**
Asia-Pacific (36) average[4]	**..**	**..**	**..**	**9.1**	**9.3**	**9.6**	**9.3**	**8.6**	**8.8**	**9.0**
LAC average[5]	**8.8**	**9.4**	**9.8**	**10.0**	**10.6**	**10.7**	**10.7**	**10.1**	**10.3**	**10.1**
OECD average[6]	**10.8**	**10.8**	**10.8**	**10.5**	**10.8**	**10.8**	**10.8**	**10.6**	**10.7**	**10.6**

.. Not available

Note: The figures include sub-national government tax revenues for Mauritius, Morocco, and Somalia (from 2019). Sub-national government tax revenues are not available in other countries.

1. The figures should be interpreted with caution for years prior to 2014 as customs revenues (representing roughly 50% of tax revenues) are estimated for these years.
2. The fiscal year for Mauritius changed in 2010 and in 2015. Figures for 2015 needed to be estimated as a result.
3. Represents an unweighted average of the 36 African countries in this publication.
4. Represents an unweighted average for 36 Asian and Pacific economies included in the publication *Revenue Statistics in Asia and the Pacific 2024*.
5. Represents an unweighted average for 26 Latin American and Caribbean (LAC) countries included in the publication *Revenue Statistics in Latin America and the Caribbean 2024*.
6. Represents an unweighted average for 38 OECD countries in the OECD publication *Revenue Statistics 2024*.

Table 4.12. Taxes on goods and services (5000) as percentage of total taxation

	1995	2000	2005	2010	2015	2018	2019	2020	2021	2022
Botswana	..	..	26.6	34.3	31.7	35.0	36.7	38.7	37.1	35.5
Burkina Faso	..	57.0	63.6	67.3	62.8	61.4	59.1	59.9	51.6	55.4
Cabo Verde	61.3	53.8	62.0	64.3	63.1	64.7	64.4	64.9	70.1	74.2
Cameroon	66.1	62.2	60.5	60.1	57.0	62.2	60.9	58.5	60.0	58.3
Chad	..	..	..	20.7	39.7	46.5	48.7	33.0	45.6	27.4
Congo	..	45.5	67.3	60.8	55.3	63.6	58.3	58.2	58.8	65.1
Congo, Dem. Rep.	..	65.3	67.4	65.5	54.2	44.0	42.2	50.7	47.2	37.9
Côte d'Ivoire	68.6	59.8	63.9	66.0	62.7	59.6	61.0	60.9	61.1	58.3
Egypt	..	..	41.1	39.8	38.8	44.0	44.4	41.9	43.2	42.8
Equatorial Guinea	..	..	8.5	9.4	10.3	19.2	15.2	16.4	18.3	16.7
Eswatini	29.9	34.8	32.2	32.6	36.6	35.0	36.3	38.0	36.4	39.0
Gabon[1]	..	..	..	56.2	51.6	43.7	38.2	39.4	46.9	39.5
Ghana	..	61.7	64.4	55.3	58.9	56.0	52.6	51.1	56.3	55.0
Guinea	..	89.4	87.1	75.2	76.3	77.4	80.5	80.2	81.1	76.0
Kenya	..	..	62.4	57.5	51.4	52.2	53.3	50.8	54.8	53.6
Lesotho	..	..	41.5	39.1	37.8	43.7	44.0	44.7	46.8	48.6
Madagascar	81.6	82.5	76.4	71.4	72.1	69.4	68.9	67.1	69.3	67.6
Malawi	..	..	57.2	55.6	51.2	51.9	52.4	52.7	53.4	54.6
Mali	59.3	72.0	68.9	60.4	57.1	55.6	54.0	49.2	51.6	47.0
Mauritania	..	..	..	54.0	55.4	62.5	63.2	55.6	56.6	60.9
Mauritius[2]	70.3	74.6	72.6	64.4	64.9	65.2	63.6	61.5	58.3	57.1
Morocco	..	55.7	45.2	46.8	42.2	42.8	42.1	40.3	42.4	41.4
Mozambique	..	..	..	79.6	68.9	50.4	53.6	46.5	50.3	47.1
Namibia	..	..	..	32.9	37.2	34.9	35.1	29.1	35.1	36.8
Niger	..	70.9	71.9	62.1	58.9	65.9	63.4	59.3	59.5	59.3
Nigeria	..	..	..	25.6	26.3	25.3	26.6	32.4	38.2	32.4
Rwanda	..	68.8	64.5	57.4	55.9	53.6	54.2	51.6	50.8	51.0
Senegal	..	69.2	67.8	63.4	63.1	58.9	60.4	57.9	61.5	61.0
Seychelles	..	..	..	57.8	62.5	59.9	61.6	59.0	57.7	62.6
Sierra Leone	..	..	70.6	68.6	58.1	48.3	50.5	47.8	46.8	43.1
Somalia	..	..	..	..	97.9	91.8	91.5	87.1	87.7	87.1
South Africa	43.4	39.9	38.9	39.5	40.4	39.9	39.1	40.1	39.5	39.2
Togo	..	74.8	73.0	78.4	80.1	76.3	75.9	77.0	74.6	75.8
Tunisia	..	51.8	45.0	39.5	35.8	39.7	35.6	34.5	36.7	37.4
Uganda	82.2	81.6	70.9	67.3	64.6	65.1	63.4	60.9	61.6	62.1
Zambia	..	..	..	..	51.4	54.5	50.2	44.0	40.5	40.0
Africa average[3]	**..**	**..**	**..**	**..**	**53.7**	**53.3**	**52.8**	**51.1**	**52.4**	**51.3**
Asia-Pacific (36) average[4]	**..**	**..**	**..**	**53.2**	**51.4**	**51.7**	**50.5**	**49.7**	**49.7**	**48.8**
LAC average[5]	**57.2**	**56.9**	**53.4**	**51.1**	**50.3**	**50.2**	**49.8**	**48.5**	**48.4**	**46.5**
OECD average[6]	**34.4**	**33.9**	**33.9**	**34.0**	**33.4**	**32.8**	**32.7**	**32.1**	**31.9**	**31.5**

.. Not available

Note: The figures include sub-national government tax revenues for Mauritius, Morocco and Somalia (from 2019). Sub-national government tax revenues are not available in other countries. See the country tables in Chapter 5 for further information.

1. The figures should be interpreted with caution for years prior to 2014 as customs revenues (representing roughly 50% of tax revenues) are estimated for these years.
2. The fiscal year for Mauritius changed in 2010 and in 2015. Figures for 2015 needed to be estimated as a result.
3. Represents an unweighted average of the 36 African countries in this publication.
4. Represents an unweighted average for 36 Asian and Pacific economies included in the publication *Revenue Statistics in Asia and the Pacific 2024*.
5. Represents an unweighted average for 26 Latin American and Caribbean (LAC) countries included in the publication *Revenue Statistics in Latin America and the Caribbean 2024*.
6. Represents an unweighted average for 38 OECD countries in the OECD publication *Revenue Statistics 2024*.

Table 4.13. Taxes on general consumption (5110) as percentage of GDP

	1995	2000	2005	2010	2015	2018	2019	2020	2021	2022
Botswana	..	..	3.6	5.0	3.8	4.1	4.5	4.3	4.4	4.1
Burkina Faso	..	2.9	4.1	4.6	4.9	5.5	5.7	4.8	2.9	4.7
Cabo Verde	0.0	0.0	6.9	6.6	6.2	7.3	6.8	7.1	6.9	7.5
Cameroon	2.7	3.5	3.5	3.6	4.6	5.2	4.9	4.0	4.3	4.6
Chad	..	..	..	1.4	0.9	0.9	1.3	1.5	1.5	0.6
Congo	..	1.5	2.2	2.4	4.0	3.0	2.8	3.3	2.4	3.5
Congo, Dem. Rep.	..	0.1	1.8	2.9	2.4	1.9	1.7	2.3	2.7	2.7
Côte d'Ivoire	2.7	2.4	2.3	2.9	2.6	2.8	2.8	2.7	3.1	3.1
Egypt	..	..	3.3	3.1	2.5	3.3	3.5	3.1	3.5	3.2
Equatorial Guinea	..	..	0.5	0.6	0.8	0.7	0.9	0.9	0.6	0.7
Eswatini	2.4	3.0	3.2	3.8	4.0	4.3	4.6	4.7	4.3	5.0
Gabon	..	..	..	3.7	4.7	2.2	2.2	2.1	2.3	2.2
Ghana	..	2.0	2.7	3.2	4.1	3.7	3.5	3.3	4.0	4.2
Guinea	..	2.1	2.4	3.1	4.1	4.0	4.2	3.7	3.9	3.6
Kenya	..	..	3.8	4.1	4.1	4.0	4.0	3.6	3.6	4.1
Lesotho	..	..	5.9	7.6	7.3	8.5	8.5	7.6	8.7	9.0
Madagascar	3.2	3.9	3.5	3.9	4.5	5.0	5.0	4.4	4.9	5.2
Malawi	..	..	2.5	2.9	3.4	3.6	3.7	3.9	3.7	3.7
Mali	1.7	3.8	5.8	4.9	4.2	3.9	5.3	4.8	5.4	4.4
Mauritania	..	..	..	3.3	4.7	4.7	4.5	3.3	3.9	4.0
Mauritius[1]	0.1	4.6	6.4	6.8	6.7	6.8	6.9	6.8	6.1	7.3
Morocco	..	4.8	5.5	7.7	7.0	7.2	7.0	6.9	7.3	8.0
Mozambique	..	..	..	6.2	8.0	7.2	7.6	6.4	7.9	7.2
Namibia	..	..	..	6.0	7.8	6.3	6.4	4.7	6.0	6.7
Niger	..	..	..	..	4.5	5.1	3.8	3.1	3.4	3.3
Nigeria	..	..	..	1.0	0.8	0.9	0.8	1.0	1.2	1.2
Rwanda	..	1.7	3.5	3.7	5.0	5.1	5.5	5.1	5.1	4.8
Senegal	..	5.2	6.1	6.0	5.9	5.7	6.4	5.7	6.1	5.7
Seychelles	..	..	..	4.0	9.9	10.5	10.3	9.1	9.6	10.2
Sierra Leone	..	..	0.0	2.4	2.7	2.7	2.8	2.6	2.8	2.5
Somalia	..	..	..	..	0.1	0.3	0.3	0.3	0.4	0.4
South Africa	5.1	4.9	5.9	5.6	6.3	6.1	5.9	6.0	6.0	6.2
Togo	..	2.6	4.0	4.9	7.4	6.6	6.9	6.9	7.1	7.2
Tunisia	..	5.9	5.3	5.8	5.8	6.8	6.5	6.2	6.9	7.4
Uganda	2.4	2.7	3.1	2.7	3.4	3.7	3.7	3.4	3.8	3.8
Zambia	..	..	..	..	4.5	6.3	5.6	4.4	4.3	4.2
Africa average[2]	**..**	**..**	**..**	**..**	**4.5**	**4.6**	**4.6**	**4.3**	**4.5**	**4.6**
Asia-Pacific (36) average[3]	**..**	**..**	**..**	**4.5**	**5.1**	**5.1**	**5.0**	**4.6**	**4.9**	**5.2**
LAC average[4]	**4.3**	**4.8**	**5.5**	**5.9**	**6.6**	**6.8**	**6.7**	**6.4**	**6.7**	**6.7**
OECD average[5]	**6.3**	**6.5**	**6.7**	**6.5**	**6.8**	**6.9**	**6.9**	**6.8**	**7.1**	**7.1**

.. Not available

Note: The figures include sub-national government tax revenues Morocco and Somalia (from 2019). Sub-national government tax revenues are not available in other countries. See the country tables in Chapter 5 for further information.

1. The fiscal year for Mauritius changed in 2010 and in 2015. Figures for 2015 needed to be estimated as a result.
2. Represents an unweighted average of the 36 African countries in this publication.
3. Represents an unweighted average for 36 Asian and Pacific economies included in the publication *Revenue Statistics in Asia and the Pacific 2024*.
4. Represents an unweighted average for 26 Latin American and Caribbean (LAC) countries included in the publication *Revenue Statistics in Latin America and the Caribbean 2024*.
5. Represents an unweighted average for 38 OECD countries in the OECD publication *Revenue Statistics 2024*.

Table 4.14. Taxes on general consumption (5110) as percentage of total taxation

	1995	2000	2005	2010	2015	2018	2019	2020	2021	2022
Botswana	..	..	23.2	31.3	28.2	31.1	32.6	35.0	29.9	30.2
Burkina Faso	..	28.7	34.7	32.8	33.7	32.9	33.1	30.1	19.1	25.5
Cabo Verde	0.0	0.0	34.0	38.2	35.3	37.5	36.3	38.0	38.6	41.1
Cameroon	29.0	32.2	31.7	31.2	32.9	36.8	35.3	31.2	31.9	32.9
Chad	..	..	..	12.3	20.0	16.2	22.2	13.5	20.6	6.0
Congo	..	40.2	37.9	34.2	30.6	39.0	34.0	33.7	29.7	39.0
Congo, Dem. Rep.	..	18.4	37.1	35.1	25.6	24.6	22.2	31.9	30.9	21.9
Côte d'Ivoire	22.4	21.8	20.5	24.1	20.3	21.4	21.7	21.0	22.8	24.2
Egypt	..	..	21.0	20.2	18.3	21.6	23.3	23.2	24.9	22.9
Equatorial Guinea	..	..	6.2	7.4	6.3	11.3	8.9	10.1	10.4	8.2
Eswatini	23.2	28.0	27.5	27.4	26.7	24.5	25.0	26.2	24.5	28.5
Gabon	..	..	..	29.3	30.5	21.5	18.0	16.4	22.1	19.3
Ghana	..	26.1	25.4	30.0	32.1	26.8	26.6	25.0	28.8	29.8
Guinea	..	28.1	29.2	31.0	31.2	33.7	34.3	31.6	35.2	33.6
Kenya	..	..	26.1	25.9	24.2	23.9	24.5	22.8	23.3	24.4
Lesotho	..	..	41.5	39.1	37.6	39.5	40.1	38.5	39.9	42.1
Madagascar	48.6	41.4	40.4	45.3	48.4	45.4	45.5	43.4	46.0	45.2
Malawi	..	..	27.8	25.4	28.3	28.1	29.7	31.4	29.6	29.5
Mali	22.3	33.7	40.2	34.8	27.2	28.3	29.3	25.9	27.0	24.5
Mauritania	..	..	..	33.4	32.5	31.2	32.4	25.9	27.0	27.6
Mauritius[1]	0.5	25.3	36.0	36.1	35.4	34.5	33.8	33.6	30.7	32.7
Morocco	..	23.6	23.7	30.1	28.4	27.5	26.7	25.4	26.8	26.8
Mozambique	..	..	..	23.9	25.3	34.0	36.3	30.9	34.7	32.9
Namibia	..	..	..	32.1	36.5	32.6	31.8	25.4	31.0	34.0
Niger	..	28.5	43.2	37.5	36.4	45.1	36.8	32.2	32.7	34.5
Nigeria	..	..	..	14.0	13.3	13.5	13.7	17.9	17.6	15.7
Rwanda	..	20.0	33.1	29.9	30.6	30.2	31.5	29.6	29.9	29.3
Senegal	..	39.6	40.0	37.7	35.8	33.1	34.4	30.8	32.6	28.9
Seychelles	..	..	..	13.0	34.6	35.0	35.6	32.9	33.6	37.4
Sierra Leone	..	..	0.0	26.5	27.8	22.0	21.1	21.0	21.3	21.6
Somalia	..	..	..	..	5.7	16.1	15.3	14.5	14.7	15.3
South Africa	26.0	24.6	26.1	24.1	23.8	22.9	22.4	23.8	22.9	23.1
Togo	..	36.9	40.1	45.9	46.9	44.6	44.5	43.6	41.3	41.2
Tunisia	..	25.2	23.1	22.3	20.3	22.8	20.4	19.1	21.3	22.1
Uganda	30.4	33.0	33.0	32.3	32.3	32.0	30.8	29.8	29.9	30.4
Zambia	..	..	..	..	31.6	39.3	34.5	28.1	26.8	26.1
Africa average[2]	**..**	**..**	**..**	**..**	**28.7**	**29.5**	**29.0**	**27.6**	**28.1**	**28.0**
Asia-Pacific (36) average[3]	**..**	**..**	**..**	**24.0**	**26.7**	**26.7**	**26.8**	**25.9**	**27.0**	**27.2**
LAC average[4]	**26.6**	**27.9**	**28.6**	**29.6**	**30.9**	**31.5**	**31.1**	**30.9**	**31.1**	**30.8**
OECD average[5]	**20.1**	**20.3**	**21.0**	**21.2**	**20.9**	**21.0**	**20.9**	**20.8**	**21.3**	**21.4**

.. Not available

Note: The figures include sub-national government tax revenues for Morocco and Somalia (from 2019). Sub-national government tax revenues are not available in other countries. See the country tables in Chapter 5 for further information.

1. The fiscal year for Mauritius changed in 2010 and in 2015. Figures for 2015 needed to be estimated as a result.
2. Represents an unweighted average of the 36 African countries in this publication.
3. Represents an unweighted average for 36 Asian and Pacific economies included in the publication *Revenue Statistics in Asia and the Pacific 2024*.
4. Represents an unweighted average for 26 Latin American and Caribbean (LAC) countries included in the publication *Revenue Statistics in Latin America and the Caribbean 2024*.
5. Represents an unweighted average for 38 OECD countries in the OECD publication *Revenue Statistics 2024*.

Table 4.15. Taxes on specific goods and services (5120) as percentage of GDP

	1995	2000	2005	2010	2015	2018	2019	2020	2021	2022
Botswana	..	..	0.3	0.2	0.3	0.2	0.3	0.2	0.8	0.4
Burkina Faso	..	2.2	2.8	2.8	3.6	4.1	3.8	3.6	4.1	4.7
Cabo Verde	9.3	8.4	5.7	4.5	4.9	5.3	5.2	5.0	5.6	6.1
Cameroon	3.4	3.2	3.1	3.3	3.4	3.6	3.5	3.5	3.7	3.5
Chad	..	..	..	0.9	0.8	1.6	1.6	2.0	1.8	2.1
Congo	..	0.2	1.7	1.9	3.3	1.8	2.0	2.3	2.3	2.3
Congo, Dem. Rep.	..	0.3	1.5	2.4	2.6	1.4	1.4	1.2	1.3	1.8
Côte d'Ivoire	5.5	4.0	4.7	4.7	5.0	4.6	4.7	4.9	5.0	4.1
Egypt	..	..	3.0	2.9	2.7	3.4	3.1	2.4	2.4	2.7
Equatorial Guinea	..	..	0.2	0.2	0.5	0.5	0.6	0.5	0.5	0.7
Eswatini	0.6	0.6	0.5	0.6	1.4	1.7	1.9	1.9	1.9	1.7
Gabon[1]	..	..	..	3.4	3.1	2.3	2.4	2.9	2.5	2.3
Ghana	..	2.8	4.1	2.7	3.5	4.0	3.4	3.4	3.9	3.5
Guinea	..	4.3	4.7	4.2	5.6	4.9	5.3	5.4	4.9	4.3
Kenya	..	..	5.1	4.9	4.5	4.6	4.7	4.4	4.8	4.8
Lesotho	..	..	..	..	0.0	0.9	0.8	1.2	1.5	1.4
Madagascar	2.2	3.9	3.1	2.2	2.2	2.6	2.6	2.4	2.5	2.6
Malawi	..	..	2.6	3.4	2.7	3.0	2.8	2.7	2.9	3.1
Mali	2.7	4.3	4.1	3.6	4.6	3.7	4.4	4.3	4.8	4.0
Mauritania	..	..	..	1.9	3.2	4.2	3.8	3.3	3.9	4.5
Mauritius[2]	11.5	8.7	5.5	4.4	4.6	5.1	5.2	4.8	4.7	4.6
Morocco	..	6.3	4.7	4.0	3.1	3.5	3.6	3.6	3.7	3.8
Mozambique	..	..	..	3.0	4.0	3.4	3.6	3.2	3.5	3.1
Namibia	..	..	..	0.1	0.1	0.4	0.7	0.7	0.8	0.5
Niger	..	2.9	2.3	2.3	2.7	2.3	2.7	2.6	2.7	2.3
Nigeria	..	..	..	0.8	0.8	0.7	0.8	0.8	1.4	1.3
Rwanda	..	4.1	3.3	3.3	4.0	3.9	3.9	3.7	3.5	3.5
Senegal	..	3.8	4.2	4.0	4.4	4.4	4.8	4.9	5.3	5.9
Seychelles	..	..	..	12.7	7.0	6.7	6.7	6.4	6.1	6.1
Sierra Leone	..	..	5.5	3.8	3.0	3.3	3.9	3.4	3.4	2.5
Somalia	..	..	..	..	1.1	1.3	1.5	1.6	1.7	1.7
South Africa	3.4	3.1	2.7	3.4	4.2	4.3	4.3	3.9	4.1	4.2
Togo	..	2.6	3.2	3.4	5.1	4.6	4.7	5.0	5.4	5.5
Tunisia	..	6.0	4.8	4.2	4.2	4.9	4.7	4.8	4.8	4.9
Uganda	3.8	3.8	3.2	2.7	3.2	3.7	3.8	3.4	3.8	3.8
Zambia	..	..	..	..	2.8	2.4	2.5	2.5	2.2	2.2
Africa average[3]	**..**	**..**	**..**	**..**	**3.1**	**3.2**	**3.2**	**3.1**	**3.3**	**3.2**
Asia-Pacific (36) average[4]	**..**	**..**	**..**	**4.2**	**3.8**	**4.1**	**4.0**	**3.6**	**3.6**	**3.5**
LAC average[5]	**4.2**	**4.3**	**4.0**	**3.7**	**3.5**	**3.6**	**3.7**	**3.4**	**3.3**	**3.1**
OECD average[6]	**3.9**	**3.7**	**3.5**	**3.4**	**3.4**	**3.3**	**3.2**	**3.1**	**2.9**	**2.8**

.. Not available

Note: The figures include sub-national government tax revenues for Mauritius, Morocco and Somalia (from 2019). Sub-national government tax revenues are not available in other countries. See the country tables in Chapter 5 for further information.

1. The figures should be interpreted with caution for years prior to 2014 as customs revenues (representing roughly 50% of tax revenues) are estimated for these years.
2. The fiscal year for Mauritius changed in 2010 and in 2015. Figures for 2015 needed to be estimated as a result.
3. Represents an unweighted average of the 36 African countries in this publication.
4. Represents an unweighted average for 36 Asian and Pacific economies included in the publication *Revenue Statistics in Asia and the Pacific 2024*.
5. Represents an unweighted average for 26 Latin American and Caribbean (LAC) countries included in the publication *Revenue Statistics in Latin America and the Caribbean 2024*.
6. Represents an unweighted average for 38 OECD countries in the OECD publication *Revenue Statistics 2024*.

Table 4.16. Taxes on specific goods and services (5120) as percentage of total taxation

	1995	2000	2005	2010	2015	2018	2019	2020	2021	2022
Botswana	..	..	1.8	1.3	2.2	1.8	2.2	2.0	5.6	3.0
Burkina Faso	..	21.7	24.0	20.3	25.0	24.6	22.1	22.7	26.3	25.8
Cabo Verde	61.3	53.8	27.9	26.2	27.8	27.1	28.1	26.9	31.5	33.1
Cameroon	36.5	29.6	28.1	28.4	23.8	25.1	25.3	27.0	28.0	25.3
Chad	..	..	..	8.1	19.1	28.4	26.1	18.2	24.4	20.0
Congo	..	5.1	29.3	26.4	24.6	24.0	23.8	23.8	28.5	25.4
Congo, Dem. Rep.	..	45.6	30.1	28.4	28.1	18.0	18.9	17.3	15.1	14.6
Côte d'Ivoire	45.3	35.8	41.3	39.5	40.0	35.7	36.9	37.7	36.1	31.8
Egypt	..	..	19.1	18.5	19.6	21.8	20.4	17.9	17.4	19.1
Equatorial Guinea	..	..	2.3	2.0	4.0	7.9	6.3	6.3	8.0	8.5
Eswatini	5.6	5.9	4.0	4.1	9.0	9.7	10.4	11.0	10.9	9.5
Gabon[1]	..	..	..	26.6	20.5	21.9	19.8	22.6	24.3	19.8
Ghana	..	35.6	39.0	25.3	26.9	29.1	25.9	26.1	27.5	25.2
Guinea	..	58.0	56.1	42.0	43.1	40.8	43.5	46.1	44.2	40.2
Kenya	..	..	35.0	30.9	26.6	27.7	28.5	27.7	31.1	28.9
Lesotho	..	..	..	..	0.2	4.2	3.9	6.2	6.9	6.5
Madagascar	33.1	41.2	36.0	26.1	23.6	23.9	23.4	23.7	23.3	22.3
Malawi	..	..	29.4	30.2	22.9	23.8	22.7	21.2	23.6	24.9
Mali	36.5	37.9	28.4	25.3	29.7	26.9	24.4	23.1	24.4	22.4
Mauritania	..	..	..	19.2	21.8	27.8	27.5	26.3	26.8	30.9
Mauritius[2]	68.8	48.3	31.3	23.4	24.3	26.2	25.2	23.8	23.4	20.7
Morocco	..	30.9	20.4	15.6	12.7	13.5	13.5	13.0	13.7	12.8
Mozambique	..	..	..	11.6	12.7	16.2	17.2	15.6	15.5	14.2
Namibia	..	..	..	0.7	0.7	2.3	3.4	3.7	4.1	2.8
Niger	..	40.7	28.4	24.2	22.2	20.4	26.1	26.6	26.2	24.3
Nigeria	..	..	..	11.5	12.7	11.5	12.6	14.2	20.3	16.5
Rwanda	..	47.9	31.0	26.9	24.4	22.9	22.3	21.6	20.5	20.9
Senegal	..	29.2	27.4	25.4	26.8	25.3	25.4	26.6	28.5	29.7
Seychelles	..	..	..	41.4	24.3	22.3	23.2	23.2	21.3	22.5
Sierra Leone	..	..	70.6	42.1	30.3	26.3	29.3	26.8	25.5	21.5
Somalia	..	..	..	..	88.5	75.7	72.0	67.9	68.5	66.9
South Africa	17.4	15.3	12.0	14.6	15.9	16.3	16.6	15.4	15.7	15.4
Togo	..	37.7	32.7	32.2	32.8	31.2	30.3	31.9	31.4	31.6
Tunisia	..	25.7	20.8	16.3	14.7	16.3	14.6	14.8	14.8	14.8
Uganda	49.2	46.4	34.6	32.9	30.7	31.9	31.5	30.1	30.6	30.6
Zambia	..	..	..	..	19.8	15.0	15.6	15.9	13.6	13.8
Africa average[3]	**..**	**..**	**..**	**..**	**23.1**	**22.9**	**22.7**	**22.4**	**23.3**	**22.1**
Asia-Pacific (36) average[4]	**..**	**..**	**..**	**26.2**	**22.6**	**23.1**	**21.9**	**21.7**	**21.1**	**20.0**
LAC average[5]	**29.0**	**27.4**	**23.2**	**19.7**	**17.4**	**16.9**	**16.9**	**16.1**	**15.8**	**14.3**
OECD average[6]	**12.5**	**11.8**	**11.1**	**10.9**	**10.5**	**9.8**	**9.7**	**9.3**	**8.7**	**8.2**

.. Not available

Note: The figures include sub-national government tax revenues for Mauritius, Morocco and Somalia (from 2019). Sub-national government tax revenues are not available in other countries. See the country tables in Chapter 5 for further information. See the country tables in Chapter 5 for further information.

1. The figures should be interpreted with caution for years prior to 2014 as customs revenues (representing roughly 50% of tax revenues) are estimated for these years.
2. The fiscal year for Mauritius changed in 2010 and in 2015. Figures for 2015 needed to be estimated as a result.
3. Represents an unweighted average of the 36 African countries in this publication.
4. Represents an unweighted average for 36 Asian and Pacific economies included in the publication *Revenue Statistics in Asia and the Pacific 2024.*
5. Represents an unweighted average for 26 Latin American and Caribbean (LAC) countries included in the publication *Revenue Statistics in Latin America and the Caribbean 2024.*
6. Represents an unweighted average for 38 OECD countries in the OECD publication *Revenue Statistics 2024.*

Table 4.17. Gross domestic product for tax reporting years at current prices, in national currency units

	1995	2000	2005	2010	2015	2018	2019	2020	2021	2022
Botswana[1]	14 054	29 719	52 191	90 222	143 894	175 189	177 446	180 217	218 741	258 295
Burkina Faso	1 335 831	2 108 160	3 240 716	5 002 182	6 995 311	8 836 569	9 392 201	10 204 283	10 892 945	11 767 628
Cabo Verde	41 215	70 536	92 325	151 963	173 911	205 986	221 708	176 824	186 237	235 003
Cameroon	5 225 059	7 504 469	10 286 733	13 610 554	19 043 067	22 203 329	23 243 662	23 486 470	25 157 753	27 702 493
Chad	1 112 897	1 520 599	4 793 729	7 064 316	8 576 280	8 513 328	8 739 824	8 399 916	8 894 126	10 218 215
Congo	1 226 473	2 580 266	3 506 269	6 505 751	7 029 660	8 206 111	8 189 066	6 601 216	7 419 748	8 689 849
Congo, Dem. Rep.	1 758	1 317 075	5 975 851	20 261 584	37 185 001	77 940 342	83 859 421	91 858 647	115 792 002	132 314 626
Côte d'Ivoire	7 589 656	10 547 189	12 456 798	17 036 258	27 086 367	32 506 103	35 379 059	36 277 950	40 366 859	44 843 177
Egypt[2]	214 501	357 607	566 220	1 268 711	2 576 700	4 666 200	5 596 000	6 152 600	6 663 100	7 842 500
Equatorial Guinea	84 131	822 850	4 316 629	8 072 293	7 795 420	7 274 689	6 658 371	5 694 742	6 803 755	7 340 020
Eswatini[1]	7 221	12 366	20 730	33 123	52 876	62 581	65 121	67 119	73 382	81 254
Gabon	2 635 849	3 842 278	4 989 260	7 111 477	8 503 445	9 343 897	9 856 684	8 814 843	11 211 460	13 118 310
Ghana	1 752	6 250	22 294	62 002	183 526	308 587	356 544	391 941	461 695	610 222
Guinea	5 095 078	7 055 304	16 422 581	39 243 500	65 829 149	106 845 292	123 457 571	134 759 570	159 336 000	170 313 000
Kenya[2]	760 609	1 347 258	1 896 029	3 436 636	6 444 076	8 911 852	9 789 019	10 475 910	11 370 876	12 698 001
Lesotho	3 742	6 395	11 071	16 950	30 356	34 007	34 355	34 239	36 039	39 516
Madagascar	3 274 385	6 265 668	11 736 269	20 863 367	33 216 184	45 886 302	51 035 217	49 435 649	55 744 386	62 607 257
Malawi	38 871	222 319	571 292	1 352 608	4 060 849	6 883 582	7 727 897	8 517 597	9 395 813	10 881 681
Mali	1 650 181	2 103 270	3 294 055	5 288 939	7 747 730	9 481 959	10 124 689	10 140 312	10 966 150	11 654 547
Mauritania	27 144	42 517	77 981	155 297	200 221	266 638	289 665	307 212	332 596	361 696
Mauritius	73 494	122 653	196 989	312 103	420 936	486 454	506 078	480 491	463 841	525 459
Morocco	360 722	446 843	598 108	849 130	1 078 119	1 195 237	1 239 836	1 152 477	1 274 727	1 330 158
Mozambique	27 629	90 308	204 516	387 549	648 075	905 940	970 297	988 863	1 058 442	1 175 292
Namibia	14 988	28 194	47 993	84 476	148 941	181 103	179 469	176 667	189 506	211 530
Niger	1 145 340	1 586 921	2 304 126	3 875 000	5 724 873	7 114 531	7 567 900	7 910 951	8 270 763	9 615 069
Nigeria	2 895 201	6 897 482	22 269 978	55 469 351	95 177 736	129 086 908	145 639 140	154 252 320	176 075 502	202 365 028
Rwanda	385 387	806 000	1 636 000	3 571 000	6 150 000	8 298 000	9 305 000	9 596 000	10 930 000	13 716 000
Senegal	3 007 532	4 270 612	5 804 605	7 976 735	10 508 650	12 840 090	13 712 800	14 101 000	15 287 932	17 268 329
Seychelles	2 420	3 513	5 055	11 705	19 071	24 822	26 224	24 356	25 164	29 373
Sierra Leone	959 634	1 941 321	4 769 788	10 255 614	21 583 301	32 401 624	36 730 876	39 938 072	44 359 565	57 519 000
Somalia	..	..	..	..	6 841	8 278	9 420	9 204	9 839	10 420
South Africa	622 901	1 053 138	1 837 000	3 055 613	4 420 793	5 363 190	5 625 207	5 567 974	6 208 786	6 628 550
Togo	1 118 314	1 429 225	1 622 674	2 348 485	3 402 694	3 904 413	4 097 073	4 253 191	4 621 478	5 068 944
Tunisia	19 497	30 874	43 920	66 140	89 802	112 985	122 969	119 633	130 466	143 596
Uganda	6 676 316	12 067 688	20 823 563	51 348 000	93 981 000	120 508 000	133 510 000	140 640 000	147 267 000	164 424 000
Zambia	..	11 201	37 189	97 216	183 381	275 175	300 450	332 721	442 337	493 964

.. Not available

Notes:

1. The GDP for Botswana, Eswatini and Namibia are adjusted using the following formula: GDP(n)*3/4+GDP(n+1))/4 in order to make them correspond more closely to an April(n)-to-March(n+1) fiscal year. The GDP for Lesotho is not adjusted because it is already reported on an April-March fiscal year basis in the IMF *World Economic Outlook*.
2. The GDP for Kenya, Malawi and Uganda in all years and for Mauritius in the years preceding 2010 and from 2016 onwards are adjusted using the formula GDP(n)/2+GDP(n-1)/2. This is done in order to make the value of the GDP correspond more closely to a July(n-1)-to-June(n) fiscal year. The GDP for Egypt is not adjusted because it is already reported on a July-June fiscal year basis in the IMF *World Economic Outlook.* The GDP for Mauritius is not adjusted from 2010 to 2015 because public finance data are reported on a calendar year for those years.

Source: World Economic Outlook April 2024, IMF.

Table 4.18. Gross domestic product for tax reporting years at current prices, in millions of US dollars

	1995	2000	2005	2010	2015	2018	2019	2020	2021	2022
Botswana[1]	4 835	5 627	9 855	13 256	13 919	16 948	16 255	15 882	19 141	20 375
Burkina Faso	2 676	2 961	6 150	10 118	11 833	15 916	16 031	17 754	19 654	18 906
Cabo Verde	536	609	1 041	1 825	1 750	2 073	2 231	1 830	1 999	2 246
Cameroon	10 075	10 245	19 534	27 530	32 213	39 992	39 673	40 863	45 391	44 508
Chad	2 230	2 142	9 097	14 289	14 508	15 334	14 917	14 615	16 047	16 417
Congo	2 457	3 624	6 654	13 159	11 891	14 781	13 977	11 485	13 387	13 961
Congo, Dem. Rep.	25 021	19 077	12 720	22 340	40 154	48 037	50 891	49 613	58 182	65 927
Côte d'Ivoire	15 205	14 851	23 626	34 431	45 815	58 522	60 383	63 119	72 833	72 046
Egypt[2]	63 250	104 752	94 127	230 024	350 119	263 156	317 894	382 525	423 300	475 231
Equatorial Guinea	169	1 159	8 187	16 314	13 185	13 097	11 364	9 894	12 269	11 767
Eswatini[1]	1 907	1 690	3 206	4 535	4 000	4 624	4 367	4 201	4 836	4 810
Gabon	5 281	5 397	9 468	14 384	14 385	16 830	16 824	15 337	20 229	21 076
Ghana	14 610	11 470	24 600	43 327	49 437	67 259	68 353	70 008	79 599	72 243
Guinea	5 139	4 039	4 506	6 858	8 790	11 857	13 443	14 089	16 320	19 589
Kenya[2]	14 226	18 400	24 549	43 877	69 383	87 088	96 270	100 620	105 394	111 788
Lesotho	1 032	922	1 730	2 356	2 202	2 472	2 323	2 092	2 427	2 325
Madagascar	3 838	4 629	5 859	9 983	11 323	13 760	14 105	13 051	14 555	15 285
Malawi	3 171	4 297	5 022	9 260	8 770	9 413	10 457	11 439	12 162	12 499
Mali	3 337	2 963	6 251	10 698	13 106	17 079	17 281	17 643	19 786	18 724
Mauritania	2 092	1 780	2 936	5 637	6 182	7 472	7 894	8 464	9 126	9 799
Mauritius	4 163	4 766	6 915	10 138	12 007	14 225	14 586	12 922	11 446	12 217
Morocco	42 238	42 053	67 468	100 881	110 414	127 341	128 920	121 354	141 818	130 913
Mozambique	3 062	5 931	8 868	11 412	16 209	15 017	15 513	14 235	16 168	18 407
Namibia	3 950	3 850	7 421	11 567	11 267	13 392	12 050	11 048	12 483	12 533
Niger	2 296	2 235	4 372	7 838	9 684	12 814	12 917	13 764	14 923	15 448
Nigeria	132 230	67 824	169 645	369 062	492 437	421 737	448 120	429 423	441 424	477 376
Rwanda	1 470	2 049	2 943	6 124	8 546	9 637	10 345	10 173	11 053	13 309
Senegal	6 026	6 016	11 015	16 134	17 777	23 127	23 405	24 534	27 584	27 744
Seychelles	508	615	919	970	1 432	1 777	1 867	1 384	1 490	2 058
Sierra Leone	1 273	941	1 610	2 578	4 252	4 085	4 074	4 059	4 148	4 095
Somalia	..	..	..	..	6 841	8 278	9 420	9 204	9 839	10 420
South Africa	171 736	151 855	288 749	417 315	346 663	405 093	389 245	338 193	420 009	405 106
Togo	2 240	2 014	3 080	4 750	5 756	7 033	6 993	7 400	8 338	8 144
Tunisia	20 616	22 524	33 851	46 210	45 779	42 687	41 905	42 540	46 688	46 265
Uganda[2]	6 857	7 790	11 605	24 395	32 438	32 858	36 010	37 897	40 324	45 157
Zambia	..	3 601	8 329	20 264	21 245	26 312	23 309	18 138	22 096	29 122

.. Not available

Note:

1. The GDP for Botswana, Eswatini and Namibia are adjusted using the following formula: GDP(n)*3/4+GDP(n+1))/4 in order to make them correspond more closely to an April(n)-to-March(n+1) fiscal year. The GDP for Lesotho is not adjusted because it is already reported on an April-March fiscal year basis in the IMF World Economic Outlook.
2. The GDP for Kenya, Malawi and Uganda in all years and for Mauritius in the years preceding 2010 and from 2016 onwards are adjusted using the formula GDP(n)/2+GDP(n-1)/2. This is done in order to make the value of the GDP correspond more closely to a July(n-1)-to-June(n) fiscal year. The GDP for Egypt is not adjusted because it is already reported on a July-June fiscal year basis in the IMF World Economic Outlook. The GDP for Mauritius is not adjusted from 2010 to 2015 because public finance data are reported on a calendar year for those years.

Source: World Economic Outlook April 2024, IMF.

Table 4.19. Exchange rates used, national currency per US dollar

	1995	2000	2005	2010	2015	2018	2019	2020	2021	2022
Botswana	2.91	5.28	5.30	6.81	10.34	10.34	10.92	11.35	11.43	12.68
Burkina Faso	499.19	711.98	526.95	494.38	591.17	555.20	585.88	574.76	554.24	622.43
Cabo Verde	76.89	115.82	88.69	83.27	99.38	99.37	99.38	96.63	93.17	104.63
Cameroon	518.62	732.50	526.61	494.39	591.16	555.19	585.88	574.76	554.25	622.42
Chad	499.06	709.90	526.96	494.39	591.14	555.19	585.90	574.75	554.25	622.42
Congo	499.18	711.99	526.94	494.40	591.17	555.18	585.90	574.77	554.25	622.44
Congo, Dem. Rep.	0.07	69.04	469.80	906.96	926.06	1622.51	1647.82	1851.50	1990.17	2006.99
Côte d'Ivoire	499.16	710.20	527.25	494.79	591.21	555.45	585.91	574.75	554.24	622.42
Egypt	3.39	3.41	6.02	5.52	7.36	17.73	17.60	16.08	15.74	16.50
Equatorial Guinea	497.82	709.97	527.25	494.81	591.23	555.45	585.92	575.58	554.55	623.78
Eswatini	3.79	7.32	6.47	7.30	13.22	13.53	14.91	15.98	15.17	16.89
Gabon	499.12	711.93	526.96	494.40	591.13	555.19	585.87	574.74	554.23	622.43
Ghana	0.12	0.54	0.91	1.43	3.71	4.59	5.22	5.60	5.80	8.45
Guinea	991.45	1746.79	3644.60	5722.30	7489.10	9011.16	9183.78	9564.88	9763.24	8694.32
Kenya	53.47	73.22	77.23	78.33	92.88	102.33	101.68	104.11	107.89	113.59
Lesotho	3.63	6.94	6.40	7.19	13.79	13.76	14.79	16.37	14.85	17.00
Madagascar	853.15	1353.57	2003.12	2089.89	2933.51	3334.76	3618.24	3787.88	3829.91	4095.99
Malawi	12.26	51.74	113.77	146.08	463.04	731.32	739.05	744.61	772.59	870.60
Mali	494.51	709.84	526.96	494.39	591.16	555.18	585.89	574.75	554.24	622.44
Mauritania	12.98	23.89	26.56	27.55	32.39	35.68	36.69	36.30	36.44	36.91
Mauritius	17.65	25.73	28.49	30.79	35.06	34.20	34.70	37.18	40.52	43.01
Morocco	8.54	10.63	8.87	8.42	9.76	9.39	9.62	9.50	8.99	10.16
Mozambique	9.02	15.23	23.06	33.96	39.98	60.33	62.55	69.47	65.47	63.85
Namibia	3.79	7.32	6.47	7.30	13.22	13.52	14.89	15.99	15.18	16.88
Niger	498.84	710.03	527.02	494.39	591.17	555.22	585.89	574.76	554.23	622.42
Nigeria	21.90	101.70	131.27	150.30	193.28	306.08	325.00	359.21	398.88	423.91
Rwanda	262.17	393.36	555.90	583.12	719.63	861.06	899.47	943.28	988.87	1030.58
Senegal	499.09	709.88	526.97	494.41	591.14	555.20	585.89	574.75	554.23	622.42
Seychelles	4.76	5.71	5.50	12.07	13.32	13.97	14.05	17.60	16.89	14.27
Sierra Leone	753.84	2063.04	2962.60	3978.13	5076.04	7931.85	9015.92	9839.39	10694.21	14046.15
Somalia	0.00	0.00	0.00	0.00	1.00	1.00	1.00	1.00	1.00	1.00
South Africa	3.63	6.94	6.36	7.32	12.75	13.24	14.45	16.46	14.78	16.36
Togo	499.25	709.64	526.84	494.42	591.16	555.16	585.88	574.76	554.27	622.41
Tunisia	0.95	1.37	1.30	1.43	1.96	2.65	2.93	2.81	2.79	3.10
Uganda	973.72	1549.22	1794.36	2104.86	2897.25	3667.54	3707.63	3711.16	3652.09	3641.16
Zambia	0.00	3.11	4.47	4.80	8.63	10.46	12.89	18.34	20.02	16.96

Note: The exchange rate is calculated by taking the ratio of the estimated fiscal year GDP in national currency for Table 4.17 to the estimated fiscal year GDP in US dollars in Table 4.18.

5 Country tables, 1995-2022 – Tax revenues

Country tables, 1995-2022

In all of the following tables, ".." indicates not available or not applicable. The main series in this volume covers the years 1995 to 2022. Figures referring to 1990-94, 1996-99, 2001-04, 2006-09, 2011-14 and 2016-17 in Tables 5.1 to 5.36 have been omitted because of lack of space. Complete series are, however, available online at the OECD Data Explorer and can be accessed at https://data-explorer.oecd.org/ within the theme Taxation/ Global tax revenue or by searching for African tax revenues.

Table 5.1. Botswana – Details of tax revenue

Million BWP

	1995	2000	2005	2010	2015	2018	2019	2020	2021	2022
Total tax revenue	..	..	**8 037**	**14 300**	**19 332**	**23 287**	**24 357**	**21 973**	**32 254**	**35 233**
1000 Taxes on income, profits and capital gains	..	..	**5 887**	**9 345**	**13 134**	**15 069**	**15 341**	**13 418**	**20 178**	**22 619**
1100 Of individuals	..	..	..	..	..	..	..	..	..	..
1110 On income and profits	..	..	..	..	..	..	..	..	..	..
1120 On capital gains	..	..	..	..	..	..	..	..	..	..
1200 Corporate	..	..	..	..	..	..	..	..	..	..
1210 On profits	..	..	..	..	..	..	..	..	..	..
1220 On capital gains of corporates	..	..	..	..	..	..	..	..	..	..
1300 Unallocable between 1100 and 1200	..	..	5 887	9 345	13 134	15 069	15 341	13 418	20 178	22 619
Assessed income tax	..	..	3 877	5 168	6 825	7 661	6 501	4 836	9 002	10 916
Income tax arrears and deductions	..	..	1 171	3 114	5 259	5 349	7 187	7 287	8 486	8 563
Withholding tax	..	..	840	1 062	1 050	2 059	1 653	1 295	2 690	3 140
PAYE taxes	..	..	0	0	0	0	0	0	0	0
2000 Social security contributions	..	..	**0**	**0**	**0**	**0**	**0**	**0**	**0**	**0**
2100 Employees	..	..	..	..	..	..	..	..	..	..
2110 On a payroll basis	..	..	..	..	..	..	..	..	..	..
2120 On an income tax basis	..	..	..	..	..	..	..	..	..	..
2200 Employers	..	..	..	..	..	..	..	..	..	..
2210 On a payroll basis	..	..	..	..	..	..	..	..	..	..
2220 On an income tax basis	..	..	..	..	..	..	..	..	..	..
2300 Self-employed or non-employed	..	..	..	..	..	..	..	..	..	..
2310 On a payroll basis	..	..	..	..	..	..	..	..	..	..
2320 On an income tax basis	..	..	..	..	..	..	..	..	..	..
2400 Unallocable between 2100, 2200 and 2300	..	..	..	..	..	..	..	..	..	..
2410 On a payroll basis	..	..	..	..	..	..	..	..	..	..
2420 On an income tax basis	..	..	..	..	..	..	..	..	..	..
3000 Taxes on payroll and workforce	..	..	**0**	**0**	**0**	**0**	**0**	**0**	**0**	**0**
4000 Taxes on property	..	..	**13**	**52**	**66**	**78**	**71**	**63**	**99**	**100**
4100 Recurrent taxes on immovable property	..	..	0	0	0	0	0	0	0	0
4110 Households	..	..	..	..	..	..	..	..	..	..
4120 Others	..	..	..	..	..	..	..	..	..	..
4200 Recurrent taxes on net wealth	..	..	0	0	0	0	0	0	0	0
4210 Individual	..	..	..	..	..	..	..	..	..	..
4220 Corporate	..	..	..	..	..	..	..	..	..	..
4300 Estate, inheritance and gift taxes	..	..	0	0	0	0	0	0	0	0
4310 Estate and inheritance taxes	..	..	..	..	..	..	..	..	..	..
4320 Gift taxes	..	..	..	..	..	..	..	..	..	..
4400 Taxes on financial and capital transactions	..	..	13	52	66	78	71	63	99	100
4500 Other non-reccurrent taxes on property	..	..	0	0	0	0	0	0	0	0
4510 On net wealth	..	..	..	..	..	..	..	..	..	..
4520 Other non-recurrent taxes	..	..	..	..	..	..	..	..	..	..
4600 Other recurrent taxes on property	..	..	0	0	0	0	0	0	0	0
5000 Taxes on goods and services	..	..	**2 136**	**4 903**	**6 132**	**8 140**	**8 944**	**8 493**	**11 977**	**12 514**
5100 Taxes on production, sale, transfer, etc	..	..	2 006	4 669	5 870	7 661	8 475	8 131	11 449	11 721
5110 General taxes on goods and services	..	..	1 862	4 481	5 448	7 253	7 939	7 687	9 639	10 654
5111 Value added taxes	..	..	1 862	4 481	5 448	7 253	7 939	7 687	9 639	10 654
VAT revenues (gross)	..	..	1 832	4 481	5 448	7 253	7 939	7 687	9 639	10 654
VAT accrued Interest	..	..	31	0	0	0	0	0	0	0
VAT refunds	..	..	- 1	0	0	0	0	0	0	0
5112 Sales tax	..	..	0	0	0	0	0	0	0	0
5113 Other	..	..	0	0	0	0	0	0	0	0
5120 Taxes on specific goods and services	..	..	144	188	422	408	536	445	1 809	1 067
5121 Excises	..	..	115	157	393	405	531	353	1 791	1 059
Alcohol levy	..	..	0	0	284	284	401	236	382	462
Fuel levy	..	..	115	157	109	121	130	117	1 312	491
Plastic levy	..	..	0	0	0	0	0	0	17	0
Sweetened beverage levy	..	..	0	0	0	0	0	0	79	106
5122 Profits of fiscal monopolies	..	..	0	0	0	0	0	0	0	0
5123 Customs and import duties	..	..	2	9	4	1	1	2	1	0

Table 5.1. Botswana – Details of tax revenue

Million BWP

	1995	2000	2005	2010	2015	2018	2019	2020	2021	2022
5124 Taxes on exports	..	..	0	2	2	2	3	1	1	3
5125 Taxes on investment goods	..	..	0	0	0	0	0	0	0	0
5126 Taxes on specific services	..	..	27	20	23	0	1	88	16	5
5127 Other taxes on international trade and transactions	..	..	0	0	0	0	0	0	0	0
5128 Other taxes	..	..	0	0	0	0	0	0	0	0
5130 Unallocable between 5110 and 5120	..	..	0	0	0	0	0	0	0	0
5200 Taxes on use of goods and to perform activities	..	..	131	234	262	479	469	361	528	792
5210 Recurrent taxes	..	..	131	234	262	479	469	361	528	792
5211 Paid by households: motor vehicles	..	..	41	62	77	115	118	120	173	176
5212 Paid by others: motor vehicles	..	..	74	144	180	317	346	196	293	507
5213 Paid in respect of other goods	..	..	15	29	5	46	5	45	62	110
5220 Non-recurrent taxes	..	..	0	0	0	0	0	0	0	0
5300 Unallocable between 5100 and 5200	..	..	0	0	0	0	0	0	0	0
6000 Other taxes	**..**	**..**	**0**	**0**	**0**	**0**	**0**	**0**	**0**	**0**
6100 Paid solely by business	..	..	..	..	..	..	..	..	..	..
6200 Other	..	..	..	..	..	..	..	..	..	..

.. Not available

Note: Data are on a fiscal year basis beginning 1st April. For example, the data for 2022 represent April 2022 to March 2023.

The data are on a cash basis.

Figures exclude tax revenues collected by sub-national governments as the data are not available.

Heading 2000: Social security contributions for Botswana are deemed to be zero as they do not meet the criteria to be classified as social security contributions set out in the OECD classification of taxes in the *Interpretative Guide*.

Source: Botswana Ministry of Finance and Economic Development, and Statistics Botswana.

Table 5.2. Burkina Faso – Details of tax revenue

Million XOF

	1995	2000	2005	2010	2015	2018	2019	2020	2021	2022
Total tax revenue	..	**214 601**	**380 161**	**698 853**	**1 018 759**	**1 484 685**	**1 622 546**	**1 623 919**	**1 680 044**	**2 166 789**
1000 Taxes on income, profits and capital gains	..	**53 109**	**79 290**	**135 056**	**236 193**	**377 120**	**450 579**	**456 645**	**576 631**	**725 812**
1100 Of individuals	..	15 371	27 639	56 429	75 300	125 405	149 467	172 403	178 426	207 072
1110 On income and profits	..	15 371	27 639	56 429	75 300	125 405	149 467	172 403	178 426	207 072
1120 On capital gains	..	..	..	..	..	..	..	..	..	..
1200 Corporate	..	36 190	48 829	76 008	157 319	246 558	295 436	278 203	390 819	508 543
1210 On profits	..	36 190	48 829	76 008	157 319	246 558	295 436	278 203	390 819	508 543
1220 On capital gains	..	..	..	..	..	..	..	..	..	..
1300 Unallocable between 1100 and 1200	..	1 549	2 821	2 619	3 574	5 157	5 675	6 039	7 386	10 196
2000 Social security contributions	..	**34 142**	**50 081**	**76 584**	**120 046**	**164 195**	**177 435**	**158 101**	**183 719**	**198 196**
2100 Employees	..	10 332	15 753	23 424	35 064	42 003	45 391	..	..	..
2110 On a payroll basis	..	10 332	15 753	23 424	35 064	42 003	45 391	..	..	..
2120 On an income tax basis	..	0	0	0	0	0	0	..	..	..
2200 Employers	..	23 810	34 329	53 160	84 983	122 192	132 044	51 556	57 968	63 370
2210 On a payroll basis	..	23 810	34 329	53 160	84 983	122 192	132 044	..	..	..
2220 On an income tax basis	..	0	0	0	0	0	0	..	..	..
2300 Self-employed or non-employed	..	0	0	0	0	0	0	0	0	0
2310 On a payroll basis	..	..	..	..	..	..	..	..	..	..
2320 On an income tax basis	..	..	..	..	..	..	..	..	..	..
2400 Unallocable between 2100, 2200 and 2300	..	0	0	0	0	0	0	106 546	125 751	134 825
2410 On a payroll basis	..	..	..	..	..	..	..	..	..	..
2420 On an income tax basis	..	..	..	..	..	..	..	..	..	..
3000 Taxes on payroll and workforce	..	**2 678**	**4 370**	**5 479**	**7 889**	**12 331**	**13 210**	**14 647**	**16 230**	**18 269**
4000 Taxes on property	..	**938**	**2 076**	**4 778**	**8 529**	**9 982**	**11 025**	**13 012**	**25 886**	**14 138**
4100 Recurrent taxes on immovable property	..	54	0	615	1 011	2 013	2 438	2 775	12 963	3 685
4110 Households	..	0	..	0	0	0	0	0	..	..
4120 Others	..	0	..	0	0	0	0	0	..	..
4200 Recurrent taxes on net wealth	..	0	0	0	0	0	0	0	0	0
4210 Individual	..	..	..	..	..	..	..	..	..	..
4220 Corporate	..	..	..	..	..	..	..	..	..	..
4300 Estate, inheritance and gift taxes	..	73	56	41	200	170	317	306	302	498
4310 Estate and inheritance taxes	..	66	38	28	179	156	265	251	258	410
4320 Gift taxes	..	7	18	13	21	13	52	55	44	88
4400 Taxes on financial and capital transactions	..	646	1 481	2 803	6 160	5 818	5 778	7 241	8 597	6 815
4500 Non-recurrent taxes	..	165	539	1 318	1 158	1 981	2 492	2 690	4 023	3 141
4510 On net wealth	..	0	0	0	0	0	0	0	0	0
4520 Other non-recurrent taxes	..	165	539	1 318	1 158	1 981	2 492	2 690	4 023	3 141
4600 Other recurrent taxes on property	..	0	0	0	0	0	0	0	0	0
5000 Taxes on goods and services	..	**122 232**	**241 776**	**470 504**	**639 524**	**911 247**	**959 602**	**973 051**	**866 818**	**1 199 901**
5100 Taxes on production, sale, transfer, etc	..	108 003	222 923	370 927	598 102	852 880	895 777	856 840	761 989	1 109 935
5110 General taxes	..	61 497	131 867	229 176	343 378	487 799	536 770	488 599	320 231	551 505
5111 Value added taxes	..	61 497	131 005	228 498	342 660	486 929	535 895	488 276	319 689	550 897
5112 Sales tax	..	0	0	0	0	0	0	0	0	0
5113 Other	..	0	862	678	719	870	874	322	542	608
5120 Taxes on specific goods and services	..	46 506	91 056	141 750	254 723	365 080	359 007	368 242	441 759	558 431
5121 Excises	..	16 129	31 956	46 912	94 105	141 049	138 068	145 014	172 758	191 743
5122 Profits of fiscal monopolies	..	2 912	5 344	7 234	15 212	22 259	24 158	22 646	23 675	23 887
5123 Customs and import duties	..	25 242	52 066	85 075	128 465	182 180	176 799	167 212	194 772	268 583
5124 Taxes on exports	..	572	322	434	601	454	422	345	315	362
5125 Taxes on investment goods	..	0	0	0	0	0	0	0	0	0
5126 Taxes on specific services	..	1 651	1 369	2 096	16 339	19 139	19 560	33 026	50 238	73 856
5127 Other taxes on internat. trade and transactions	..	0	0	0	0	0	0	0	0	0
5128 Other taxes	..	0	0	0	0	0	0	0	0	0
5130 Unallocable between 5110 and 5120	..	0	0	0	0	0	0	0	0	0
5200 Taxes on use of goods and to perform activities	..	10 503	15 876	98 077	38 970	53 794	58 412	114 498	103 126	82 572
5210 Recurrent taxes	..	3 837	648	70 529	12 022	19 339	21 043	73 348	58 691	35 040
5211 Paid by households: motor vehicles	..	0	0	0	0	0	942	900	1 048	1 258
5212 Paid by others: motor vehicles	..	0	0	0	0	0	0	0	0	0

Table 5.2. Burkina Faso – Details of tax revenue (continued)

Million XOF

	1995	2000	2005	2010	2015	2018	2019	2020	2021	2022
5213 Paid in respect of other goods	..	3 837	648	70 529	12 022	19 339	20 101	72 448	57 643	33 783
5220 Non-recurrent taxes	..	6 666	15 228	27 547	26 948	34 456	37 369	41 150	44 436	47 531
5300 Unallocable between 5100 and 5200	..	3 726	2 977	1 501	2 452	4 573	5 413	1 713	1 702	7 394
6000 Other taxes	**..**	**1 502**	**2 568**	**6 452**	**6 579**	**9 810**	**10 695**	**8 462**	**10 760**	**10 472**
6100 Paid solely by business	..	..	..	..	..	..	..	..	..	..
6200 Other	..	..	..	..	..	..	..	..	..	..

.. Not available

Note: Year ending 31st December.

The data are on a cash basis.

Figures exclude tax revenues collected by sub-national governments as the data are not available. They do however include revenues collected by the central administration for sub-national governments.

Revenues from property rental tax, mining title fees, mining royalties and administrative fees are included in non-tax revenue following the OECD classification of taxes (see the *Interpretative Guide* in Annex A). Under Burkina Faso's national classification they are included in tax revenues.

The higher revenues in 2010 and 2020 under heading 5213 are attributable to revenues from mobile telephone licences, most of which were collected in those two years.

Source: Ministry of Economy, Finance and Planning, Burkina Faso.

Table 5.3. Cabo Verde – Details of tax revenue

Million CPV

	1995	2000	2005	2010	2015	2018	2019	2020	2021	2022
Total tax revenue	**6 290**	**10 974**	**18 828**	**26 290**	**30 692**	**40 338**	**41 447**	**33 130**	**33 127**	**42 904**
1000 Taxes on income, profits and capital gains	**2 105**	**3 913**	**5 815**	**7 892**	**9 669**	**12 300**	**12 806**	**9 990**	**9 200**	**10 215**
1100 Of individuals	1 579	2 958	3 516	4 645	5 327	6 927	7 334	6 581	6 073	6 466
1110 On income and profits	..	..	..	..	..	..	..	..	..	..
1120 On capital gains	..	..	..	..	..	..	..	..	..	..
1200 Corporate	526	955	2 299	3 247	4 342	5 374	5 472	3 410	2 738	3 207
1210 On profits	..	..	..	..	..	..	..	..	..	..
1220 On capital gains of corporates	..	..	..	..	..	..	..	..	..	..
1300 Unallocable between 1100 and 1200	0	0	0	0	0	0	0	0	389	542
2000 Social security contributions	**0**	**569**	**533**	**42**	**46**	**77**	**76**	**77**	**79**	**81**
2100 Employees	..	..	..	..	..	..	..	..	..	..
2110 On a payroll basis	..	..	..	..	..	..	..	..	..	..
2120 On an income tax basis	..	..	..	..	..	..	..	..	..	..
2200 Employers	..	..	..	..	..	..	..	..	..	..
2210 On a payroll basis	..	..	..	..	..	..	..	..	..	..
2220 On an income tax basis	..	..	..	..	..	..	..	..	..	..
2300 Self-employed or non-employed	..	..	..	..	..	..	..	..	..	..
2310 On a payroll basis	..	..	..	..	..	..	..	..	..	..
2320 On an income tax basis	..	..	..	..	..	..	..	..	..	..
2400 Unallocable between 2100, 2200 and 2300	..	569	533	42	46	77	76	77	79	81
2410 On a payroll basis	..	569	533	42	46	77	76	77	79	81
Social security contributions	..	11	1	28	40	77	76	77	78	81
Unique social tax	..	558	532	14	5	0	0	0	0	0
2420 On an income tax basis	..	0	0	0	0	0	0	0	0	0
3000 Taxes on payroll and workforce	**0**	**0**	**0**	**0**	**0**	**0**	**0**	**0**	**0**	**0**
4000 Taxes on property	**332**	**584**	**810**	**1 439**	**1 606**	**1 882**	**1 884**	**1 556**	**642**	**755**
4100 Recurrent taxes on immovable property	..	..	..	738	1 024	1 140	1 250	905	0	0
Single property tax	..	..	..	738	1 024	1 140	1 250	905	0	0
4110 Households	..	..	..	..	..	..	..	..	..	..
4120 Others	..	..	..	..	..	..	..	..	..	..
4200 Recurrent taxes on net wealth	0	0	0	0	0	0	0	0	0	0
4210 Individual	..	..	..	..	..	..	..	..	..	..
4220 Corporate	..	..	..	..	..	..	..	..	..	..
4300 Estate, inheritance and gift taxes	0	0	0	0	0	0	0	0	0	0
4310 Estate and inheritance taxes	..	..	..	..	..	..	..	..	..	..
4320 Gift taxes	..	..	..	..	..	..	..	..	..	..
4400 Taxes on financial and capital transactions	332	584	810	701	582	742	634	651	642	755
4500 Other non-reccurrent taxes on property	0	0	0	0	0	0	0	0	0	0
4510 On net wealth	..	..	..	..	..	..	..	..	..	..
4520 Other non-recurrent taxes	..	..	..	..	..	..	..	..	..	..
4600 Other recurrent taxes on property	0	0	0	0	0	0	0	0	0	0
5000 Taxes on goods and services	**3 853**	**5 908**	**11 670**	**16 917**	**19 370**	**26 079**	**26 681**	**21 507**	**23 207**	**31 854**
5100 Taxes on production, sale, transfer, etc	3 853	5 908	11 670	16 917	19 370	26 079	26 681	21 507	23 207	31 854
5110 General taxes on goods and services	0	0	6 409	10 035	10 824	15 139	15 048	12 589	12 784	17 633
5111 Value added taxes	..	..	6 409	10 035	10 824	15 139	15 048	12 589	12 784	17 633
VAT on imports (gross) - DGA	..	..	4 192	6 180	6 358	7 801	8 260	6 670	8 319	10 918
Interior VAT (gross) - DGCI	..	..	2 359	4 341	4 935	8 412	8 468	6 371	4 798	7 002
VAT refunds	..	..	- 143	- 486	- 469	-1 074	-1 679	- 452	- 333	- 287
5112 Sales tax	..	..	0	0	0	0	0	0	0	0
5113 Other	..	..	0	0	0	0	0	0	0	0
5120 Taxes on specific goods and services	3 853	5 908	5 261	6 882	8 546	10 940	11 633	8 918	10 423	14 221
5121 Excises	1 197	1 938	1 030	1 494	2 073	2 680	2 931	2 295	2 685	3 832
Special tax on consumption	1 197	1 812	838	1 227	1 478	1 963	2 192	1 702	2 010	3 146
Ecological tax	0	126	192	267	595	717	739	593	675	685
5122 Profits of fiscal monopolies	0	0	0	0	0	0	0	0	0	0
5123 Customs and import duties	2 656	3 971	4 231	5 388	5 827	7 409	7 672	6 296	7 565	9 593
5124 Taxes on exports	0	0	0	0	0	0	0	0	0	0
5125 Taxes on investment goods	0	0	0	0	0	0	0	0	0	0
5126 Taxes on specific services	0	0	0	0	645	851	1 030	327	172	796

Table 5.3. Cabo Verde – Details of tax revenue (continued)

Million CPV

	1995	2000	2005	2010	2015	2018	2019	2020	2021	2022
Contribution for tourism	..	..	..	..	645	811	992	297	145	735
Other (fire tax, tourist tax)	..	..	..	..	0	40	38	30	27	61
5127 Other taxes on internat. trade and transactions	0	0	0	0	0	0	0	0	0	0
5128 Other taxes	0	0	0	0	0	0	0	0	0	0
5130 Unallocable between 5110 and 5120	0	0	0	0	0	0	0	0	0	0
5200 Taxes on use of goods and to perform activities	0	0	0	0	0	0	0	0	0	0
5210 Recurrent taxes	..	..	..	..	..	..	..	..	..	..
5211 Paid by households: motor vehicles	..	..	..	..	..	..	..	..	..	..
5212 Paid by others: motor vehicles	..	..	..	..	..	..	..	..	..	..
5213 Paid in respect of other goods	..	..	..	..	..	..	..	..	..	..
5220 Non-recurrent taxes	..	..	..	..	..	..	..	..	..	..
5300 Unallocable between 5100 and 5200	0	0	0	0	0	0	0	0	0	0
6000 Other taxes	**0**	**0**	**0**	**0**	**0**	**0**	**0**	**0**	**0**	**0**
6100 Paid solely by business	..	..	..	..	..	..	..	..	..	..
6200 Other	..	..	..	..	..	..	..	..	..	..
Memo item:	..	..	..	..	..	..	..	..	..	..
ECOWAS Community rate	0	67	156	245	254	324	339	297	328	433

.. Not available

Note: Year ending 31st December.

The data are on a cash basis.

Heading 4100: This heading includes revenue from the Single Property Tax (*Imposto Único sobre o Património*) collected by Cabo Verde municipalities.

Heading 4400: This heading includes stamp duty, included in the heading "Other taxes" under Cabo Verde's national classification.

Heading 5126: The fire tax and the tourist tax are included in the heading "Other taxes" under Cabo Verde's national classification.

The ECOWAS (Economic Community of West African States) community levy is not considered as a revenue of the government of Cabo Verde following the OECD *Interpretative Guide* (see § 4). Under Cabo Verde's national classification, it is included in tax revenues. This revenue, which is not included in total tax revenues or non-tax revenues, is presented separately under the heading "Memo item".

Source: Ministry of Finance and Planning, Cabo Verde.

Table 5.4. Cameroon – Details of tax revenue

Million XAF

	1995	2000	2005	2010	2015	2018	2019	2020	2021	2022
Total tax revenue	**481 383**	**810 500**	**1 135 257**	**1 571 695**	**2 687 926**	**3 146 494**	**3 222 162**	**3 014 088**	**3 355 315**	**3 889 586**
1000 Taxes on income, profits and capital gains	**115 300**	**228 100**	**325 764**	**425 741**	**867 834**	**848 398**	**882 190**	**863 643**	**916 953**	**1 174 494**
1100 Of individuals	55 400	87 100	66 598	102 793	185 512	247 546	226 293	221 249	237 798	248 351
1110 On income and profits	55 400	87 100	66 548	102 728	184 213	246 321	225 213	219 377	235 261	246 261
Salaries, wages, pensions and annuities	37 100	60 800	17 722	86 440	135 738	165 187	150 396	152 945	162 710	184 152
Property income	0	0	2 225	2 402	12 405	14 401	12 442	12 865	11 469	13 219
Artisanal profits, both industrial and commercial	0	0	3 904	5 342	21 010	29 610	35 745	28 826	30 363	30 172
Agricultural profits	0	0	77	47	56	161	253	23	21	31
Profits of non-commercial professions	0	0	249	295	2 875	24 643	14 865	13 387	18 076	11 213
Other income taxes	18 300	26 300	42 372	8 202	12 130	12 319	11 511	11 332	12 622	7 474
1120 On capital gains	..	..	50	65	1 299	1 225	1 079	1 872	2 538	2 090
Taxes on capital gains on land transfers	..	..	46	46	1 297	1 223	1 079	1 871	2 538	2 083
Other capital gains taxes	..	..	3	19	2	2	0	1	0	8
1200 Corporate	58 800	119 400	217 495	256 404	538 969	441 882	457 428	459 160	467 457	663 860
1210 On profits	58 800	119 400	217 495	256 404	538 969	441 882	457 428	459 160	467 457	663 860
Oil company profits	28 600	39 000	76 523	83 764	171 891	86 948	113 018	106 845	73 159	199 333
Profits of non-oil companies	30 200	80 400	140 972	172 639	367 078	354 934	344 410	352 315	394 299	464 527
1220 On capital gains	..	..	..	..	..	..	..	..	..	..
1300 Unallocable between 1100 and 1200	1 100	21 600	41 671	66 544	143 352	158 970	198 470	183 234	211 697	262 283
Special tax on revenues paid abroad	0	12 400	19 198	38 877	84 412	67 809	91 879	85 517	82 502	124 228
Taxes on income from movable capital	1 100	9 200	21 619	27 629	48 774	42 715	47 612	54 227	45 549	60 624
Municipal income tax surcharges	0	0	854	39	10 166	48 446	58 978	43 490	83 646	77 432
2000 Social security contributions	**40 183**	**65 500**	**83 903**	**135 747**	**160 992**	**226 610**	**235 937**	**243 702**	**256 642**	**265 682**
2100 Employees	11 294	19 747	24 123	33 297	44 669	48 105	45 565	55 342	55 371	56 258
2110 On a payroll basis	11 294	19 747	24 123	33 297	44 669	48 105	45 565	55 342	55 371	56 258
2120 On an income tax basis	0	0	0	0	0	0	0	0	0	0
2200 Employers	..	..	..	..	..	..	..	..	..	..
2210 On a payroll basis	..	..	..	..	..	..	..	..	..	..
2220 On an income tax basis	..	..	..	..	..	..	..	..	..	..
2300 Self-employed or non-employed	..	..	..	..	..	..	..	..	..	..
2310 On a payroll basis	..	..	..	..	..	..	..	..	..	..
2320 On an income tax basis	..	..	..	..	..	..	..	..	..	..
2400 Unallocable between 2100, 2200 and 2300	28 889	45 753	59 780	102 450	116 323	178 505	190 372	188 360	201 271	209 424
2410 On a payroll basis	28 889	45 753	59 780	102 450	116 323	178 505	190 372	188 360	201 271	209 424
2420 On an income tax basis	0	0	0	0	0	0	0	0	0	0
3000 Taxes on payroll and workforce	**0**	**0**	**8 644**	**17 860**	**53 572**	**32 131**	**36 046**	**35 521**	**52 977**	**67 092**
4000 Taxes on property	**7 900**	**13 100**	**13 361**	**18 003**	**25 437**	**25 311**	**27 113**	**25 639**	**29 116**	**26 857**
4100 Recurrent taxes on immovable property	500	500	1 318	1 552	1 743	2 443	2 249	2 044	1 893	2 209
4110 Households	..	..	..	..	..	..	..	..	..	..
4120 Others	..	..	..	..	..	..	..	..	..	..
4200 Recurrent taxes on net wealth	0	0	0	0	0	0	0	0	0	0
4210 Individual	..	..	..	..	..	..	..	..	..	..
4220 Corporate	..	..	..	..	..	..	..	..	..	..
4300 Estate, inheritance and gift taxes	0	0	33	39	62	86	38	180	122	97
4310 Estate and inheritance taxes	..	..	33	39	62	86	38	180	122	97
4320 Gift taxes	..	..	0	0	0	0	0	0	0	0
4400 Taxes on financial and capital transactions	7 400	12 600	12 010	16 412	23 632	22 782	24 827	23 415	27 101	24 551
Registration fees on transfers fo livestock	..	..	82	32	391	76	301	46	129	87
Registration duties on real estate transactions	..	..	1 909	2 747	3 080	3 924	4 991	5 005	4 444	5 987
Bail fees	..	..	3 976	4 602	2 364	2 395	2 802	2 517	3 125	2 258
Other fees for transactions and transfers	..	..	6 043	9 031	17 797	16 388	16 733	15 847	19 403	16 218
4500 Non-recurrent taxes	0	0	0	0	0	0	0	0	0	0
4510 On net wealth	..	..	..	..	..	..	..	..	..	..
4520 Other non-recurrent taxes	..	..	..	..	..	..	..	..	..	..
4600 Other recurrent taxes on property	0	0	0	0	0	0	0	0	0	0
5000 Taxes on goods and services	**318 000**	**503 800**	**686 416**	**944 412**	**1 532 668**	**1 958 026**	**1 963 031**	**1 763 852**	**2 014 841**	**2 269 539**
5100 Taxes on production, sale, transfer, etc	315 100	501 100	679 379	936 564	1 522 834	1 948 068	1 952 839	1 754 298	2 007 632	2 262 071
5110 General taxes	139 600	260 900	360 218	490 521	883 618	1 158 458	1 138 354	941 804	1 069 636	1 278 783

Table 5.4. Cameroon – Details of tax revenue (continued)

Million XAF

	1995	2000	2005	2010	2015	2018	2019	2020	2021	2022
5111 Value added taxes	0	260 900	360 218	490 513	883 580	1 158 458	1 138 354	941 804	1 069 636	1 258 795
VAT revenues (gross) - Domestic	..	186 500	251 019	299 504	604 046	846 136	810 285	700 919	740 597	869 844
VAT revenues (gross) - Paid at the border	..	107 300	157 799	259 343	354 701	384 310	394 070	319 879	396 054	468 958
VAT refunds	..	- 32 900	- 48 600	- 68 334	- 75 167	- 71 988	- 66 002	- 78 995	- 67 015	- 80 007
5112 Sales tax	0	0	0	0	0	0	0	0	0	0
5113 Other	139 600	0	0	8	39	0	0	0	0	19 988
5120 Taxes on specific goods and services	175 500	240 200	319 161	446 043	639 216	789 609	814 485	812 494	937 996	983 289
5121 Excises	55 800	84 000	114 306	164 943	289 280	337 533	380 616	430 287	486 202	529 742
Interior excise tax	18 300	26 500	42 754	68 414	170 164	192 954	217 381	255 610	280 401	289 499
Excise tax paid at the border	800	1 900	2 198	12 936	14 608	16 655	33 798	38 440	58 147	89 140
Special tax on petroleum products	36 700	55 600	69 345	82 962	103 773	127 456	128 709	135 652	146 842	150 253
Stamp fee for tobacco and manufactured products	0	0	8	632	736	469	728	585	812	851
5122 Profits of fiscal monopolies	0	0	0	0	0	0	0	0	0	0
5123 Customs and import duties	62 400	119 900	189 364	261 731	320 314	394 169	386 778	336 729	383 011	394 172
5124 Taxes on exports	56 400	24 300	1 725	8 793	17 133	36 581	31 799	38 440	58 147	42 891
5125 Taxes on investment goods	0	0	0	0	0	0	0	0	0	0
5126 Taxes on specific services	900	1 100	3 108	3 600	5 035	12 271	13 889	6 387	9 925	13 996
5127 Other taxes on internat. trade and transactions	0	0	0	0	0	0	0	0	0	0
5128 Other taxes	0	10 900	10 658	6 977	7 454	9 054	1 403	650	710	2 489
5130 Unallocable between 5110 and 5120	0	0	0	0	0	0	0	0	0	0
5200 Taxes on use of goods and to perform activities	2 900	2 700	7 037	7 848	9 835	9 959	10 193	9 553	7 209	7 468
5210 Recurrent taxes	2 900	2 700	7 037	7 848	9 835	9 959	10 193	9 553	7 209	7 468
5211 Paid by households: motor vehicles	2 200	1 600	4 987	6 111	7 539	7 000	7 000	7 000	7 000	7 000
5212 Paid by others: motor vehicles	700	1 100	1 902	1 663	2 213	2 710	2 859	2 418	121	15
5213 Paid in respect of other goods	0	0	149	74	83	248	334	136	88	452
5220 Non-recurrent taxes	0	0	0	0	0	0	0	0	0	0
5300 Unallocable between 5100 and 5200	0	0	0	0	0	0	0	0	0	0
6000 Other taxes	**0**	**0**	**17 169**	**29 932**	**47 424**	**56 018**	**77 845**	**81 731**	**84 787**	**85 922**
6100 Paid solely by business	..	..	..	..	..	..	..	..	..	..
6200 Other	..	..	..	..	..	..	..	..	..	..

.. Not available

Note: Year ending 31st December.

The data are on a cash basis.

Figures exclude tax revenues collected by sub-national governments as the data are not available.

Heading 2000: Social security contributions from the public sector (APU) only include pension contributions and do not cover family and disability benefits.

Heading 5111: Data prior to 1999 correspond to revenues from the turnover tax (*TCA: taxe sur le chiffre d'affaire*) and have been reclassified under heading "5113 Turnover and other general taxes on goods and services". VAT was introduced in Cameroon in 1999. Data on VAT revenues are presented net of VAT refunds following the OECD classification of taxes (see the *Interpretative Guide* in Annex A).

Source: Ministry of Finance, Cameroon.

Table 5.5. Chad – Details of tax revenue

Million XAF

	1995	2000	2005	2010	2015	2018	2019	2020	2021	2022
Total tax revenue	..	..	..	**773 264**	**374 179**	**482 783**	**519 374**	**901 916**	**652 288**	**1088 274**
1000 Taxes on income, profits and capital gains	..	..	..	**580 929**	**202 651**	**249 670**	**234 826**	**560 468**	**318 624**	**757 122**
1100 Of individuals	..	..	..	55 020	94 216	88 445	105 077	124 911	105 113	98 582
1110 On income and profits	..	..	..	55 020	94 216	88 445	105 077	124 911	105 113	98 582
Employees, beneficiaries of pensions and annuities	..	..	..	45 127	62 041	45 048	75 996	66 857	70 419	64 573
Profits from liberal professions (non-commercial)	..	..	..	4 877	21 221	18 587	19 740	48 205	11 738	13 289
Industrial and commercial profit	..	..	..	0	82	1 059	96	1 908	48	2 050
Landowners	..	..	..	1 470	2 434	7 077	2 098	1 337	1 901	1 709
Income from capital and securities	..	..	..	3 546	8 438	16 674	7 147	6 604	21 007	16 961
1120 On capital gains	..	..	..	0	0	0	0	0	0	0
1200 Corporate	..	..	..	525 628	108 316	161 222	129 631	435 557	213 511	658 540
1210 On profits	..	..	..	525 628	108 316	161 222	129 631	435 557	213 511	658 540
Income tax on oil companies	..	..	..	464 428	41 797	115 930	93 866	415 990	195 747	588 469
Tax on profits of non-oil companies	..	..	..	53 381	60 901	39 784	30 091	13 907	11 969	67 677
4% domestic withholding tax	..	..	..	7 819	5 618	5 508	5 674	5 660	5 795	2 393
1220 On capital gains of corporates	..	..	..	0	0	0	0	0	0	0
1300 Unallocable between 1100 and 1200	..	..	..	281	119	3	118	0	0	0
2000 Social security contributions	..	..	..	..	..	..	..	..	..	..
2100 Employees	..	..	..	..	..	..	..	..	..	..
2110 On a payroll basis	..	..	..	..	..	..	..	..	..	..
2120 On an income tax basis	..	..	..	..	..	..	..	..	..	..
2200 Employers	..	..	..	..	..	..	..	..	..	..
2210 On a payroll basis	..	..	..	..	..	..	..	..	..	..
2220 On an income tax basis	..	..	..	..	..	..	..	..	..	..
2300 Self-employed or non-employed	..	..	..	..	..	..	..	..	..	..
2310 On a payroll basis	..	..	..	..	..	..	..	..	..	..
2320 On an income tax basis	..	..	..	..	..	..	..	..	..	..
2400 Unallocable between 2100, 2200 and 2300	..	..	..	..	..	..	..	..	..	..
2410 On a payroll basis	..	..	..	..	..	..	..	..	..	..
2420 On an income tax basis	..	..	..	..	..	..	..	..	..	..
3000 Taxes on payroll and workforce	..	..	..	**8 304**	**10 856**	**628**	**7 968**	**12 389**	**9 482**	**10 322**
Flat-rate payroll tax	..	..	..	8 304	10 856	437	7 304	12 259	9 368	10 192
Employers' apprenticeship tax	..	..	..	0	0	191	664	130	114	130
4000 Taxes on property	..	..	..	**23 875**	**11 922**	**7 926**	**23 710**	**31 318**	**26 585**	**22 391**
4100 Recurrent taxes on immovable property	..	..	..	0	0	0	0	0	0	0
4110 Households	..	..	..	..	..	..	..	..	..	..
4120 Others	..	..	..	..	..	..	..	..	..	..
4200 Recurrent taxes on net wealth	..	..	..	0	0	0	0	0	0	0
4210 Individual	..	..	..	..	..	..	..	..	..	..
4220 Corporate	..	..	..	..	..	..	..	..	..	..
4300 Estate, inheritance and gift taxes	..	..	..	71	0	13	1	0	0	0
4310 Estate and inheritance taxes	..	..	..	8	..	1	0	..	..	..
4320 Gift taxes	..	..	..	63	..	12	1	..	..	..
4400 Taxes on financial and capital transactions	..	..	..	23 651	11 473	6 911	23 386	31 022	26 219	20 731
4500 Other non-reccurrent taxes on property	..	..	..	153	449	1 002	323	296	366	1 660
4510 On net wealth	..	..	..	0	0	0	0	0	0	0
4520 Other non-recurrent taxes	..	..	..	153	449	1 002	323	296	366	1 660
4600 Other recurrent taxes on property	..	..	..	0	0	0	0	0	0	0
5000 Taxes on goods and services	..	..	..	**160 089**	**148 688**	**224 500**	**252 787**	**297 511**	**297 534**	**298 439**
5100 Taxes on production, sale, transfer, etc	..	..	..	157 944	146 538	215 386	250 633	285 719	293 580	283 170
5110 General taxes on goods and services	..	..	..	95 467	74 894	78 311	115 074	121 831	134 693	65 492
5111 Value added taxes	..	..	..	76 549	66 730	72 160	98 038	103 449	108 955	63 129
Domestic value-added tax	..	..	..	46 148	45 476	39 374	55 598	59 254	56 652	60 698
VAT imports	..	..	..	30 401	21 254	32 786	42 440	44 195	52 303	2 431
5112 Sales tax	..	..	..	0	0	0	0	0	0	0
5113 Other	..	..	..	18 918	8 164	6 151	17 036	18 382	25 738	2 363
Minimum tax (IMF)	..	..	..	13 781	6 165	3 821	10 569	16 844	18 504	0
General withholding tax (IGL)	..	..	..	5 137	1 999	2 330	6 467	1 538	7 234	2 363

Table 5.5. Chad – Details of tax revenue (continued)

Million XAF

	1995	2000	2005	2010	2015	2018	2019	2020	2021	2022
5121 Excises	..	..	..	9 388	10 161	31 307	34 947	30 234	34 798	41 822
Domestic excise duties	..	..	..	2 356	7 045	7 111	11 575	5 412	485	0
Import excise duty	..	..	..	243	125	1 261	3 917	1 808	2 089	0
Fuels and lubricants	..	..	..	6 168	1 814	16 888	13 751	21 692	30 453	0
Livestock sales tax	..	..	..	621	1 177	1 581	1 734	1 322	1 771	1 727
Livestock sales tax	..	..	..	621	1 177	1 581	1 734	1 322	1 771	1 727
Domestic tax on petroleum products	..	..	..	0	0	4 466	3 970	0	0	14 342
Unallocated excise duties	..	..	..	0	0	0	0	0	0	25 753
5122 Profits of fiscal monopolies	..	..	..	0	0	0	0	0	0	0
5123 Customs and import duties	..	..	..	33 150	48 642	79 650	82 129	89 397	101 355	168 308
Customs duties	..	..	..	26 441	44 056	51 448	54 869	67 357	80 985	127 899
Statistical fees	..	..	..	6 709	4 586	28 202	27 260	22 040	20 370	40 409
5124 Taxes on exports	..	..	..	19 078	12 375	8 152	5 224	24 960	7 633	2 724
Statistical royalty consortium	..	..	..	16 821	9 611	3 816	2 505	23 220	3 495	0
Exit duties	..	..	..	2 257	2 764	4 336	2 719	1 740	4 138	2 724
5125 Taxes on investment goods	..	..	..	0	0	0	0	0	0	0
5126 Taxes on specific services	..	..	..	775	431	17 851	13 126	19 167	14 961	0
Telephone excise duty 18 %	..	..	..	0	0	17 131	12 452	18 387	14 101	..
Insurance convention tax	..	..	..	775	431	720	674	755	789	..
4% royalty on sales	..	..	..	0	0	0	0	25	71	..
5127 Other taxes on internat. trade and transactions	..	..	..	0	0	0	0	0	0	4 824
5128 Other taxes	..	..	..	86	35	115	133	130	140	0
5130 Unallocable between 5110 and 5120	..	..	..	0	0	0	0	0	0	0
5200 Taxes on use of goods and to perform activities	..	..	..	2 145	2 150	9 114	2 154	11 792	3 954	5 818
5210 Recurrent taxes	..	..	..	2 145	2 150	9 114	2 154	11 792	3 954	5 818
5211 Paid by households: motor vehicles	..	..	..	1 567	1 929	8 829	519	8 317	70	0
5212 Paid by others: motor vehicles	..	..	..	204	144	74	313	35	66	0
5213 Paid in respect of other goods	..	..	..	374	77	211	1 322	3 440	3 818	5 818
Contribution from patents and licenses	..	..	..	374	77	211	1 322	3 440	3 818	5 818
5220 Non-recurrent taxes	..	..	..	0	0	0	0	0	0	0
5300 Unallocable between 5100 and 5200	..	..	..	0	0	0	0	0	0	9 451
6000 Other taxes	**..**	**..**	**..**	**67**	**62**	**59**	**83**	**230**	**63**	**0**
6100 Paid solely by business	..	..	..	..	..	..	..	..	..	..
6200 Other	..	..	..	..	..	..	..	..	..	..

.. Not available

Note: Year ending 31st December.

The data are on a cash basis.

Figures exclude tax revenues collected by sub-national governments as the data are not available.

Chad adopted a new budgetary nomenclature from 2022, so the data in this edition are presented differently, mainly in relation to taxes on goods and services.

Heading 5113: Revenues from the "minimum tax" (*IMF: Impôt Minimal Fiscal*) and the "General withholding tax" (*IGL: Impôt Général Libératoire*) are classified under this heading because the tax base for these taxes is turnover. Under Chad's new nomenclature, revenues from the minimum tax are not reported separately and are grouped with taxes on the profits of non-oil companies (Heading 1210).

Heading 5121: Details of excise duties are not available for 2022. In this edition they are grouped under "Unallocated excise duties".

Heading 5127: This heading includes revenues from "Other taxes on foreign exchange transactions", which are reported separately under Chad's new budgetary nomenclature.

Heading 5213: The category "Contribution from patents and licences" also includes revenues from the tax on transport of fish, transporters' licences and firearms licences.

Heading 5300: This heading includes revenues from the non-itemised categories of other taxes on goods and services under the new budgetary nomenclature.

Source: Ministry of Finance and Budget, Chad.

Table 5.6. Congo – Details of tax revenue

Million XAF

	1995	2000	2005	2010	2015	2018	2019	2020	2021	2022
Total tax revenue	..	**98 684**	**206 416**	**462 923**	**931 417**	**622 962**	**672 862**	**648 016**	**610 767**	**772 627**
1000 Taxes on income, profits and capital gains	..	**47 544**	**62 458**	**150 792**	**342 763**	**138 956**	**183 900**	**179 210**	**160 325**	**176 981**
1100 Of individuals	..	22 850	28 265	64 364	145 622	114 722	111 996	107 221	113 258	127 814
1110 On income and profits	..	22 850	28 265	64 364	145 622	114 722	111 996	107 221	113 258	127 814
Salaries and wages	..	21 836	22 581	54 763	103 818	103 858	101 282	94 784	86 669	93 318
Property income	..	549	1 079	2 259	5 531	3 658	3 433	3 582	2 755	3 250
Non-commercial profits (BNC)	..	0	62	112	50	1 377	2 098	7 881	6 358	956
Industrial and commercial benefits (BIC)	..	0	468	25	152	175	1 119	339	883	61
Securities Income (IRVM)	..	466	4 075	7 176	35 441	5 427	0	0	2 189	0
Withholding taxes	..	0	0	0	471	221	1 817	633	14 404	16 527
Other income from personal income	..	0	0	29	159	6	2 247	2	0	13 703
1120 On capital gains	..	..	..	..	..	..	..	..	..	..
1200 Corporate	..	24 694	34 193	86 428	197 141	24 233	71 904	71 990	47 067	49 167
1210 On profits	..	24 694	34 193	86 428	197 141	24 233	71 904	71 990	47 067	49 167
1220 On capital gains of corporates	..	..	..	..	..	..	..	..	..	..
1300 Unallocable between 1100 and 1200	..	0	0	0	0	0	0	0	0	0
2000 Social security contributions	..	..	..	..	..	**49 600**	**54 897**	**54 897**	**52 800**	**53 600**
2100 Employees	..	..	..	..	..	..	..	..	..	..
2110 On a payroll basis	..	..	..	..	..	..	..	..	..	..
2120 On an income tax basis	..	..	..	..	..	..	..	..	..	..
2200 Employers	..	..	..	..	..	..	..	..	..	..
2210 On a payroll basis	..	..	..	..	..	..	..	..	..	..
2220 On an income tax basis	..	..	..	..	..	..	..	..	..	..
2300 Self-employed or non-employed	..	..	..	..	..	..	..	..	..	..
2310 On a payroll basis	..	..	..	..	..	..	..	..	..	..
2320 On an income tax basis	..	..	..	..	..	..	..	..	..	..
2400 Unallocable between 2100, 2200 and 2300	..	..	..	..	..	49 600	54 897	54 897	52 800	53 600
2410 On a payroll basis	..	..	..	..	..	..	..	..	..	..
2420 On an income tax basis	..	..	..	..	..	..	..	..	..	..
3000 Taxes on payroll and workforce	..	**4 965**	**3 455**	**16 585**	**24 528**	**20 436**	**17 356**	**16 466**	**13 454**	**14 873**
4000 Taxes on property	..	**1 299**	**1 571**	**12 012**	**47 399**	**17 052**	**23 129**	**19 305**	**23 855**	**23 046**
4100 Recurrent taxes on immovable property	..	0	0	0	0	0	0	0	0	0
4110 Households	..	..	..	..	..	..	..	..	..	..
4120 Others	..	..	..	..	..	..	..	..	..	..
4200 Recurrent taxes on net wealth	..	0	0	0	0	0	0	0	0	0
4210 Individual	..	..	..	..	..	..	..	..	..	..
4220 Corporate	..	..	..	..	..	..	..	..	..	..
4300 Estate, inheritance and gift taxes	..	0	0	0	0	0	0	0	0	0
4310 Estate and inheritance taxes	..	..	..	..	..	..	..	..	..	..
4320 Gift taxes	..	..	..	..	..	..	..	..	..	..
4400 Taxes on financial and capital transactions	..	1 299	1 571	12 012	47 399	17 052	23 129	19 305	23 855	23 046
4500 Other non-recurrent taxes on property	..	0	0	0	0	0	0	0	0	0
4510 On net wealth	..	..	..	..	..	..	..	..	..	..
4520 Other non-recurrent taxes	..	..	..	..	..	..	..	..	..	..
4600 Other recurrent taxes on property	..	0	0	0	0	0	0	0	0	0
5000 Taxes on goods and services	..	**44 876**	**138 932**	**281 274**	**515 385**	**396 133**	**391 993**	**377 294**	**359 352**	**503 020**
5100 Taxes on production, sale, transfer, etc	..	44 809	138 834	280 869	513 854	394 360	389 284	372 668	355 394	497 729
5110 General taxes on goods and services	..	39 641	78 187	158 512	284 586	242 924	228 784	218 280	181 115	301 196
5111 Value added taxes	..	36 889	75 247	147 032	253 875	149 926	156 262	154 519	154 091	197 149
Domestic VAT (gross)	..	38 962	54 294	92 054	163 875	95 165	93 529	93 963	92 786	127 369
Customs VAT (gross)	..	..	23 744	57 110	90 000	54 761	62 733	60 556	61 305	69 781
VAT refunds	..	-2 073	-2 791	-2 132	0	0	0	0	0	0
5112 Sales tax	..	0	0	1 742	2 214	2 568	1 980	2 146	2 326	2 224
ASDI (Advance payment on various taxes)	..	..	..	1 742	2 214	2 568	1 980	2 146	2 326	2 224
5113 Other	..	2 753	2 940	9 738	28 497	90 430	70 542	61 616	24 699	101 823
Special corporate tax (TSS)	..	2 753	2 940	9 738	26 248	23 758	24 907	25 107	12 307	43 888
Global flat-rate tax	..	0	0	0	2 250	830	850	899	483	1 639
Flat-rate corporate tax	..	0	0	0	0	57 916	36 860	31 097	9 986	47 630
Flat-rate tax on income from securities	..	0	0	0	0	7 925	7 925	4 513	1 922	8 667

Table 5.6. Congo – Details of tax revenue (continued)

Million XAF

	1995	2000	2005	2010	2015	2018	2019	2020	2021	2022
5120 Taxes on specific goods and services	..	5 059	60 506	122 357	229 268	149 746	159 863	154 155	173 793	196 282
5121 Excises	..	4 966	8 313	17 603	24 337	22 207	21 356	15 214	19 437	16 937
Special tax on alcoholic beverages and tobacco	..	0	0	0	11 140	9 351	8 649	2 073	482	267
Excise duties	..	4 966	8 313	17 603	13 197	12 855	12 566	12 955	18 679	16 487
Excise on beverages - Customs	..	0	0	0	0	0	140	186	255	179
Excise on tobacco - Customs	..	0	0	0	0	0	1	0	21	5
5122 Profits of fiscal monopolies	..	0	0	0	0	0	0	0	0	0
5123 Customs and import duties	..	..	44 446	85 775	166 613	91 286	104 670	106 173	118 387	144 481
Import receipts	..	..	41 022	77 852	148 444	80 210	92 640	93 544	104 042	127 376
Customs revenue off budget	..	..	3 424	7 923	18 169	11 076	12 030	12 629	14 345	17 105
5124 Taxes on exports	..	0	0	0	0	5 380	3 220	1 502	1 213	1 467
5125 Taxes on investment goods	..	0	0	0	0	0	0	0	0	0
5126 Taxes on specific services	..	93	7 746	18 979	38 318	30 873	30 618	31 266	34 756	33 397
Air ticket tax	..	0	0	597	849	634	624	256	443	539
Electronic telecommunications tax	..	0	0	0	0	5 564	6 378	6 947	7 986	7 486
Insurance tax	..	93	687	1 526	2 703	2 741	3 639	3 567	3 327	3 064
Funds transfer tax	..	0	7 060	16 856	34 766	21 906	19 912	20 474	22 919	22 117
Tax on games of chance	..	0	0	0	0	27	64	21	81	192
5127 Other taxes on internat. trade and transactions	..	0	0	0	0	0	0	0	0	0
5128 Other taxes	..	0	0	0	0	0	0	0	0	0
5130 Unallocable between 5110 and 5120	..	109	141	0	0	1 690	637	232	485	251
5200 Taxes on use of goods and to perform activities	..	67	98	405	1 531	1 774	2 709	4 626	3 958	5 292
5210 Recurrent taxes	..	67	98	405	1 531	1 598	2 368	4 288	3 574	4 963
5211 Paid by households: motor vehicles	..	0	0	0	0	0	0	0	0	0
5212 Paid by others: motor vehicles	..	67	98	343	1 405	814	746	1 174	556	572
5213 Paid in respect of other goods	..	0	0	62	126	784	1 622	3 114	3 019	4 390
Tax on television subscriptions and re-subscriptions	..	..	..	0	0	0	1 495	2 966	2 886	3 261
Audiovisual licence fee	..	..	..	52	126	764	127	148	132	1 129
Hunting rights	..	..	..	10	0	20	0	0	0	0
5220 Non-recurrent taxes	..	0	0	0	0	176	341	339	383	329
Stamps on motor vehicles	..	..	..	..	..	176	341	339	383	329
5300 Unallocable between 5100 and 5200	..	0	0	0	0	0	0	0	0	0
6000 Other taxes	**..**	**..**	**..**	**2 259**	**1 340**	**785**	**1 587**	**844**	**981**	**1 107**
6100 Paid solely by business	..	..	..	..	..	..	..	..	..	..
6200 Other	..	..	..	..	..	..	..	..	..	..

.. Not available

Note: Year ending 31st December.

The data are on a cash basis.

Figures exclude tax revenues collected by sub-national governments as the data are not available.

Heading 1210: This heading includes revenues from flat-rate corporation tax and flat-rate tax on income from corporate securities for the years from 1998 to 2017 as it was not possible to distinguish them from corporation tax revenues.

Heading 2000: For the first time this edition presents contributions to the *Caisse de Retraite des Fonctionnaires* (CRF) and the *Caisse Nationale de Sécurité Sociale* (CNSS) in this heading. The figures are taken from various public documents (Table of government financial operations (TOFE) 2018, *Perspective de l'économie Congolaise*, Loi de finances).

Heading 5113: This heading includes revenues from the flat-rate corporation tax and the flat-rate tax on income from corporate securities from 2018 following the OECD classification of taxes (see the *Interpretative Guide* in Annex A). Under the Republic of Congo's national classification, they are included in revenues from corporate profits.

Heading 5123: Export duties and excise duties collected at customs for the period 2002-2016 are included in heading 5123 as it was not possible to break down these revenues.

Source: Ministry of Economy and Finance, Republic of the Congo.

Table 5.7. Democratic Republic of the Congo – Details of tax revenue

Million CDF

	1995	2000	2005	2010	2015	2018	2019	2020	2021	2022
Total tax revenue	..	**7 551**	**295 581**	**1 684 363**	**3 487 560**	**5 929 744**	**6 380 522**	**6 613 477**	**10 262 695**	**16 547 194**
1000 Taxes on income, profits and capital gains	..	**2 565**	**54 761**	**447 039**	**1 225 021**	**2 564 782**	**2 697 780**	**2 179 654**	**4 013 298**	**8 520 399**
1100 Of individuals	..	996	24 243	208 715	515 851	821 801	834 587	993 999	1 301 948	1 451 466
1110 On income and profits	..	996	24 243	208 715	515 851	821 801	834 587	993 999	1 301 948	1 451 466
Domestic personal income tax - excluding natural resources (from 2022)	..	899	15 444	162 931	417 442	589 377	631 366	629 181	647 657	653 842
Domestic personal income tax - mining	..	..	..	..	..	..	..	..	..	272 366
Domestic personal income tax - hydrocarbons	..	..	..	..	..	..	..	..	..	3 765
Domestic personal income tax - forests	..	..	..	..	..	..	..	..	..	1 013
Income tax - Political institutions	..	..	..	1 842	16 698	21 901	27 224	44 541	76 941	102 292
Income tax - Civil servants and public officials	..	..	..	..	12 825	10 968	8 855	156 720	306 093	110 021
Income tax - Financial authorities	..	..	..	..	8 186	27 654	18 094	21 965	75 904	33 649
Personal income tax - expatriates - excluding natural resources (from 2022)	..	81	7 513	43 779	59 921	170 926	148 489	140 484	195 347	109 312
Personal income tax - expatriates - mines	..	..	..	..	..	..	..	..	..	162 206
Personal income tax - expatriates - hydrocarbons	..	..	..	..	..	..	..	..	..	541
Personal income tax - expatriates - forests	..	..	..	..	..	..	..	..	..	96
Income tax - Liberal professions	..	15	1 286	44	0	0	0	0	0	0
Ad valorem tax on winnings from bets (DGRAD)	..	..	..	119	779	975	558	1 108	5	2 363
1120 On capital gains	..	..	..	..	..	..	..	..	..	..
1200 Corporate	..	1 569	30 518	237 937	709 095	1 742 853	1 862 769	1 185 045	2 710 199	7 067 788
Investment income tax - excluding natural resources (from 2022)	..	30	2 065	23 356	53 212	164 586	130 849	117 911	343 684	286 447
Investment income tax - mining	..	..	..	..	..	..	..	..	..	370 967
Investment income tax - hydrocarbons	..	..	..	..	..	..	..	..	..	53
Investment income tax - forests	..	..	..	..	..	..	..	..	..	34
1210 On profits	..	1 539	28 453	214 582	655 884	1 578 267	1 731 920	804 482	2 366 515	6 410 267
Corporate income tax - non-oil companies - excluding natural resources (from 2022)	..	1 061	22 942	194 758	607 004	1 466 176	1 603 430	695 141	2 193 793	947 834
Corporate income tax - non-oil companies - mining	..	..	..	..	..	..	..	..	..	4 181 469
Corporate income tax - non-oil companies - hydrocarbons	..	..	..	..	..	..	..	..	..	189 105
Corporate income tax - non-oil companies - forests	..	..	..	..	..	..	..	..	..	747
Corporate income tax - Non-residents - excluding natural resources (from 2022)	..	0	0	0	46 124	102 597	97 818	100 534	164 043	118 180
Corporate income tax - Non-residents - mining	..	..	..	..	..	..	..	..	..	93 791
Corporate income tax - Non-residents - forests	..	..	..	..	..	..	..	..	..	42
Tax on profits - Individual corporations	..	410	3 523	19 823	2 756	9 494	6 747	8 807	8 520	11 416
Rental income tax	..	69	1 988	0	0	0	0	0	0	0
Special tax on excess mining profits	..	0	0	0	0	0	23 925	0	159	867 684
1220 On capital gains of corporates	..	..	..	..	..	..	..	262 652	0	20
1300 Unallocable between 1100 and 1200	..	..	..	386	75	128	424	610	1 151	1 145
2000 Social security contributions	..	..	..	..	**201 761**	**371 835**	**653 773**	**763 148**	**891 632**	**1 105 014**
2100 Employees	..	..	..	..	56 493	117 412	176 369	202 733	238 202	293 664
2110 On a payroll basis	..	..	..	..	56 493	117 412	176 369	202 733	238 202	293 664
2120 On an income tax basis	..	..	..	..	0	0	0	0	0	0
2200 Employers	..	..	..	..	145 268	235 521	452 793	527 105	619 326	765 128
2210 On a payroll basis	..	..	..	..	145 268	235 521	452 793	527 105	619 326	765 128
2220 On an income tax basis	..	..	..	..	0	0	0	0	0	0
2300 Self-employed or non-employed	..	..	..	..	0	0	0	0	0	0
2310 On a payroll basis	..	..	..	..	..	..	..	..	..	..
2320 On an income tax basis	..	..	..	..	..	..	..	..	..	..
2400 Unallocable between 2100, 2200 and 2300	..	..	..	..	0	18 902	24 611	33 311	34 103	46 222
2410 On a payroll basis	..	..	..	..	..	..	..	..	..	..
2420 On an income tax basis	..	..	..	..	..	..	..	..	..	..
3000 Taxes on payroll and workforce	..	**56**	**4 266**	**25 904**	**79 248**	**143 254**	**172 187**	**180 583**	**314 440**	**361 350**
Tax on earnings of expatriates - excluding natural resources (from 2022)	..	56	2 630	15 370	48 503	91 777	121 128	125 228	229 128	169 251
Tax on earnings of expatriates - mining	..	..	..	..	..	..	..	..	..	137 841
Tax on earnings of expatriates - forests	..	..	..	..	..	..	..	..	..	135

Table 5.7. Democratic Republic of the Congo – Details of tax revenue (continued)

Million CDF

	1995	2000	2005	2010	2015	2018	2019	2020	2021	2022
Contributions to the National Institute for Professional Preparation (INPP)	..	0	1 636	10 534	28 447	46 030	44 570	48 254	76 069	43 603
Contributions to the National Employment Office (ONEM)	..	..	..	..	2 298	5 447	6 488	7 102	9 243	10 520
4000 Taxes on property	**..**	**..**	**..**	**9 644**	**12 983**	**38 796**	**44 567**	**55 764**	**62 643**	**89 581**
4100 Recurrent taxes on immovable property	..	..	..	3 695	8 817	28 719	31 985	38 687	42 630	49 699
4110 Households	..	..	..	..	..	..	..	..	..	..
4120 Others	..	..	..	..	..	..	..	..	..	..
4200 Recurrent taxes on net wealth	..	..	..	..	..	..	..	..	..	..
4210 Individual	..	..	..	..	..	..	..	..	..	..
4220 Corporate	..	..	..	..	..	..	..	..	..	..
4300 Estate, inheritance and gift taxes	..	..	..	..	..	..	..	..	..	..
4310 Estate and inheritance taxes	..	..	..	..	..	..	..	..	..	..
4320 Gift taxes	..	..	..	..	..	..	..	..	..	..
4400 Taxes on financial and capital transactions	..	..	..	5 949	4 166	10 078	12 582	17 077	20 013	39 882
4500 Other non-reccurrent taxes on property	..	..	..	..	..	..	..	..	..	..
4510 On net wealth	..	..	..	..	..	..	..	..	..	..
4520 Other non-recurrent taxes	..	..	..	..	..	..	..	..	..	..
4600 Other recurrent taxes on property	..	..	..	..	..	..	..	..	..	..
5000 Taxes on goods and services	**..**	**4 931**	**199 076**	**1 102 691**	**1 889 732**	**2 610 568**	**2 689 499**	**3 354 923**	**4 847 640**	**6 279 616**
5100 Taxes on production, sale, transfer, etc	..	4 833	198 497	1 068 789	1 870 291	2 525 463	2 622 648	3 254 548	4 720 902	6 051 251
5110 General taxes on goods and services	..	1 390	109 602	590 594	891 546	1 456 884	1 417 107	2 110 167	3 168 331	3 631 298
5111 Value added taxes	..	0	0	0	891 404	1 456 766	1 417 090	2 109 867	3 168 321	3 631 298
VAT revenues - Domestic - excluding natural resources (from 2022)	..	..	..	..	639 995	939 202	1 055 667	1 227 594	1 802 284	1 859 181
VAT revenues - Domestic - mining	..	..	..	..	..	..	..	..	..	347 235
VAT revenues - Domestic - forests	..	..	..	..	..	..	..	..	..	30
VAT on imports	..	..	..	..	879 549	766 232	803 860	882 273	1 366 037	1 424 852
VAT refunds	..	..	..	..	- 628 140	- 248 668	- 442 438	0	0	0
5112 Sales tax	..	..	..	110	0	0	0	215	0	0
5113 Other	..	1 390	109 602	590 484	143	119	18	85	11	0
Turnover tax / domestic sales	..	194	20 440	110 004	143	118	14	0	0	0
Turnover tax - Delivery service	..	409	28 534	181 338	0	0	0	84	11	0
Turnover tax - Construction	..	14	3 971	5 969	0	0	0	0	0	0
Turnover tax - Mineral exports	..	0	2	0	0	0	0	0	0	0
Turnover tax - Exports excl. Minerals	..	6	0	0	0	0	0	0	0	0
Turnover tax (ICA) on imports	..	768	56 654	291 557	0	0	0	0	0	0
Other general taxes on goods and services (DGRAD)	..	0	0	1 616	0	0	3	1	0	0
5120 Taxes on specific goods and services	..	3 442	88 896	478 194	978 745	1 068 579	1 205 541	1 144 381	1 552 570	2 419 953
5121 Excises	..	1 417	26 357	195 837	409 441	482 304	526 419	583 713	774 644	948 790
Dedicated product royalties (DGRAD)	..	..	..	12 259	3 256	563	630	560	0	129
Domestic excises - Beers	..	..	..	57 301	131 359	169 694	172 880	183 894	231 777	272 746
Domestic excises - Drinking water and lemonades	..	..	..	5 336	13 457	21 246	21 593	24 015	37 247	39 835
Domestic excises - Alcohol and alcoholic beverages	..	..	..	147	3 363	7 818	9 530	7 823	11 459	15 048
Domestic excises - Tobacco and matches	..	..	..	40 034	2 643	4 901	10 448	14 546	29 356	27 039
Domestic excises - Telecommunications	..	..	..	49 338	86 315	145 710	168 852	194 138	237 314	292 477
Domestic excises - Other products	..	..	..	848	4 339	2 875	4 245	6 185	8 749	12 611
Excises on imports - Beers	..	..	..	483	3 545	10 751	5 504	3 707	1 981	2 017
Excises on imports - Table water and limonade	..	..	..	467	4 631	1 384	1 315	2 429	1 905	2 728
Excises on imports - Alcohol and alcoholic beverages	..	..	..	1 481	5 380	8 577	5 168	3 824	7 960	10 254
Excises on imports - Tobacco and matches	..	..	..	4 739	59 422	54 475	66 304	66 184	75 895	83 206
Excises on imports - Petroleum products	..	..	..	9 257	53 350	0	0	10 535	0	0
Excises on imports - Vehicles	..	..	..	9 901	15 878	23 427	22 940	38 355	70 687	111 330
Excises on imports - Other products	..	..	..	4 246	22 504	30 883	37 011	27 517	60 314	79 371
5122 Profits of fiscal monopolies	..	0	0	0	0	0	0	0	0	0
5123 Customs and import duties	..	1 942	56 349	270 089	560 340	569 751	670 378	549 396	763 240	1 441 556
5124 Taxes on exports	..	83	6 190	7 725	5 446	9 505	7 984	10 216	13 416	28 756
Mineral export fee	..	82	5 623	3 850	3 238	4 780	2 713	1 933	3 580	17 197

Table 5.7. Democratic Republic of the Congo – Details of tax revenue (continued)

Million CDF

	1995	2000	2005	2010	2015	2018	2019	2020	2021	2022
Agricultural product export fee	..	1	567	3 046	2 208	4 725	5 271	8 283	9 837	11 559
Other products export fee	..	0	0	829	0	0	0	0	0	0
5125 Taxes on investment goods	..	0	0	0	0	0	0	0	0	0
5126 Taxes on specific services	..	0	0	4 543	3 518	7 019	759	1 056	1 269	851
5127 Other taxes on internat. trade and transactions	..	..	..	..	..	..	..	..	..	..
5128 Other taxes	..	0	0	0	0	0	0	0	1	0
5130 Unallocable between 5110 and 5120	..	0	0	0	0	0	0	0	0	0
5200 Taxes on use of goods and to perform activities	..	98	579	33 903	19 441	85 104	66 852	100 375	126 738	228 364
5210 Recurrent taxes	..	0	0	822	619	1 448	887	6 620	1 066	4 409
5211 Paid by households: motor vehicles	..	..	..	0	0	0	0	0	0	0
5212 Paid by others: motor vehicles	..	..	..	0	0	0	0	0	0	0
5213 Paid in respect of other goods	..	..	..	822	619	1 448	887	6 620	1 066	4 409
5220 Non-recurrent taxes	..	98	579	33 081	18 821	83 656	65 964	93 755	125 672	223 956
Truck registration (plates)	..	98	579	2 681	1 366	3 734	3 476	3 032	3 932	4 176
Export and import authorisation	..	0	0	3 212	3 571	9 303	9 146	14 804	21 079	4 936
Implementation tax for dangerous, unhealthy and incommodious establishments	..	0	0	1 225	2 939	46 159	32 995	49 963	63 513	145 014
Other authorisations	..	0	0	25 963	10 945	24 461	20 347	25 956	37 149	69 830
5300 Unallocable between 5100 and 5200	..	0	0	0	0	0	0	0	0	0
6000 Other taxes	**..**	**0**	**37 477**	**99 085**	**78 815**	**200 509**	**122 716**	**79 405**	**133 043**	**191 233**
Petrol revenues	..	..	37 477	98 431	78 417	106 245	121 703	77 670	131 834	189 105
Proportional fees on LLC (Direction générale des recettes administratives, judiciaires, domaniales et de participation, DGRAD)	..	..	0	654	398	94 264	1 013	1 734	1 209	2 128
6100 Paid solely by business	..	..	..	..	..	..	..	..	..	..
6200 Other	..	..	..	..	..	..	..	..	..	..

.. Not available

Note: Year ending 31st December.

The data are on a cash basis.

Figures exclude tax revenues collected by sub-national governments as the data are not available.

Data between 2000 and 2003 should be interpreted with caution as they are significantly affected by high inflation rates.

For the first time this edition presents the breakdown between revenues from natural resources and revenues excluding natural resources for the year 2022. Revenues labelled "excluding natural resources (from 2022)" include revenues from natural resources for years prior to 2022, as the breakdown is not available.

Headings 1110, 5113, 5121, 5220, 6000: For 2008 and subsequent years, these headings contain revenues from the *Direction Générale des Recettes Administratives, Judiciaires, Domaniales et de Participation* (DGRAD) and are indicated as such.

Headings 1300, 4100, 4400, 5112, 5126, 5128: For 2008 and subsequent years, these headings contain revenues exclusively from DGRAD.

Source: Ministry of Finance, Democratic Republic of Congo.

Table 5.8. Côte d'Ivoire – Details of tax revenue

Million XOF

	1995	2000	2005	2010	2015	2018	2019	2020	2021	2022
Total tax revenue	**924 472**	**1 169 607**	**1 407 277**	**2 035 468**	**3 414 418**	**4 194 689**	**4 527 842**	**4 734 486**	**5 542 132**	**5 772 577**
1000 Taxes on income, profits and capital gains	**138 299**	**192 282**	**192 895**	**260 799**	**408 880**	**574 179**	**557 445**	**580 534**	**730 313**	**868 901**
1100 Of individuals	3 397	5 108	6 184	6 970	10 054	13 894	13 089	14 508	19 601	23 455
1110 On income and profits	3 397	5 093	6 164	6 937	10 011	13 822	13 023	14 435	19 499	23 367
General income tax	0	0	323	1 420	817	114	57	12	2	2
Industrial and commercial profit tax, excluding gas and oil (individuals)	3 397	5 045	5 770	5 431	9 008	13 457	12 760	14 141	19 208	22 998
Transferable securities tax (persons)	0	48	71	86	186	252	206	282	289	367
1120 On capital gains	0	16	20	33	42	72	67	73	102	88
Capital gains tax (individuals)	..	16	20	33	42	72	67	73	102	88
1200 Corporate	86 005	148 900	176 272	240 768	375 893	534 279	517 653	541 288	691 426	827 184
1210 On profits	86 005	143 602	169 683	229 732	361 782	510 483	495 535	517 177	657 565	797 996
Industrial and commercial profit tax on gas and oil	0	0	0	63 649	71 985	86 071	104 181	65 361	75 334	93 848
Industrial and commercial profit tax, excluding gas and oil (corporations)	86 005	127 710	146 074	137 500	228 043	340 667	323 022	357 997	486 277	582 215
Transferable securities tax (corporations)	0	15 892	23 609	28 583	61 753	83 745	68 332	93 819	95 954	121 933
1220 On capital gains of corporates	0	5 297	6 589	11 036	14 111	23 796	22 118	24 112	33 861	29 188
Capital gains tax (corporations)	..	5 297	6 589	11 036	14 111	23 796	22 118	24 112	33 861	29 188
1300 Unallocable between 1100 and 1200	48 897	38 274	10 439	13 061	22 934	26 006	26 703	24 738	19 286	18 261
Tax payment on income from the informal sector	45 763	33 983	5 882	7 624	14 637	15 845	16 023	16 124	16 588	17 382
Synthetic tax	3 134	4 291	4 557	5 437	8 296	10 162	10 680	8 614	2 697	879
2000 Social security contributions	**52 200**	**102 700**	**116 818**	**162 754**	**383 540**	**479 197**	**509 592**	**549 890**	**617 150**	**645 516**
2100 Employees	..	..	..	64 364	151 728	189 616	201 522	218 051	247 493	259 078
Caisse nationale de prévoyance sociale (CNPS)	..	..	..	39 044	92 206	115 381	122 230	134 183	161 271	169 489
Caisse générale de retraite des agents de l'État (CGRAE)	..	..	..	25 320	59 522	74 235	79 292	83 868	86 222	89 589
2110 On a payroll basis	..	..	..	0	0	0	0	0	0	0
2120 On an income tax basis	..	..	..	0	0	0	0	0	0	0
2200 Employers	..	..	..	98 390	231 812	289 581	308 070	331 839	369 657	386 438
Caisse nationale de prévoyance sociale (CNPS)	..	..	..	47 721	112 697	141 022	149 392	164 002	197 109	207 153
Caisse générale de retraite des agents de l'État (CGRAE)	..	..	..	50 669	119 115	148 559	158 678	167 837	172 548	179 285
2210 On a payroll basis	..	..	..	0	0	0	0	0	0	0
2220 On an income tax basis	..	..	..	0	0	0	0	0	0	0
2300 Self-employed or non-employed	..	..	..	0	0	0	0	0	0	0
2310 On a payroll basis	..	..	..	..	..	..	..	..	..	..
2320 On an income tax basis	..	..	..	..	..	..	..	..	..	..
2400 Unallocable between 2100, 2200 and 2300	52 200	102 700	116 818	0	0	0	0	0	0	0
2410 On a payroll basis	..	..	..	..	..	..	..	..	..	..
2420 On an income tax basis	..	..	..	..	..	..	..	..	..	..
3000 Taxes on payroll and workforce	**84 393**	**138 023**	**148 912**	**207 243**	**372 524**	**497 124**	**527 045**	**549 630**	**591 639**	**661 642**
Professional training fund	0	6 990	7 473	9 776	11 805	22 674	23 966	25 144	26 755	29 773
Income and salary tax, balance of wages and salaries tax	84 393	131 033	141 439	197 467	360 719	474 449	503 079	524 487	564 884	631 868
4000 Taxes on property	**15 825**	**32 732**	**43 879**	**49 706**	**89 040**	**120 153**	**139 654**	**135 324**	**172 208**	**190 254**
4100 Recurrent taxes on immovable property	15 825	24 664	34 032	38 009	72 299	99 417	113 362	106 889	132 394	146 262
4110 Households	..	..	..	..	..	..	..	..	..	..
4120 Others	..	..	..	..	..	..	..	..	..	..
4200 Recurrent taxes on net wealth	0	0	0	0	0	0	0	0	0	0
4210 Individual	..	..	..	..	..	..	..	..	..	..
4220 Corporate	..	..	..	..	..	..	..	..	..	..
4300 Estate, inheritance and gift taxes	0	0	0	0	0	0	0	0	0	0
4310 Estate and inheritance taxes	..	..	..	..	..	..	..	..	..	..
4320 Gift taxes	..	..	..	..	..	..	..	..	..	..
4400 Taxes on financial and capital transactions	0	8 068	9 847	11 697	16 741	20 735	26 292	28 435	39 814	43 992
4500 Other non-reccurrent taxes on property	0	0	0	0	0	0	0	0	0	0
4510 On net wealth	..	..	..	..	..	..	..	..	..	..
4520 Other non-recurrent taxes	..	..	..	..	..	..	..	..	..	..

Table 5.8. Côte d'Ivoire – Details of tax revenue (continued)

Million XOF

	1995	2000	2005	2010	2015	2018	2019	2020	2021	2022
5000 Taxes on goods and services	**633 755**	**699 518**	**899 720**	**1 344 201**	**2 139 379**	**2 499 839**	**2 760 029**	**2 885 098**	**3 388 228**	**3 364 440**
5100 Taxes on production, sale, transfer, etc	625 607	674 206	870 745	1 294 835	2 057 991	2 396 326	2 650 639	2 776 423	3 267 425	3 232 563
5110 General taxes on goods and services	206 914	255 297	288 886	490 521	692 417	897 334	982 115	993 540	1 265 875	1 397 309
5111 Value added taxes	206 914	255 297	267 107	473 712	680 081	883 175	963 541	960 051	1 213 233	1 313 225
VAT receipts (gross) - DGI	67 614	106 797	112 304	194 241	327 995	471 327	516 161	505 522	615 258	660 571
VAT credit refunds (DGI)	0	0	- 8 100	- 15 480	- 41 825	- 42 599	- 49 349	- 44 080	- 58 900	- 53 500
VAT revenue (gross) DGD	139 300	148 500	172 802	313 870	445 028	504 893	547 827	544 935	720 476	767 355
VAT credit refunds (DGD)	0	0	- 9 899	- 18 919	- 51 118	- 50 446	- 51 099	- 46 326	- 63 600	- 61 200
5112 Sales tax	0	0	0	0	0	0	0	0	0	0
5113 Other	0	0	21 779	16 809	12 336	14 159	18 575	33 488	52 641	84 084
Ad valorem tax (national tax)	..	..	0	0	12 185	13 932	18 565	33 483	35 229	54 018
Contribution pour la reconstruction nationale	..	..	21 779	1 567	71	98	10	6	9	3
Solidarity tax for post - crisis measures	..	..	0	15 243	80	128	0	0	0	0
Entrepreneur State Tax (TEE)	..	..	0	0	0	0	0	0	10 437	17 157
Micro - Enterprise Tax	..	..	0	0	0	0	0	0	6 966	12 907
5120 Taxes on specific goods and services	418 693	418 909	581 859	804 314	1 365 574	1 498 991	1 668 523	1 782 884	2 001 550	1 835 253
5121 Excises	71 495	74 908	59 977	128 698	243 151	308 095	376 839	558 188	517 655	266 792
Tax for aids funding	0	0	0	740	821	1 048	1 299	1 568	1 824	1 947
Tax on rubber	0	0	0	0	78	5	66	12	241	0
Tax on tobacco for sports development	0	0	0	1 708	2 029	2 621	3 246	3 924	4 559	4 867
Tax on plastic bags and plastic material	0	0	0	0	113	107	122	249	173	415
Tax on drinks	1 402	3 642	2 986	5 050	18 213	24 536	25 343	26 133	38 480	39 565
Tax on fuel	267	290	122	81	105	173	310	101	7	8
Tax on tobacco	10 626	15 518	10 933	12 040	14 771	18 786	23 971	31 056	35 656	39 348
Various taxes specific to the DGD	59 200	50 300	38 391	96 560	183 719	224 397	281 613	456 135	389 525	135 792
Various excise taxes specific to the DGD	0	5 158	7 545	12 520	23 302	36 420	40 803	38 893	45 055	42 345
Special tax for forest preservation and development (TSPDF)	0	0	0	0	0	0	66	118	700	672
Tax on perfumery and cosmetic products	0	0	0	0	0	0	0	0	1 435	1 832
5122 Profits of fiscal monopolies	0	0	0	0	0	0	0	0	0	0
5123 Customs and import duties	152 200	126 512	167 701	288 039	486 862	586 581	607 626	574 910	751 556	824 079
5124 Taxes on exports	177 400	185 114	320 201	331 261	473 333	417 137	477 488	439 701	489 882	484 001
Registration fees for coffee and cocoa	0	21 114	58 039	103 669	86 244	12 901	39 240	37 686	74 810	78 205
Tax on cocoa and coffee (DGD)	162 700	156 700	253 148	221 180	377 418	343 058	394 161	359 206	366 966	345 557
Tax on wood and other products (DGD)	14 700	7 300	9 014	6 412	9 671	2 103	2 236	2 229	2 437	18 487
Cashew nut duty (DGD)	0	0	0	0	0	59 076	41 850	40 580	45 669	41 752
5125 Taxes on investment goods	0	0	0	0	0	0	0	0	0	0
5126 Taxes on specific services	17 598	32 375	33 980	56 315	162 229	187 178	206 570	210 085	242 457	260 381
Social contribution on airline tickets	0	0	0	216	3 088	47	0	0	0	0
Tax on airline transport	0	0	0	799	2 569	2 101	2 014	1 037	1 681	2 148
Cultural promotion tax	0	0	0	1 598	1 884	1 849	2 169	2 245	2 431	2 329
Tax for the development of it in rural areas	0	0	0	11 486	16 977	20 318	20 830	22 263	22 870	26 044
Tax on telecommunications	0	0	0	0	50 618	46 893	52 160	55 815	60 918	60 813
Urban transportation tax	0	0	0	1 019	3	0	0	0	0	0
Debit on casino games	359	168	339	378	163	1 080	2 324	1 002	2 460	3 175
Stumpage tax	1 240	2 434	1 810	1 125	1 299	659	1 309	1 232	1 541	1 647
Tax on advertising	0	137	93	300	437	1 051	940	649	1 294	1 285
Tourism development tax	560	0	0	0	1 298	1 609	1 908	1 053	1 569	2 047
Telephone communications tax	0	0	0	0	20 425	20 659	20 091	21 676	28 698	27 572
Insurance tax	0	6 942	8 666	7 739	14 435	19 228	20 445	21 134	23 416	26 985
Tax on bank loans	1 464	2 002	2 030	3 627	0	0	0	0	0	0
Tax on bank operations	13 975	20 692	21 042	28 028	49 023	66 122	70 418	76 919	87 867	97 750
Health and Environmental Protection Tax	0	0	0	0	11	2	2	1	3	0
Tax for household waste collection	0	0	0	0	0	5 559	11 307	4 819	7 254	7 909
Port and airport tax	0	0	0	0	0	0	655	239	453	596
Video-on-demand tax	0	0	0	0	0	0	0	0	2	82
5127 Other taxes on internat. trade and transactions	0	0	0	0	0	0	0	0	0	0
5128 Other taxes	0	0	0	0	0	0	0	0	0	0
5130 Unallocable between 5110 and 5120	0	0	0	0	0	0	0	0	0	0

Table 5.8. Côte d'Ivoire – Details of tax revenue (continued)

Million XOF

	1995	2000	2005	2010	2015	2018	2019	2020	2021	2022
5200 Taxes on use of goods and to perform activities	8 148	25 312	28 975	49 366	81 388	103 513	109 390	108 675	120 804	131 877
5210 Recurrent taxes	8 148	25 312	28 975	49 366	81 388	103 513	109 390	108 675	120 804	131 877
5211 Paid by households: motor vehicles	0	4 176	5 942	9 171	14 926	18 423	17 592	18 206	21 331	22 097
5212 Paid by others: motor vehicles	0	0	0	0	0	0	0	0	0	0
5213 Paid in respect of other goods	8 148	21 136	23 033	40 195	66 462	85 091	91 798	90 468	99 473	109 780
5220 Non-recurrent taxes	0	0	0	0	0	0	0	0	0	0
5300 Unallocable between 5100 and 5200	0	0	0	0	0	0	0	0	0	0
6000 Other taxes	**0**	**4 352**	**5 053**	**10 765**	**21 055**	**24 197**	**34 077**	**34 009**	**42 594**	**41 825**
6100 Paid solely by business	..	0	0	3 732	6 979	10 275	10 657	11 164	14 229	9 178
Housing support tax	..	..	..	45	0	0	0	0	0	0
Interprofessional funds	..	..	..	3 687	6 979	10 275	10 657	11 164	14 229	9 178
6200 Other	..	4 352	5 053	7 033	14 076	13 922	23 420	22 846	28 365	32 648

.. Not available

Note: Year ending 31st December.

The data are on a cash basis.

Figures exclude tax revenues collected by sub-national governments as the data are not available.

Heading 5113 includes the ad-valorem tax, which is a property tax. Revenues collected other than from the ad-valorem tax are included in non-tax revenues following the OECD classification of taxes (see the *Interpretative Guide* in Annex A). Under Côte d'Ivoire's national classification, they are included in tax revenues.

Heading 5113 includes the "National Reconstruction Levy" (*CRN* : *Contribution à la reconstruction nationale*), which was introduced in 2004 for five years and expired in 2009. It has been replaced by the Solidarity tax for post-crisis measures (*Taxe de solidarité pour la sortie de crise.*), based on the operating costs of companies with an annual turnover of 1 billion CFA francs or more for the year ended 31 December 2009. This heading also includes the "State Entrepreneurs' Tax" (*TEE*: *Taxe d'État de l'Entreprenant*) and the Micro-Business Tax (*Taxe des Micro-Entreprises*), both of which were introduced in 2021.

Heading 6100 includes the "Housing Support Fund" (*FSH: Fonds de soutien à l'habitat*), which is financed by allocated tax revenues (employer payroll contribution, taxes on specified services and the fuel tax). It is not possible to distinguish between these different revenues, hence their classification under heading 6100. This tax was abolished in 2010.

Revenues from the audiovisual tax and the "Ivoirian radio and television" (*RTI: Radiodiffusion télévision ivoirienne*) royalties are included in non-tax revenues following the OECD classification of taxes (see the *Interpretative Guide* in Annex A) and have been included under the heading "Sales of goods and services". Under Côte d'Ivoire's national classification, they are included in tax revenues.

Source: Ministry of Economy and Finance, Côte d'Ivoire.

Table 5.9. Egypt – Details of tax revenue

Million EGP

	1995	2000	2005	2010	2015	2018	2019	2020	2021	2022
Total tax revenue	..	..	**88 969**	**196 967**	**358 658**	**724 105**	**850 042**	**835 064**	**939 710**	**1 112 732**
1000 Taxes on income, profits and capital gains	..	..	**35 551**	**85 867**	**157 041**	**289 904**	**332 239**	**366 875**	**398 224**	**479 806**
1100 Of individuals	..	..	9 315	16 403	38 215	64 578	87 306	98 032	123 711	151 918
1110 On income and profits	..	..	9 310	16 319	37 936	64 128	86 382	96 978	122 513	149 973
Tax on salaries	..	..	3 997	9 623	23 803	40 976	56 938	64 022	75 562	89 163
Taxes on industrial and commercial profits	..	..	3 715	4 570	10 589	16 815	24 657	28 672	39 997	52 396
Stamp duty on salaries	..	..	1 180	1 778	2 998	4 683	2 243	1 486	2 511	2 762
Tax on professionals income	..	..	150	314	544	1 650	2 506	2 798	4 170	5 629
Other taxes on activity other than employment	..	..	268	35	2	3	37	0	273	23
1120 On capital gains	..	..	5	84	279	450	924	1 054	1 198	1 945
1200 Corporate	..	..	22 257	66 022	108 285	186 374	209 702	237 846	254 696	309 556
1210 On profits	..	..	22 257	66 022	108 285	186 374	209 702	237 846	254 696	309 556
Egyptian General Petroleum Corporation (EGPC) and foreign partner	..	..	4 030	32 181	36 000	51 976	42 532	26 337	39 817	30 552
Suez Canal Authority (SCA)	..	..	7 343	9 443	13 400	29 900	34 480	42 913	32 450	38 952
Central Bank of Egypt (CBE)	..	..	212	0	3 691	0	0	0	0	0
Other companies	..	..	10 672	18 591	38 512	60 776	85 763	119 625	125 268	164 971
Interest income from T-Bills and Bonds	..	..	0	5 808	16 682	43 722	46 928	48 972	57 161	75 081
1220 On capital gains of corporates	..	..								
1300 Unallocable between 1100 and 1200	..	..	3 979	3 442	10 542	38 952	35 231	30 996	19 817	18 331
Tax on movable capital revenues from CBE and other entities	..	..	3 979	3 309	10 235	38 497	34 538	30 579	19 300	17 621
Delayed tax income	..	..	0	134	306	455	693	417	517	710
2000 Social security contributions	..	..	**16 252**	**31 570**	**60 404**	**111 516**	**134 425**	**113 756**	**128 422**	**149 697**
2100 Employees	..	..	..	..	..	..	..	..	..	..
2110 On a payroll basis	..	..	..	..	..	..	..	..	..	..
2120 On an income tax basis	..	..	..	..	..	..	..	..	..	..
2200 Employers	..	..	..	..	..	..	..	..	..	..
2210 On a payroll basis	..	..	..	..	..	..	..	..	..	..
2220 On an income tax basis	..	..	..	..	..	..	..	..	..	..
2300 Self-employed or non-employed	..	..	..	..	..	..	..	..	..	..
2310 On a payroll basis	..	..	..	..	..	..	..	..	..	..
2320 On an income tax basis	..	..	..	..	..	..	..	..	..	..
2400 Unallocable between 2100, 2200 and 2300	..	..	16 252	31 570	60 404	111 516	134 425	113 756	128 422	149 697
2410 On a payroll basis	..	..	..	..	..	..	..	..	..	..
2420 On an income tax basis	..	..	..	..	..	..	..	..	..	..
3000 Taxes on payroll and workforce	..	..	**0**	**0**	**0**	**0**	**0**	**0**	**1**	**1**
4000 Taxes on property	..	..	**640**	**1 128**	**2 224**	**4 214**	**6 281**	**4 836**	**6 957**	**6 511**
4100 Recurrent taxes on immovable property	..	..	327	518	637	2 976	4 871	3 393	5 159	4 599
4110 Households	..	..	..	..	..	..	..	..	..	..
4120 Others	..	..	..	..	..	..	..	..	..	..
4200 Recurrent taxes on net wealth	..	..	0	0	0	0	0	0	0	0
4210 Individual	..	..								
4220 Corporate	..	..								
4300 Estate, inheritance and gift taxes	..	..	0	0	0	0	0	0	0	0
4310 Estate and inheritance taxes	..	..	..	..	..	..	..	..	..	..
4320 Gift taxes	..	..	..	..	..	..	..	..	..	..
4400 Taxes on financial and capital transactions	..	..	312	610	1 588	1 238	1 410	1 443	1 798	1 912
Property transferring fees	..	..	312	607	948	1 235	1 407	1 443	1 770	1 887
Stamps taxes	..	..	0	3	640	3	3	0	28	26
4500 Other non-reccurrent taxes on property	..	..	..	..	..	..	..	..	..	..
4510 On net wealth	..	..	..	..	..	..	..	..	..	..
4520 Other non-recurrent taxes	..	..	..	..	..	..	..	..	..	..
4600 Other recurrent taxes on property	..	..	0	0	0	0	0	0	0	0
5000 Taxes on goods and services	..	..	**36 527**	**78 401**	**138 988**	**318 471**	**377 097**	**349 598**	**406 106**	**476 717**
5100 Taxes on production, sale, transfer, etc	..	..	35 697	76 232	135 761	314 484	370 724	343 359	396 906	467 313
5110 General taxes on goods and services	..	..	18 725	39 864	65 523	156 276	197 679	193 730	233 704	254 777
5111 Value added taxes	..	..	18 725	39 864	65 523	156 276	197 679	193 730	233 704	254 777
Local commodities	..	..	5 257	11 735	18 415	43 100	50 351	53 017	67 544	74 408

Table 5.9. Egypt – Details of tax revenue (continued)

Million EGP

	1995	2000	2005	2010	2015	2018	2019	2020	2021	2022
Imported goods	..	..	8 548	18 977	35 010	83 939	105 000	95 249	112 849	122 652
Hotel and restaurant services for tourists	..	..	1 126	2 172	2 334	5 894	7 127	5 478	2 792	5 662
Operating services for others	..	..	1 555	2 936	4 844	15 819	24 048	28 190	36 706	36 644
International and local communication services	..	..	1 911	3 700	4 393	6 065	8 915	10 393	11 338	13 087
Other services	..	..	328	345	527	1 460	2 238	1 403	2 475	2 324
5112 Sales tax	..	..	0	0	0	0	0	0	0	0
5113 Other	..	..	0	0	0	0	0	0	0	0
5120 Taxes on specific goods and services	..	..	16 971	36 369	70 238	158 208	173 045	149 629	163 203	212 536
5121 Excises	..	..	6 539	17 170	41 207	106 447	114 977	100 726	108 361	142 945
Tobacco and cigarettes	..	..	3 987	6 997	26 463	51 654	56 389	61 141	73 390	74 944
Petroleum products	..	..	818	7 563	12 004	40 470	41 484	27 599	23 345	57 223
Alcohol	..	..	95	198	181	218	315	250	59	2
Beer	..	..	170	241	499	960	1 113	1 602	1 254	1 903
Fizz water	..	..	510	0	0	1 550	2 128	2 836	2 976	3 878
Stamp taxes on specific goods	..	..	536	1 603	1 198	1 214	3 687	443	2 354	140
Other excises	..	..	422	567	864	10 381	9 861	6 857	4 984	4 855
5122 Profits of fiscal monopolies	..	..	80	0	0	0	0	0	0	0
5123 Customs and import duties	..	..	7 664	13 733	21 460	36 848	40 995	31 644	35 530	42 179
Valued customs taxes	..	..	7 285	13 242	20 955	36 246	40 344	31 106	35 039	41 979
Customs taxes on imported cigarettes and tobacco	..	..	379	491	506	603	651	538	491	201
5124 Taxes on exports	..	..	1	819	180	429	427	190	116	0
5125 Taxes on investment goods	..	..	0	0	0	0	0	0	0	0
5126 Taxes on specific services	..	..	1 952	2 729	3 699	7 414	5 261	6 948	1 931	2 528
Stamp taxes on specific services	..	..	1 114	1 950	2 700	5 487	3 517	5 517	1 157	868
Other taxes on specific services	..	..	838	779	999	1 927	1 744	1 431	774	1 661
5127 Other taxes on internat. trade and transactions	..	..	0	0	0	0	0	0	0	0
5128 Other taxes	..	..	736	1 919	3 690	7 070	11 386	10 121	17 265	24 884
5130 Unallocable between 5110 and 5120	..	..	0	0	0	0	0	0	0	0
5200 Taxes on use of goods and to perform activities	..	..	830	2 169	3 227	3 987	6 373	6 239	9 200	9 404
5210 Recurrent taxes	..	..	830	2 169	3 227	3 987	6 373	6 239	9 200	9 404
5211 Paid by households: motor vehicles	..	..	394	1 837	2 841	3 477	5 702	5 789	8 314	8 654
5212 Paid by others: motor vehicles	..	..	0	0	0	0	0	0	0	0
5213 Paid in respect of other goods	..	..	436	332	386	509	672	450	886	750
5220 Non-recurrent taxes	..	..	0	0	0	0	0	0	0	0
5300 Unallocable between 5100 and 5200	..	..	0	0	0	0	0	0	0	0
6000 Other taxes	**..**	**..**	**0**	**0**	**0**	**0**	**0**	**0**	**0**	**0**
6100 Paid solely by business	..	..	..	..	..	..	..	..	..	..
6200 Other	..	..	..	..	..	..	..	..	..	..
Memo items:	..	..	..	..	..	..	..	..	..	..
VAT revenues (net)	..	..	18 725	39 864	65 523	156 276	197 679	193 730	233 704	254 777
VAT revenues (gross)	..	..	19 544	40 487	66 235	157 025	198 876	194 570	235 017	257 218
VAT refunds	..	..	- 819	- 623	- 712	- 749	-1 197	- 840	-1 314	-2 441

.. Not available

Note: Fiscal year ends on 30 June. For example, the data for 2022 represent July 2021 to June 2022.

The data are on a cash basis.

Figures exclude tax revenues collected by sub-national governments as the data are not available. These data are estimated to be insignificant.

Heading 2000: Egypt does not include social security contributions in its tax revenue data as the Egyptian authorities do not consider them as taxes.

Royalties on the Suez Canal as well as other royalties and administrative fees are reported as taxes in Egypt. These revenues are considered as non-tax revenues according to the OECD classification, described in the *Interpretative Guide* in Annex A.

Source: Ministry of Finance.

Table 5.10. Equatorial Guinea – Details of tax revenue

Million XAF

	1995	2000	2005	2010	2015	2018	2019	2020	2021	2022
Total tax revenue	..	..	**356 040**	**612 377**	**935 907**	**480 100**	**651 421**	**490 389**	**404 055**	**597 171**
1000 Taxes on income, profits and capital gains	..	..	**324 934**	**545 376**	**772 421**	**320 639**	**497 079**	**351 160**	**279 837**	**447 462**
1100 Of individuals	..	..	18 417	59 938	85 021	57 188	60 285	53 978	49 754	58 617
1110 On income and profits	..	..	18 417	59 938	85 021	57 188	60 285	53 978	49 754	58 617
Petroleum tax on physical persons	..	..	25 926	44 339	64 217	39 652	41 720	39 403	33 848	38 868
Personal income tax	..	..	7 390	15 325	20 421	17 201	18 245	14 299	15 459	19 203
Taxes on urban farms	..	..	101	129	379	305	297	272	435	528
Taxes on rural farms	..	..	- 15 000	145	4	30	22	5	12	18
1120 On capital gains	..	..	0	0	0	0	0	0	0	0
1200 Corporate	..	..	306 517	485 438	687 400	263 451	436 794	297 182	230 083	388 845
1210 On profits	..	..	306 517	485 438	687 400	263 451	436 794	297 182	230 083	388 845
Oil companies - Contractors	..	..	32 454	406 163	546 181	184 343	331 801	216 081	145 418	301 718
Oil companies - Subcontractors	..	..	218 977	29 619	51 317	36 969	52 261	52 375	54 420	65 249
Non-oil companies - Taxes on companies	..	..	18 251	38 659	86 658	36 571	51 395	26 796	28 172	21 045
Oil companies - Year end (PNT)	..	..	34 763	9 765	573	609	172	1 777	1 394	190
OCIPEF Tax on wood exporters	..	..	2 072	1 233	2 671	4 958	1 166	153	678	643
1220 On capital gains of corporates	..	..	0	0	0	0	0	0	0	0
1300 Unallocable between 1100 and 1200	..	..	0	0	0	0	0	0	0	0
2000 Social security contributions	..	..	**0**	**0**	**58 868**	**47 725**	**48 881**	**49 925**	**44 870**	**48 415**
2100 Employees	..	..	..	..	7 935	7 054	7 612	7 806	7 195	7 629
2110 On a payroll basis	..	..	..	..	0	0	0	0	0	0
2120 On an income tax basis	..	..	..	..	7 935	7 054	7 612	7 806	7 195	7 629
2200 Employers	..	..	..	..	41 793	36 711	36 370	37 294	34 345	36 450
2210 On a payroll basis	..	..	..	..	0	0	0	0	0	0
2220 On an income tax basis	..	..	..	..	41 793	36 711	36 370	37 294	34 345	36 450
2300 Self-employed or non-employed	..	..	..	..	0	0	0	0	0	0
2310 On a payroll basis	..	..	..	..	..	..	..	..	..	..
2320 On an income tax basis	..	..	..	..	..	..	..	..	..	..
2400 Unallocable between 2100, 2200 and 2300	..	..	..	..	9 140	3 960	4 900	4 826	3 330	4 336
2410 On a payroll basis	..	..	..	..	0	0	0	0	0	0
2420 On an income tax basis	..	..	..	..	9 140	3 960	4 900	4 826	3 330	4 336
3000 Taxes on payroll and workforce	..	..	**0**	**0**	**0**	**0**	**0**	**0**	**0**	**0**
4000 Taxes on property	..	..	**27**	**160**	**211**	**278**	**227**	**139**	**97**	**178**
4100 Recurrent taxes on immovable property	..	..	0	0	0	0	0	0	0	0
4110 Households	..	..	..	..	..	..	..	..	..	..
4120 Others	..	..	..	..	..	..	..	..	..	..
4200 Recurrent taxes on net wealth	..	..	0	0	0	0	0	0	0	0
4210 Individual	..	..	..	..	..	..	..	..	..	..
4220 Corporate	..	..	..	..	..	..	..	..	..	..
4300 Estate, inheritance and gift taxes	..	..	0	0	0	0	0	0	0	0
4310 Estate and inheritance taxes	..	..	..	..	..	..	..	..	..	..
4320 Gift taxes	..	..	..	..	..	..	..	..	..	..
4400 Taxes on financial and capital transactions	..	..	27	160	211	278	227	139	97	178
4500 Other non-reccurrent taxes on property	..	..	0	0	0	0	0	0	0	0
4510 On net wealth	..	..	..	..	..	..	..	..	..	..
4520 Other non-recurrent taxes	..	..	..	..	..	..	..	..	..	..
4600 Other recurrent taxes on property	..	..	0	0	0	0	0	0	0	0
5000 Taxes on goods and services	..	..	**30 243**	**57 852**	**96 353**	**92 399**	**98 695**	**80 589**	**74 106**	**99 622**
5100 Taxes on production, sale, transfer, etc	..	..	30 243	57 852	96 353	92 399	98 695	80 589	74 106	99 622
5110 General taxes on goods and services	..	..	22 122	45 607	58 761	54 466	57 859	49 509	41 943	48 691
5111 Value added taxes	..	..	22 122	45 607	58 761	54 466	57 859	49 509	41 943	48 691
VAT on domestic activities	..	..	0	0	0	0	0	43 181	34 389	40 079
VAT on imports	..	..	0	0	0	0	0	4 200	5 792	5 619
VAT revenues on petroleum products	..	..	7 132	15 066	6 799	2 355	2 160	2 129	1 762	2 993
VAT revenues on other products and services	..	..	14 990	30 541	51 962	52 111	55 699	0	0	0
5112 Sales tax	..	..	0	0	0	0	0	0	0	0
5113 Other	..	..	0	0	0	0	0	0	0	0
5120 Taxes on specific goods and services	..	..	8 121	12 245	37 592	37 933	40 836	31 079	32 163	50 931
5121 Excises	..	..	0	0	19 961	18 570	20 904	19 155	19 003	27 478

Table 5.10. Equatorial Guinea – Details of tax revenue (continued)

Million XAF

	1995	2000	2005	2010	2015	2018	2019	2020	2021	2022
Taxes on petroleum products	..	..	..	..	19 961	18 570	17 604	17 504	17 425	25 733
Tax on alcoholic beverages and other drinks	..	..	..	..	0	0	3 300	1 515	899	989
Other excise taxes	..	..	..	..	0	0	0	136	679	756
5122 Profits of fiscal monopolies	..	..	0	0	0	0	0	0	0	0
5123 Customs and import duties	..	..	3 974	9 667	13 434	13 015	15 438	9 952	9 874	20 294
Imports of petroleum products	..	..	618	1 446	2 009	1 448	1 297	1 245	1 308	12 580
Imports of other products	..	..	3 356	8 221	11 425	11 567	14 141	8 707	8 566	7 714
5124 Taxes on exports	..	..	4 147	2 578	4 197	6 348	4 494	1 972	3 286	3 159
Wood exports	..	..	3 916	2 517	4 088	6 253	4 294	1 906	3 205	2 915
Exports of other products	..	..	91	21	91	89	193	64	71	65
Re-exports	..	..	140	40	18	6	6	2	10	179
5125 Taxes on investment goods	..	..	0	0	0	0	0	0	0	0
5126 Taxes on specific services	..	..	0	0	0	0	0	0	0	0
5127 Other taxes on internat. trade and transactions	..	..	0	0	0	0	0	0	0	0
5128 Other taxes	..	..	0	0	0	0	0	0	0	0
5130 Unallocable between 5110 and 5120	..	..	0	0	0	0	0	0	0	0
5200 Taxes on use of goods and to perform activities	..	..	0	0	0	0	0	0	0	0
5210 Recurrent taxes	..	..	..	..	..	..	..	..	..	..
5211 Paid by households: motor vehicles	..	..	..	..	..	..	..	..	..	..
5212 Paid by others: motor vehicles	..	..	..	..	..	..	..	..	..	..
5213 Paid in respect of other goods	..	..	..	..	..	..	..	..	..	..
5220 Non-recurrent taxes	..	..	..	..	..	..	..	..	..	..
5300 Unallocable between 5100 and 5200	..	..	0	0	0	0	0	0	0	0
6000 Other taxes	**..**	**..**	**836**	**8 989**	**8 054**	**19 060**	**6 538**	**8 575**	**5 145**	**1 495**
6100 Paid solely by business	..	..	..	..	..	..	..	..	..	..
6200 Other	..	..	..	..	..	..	..	..	..	..

.. Not available

Note: Year ending 31st December.

The data are on a cash basis.

Heading 2000: Social security contributions to the *Instituto Nacional de Seguridad Social de Guinea Ecuatorial* (INSESO) are reported under this heading for the years 2013-21.

Source: Ministry of Finance, Economy and Planning; *Instituto Nacional de Seguridad Social de Guinea Ecuatorial* (INSESO).

Table 5.11. Eswatini – Details of tax revenue

Million SZL

	1995	2000	2005	2010	2015	2018	2019	2020	2021	2022
Total tax revenue	**745**	**1 327**	**2 406**	**4 588**	**7 907**	**10 891**	**11 893**	**11 916**	**12 784**	**14 304**
1000 Taxes on income, profits and capital gains	**392**	**677**	**1 289**	**2 373**	**3 854**	**5 259**	**5 732**	**5 624**	**6 207**	**6 604**
1100 Of individuals	165	428	804	1 449	2 278	3 289	3 513	3 586	3 820	4 254
1110 On income and profits	165	428	804	1 449	2 278	3 289	3 513	3 586	3 820	4 254
Pay-as-you-earn tax (PAYE)	162	421	733	1 321	2 176	3 181	3 407	3 466	3 700	4 135
Provisional income tax (farmers, directors, individuals)	0	2	16	75	24	44	38	40	42	39
Taxes on interest, dividends and trust income	0	0	8	35	1	0	0	0	0	0
Personal income tax on non-residents	0	0	0	3	1	0	0	0	0	0
Tax on benefits	0	0	5	11	15	18	18	19	19	19
Withholding tax on resident suppliers of goods and services	0	0	40	0	0	0	0	0	0	0
Personal income tax on the self employed	2	4	0	1	59	43	47	56	53	58
Lottery levy	0	1	1	2	2	3	3	5	5	3
1120 On capital gains	0	0	0	0	0	0	0	0	0	0
1200 Corporate	202	236	461	905	1 507	1 969	2 218	2 036	2 385	2 348
1210 On profits	202	236	461	905	1 507	1 969	2 218	2 036	2 385	2 348
Corporate income tax on resident companies	201	233	394	739	1 358	1 479	1 734	1 462	1 857	1 603
Taxes on royalties	0	0	54	144	42	0	0	0	0	0
Corporate income tax on non-resident companies	0	3	13	22	107	490	483	574	528	745
1220 On capital gains of corporates	0	0	0	0	0	0	0	0	0	0
1300 Unallocable between 1100 and 1200	26	14	23	20	68	1	1	2	2	2
Income taxes on non-residents	23	11	20	15	67	0	0	0	0	0
Other taxes on income	2	3	3	4	2	1	1	2	2	2
2000 Social security contributions	**115**	**154**	**287**	**626**	**1 028**	**1 536**	**1 542**	**1 589**	**1 695**	**1 714**
2100 Employees	29	38	72	157	309	472	475	495	511	541
2110 On a payroll basis	..	..	..	..	..	..	..	..	..	..
2120 On an income tax basis	..	..	..	..	..	..	..	..	..	..
2200 Employers	87	115	215	469	719	1 065	1 067	1 094	1 184	1 173
2210 On a payroll basis	..	..	..	..	..	..	..	..	..	..
2220 On an income tax basis	..	..	..	..	..	..	..	..	..	..
2300 Self-employed or non-employed	0	0	0	0	0	0	0	0	0	0
2310 On a payroll basis	..	..	..	..	..	..	..	..	..	..
2320 On an income tax basis	..	..	..	..	..	..	..	..	..	..
2400 Unallocable between 2100, 2200 and 2300	0	0	0	0	0	0	0	0	0	0
2410 On a payroll basis	..	..	..	..	..	..	..	..	..	..
2420 On an income tax basis	..	..	..	..	..	..	..	..	..	..
3000 Taxes on payroll and workforce	**0**	**0**	**0**	**0**	**0**	**0**	**0**	**0**	**0**	**0**
4000 Taxes on property	**15**	**34**	**55**	**92**	**133**	**285**	**306**	**174**	**234**	**403**
4100 Recurrent taxes on immovable property	8	24	30	54	78	212	236	118	139	303
Local property taxes	8	24	30	54	78	212	236	118	139	303
4110 Households	0	0	0	0	0	0	0	0	0	0
4120 Others	0	0	0	0	0	0	0	0	0	0
4200 Recurrent taxes on net wealth	0	0	0	0	0	0	0	0	0	0
4210 Individual	..	..	..	..	..	..	..	..	..	..
4220 Corporate	..	..	..	..	..	..	..	..	..	..
4300 Estate, inheritance and gift taxes	0	0	0	0	0	0	0	0	0	0
4310 Estate and inheritance taxes	..	..	..	..	..	..	..	..	..	..
Tax on trust beneficiaries	..	..	..	..	..	..	..	..	..	..
4320 Gift taxes	..	..	..	..	..	..	..	..	..	..
4400 Taxes on financial and capital transactions	7	10	25	39	56	73	70	56	95	99
Transfer duties	3	5	13	26	30	49	37	30	45	39
Stamp duties	4	5	12	12	25	23	34	27	50	60
4500 Other non-reccurrent taxes on property	0	0	0	0	0	0	0	0	0	0
4510 On net wealth	..	..	..	..	..	..	..	..	..	..
4520 Other non-recurrent taxes	..	..	..	..	..	..	..	..	..	..
4600 Other recurrent taxes on property	0	0	0	0	0	0	0	0	0	0
5000 Taxes on goods and services	**223**	**462**	**776**	**1 496**	**2 892**	**3 811**	**4 313**	**4 529**	**4 648**	**5 583**
5100 Taxes on production, sale, transfer, etc	214	449	758	1 442	2 823	3 729	4 205	4 429	4 524	5 438
5110 General taxes on goods and services	173	372	661	1 255	2 109	2 668	2 972	3 123	3 134	4 074

Table 5.11. Eswatini – Details of tax revenue (continued)

Million SZL

	1995	2000	2005	2010	2015	2018	2019	2020	2021	2022
5111 Value added taxes	0	0	0	0	2 107	2 668	2 965	3 119	3 134	4 073
VAT revenues (gross)	..	..	..	..	3 048	3 753	4 349	4 595	4 823	5 675
VAT refunds	..	..	..	..	- 941	-1 085	-1 384	-1 475	-1 689	-1 601
5112 Sales tax	173	372	661	1 255	2	0	7	4	0	1
5113 Other	0	0	0	0	0	0	0	0	0	0
5120 Taxes on specific goods and services	41	78	97	186	714	1 061	1 232	1 306	1 390	1 364
5121 Excises	40	75	73	148	667	1 050	1 218	1 291	1 334	1 305
Fuel taxes	40	75	73	148	667	1 050	1 202	1 261	1 290	1 259
Levy on alcohol and tobacco	0	0	0	0	0	0	16	29	44	46
5122 Profits of fiscal monopolies	0	0	0	0	0	0	0	0	0	0
5123 Customs and import duties	0	0	0	0	0	5	9	12	9	7
5124 Taxes on exports	0	0	0	0	0	0	0	0	0	0
Cattle export tax	0	0	0	0	0	0	0	0	0	0
5125 Taxes on investment goods	0	0	0	0	0	0	0	0	0	0
5126 Taxes on specific services	1	2	23	39	47	5	6	3	47	52
Tax on management fees	0	0	17	37	42	0	0	0	2	0
Taxes on lotteries, gaming and betting	1	2	7	2	5	5	6	3	46	52
Other taxes on services and hospitality	0	0	0	0	0	0	0	0	0	0
5127 Other taxes on internat. trade and transactions	0	0	0	0	0	0	0	0	0	0
5128 Other taxes	0	0	0	0	0	0	0	0	0	0
5130 Unallocable between 5110 and 5120	0	0	0	0	0	0	0	0	0	0
5200 Taxes on use of goods and to perform activities	8	12	18	54	68	82	108	100	124	145
5210 Recurrent taxes	4	8	13	30	38	48	51	51	67	68
5211 Paid by households: motor vehicles	2	4	1	11	16	20	22	25	35	35
5212 Paid by others: motor vehicles	0	0	0	0	0	0	0	0	0	0
5213 Paid in respect of other goods	2	3	11	19	22	28	29	26	32	33
Trading licences	1	1	8	11	14	18	19	20	21	22
Company licences	1	1	2	7	7	9	9	5	9	10
Special activities licences (gaming, casino, labor agents, cattle slaughter)	0	1	1	1	1	1	1	1	2	1
5220 Non-recurrent taxes	4	5	5	25	31	34	57	49	57	77
Road tolls	4	4	4	24	30	33	56	48	56	77
Firearm registration fees	0	0	1	1	1	1	1	1	1	1
5300 Unallocable between 5100 and 5200	0	0	0	0	0	0	0	0	0	0
6000 Other taxes	**0**	**0**	**0**	**0**	**0**	**0**	**0**	**0**	**0**	**0**
6100 Paid solely by business	..	..	..	..	..	..	..	..	..	..
6200 Other	..	..	..	..	..	..	..	..	..	..

.. Not available

Note: Data are reported on a fiscal year basis beginning 1st April. For example, the data for 2022 represent April 2022 to March 2023.

The data are on a cash basis.

Heading 5211: This heading includes revenue from motor vehicle licences, the change of ownership fees and the registration of new motor vehicles. These revenues are considered as tax revenue according to the OECD classification, described in the interpretative guide in Annex A. The national classification of Eswatini classifies these revenues as non-tax revenues.

Heading 5213: This heading includes revenue from business and sundry licences. These revenues are considered as tax revenues according to the OECD classification, described in the interpretative guide in Annex A. The national classification of Eswatini classifies them as nontax revenues.

Heading 5220: This heading includes revenue from the registrations of specific goods (e.g firearms). These revenues are considered as tax revenues under the OECD classification, as set out in the Interpretative Guide in Annex A. The national classification of Eswatini classifies these revenues as non-tax revenues.

Revenue from PAYE Penalties, tax interest and penalties on taxes are considered as non-tax revenue under the OECD classification, as set out in the Interpretative Guide in Annex A. The national classification of Eswatini classifies these revenues as tax revenues.

Source: Eswatini Revenue Service; Local Government; Eswatini National Provident Fund and Public Service Pension Fund; Ministry of Economic Planning and Development; Central Government.

Table 5.12. Gabon – Details of tax revenue

Million XAF

	1995	2000	2005	2010	2015	2018	2019	2020	2021	2022
Total tax revenue	..	..	..	**903 847**	**1 302 204**	**969 109**	**1 191 698**	**1 131 616**	**1 157 115**	**1 497 936**
1000 Taxes on income, profits and capital gains	..	..	..	**282 644**	**513 891**	**377 016**	**561 846**	**508 963**	**398 915**	**702 269**
1100 Of individuals	..	..	..	66 984	138 542	90 579	109 639	110 446	111 585	135 765
1110 On income and profits	..	..	..	66 984	138 542	90 579	109 639	110 446	111 585	135 765
Personal income tax (IRPP)	..	..	..	5 514	16 807	17 067	21 382	18 909	22 423	30 627
Personal income tax - employer's levy	..	..	..	45 315	91 116	54 009	65 722	69 834	67 378	79 099
Flat-rate tax and additional wage tax	..	..	..	16 155	30 619	19 503	22 534	21 703	21 784	26 039
1120 On capital gains	..	..	..	0	0	0	0	0	0	0
1200 Corporate	..	..	..	180 820	343 535	273 390	436 010	384 452	270 815	548 723
1210 On profits	..	..	..	180 820	343 535	273 390	436 010	384 452	270 815	548 723
Corporate income tax excluding mining and oil	..	..	..	154 072	241 835	111 691	182 567	119 542	137 882	167 740
Corporate income tax - mining	..	..	..	144	14 319	50 000	102 003	11 304	48 759	48 600
Corporate income tax - oil	..	..	..	11 787	44 326	86 587	122 898	224 470	56 045	298 001
Corporate income tax - withholding tax	..	..	..	14 816	43 055	25 113	28 542	29 136	28 129	34 382
1220 On capital gains of corporates	..	..	..	0	0	0	0	0	0	0
1300 Unallocable between 1100 and 1200	..	..	..	34 840	31 814	13 047	16 198	14 065	16 514	17 780
Income from movable capital	..	..	..	31 658	22 408	9 691	13 814	11 294	13 064	14 421
Special property tax on rental income	..	..	..	3 182	9 407	3 356	2 384	2 770	3 450	3 360
2000 Social security contributions	..	..	..	**103 354**	**87 655**	**143 026**	**148 925**	**146 152**	**152 901**	**160 131**
2100 Employees	..	..	..	..	..	17 426	20 462	19 775	21 797	22 225
2110 On a payroll basis	..	..	..	..	..	..	..	..	..	..
2120 On an income tax basis	..	..	..	..	..	..	..	..	..	..
2200 Employers	..	..	..	..	..	8 509	9 982	9 646	10 633	10 841
2210 On a payroll basis	..	..	..	..	..	..	..	..	..	..
2220 On an income tax basis	..	..	..	..	..	..	..	..	..	..
2300 Self-employed or non-employed	..	..	..	..	..	..	..	..	..	..
2310 On a payroll basis	..	..	..	..	..	..	..	..	..	..
2320 On an income tax basis	..	..	..	..	..	..	..	..	..	..
2400 Unallocable between 2100, 2200 and 2300	..	..	..	103 354	87 655	117 091	118 480	116 731	120 471	127 065
2410 On a payroll basis	..	..	..	..	..	..	..	..	..	..
2420 On an income tax basis	..	..	..	..	..	..	..	..	..	..
3000 Taxes on payroll and workforce	..	..	..	**5 830**	**9 847**	**8 597**	**10 172**	**9 496**	**9 999**	**10 966**
National housing fund	..	..	..	5 613	9 847	6 770	7 913	7 435	7 855	8 525
Vocational training contribution	..	..	..	217	0	1 827	2 258	2 061	2 144	2 441
4000 Taxes on property	..	..	..	**3 202**	**19 163**	**15 003**	**13 461**	**19 376**	**17 480**	**23 825**
4100 Recurrent taxes on immovable property	..	..	..	2 765	10 610	9 055	8 812	13 651	12 170	18 059
Land taxes	..	..	..	2 720	10 610	9 055	8 812	13 615	12 142	18 032
Other property taxes	..	..	..	45	0	0	0	36	29	27
4110 Households	..	..	..	0	0	0	0	0	0	0
4120 Others	..	..	..	0	0	0	0	0	0	0
4200 Recurrent taxes on net wealth	..	..	..	0	0	0	0	0	0	0
4210 Individual	..	..	..	..	..	..	..	..	..	..
4220 Corporate	..	..	..	..	..	..	..	..	..	..
4300 Estate, inheritance and gift taxes	..	..	..	0	0	0	0	0	0	0
4310 Estate and inheritance taxes	..	..	..	..	..	..	..	..	..	..
4320 Gift taxes	..	..	..	..	..	..	..	..	..	..
4400 Taxes on financial and capital transactions	..	..	..	437	8 553	5 948	4 649	5 725	5 310	5 766
Registration duty on transfer deeds	..	..	..	426	7 263	5 295	4 483	4 795	4 872	4 936
Other property registration fees	..	..	..	11	1 289	653	166	931	438	829
4500 Other non-reccurrent taxes on property	..	..	..	0	0	0	0	0	0	0
4510 On net wealth	..	..	..	..	..	..	..	..	..	..
4520 Other non-recurrent taxes	..	..	..	..	..	..	..	..	..	..
4600 Other recurrent taxes on property	..	..	..	0	0	0	0	0	0	0
5000 Taxes on goods and services	..	..	..	**507 897**	**671 600**	**423 444**	**454 919**	**445 895**	**542 365**	**591 115**
5100 Taxes on production, sale, transfer, etc	..	..	..	507 014	667 296	420 782	451 032	441 785	537 769	586 466
5110 General taxes on goods and services	..	..	..	265 000	397 207	208 053	214 426	185 150	255 583	289 263
5111 Value added taxes	..	..	..	265 000	397 207	208 053	214 426	185 150	255 583	289 263
Value-added tax - domestic	..	..	..	175 231	303 966	189 534	187 156	204 468	212 754	214 343
Value-added tax - import	..	..	..	144 480	143 213	94 622	101 673	117 868	115 751	132 526

Table 5.12. Gabon – Details of tax revenue (continued)

Million XAF

	1995	2000	2005	2010	2015	2018	2019	2020	2021	2022
VAT refunds	..	..	..	-54 710	-49 972	-76 103	-74 404	-137 186	-72 923	-57 606
5112 Sales tax	..	..	..	0	0	0	0	0	0	0
5113 Other	..	..	..	0	0	0	0	0	0	0
5120 Taxes on specific goods and services	..	..	..	240 296	266 498	211 929	235 407	255 190	281 277	296 934
5121 Excises	..	..	..	22 222	61 532	38 895	38 067	52 194	54 477	30 519
Excise duties, domestic	..	..	..	8 406	14 875	12 950	17 563	18 685	21 122	17 885
Tax on butane gas and bitumen	..	..	..	0	0	441	459	696	615	550
Vehicle tax	..	..	..	0	0	0	12	30	75	44
Municipal fuel tax	..	..	..	1 234	2 929	2 315	2 296	1 837	2 238	2 359
Road wear charge	..	..	..	619	35 073	8 643	8 909	21 280	20 366	7
Excise duty on imports	..	..	..	11 963	8 656	14 546	8 829	9 668	10 063	9 674
5122 Profits of fiscal monopolies	..	..	..	0	0	0	0	0	0	0
5123 Customs and import duties	..	..	..	148 649	148 886	102 230	123 249	121 916	123 463	151 979
5124 Taxes on exports	..	..	..	24 912	13 193	21 823	24 109	26 058	37 922	27 286
Exit duty on mines	..	..	..	17 843	10 471	17 325	19 307	21 622	24 530	11 178
Slaughter tax and exit fee	..	..	..	6 944	2 633	4 407	4 716	4 253	13 143	16 074
Customs stamp	..	..	..	18	24	10	5	70	8	0
Tax on mineral products	..	..	..	107	65	80	81	113	241	34
5125 Taxes on investment goods	..	..	..	0	0	0	0	0	0	0
5126 Taxes on specific services	..	..	..	44 513	42 887	48 982	49 982	55 022	65 415	87 150
Special solidarity contribution L01	..	..	..	10 435	16 436	18 600	18 666	18 246	22 359	23 369
Computer fee	..	..	..	18 070	16 006	14 393	13 175	14 967	14 724	21 024
Passenger fee	..	..	..	0	0	0	0	0	1 695	12 300
Special solidarity contribution L04	..	..	..	6 343	0	7 483	8 181	8 682	8 980	9 054
Household waste contribution	..	..	..	0	0	0	2 534	5 635	6 318	7 683
Withdrawal tax	..	..	..	0	0	0	0	0	3 489	5 678
Tax on insurance contracts	..	..	..	3 942	5 793	5 042	4 715	5 473	5 493	5 168
Tax on fund transfers	..	..	..	4 267	3 736	2 879	1 957	1 652	1 331	2 034
Other taxes on services	..	..	..	1 455	917	585	755	366	1 027	840
5127 Other taxes on internat. trade and transactions	..	..	..	0	0	0	0	0	0	0
5128 Other taxes	..	..	..	0	0	0	0	0	0	0
5130 Unallocable between 5110 and 5120	..	..	..	1 718	3 591	800	1 200	1 445	909	269
Credit interest and surtax	..	..	..	1 718	3 591	800	1 200	1 445	909	269
5200 Taxes on use of goods and to perform activities	..	..	..	883	4 304	2 662	3 887	4 110	4 596	4 649
5210 Recurrent taxes	..	..	..	883	4 304	2 662	3 887	4 110	4 596	4 649
5211 Paid by households: motor vehicles	..	..	..	15	24	12	15	10	38	2
5212 Paid by others: motor vehicles	..	..	..	0	0	0	0	0	0	0
5213 Paid in respect of other goods	..	..	..	868	4 280	2 650	3 872	4 100	4 558	4 647
Licence contributions	..	..	..	843	4 278	2 648	2 297	2 220	2 699	2 826
Audiov, cinema and hunting royalties	..	..	..	25	3	2	1 575	1 880	1 860	1 821
5220 Non-recurrent taxes	..	..	..	0	0	0	0	0	0	0
5300 Unallocable between 5100 and 5200	..	..	..	0	0	0	0	0	0	0
6000 Other taxes	**..**	**..**	**..**	**921**	**47**	**2 023**	**2 375**	**1 735**	**35 454**	**9 630**
Synthetic tax and other taxes	..	..	..	921	47	2 023	2 375	1 735	2 435	3 631
Revenues to be allocated	..	..	..	0	0	0	0	0	33 019	5 999
6100 Paid solely by business	..	..	..	0	0	0	0	0	0	0
6200 Other	..	..	..	0	0	0	0	0	0	0
Memo items :	..	..	..	..	..	..	..	..	..	..
Community contributions	..	..	..	10 786	9 726	5 367	10 954	7 964	10 627	11 205

.. Not available

Note: Year ending 31st December.The data are on a cash basis.

Figures exclude tax revenues collected by sub-national governments as the data are not available.

Total tax revenues prior to 2016 should be interpreted with caution as they exclude social security contributions which are only available from 2016.

Tax revenues include certain tax revenues allocated to sub-national governments and special funds (e.g. *Fonds National de l'Habitat, or* "National Housing Fund"). These revenues are included in headings 4100, 5121, 5126, 5213 and 6000.

Revenues from fines and penalties relating to taxes and certain registration fees are included in non-tax revenues following the OECD classification of taxes (see the *Interpretative Guide* in Annexes A and B). Under Gabon's national classification they are included in tax revenues.

Source: Ministry of Economy and Participations, Gabon.

Table 5.13. Ghana – Details of tax revenue

Million GHS

	1995	2000	2005	2010	2015	2018	2019	2020	2021	2022
Total tax revenue	..	**487**	**2 342**	**6 695**	**23 592**	**42 184**	**47 039**	**51 467**	**64 858**	**85 196**
1000 Taxes on income, profits and capital gains	..	**141**	**642**	**2 417**	**7 570**	**16 344**	**19 853**	**21 075**	**24 979**	**33 383**
1100 Of individuals	..	56	269	1 115	3 570	6 649	7 734	7 901	9 725	12 649
1110 On income and profits	..	56	269	1 115	3 570	6 649	7 734	7 901	9 725	12 649
Employees income tax	..	48	232	1 015	3 310	6 270	7 313	7 507	9 250	0
Self employers income / profit tax	..	8	37	100	260	379	421	394	474	654
Pay-as-you-earn (PAYE) taxes	..	0	0	0	0	0	0	0	0	11 995
1120 On capital gains	..	..	..	..	..	..	..	..	..	..
1200 Corporate	..	70	303	1 080	3 837	9 563	11 833	12 860	14 819	20 420
1210 On profits	..	70	303	1 080	3 837	9 563	11 833	12 860	14 819	20 420
Income / profit tax on companies (excl. oil)	..	70	303	988	3 620	8 528	10 567	11 426	13 066	16 002
Income / profit tax on oil companies	..	0	0	0	45	736	926	951	933	3 499
National Fiscal Stabilisation Levy (NFSL)	..	0	0	85	172	299	340	483	558	553
National Reconstruction Levy (NRL)	..	0	0	7	0	0	0	0	0	0
Financial Sector Recovery Levy	..	0	0	0	0	0	0	0	263	366
1220 On capital gains of corporates	..	..	..	..	..	..	..	..	..	..
1300 Unallocable between 1100 and 1200	..	15	70	222	163	132	286	314	435	314
Other direct taxes aside from oil and mineral royalties	..	15	70	222	163	132	286	314	435	314
2000 Social security contributions	..	**46**	**191**	**577**	**2 122**	**2 213**	**2 466**	**4 107**	**3 368**	**4 360**
2100 Employees	..	..	..	..	..	..	..	..	..	..
2110 On a payroll basis	..	..	..	..	..	..	..	..	..	..
2120 On an income tax basis	..	..	..	..	..	..	..	..	..	..
2200 Employers	..	..	..	..	..	..	..	..	..	..
2210 On a payroll basis	..	..	..	..	..	..	..	..	..	..
2220 On an income tax basis	..	..	..	..	..	..	..	..	..	..
2300 Self-employed or non-employed	..	..	..	..	..	..	..	..	..	..
2310 On a payroll basis	..	..	..	..	..	..	..	..	..	..
2320 On an income tax basis	..	..	..	..	..	..	..	..	..	..
2400 Unallocable between 2100, 2200 and 2300	..	46	191	577	2 122	2 213	2 466	4 107	3 368	4 360
SSNIT revenue - Social security contributions	..	46	191	577	2 122	2 213	2 466	4 107	3 368	4 360
2410 On a payroll basis	..	..	..	..	..	..	..	..	..	..
2420 On an income tax basis	..	..	..	..	..	..	..	..	..	..
3000 Taxes on payroll and workforce	..	**0**	**0**	**0**	**0**	**0**	**0**	**0**	**0**	**0**
4000 Taxes on property	..	..	..	..	..	..	..	..	..	**592**
4100 Recurrent taxes on immovable property	..	..	..	..	..	..	..	..	..	0
4110 Households	..	..	..	..	..	..	..	..	..	0
4120 Others	..	..	..	..	..	..	..	..	..	0
4200 Recurrent taxes on net wealth	..	..	..	..	..	..	..	..	..	0
4210 Individual	..	..	..	..	..	..	..	..	..	0
4220 Corporate	..	..	..	..	..	..	..	..	..	0
4300 Estate, inheritance and gift taxes	..	..	..	..	..	..	..	..	..	0
4310 Estate and inheritance taxes	..	..	..	..	..	..	..	..	..	0
4320 Gift taxes	..	..	..	..	..	..	..	..	..	0
4400 Taxes on financial and capital transactions	..	..	..	..	..	..	..	..	..	592
Electronic Transfer Levy	..	..	..	..	..	..	..	..	..	592
4500 Other non-reccurrent taxes on property	..	..	..	..	..	..	..	..	..	0
4510 On net wealth	..	..	..	..	..	..	..	..	..	..
4520 Other non-recurrent taxes	..	..	..	..	..	..	..	..	..	..
4600 Other recurrent taxes on property	..	..	..	..	..	..	..	..	..	0
5000 Taxes on goods and services	..	**301**	**1 509**	**3 701**	**13 900**	**23 627**	**24 720**	**26 286**	**36 511**	**46 861**
5100 Taxes on production, sale, transfer, etc	..	301	1 509	3 701	13 900	23 606	24 659	26 286	36 511	46 861
5110 General taxes on goods and services	..	127	595	2 006	7 562	11 326	12 498	12 875	18 695	25 417
5111 Value added taxes	..	127	595	2 006	7 562	11 326	12 498	12 875	18 695	25 417
VAT revenues (external collection)	..	89	399	970	3 489	4 912	4 121	3 906	5 301	7 010
VAT revenues (domestic)	..	39	196	649	2 766	3 980	5 209	5 302	7 179	8 941
National Health Insurance Levy (NHIL - customs collection)	..	0	0	183	558	810	715	744	921	1 256
National Health Insurance Levy (NHIL - domestic)	..	0	0	133	461	691	1 030	1 060	1 574	2 520

Table 5.13. Ghana – Details of tax revenue (continued)

Million GHS

	1995	2000	2005	2010	2015	2018	2019	2020	2021	2022
Social Security and National Insurance Trust (SSNIT) contributions to the National Health Insurance Scheme (NHIS)	..	0	0	72	289	377	153	46	448	350
GETFund Levy (external collection)	..	0	0	0	0	289	834	757	923	1 257
GETFund Levy (domestic)	..	0	0	0	0	267	435	1 060	1 574	2 520
COVID-19 Health Recovery Levy	..	0	0	0	0	0	0	0	776	1 565
5112 Sales tax	..	0	0	0	0	0	0	0	0	0
5113 Other	..	0	0	0	0	0	0	0	0	0
5120 Taxes on specific goods and services	..	173	915	1 695	6 337	12 279	12 161	13 411	17 815	21 444
5121 Excises	..	75	477	374	2 402	5 282	5 817	7 153	9 982	10 093
Petroleum taxes aside from EFL and RFL	..	53	403	221	2 163	1 975	1 952	2 170	3 215	2 333
Energy Fund Levy (EFL)	..	0	0	36	0	35	39	38	48	44
Road Fund Levy (RFL)	..	0	0	0	0	1 331	1 541	1 780	2 152	2 102
Energy Debt Recovery Levy (EDRL)	..	0	0	0	0	876	1 665	2 040	2 329	2 166
Price Stabilisation and Recovery Levy	..	0	0	0	0	548	125	484	629	1 342
Public Lighting Levy (PLL)	..	0	0	0	0	119	63	134	141	93
National Electrification Scheme Levy (NESL)	..	0	0	0	0	78	44	90	94	66
Energy Sector Recovery Levy (Delta Fund)	..	0	0	0	0	0	0	0	566	956
Sanitation and Pollution Levy	..	0	0	0	0	0	0	0	265	450
Other excise duties	..	21	74	118	239	319	387	415	543	540
5122 Profits of fiscal monopolies	..	0	0	0	0	0	0	0	0	0
5123 Customs and import duties	..	81	377	1 051	3 078	6 102	5 410	5 514	6 945	9 848
Import Duty	..	81	377	1 051	3 078	6 102	5 410	5 514	6 945	9 848
5124 Taxes on exports	..	18	61	95	371	0	0	0	0	0
Levies on cocoa exports	..	18	61	95	371	..	..	..	..	..
5125 Taxes on investment goods	..	0	0	0	0	0	0	0	0	0
5126 Taxes on specific services	..	0	0	174	486	896	934	745	888	1 502
Communication Service Tax	..	..	..	137	252	420	412	559	528	713
Airport Tax	..	..	..	37	235	476	521	185	360	790
5127 Other taxes on internat. trade and transactions	..	0	0	0	0	0	0	0	0	0
5128 Other taxes	..	0	0	0	0	0	0	0	0	0
5130 Unallocable between 5110 and 5120	..	0	0	0	0	0	0	0	0	0
5200 Taxes on use of goods and to perform activities	..	0	0	0	0	21	61	0	0	0
5210 Recurrent taxes	..	..	..	..	..	21	61	..	..	..
5211 Paid by households: motor vehicles	..	..	..	..	..	21	61	..	..	..
Luxury Vehicle Levy	..	..	..	..	..	21	61	..	..	..
5212 Paid by others: motor vehicles	..	..	..	..	..	0	0	..	..	..
5213 Paid in respect of other goods	..	..	..	..	..	0	0	..	..	..
Licences	..	..	..	..	..	..	..	..	..	..
5220 Non-recurrent taxes	..	..	..	..	..	0	0	..	..	..
5300 Unallocable between 5100 and 5200	..	0	0	0	0	0	0	0	0	0
6000 Other taxes	**..**	**0**	**0**	**0**	**0**	**0**	**0**	**0**	**0**	**0**
6100 Paid solely by business	..	..	..	..	..	..	..	..	..	..
6200 Other	..	..	..	..	..	..	..	..	..	..
Memo Items:	..	..	..	..	..	..	..	..	..	..
VAT refunds	..	0	12	45	627	2 125	2 470	2 587	3 117	4 116

.. Not available

Note: Year ending 31st December. The data are on a cash basis.

Figures exclude tax revenues collected by sub-national governments as the data are not available.

Heading 1210: The Financial Sector Recovery Levy was introduced in 2021 as a tax on bank profits to raise revenue for financial sector reforms.

Heading 2000: The data are not available from 2000 to 2007.

Heading 5111: The national health insurance levy is a tax on goods and services whose funds are allocated to the National Health Insurance Scheme (NHIS). For 2019, the division of GETFund Levy revenues between domestic and external collections are estimates based on programmed budget figures. The COVID-19 Health Recovery Levy was a special levy introduced in 2021 on goods and services outside of a set of exempted goods and services to support COVID-19 expenditures and related matters.

Heading 5121: The Energy Sector Recovery levy and the Sanitation and Pollution Levy are both excise taxes on fuel that were introduced in 2021.

Source: Ghana Statistical Service. Annual reports of the Social Security and National Insurance Trust (SSNIT) for social security revenues up to 2021, and the Annual Report of the National Pensions Regulatory Authority (NPRA) for 2022 social security revenues. Figures for social security revenues aside from contributions were not available for 2022.

Table 5.14. Guinea – Details of tax revenue

Million GNF

	1995	2000	2005	2010	2015	2018	2019	2020	2021	2022
Total tax revenue	..	**527 123**	**1 376 744**	**3 932 265**	**8 576 406**	**12 796 661**	**15 080 304**	**15 773 897**	**17 674 852**	**18 335 191**
1000 Taxes on income, profits and capital gains	..	**47 869**	**164 416**	**919 627**	**1 832 392**	**2 427 218**	**2 360 363**	**2 556 435**	**2 800 567**	**3 732 226**
1100 Of individuals	..	30 159	66 951	308 546	328 821	670 040	694 825	827 524	1 037 585	930 885
1110 On income and profits	..	30 159	66 951	308 546	328 821	670 040	694 825	827 524	1 037 585	930 885
Withholding on salaries and wages	..	27 313	53 946	242 641	168 830	359 467	414 711	474 144	636 766	573 773
Withholding on non-wage income	..	1 607	11 559	62 964	154 934	294 228	260 806	328 346	378 569	353 660
BIC and BNC withholding tax	..	1 106	877	1 930	3 167	14 166	18 644	21 837	12 978	3 452
Other income tax	..	133	569	1 011	1 891	2 179	665	3 197	9 272	0
1120 On capital gains	..	0	0	0	0	0	0	0	0	0
1200 Corporate	..	15 877	90 724	564 935	1 435 774	1 668 785	1 520 784	1 585 204	1 662 129	2 541 766
1210 On profits	..	15 877	90 724	564 935	1 435 774	1 668 785	1 520 784	1 585 204	1 662 129	2 541 766
Tax on non-mining companies	..	9 925	57 909	204 831	636 828	1 013 069	1 133 307	1 340 928	1 405 551	2 069 590
Tax on mining companies	..	5 953	32 593	359 510	791 739	653 363	385 990	243 782	256 579	472 177
Other corporate taxes	..	0	222	594	7 208	2 354	1 488	494	0	0
1220 On capital gains of corporates	..	0	0	0	0	0	0	0	0	0
1300 Unallocable between 1100 and 1200	..	1 833	6 742	46 146	67 797	88 393	144 754	143 707	100 853	259 575
Withholding tax on capital income	..	581	5 800	35 899	62 197	88 393	144 754	143 707	100 853	259 575
Other income tax deductions	..	1 252	942	10 247	5 600	0	0	0	0	0
2000 Social security contributions	..	..	..	..	..	..	..	..	..	..
2100 Employees	..	0	0	0	0	0	0	0	0	..
2110 On a payroll basis	..	..	..	..	..	..	..	..	..	..
2120 On an income tax basis	..	..	..	..	..	..	..	..	..	..
2200 Employers	..	0	0	0	0	0	0	0	0	..
2210 On a payroll basis	..	..	..	..	..	..	..	..	..	..
2220 On an income tax basis	..	..	..	..	..	..	..	..	..	..
2300 Self-employed or non-employed	..	..	..	..	..	..	..	..	..	..
2310 On a payroll basis	..	..	..	..	..	..	..	..	..	..
2320 On an income tax basis	..	..	..	..	..	..	..	..	..	..
2400 Unallocable between 2100, 2200 and 2300	..	0	0	0	0	0	0	0	0	..
2410 On a payroll basis	..	..	..	..	..	..	..	..	..	..
2420 On an income tax basis	..	..	..	..	..	..	..	..	..	..
3000 Taxes on payroll and workforce	..	**5 679**	**11 662**	**47 962**	**136 549**	**209 033**	**288 489**	**298 480**	**198 899**	**369 292**
Lump sum payments	..	5 030	10 094	45 545	130 904	199 549	278 521	286 564	189 842	366 427
Apprenticeship tax	..	649	1 568	2 417	5 645	9 485	9 968	11 916	9 057	2 865
4000 Taxes on property	..	**2 206**	**1 457**	**7 276**	**13 041**	**55 673**	**28 913**	**28 240**	**22 391**	**45 661**
4100 Recurrent taxes on immovable property	..	2 194	1 083	282	13 041	14 605	21 183	17 958	14 250	45 263
One-time property tax	..	2 194	1 083	282	13 041	14 605	21 183	17 958	14 250	45 263
4110 Households	..	0	0	0	0	0	0	0	0	0
4120 Others	..	0	0	0	0	0	0	0	0	0
4200 Recurrent taxes on net wealth	..	0	0	0	0	0	0	0	0	0
4210 Individual	..	..	..	..	..	..	..	..	..	..
4220 Corporate	..	..	..	..	..	..	..	..	..	..
4300 Estate, inheritance and gift taxes	..	0	0	0	0	0	0	0	0	0
4310 Estate and inheritance taxes	..	..	..	..	..	..	..	..	..	..
4320 Gift taxes	..	..	..	..	..	..	..	..	..	..
4400 Taxes on financial and capital transactions	..	12	374	6 994	0	41 068	7 730	10 283	8 141	398
4500 Other non-reccurrent taxes on property	..	0	0	0	0	0	0	0	0	0
4510 On net wealth	..	..	..	..	..	..	..	..	..	..
4520 Other non-recurrent taxes	..	..	..	..	..	..	..	..	..	..
4600 Other recurrent taxes on property	..	0	0	0	0	0	0	0	0	0
5000 Taxes on goods and services	..	**471 273**	**1 199 201**	**2 955 138**	**6 540 619**	**9 900 600**	**12 141 993**	**12 642 991**	**14 336 047**	**13 927 769**
5100 Taxes on production, sale, transfer, etc	..	464 802	1 189 907	2 943 009	6 530 520	9 864 107	12 110 843	12 610 018	14 305 228	13 862 784
5110 General taxes on goods and services	..	148 227	402 015	1 218 114	2 677 114	4 314 120	5 175 643	4 983 043	6 215 677	6 161 987
5111 Value added taxes	..	143 178	387 826	1 157 032	2 585 659	4 151 235	5 063 743	4 844 745	6 066 433	5 902 403
VAT domestic (gross)	..	28 086	66 379	421 411	831 832	1 431 169	1 900 231	1 771 872	2 131 501	2 807 518
Gross import VAT excluding petroleum products	..	115 092	321 447	514 935	1 019 501	1 580 672	1 783 029	1 820 946	2 549 165	2 245 273
Gross import VAT on petroleum products	..	0	0	220 686	734 327	1 139 394	1 380 483	1 251 927	1 385 767	849 612
VAT withholding	..	0	0	0	0	0	0	0	0	0
5112 Sales tax	..	1 638	7 114	50 414	51 293	58 713	52 779	62 699	72 252	157 245

Table 5.14. Guinea – Details of tax revenue (continued)

Million GNF

	1995	2000	2005	2010	2015	2018	2019	2020	2021	2022
5113 Other	..	3 411	7 074	10 667	40 162	104 171	59 121	75 599	76 993	102 339
Flat-rate minimum tax	..	3 411	7 074	10 667	40 162	104 171	59 121	75 599	76 993	102 339
5120 Taxes on specific goods and services	..	305 475	772 462	1 651 738	3 697 777	5 215 342	6 565 685	7 274 618	7 820 698	7 363 922
5121 Excises	..	54 382	133 113	250 500	701 047	442 539	1 006 425	1 779 536	999 182	846 040
Road maintenance fees	..	0	22 185	98 683	182 481	264 943	285 326	427 044	565 089	637 709
Excise duties	..	7 227	7 470	51 294	27 425	98 599	116 278	146 423	204 237	204 534
Tax on petroleum products	..	47 155	103 459	100 523	491 141	78 997	604 820	1 206 069	229 856	3 797
5122 Profits of fiscal monopolies	..	2	1 095	5 873	43 226	24 223	19 300	27 913	16 599	19 452
5123 Customs and import duties	..	101 716	324 491	533 184	1 833 780	2 460 416	3 184 000	2 954 696	3 618 894	3 171 814
Tax on imports excluding petroleum products	..	84 333	256 856	268 302	947 153	1 339 729	1 519 535	1 471 508	1 958 844	2 085 478
Import tax on petroleum products	..	0	0	144 470	492 579	548 311	1 020 510	842 111	859 854	366 228
Liquidation royalty excluding petroleum products	..	12 828	44 940	49 852	200 141	289 279	334 424	373 407	447 855	399 729
Liquidation royalty on petroleum products	..	0	0	26 350	54 130	94 308	115 310	92 640	137 003	92 889
Tax on storage excluding petroleum products	..	1 277	6 018	0	3 748	6 265	5 238	4 823	9 053	19 846
Storage tax on petroleum products	..	0	0	0	33 565	60 961	66 907	53 943	81 637	93 228
Flat-rate import levy	..	2 847	15 169	40 051	71 891	67 471	65 852	65 810	70 311	63 014
Customs registration fees	..	394	762	3 130	6 642	29 636	33 498	26 437	28 796	25 732
Degressive production tax	..	0	0	0	23 617	24 066	22 259	23 526	24 559	24 580
Other customs duties	..	37	745	1 030	315	390	467	492	981	1 089
5124 Taxes on exports	..	12 593	30 081	193 059	217 856	918 669	909 009	1 060 068	1 520 840	1 901 946
Exit tax (mining sector)	..	3 975	5 057	177 423	211 221	918 669	909 009	1 060 068	1 520 840	1 901 946
Diamond export tax	..	4 756	3 486	2 023	6 635	0	0	0	0	0
Tax on the export of precious metals	..	3 862	21 539	13 613	0	0	0	0	0	0
5125 Taxes on investment goods	..	0	0	0	0	0	0	0	0	0
5126 Taxes on specific services	..	5 389	13 818	44 867	376 136	932 686	1 128 146	1 257 693	1 448 766	1 424 670
Telephone consumption tax (TCT)	..	0	0	0	128 737	574 656	679 798	869 972	982 245	1 005 473
Telecommunications network access tax (TART)	..	0	0	0	120 856	171 660	216 014	136 445	168 233	192 214
Tax on financial affairs	..	4 884	12 878	39 663	115 399	169 946	206 523	227 195	272 159	193 579
Tax on insurance contracts	..	504	941	5 204	11 144	16 424	25 811	24 080	26 128	33 405
5127 Other taxes on internat. trade and transactions	..	0	0	0	0	0	0	0	0	0
5128 Other taxes	..	131 393	269 863	624 255	525 733	436 809	318 805	194 712	216 418	0
Tax on mining products	..	131 393	269 863	624 255	525 733	436 809	318 805	194 712	216 418	0
5130 Unallocable between 5110 and 5120	..	11 100	15 431	73 157	155 630	334 645	369 516	352 358	268 852	336 875
Tax borne by the State Achat finex (DND)	..	7 269	4 000	31 324	97 200	241 467	195 578	175 964	193 220	202 015
Tax borne by the State Achat finex (DNI)	..	3 250	10 640	40 878	47 442	88 535	147 566	144 267	38 193	88 186
Tax surcharge	..	581	791	955	10 988	4 642	26 372	32 127	37 439	46 675
5200 Taxes on use of goods and to perform activities	..	2 816	5 368	12 016	8 422	24 900	30 953	32 973	30 820	64 984
5210 Recurrent taxes	..	2 359	2 094	5 504	8 130	0	3 961	0	0	4 009
5211 Paid by households: motor vehicles	..	2 359	2 094	5 504	8 130	..	3 961	..	..	4 009
5212 Paid by others: motor vehicles	..	0	0	0	0	..	0	..	..	0
5213 Paid in respect of other goods	..	0	0	0	0	..	0	..	..	0
5220 Non-recurrent taxes	..	457	3 274	6 512	292	24 900	26 991	32 973	30 820	60 975
5300 Unallocable between 5100 and 5200	..	3 655	3 926	113	1 677	11 594	197	0	0	0
6000 Other taxes	**..**	**95**	**7**	**2 263**	**53 805**	**204 136**	**260 545**	**247 749**	**316 947**	**260 243**
Tax stamps	..	0	0	0	0	40 387	37 488	26 736	24 852	20 391
Recovery from previous years	..	95	7	2 263	53 805	163 749	223 057	221 013	292 095	239 851

.. Not available

Note: Year ending 31st December.

The data are on a cash basis.

Figures exclude tax revenues collected by sub-national governments as the data are not available.

Revenues from mining taxes on extraction, fees for administrative services, auction proceeds, and fines and penalties relating to taxes are included in non-tax revenues following the OECD classification of taxes (see the *Interpretative Guide* in Annexes A and B). Under Guinea's national classification they are included in tax revenues.

Heading 5111: The breakdown of gross VAT import revenues between petroleum products and non-petroleum products is not available before 2007. The category "Gross import VAT excluding petroleum products" therefore also includes VAT revenues on petroleum products for the period 2000 to 2006.

Heading 5121: Includes revenues from "Road maintenance charges" (*RER*: *Redevance entretien routier*) allocated to the "Special Road Maintenance Fund" (*FER*: *Fonds d'Entretien Routier*).

Heading 5123: The breakdown of revenues from import duty, storage tax and liquidation charge between petroleum products and non-petroleum products is not available until 2007. The categories labelled "excluding petroleum products" therefore also include revenues from petroleum products for the period 2000 to 2006.
Source: Ministry of Budget, Guinea.

Table 5.15. Kenya – Details of tax revenue

Million KES

	1995	2000	2005	2010	2015	2018	2019	2020	2021	2022
Total tax revenue	..	..	**278 714**	**545 519**	**1 096 626**	**1 494 360**	**1 614 857**	**1 676 077**	**1 753 261**	**2 131 709**
1000 Taxes on income, profits and capital gains	..	..	**100 129**	**219 227**	**504 077**	**654 609**	**687 055**	**753 861**	**717 660**	**895 727**
1100 Of individuals	..	..	56 376	124 392	284 222	377 353	410 193	419 325	382 519	483 817
1110 On income and profits	..	..	56 376	124 392	284 222	377 353	410 193	419 325	382 519	483 817
Pay-as-you-earn (PAYE) tax	..	..	53 325	120 593	277 068	364 104	392 693	400 508	363 349	461 816
of which pay-as-you-earn (PAYE) on extractive industry	..	..	..	..	..	3 682	2 698	2 456	2 299	2 439
Individual income tax	..	..	3 051	3 799	7 154	7 191	8 916	8 672	8 406	9 682
Tax on rental income	..	..	0	0	0	6 058	8 584	10 145	10 764	12 320
1120 On capital gains	..	..	..	..	..	..	..	..	..	..
1200 Corporate	..	..	31 947	67 661	126 541	159 993	168 655	175 905	182 214	242 018
1210 On profits	..	..	31 947	67 661	126 541	159 993	168 655	175 905	182 214	242 018
Corporation tax	..	..	31 947	67 661	126 541	159 993	168 655	175 905	182 214	242 018
of which corporation tax on extractive industry	..	..	..	..	..	656	714	3 466	1 994	3 719
1220 On capital gains of corporates	..	..	..	..	..	..	..	..	..	..
1300 Unallocable between 1100 and 1200	..	..	11 806	27 174	93 314	117 263	108 207	158 631	152 927	169 892
Withholding tax	..	..	11 792	27 174	92 678	100 623	105 256	121 511	126 127	151 160
of which withholding tax on extractive industry	..	..	..	..	..	916	802	1 330	889	3 221
Capital gains tax	..	..	14	0	636	16 640	2 951	37 120	26 800	18 732
2000 Social security contributions	..	..	**3 675**	**6 026**	**15 826**	**47 600**	**55 600**	**60 815**	**60 775**	**78 843**
2100 Employees	..	..	558	..	..	..	..	..	..	..
Women and children's pension	..	..	558	..	..	..	..	..	..	..
2110 On a payroll basis	..	..	..	..	..	..	..	..	..	..
2120 On an income tax basis	..	..	..	..	..	..	..	..	..	..
2200 Employers	..	..	..	..	..	..	..	..	..	..
2210 On a payroll basis	..	..	..	..	..	..	..	..	..	..
2220 On an income tax basis	..	..	..	..	..	..	..	..	..	..
2300 Self-employed or non-employed	..	..	..	..	..	..	..	..	..	..
2310 On a payroll basis	..	..	..	..	..	..	..	..	..	..
2320 On an income tax basis	..	..	..	..	..	..	..	..	..	..
2400 Unallocable between 2100, 2200 and 2300	..	..	3 117	6 026	15 826	47 600	55 600	60 815	60 775	78 843
2410 On a payroll basis	..	..	..	..	..	..	..	..	..	..
2420 On an income tax basis	..	..	..	..	..	..	..	..	..	..
3000 Taxes on payroll and workforce	..	..	**0**	**0**	**0**	**0**	**0**	**0**	**0**	**0**
4000 Taxes on property	..	..	**185**	**1 133**	**1 051**	**629**	**682**	**567**	**682**	**827**
4100 Recurrent taxes on immovable property	..	..	185	1 133	1 051	629	682	567	682	827
Immovable property (stand premia on town plots)	..	..	7	86	6	28	94	93	67	86
Land rates	..	..	178	0	0	0	0	0	102	431
Land rent	..	..	0	1 047	1 045	601	588	474	513	310
4110 Households	..	..	..	..	..	..	..	..	..	..
4120 Others	..	..	..	..	..	..	..	..	..	..
4200 Recurrent taxes on net wealth	..	..	0	0	0	0	0	0	0	0
4210 Individual	..	..	..	..	..	..	..	..	..	..
4220 Corporate	..	..	..	..	..	..	..	..	..	..
4300 Estate, inheritance and gift taxes	..	..	0	0	0	0	0	0	0	0
4310 Estate and inheritance taxes	..	..	..	..	..	..	..	..	..	..
4320 Gift taxes	..	..	..	..	..	..	..	..	..	..
4400 Taxes on financial and capital transactions	..	..	0	0	0	0	0	0	0	0
4500 Other non-reccurrent taxes on property	..	..	0	0	0	0	0	0	0	0
4510 On net wealth	..	..	..	..	..	..	..	..	..	..
4520 Other non-recurrent taxes	..	..	..	..	..	..	..	..	..	..
4600 Other recurrent taxes on property	..	..	0	0	0	0	0	0	0	0
5000 Taxes on goods and services	..	..	**173 785**	**313 615**	**564 115**	**779 319**	**861 339**	**851 741**	**961 179**	**1 142 933**
5100 Taxes on production, sale, transfer, etc	..	..	170 235	309 829	557 630	771 150	855 354	845 941	954 091	1 136 017
5110 General taxes on goods and services	..	..	72 656	141 152	265 501	356 881	395 121	382 053	408 421	520 523
5111 Value added taxes	..	..	72 656	141 041	264 872	356 777	395 033	382 029	408 359	520 423
VAT - Ordinary imports	..	..	28 287	57 594	127 744	144 035	157 496	146 482	182 557	226 937
VAT - Oil imports	..	..	4 186	5 352	7 894	7 643	7 189	5 506	6 075	12 835

Table 5.15. Kenya – Details of tax revenue (continued)

Million KES

	1995	2000	2005	2010	2015	2018	2019	2020	2021	2022
VAT - Domestic (gross)	..	..	48 583	92 255	143 922	219 499	244 748	228 515	217 687	264 746
of which VAT - Domestic (gross) on extractive industry	..	..	..	..	..	1 284	1 371	1 148	1 490	1 474
VAT - Domestic (refunds)	..	..	- 8 400	- 14 160	- 14 688	- 14 400	- 14 400	- 14 400	- 20 400	- 20 040
VAT - Oil imports at 8%	..	..	0	0	0	0	0	15 926	22 440	35 945
5112 Sales tax	..	..	0	0	0	0	0	0	0	0
5113 Other	..	..	0	111	630	103	88	24	62	100
Turnover tax	..	..	..	111	630	103	88	24	62	100
5120 Taxes on specific goods and services	..	..	97 579	168 677	292 129	414 270	460 233	463 888	545 670	615 494
5121 Excises	..	..	58 254	99 135	142 489	225 319	239 516	231 392	296 029	303 706
Excise duty - Oil	..	..	24 876	35 780	42 687	61 216	63 834	65 065	79 338	79 907
Excise duty - Domestic	..	..	15 744	23 755	38 246	53 011	59 509	55 721	62 405	66 264
Road Maintenance Levy	..	..	9 645	23 780	30 890	73 668	78 159	74 458	87 316	86 396
Excise duty - Imports	..	..	4 235	6 994	15 175	22 311	24 622	23 739	26 639	29 445
Sugar Levy	..	..	1 587	1 590	1 329	16	0	0	1	1
Petroleum Development Levy	..	..	1 041	1 585	1 817	2 262	2 165	2 044	25 880	26 849
Petroleum regulatory levy	..	..	0	134	301	521	1 087	1 073	1 252	1 232
Second hand motor vehicles purchase tax	..	..	186	183	466	171	192	186	243	260
Stamp duty - Domestic taxes	..	..	940	5 332	11 579	12 143	9 947	9 105	12 955	13 351
5122 Profits of fiscal monopolies	..	..	0	0	0	0	0	0	0	0
5123 Customs and import duties	..	..	32 992	57 047	120 612	142 194	154 748	159 265	185 560	215 024
Import duty - Ordinary	..	..	22 722	40 382	72 346	92 076	103 511	96 494	106 800	116 217
Import declaration fees	..	..	9 724	15 836	27 119	26 189	26 782	33 560	44 183	56 017
Railway Development Levy	..	..	0	0	18 940	20 780	21 303	23 258	28 504	36 361
Import duty - Oil	..	..	427	797	1 387	1 638	1 698	1 656	1 627	2 571
Merchant superintendent shipping levy	..	..	0	32	820	1 512	1 454	1 535	1 686	1 607
Stamp duty - Customs services	..	..	119	0	0	0	0	0	0	0
Anti-adulteration Levy	..	..	0	0	0	0	0	2 762	2 760	2 252
5124 Taxes on exports	..	..	0	0	0	0	0	0	0	0
5125 Taxes on investment goods	..	..	0	0	0	0	0	0	0	0
5126 Taxes on specific services	..	..	6 333	12 495	29 028	46 756	65 969	73 232	64 082	96 764
Excise on air time	..	..	2 982	7 893	13 122	15 626	25 120	28 841	29 297	37 370
Airport revenue	..	..	1 846	2 464	6 619	10 414	12 291	11 176	3 059	8 184
Aviation revenue	..	..	1 505	2 138	3 565	4 819	5 912	4 860	3 319	4 172
Excise on financial services	..	..	0	0	5 722	15 898	22 646	24 351	21 648	38 228
Excise on Betting Services	..	..	0	0	0	0	0	2 045	759	5 109
Betting Tax	..	..	0	0	0	0	0	1 960	3 000	3 389
Digital Service Tax (DST)	..	..	0	0	0	0	0	0	3 000	312
5127 Other taxes on internat. trade and transactions	..	..	0	0	0	0	0	0	0	0
5128 Other taxes	..	..	0	0	0	0	0	0	0	0
5130 Unallocable between 5110 and 5120	..	..	0	0	0	0	0	0	0	0
5200 Taxes on use of goods and to perform activities	..	..	3 550	3 786	6 485	8 169	5 985	5 800	7 088	6 916
5210 Recurrent taxes	..	..	3 550	3 786	6 485	8 169	5 985	5 800	7 088	6 916
5211 Paid by households: motor vehicles	..	..	3 266	3 367	6 010	7 678	5 474	5 284	6 584	6 387
Road transport fees	..	..	2 793	2 499	3 947	3 366	4 302	4 010	5 170	4 932
Foreign motor vehicles tax	..	..	0	0	0	69	0	0	0	0
Advance and other taxes	..	..	473	868	2 064	4 243	1 172	1 274	1 414	1 456
5212 Paid by others: motor vehicles	..	..	0	0	0	0	0	0	0	0
5213 Paid in respect of other goods	..	..	284	419	475	491	511	516	503	529
Kenya Bureau of Standards (KEBS) tax	..	..	284	419	475	491	511	516	503	529
5220 Non-recurrent taxes	..	..	0	0	0	0	0	0	0	0
5300 Unallocable between 5100 and 5200	..	..	0	0	0	0	0	0	0	0
6000 Other taxes	**..**	**..**	**940**	**5 519**	**11 556**	**12 204**	**10 181**	**9 093**	**12 965**	**13 379**
Other taxes	..	..	..	164	150	86	66	6	10	13
6100 Paid solely by business	..	..	0	0	0	0	0	0	0	0
6200 Other	..	..	940	5 356	11 406	12 118	10 115	9 087	12 955	13 366

.. Not available

Note: Data are reported on a fiscal year basis beginning 1st July. For example, the data for 2022 represent the period July 2021 to June 2022.

The data are on a cash basis.
Figures exclude tax revenues collected by sub-national governments as the data are not available.
Heading 4100: The data for the immovable property (stand premia on town plots) tax are not readily available for the years 2001-04 and 2006. No estimation was undertaken given the magnitude of the figures.
Heading 5121: Data for the second-hand motor vehicles purchase tax are not readily available for the years 2001-04, 2006, 2013 and 2014. No estimation was undertaken given the magnitude of the figures. Stamp duties on domestic taxes are classified under this heading in this edition; In the previous edition they were classified under 4400 taxes on financial and capital transactions.
These revenues are collected by the Kenya Revenue Authority (KRA) on behalf of other agencies. The national classification of Kenya classifies all agency revenues as non-tax revenues.
Source: Kenya Revenue Authority (KRA).

Table 5.16. Lesotho – Details of tax revenue

Million LSL

	1995	2000	2005	2010	2015	2018	2019	2020	2021	2022
Total tax revenue	..	..	**1 462**	**2 933**	**5 872**	**7 289**	**7 248**	**6 771**	**7 826**	**8 422**
1000 Taxes on income, profits and capital gains	..	..	**807**	**1 652**	**3 651**	**4 103**	**4 056**	**3 743**	**4 161**	**4 328**
1100 Of individuals	..	..	618	1 180	2 484	3 112	3 142	2 851	3 235	3 455
1110 On income and profits	..	..	618	1 180	2 484	3 112	3 142	2 851	3 235	3 455
Personal income tax	..	..	618	1 180	1 737	2 212	2 296	2 023	2 373	2 829
Withholding tax	..	..	0	0	748	900	847	828	862	626
1120 On capital gains	..	..	0	0	0	0	0	0	0	0
1200 Corporate	..	..	189	472	1 133	959	884	862	885	840
1210 On profits	..	..	189	472	1 133	959	884	862	885	840
Corporate income tax	..	..	189	472	1 126	955	877	858	881	834
Gambling levy	..	..	0	0	8	4	7	3	4	7
1220 On capital gains of corporates	..	..	0	0	0	0	0	0	0	0
1300 Unallocable between 1100 and 1200	..	..	0	0	34	33	29	31	41	33
2000 Social security contributions	..	..	**0**	**0**	**0**	**0**	**0**	**0**	**0**	**0**
2100 Employees	..	..	..	..	..	..	..	..	..	..
2110 On a payroll basis	..	..	..	..	..	..	..	..	..	..
2120 On an income tax basis	..	..	..	..	..	..	..	..	..	..
2200 Employers	..	..	..	..	..	..	..	..	..	..
2210 On a payroll basis	..	..	..	..	..	..	..	..	..	..
2220 On an income tax basis	..	..	..	..	..	..	..	..	..	..
2300 Self-employed or non-employed	..	..	..	..	..	..	..	..	..	..
2310 On a payroll basis	..	..	..	..	..	..	..	..	..	..
2320 On an income tax basis	..	..	..	..	..	..	..	..	..	..
2400 Unallocable between 2100, 2200 and 2300	..	..	..	..	..	..	..	..	..	..
2410 On a payroll basis	..	..	..	..	..	..	..	..	..	..
2420 On an income tax basis	..	..	..	..	..	..	..	..	..	..
3000 Taxes on payroll and workforce	..	..	**0**	**0**	**0**	**0**	**0**	**0**	**0**	**0**
4000 Taxes on property	..	..	..	..	..	..	..	..	..	..
4100 Recurrent taxes on immovable property	..	..	..	..	..	..	..	..	..	..
4110 Households	..	..	..	..	..	..	..	..	..	..
4120 Others	..	..	..	..	..	..	..	..	..	..
4200 Recurrent taxes on net wealth	..	..	..	..	..	..	..	..	..	..
4210 Individual	..	..	..	..	..	..	..	..	..	..
4220 Corporate	..	..	..	..	..	..	..	..	..	..
4300 Estate, inheritance and gift taxes	..	..	..	..	..	..	..	..	..	..
4310 Estate and inheritance taxes	..	..	..	..	..	..	..	..	..	..
4320 Gift taxes	..	..	..	..	..	..	..	..	..	..
4400 Taxes on financial and capital transactions	..	..	..	..	..	..	..	..	..	..
4500 Other non-reccurrent taxes on property	..	..	..	..	..	..	..	..	..	..
4510 On net wealth	..	..	..	..	..	..	..	..	..	..
4520 Other non-recurrent taxes	..	..	..	..	..	..	..	..	..	..
4600 Other recurrent taxes on property	..	..	..	..	..	..	..	..	..	..
5000 Taxes on goods and services	..	..	**656**	**1 281**	**2 221**	**3 185**	**3 192**	**3 028**	**3 665**	**4 095**
5100 Taxes on production, sale, transfer, etc	..	..	656	1 281	2 221	3 185	3 192	3 028	3 665	4 095
5110 General taxes on goods and services	..	..	656	1 281	2 210	2 880	2 907	2 608	3 122	3 544
5111 Value added taxes	..	..	656	1 281	2 210	2 880	2 907	2 608	3 122	3 544
VAT on imports	..	..	252	473	780	880	896	662	841	2 116
VAT - Domestic (Net)	..	..	403	808	1 430	2 000	2 011	1 946	2 281	1 428
VAT - Domestic (Gross)	..	..	463	1 046	1 996	2 681	2 877	2 668	3 141	2 160
VAT - Domestic (Refunds)	..	..	- 59	- 238	- 566	- 682	- 867	- 722	- 860	- 732
5112 Sales tax	..	..	0	0	0	0	0	0	0	0
5113 Other	..	..	0	0	0	0	0	0	0	0
5120 Taxes on specific goods and services	..	..	0	0	11	305	285	420	544	551
5121 Excises	..	..	..	..	11	305	285	420	544	551
Oil levy	..	..	..	..	11	17	22	229	340	311
Motor vehicle insurance	..	..	..	..	..	189	147	8	11	21
Petroleum levy	..	..	..	..	..	61	22	72	38	36
Road maintenance levy	..	..	..	..	..	39	93	111	154	182

Table 5.16. Lesotho – Details of tax revenue (continued)

Million LSL

	1995	2000	2005	2010	2015	2018	2019	2020	2021	2022
5122 Profits of fiscal monopolies	..	..	..	..	0	0	0	0	0	0
5123 Customs and import duties	..	..	..	..	0	0	0	0	0	0
5124 Taxes on exports	..	..	..	..	0	0	0	0	0	0
5125 Taxes on investment goods	..	..	..	..	0	0	0	0	0	0
5126 Taxes on specific services	..	..	..	..	0	0	0	0	0	0
5127 Other taxes on internat. trade and transactions	..	..	..	..	0	0	0	0	0	0
5128 Other taxes	..	..	..	..	0	0	0	0	0	0
5130 Unallocable between 5110 and 5120	..	..	0	0	0	0	0	0	0	0
5200 Taxes on use of goods and to perform activities	..	..	0	0	0	0	0	0	0	0
5210 Recurrent taxes	..	..	..	..	..	..	..	..	..	..
5211 Paid by households: motor vehicles	..	..	..	..	..	..	..	..	..	..
5212 Paid by others: motor vehicles	..	..	..	..	..	..	..	..	..	..
5213 Paid in respect of other goods	..	..	..	..	..	..	..	..	..	..
5220 Non-recurrent taxes	..	..	..	..	..	..	..	..	..	..
5300 Unallocable between 5100 and 5200	..	..	0	0	0	0	0	0	0	0
6000 Other taxes	**..**	**..**	**0**	**0**	**0**	**0**	**0**	**0**	**0**	**0**
6100 Paid solely by business	..	..	..	..	..	..	..	..	..	..
6200 Other	..	..	..	..	..	..	..	..	..	..
Memo items:	..	..	..	..	..	..	..	..	..	..
Excise taxes collected on behalf of the SACU Common Revenue Pool	..	..	53	110	102	212	215	82	266	312
Import duties collected on behalf of the SACU Common Revenue Pool	..	..	18	32	145	145	147	107	134	340

.. Not available

Note: Data are on a fiscal year basis beginning 1st April. For example, the data for 2022 represent April 2022 to March 2023.

Data are reported on a cash basis.

Heading 2000: Social security contributions for Lesotho are deemed to be zero as they do not meet the criteria to be classified as social security contributions set out in the OECD classification of taxes in the *Interpretative Guide*.

Source: Revenue Services Lesotho.

Table 5.17. Madagascar – Details of tax revenue

Million MGA

	1995	2000	2005	2010	2015	2018	2019	2020	2021	2022
Total tax revenue	**215 420**	**591 900**	**1 016 402**	**1 776 183**	**3 105 267**	**5 006 524**	**5 645 481**	**5 011 290**	**5 949 864**	**7 183 000**
1000 Taxes on income, profits and capital gains	**33 100**	**92 960**	**219 944**	**490 294**	**706 768**	**1 174 775**	**1 437 601**	**1 305 414**	**1 546 901**	**1 922 818**
1100 Of individuals	12 600	36 080	77 147	253 868	366 621	547 827	687 985	620 915	661 014	753 513
1110 On income and profits	12 120	35 540	75 254	252 027	362 771	541 733	680 183	612 579	650 990	742 900
Tax on wage and similar income (IRSA)	9 180	25 260	56 673	201 077	315 570	446 571	549 317	490 419	484 484	594 720
Synthetic tax (IS)	0	0	2 079	13 497	19 140	39 344	69 167	69 004	78 088	86 361
Tax on capital income (IRCM)	2 940	10 280	16 502	37 453	28 040	55 807	61 699	53 156	88 417	61 820
Fees and gaming income	..	..	..	..	21	11	0	0	0	0
1120 On capital gains	480	540	1 893	1 841	3 850	6 094	7 802	8 336	10 024	10 612
Capital gains tax on real estate (IPVI)	480	540	1 893	1 841	3 850	6 094	7 802	8 336	10 024	10 612
1200 Corporate	20 500	56 880	142 797	236 426	340 147	626 948	749 616	684 499	808 626	1 054 107
1210 On profits	20 500	56 880	142 797	236 426	340 147	626 948	749 616	684 499	808 626	1 054 107
Income tax (IR)	20 500	56 880	142 797	236 426	339 001	566 723	680 654	584 277	672 929	862 068
Tax on non-resident income	..	..	..	..	0	60 130	68 958	99 267	135 697	192 022
Tax on non-wage income (IRNS)	..	..	..	..	1 030	1	3	9	0	5
Other corporate income taxes	..	..	..	..	116	95	1	946	1	11
1220 On capital gains of corporates	0	0	0	0	0	0	0	0	0	0
1300 Unallocable between 1100 and 1200	0	0	0	0	0	0	0	0	77 261	115 198
Public contract tax (IMP)	..	..	..	..	..	..	..	..	77 261	115 198
2000 Social security contributions	**..**	**..**	**..**	**..**	**133 072**	**295 800**	**260 981**	**304 656**	**242 517**	**356 991**
2100 Employees	..	..	..	..	0	0	0	0	0	0
2110 On a payroll basis	..	..	..	..	..	..	..	..	..	..
2120 On an income tax basis	..	..	..	..	..	..	..	..	..	..
2200 Employers	..	..	..	..	0	0	0	0	0	0
2210 On a payroll basis	..	..	..	..	..	..	..	..	..	..
2220 On an income tax basis	..	..	..	..	..	..	..	..	..	..
2300 Self-employed or non-employed	..	..	..	..	0	0	0	0	0	0
2310 On a payroll basis	..	..	..	..	..	..	..	..	..	..
2320 On an income tax basis	..	..	..	..	..	..	..	..	..	..
2400 Unallocable between 2100, 2200 and 2300	..	..	..	..	133 072	295 800	260 981	304 656	242 517	356 991
2410 On a payroll basis	..	..	..	..	..	..	..	..	..	..
2420 On an income tax basis	..	..	..	..	..	..	..	..	..	..
3000 Taxes on payroll and workforce	**0**	**0**	**0**	**0**	**0**	**0**	**0**	**0**	**0**	**0**
4000 Taxes on property	**2 380**	**4 340**	**8 514**	**10 560**	**24 150**	**41 045**	**31 454**	**30 321**	**36 426**	**40 898**
4100 Recurrent taxes on immovable property	0	0	0	0	0	0	0	0	0	0
4110 Households	..	..	..	..	..	..	..	..	..	..
4120 Others	..	..	..	..	..	..	..	..	..	..
4200 Recurrent taxes on net wealth	0	0	0	0	0	0	0	0	0	0
4210 Individual	..	..	..	..	..	..	..	..	..	..
4220 Corporate	..	..	..	..	..	..	..	..	..	..
4300 Estate, inheritance and gift taxes	0	0	0	0	0	0	0	0	0	0
4310 Estate and inheritance taxes	..	..	..	..	..	..	..	..	..	..
4320 Gift taxes	..	..	..	..	..	..	..	..	..	..
4400 Taxes on financial and capital transactions	2 380	4 340	8 514	10 560	24 150	41 045	31 454	30 321	36 426	40 898
Transfer tax	2 380	4 340	8 514	10 560	24 150	41 045	31 454	30 321	36 426	40 898
4500 Other non-reccurrent taxes on property	0	0	0	0	0	0	0	0	0	0
4510 On net wealth	..	..	..	..	..	..	..	..	..	..
4520 Other non-recurrent taxes	..	..	..	..	..	..	..	..	..	..
4600 Other recurrent taxes on property	0	0	0	0	0	0	0	0	0	0
5000 Taxes on goods and services	**175 880**	**488 480**	**776 544**	**1 268 030**	**2 238 127**	**3 473 452**	**3 889 145**	**3 364 916**	**4 120 768**	**4 852 959**
5100 Taxes on production, sale, transfer, etc	175 880	488 480	776 544	1 268 030	2 238 127	3 473 452	3 889 145	3 364 916	4 120 768	4 852 959
5110 General taxes on goods and services	104 600	244 860	410 256	803 932	1 504 330	2 274 724	2 567 663	2 175 841	2 734 186	3 247 844
5111 Value added taxes	104 600	244 860	410 256	803 932	1 504 330	2 274 724	2 567 663	2 175 841	2 734 186	3 247 844
VAT domestic	48 460	102 560	196 922	437 348	544 130	906 711	953 565	911 289	1 141 022	1 125 007
VAT imports	56 140	142 300	213 334	387 092	728 300	1 232 623	1 346 233	1 135 945	1 302 641	1 598 978
VAT import petroleum products	..	..	..	179 592	272 700	427 632	511 256	320 159	496 323	811 027
Domestic VAT refunds	..	..	..	- 200 100	- 40 800	- 255 753	- 212 833	- 132 197	- 175 001	- 283 169

Table 5.17. Madagascar – Details of tax revenue (continued)

Million MGA

	1995	2000	2005	2010	2015	2018	2019	2020	2021	2022
VAT import refunds on petroleum products	..	..	..	0	0	- 36 490	- 30 557	- 59 355	- 30 800	- 4 000
5112 Sales tax	0	0	0	0	0	0	0	0	0	0
5113 Other	0	0	0	0	0	0	0	0	0	0
5120 Taxes on specific goods and services	71 280	243 620	366 288	464 098	733 797	1 198 728	1 321 482	1 189 074	1 386 582	1 605 115
5121 Excises	9 460	79 540	99 115	201 039	253 819	365 226	386 891	385 698	454 624	466 241
Domestic excise taxes	9 440	67 760	88 586	201 039	253 819	365 226	386 891	385 698	454 624	466 241
Domestic excise duties - intermittent	..	..	..	..	25 923	54 128	52 284	53 263	97 567	89 867
Domestic excise duty - spirits	..	..	..	..	37 975	62 773	57 150	71 274	83 747	126 731
Domestic excise duty - hygienic beverages	..	..	..	..	0	2 803	2 758	2 862	4 113	4 517
Domestic excise duty - tobacco	..	..	..	..	185 571	224 113	248 696	244 949	253 627	231 882
Domestic excise duty - non-disaggregable	..	..	..	..	4 349	21 408	26 003	13 350	15 570	13 244
Customs excise duties	20	11 780	10 529	0	0	0	0	0	0	0
5122 Profits of fiscal monopolies	0	0	0	0	0	0	0	0	0	0
5123 Customs and import duties	61 820	152 380	266 588	262 726	458 100	767 173	890 053	730 087	856 644	1 054 304
Customs duties	16 260	24 700	112 160	172 369	331 400	535 458	604 739	498 342	591 679	780 016
Import tax	29 780	48 140	0	0	0	0	0	0	0	0
Taxes on petroleum products	15 780	79 540	154 428	90 357	126 700	231 715	285 314	231 745	264 965	274 287
5124 Taxes on exports	0	0	0	0	0	0	0	0	0	0
5125 Taxes on investment goods	0	0	0	0	0	0	0	0	0	0
5126 Taxes on specific services	..	..	..	..	21 778	65 819	43 738	72 098	73 911	83 235
Telecommunications	..	..	..	..	14 673	57 127	34 260	61 919	63 677	73 221
Insurance tax	..	..	..	..	6 220	7 540	8 268	8 983	8 852	8 517
Additional tax on motor vehicle insurance contracts	..	..	..	..	885	1 152	1 211	1 196	1 382	1 496
5127 Other taxes on internat. trade and transactions	0	11 700	585	333	100	510	799	1 192	1 404	1 335
Statistical tax on imports	..	8 040	0	0	0	0	0	0	0	0
Other	..	3 660	585	333	100	510	799	1 192	1 404	1 335
5128 Other taxes	0	0	0	0	0	0	0	0	0	0
5130 Unallocable between 5110 and 5120	0	0	0	0	0	0	0	0	0	0
5200 Taxes on use of goods and to perform activities	0	0	0	0	0	0	0	0	0	0
5210 Recurrent taxes	..	..	..	..	..	..	..	..	..	..
5211 Paid by households: motor vehicles	..	..	..	..	..	..	..	..	..	..
5212 Paid by others: motor vehicles	..	..	..	..	..	..	..	..	..	..
5213 Paid in respect of other goods	..	..	..	..	..	..	..	..	..	..
5220 Non-recurrent taxes	..	..	..	..	..	..	..	..	..	..
5300 Unallocable between 5100 and 5200	0	0	0	0	0	0	0	0	0	0
6000 Other taxes	**4 060**	**6 120**	**11 400**	**7 299**	**3 150**	**21 453**	**26 300**	**5 984**	**3 252**	**9 334**
6100 Paid solely by business	2 720	2 540	4 349	3 739	650	687	1 178	872	1 085	1 015
6200 Other	1 340	3 580	7 051	3 560	2 500	20 766	25 123	5 112	2 167	8 320

.. Not available

Note: Year ending 31st December.

The data are on a cash basis.

Figures exclude tax revenues collected by sub-national governments as the data are not available.

Social security contributions under heading 2000 are not considered as tax revenues in Madagascar.

Heading 5121: The breakdown of domestic excise duties is presented from 2013. Domestic excise duties on telecommunications are reported under heading 5126 "Taxes on specific services" following the *Interpretive Guide* in Annex A. From 2009, customs excise duties are included in the categories of intermittent excise duties or other categories of excise duties collected by the tax authorities, i.e. they are included in domestic tax revenues.

Heading 5126: This heading includes insurance tax revenues and revenues from the supplementary tax on motor vehicle insurance contracts.

Heading 6100: This heading includes revenues from stamps. Revenues from visa stamps are included in this heading until 2014 because it was not possible to separate them from other stamp revenues; from 2015 they are classified as non-tax revenues following the OECD classification of taxes (see the *Interpretative Guide* in Annexes A and B).

Heading 6200: Revenues from tax penalties and revenues from levies on fees and gaming products are included in this heading until 2014 because it was not possible to separate them from other revenues. From 2015 revenues from tax penalties are classified as non-tax revenues and revenues from fees and gaming products are reported under heading 1110 "On income and profits of individuals" following the OECD classification of taxes (see the *Interpretative Guide* in Annexes A and B).

Source: Ministry of Economy and Finance, Madagascar.

Table 5.18. Malawi – Details of tax revenue

Million MWK

	1995	2000	2005	2010	2015	2018	2019	2020	2021	2022
Total tax revenue	..	..	**51 183**	**152 744**	**485 326**	**880 895**	**968 929**	**1 070 917**	**1 160 482**	**1 362 482**
1000 Taxes on income, profits and capital gains	..	..	**21 837**	**67 576**	**236 126**	**423 259**	**460 724**	**506 568**	**539 925**	**616 577**
1100 Of individuals	..	..	12 152	36 525	139 074	256 576	302 061	335 991	326 626	340 276
1110 On income and profits	..	..	12 152	36 525	139 074	256 576	302 061	335 991	326 626	340 276
Pay-as-you-earn (PAYE) tax	..	..	11 098	32 849	126 367	228 697	269 244	296 370	283 610	290 173
Fringe benefits	..	..	844	1 675	5 350	10 749	12 111	11 947	12 966	14 657
Non-resident tax	..	..	196	835	4 585	13 116	16 350	22 479	22 576	23 541
Dividends	..	..	14	1 165	2 772	4 013	4 355	5 195	7 474	11 905
1120 On capital gains	..	..	0	0	0	0	0	0	0	0
1200 Corporate	..	..	9 685	31 051	97 052	166 683	158 664	170 577	213 300	276 301
1210 On profits	..	..	9 685	31 051	97 052	166 683	158 664	170 577	213 300	276 301
Company assessments	..	..	1 984	6 981	14 186	28 858	19 619	16 369	30 780	22 805
Provisional corporate income tax	..	..	3 957	16 253	43 723	64 987	55 936	65 470	78 331	120 184
Withholding tax on corporations	..	..	3 745	7 817	39 143	72 839	83 109	88 738	104 189	131 204
Capital gains tax	..	..	0	0	0	0	0	0	0	0
Advance Income Tax (AIT)	..	..	0	0	0	0	0	0	0	2 108
1220 On capital gains of corporates	..	..	0	0	0	0	0	0	0	0
1300 Unallocable between 1100 and 1200	..	..	0	0	0	0	0	0	0	0
2000 Social security contributions	..	..	**0**	**0**	**0**	**0**	**0**	**0**	**0**	**0**
2100 Employees	..	..	..	..	..	..	..	..	..	..
2110 On a payroll basis	..	..	..	..	..	..	..	..	..	..
2120 On an income tax basis	..	..	..	..	..	..	..	..	..	..
2200 Employers	..	..	..	..	..	..	..	..	..	..
2210 On a payroll basis	..	..	..	..	..	..	..	..	..	..
2220 On an income tax basis	..	..	..	..	..	..	..	..	..	..
2300 Self-employed or non-employed	..	..	..	..	..	..	..	..	..	..
2310 On a payroll basis	..	..	..	..	..	..	..	..	..	..
2320 On an income tax basis	..	..	..	..	..	..	..	..	..	..
2400 Unallocable between 2100, 2200 and 2300	..	..	..	..	..	..	..	..	..	..
2410 On a payroll basis	..	..	..	..	..	..	..	..	..	..
2420 On an income tax basis	..	..	..	..	..	..	..	..	..	..
3000 Taxes on payroll and workforce	..	..	**0**	**0**	**0**	**0**	**0**	**0**	**0**	**0**
4000 Taxes on property	..	..	**0**	**0**	**0**	**0**	**0**	**0**	**0**	**0**
4100 Recurrent taxes on immovable property	..	..	..	..	..	..	..	..	..	..
4110 Households	..	..	..	..	..	..	..	..	..	..
4120 Others	..	..	..	..	..	..	..	..	..	..
4200 Recurrent taxes on net wealth	..	..	..	..	..	..	..	..	..	..
4210 Individual	..	..	..	..	..	..	..	..	..	..
4220 Corporate	..	..	..	..	..	..	..	..	..	..
4300 Estate, inheritance and gift taxes	..	..	..	..	..	..	..	..	..	..
4310 Estate and inheritance taxes	..	..	..	..	..	..	..	..	..	..
4320 Gift taxes	..	..	..	..	..	..	..	..	..	..
4400 Taxes on financial and capital transactions	..	..	..	..	..	..	..	..	..	..
4500 Other non-reccurrent taxes on property	..	..	..	..	..	..	..	..	..	..
4510 On net wealth	..	..	..	..	..	..	..	..	..	..
4520 Other non-recurrent taxes	..	..	..	..	..	..	..	..	..	..
4600 Other recurrent taxes on property	..	..	..	..	..	..	..	..	..	..
5000 Taxes on goods and services	..	..	**29 263**	**84 865**	**248 646**	**457 223**	**507 491**	**564 313**	**619 701**	**744 589**
5100 Taxes on production, sale, transfer, etc	..	..	29 263	84 865	248 646	457 223	507 491	563 043	617 070	741 370
5110 General taxes on goods and services	..	..	14 216	38 751	137 551	247 658	287 974	336 128	343 184	402 039
5111 Value added taxes	..	..	14 216	38 751	137 539	247 632	287 926	336 101	343 158	401 940
VAT revenues (domestic)	..	..	6 880	21 932	67 149	132 750	163 852	176 801	197 059	241 272
VAT on imports	..	..	8 279	22 482	80 007	139 080	152 835	138 453	166 486	195 855
VAT refunds	..	..	- 942	- 5 663	- 9 618	- 24 199	- 28 761	20 847	- 20 386	- 35 187
5112 Sales tax	..	..	0	0	0	0	0	0	0	0
5113 Other	..	..	0	0	12	26	48	27	26	98
Turnover tax	..	..	..	..	12	26	48	27	26	98
5120 Taxes on specific goods and services	..	..	15 047	46 115	111 094	209 565	219 517	226 915	273 886	339 331
5121 Excises	..	..	8 097	31 122	64 856	133 326	131 225	142 242	181 387	216 173

Table 5.18. Malawi – Details of tax revenue (continued)

Million MWK

	1995	2000	2005	2010	2015	2018	2019	2020	2021	2022
Local excise taxes	..	..	1 294	5 805	15 368	32 208	36 215	40 042	47 363	50 505
Excise taxes on imports	..	..	5 401	14 233	26 419	48 544	55 172	52 302	53 186	78 206
Road Levy (fuel tax)	..	..	1 402	7 507	9 312	26 277	31 218	39 055	36 597	55 690
Road tax (fuel tax)	..	..	0	0	3 837	5 580	6 662	7 941	9 213	9 526
Rural Electrification Levy (fuel tax)	..	..	0	3 577	8 681	18 950	0	0	33 231	19 665
Storage Levy (fuel tax)	..	..	0	0	1 240	1 768	1 958	2 902	1 797	2 580
5122 Profits of fiscal monopolies	..	..	0	0	0	0	0	0	0	0
5123 Customs and import duties	..	..	6 950	14 993	46 238	76 239	88 292	84 672	92 498	123 159
Import duty	..	..	6 229	15 775	46 121	76 179	88 213	82 528	87 702	116 839
Prepayments collected on import duties	..	..	721	- 783	117	60	79	33	1 323	66
Surcharges on import duties	..	..	0	0	0	0	0	2 112	3 474	6 253
5124 Taxes on exports	..	..	0	0	0	0	0	0	0	0
5125 Taxes on investment goods	..	..	0	0	0	0	0	0	0	0
5126 Taxes on specific services	..	..	0	0	0	0	0	0	0	0
5127 Other taxes on internat. trade and transactions	..	..	0	0	0	0	0	0	0	0
5128 Other taxes	..	..	0	0	0	0	0	0	0	0
5130 Unallocable between 5110 and 5120	..	..	0	0	0	0	0	0	0	0
5200 Taxes on use of goods and to perform activities	..	..	0	0	0	0	0	1 271	2 631	3 219
5210 Recurrent taxes	..	..	..	..	..	..	..	1 271	2 631	3 219
5211 Paid by households: motor vehicles	..	..	..	..	..	..	..	0	0	0
5212 Paid by others: motor vehicles	..	..	..	..	..	..	..	1 271	2 631	3 219
Carbon tax on vehicle ownership	..	..	..	..	..	..	..	1 271	2 631	3 219
5213 Paid in respect of other goods	..	..	..	..	..	..	..	0	0	0
5220 Non-recurrent taxes	..	..	..	..	..	..	..	0	0	0
5300 Unallocable between 5100 and 5200	..	..	0	0	0	0	0	0	0	0
6000 Other taxes	**..**	**..**	**82**	**303**	**554**	**413**	**714**	**36**	**855**	**1 316**
6100 Paid solely by business	..	..	82	303	554	413	714	36	855	1 316
Miscellaneous duties	..	..	82	303	554	413	714	36	855	1 316
6200 Other	..	..	0	0	0	0	0	0	0	0

.. Not available

Note: Data for Malawi are on a fiscal year basis beginning 1st July for all years. For example, the data for 2022 represent July 1, 2021 to June 30, 2022. In the year 2021, Malawi changed its fiscal year from a July-June fiscal year to an April-March fiscal year. This means that while *Revenue Statistics in Africa* uses the same fiscal year basis that's used in Malawi's national reporting for all years up to 2021, this is not the case for 2022. Since Malawi's 2021/22 fiscal year is shortened to nine months and goes from July 2021 to March 2022, for the sake of better year-over-year comparability, a 12-month fiscal year is used for Malawi in *Revenue Statistics in Africa* for the year 2022.

Figures exclude revenues from business licenses and permits collected by city and district councils from business entities within their jurisdictions.

Heading 2000: Social security contributions for Malawi are deemed to be zero as they do not meet the criteria to be classified as social security contributions set out in the OECD classification of taxes in the *Interpretative Guide*.

Heading 4000: Revenues from property taxes are mainly levied by local governments for which data on revenue are not available.

Source: Ministry of Finance, Economic Planning and Development of Malawi.

Table 5.19. Mali – Details of tax revenue

Million XOF

	1995	2000	2005	2010	2015	2018	2019	2020	2021	2022
Total tax revenue	**124 203**	**239 362**	**476 775**	**748 245**	**1 207 241**	**1 310 703**	**1 833 214**	**1 886 935**	**2 175 585**	**2 088 160**
1000 Taxes on income, profits and capital gains	**26 399**	**34 698**	**78 979**	**184 760**	**296 284**	**313 752**	**410 014**	**495 867**	**525 539**	**529 216**
1100 Of individuals	10 053	16 061	33 283	50 375	88 233	90 875	125 158	133 257	137 752	147 879
1110 On income and profits	10 053	16 061	33 283	50 375	88 233	90 875	125 158	133 257	137 752	147 879
Retained tax on salaries and wages, private sector	5 853	12 374	25 119	39 859	71 153	74 395	101 950	109 256	119 803	109 997
Retained tax on salaries and wages, public sector	2 723	3 311	7 125	8 624	13 904	12 004	18 066	19 624	11 535	31 105
Capital gains tax	0	0	0	0	862	1 371	1 599	989	2 955	2 925
Taxes on property income	1 477	376	1 039	1 892	2 314	3 105	3 543	3 388	3 459	3 851
1120 On capital gains	0	0	0	0	0	0	0	0	0	0
1200 Corporate	10 840	16 034	38 386	118 346	179 458	201 763	253 131	326 412	332 699	341 121
1210 On profits	10 840	16 034	38 386	118 346	179 458	201 763	253 131	326 412	332 699	341 121
Corporate tax (private)	..	..	31 767	107 582	174 433	197 499	249 245	322 380	306 584	332 838
Corporate tax (public)	..	..	0	121	1	157	26	108	20 341	30
Tax on industrial and commercial profits, private sector	10 840	15 996	6 589	10 643	5 024	4 107	3 859	3 925	5 775	8 253
Tax on industrial and commercial profits, public sector	0	38	30	0	0	0	0	0	0	0
1220 On capital gains	..	..	..	..	..	..	..	..	..	..
1300 Unallocable between 1100 and 1200	5 506	2 603	7 310	16 039	28 593	21 115	31 725	36 197	55 089	40 217
Synthetic tax	0	480	1 449	1 212	1 441	1 469	1 486	1 399	1 544	0
Tax on income and securities	5 506	2 123	5 861	14 827	27 152	19 646	30 239	34 798	53 545	40 217
2000 Social security contributions	**13 169**	**18 442**	**45 497**	**73 600**	**149 083**	**205 344**	**297 236**	**333 298**	**403 322**	**460 568**
2100 Employees	..	..	..	..	..	..	..	..	..	..
2110 On a payroll basis	..	..	..	..	..	..	..	..	..	..
2120 On an income tax basis	..	..	..	..	..	..	..	..	..	..
2200 Employers	..	..	..	..	..	..	..	..	..	..
2210 On a payroll basis	..	..	..	..	..	..	..	..	..	..
2220 On an income tax basis	..	..	..	..	..	..	..	..	..	..
2300 Self-employed or non-employed	..	..	..	..	..	..	..	..	..	..
2310 On a payroll basis	..	..	..	..	..	..	..	..	..	..
2320 On an income tax basis	..	..	..	..	..	..	..	..	..	..
2400 Unallocable between 2100, 2200 and 2300	13 169	18 442	45 497	73 600	149 083	205 344	297 236	333 298	403 322	460 568
Social security contributions (CMSS)	..	..	9 259	12 834	26 550	34 758	98 520	114 470	153 307	150 502
Social security contributions (INPS)	13 169	18 442	36 238	60 766	90 152	123 801	136 492	154 189	165 462	222 503
Social security contributions (CANAM - CMSS)	..	..	..	..	18 393	22 468	25 253	26 596	38 313	38 503
Social security contributions (CANAM - INPS)	..	..	..	..	13 871	24 315	36 971	38 041	46 236	49 060
Social security contributions (CANAM - ANICT / AR / PGT)	..	..	..	..	118	2	2	2	4	0
2410 On a payroll basis	..	..	..	..	..	..	..	..	..	..
2420 On an income tax basis	..	..	..	..	..	..	..	..	..	..
3000 Taxes on payroll and workforce	**2 470**	**4 671**	**8 381**	**6 278**	**11 567**	**11 938**	**14 737**	**5 724**	**12 197**	**14 882**
Fixed contribution	2 470	4 671	8 381	6 278	11 567	11 938	14 737	5 724	12 197	14 882
Counterpart of salaries paid / foreign mineral companies	0	0	0	0	0	0	0	0	0	0
4000 Taxes on property	**2 724**	**3 149**	**7 909**	**12 062**	**17 933**	**26 353**	**30 862**	**27 441**	**30 802**	**29 307**
4100 Recurrent taxes on immovable property	54	119	930	979	1 561	1 779	1 957	2 074	2 193	2 504
Property retention tax	54	119	930	979	1 549	1 764	1 914	2 025	2 144	2 474
Tax on private rentals	0	0	0	0	12	15	42	49	49	30
4110 Households	..	..	..	..	..	..	..	..	..	..
4120 Others	..	..	..	..	..	..	..	..	..	..
4200 Recurrent taxes on net wealth	0	0	0	0	0	0	0	0	0	0
4210 Individual	..	..	..	..	..	..	..	..	..	..
4220 Corporate	..	..	..	..	..	..	..	..	..	..
4300 Estate, inheritance and gift taxes	0	0	0	0	0	0	0	0	0	0
4310 Estate and inheritance taxes	..	..	..	..	..	..	..	..	..	..
4320 Gift taxes	..	..	..	..	..	..	..	..	..	..
4400 Taxes on financial and capital transactions	2 670	3 030	6 979	11 083	16 372	24 573	28 905	25 366	28 610	26 803
Registration fees (DGI)	2 600	2 934	3 414	6 928	11 023	16 754	13 027	12 158	14 018	11 382
Registration fees (DND)	0	0	3 055	4 107	5 321	7 499	15 583	13 174	14 544	15 411

Table 5.19. Mali – Details of tax revenue (continued)

Million XOF

	1995	2000	2005	2010	2015	2018	2019	2020	2021	2022
Transfer letter and land occupancy permit in land registry	70	96	510	0	0	0	0	0	0	0
Land occupancy fees	0	0	0	48	28	320	295	35	48	10
4500 Non-recurrent taxes	0	0	0	0	0	0	0	0	0	0
4510 On net wealth	..	..	..	..	..	..	..	..	..	..
4520 Other non-recurrent taxes	..	..	..	..	..	..	..	..	..	..
4600 Other recurrent taxes on property	0	0	0	0	0	0	0	0	0	0
5000 Taxes on goods and services	**73 710**	**172 271**	**328 545**	**451 942**	**689 931**	**728 932**	**989 465**	**927 742**	**1 123 085**	**981 871**
5100 Taxes on production, sale, transfer, etc	73 011	171 443	327 388	450 213	687 273	724 619	985 878	924 163	1 119 433	978 063
5110 General taxes	27 647	80 633	191 827	260 599	328 157	371 539	537 907	488 545	588 033	511 180
5111 Value added taxes	27 647	80 633	191 827	260 599	328 157	371 539	537 907	488 545	588 033	511 180
VAT on imports	13 863	46 622	119 548	161 656	210 431	268 881	316 487	328 676	401 303	309 147
VAT revenues (private sector)	9 332	31 218	67 629	95 383	113 512	100 982	220 473	159 346	186 359	197 202
VAT revenues (government)	4 452	2 793	4 650	3 560	4 214	1 677	947	522	371	4 831
5112 Sales tax	0	0	0	0	0	0	0	0	0	0
5113 Other	0	0	0	0	0	0	0	0	0	0
General Solidarity Contribution (Sustainable Development Fund - FDD)	0	0	0	0	0	0	0	0	0	0
5120 Taxes on specific goods and services	45 364	90 810	135 561	189 614	359 116	353 080	447 970	435 618	531 400	466 883
5121 Excises	23 257	45 791	42 725	56 909	136 898	103 676	118 607	127 286	81 985	126 260
Domestic taxes on petroleum products (TIPP)	9 133	33 694	26 389	25 660	93 264	48 611	43 626	55 127	20 814	35 805
Ad Valorem Tax (Mining Companies) (DNDC)	439	4 233	9 811	20 479	25 253	27 246	45 845	40 165	32 556	61 527
Local taxes on tobacco	981	816	3 285	5 385	8 264	14 405	13 420	14 571	12 794	6 915
Taxes on alcoholic beverages	867	1 169	1 317	1 777	3 611	4 750	6 037	4 430	2 256	1 135
Special tax on drinks	133	1 519	708	2 088	4 237	5 459	5 144	5 670	6 554	10 386
Tax on other products	11 704	4 360	1 215	1 520	2 269	3 205	4 535	7 325	7 011	10 492
5122 Profits of fiscal monopolies	0	0	0	0	0	0	0	0	0	0
5123 Customs and import duties	19 055	30 734	67 175	86 853	124 049	147 355	173 683	173 257	211 063	190 290
Customs duties	19 029	29 328	60 305	76 287	111 062	129 869	154 469	153 294	188 338	167 841
Statistical fees	0	315	6 485	9 702	12 940	16 939	19 148	19 924	22 707	22 194
Degressive compensatory tax (TDP)	0	6	373	831	0	0	0	0	0	0
Cyclical tax on imports	26	1 085	12	33	47	547	67	38	19	254
5124 Taxes on exports	102	4 046	9 922	20 503	30 243	33 887	53 055	42 532	124 889	55 719
Contribution pour prestation de service (CPS) on gold	102	4 046	9 922	20 503	30 243	33 887	53 055	42 532	50 722	55 719
Export tax on cotton (Fonds pour le développement durable - FDD)	0	0	0	0	0	0	0	0	74 167	0
5125 Taxes on investment goods	0	0	0	0	0	0	0	0	0	0
5126 Taxes on specific services	2 950	10 239	15 739	25 349	67 926	68 162	102 625	92 543	113 463	94 613
Taxes on financial activities	0	5 785	9 995	17 828	39 608	32 993	59 838	53 412	67 968	49 370
Gambling revenues from PMU and casinos	1 497	1 515	1 955	3 061	5 966	7 069	7 478	5 580	9 413	12 585
Taxes on road carriers	620	1 676	2 287	2 659	3 499	4 212	3 505	2 712	2 181	1 841
Taxes on insurance contracts	830	1 261	1 475	1 787	3 321	4 066	4 852	5 149	6 638	8 008
Other taxes on specified services	3	2	27	14	2	1	3	1	1	1
Tax on Access to the Telecom Network Open to the Public (TARTOP)	0	0	0	0	15 530	19 822	26 950	25 688	27 261	22 808
5127 Other taxes on internat. trade and transactions	0	0	0	0	0	0	0	0	0	0
5128 Other taxes	0	0	0	0	0	0	0	0	0	0
5130 Unallocable between 5110 and 5120	0	0	0	0	0	0	0	0	0	0
5200 Taxes on use of goods and to perform activities	699	828	1 157	1 729	2 658	4 313	3 588	3 579	3 652	3 808
5210 Recurrent taxes	699	828	1 157	1 729	2 658	4 313	3 588	3 579	3 652	3 808
5211 Paid by households: motor vehicles	583	716	1 140	1 715	2 658	3 389	3 588	3 579	3 652	3 808
Motor vehicle taxes	583	716	1 140	1 715	2 658	3 389	3 588	3 579	3 652	3 808
5212 Paid by others: motor vehicles	0	0	0	0	0	0	0	0	0	0
5213 Paid in respect of other goods	116	112	17	14	0	924	0	0	0	0
Forestry and wildlife licences	116	112	17	14	..	924	..	..	..	..
5220 Non-recurrent taxes	0	0	0	0	0	0	0	0	0	0
5300 Unallocable between 5100 and 5200	0	0	0	0	0	0	0	0	0	0
6000 Other taxes	**5 731**	**6 131**	**7 464**	**19 603**	**42 443**	**24 385**	**90 899**	**96 863**	**80 641**	**72 316**
Stamp fees (DGI)	4 839	4 188	6 172	10 797	16 840	17 702	20 027	19 492	22 112	19 569

Table 5.19. Mali – Details of tax revenue (continued)

Million XOF

	1995	2000	2005	2010	2015	2018	2019	2020	2021	2022
Stamp duties (DND)	0	0	911	143	235	406	550	509	579	553
Revenues from previous years	892	1 943	381	8 663	25 368	6 277	70 323	76 862	57 950	52 195
6100 Paid solely by business	..	..	..	..	..	..	..	..	..	..
6200 Other	..	..	..	..	..	..	..	..	..	..
Memo items:	..	..	..	..	..	..	..	..	..	..
Community collections (CP) (UEMOA tax)	1 978	1 394	0	0	0	0	0	0	0	0

.. Not available

Note: Year ending 31st December.

ANICT = "*Agence Nationale d'Investissement des Collectivités Territoriales*"; AR = "*Autorités Régionales*"; PGT = "*Paierie Générale du Trésor*". The data are on a cash basis.

Figures exclude tax revenues collected by sub-national governments as the data are not available.

Data on contributions from the *Caisse Malienne de Sécurité Sociale* (CMSS), the *Caisse Nationale d'Assurance Maladie* (CANAM), and the *Institut National de Prévoyance Sociale* (INPS) are only available from 2004, 2011, and 2006 respectively. These revenues are not included in Malian state revenues.

Heading 2400: This heading includes data from CANAM. Part of CANAM's revenues is collected by CMSS and INPS. These revenues do not form part of the revenues of CMSS or INPS.

Heading 5123: Revenues from ECOWAS (Economic Community of West African States), including statistical fees, the community levy, and the degressive protection tax, are not considered tax revenues or non-tax revenues of the government of Mali following the OECD *Interpretative Guide* (see § 4).

Heading 5126: Revenues from the "Tax on Access to the Public Telecommunications Network" (*TARTOP: Taxe sur Accès au Reseau de Télécom Ouvert au Public*) were included in non-tax revenues (Sales of goods and services) in previous editions.

Source: Ministry of Economy and Finance and the National Treasury and Public Accounting Directorate, Mali.

Table 5.20. Mauritania – Details of tax revenue

Million MRU

	1995	2000	2005	2010	2015	2018	2019	2020	2021	2022
Total tax revenue	..	..	..	**15 182**	**29 093**	**40 366**	**39 933**	**38 601**	**47 883**	**53 072**
1000 Taxes on income, profits and capital gains	..	..	..	**5 282**	**9 722**	**11 853**	**12 566**	**14 906**	**18 416**	**18 057**
1100 Of individuals	..	..	..	2 266	4 324	4 586	5 081	5 812	6 870	7 232
1110 On income and profits	..	..	..	2 266	4 324	4 586	5 081	5 812	6 870	7 232
Tax on wages and salaries	..	..	..	1 396	3 819	3 936	4 325	4 865	5 544	5 316
of which: ITS Pétrole	..	..	..	94	129	342	..	..	..	..
Capital gains tax	..	..	..	777	400	526	635	834	1 197	1 795
Property income tax	..	..	..	45	101	124	121	112	129	121
General income tax	..	..	..	48	4	0	0	0	0	0
1120 On capital gains	..	..	..	0	0	0	0	0	0	0
1200 Corporate	..	..	..	3 015	5 398	7 267	7 485	9 094	11 546	10 824
1210 On profits	..	..	..	3 015	5 398	7 267	7 485	9 094	11 546	10 824
Industrial and commercial profits (BIC), non-commercial profits (BNC) and flat-rate minimum tax (IMF)	..	..	..	1 400	3 400	3 398	3 759	3 909	4 677	5 222
of which: BIC Pétrole	..	..	..	144	43	296	..	..	..	..
Single tax on Société Nationale Industrielle et Minière (SNIM)	..	..	..	921	223	408	1 196	1 890	4 696	2 847
Flat-rate minimum tax (IMF)- customs	..	..	..	695	1 452	1 850	1 946	1 504	1 633	2 262
Simplified taxation system	..	..	..	0	323	1 610	585	1 792	540	494
1220 On capital gains of corporates	..	..	..	0	0	0	0	0	0	0
1300 Unallocable between 1100 and 1200	..	..	..	0	0	0	0	0	0	0
2000 Social security contributions	..	..	..	**1 026**	**1 818**	**2 061**	**2 015**	**2 100**	..	**2 250**
2100 Employees	..	..	..	..	..	..	..	..	..	..
2110 On a payroll basis	..	..	..	..	..	..	..	..	..	..
2120 On an income tax basis	..	..	..	..	..	..	..	..	..	..
2200 Employers	..	..	..	..	..	..	..	..	..	..
2210 On a payroll basis	..	..	..	..	..	..	..	..	..	..
2220 On an income tax basis	..	..	..	..	..	..	..	..	..	..
2300 Self-employed or non-employed	..	..	..	..	..	..	..	..	..	..
2310 On a payroll basis	..	..	..	..	..	..	..	..	..	..
2320 On an income tax basis	..	..	..	..	..	..	..	..	..	..
2400 Unallocable between 2100, 2200 and 2300	..	..	..	1 026	1 818	2 061	2 015	2 100	2 160	2 250
CNSS contributions	..	..	..	424	592	650	686	707	730	750
CNAM contributions	..	..	..	602	1 227	1 411	1 329	1 393	1 430	1 500
2410 On a payroll basis	..	..	..	..	..	..	..	..	..	..
2420 On an income tax basis	..	..	..	..	..	..	..	..	..	..
3000 Taxes on payroll and workforce	..	..	..	**32**	**48**	**41**	**50**	**45**	**51**	**53**
4000 Taxes on property	..	..	..	**646**	**1 387**	**1 172**	**45**	**58**	**76**	**44**
4100 Recurrent taxes on immovable property	..	..	..	622	1 346	1 113	..	..	..	..
4110 Households	..	..	..	..	..	..	..	..	..	..
4120 Others	..	..	..	..	..	..	..	..	..	..
4200 Recurrent taxes on net wealth	..	..	..	0	0	0	0	0	0	0
4210 Individual	..	..	..	..	..	..	..	..	..	..
4220 Corporate	..	..	..	..	..	..	..	..	..	..
4300 Estate, inheritance and gift taxes	..	..	..	0	0	0	0	0	0	0
4310 Estate and inheritance taxes	..	..	..	..	..	..	..	..	..	..
4320 Gift taxes	..	..	..	..	..	..	..	..	..	..
4400 Taxes on financial and capital transactions	..	..	..	25	41	59	45	58	76	44
Land conservation rights	..	..	..	25	41	59	45	58	76	44
4500 Other non-reccurrent taxes on property	..	..	..	0	0	0	0	0	0	0
4510 On net wealth	..	..	..	..	..	..	..	..	..	..
4520 Other non-recurrent taxes	..	..	..	..	..	..	..	..	..	..
4600 Other recurrent taxes on property	..	..	..	0	0	0	0	0	0	0
5000 Taxes on goods and services	..	..	..	**8 196**	**16 118**	**25 240**	**25 257**	**21 472**	**27 121**	**32 319**
5100 Taxes on production, sale, transfer, etc	..	..	..	7 983	15 785	23 826	23 925	20 160	25 740	31 012
5110 General taxes on goods and services	..	..	..	5 069	9 454	12 605	12 951	10 014	12 918	14 631
5111 Value added taxes	..	..	..	5 069	9 454	12 605	12 951	10 014	12 918	14 631
Domestic VAT revenue	..	..	..	1 290	3 500	3 643	3 937	3 339	3 883	3 187
Import VAT receipts	..	..	..	3 779	5 954	8 963	9 014	6 675	9 034	11 444

Table 5.20. Mauritania – Details of tax revenue (continued)

Million MRU

	1995	2000	2005	2010	2015	2018	2019	2020	2021	2022
5112 Sales tax	..	..	..	0	0	0	0	0	0	0
5113 Other	..	..	..	0	0	0	0	0	0	0
5120 Taxes on specific goods and services	..	..	..	2 915	6 330	11 220	10 974	10 146	12 822	16 381
5121 Excises	..	..	..	188	586	1 256	1 027	983	1 024	1 112
5122 Profits of fiscal monopolies	..	..	..	0	0	0	0	0	0	0
5123 Customs and import duties	..	..	..	2 463	5 145	9 250	9 150	8 363	10 960	14 246
Import tax duty	..	..	..	1 631	3 313	5 502	5 381	4 827	6 696	8 626
Tax on petroleum products	..	..	..	494	1 042	2 277	2 369	2 103	2 294	2 565
Consumption taxes	..	..	..	0	0	0	0	528	695	..
Statistical tax	..	..	..	319	553	810	808	648	934	1 213
Tax for the promotion of culture and sport	..	..	..	0	199	266	264	229	305	397
Other import duties and charges	..	..	..	20	39	395	328	29	35	1 445
5124 Taxes on exports	..	..	..	0	0	0	0	1	0	0
5125 Taxes on investment goods	..	..	..	0	0	0	0	0	0	0
5126 Taxes on specific services	..	..	..	264	599	714	798	799	839	1 023
Tax on financial transactions	..	..	..	208	538	642	722	749	748	898
Airport and foreign destination tax	..	..	..	56	61	72	76	33	75	125
Consumption tax on scratch cards (TCG)	..	..	..	0	0	0	0	17	15	..
5127 Other taxes on internat. trade and transactions	..	..	..	0	0	0	0	0	0	0
5128 Other taxes	..	..	..	0	0	0	0	0	0	0
5130 Unallocable between 5110 and 5120	..	..	..	0	0	0	0	0	0	0
5200 Taxes on use of goods and to perform activities	..	..	..	213	333	1 414	1 332	1 312	1 381	1 307
5210 Recurrent taxes	..	..	..	213	333	1 414	1 332	1 312	1 381	1 307
5211 Paid by households: motor vehicles	..	..	..	153	236	235	231	205	225	196
5212 Paid by others: motor vehicles	..	..	..	0	0	0	0	110	178	0
5213 Paid in respect of other goods	..	..	..	60	97	1 179	1 102	997	979	1 111
Patent	..	..	..	0	76	80	75	73	83	78
Fishing duty	..	..	..	60	21	1 098	1 027	600	369	1 033
Exploitation royalties (RE)	..	..	..	..	..	..	..	324	527	..
5220 Non-recurrent taxes	..	..	..	0	0	0	0	0	0	0
5300 Unallocable between 5100 and 5200	..	..	..	0	0	0	0	0	0	0
6000 Other taxes	**..**	**..**	**..**	**0**	**0**	**0**	**0**	**20**	**59**	**349**
6100 Paid solely by business	..	..	..	..	..	..	..	..	..	..
6200 Other	..	..	..	..	..	..	..	..	..	..
Memo Items	..	..	..	..	..	..	..	..	..	..
ECOWAS community levy	..	..	..	..	..	..	..	*283*	*320*	..

.. Not available

Note: Year ending 31st December.

The data are on a cash basis.

Heading 2400: Social security contributions have been estimated for 2021 and 2022 by applying a five-year average growth rate to the 2020 data.

Heading 4100: This heading includes municipal revenues. These revenues come from the various communal taxes and municipal levies, which include in particular the property tax on developed property, the property tax on agricultural land used for crops, the council tax, the community contribution, the patent tax, the communal tax and public domain occupation fees and royalties. It has not been possible to identify each of these revenues separately so all of them are reported under this heading, given that the majority are derived from taxes on property. These revenues are not included from 2019 onwards.

Heading 4400: This heading includes revenues from land conservation fees. They are included in tax revenues following the OECD classification of taxes (see the *Interpretative Guide* in Annex A) but are included in non-tax revenues in Mauritania.

Heading 5121: This heading includes revenues from the scratch card tax for the years 2007-2019 and 2022.

Heading 5213: Revenues from operating royalties are included in revenues from fishing rights for the years 2007-2019 and 2022.

Source: Ministry of Finance, Mauritania.

Table 5.21. Mauritius – Details of tax revenue

Million MUR

	1995	2000	2005	2010	2015	2018	2019	2020	2021	2022
Total tax revenue	**12 262**	**22 146**	**34 828**	**58 404**	**79 225**	**95 752**	**103 385**	**97 275**	**92 675**	**117 028**
1000 Taxes on income, profits and capital gains	**1 804**	**2 881**	**5 829**	**15 005**	**19 793**	**24 325**	**27 810**	**27 940**	**27 562**	**34 959**
1100 Of individuals	863	1 540	2 553	4 583	7 614	9 527	10 453	11 221	11 450	13 944
1110 On income and profits	..	..	..	..	..	..	..	..	..	..
1120 On capital gains	..	..	..	..	..	..	..	..	..	..
1200 Corporate	941	1 341	3 276	9 457	10 993	13 407	15 648	15 000	14 306	18 842
1210 On profits	941	1 341	3 276	9 457	10 993	13 407	15 648	15 000	14 306	18 842
Income tax - Companies and corporate bodies	..	..	..	8 428	9 788	12 403	14 556	13 876	11 760	16 446
Special levy on banks	..	..	..	455	748	846	934	939	950	1 028
Solidarity levy on telecommunication companies	..	..	..	424	331	158	158	185	157	148
Corporate social responsibility	..	..	..	150	126	0	0	0	0	0
Special contribution from hotels	..	..	..	0	0	0	0	0	0	0
COVID-19 Levy	..	..	..	0	0	0	0	0	1 439	1 219
1220 On capital gains of corporates	..	..	..	..	..	..	..	..	..	..
1300 Unallocable between 1100 and 1200	..	..	..	965	1 186	1 392	1 709	1 720	1 806	2 173
Tax deduction at source	..	..	..	965	1 186	1 392	1 709	1 720	1 806	2 173
2000 Social security contributions	**689**	**986**	**1 314**	**2 113**	**3 252**	**3 630**	**4 239**	**4 560**	**6 026**	**8 348**
2100 Employees	230	329	438	704	1 084	1 210	1 413	1 520	1 541	2 270
2110 On a payroll basis	230	329	438	704	1 084	1 210	1 413	1 520	1 541	2 270
Contributions by employees to National Pension fund (NPF)	230	329	438	704	1 084	1 210	1 413	1 520	260	0
Contribution Sociale Généralisée (CSG) - private sector employees	0	0	0	0	0	0	0	0	1 281	2 008
Contribution Sociale Généralisée (CSG) - public sector employees	0	0	0	0	0	0	0	0	0	262
2120 On an income tax basis	0	0	0	0	0	0	0	0	0	0
2200 Employers	459	657	876	1 408	2 168	2 420	2 826	3 040	4 482	5 991
2210 On a payroll basis	459	657	876	1 408	2 168	2 420	2 826	3 040	4 482	5 991
Contributions by employers to National Pension fund (NPF)	459	657	876	1 408	2 168	2 420	2 826	3 040	519	0
Contribution Sociale Généralisée (CSG) - private sector employers	0	0	0	0	0	0	0	0	2 562	4 061
Contribution Sociale Généralisée (CSG) - public sector employers	0	0	0	0	0	0	0	0	1 400	1 930
2220 On an income tax basis	0	0	0	0	0	0	0	0	0	0
2300 Self-employed or non-employed	0	0	0	0	0	0	0	0	3	87
2310 On a payroll basis	..	..	..	..	..	..	..	..	3	87
Contribution Sociale Généralisée (CSG) - self - employed	..	..	..	..	..	..	..	..	3	87
2320 On an income tax basis	..	..	..	..	..	..	..	..	0	0
2400 Unallocable between 2100, 2200 and 2300	0	0	0	0	0	0	0	0	0	0
2410 On a payroll basis	..	..	..	..	..	..	..	..	..	..
2420 On an income tax basis	..	..	..	..	..	..	..	..	..	..
3000 Taxes on payroll and workforce	**77**	**140**	**204**	**176**	**474**	**549**	**777**	**798**	**409**	**860**
Extra-budgetary taxes on payroll and workforce	77	140	204	176	474	549	777	798	409	860
4000 Taxes on property	**945**	**1 411**	**1 920**	**3 328**	**4 095**	**4 711**	**4 706**	**4 084**	**4 538**	**5 847**
4100 Recurrent taxes on immovable property	135	205	240	417	146	306	294	321	296	305
4110 Households	0	0	0	0	0	0	0	0	0	0
4120 Others	135	205	240	417	146	306	294	321	296	305
Local taxes on immovable property	135	205	240	410	143	299	288	313	293	302
Campement taxes	..	..	..	6	3	7	6	8	3	3
4200 Recurrent taxes on net wealth	0	0	0	0	0	0	0	0	0	0
4210 Individual	..	..	..	..	..	..	..	..	..	..
4220 Corporate	..	..	..	..	..	..	..	..	..	..
4300 Estate, inheritance and gift taxes	0	0	0	0	0	0	0	0	0	0
4310 Estate and inheritance taxes	..	..	..	..	..	..	..	..	..	..
4320 Gift taxes	..	..	..	..	..	..	..	..	..	..
4400 Taxes on financial and capital transactions	809	1 206	1 680	2 902	3 907	4 385	4 376	3 754	4 216	5 496
Land transfer tax	..	..	409	1 190	1 650	1 971	1 964	1 693	1 939	2 640
Registration duty on transfer of immovable property	..	..	562	1 180	1 708	1 884	1 859	1 619	1 780	2 296

Table 5.21. Mauritius – Details of tax revenue (continued)

Million MUR

	1995	2000	2005	2010	2015	2018	2019	2020	2021	2022
Tax on transfer of leasehold rights in state lands	..	..	0	175	157	168	164	144	128	191
Registration duty on transfer of shares	..	..	0	84	122	50	53	25	56	63
Registration duty on fixed and floating charges	..	..	116	180	157	204	220	181	211	306
Stamp duties	..	..	14	75	112	109	115	91	102	0
Registration duty on loans	..	..	0	9	0	0	0	0	0	0
Mortgages, inscriptions and transcriptions	..	..	10	11	0	0	0	0	0	0
Other taxes on financial and capital transactions	..	..	568	0	0	0	0	0	0	0
4500 Other non-reccurrent taxes on property	0	0	0	10	42	20	36	10	27	46
4510 On net wealth	..	..	..	0	0	0	0	0	0	0
4520 Other non-recurrent taxes	..	..	..	10	42	20	36	10	27	46
4600 Other recurrent taxes on property	0	0	0	0	0	0	0	0	0	0
5000 Taxes on goods and services	**8 617**	**16 514**	**25 300**	**37 618**	**51 422**	**62 410**	**65 719**	**59 781**	**54 017**	**66 832**
5100 Taxes on production, sale, transfer, etc	8 499	16 312	23 445	34 755	47 254	58 041	61 018	55 784	50 151	62 488
5110 General taxes on goods and services	64	5 604	12 529	21 094	28 036	32 989	34 941	32 658	28 490	38 273
5111 Value added taxes	0	5 604	12 529	21 094	28 036	32 989	34 941	32 658	28 490	38 273
VAT revenues (gross)	..	..	..	26 590	33 302	39 176	41 948	39 061	35 716	46 949
VAT refunds	..	..	..	- 5 495	- 5 267	- 6 187	- 7 007	- 6 403	- 7 226	- 8 676
5112 Sales tax	64	0	0	0	0	0	0	0	0	0
5113 Other	0	0	0	0	0	0	0	0	0	0
Extra-budgetary taxes on goods and services	..	..	..	..	..	..	..	..	..	..
Local taxes on goods and services	..	..	..	..	..	..	..	..	..	..
5120 Taxes on specific goods and services	8 435	10 707	10 916	13 660	19 218	25 052	26 077	23 125	21 660	24 215
Unallocated budgetary taxes on goods and services	..	..	3 279	0	0	0	0	0	0	0
5121 Excises	..	..	2 840	9 331	14 834	20 109	20 871	18 925	18 680	20 144
Spirits, liquors and alcoholic beverages	..	..	1 220	2 351	4 448	5 349	5 221	5 307	5 068	5 691
Tobacco products	..	..	1 617	2 371	3 851	5 333	5 233	5 620	5 845	6 346
Motor vehicles and motor cycles	..	..	0	1 928	2 471	3 384	3 756	3 120	2 636	2 510
Petroleum products (including MID Levy)	..	..	0	2 421	3 292	5 141	5 700	3 938	3 859	4 287
PET bottles and other plastic products	..	..	0	159	250	252	270	273	236	228
Sugar content of soft drinks	..	..	0	0	344	404	445	428	813	792
Energy inefficient products	..	..	0	0	3	4	4	19	12	29
Sugar brokerage	..	..	1	0	0	0	0	0	0	0
Extra-budgetary excise taxes	..	..	0	0	0	0	0	0	0	0
Other excises	..	..	1	101	175	241	242	219	210	262
5122 Profits of fiscal monopolies	..	..	0	0	0	0	0	0	0	0
5123 Customs and import duties	..	..	3 899	1 525	1 302	1 344	1 379	1 216	1 180	1 528
5124 Taxes on exports	..	..	0	0	0	0	0	0	0	0
5125 Taxes on investment goods	..	..	0	0	0	0	0	0	0	0
5126 Taxes on specific services	..	..	898	2 731	3 083	3 599	3 827	2 984	1 800	2 543
Taxes on the national lottery and other lotteries	..	..	14	693	436	221	309	285	275	310
Betting taxes on horse racing, football, etc.	..	..	269	658	837	971	1 047	740	928	1 012
Gaming taxes on casinos and gaming houses	..	..	614	818	591	778	797	695	571	608
Passenger fee on air tickets	..	..	0	561	1 173	1 630	1 673	1 264	26	613
Levy on messaging services	..	..	0	0	46	0	0	0	0	0
Hotel and restaurant tax	..	..	0	0	0	0	0	0	0	0
5127 Other taxes on internat. trade and transactions	..	..	0	0	0	0	0	0	0	0
5128 Other taxes	..	..	0	73	0	0	0	0	0	0
Temporary solidarity tax on hotels	..	..	..	0	..	..	..	..	..	..
Local government taxes on goods and services	..	..	..	73	..	..	..	..	..	..
5130 Unallocable between 5110 and 5120	..	..	0	0	0	0	0	0	0	0
5200 Taxes on use of goods and to perform activities	118	203	1 750	2 765	4 168	4 369	4 701	3 998	3 867	4 344
5210 Recurrent taxes	118	203	1 287	1 934	2 702	2 922	3 019	2 770	2 513	2 963
5211 Paid by households: motor vehicles	0	0	652	1 117	1 362	1 526	1 604	1 587	1 704	1 802
5212 Paid by others: motor vehicles	0	0	0	0	0	0	0	0	0	0
5213 Paid in respect of other goods	118	203	635	816	1 341	1 396	1 415	1 183	808	1 161
Company licences	..	..	103	148	306	200	200	203	213	217

Table 5.21. Mauritius – Details of tax revenue (continued)

Million MUR

	1995	2000	2005	2010	2015	2018	2019	2020	2021	2022
Incorporation and lodging fees, search duty, etc.	..	..	5	9	18	14	13	12	10	12
Tourist enterprise licences	..	..	33	74	91	104	112	73	24	49
Gambling licences	..	..	48	100	368	465	439	344	305	286
Liquor licences	..	..	10	10	25	23	23	22	22	22
Freeport licences	..	..	0	0	6	7	1	9	5	5
Pharmacy licences	..	..	0	1	2	1	1	1	1	2
Fishing vessel licences	..	..	38	52	43	63	82	85	23	92
Registration of factories	..	..	2	2	3	3	3	2	2	2
Registration of associations	..	..	1	2	1	1	1	1	1	0
Recruitment licences	..	..	0	2	0	0	0	0	0	0
Environment protection fee	..	..	132	141	391	400	424	330	89	326
Advertising structure fee	..	..	0	0	63	52	58	44	46	35
Regional taxes on permission to use goods	..	..	2	2	2	3	0	3	3	3
Local taxes on permission to use goods	118	203	244	255	0	21	21	18	30	28
Other recurrent taxes on goods and activities	..	..	16	20	23	39	36	34	34	81
5220 Non-recurrent taxes	0	0	463	832	1 466	1 447	1 682	1 228	1 354	1 381
Processing fee on acquisitions schemes	..	..	0	0	4	5	1	7	7	4
Registration duty on transfer of motor vehicles	..	..	463	794	1 277	1 378	1 462	1 175	1 322	1 347
Land conversion tax	..	..	0	38	185	64	219	45	25	30
5300 Unallocable between 5100 and 5200	0	0	105	98	0	0	0	0	0	0
Extra-budgetary taxes on goods and services	..	..	105	98	..	..	..	..	..	..
6000 Other taxes	**130**	**215**	**260**	**164**	**188**	**126**	**134**	**112**	**122**	**181**
Mauritius Revenue Authority penalties	0	0	0	0	74	24	36	31	23	30
Unidentified local government taxes	0	0	0	0	0	0	0	0	0	0
Unidentified taxes	130	215	260	164	114	102	98	80	99	150
6100 Paid solely by business	..	..	..	..	..	..	..	..	..	..
6200 Other	..	..	..	..	..	..	..	..	..	..

.. Not available

Note: Data for 2016 onwards and for years prior to 2010 are on a fiscal year basis beginning 1st July. For example, the data for 2009 represent July 2008 to June 2009 and 2022 represents July 2021 to June 2022. The data for years 2010-15 are on a calendar year (January-December) basis. Mauritius budget statements cover January-June 2015 and July 2015 to June 2016, but neither the fiscal nor the calendar year for 2015. Figures for 2015 are therefore estimated using quarterly revenue figures at the aggregate level and fiscal year revenue data.

Data are reported on a cash basis.

Data for the central government budgetary tax prior to 2007 and all extra-budgetary, regional and local data were classified according to the IMF *Government Finance Statistics Manual*. The 1986 manual was used for data up to 2009 and the 2001 manual for data up to 2009 onwards. Data from 2007 onwards are classified under the OECD classification, as set out in the *Interpretative Guide* in Annex A.

Heading 2000: revenues under this heading refer to revenues reported as contributions to the National Pension Fund (NPF) in the *Digest of Social Security Statistics*. Employer contributions and employee contributions are calculated by taking respectively one third and two thirds of total NPF contributions since employer contributions rates are set at twice those of employees. Contributions to the National Savings Fund (NSF) are not included in *Revenue Statistics in Africa*, since they do not meet the definition of social security contributions. In 2020, the *Contribution Sociale Généralisée* was introduced by the Finance (Miscellaneous Provisions) Act 2020, which replaced the National Pensions Fund (NPF) beginning in September 2020. The NPF contributions for 2020/21 therefore consist only of the amount received for July and August.

Heading 3000: revenues under this heading include revenues collected by the Ministry of Social Services under the Training Levy.

Heading 1210: The solidarity levy on telecommunications companies, the corporate social responsibility tax and the special contribution from hotels are classified as "other taxes" by the Mauritius Revenue Authority.

Heading 5213: The Environment protection fee and advertising structure fee are classified as other taxes by the Mauritius Revenue Authority.

Heading 5220: Includes the registration duty on transfer of motor vehicles and the land conversion tax that are classified as taxes on property by the Mauritius Revenue Authority.

Source: Mauritius Revenue Authority for the central government budgetary tax data from 2007 to 2014. Statistics Mauritius for extra-budgetary, local government, regional government and social security revenues from 1990 to 2022, as well as for budgetary central government tax revenues up to 2006; Ministry of Finance budget estimates for detailed revenue figures for the periods July 2005-June 2008, for 2016-22, and for the figures used to estimate calendar year 2015 revenues.

Table 5.22. Morocco – Details of tax revenue

Million MAD

	1995	2000	2005	2010	2015	2018	2019	2020	2021	2022
Total tax revenue	**..**	**90 900**	**137 440**	**216 769**	**265 069**	**313 217**	**327 338**	**314 334**	**347 401**	**397 942**
1000 Taxes on income, profits and capital gains	**..**	**23 656**	**42 613**	**62 646**	**78 952**	**96 026**	**98 276**	**95 427**	**98 265**	**122 588**
1100 Of individuals	..	14 540	23 661	26 598	37 214	43 889	44 353	42 206	47 905	50 855
1110 On income and profits	..	12 473	21 009	22 391	32 797	43 462	42 823	41 568	47 416	49 957
Salaries	..	10 829	18 830	19 409	28 277	32 561	32 865	32 516	35 317	39 247
Professional income	..	1 645	2 179	2 982	4 519	6 374	6 112	5 251	5 627	4 932
Other personal income taxes	..	0	0	0	0	4 527	3 846	3 801	6 472	5 777
1120 On capital gains	..	2 067	2 653	4 207	4 417	427	1 530	637	489	898
1200 Corporate	..	9 116	18 952	36 049	41 738	52 137	53 924	53 221	50 361	71 733
1210 On profits	..	8 330	16 962	31 164	32 693	52 130	53 920	53 221	50 354	71 726
Profits	..	8 084	16 494	29 381	30 553	49 529	51 396	50 971	47 912	69 015
Gross profits distributed to foreign companies	..	246	468	1 783	2 140	2 601	2 524	2 250	2 442	2 712
1220 On capital gains of corporates	..	786	1 990	4 884	9 045	7	4	0	6	7
1300 Unallocable between 1100 and 1200	..	0	0	0	0	0	0	0	0	0
2000 Social security contributions	**..**	**9 982**	**22 983**	**37 924**	**52 418**	**65 143**	**73 616**	**77 978**	**82 188**	**89 572**
2100 Employees	..	2 803	8 313	13 208	17 730	22 401	24 847	25 799	27 807	29 453
2110 On a payroll basis	..	..	..	..	..	..	..	..	..	..
2120 On an income tax basis	..	..	..	..	..	..	..	..	..	..
2200 Employers	..	7 179	14 644	24 524	34 385	42 310	48 265	51 630	53 691	59 524
2210 On a payroll basis	..	..	..	..	..	..	..	..	..	..
2220 On an income tax basis	..	..	..	..	..	..	..	..	..	..
2300 Self-employed or non-employed	..	0	0	0	0	0	0	0	0	0
2310 On a payroll basis	..	..	..	..	..	..	..	..	..	..
2320 On an income tax basis	..	..	..	..	..	..	..	..	..	..
2400 Unallocable between 2100, 2200 and 2300	..	0	25	192	302	432	505	549	690	594
2410 On a payroll basis	..	..	..	..	..	..	..	..	..	..
2420 On an income tax basis	..	..	..	..	..	..	..	..	..	..
3000 Taxes on payroll and workforce	**..**	**0**	**0**	**0**	**0**	**0**	**0**	**0**	**0**	**0**
4000 Taxes on property	**..**	**5 405**	**8 403**	**12 702**	**19 536**	**16 679**	**16 536**	**13 445**	**18 590**	**19 843**
4100 Recurrent taxes on immovable property	..	3 340	4 415	5 740	6 859	7 947	8 182	7 487	9 713	9 233
4110 Households	..	1 989	2 866	3 898	4 414	5 143	5 324	4 855	6 325	6 014
Housing tax	..	517	696	382	364	402	443	292	412	378
Tax on undeveloped land	..	135	236	839	1 113	1 439	1 577	1 342	1 817	1 719
Communal services tax	..	1 337	1 934	2 677	2 937	3 302	3 304	3 221	4 096	3 917
4120 Others	..	1 351	1 549	1 842	2 445	2 804	2 858	2 632	3 388	3 219
4200 Recurrent taxes on net wealth	..	0	0	0	0	0	0	0	0	0
4210 Individual	..	..	..	..	..	..	..	..	..	..
4220 Corporate	..	..	..	..	..	..	..	..	..	..
4300 Estate, inheritance and gift taxes	..	0	0	0	0	0	0	0	0	0
4310 Estate and inheritance taxes	..	..	..	..	..	..	..	..	..	..
4320 Gift taxes	..	..	..	..	..	..	..	..	..	..
4400 Taxes on financial and capital transactions	..	2 065	3 988	6 962	12 677	8 732	8 354	5 958	8 877	10 610
4500 Other non-reccurrent taxes on property	..	0	0	0	0	0	0	0	0	0
4510 On net wealth	..	..	..	..	..	..	..	..	..	..
4520 Other non-recurrent taxes	..	..	..	..	..	..	..	..	..	..
4600 Other recurrent taxes on property	..	0	0	0	0	0	0	0	0	0
5000 Taxes on goods and services	**..**	**50 655**	**62 100**	**101 384**	**111 766**	**134 189**	**137 937**	**126 572**	**147 284**	**164 796**
5100 Taxes on production, sale, transfer, etc	..	49 539	60 701	99 056	108 848	128 153	131 538	120 742	140 511	157 772
5110 General taxes on goods and services	..	21 476	32 607	65 247	75 271	86 024	87 396	79 781	93 043	106 826
5111 Value added taxes	..	21 476	32 607	65 247	75 271	86 024	87 396	79 781	93 043	106 826
5112 Sales tax	..	0	0	0	0	0	0	0	0	0
5113 Other	..	0	0	0	0	0	0	0	0	0
5120 Taxes on specific goods and services	..	28 063	28 094	33 809	33 577	42 128	44 142	40 961	47 468	50 945
5121 Excises	..	15 223	15 631	21 382	25 661	28 674	30 276	27 633	31 235	31 994
Domestic excises	..	15 183	15 544	21 132	25 366	28 318	29 900	27 390	30 960	31 605
Tax on the sale of forestry products	..	4	18	26	29	8	- 3	4	10	20
Tax on the sale of beverages	..	23	37	143	162	203	221	117	126	199
Tax on mineral and drinking water	..	13	31	81	104	145	157	122	139	170
5122 Profits of fiscal monopolies	..	0	0	0	0	0	0	0	0	0

Table 5.22. Morocco – Details of tax revenue (continued)

Million MAD

	1995	2000	2005	2010	2015	2018	2019	2020	2021	2022
5123 Customs and import duties	..	12 810	12 386	12 242	7 715	9 693	9 768	9 488	11 885	13 895
5124 Taxes on exports	..	0	0	0	0	0	0	0	0	0
5125 Taxes on investment goods	..	0	0	0	0	0	0	0	0	0
5126 Taxes on specific services	..	30	77	184	201	3 762	4 098	3 840	4 348	5 056
Tax on visitors	..	26	67	160	173	228	258	109	82	164
Tax on public passenger transport	..	4	10	24	28	35	38	23	30	32
Stamp duty on screen advertising	..	0	0	0	0	3 499	3 803	3 708	4 236	4 860
5127 Other taxes on internat. trade and transactions	..	0	0	0	0	0	0	0	0	0
5128 Other taxes	..	0	0	0	0	0	0	0	0	0
5130 Unallocable between 5110 and 5120	..	0	0	0	0	0	0	0	0	0
5200 Taxes on use of goods and to perform activities	..	1 116	1 398	2 328	2 918	6 036	6 399	5 830	6 773	7 024
5210 Recurrent taxes	..	964	1 134	1 385	1 955	3 158	3 459	3 470	3 756	4 009
5211 Paid by households: motor vehicles	..	959	1 119	1 351	1 920	2 570	2 846	2 805	3 047	3 244
5212 Paid by others: motor vehicles	..	0	0	0	0	556	583	629	669	722
5213 Paid in respect of other goods	..	5	15	33	35	32	29	36	40	43
Tax on hunting licences	..	5	15	33	35	32	29	36	40	43
5220 Non-recurrent taxes	..	152	265	943	963	2 878	2 941	2 359	3 017	3 016
Tax on building operations	..	113	230	703	709	723	730	618	829	793
Tax on subdivision operations	..	39	35	240	254	285	313	215	229	258
Other	..	0	0	0	0	1 870	1 898	1 526	1 959	1 965
5300 Unallocable between 5100 and 5200	..	0	0	0	0	0	0	0	0	0
6000 Other taxes	**..**	**1 201**	**1 341**	**2 112**	**2 398**	**1 179**	**972**	**912**	**1 074**	**1 143**
Stamp duties	..	1 132	1 260	1 683	2 092	965	801	733	868	910
Local taxes	..	69	81	429	306	214	171	179	206	233
6100 Paid solely by business	..	..	..	..	..	..	..	..	..	..
6200 Other	..	..	..	..	..	..	..	..	..	..

.. Not available

Note: Year ending 31st December.

The data are on a cash basis.

The data include taxes allocated to the Special Treasury Accounts (*Fonds Spéciaux du Trésor*).

Heading 2000: Data for social security contributions are estimated for the years 2000 and 2001. Revenues from tax surcharges and penalties are considered as non-tax revenues following the OECD classification of taxes (see the *Interpretative Guide* in Annexes A and B). Under Morocco's national classification they are included in tax revenues.

Source: Ministry of Economy and Finance, Morocco.

Table 5.23. Mozambique – Details of tax revenue

Million MZN

	1995	2000	2005	2010	2015	2018	2019	2020	2021	2022
Total tax revenue	..	..	..	**101 153**	**205 303**	**191 986**	**203 808**	**204 456**	**239 979**	**256 651**
1000 Taxes on income, profits and capital gains	..	..	..	**18 430**	**57 810**	**90 910**	**90 534**	**100 018**	**109 469**	**128 992**
1100 Of individuals	..	..	..	8 631	21 311	33 151	37 328	40 995	44 836	50 911
1110 On income and profits	..	..	..	8 631	21 311	33 151	37 328	40 995	44 836	50 911
Employees and others - *Imposto Rendimento de Pessoas Singulares* (IRPS)	..	..	..	7 888	20 056	31 550	35 579	39 318	43 275	49 435
Business and professional income - IRPS	..	..	..	741	1 255	1 600	1 749	1 676	1 557	1 473
Withholding tax - IRPS	..	..	..	0	0	0	1	1	4	3
Labor Income Tax Section A	..	..	..	1	0	0	0	0	0	0
Complementary tax	..	..	..	0	0	0	0	0	0	0
1120 On capital gains	..	..	..	0	0	0	0	0	0	0
1200 Corporate	..	..	..	9 799	36 498	57 759	53 206	59 023	64 633	78 081
1210 On profits	..	..	..	9 799	36 498	57 759	53 206	59 023	64 633	78 081
Corporate income tax - *Imposto sobre o Rendimento das Pessoas* Colectivas (IRPC)	..	..	..	9 467	36 092	45 067	43 218	46 838	50 881	64 730
Final settlement -IRPC	..	..	..	0	0	11 813	9 216	11 369	12 657	12 298
Withholding tax - free zones	..	..	..	327	406	874	764	811	1 089	1 046
Withholding tax - IRPC	..	..	..	0	0	6	8	5	6	8
Industrial contribution groups A ans B	..	..	..	5	0	0	0	0	0	0
1220 On capital gains of corporates	..	..	..	0	0	0	0	0	0	0
1300 Unallocable between 1100 and 1200	..	..	..	0	0	0	0	0	0	0
2000 Social security contributions	..	..	..	**1 161**	**3 445**	**539**	**518**	**1 549**	**941**	**1 776**
2100 Employees	..	..	..	..	..	..	..	..	..	..
2110 On a payroll basis	..	..	..	..	..	..	..	..	..	..
2120 On an income tax basis	..	..	..	..	..	..	..	..	..	..
2200 Employers	..	..	..	..	..	..	..	..	..	..
2210 On a payroll basis	..	..	..	..	..	..	..	..	..	..
Public sector employer contribution	..	..	..	..	..	..	..	..	..	..
2220 On an income tax basis	..	..	..	..	..	..	..	..	..	..
2300 Self-employed or non-employed	..	..	..	..	..	..	..	..	..	..
2310 On a payroll basis	..	..	..	..	..	..	..	..	..	..
2320 On an income tax basis	..	..	..	..	..	..	..	..	..	..
2400 Unallocable between 2100, 2200 and 2300	..	..	..	1 161	3 445	539	518	1 549	941	1 776
Retirement compensation and survivor's pension	..	..	..	1 161	3 445	0	0	0	0	0
Other public sector social contributions	..	..	..	0	0	256	200	1 118	208	1 241
Funeral allowance	..	..	..	0	0	216	241	312	338	428
State employee contributions	..	..	..	0	0	67	76	119	396	107
2410 On a payroll basis	..	..	..	..	..	..	..	..	..	..
2420 On an income tax basis	..	..	..	..	..	..	..	..	..	..
3000 Taxes on payroll and workforce	..	..	..	**0**	**0**	**0**	**0**	**0**	**0**	**0**
4000 Taxes on property	..	..	..	**599**	**1 401**	**3 119**	**2 666**	**4 088**	**6 674**	**3 048**
4100 Recurrent taxes on immovable property	..	..	..	0	1	0	0	0	0	0
4110 Households	..	..	..	0	1	..	..	..	..	..
Property tax	..	..	..	0	1	..	..	..	..	..
4120 Others	..	..	..	..	..	..	..	..	..	..
4200 Recurrent taxes on net wealth	..	..	..	0	0	0	0	0	0	0
4210 Individual	..	..	..	..	..	..	..	..	..	..
4220 Corporate	..	..	..	..	..	..	..	..	..	..
4300 Estate, inheritance and gift taxes	..	..	..	0	0	14	14	0	13	0
Inheritance and donations tax	..	..	..	..	..	14	14	..	13	..
4310 Estate and inheritance taxes	..	..	..	..	..	..	..	..	..	..
4320 Gift taxes	..	..	..	..	..	..	..	..	..	..
4400 Taxes on financial and capital transactions	..	..	..	598	1 401	3 105	2 652	4 088	6 661	3 048
Stamp duties	..	..	..	598	1 401	3 028	2 629	4 088	6 652	3 048
Property transfer tax	..	..	..	0	0	77	23	0	9	0
4500 Other non-reccurrent taxes on property	..	..	..	0	0	0	0	0	0	0
4510 On net wealth	..	..	..	..	..	..	..	..	..	..
4520 Other non-recurrent taxes	..	..	..	..	..	..	..	..	..	..
4600 Other recurrent taxes on property	..	..	..	0	0	0	0	0	0	0
5000 Taxes on goods and services	..	..	..	**80 550**	**141 548**	**96 723**	**109 336**	**95 133**	**120 712**	**120 804**

Table 5.23. Mozambique – Details of tax revenue (continued)

Million MZN

	1995	2000	2005	2010	2015	2018	2019	2020	2021	2022
5100 Taxes on production, sale, transfer, etc	..	..	..	35 950	77 916	96 524	109 164	95 132	120 563	120 801
5110 General taxes on goods and services	..	..	..	24 188	51 905	65 345	74 037	63 277	83 367	84 403
5111 Value added taxes	..	..	..	24 165	51 719	65 096	73 791	63 041	83 076	84 072
VAT on domestic transactions	..	..	..	9 798	21 877	29 131	31 836	36 996	39 021	37 881
VAT on imports	..	..	..	14 366	29 842	35 966	41 955	38 503	44 055	46 206
VAT refunds	..	..	..	0	0	0	0	- 12 457	0	- 14
5112 Sales tax	..	..	..	0	0	0	0	0	0	0
5113 Turnover and other	..	..	..	24	185	249	246	236	291	330
Simplified tax for small taxpayers	..	..	..	24	185	249	246	236	291	330
5120 Taxes on specific goods and services	..	..	..	11 762	26 012	31 178	35 127	31 854	37 196	36 398
5121 Excises	..	..	..	6 394	12 876	15 610	17 340	16 059	18 382	16 955
Excises - imports	..	..	..	1 241	3 769	4 236	5 078	4 388	4 596	5 299
Beer - domestic production	..	..	..	1 811	2 910	3 398	3 376	0	3 373	3 167
Tobacco - domestic production	..	..	..	271	735	875	731	0	658	426
Other excises - domestic production	..	..	..	137	425	608	689	5 152	1 624	1 950
Fuel tax (earmarked)	..	..	..	2 935	5 037	0	0	0	0	0
Petrol	..	..	..	0	0	2 655	3 000	2 693	4 175	3 484
Diesel	..	..	..	0	0	3 838	4 394	3 728	3 693	2 625
Other fuels	..	..	..	0	0	0	71	98	263	4
5122 Profits of fiscal monopolies	..	..	..	0	0	0	0	0	0	0
5123 Customs and import duties	..	..	..	5 264	12 643	15 177	17 416	15 579	18 620	19 131
Customs duties	..	..	..	5 254	12 641	13 739	16 265	15 083	17 954	18 324
Surcharge (trade tax)	..	..	..	10	2	1 000	800	2	24	79
Customs service Fee	..	..	..	0	0	146	130	352	543	727
Maritime trade tax	..	..	..	0	0	292	221	142	99	0
5124 Taxes on exports	..	..	..	47	382	0	0	0	0	0
Madeira overvaluation tax	..	..	..	0	296	..	..	..	..	..
Cashew nut overvaluation tax	..	..	..	47	86	..	..	..	..	..
5125 Taxes on investment goods	..	..	..	0	0	0	0	0	0	0
5126 Taxes on specific services	..	..	..	56	109	391	371	216	194	312
Special tax on gambling	..	..	..	56	109	391	371	216	194	312
5127 Other taxes on internat. trade and transactions	..	..	..	0	0	0	0	0	0	0
5128 Other taxes	..	..	..	0	0	0	0	0	0	0
5130 Unallocable between 5110 and 5120	..	..	..	0	0	0	0	0	0	0
5200 Taxes on use of goods and to perform activities	..	..	..	44 600	63 632	199	172	1	149	3
5210 Recurrent taxes	..	..	..	44 600	63 632	0	1	1	1	3
5211 Paid by households: motor vehicles	..	..	..	62	4	0	1	1	1	3
Vehicle tax	..	..	..	62	4	0	1	1	1	3
5212 Paid by others: motor vehicles	..	..	..	..	..	..	..	..	..	..
5213 Paid in respect of other goods	..	..	..	44 538	63 628	0	0	0	0	0
Fishing License	..	..	..	44 538	63 628	..	..	..	..	..
5220 Non-recurrent taxes	..	..	..	0	0	199	171	0	148	0
Land use tax	..	..	..	..	..	133	75	..	77	..
Contractor registration Fee	..	..	..	..	..	38	55	..	41	..
Concession and exploitation application fee	..	..	..	..	..	9	6	..	26	..
Customs transit fee	..	..	..	..	..	9	26	..	0	..
Operator and tobacco production registration fees	..	..	..	..	..	10	8	..	3	..
5300 Unallocable between 5100 and 5200	..	..	..	0	0	0	0	0	0	0
6000 Other taxes	**..**	**..**	**..**	**414**	**1 098**	**694**	**754**	**3 669**	**2 183**	**2 031**
National reconstruction tax	..	..	..	0	0	17	22	50	24	23
Other national taxes	..	..	..	0	0	677	732	3 619	2 160	2 008
Miscellaneous other taxes	..	..	..	414	1 098	0	0	0	0	0
6100 Paid solely by business	..	..	..	..	..	..	..	..	..	..
6200 Other	..	..	..	..	..	..	..	..	..	..

.. Not available

Note: Year ending 31st December.The data are on a cash basis.

Figures exclude tax revenues collected by sub-national governments as the data are not available.

Revenue from "Special Tax on Gambling" are considered a tax on specific services under the OECD classification, as set out in the *Interpretative Guide* in Annex A. The national classification of Mozambique classifies it as income tax.

Source: Mozambique Revenue Authority.

Table 5.24. Namibia – Details of tax revenue

Million NAD

	1995	2000	2005	2010	2015	2018	2019	2020	2021	2022
Total tax revenue	..	..	..	**15 734**	**31 974**	**35 168**	**36 247**	**32 762**	**36 863**	**41 680**
1000 Taxes on income, profits and capital gains	..	..	..	**9 912**	**19 006**	**21 855**	**22 611**	**22 295**	**22 949**	**25 362**
1100 Of individuals	..	..	..	6 156	10 982	13 923	14 557	14 077	14 953	16 531
1110 On income and profits	..	..	..	6 156	10 982	13 923	14 557	14 077	14 953	16 531
Income tax on individuals	..	..	..	5 945	10 794	13 588	14 147	13 768	14 629	16 137
Non-resident shareholders tax	..	..	..	189	147	265	307	207	227	279
Tax on royalty	..	..	..	21	41	70	103	102	97	115
1120 On capital gains	..	..	..	0	0	0	0	0	0	0
1200 Corporate	..	..	..	3 756	8 024	7 932	8 054	8 218	7 995	8 831
1210 On profits	..	..	..	3 756	8 024	7 932	8 054	8 218	7 995	8 831
Diamond mining companies	..	..	..	354	2 199	1 496	1 143	1 367	933	1 579
Other mining companies	..	..	..	213	99	445	187	849	743	511
Non-mining companies	..	..	..	3 018	5 425	5 384	5 927	5 342	5 810	6 071
Withholding taxes	..	..	..	156	280	607	797	653	509	665
Annual levy on gambling income	..	..	..	15	21	0	0	6	1	5
1220 On capital gains of corporates	..	..	..	0	0	0	0	0	0	0
1300 Unallocable between 1100 and 1200	..	..	..	0	0	0	0	0	0	0
2000 Social security contributions	..	..	..	**305**	**537**	**621**	**621**	**650**	**603**	**595**
2100 Employees	..	..	..	..	..	..	..	..	..	..
2110 On a payroll basis	..	..	..	..	..	..	..	..	..	..
2120 On an income tax basis	..	..	..	..	..	..	..	..	..	..
2200 Employers	..	..	..	..	..	..	..	..	..	..
2210 On a payroll basis	..	..	..	..	..	..	..	..	..	..
2220 On an income tax basis	..	..	..	..	..	..	..	..	..	..
2300 Self-employed or non-employed	..	..	..	..	..	..	..	..	..	..
2310 On a payroll basis	..	..	..	..	..	..	..	..	..	..
2320 On an income tax basis	..	..	..	..	..	..	..	..	..	..
2400 Unallocable between 2100, 2200 and 2300	..	..	..	305	537	621	621	650	603	595
2410 On a payroll basis	..	..	..	..	..	..	..	..	..	..
2420 On an income tax basis	..	..	..	..	..	..	..	..	..	..
3000 Taxes on payroll and workforce	..	..	..	**0**	**0**	**0**	**0**	**0**	**0**	**0**
4000 Taxes on property	..	..	..	**139**	**313**	**221**	**174**	**173**	**242**	**247**
4100 Recurrent taxes on immovable property	..	..	..	0	0	0	0	0	5	2
4110 Households	..	..	..	..	..	..	..	..	..	..
4120 Others	..	..	..	..	..	..	..	..	..	..
4200 Recurrent taxes on net wealth	..	..	..	0	0	0	0	0	0	0
4210 Individual	..	..	..	..	..	..	..	..	..	..
4220 Corporate	..	..	..	..	..	..	..	..	..	..
4300 Estate, inheritance and gift taxes	..	..	..	0	0	0	0	0	0	0
4310 Estate and inheritance taxes	..	..	..	..	..	..	..	..	..	..
4320 Gift taxes	..	..	..	..	..	..	..	..	..	..
4400 Taxes on financial and capital transactions	..	..	..	139	313	221	174	173	237	245
4500 Other non-reccurrent taxes on property	..	..	..	0	0	0	0	0	0	0
4510 On net wealth	..	..	..	..	..	..	..	..	..	..
4520 Other non-recurrent taxes	..	..	..	..	..	..	..	..	..	..
4600 Other recurrent taxes on property	..	..	..	0	0	0	0	0	0	0
5000 Taxes on goods and services	..	..	..	**5 169**	**11 902**	**12 274**	**12 732**	**9 547**	**12 937**	**15 331**
5100 Taxes on production, sale, transfer, etc	..	..	..	5 169	11 901	12 274	12 732	9 544	12 935	15 328
5110 General taxes on goods and services	..	..	..	5 057	11 678	11 461	11 516	8 326	11 431	14 176
5111 Value added taxes	..	..	..	5 057	11 678	11 461	11 516	8 326	11 431	14 176
5112 Sales tax	..	..	..	0	0	0	0	0	0	0
5113 Other	..	..	..	0	0	0	0	0	0	0
5120 Taxes on specific goods and services	..	..	..	113	223	813	1 216	1 218	1 504	1 152
5121 Excises	..	..	..	0	0	0	0	0	0	0
5122 Profits of fiscal monopolies	..	..	..	0	0	0	0	0	0	0
5123 Customs and import duties	..	..	..	102	209	813	1 201	1 207	1 477	1 141
Levy on fuel	..	..	..	102	209	730	1 107	1 152	1 324	1 043
Environmental levies and carbon emission taxes	..	..	..	0	0	83	94	55	153	98
5124 Taxes on exports	..	..	..	0	0	0	0	0	0	0

Table 5.24. Namibia – Details of tax revenue (continued)

Million NAD

	1995	2000	2005	2010	2015	2018	2019	2020	2021	2022
5125 Taxes on investment goods	..	..	..	0	0	0	0	0	0	0
5126 Taxes on specific services	..	..	..	0	0	0	0	0	0	0
5127 Other taxes on internat. trade and transactions	..	..	..	0	0	0	0	0	0	0
5128 Other taxes	..	..	..	11	14	0	15	11	27	11
5130 Unallocable between 5110 and 5120	..	..	..	0	0	0	0	0	0	0
5200 Taxes on use of goods and to perform activities	..	..	..	0	1	0	0	3	2	3
5210 Recurrent taxes	..	..	..	0	1	0	0	3	2	3
5211 Paid by households: motor vehicles	..	..	..	0	0	0	0	0	0	0
5212 Paid by others: motor vehicles	..	..	..	0	0	0	0	0	0	0
5213 Paid in respect of other goods	..	..	..	0	1	0	0	3	2	3
5220 Non-recurrent taxes	..	..	..	0	0	0	0	0	0	0
5300 Unallocable between 5100 and 5200	..	..	..	0	0	0	0	0	0	0
6000 Other taxes	**..**	**..**	**..**	**208**	**216**	**197**	**109**	**97**	**133**	**145**
6100 Paid solely by business	..	..	..	..	..	..	..	..	..	..
6200 Other	..	..	..	..	..	..	..	..	..	..

.. Not available

Note: Data are on a fiscal year basis beginning 1st April. For example, the data for 2022 represent April 2022 to March 2023.

Data are on a cash basis.

Figures exclude tax revenues collected by sub-national governments as the data are not available.

Heading 2000: Data are not available prior to 2009.

Heading 5111: Value added taxes include revenue from VAT, additional sales tax and the general sales tax.

Source: Namibia Revenue Agency.

Table 5.25. Niger – Details of tax revenue

Million XOF

	1995	2000	2005	2010	2015	2018	2019	2020	2021	2022
Total tax revenue	..	**111 372**	**185 002**	**365 431**	**704 416**	**796 671**	**786 351**	**773 976**	**864 510**	**921 496**
1000 Taxes on income, profits and capital gains	..	**20 891**	**34 848**	**94 839**	**177 695**	**167 981**	**172 209**	**181 800**	**210 467**	**232 780**
1100 Of individuals	..	9 634	12 268	19 756	45 501	55 069	61 154	62 628	75 487	74 689
1110 On income and profits	..	9 634	12 217	19 623	45 294	54 567	60 807	62 342	75 066	73 801
Tax on wages and salaries - excluding oil and mining from 2022	..	8 000	11 207	18 575	44 198	51 539	58 686	60 552	73 155	62 136
Tax on wages and salaries - oil	..	..	..	..	..	..	..	..	..	7 433
Tax on wages and salaries - mining	..	..	..	..	..	..	..	..	..	2 002
Synthetic tax	..	1 530	803	974	1 030	2 775	2 060	1 741	1 862	2 187
General income tax (IGR)	..	103	207	74	66	253	62	49	49	44
1120 On capital gains	..	0	51	133	208	502	347	285	421	888
Capital gains on real estate sales (IPVCI)	..	0	51	133	208	502	347	285	421	888
1200 Corporate	..	11 257	22 580	75 083	132 194	112 913	111 055	119 173	134 980	158 091
1210 On profits	..	11 257	22 580	75 083	132 194	112 913	111 055	119 173	134 980	158 091
Income tax on profits (ISB) - excluding oil and mining from 2022	..	10 933	21 605	67 863	121 448	102 484	102 851	110 263	123 967	99 513
Income tax on profits (ISB) - oil	..	..	..	..	..	..	..	..	..	22 091
Income tax on profits (ISB) - mining	..	..	..	..	..	..	..	..	..	1 237
Tax Oil	..	..	..	..	..	..	..	..	..	22 060
Non-commercial profits (BNC)	..	126	239	0	0	140	217	77	0	0
Income tax on securities (IRVM)	..	198	736	5 695	7 900	8 665	7 776	6 927	8 581	12 015
Port revenues	..	0	0	1 525	2 846	1 623	212	1 907	2 432	1 175
1220 On capital gains of corporates	..	0	0	0	0	0	0	0	0	0
1300 Unallocable between 1100 and 1200	..	0	0	0	0	0	0	0	0	0
2000 Social security contributions	..	**6 216**	**7 305**	**19 950**	**34 117**	**37 840**	**42 272**	**43 370**	**46 004**	**50 110**
2100 Employees	..	..	..	..	..	..	..	..	..	..
2110 On a payroll basis	..	..	..	..	..	..	..	..	..	..
2120 On an income tax basis	..	..	..	..	..	..	..	..	..	..
2200 Employers	..	..	..	..	..	..	..	..	..	..
2210 On a payroll basis	..	..	..	..	..	..	..	..	..	..
2220 On an income tax basis	..	..	..	..	..	..	..	..	..	..
2300 Self-employed or non-employed	..	..	..	..	..	..	..	..	..	..
2310 On a payroll basis	..	..	..	..	..	..	..	..	..	..
2320 On an income tax basis	..	..	..	..	..	..	..	..	..	..
2400 Unallocable between 2100, 2200 and 2300	..	6 216	7 305	19 950	34 117	37 840	42 272	43 370	46 004	50 110
2410 On a payroll basis	..	..	..	..	..	..	..	..	..	..
2420 On an income tax basis	..	..	..	..	..	..	..	..	..	..
3000 Taxes on payroll and workforce	..	**401**	**533**	**1 121**	**3 978**	**3 726**	**4 348**	**1 927**	**6 010**	**5 306**
Apprenticeship tax (TAP)	..	401	533	1 121	3 978	3 726	4 348	1 927	6 010	5 306
4000 Taxes on property	..	**1 252**	**1 590**	**2 906**	**2 742**	**5 564**	**9 804**	**13 569**	**14 303**	**17 683**
4100 Recurrent taxes on immovable property	..	1 252	1 590	2 906	2 742	5 564	9 804	13 569	14 303	17 683
Real estate tax	..	1 015	1 150	2 904	2 742	2 366	1 684	995	1 080	3
Property tax	..	238	440	0	0	2	0	60	0	2
Flat-rate property tax	..	0	0	2	0	25	5	35	0	0
Income tax on residential leases	..	0	0	0	0	207	386	317	317	578
Income tax on professional leases	..	0	0	0	0	704	1 548	1 165	1 151	2 902
Council tax	..	0	0	0	0	2 184	3 141	2 433	3 547	4 171
4110 Households	..	..	..	..	..	..	..	..	..	..
4120 Others	..	0	0	0	0	77	3 040	8 563	8 207	10 026
Real estate tax on companies - excluding oil and mining from 2022	..	0	0	0	0	77	3 040	8 563	8 207	4 963
Real estate tax on companies - oil	..	..	..	..	..	..	..	..	..	5 041
Real estate tax on companies - mining	..	..	..	..	..	..	..	..	..	22
4200 Recurrent taxes on net wealth	..	0	0	0	0	0	0	0	0	0
4210 Individual	..	..	..	..	..	..	..	..	..	..
4220 Corporate	..	..	..	..	..	..	..	..	..	..
4300 Estate, inheritance and gift taxes	..	0	0	0	0	0	0	0	0	0
4310 Estate and inheritance taxes	..	..	..	..	..	..	..	..	..	..
4320 Gift taxes	..	..	..	..	..	..	..	..	..	..
4400 Taxes on financial and capital transactions	..	0	0	0	0	0	0	0	0	0

Table 5.25. Niger (continued) – Details of tax revenue

Million XOF

	1995	2000	2005	2010	2015	2018	2019	2020	2021	2022
4500 Other non-reccurrent taxes on property	..	0	0	0	0	0	0	0	0	0
4510 On net wealth	..	..	..	..	..	..	..	..	..	..
4520 Other non-recurrent taxes	..	..	..	..	..	..	..	..	..	..
4600 Other recurrent taxes on property	..	0	0	0	0	0	0	0	0	0
5000 Taxes on goods and services	**..**	**78 935**	**133 096**	**226 808**	**415 109**	**525 172**	**498 790**	**459 045**	**514 302**	**546 651**
5100 Taxes on production, sale, transfer, etc	..	77 041	132 459	225 447	412 767	521 777	494 738	454 784	509 309	541 915
5110 General taxes on goods and services	..	31 766	79 938	136 966	256 546	359 611	289 733	249 180	282 893	318 218
5111 Value added taxes	..	31 766	79 938	136 966	237 621	341 450	269 488	230 633	264 252	291 956
VAT domestic (gross)	..	12 375	31 686	76 999	145 529	259 228	183 386	137 964	163 310	139 996
VAT domestic (gross) - oil	..	..	..	..	..	..	..	..	..	40 362
VAT domestic (gross) - mining	..	..	..	..	..	..	..	..	..	3 155
Import VAT (gross)	..	19 391	48 252	59 967	92 092	82 222	86 103	92 669	100 942	108 444
5112 Sales tax	..	..	..	..	0	0	0	0	0	0
5113 Other	..	0	0	0	18 925	18 161	20 245	18 547	18 640	26 262
Ad Valorem royalty	..	0	0	0	18 925	18 161	20 245	18 547	18 640	26 262
5120 Taxes on specific goods and services	..	45 275	52 521	88 480	156 221	162 166	205 004	205 605	226 416	223 697
5121 Excises	..	9 306	12 500	20 475	34 957	41 203	36 661	41 827	43 790	45 376
Domestic tax on petroleum products (TIPP) (including DGD)	..	4 313	6 654	11 694	19 375	18 804	15 673	17 226	14 482	16 407
Tobacco and cigarette tax	..	2 300	2 485	5 566	9 061	11 451	10 795	4 133	15 698	18 056
Tax on alcoholic beverages (TBA)	..	713	583	701	701	1 074	1 036	3 254	1 532	280
Artisanal exploitation tax (TEA)	..	0	0	0	22	182	390	1 042	975	879
Other excise duties	..	1 979	2 778	2 514	5 798	9 693	8 767	16 172	11 104	9 754
5122 Profits of fiscal monopolies	..	0	0	0	0	0	0	0	0	0
5123 Customs and import duties	..	22 930	26 854	36 286	59 517	62 450	72 842	87 045	90 497	100 493
Customs duties	..	14 722	24 354	28 141	53 226	56 383	64 396	77 464	80 555	86 323
Statistical import fee	..	1 652	2 493	8 144	6 283	6 026	8 255	9 456	9 855	14 062
Miscellaneous duties (including T.C.I)	..	6 556	7	0	8	41	192	124	87	109
5124 Taxes on exports	..	11 671	12 012	27 567	31 025	48 130	48 086	33 725	28 030	20 502
Taxes on re-exports	..	9 997	11 069	25 405	25 657	41 097	41 039	26 933	21 882	15 743
Statistical export fee	..	1 673	943	1 465	5 342	6 671	6 982	6 427	6 116	4 758
Flat-rate tax on re-export and/or transit of tobacco and cigarettes (TFEAR)	..	0	0	696	25	363	64	365	32	1
5125 Taxes on investment goods	..	0	0	0	0	0	0	0	0	0
5126 Taxes on specific services	..	1 238	901	3 080	30 399	10 224	46 982	42 432	63 680	56 942
Tax on the termination of incoming international traffic (TATTIE)	..	0	0	0	18 666	1 452	18 419	10 866	27 820	15 231
Tax on the use of the telecommunications network (TURTEL)	..	0	0	0	5 349	4 220	5 853	4 076	6 082	8 631
Tax on lottery revenues	..	877	104	1 303	3 377	1 778	2 716	3 084	3 599	5 469
Single insurance tax (TUA)	..	361	792	1 490	2 310	2 338	2 852	2 804	3 143	3 422
Tax on lottery winnings	..	0	5	0	550	0	31	1	3	1
Tax on gambling (TJH)	..	0	0	246	140	435	33	24	347	64
Tax on outdoor commercial advertising (TPCE)	..	0	0	41	8	1	0	2	0	0
Tax on financial activities (TAFI)	..	0	0	0	0	0	17 078	21 575	22 686	24 124
5127 Other taxes on internat. trade and transactions	..	0	0	0	0	0	0	0	0	0
5128 Other taxes	..	130	254	1 074	324	158	433	576	418	384
Mining duties	..	130	254	1 074	295	3	2	0	0	0
Fixed fee Mine	..	0	0	0	28	155	428	572	388	379
Oil duty	..	0	0	0	1	0	3	5	30	5
5130 Unallocable between 5110 and 5120	..	0	0	0	0	0	0	0	0	0
5200 Taxes on use of goods and to perform activities	..	894	637	1 362	2 341	3 394	4 052	4 261	4 993	4 736
5210 Recurrent taxes	..	529	637	1 362	2 316	3 390	4 050	4 081	4 476	4 736
Stickers	..	520	625	1 354	2 310	2 918	3 072	3 225	3 257	3 634
5211 Paid by households: motor vehicles	..	0	0	0	0	0	0	0	0	0
5212 Paid by others: motor vehicles	..	0	0	0	0	0	0	0	0	0
5213 Paid in respect of other goods	..	9	12	8	6	472	977	855	1 219	1 102
Hunting and visiting permits	..	0	1	0	2	3	18	10	0	2
Tax on firearms (TAF)	..	9	11	8	4	4	13	1	2	1
Tax on audiovisual subscriptions	..	0	0	0	0	465	946	844	1 217	1 099

Table 5.25. Niger – Details of tax revenue (continued)

Million XOF

	1995	2000	2005	2010	2015	2018	2019	2020	2021	2022
5220 Non-recurrent taxes	..	365	0	0	25	5	3	180	517	0
Road tolls	..	365	..	..	0	0	0	0	0	..
Licence plate royalty	..	0	..	..	25	5	3	180	517	..
5300 Unallocable between 5100 and 5200	..	1 000	0	0	0	0	0	0	0	0
6000 Other taxes	**..**	**3 676**	**7 630**	**19 807**	**70 775**	**56 389**	**58 927**	**74 264**	**73 423**	**68 966**
Registration fees	..	2 166	4 834	8 048	51 113	34 344	35 469	45 326	43 108	36 695
Levy on behalf of local authorities	..	0	0	6 512	11 727	12 312	12 304	17 064	17 459	15 675
Tax on certain corporate overheads (TCFGE)	..	310	776	1 963	4 132	4 729	5 788	5 955	6 645	6 869
Stamp duties	..	1 201	2 019	3 283	3 803	5 003	5 366	5 920	6 212	9 726
6100 Paid solely by business	..	..	..	..	..	..	..	..	..	..
6200 Other	..	..	..	..	..	..	..	..	..	..
Memo items:	..	..	..	..	..	..	..	..	..	..
ECOWAS community levy	..	448	1 479	5 302	4 893	0	7 651	4 191	4 187	6 382
WAEMU community levy	..	866	0	0	0	0	6 540	7 041	7 481	10 540
AU community levy	..	0	0	0	0	0	0	1 451	1 455	2 243

.. Not available

Note: Year ending 31st December.

The data are on a cash basis.

Figures exclude tax revenues collected by sub-national governments as the data are not available.

Revenues from the public domain, mining royalties, surface royalties from mines and petroleum and fines and penalties relating to taxes are included in non-tax revenues in this edition following the OECD classification of taxes (see the *Interpretative Guide* in Annexes A and B). Under Niger's national classification, they are included in tax revenues.

Headings 1110, 1210, 4120 and 5111: For the first time in this edition these headings contain details of revenues from the oil and mining sectors.

Heading 5121: These headings contain revenues from the Directorate General of Customs (DGD) and are annotated as such.

Heading 5220: This heading includes revenues from licence plate fees collected by the *Direction Générale du Trésor et de la Comptabilité Publique* (DGTCP) between 2005 and 2018 following the OECD classification of taxes (see the *Interpretative Guide* in Annex A). Under Niger's national classification, they are included in non-tax revenues.

Heading 6000: A percentage of some taxes is retroceded to sub-national governments, namely the tax on income from residential leases (50%), the tax on income from professional leases (50%), the synthetic tax (40%) and the business tax (100%) and these revenues are reported under the sub-heading "Levy on behalf of local authorities".

Community levies for the benefit of African regional organisations (ECOWAS, UEMOA, AU) are not considered as revenues of the government of Niger following the OECD *Interpretative Guide* (see § 4). Under Niger's national classification, they are included in tax revenues. Revenues that are not included in total tax revenues or non-tax revenues are shown separately under the "Memo items" heading.

Source: Directorate General of Taxes, Niger.

Table 5.26. Nigeria – Details of tax revenue

Million NGN

	1995	2000	2005	2010	2015	2018	2019	2020	2021	2022
Total tax revenue	..	..	..	**4 046 327**	**5 783 735**	**8 199 097**	**8 714 796**	**8 560 996**	**11 775 692**	**16 005 109**
1000 Taxes on income, profits and capital gains	..	..	..	**2 568 348**	**3 485 925**	**4 960 571**	**4 965 170**	**4 259 653**	**5 454 007**	**8 623 424**
1100 Of individuals	..	..	..	333 381	576 327	848 941	982 057	1 052 108	1 331 127	1 172 185
1110 On income and profits	..	..	..	333 381	576 327	848 941	982 057	1 052 108	1 331 127	1 172 185
Personal Income Tax (Federal)	..	..	..	32 564	57 377	85 146	70 307	93 371	61 198	37 402
State pay-as-you-earn (PAYE) Tax	..	..	..	268 821	456 595	669 218	809 320	851 731	1 124 694	994 400
Personal Income Tax (State)	..	..	..	19 386	29 589	44 266	47 670	37 056	60 495	52 350
National Housing Fund contributions	..	..	..	12 610	32 766	50 310	54 760	69 950	84 740	88 033
1120 On capital gains	..	..	..	0	0	0	0	0	0	0
1200 Corporate	..	..	..	2 234 967	2 909 598	4 111 631	3 983 113	3 207 545	4 122 880	7 451 239
1210 On profits	..	..	..	2 233 931	2 892 796	4 099 036	3 977 136	3 204 027	4 105 382	7 405 667
Petroleum Profits Tax	..	..	..	1 480 364	1 289 961	2 467 581	2 114 268	1 516 979	2 008 454	4 209 019
Companies Income Tax	..	..	..	658 503	1 268 977	1 340 329	1 604 699	1 275 370	1 747 992	2 649 191
Education Tax	..	..	..	89 178	206 040	203 285	221 058	259 563	189 535	328 674
Income tax on gas exploration companies	..	..	..	0	115 569	75 988	21 930	134 063	140 095	193 768
National Information Technology Development Fund	..	..	..	5 886	12 249	11 853	15 181	18 051	19 307	22 574
National Agency for Science and Engineering Infrastructure (NASENI) Levy	..	..	..	..	..	..	..	..	..	2 375
Police Trust Fund (PTF)	..	..	..	..	..	..	..	..	..	66
1220 On capital gains of corporates	..	..	..	1 037	16 802	12 595	5 977	3 519	17 498	45 572
Capital Gains Tax	..	..	..	1 037	16 802	12 595	5 977	3 519	17 498	45 572
1300 Unallocable between 1100 and 1200	..	..	..	0	0	0	0	0	0	0
2000 Social security contributions	..	..	..	**305 163**	**569 879**	**687 080**	**931 600**	**982 909**	**966 200**	**1 124 262**
2100 Employees	..	..	..	172 418	269 328	324 012	430 691	452 199	443 524	510 880
2110 On a payroll basis	..	..	..	172 418	269 328	324 012	430 691	452 199	443 524	510 880
National Pension Commission (employee-side)	..	..	..	132 745	226 596	270 022	378 511	403 606	391 404	456 710
National Health Insurance Scheme	..	..	..	39 673	42 732	53 990	52 180	48 593	52 120	54 170
2120 On an income tax basis	..	..	..	0	0	0	0	0	0	0
2200 Employers	..	..	..	132 745	300 551	363 068	500 909	530 710	522 676	613 382
2210 On a payroll basis	..	..	..	132 745	300 551	363 068	500 909	530 710	522 676	613 382
National Pension Commission (employer-side)	..	..	..	132 745	283 244	337 528	473 139	504 507	489 256	581 260
Nigerian Social Insurance Trust Fund	..	..	..	0	17 307	25 540	27 770	26 203	33 420	32 122
2220 On an income tax basis	..	..	..	0	0	0	0	0	0	0
2300 Self-employed or non-employed	..	..	..	0	0	0	0	0	0	0
2310 On a payroll basis	..	..	..	..	..	..	..	..	..	..
2320 On an income tax basis	..	..	..	..	..	..	..	..	..	..
2400 Unallocable between 2100, 2200 and 2300	..	..	..	0	0	0	0	0	0	0
2410 On a payroll basis	..	..	..	..	..	..	..	..	..	..
2420 On an income tax basis	..	..	..	..	..	..	..	..	..	..
3000 Taxes on payroll and workforce	..	..	..	**22 730**	**22 310**	**32 060**	**35 120**	**34 880**	**40 230**	**46 230**
Industrial Training Fund contributions	..	..	..	22 730	22 310	32 060	35 120	34 880	40 230	46 230
4000 Taxes on property	..	..	..	..	..	..	..	..	**111 835**	**125 669**
4100 Recurrent taxes on immovable property	..	..	..	..	..	..	..	..	0	0
4110 Households	..	..	..	..	..	..	..	..	..	..
4120 Others	..	..	..	..	..	..	..	..	..	..
4200 Recurrent taxes on net wealth	..	..	..	..	..	..	..	..	0	0
4210 Individual	..	..	..	..	..	..	..	..	..	..
4220 Corporate	..	..	..	..	..	..	..	..	..	..
4300 Estate, inheritance and gift taxes	..	..	..	..	..	..	..	..	0	0
4310 Estate and inheritance taxes	..	..	..	..	..	..	..	..	..	..
4320 Gift taxes	..	..	..	..	..	..	..	..	..	..
4400 Taxes on financial and capital transactions	..	..	..	..	..	..	..	..	111 835	125 669
Electronic Money Transfer Levy	..	..	..	..	..	..	..	..	111 835	125 669
4500 Other non-reccurrent taxes on property	..	..	..	..	..	..	..	..	0	0
4510 On net wealth	..	..	..	..	..	..	..	..	..	..
4520 Other non-recurrent taxes	..	..	..	..	..	..	..	..	..	..
4600 Other recurrent taxes on property	..	..	..	..	..	..	..	..	0	0
5000 Taxes on goods and services	..	..	..	**1 036 386**	**1 520 489**	**2 072 094**	**2 317 754**	**2 774 503**	**4 503 583**	**5 177 708**

Table 5.26. Nigeria – Details of tax revenue (continued)

Million NGN

	1995	2000	2005	2010	2015	2018	2019	2020	2021	2022
5100 Taxes on production, sale, transfer, etc	..	..	..	1 029 896	1 501 713	2 047 860	2 287 161	2 746 109	4 458 882	5 153 138
5110 General taxes on goods and services	..	..	..	564 892	767 334	1 108 040	1 189 981	1 531 171	2 072 852	2 511 518
5111 Value added taxes	..	..	..	564 892	767 334	1 108 040	1 189 981	1 531 171	2 072 852	2 511 518
VAT revenues (domestic)	..	..	..	436 610	597 412	859 018	945 464	1 183 446	1 605 174	1 990 021
VAT revenues (imports)	..	..	..	128 281	169 921	249 022	244 517	347 725	467 678	521 497
5112 Sales tax	..	..	..	0	0	0	0	0	0	0
5113 Other	..	..	..	0	0	0	0	0	0	0
5120 Taxes on specific goods and services	..	..	..	465 005	734 380	939 820	1 097 180	1 214 938	2 386 030	2 641 620
5121 Excises	..	..	..	35 449	39 784	55 060	91 690	120 854	145 150	173 900
Excise tax revenue (tobacco, alcohol and other)	..	..	..	35 449	39 784	55 060	91 690	120 854	145 150	173 900
5122 Profits of fiscal monopolies	..	..	..	0	0	0	0	0	0	0
5123 Customs and import duties	..	..	..	429 555	694 596	884 760	1 005 490	1 094 084	2 240 880	2 467 720
Import duties	..	..	..	272 248	468 382	604 990	693 490	746 154	1 049 750	1 234 610
Other customs taxes	..	..	..	157 307	226 214	279 770	312 000	347 930	1 191 130	1 233 110
5124 Taxes on exports	..	..	..	0	0	0	0	0	0	0
5125 Taxes on investment goods	..	..	..	0	0	0	0	0	0	0
5126 Taxes on specific services	..	..	..	0	0	0	0	0	0	0
5127 Other taxes on internat. trade and transactions	..	..	..	0	0	0	0	0	0	0
5128 Other taxes	..	..	..	0	0	0	0	0	0	0
5130 Unallocable between 5110 and 5120	..	..	..	0	0	0	0	0	0	0
5200 Taxes on use of goods and to perform activities	..	..	..	6 490	18 775	24 234	30 593	28 394	44 701	24 570
5210 Recurrent taxes	..	..	..	6 490	18 775	24 234	30 593	28 394	44 701	24 570
5211 Paid by households: motor vehicles	..	..	..	6 121	18 412	23 957	30 270	28 394	44 701	24 570
Road Taxes	..	..	..	6 121	18 412	23 957	30 270	28 394	44 701	24 570
5212 Paid by others: motor vehicles	..	..	..	0	0	0	0	0	0	0
5213 Paid in respect of other goods	..	..	..	368	364	277	323	0	0	0
Pre-operational Levy	..	..	..	368	364	277	323	..	..	..
5220 Non-recurrent taxes	..	..	..	0	0	0	0	0	0	0
5300 Unallocable between 5100 and 5200	..	..	..	0	0	0	0	0	0	0
6000 Other taxes	..	..	..	**113 700**	**185 133**	**447 292**	**465 152**	**509 051**	**699 837**	**907 816**
6100 Paid solely by business	..	..	..	0	0	0	0	0	0	0
6200 Other	..	..	..	113 700	185 133	447 292	465 152	509 051	699 837	907 816
Other tax revenue from states	..	..	..	107 106	178 048	431 493	446 960	388 894	665 897	854 290
Stamp duties	..	..	..	6 593	7 085	15 798	18 192	120 157	33 940	53 526

.. Not available

Note: Year ending 31st December.

The data are on a cash basis.

Some personal income taxes, capital gains taxes, road taxes, and other taxes are collected at the state level.

Statistics on state level revenues were not available in disaggregated form for 2017 and 2018. For these years, revenues for the categories "State PAYE ('Pay as You Earn') Tax", "Personal Income Tax (State)", and "Other tax revenue from states" were estimations.

Revenues collected by Local Government Areas (LGAs) are reported under "Non-tax revenue: Miscellaneous and unidentified revenue" although they include some tax revenues.

Heading 1110: State level income taxes on individuals on paid employment are collected on a PAYE ("Pay as you earn") basis, while those who are self-employed or receive business income on a non-salary basis are charged under direct assessment. These are reported separately in this table, but the tax basis is the same for both cases. In previous editions the contributions to the National Housing Fund were reported as payroll taxes under Heading 3000.

Heading 1210: The Petroleum Profits Tax includes all tax revenue payments by oil exploration companies irrespective of the type of exploration arrangement (production sharing, joint ventures, etc) despite the fact that different types of arrangements could give rise to different tax rates. This heading does not include the government's share of company revenue arising from the revenue-sharing component of the exploration arrangements. These latter funds are reported as oil revenues in the non-tax revenue table. The Finance Act 2021 (FA 21) recently amended the National Agency for Science and Engineering Infrastructure (NASENI) Act and imposed a levy of 0.25% of profits before tax of commercial companies and firms with turnovers of N100,000,000 and above in the banking, telecommunications, ICT, aviation, maritime, and oil and gas sectors. The Nigerian Police Trust Fund Act was signed into law in 2019. It imposes a levy of 0.005% of the "net profit" of companies 'operating business' in Nigeria.

Heading 1220: Capital gains tax for resident companies and non-residents is collected at the federal level while capital gains tax for individuals is collected at the state level.

Heading 2000: The Pension Reform Act was passed in 2004 and mandated both employees and employers to contribute 7.5% each to the pension retirement savings account. However, in 2014 there was an amendment after which the employee was mandated to contribute 8% while the employer contributed a minimum of 10% thereby bringing the total contribution to at least 18%. For the years up to and including 2014, therefore, 50% of social security contributions are reported under heading 2110 and the other half under heading 2210. Starting in 2015, 4/9 of total pension contributions are reported under heading 2110 and 5/9 of total pension contributions are reported under heading 2210.

Heading 3000: This heading includes a 1% payroll tax used to fund the Industrial Training Fund.
Heading 4000: Revenues from property taxes are mainly levied by local governments for which data on revenue are not available. The Electronic Money Transfer Levy (EMTL) was introduced in the Finance Act 2020. It amended the Stamp Duty Act and introduced a single, one-off charge of N50 on electronic receipt or transfer of money deposited in any deposit money bank or financial institution on any type of account on sums of N10,000 and above.
Heading 5211: Road Taxes, or taxes charged on the issuance of motor vehicle licenses, are collected at the state level.
Heading 5213: This heading contains taxes collected under the Pre-operational Levy. This is a tax charged each year to companies that, more than 18 months after being registered, still have not commenced operations.
Heading 6000: Other state taxes include stamp duties, capital gains taxes, business premise registration, Land Use Charge, market taxes, and levies that are collected by state governments.
Source: Federal Inland Revenue Service.

Table 5.27. Rwanda – Details of tax revenue

Million RWF

	1995	2000	2005	2010	2015	2018	2019	2020	2021	2022
Total tax revenue	**..**	**68 909**	**174 606**	**440 724**	**997 232**	**1 401 503**	**1 611 730**	**1 642 978**	**1 860 162**	**2 266 481**
1000 Taxes on income, profits and capital gains	**..**	**17 943**	**49 911**	**159 567**	**379 676**	**565 235**	**640 854**	**678 516**	**792 701**	**966 136**
1100 Of individuals	..	6 621	24 587	102 037	224 553	312 070	354 545	363 018	406 257	491 454
1110 On income and profits	..	6 621	24 587	102 037	224 553	312 070	354 545	363 018	406 257	491 454
Pay-as-you-earn (PAYE) tax	..	..	..	..	216 750	300 751	343 064	351 474	394 931	479 570
Rental Income Tax	..	..	..	..	7 803	11 319	11 481	11 544	11 327	11 884
1120 On capital gains	..	0	0	0	0	0	0	0	0	0
1200 Corporate	..	11 322	25 324	57 530	155 123	253 165	286 309	315 499	386 444	474 681
1210 On profits	..	11 322	25 324	57 530	155 123	253 165	286 309	315 499	386 444	474 681
Corporation income tax	..	3 603	11 606	26 459	49 571	94 656	95 881	118 183	136 928	188 555
Withholding tax	..	59	605	10 764	58 422	71 474	96 990	137 450	185 074	210 817
Personal income tax	..	868	2 210	7 316	7 358	10 991	10 291	10 042	10 361	12 929
Other taxes on profits	..	6 792	10 903	12 991	39 772	76 044	83 147	49 824	54 081	62 380
1220 On capital gains of corporates	..	0	0	0	0	0	0	0	0	0
1300 Unallocable between 1100 and 1200	..	0	0	0	0	0	0	0	0	0
2000 Social security contributions	**..**	**3 423**	**11 988**	**28 235**	**59 687**	**83 344**	**94 371**	**102 178**	**106 821**	**125 777**
2100 Employees	..	1 283	4 493	10 586	22 379	31 249	35 384	38 311	40 052	47 159
2110 On a payroll basis	..	1 283	4 493	10 586	22 379	31 249	35 384	38 311	40 052	47 159
2120 On an income tax basis	..	0	0	0	0	0	0	0	0	0
2200 Employers	..	2 138	7 488	17 644	37 299	52 082	58 973	63 851	66 753	78 599
2210 On a payroll basis	..	2 138	7 488	17 644	37 299	52 082	58 973	63 851	66 753	78 599
2220 On an income tax basis	..	0	0	0	0	0	0	0	0	0
2300 Self-employed or non-employed	..	3	6	4	9	13	14	16	16	19
2310 On a payroll basis	..	3	6	4	9	13	14	16	16	19
2320 On an income tax basis	..	0	0	0	0	0	0	0	0	0
2400 Unallocable between 2100, 2200 and 2300	..	0	0	0	0	0	0	0	0	0
2410 On a payroll basis	..	..	..	..	..	..	..	..	..	..
2420 On an income tax basis	..	..	..	..	..	..	..	..	..	..
3000 Taxes on payroll and workforce	**..**	**0**	**0**	**0**	**0**	**0**	**0**	**0**	**0**	**0**
4000 Taxes on property	**..**	**130**	**43**	**97**	**632**	**1 293**	**2 142**	**14 957**	**14 941**	**19 641**
4100 Recurrent taxes on immovable property	..	130	42	96	632	1 293	2 142	14 957	14 941	19 641
4110 Households	..	130	42	96	632	1 293	2 142	14 957	14 941	19 641
4120 Others	..	0	0	0	0	0	0	0	0	0
4200 Recurrent taxes on net wealth	..	0	0	0	0	0	0	0	0	0
4210 Individual	..	..	..	..	..	..	..	..	..	..
4220 Corporate	..	..	..	..	..	..	..	..	..	..
4300 Estate, inheritance and gift taxes	..	0	0	0	0	0	0	0	0	0
4310 Estate and inheritance taxes	..	..	..	..	..	..	..	..	..	..
4320 Gift taxes	..	..	..	..	..	..	..	..	..	..
4400 Taxes on financial and capital transactions	..	0	0	0	0	0	0	0	0	0
4500 Other non-reccurrent taxes on property	..	0	0	0	0	0	0	0	0	0
4510 On net wealth	..	..	..	..	..	..	..	..	..	..
4520 Other non-recurrent taxes	..	..	..	..	..	..	..	..	..	..
4600 Other recurrent taxes on property	..	0	1	0	0	0	0	0	0	0
5000 Taxes on goods and services	**..**	**47 413**	**112 664**	**252 826**	**557 238**	**751 631**	**874 363**	**847 327**	**945 698**	**1 154 927**
5100 Taxes on production, sale, transfer, etc	..	46 777	111 848	250 214	549 277	744 296	867 102	840 735	936 207	1 137 453
5110 General taxes on goods and services	..	13 777	57 747	131 665	305 544	422 903	507 719	486 043	555 282	663 668
5111 Value added taxes	..	13 777	57 747	131 665	305 544	422 903	507 719	486 043	555 282	663 668
VAT revenues (gross)	..	..	64 163	146 295	339 493	476 671	576 953	552 322	631 003	754 168
VAT refunds	..	..	-6 416	-14 629	-33 949	-53 768	-69 234	-66 279	-75 720	-90 500
5112 Sales tax	..	0	0	0	0	0	0	0	0	0
5113 Other	..	0	0	0	0	0	0	0	0	0
5120 Taxes on specific goods and services	..	32 999	54 101	118 548	243 733	321 393	359 383	354 692	380 924	473 785
5121 Excises	..	18 849	22 614	75 236	138 261	169 237	183 714	187 024	218 015	267 328
Excise tax on beers	..	7 146	9 371	22 548	45 950	54 801	61 170	64 892	78 007	92 109
Excise tax on petroleum	..	7 857	6 515	30 941	47 043	55 791	59 311	54 865	59 884	72 323
Strategic reserves levy	..	0	0	0	4 185	10 502	11 386	10 531	12 107	14 571
Other excises taxes	..	3 846	6 728	21 746	41 084	48 143	51 848	56 736	68 016	88 326
5122 Profits of fiscal monopolies	..	0	0	0	0	0	0	0	0	0

Table 5.27. Rwanda – Details of tax revenue (continued)

Million RWF

	1995	2000	2005	2010	2015	2018	2019	2020	2021	2022
5123 Customs and import duties	..	14 151	31 488	43 313	105 472	152 155	175 669	167 667	162 910	206 457
Import duties	..	9 260	22 071	26 215	69 731	83 601	100 742	99 674	100 371	130 427
Rwanda road maintenance fund	..	2 531	3 644	14 843	29 620	48 805	53 109	48 166	39 597	42 490
Infrastructure development levy	..	0	0	0	3 837	12 228	14 039	13 254	15 241	22 145
African Union Levy	..	0	0	0	0	1 579	1 835	1 676	1 923	2 843
Other customs and import duties	..	2 360	5 773	2 254	2 284	5 942	5 943	4 896	5 777	8 553
5124 Taxes on exports	..	0	0	0	0	0	0	0	0	0
5125 Taxes on investment goods	..	0	0	0	0	0	0	0	0	0
5126 Taxes on specific services	..	0	0	0	0	0	0	0	0	0
5127 Other taxes on internat. trade and transactions	..	0	0	0	0	0	0	0	0	0
5128 Other taxes	..	0	0	0	0	0	0	0	0	0
5130 Unallocable between 5110 and 5120	..	0	0	0	0	0	0	0	0	0
5200 Taxes on use of goods and to perform activities	..	636	816	2 612	7 961	7 335	7 261	6 592	9 491	17 473
5210 Recurrent taxes	..	636	816	2 612	7 961	7 335	7 261	6 592	9 491	17 473
5211 Paid by households: motor vehicles	..	636	816	2 612	3 252	2 269	3 473	3 563	3 798	4 506
5212 Paid by others: motor vehicles	..	0	0	0	0	0	0	0	0	0
5213 Paid in respect of other goods	..	0	0	0	4 709	5 066	3 788	3 029	5 693	12 967
5220 Non-recurrent taxes	..	0	0	0	0	0	0	0	0	0
5300 Unallocable between 5100 and 5200	..	0	0	0	0	0	0	0	0	0
6000 Other taxes	**..**	**0**	**0**	**0**	**0**	**0**	**0**	**0**	**0**	**0**
6100 Paid solely by business	..	..	..	..	..	..	..	..	..	..
6200 Other	..	..	..	..	..	..	..	..	..	..

.. Not available

Note: Year ending 31st December. From 2008, the figures for social security contributions are on a fiscal year basis beginning 1st July. For example, data for 2022 represent July 2021 to June 2022.

The data are on a cash basis.

Figures exclude tax revenues collected by sub-national governments as the data are not available.

Figures include fines related to tax revenues as it is not possible to split these out from tax revenues. These revenues are now classified as non-tax revenues following a change in the OECD classification. Rwanda considers these revenues as tax revenues.

Heading 2000: Rwanda does not include social security contributions in their tax revenue data as the Rwandan authorities do not consider them as taxes.

Source: Rwanda Revenue Authority.

Table 5.28. Senegal – Details of tax revenue

Million XOF

	1995	2000	2005	2010	2015	2018	2019	2020	2021	2022
Total tax revenue	..	**559 295**	**887 248**	**1 267 799**	**1 723 131**	**2 219 816**	**2 566 168**	**2 611 991**	**2 864 429**	**3 416 515**
1000 Taxes on income, profits and capital gains	..	**123 771**	**204 800**	**328 200**	**435 600**	**603 331**	**710 593**	**717 193**	**781 189**	**1 011 422**
1100 Of individuals	..	64 021	102 600	192 900	261 000	313 626	352 187	354 323	433 817	550 368
1110 On income and profits	..	63 370	101 100	191 000	257 900	313 626	352 187	354 323	433 817	550 368
1120 On capital gains	..	651	1 500	1 900	3 100	..	..	..	0	0
1200 Corporate	..	49 418	83 900	106 100	147 300	280 643	349 962	353 879	340 458	451 037
1210 On profits	..	49 418	83 900	106 100	147 300	280 643	349 962	353 879	340 458	451 037
1220 On capital gains of corporates	..	..	..	..	..	..	..	..	..	..
1300 Unallocable between 1100 and 1200	..	10 332	18 300	29 200	27 300	9 062	8 444	8 991	6 914	10 017
2000 Social security contributions	..	**22 215**	**36 568**	**72 999**	**116 260**	**150 000**	**163 100**	**154 000**	**149 066**	**159 423**
2100 Employees	..	..	..	..	..	..	..	..	..	..
2110 On a payroll basis	..	..	..	..	..	..	..	..	..	..
2120 On an income tax basis	..	..	..	..	..	..	..	..	..	..
2200 Employers	..	..	..	..	..	..	..	..	..	..
2210 On a payroll basis	..	..	..	..	..	..	..	..	..	..
2220 On an income tax basis	..	..	..	..	..	..	..	..	..	..
2300 Self-employed or non-employed	..	..	..	..	..	..	..	..	..	..
2310 On a payroll basis	..	..	..	..	..	..	..	..	..	..
2320 On an income tax basis	..	..	..	..	..	..	..	..	..	..
2400 Unallocable between 2100, 2200 and 2300	..	22 215	36 568	72 999	116 260	150 000	163 100	154 000	149 066	159 423
Senegal Pension Fund (IRPES)	..	22 215	36 568	72 999	93 400	..	..	..	149 066	..
Social Security Funds (CSS)	..	0	0	0	22 860	..	..	..	..	..
2410 On a payroll basis	..	..	..	..	..	..	..	..	..	..
2420 On an income tax basis	..	..	..	..	..	..	..	..	..	..
3000 Taxes on payroll and workforce	..	**6 668**	**9 440**	**10 800**	**20 200**	**5 283**	**8 952**	**7 996**	**33 063**	**39 267**
4000 Taxes on property	..	**11 200**	**23 200**	**39 100**	**41 500**	**56 174**	**60 876**	**62 620**	**91 854**	**77 831**
4100 Recurrent taxes on immovable property	..	0	0	0	0	0	0	0	4 835	0
4110 Households	..	..	..	..	..	..	..	..	..	..
4120 Others	..	..	..	..	..	..	..	..	..	..
4200 Recurrent taxes on net wealth	..	0	0	0	0	0	0	0	0	0
4210 Individual	..	..	..	..	..	..	..	..	..	..
4220 Corporate	..	..	..	..	..	..	..	..	..	..
4300 Estate, inheritance and gift taxes	..	2 464	5 104	12 445	8 465	4 174	3 876	6 620	6 020	3 823
4310 Estate and inheritance taxes	..	..	..	..	..	..	..	..	..	..
4320 Gift taxes	..	..	..	..	..	..	..	..	..	..
4400 Taxes on financial and capital transactions	..	8 736	18 096	26 655	33 035	52 000	57 000	56 000	81 000	74 008
Transfer duties on sale or exchange of real estate	..	..	..	15 418	15 863	27 000	31 000	22 000	35 000	25 166
Registration fees other than for property	..	..	..	11 237	17 172	25 000	26 000	34 000	46 000	48 842
4500 Other non-reccurrent taxes on property	..	0	0	0	0	0	0	0	0	0
4510 On net wealth	..	..	..	..	..	..	..	..	..	..
4520 Other non-recurrent taxes	..	..	..	..	..	..	..	..	..	..
4600 Other recurrent taxes on property	..	0	0	0	0	0	0	0	0	0
5000 Taxes on goods and services	..	**386 940**	**601 700**	**804 400**	**1 086 871**	**1 308 349**	**1 548 797**	**1 512 371**	**1 761 793**	**2 084 665**
5100 Taxes on production, sale, transfer, etc	..	384 590	597 700	799 400	1 078 171	1 297 281	1 535 951	1 499 632	1 749 793	1 999 273
5110 General taxes on goods and services	..	221 410	354 800	478 000	617 000	734 853	883 270	805 539	933 834	986 224
5111 Value added taxes	..	221 410	354 800	478 000	617 000	734 853	883 270	805 539	913 501	956 346
5112 Sales tax	..	0	0	0	0	0	0	0	0	0
5113 Other	..	0	0	0	0	0	0	0	20 333	29 878
5120 Taxes on specific goods and services	..	163 180	242 900	321 400	461 171	562 428	652 681	694 093	815 959	1 013 049
5121 Excises	..	61 100	82 700	82 600	88 821	148 561	107 789	173 475	252 349	307 624
Tax on petroleum products	..	..	62 600	63 900	61 520	91 039	69 286	97 300	91 995	126 115
Taxes on tobacco	..	..	8 483	9 647	14 565	16 403	19 672	20 250	20 686	19 247
Taxes on fats	..	..	4 148	978	1 964	6 413	4 034	13 953	11 481	12 291
Taxes on alcohols	..	..	3 535	5 297	5 516	7 854	6 056	7 630	8 494	9 882
Tax on colas	..	..	278	273	19	19	- 6	23	92	953
Tax on teas	..	..	121	154	153	70	269	123	107	262
Tax on coffee	..	..	140	175	428	442	673	348	413	547
Tax on cosmetics	..	..	0	0	1 465	2 544	1 725	2 618	3 178	3 666
Tax on cement	..	..	0	0	0	14 087	0	15 369	14 904	15 614

Table 5.28. Senegal – Details of tax revenue (continued)

Million XOF

	1995	2000	2005	2010	2015	2018	2019	2020	2021	2022
Excises not classified elsewhere	..	..	3 395	2 176	3 189	9 690	6 082	15 862	101 000	119 047
5122 Profits of fiscal monopolies	..	0	0	0	0	0	0	0	0	0
5123 Customs and import duties	..	90 340	138 900	181 600	227 600	290 339	365 538	337 908	392 610	488 410
5124 Taxes on exports	..	0	0	0	0	0	0	0	0	0
5125 Taxes on investment goods	..	0	0	0	0	0	0	0	0	0
5126 Taxes on specific services	..	11 740	21 300	45 000	71 200	105 378	78 000	100 538	91 000	128 567
Financial Activities Tax (FAT)	..	9 340	17 600	30 600	47 700	62 534	55 300	71 462	65 000	95 000
Telecommunications usage fee	..	0	0	10 000	19 500	22 289	22 700	21 214	20 000	24 567
Tax on insurance contracts	..	2 400	3 700	4 400	4 000	6 905	0	7 862	6 000	9 000
Contribution to economic development (CODEC)	..	0	0	0	0	13 649	0	0	0	0
5127 Other taxes on internat. trade and transactions	..	0	0	0	0	0	0	0	0	0
5128 Other taxes	..	0	0	12 200	73 551	18 150	101 354	82 171	80 000	88 448
Fund to secure imports of petroleum products	..	..	..	12 200	69 451	17 266	96 854	81 826	80 000	88 448
Special contribution from mining and quarrying products	..	..	..	0	4 100	884	4 500	345	0	0
5130 Unallocable between 5110 and 5120	..	0	0	0	0	0	0	0	0	0
5200 Taxes on use of goods and to perform activities	..	2 350	4 000	5 000	8 700	11 068	12 846	12 738	12 000	85 391
5210 Recurrent taxes	..	2 350	4 000	5 000	8 700	11 068	12 846	12 738	12 000	85 391
5211 Paid by households: motor vehicles	..	..	..	..	..	..	..	..	..	..
5212 Paid by others: motor vehicles	..	..	..	..	..	..	..	..	..	..
5213 Paid in respect of other goods	..	..	..	..	..	..	..	..	..	..
5220 Non-recurrent taxes	..	0	0	0	0	0	0	0	0	0
5300 Unallocable between 5100 and 5200	..	0	0	0	0	0	0	0	0	0
6000 Other taxes	**..**	**8 500**	**11 540**	**12 300**	**22 700**	**96 678**	**73 851**	**157 811**	**47 464**	**43 908**
6100 Paid solely by business	..	..	..	..	..	..	..	..	..	..
6200 Other	..	..	..	..	..	..	..	..	..	..

.. Not available

Note: Year ending 31st December.

The data are on a cash basis.

Figures exclude tax revenues collected by sub-national governments as the data are not available.

Figures exclude parafiscal charges as the data are not available.

Heading 2000 includes social security contributions from the *Institution de prévoyance retraite du Sénégal* (IPRES) from 2006 and social security contributions from the *Caisse de Sécurité* Sociale (CSS) from 2012. Social security contributions in Senegal prior to 2006 are estimated.

Heading 5126 includes the fee for access to or use of the public telecommunications network (*Redevance sur l'accès ou l'utilisation du réseau des télécommunications publiques*, or RUTEL) classified as an excise duty in Senegal.

Tax revenues include fines and penalties on taxes. These revenues are considered as non-tax revenues following the OECD classification of taxes (see the *Interpretative Guide* in Annexes A and B). In this edition, it has not been possible to separate the payment of fines and penalties from the revenues corresponding to the taxes to which these fines and penalties relate. Under Senegal's national classification they are included in tax revenues.

Source: Ministry of Economy, Finance and Planning, Senegal.

Table 5.29. Seychelles – Details of tax revenue

Million SCR

	1995	2000	2005	2010	2015	2018	2019	2020	2021	2022
Total tax revenue	..	..	..	**3 595**	**5 474**	**7 477**	**7 617**	**6 772**	**7 153**	**7 999**
1000 Taxes on income, profits and capital gains	..	..	..	**1 062**	**1 696**	**2 329**	**2 360**	**2 216**	**2 481**	**2 293**
1100 Of individuals	..	..	..	254	948	965	975	1 023	1 023	1 086
1110 On income and profits	..	..	..	254	948	965	975	1 023	1 023	1 086
Personal income tax - Central government	..	..	..	71	254	236	211	242	242	245
Personal income tax - Other public sectors	..	..	..	30	119	122	123	113	112	99
Personal income tax - Private sectors	..	..	..	153	575	607	641	668	669	742
1120 On capital gains	..	..	..	0	0	0	0	0	0	0
1200 Corporate	..	..	..	808	748	1 364	1 385	1 193	1 457	1 207
1210 On profits	..	..	..	808	748	1 364	1 385	1 193	1 457	1 207
Companies	..	..	..	703	563	1 155	1 160	1 016	1 206	1 013
Sole traders	..	..	..	14	43	37	38	36	85	51
Partnerships	..	..	..	9	11	16	18	17	24	22
Withholding tax	..	..	..	58	88	96	104	103	122	100
Residential dwellings	..	..	..	0	43	59	65	22	20	22
Others	..	..	..	0	0	0	0	0	0	0
Goods and services tax on rental income	..	..	..	24	0	0	0	0	0	0
1220 On capital gains of corporates	..	..	..	0	0	0	0	0	0	0
1300 Unallocable between 1100 and 1200	..	..	..	0	0	0	0	0	0	0
2000 Social security contributions	..	..	..	**329**	**215**	**540**	**398**	**436**	**440**	**622**
2100 Employees	..	..	..	21	93	185	199	213	214	277
2110 On a payroll basis	..	..	..	21	93	185	199	213	214	277
SPF - Mandatory employee contributions	..	..	..	21	93	185	199	213	214	277
2120 On an income tax basis	..	..	..	0	0	0	0	0	0	0
2200 Employers	..	..	..	21	102	148	196	212	214	333
2210 On a payroll basis	..	..	..	21	102	148	196	212	214	333
SPF - Mandatory employer contributions	..	..	..	21	102	148	196	212	214	333
2220 On an income tax basis	..	..	..	0	0	0	0	0	0	0
2300 Self-employed or non-employed	..	..	..	0	0	0	0	0	0	0
2310 On a payroll basis	..	..	..	..	..	..	..	..	..	..
2320 On an income tax basis	..	..	..	..	..	..	..	..	..	..
2400 Unallocable between 2100, 2200 and 2300	..	..	..	287	20	208	3	10	11	12
2410 On a payroll basis	..	..	..	0	0	0	0	0	0	0
2420 On an income tax basis	..	..	..	287	20	208	3	10	11	12
Social Security Tax	..	..	..	287	20	208	3	10	11	12
3000 Taxes on payroll and workforce	..	..	..	**0**	**0**	**0**	**0**	**0**	**0**	**0**
4000 Taxes on property	..	..	..	**126**	**140**	**126**	**168**	**124**	**103**	**73**
4100 Recurrent taxes on immovable property	..	..	..	0	0	0	0	0	0	0
4110 Households	..	..	..	..	..	..	..	..	..	..
4120 Others	..	..	..	..	..	..	..	..	..	..
4200 Recurrent taxes on net wealth	..	..	..	0	0	0	0	0	0	0
4210 Individual	..	..	..	..	..	..	..	..	..	..
4220 Corporate	..	..	..	..	..	..	..	..	..	..
4300 Estate, inheritance and gift taxes	..	..	..	0	0	0	0	0	0	0
4310 Estate and inheritance taxes	..	..	..	..	..	..	..	..	..	..
4320 Gift taxes	..	..	..	..	..	..	..	..	..	..
4400 Taxes on financial and capital transactions	..	..	..	126	140	126	168	124	103	73
Stamp Duty	..	..	..	126	140	126	168	124	103	73
4500 Other non-reccurrent taxes on property	..	..	..	0	0	0	0	0	0	0
4510 On net wealth	..	..	..	..	..	..	..	..	..	..
4520 Other non-recurrent taxes	..	..	..	..	..	..	..	..	..	..
4600 Other recurrent taxes on property	..	..	..	0	0	0	0	0	0	0
5000 Taxes on goods and services	..	..	..	**2 079**	**3 422**	**4 482**	**4 691**	**3 996**	**4 130**	**5 010**
5100 Taxes on production, sale, transfer, etc	..	..	..	1 958	3 226	4 280	4 480	3 793	3 930	4 795
5110 General taxes on goods and services	..	..	..	468	1 893	2 615	2 710	2 225	2 404	2 994
5111 Value added taxes	..	..	..	0	1 799	2 493	2 586	2 111	2 324	2 965
VAT - Domestic	..	..	..	..	990	1 550	1 587	1 203	1 430	1 855
VAT - Imported goods	..	..	..	..	833	968	1 003	910	893	1 112
VAT - Exemptions	..	..	..	..	- 24	- 25	- 4	- 3	0	- 2

Table 5.29. Seychelles – Details of tax revenue (continued)

Million SCR

	1995	2000	2005	2010	2015	2018	2019	2020	2021	2022
5112 Sales tax	..	..	..	468	4	3	3	2	2	1
Goods and services tax on locally manufactured goods (Alcohol)	..	..	..	27	0	0	0	0	0	0
Goods and services tax on locally manufactured goods (tobacco)	..	..	..	12	0	0	0	0	0	0
Goods and services tax on locally manufactured goods (other)	..	..	..	42	0	0	0	0	0	0
Goods and services tax - Fuel / petroleum products	..	..	..	10	0	0	0	0	0	0
Goods and services tax - Imported goods	..	..	..	377	0	0	0	0	0	0
Goods and services tax - Arrears	..	..	..	0	4	3	3	2	2	1
5113 Other	..	..	..	0	90	119	121	113	78	29
Corporate Social Responsibility Tax (CSR)	..	..	..	..	79	106	109	102	61	10
Presumptive taxes	..	..	..	..	10	13	12	11	17	19
5120 Taxes on specific goods and services	..	..	..	1 490	1 333	1 666	1 770	1 568	1 526	1 800
5121 Excises	..	..	..	570	961	1 281	1 385	1 268	1 207	1 416
Alcohol (beverages spirits and vinegar)	..	..	..	180	278	382	419	372	358	429
Petroleum (mineral products)	..	..	..	242	493	609	628	552	575	640
Motor Vehicles (vehicles, aircraft, vessels)	..	..	..	47	44	123	148	98	33	107
Tobacco	..	..	..	102	146	166	164	202	200	186
Sugar tax on beverages	..	..	..	0	0	0	25	44	41	54
5122 Profits of fiscal monopolies	..	..	..	0	0	0	0	0	0	0
5123 Customs and import duties	..	..	..	355	326	315	313	238	260	302
Alcohol (beverages spirits and vinegar)	..	..	..	29	97	128	110	79	79	107
Petroleum (mineral products)	..	..	..	151	0	0	0	0	0	0
Textiles and textile articles	..	..	..	11	26	15	7	7	7	7
Motor Vehicles (vehicles, aircraft, vessels)	..	..	..	63	57	1	0	0	0	0
Tobacco (tobacco and manufactured tobacco)	..	..	..	2	2	2	2	3	3	3
Prepared Food (prepared foodstuffs)	..	..	..	19	19	11	13	14	14	12
Documentary Charges	..	..	..	2	2	2	3	3	3	4
Livestock Trust Fund	..	..	..	0	0	0	22	5	26	24
Other customs duties	..	..	..	79	128	160	160	129	129	144
Custom duties exemptions	..	..	..	- 3	- 5	- 4	- 4	- 2	- 1	- 0
5124 Taxes on exports	..	..	..	0	0	0	0	0	0	0
5125 Taxes on investment goods	..	..	..	0	0	0	0	0	0	0
5126 Taxes on specific services	..	..	..	565	45	70	71	62	60	82
Gaming Tax (casino)	..	..	..	6	0	0	0	0	0	0
Tourism Marketing Tax (TMT)	..	..	..	0	45	70	71	62	60	82
Goods and services tax - Professional services	..	..	..	27	0	0	0	0	0	0
Goods and services tax - Tourism	..	..	..	411	0	0	0	0	0	0
Goods and services tax - Telecom and utilities	..	..	..	97	0	0	0	0	0	0
Goods and services tax - Insurance	..	..	..	22	0	0	0	0	0	0
5127 Other taxes on internat. trade and transactions	..	..	..	0	0	0	0	0	0	0
5128 Other taxes	..	..	..	0	0	0	0	0	0	0
5130 Unallocable between 5110 and 5120	..	..	..	0	0	0	0	0	0	0
5200 Taxes on use of goods and to perform activities	..	..	..	121	197	202	211	204	201	216
5210 Recurrent taxes	..	..	..	121	197	202	211	204	201	216
5211 Paid by households: motor vehicles	..	..	..	42	95	117	129	125	125	134
Road tax and other licences	..	..	..	42	88	108	120	117	116	125
Vehicle testing	..	..	..	0	7	8	9	9	9	9
5212 Paid by others: motor vehicles	..	..	..	0	0	0	0	0	0	0
5213 Paid in respect of other goods	..	..	..	79	102	85	82	78	76	82
Trade / industry licences	..	..	..	8	8	10	10	10	11	11
Licences and other licence registration	..	..	..	5	3	4	6	3	4	5
Telecommunications and radio broadcasting licences	..	..	..	62	88	71	66	65	61	63
Casino and hotel licences	..	..	..	3	3	1	0	0	0	1
Liquor and toddy licences	..	..	..	0	0	0	0	0	0	2
5220 Non-recurrent taxes	..	..	..	0	0	0	0	0	0	0
5300 Unallocable between 5100 and 5200	..	..	..	0	0	0	0	0	0	0

Table 5.29. Seychelles – Details of tax revenue (continued)

Million SCR

	1995	2000	2005	2010	2015	2018	2019	2020	2021	2022
6000 Other taxes	**..**	**..**	**..**	**0**	**0**	**0**	**0**	**0**	**0**	**0**
6100 Paid solely by business	..	..	..	..	..	..	..	..	..	..
6200 Other	..	..	..	..	..	..	..	..	..	..

.. Not available

Note: Year ending 31st December.

The data are on a cash basis.

Heading 1210: The Goods and Services Tax in Seychelles was also applied to rental payments, which according to *Revenue Statistics in Africa* definitions are properly classified as business taxes. These revenues are reported under the Goods and Services Tax heading in budget documents for the Seychelles.

Heading 2000: This edition includes revenues collected by the Seychelles Pensions Fund (SPF), which includes mandatory contributions classified by the OECD as social security contributions (reported under Headings 2110 and 2210). Seychelles also collected a social security tax based on income (reported under Heading 2420) which was phased out in 2010, but with a significant collection of arrears in 2018. SPF revenues are not reported as government revenues in Seychelles government documents.

Heading 5112: The Goods and Services Tax in Seychelles existed until it was replaced by a VAT in 2013. This tax imposed a 15% tax rate on sales of products and services in a long list of items enumerated in the Goods and Services Tax Act. Arrears on the Goods and Services Tax includes arrears on goods and services taxes professional services, tourism, telecom and utilities and insurance, which are reported under Heading 5126.

Heading 5113: In previous editions, the Presumptive Tax was reported under 1210, taxes on the profits of corporations.

Heading 5123: "Other customs duties" includes the Levy on Pet Bottles, the Levy on Poultry, the Levy on Cans, and the Levy on Glass Bottles. Collections of revenues for the Livestock Trust Fund began in 2019.

Figures exclude tax revenues collected by sub-national governments as the data are not available.

Source: Seychelles Revenue Commission; Seychelles Ministry of Finance, Economic Planning and Trade; Financial Services Authority Seychelles Annual Reports; and Seychelles Pension Fund Annual Reports.

Table 5.30. Sierra Leone – Details of tax revenue

Million SLL

	1995	2000	2005	2010	2015	2018	2019	2020	2021	2022
Total tax revenue	..	..	**374 356**	**929 507**	**2 135 262**	**4 038 907**	**4 874 158**	**4 990 560**	**5 895 479**	**6 570 458**
1000 Taxes on income, profits and capital gains	..	..	**110 153**	**291 747**	**895 337**	**1 595 948**	**1 866 079**	**1 992 218**	**2 435 025**	**2 904 693**
1100 Of individuals	..	..	48 458	155 237	650 329	1 157 616	1 327 986	1 407 927	1 669 755	1 791 124
1110 On income and profits	..	..	48 458	155 237	650 329	1 157 616	1 327 986	1 407 927	1 669 755	1 791 124
Personal Income Tax - excluding mining from 2010	..	..	48 458	126 044	539 469	996 003	1 171 663	1 248 294	1 586 675	1 666 333
Personal Income Tax - mining	..	..	..	29 193	110 860	161 614	156 323	159 634	83 080	124 791
1120 On capital gains	..	..	0	0	0	0	0	0	0	0
1200 Corporate	..	..	61 696	136 510	245 008	438 331	538 093	584 291	765 270	1 113 569
1210 On profits	..	..	61 696	136 510	245 008	438 331	538 093	584 291	765 270	1 113 569
Corporate Tax - excluding mining from 2010	..	..	61 696	94 890	227 668	396 717	417 012	581 973	697 469	1 079 888
Corporate Tax - mining	..	..	..	8 016	2 360	26 324	57 789	2 316	49 895	14 952
Withholding tax contract payments - mining	..	..	..	33 604	14 979	15 291	63 293	2	17 906	18 729
1220 On capital gains of corporates	..	..	0	0	0	0	0	0	0	0
1300 Unallocable between 1100 and 1200	..	..	0	0	0	0	0	0	0	0
2000 Social security contributions	..	..	..	..	..	**492 794**	**547 253**	**613 578**	**702 106**	**834 024**
2100 Employees	..	..	..	..	..	..	..	..	..	..
2110 On a payroll basis	..	..	..	..	..	..	..	..	..	..
2120 On an income tax basis	..	..	..	..	..	..	..	..	..	..
2200 Employers	..	..	..	..	..	..	..	..	..	..
2210 On a payroll basis	..	..	..	..	..	..	..	..	..	..
2220 On an income tax basis	..	..	..	..	..	..	..	..	..	..
2300 Self-employed or non-employed	..	..	..	..	..	..	..	..	..	..
2310 On a payroll basis	..	..	..	..	..	..	..	..	..	..
2320 On an income tax basis	..	..	..	..	..	..	..	..	..	..
2400 Unallocable between 2100, 2200 and 2300	..	..	..	..	..	492 794	547 253	613 578	702 106	834 024
2410 On a payroll basis	..	..	..	..	..	..	..	..	..	..
2420 On an income tax basis	..	..	..	..	..	..	..	..	..	..
3000 Taxes on payroll and workforce	..	..	..	**115**	**159**	**1 068**	**9 949**	**0**	**0**	**1 073**
Payroll Tax - mining	..	..	..	115	159	1 068	586	..	..	1 073
4000 Taxes on property	..	..	..	..	..	..	..	..	..	..
4100 Recurrent taxes on immovable property	..	..	..	..	..	..	..	..	..	..
4110 Households	..	..	..	..	..	..	..	..	..	..
4120 Others	..	..	..	..	..	..	..	..	..	..
4200 Recurrent taxes on net wealth	..	..	..	..	..	..	..	..	..	..
4210 Individual	..	..	..	..	..	..	..	..	..	..
4220 Corporate	..	..	..	..	..	..	..	..	..	..
4300 Estate, inheritance and gift taxes	..	..	..	..	..	..	..	..	..	..
4310 Estate and inheritance taxes	..	..	..	..	..	..	..	..	..	..
4320 Gift taxes	..	..	..	..	..	..	..	..	..	..
4400 Taxes on financial and capital transactions	..	..	..	..	..	..	..	..	..	..
4500 Other non-reccurrent taxes on property	..	..	..	..	..	..	..	..	..	..
4510 On net wealth	..	..	..	..	..	..	..	..	..	..
4520 Other non-recurrent taxes	..	..	..	..	..	..	..	..	..	..
4600 Other recurrent taxes on property	..	..	..	..	..	..	..	..	..	..
5000 Taxes on goods and services	..	..	**264 203**	**637 645**	**1 239 766**	**1 949 097**	**2 450 877**	**2 384 764**	**2 758 348**	**2 830 668**
5100 Taxes on production, sale, transfer, etc	..	..	264 203	637 645	1 239 766	1 949 097	2 450 877	2 384 764	2 758 348	2 830 668
5110 General taxes on goods and services	..	..	0	246 362	593 048	886 383	1 030 686	1 046 227	1 257 858	1 420 358
5111 Value added taxes	..	..	..	246 362	593 048	886 383	1 030 686	1 046 227	1 257 858	1 420 358
Domestic GST - non - mining	..	..	..	100 067	238 819	335 798	411 886	465 502	580 004	585 001
Domestic GST - mining	..	..	..	9 590	18	5	33 075	1 956	669	940
Import GST - non - mining	..	..	..	136 698	354 112	545 030	583 356	577 748	677 051	831 484
Import GST - mining	..	..	..	7	99	5 550	2 369	1 020	134	2 933
5112 Sales tax	..	..	..	0	0	0	0	0	0	0
5113 Other	..	..	..	0	0	0	0	0	0	0
5120 Taxes on specific goods and services	..	..	264 203	391 283	646 718	1 062 713	1 420 191	1 338 537	1 500 490	1 410 310
5121 Excises	..	..	73 925	190 307	311 155	412 226	709 116	694 405	693 127	561 767
Excise on petroleum	..	..	42 347	123 439	193 084	347 155	567 476	520 115	404 573	310 696
Other excises	..	..	7 643	9 568	23 361	10 877	35 354	56 409	76 715	78 840
Road user charges	..	..	23 935	57 300	94 710	54 194	106 286	117 881	211 839	172 231

Table 5.30. Sierra Leone – Details of tax revenue (continued)

Million SLL

	1995	2000	2005	2010	2015	2018	2019	2020	2021	2022
5122 Profits of fiscal monopolies	..	..	0	0	0	0	0	0	0	0
5123 Customs and import duties	..	..	185 990	189 811	329 368	650 487	711 075	644 133	807 363	848 543
Import duties - excluding mining from 2010	..	..	172 283	186 621	318 962	614 576	678 356	618 273	801 949	820 344
Import duty - mining	..	..	..	3 190	10 405	35 912	32 719	25 859	5 414	28 199
Other customs duties - non mining	..	..	13 707	0	0	0	0	0	0	0
5124 Taxes on exports	..	..	0	0	0	0	0	0	0	0
5125 Taxes on investment goods	..	..	0	0	0	0	0	0	0	0
5126 Taxes on specific services	..	..	4 288	11 164	6 195	0	0	0	0	0
Foreign travel tax	..	..	4 288	11 164	6 195	..	..	..	..	..
5127 Other taxes on internat. trade and transactions	..	..	0	0	0	0	0	0	0	0
5128 Other taxes	..	..	0	0	0	0	0	0	0	0
5130 Unallocable between 5110 and 5120	..	..	0	0	0	0	0	0	0	0
5200 Taxes on use of goods and to perform activities	..	..	0	0	0	0	0	0	0	0
5210 Recurrent taxes	..	..	..	..	..	..	..	..	..	..
5211 Paid by households: motor vehicles	..	..	..	..	..	..	..	..	..	..
5212 Paid by others: motor vehicles	..	..	..	..	..	..	..	..	..	..
5213 Paid in respect of other goods	..	..	..	..	..	..	..	..	..	..
5220 Non-recurrent taxes	..	..	..	..	..	..	..	..	..	..
5300 Unallocable between 5100 and 5200	..	..	0	0	0	0	0	0	0	0
6000 Other taxes	**..**	**..**	**0**	**0**	**0**	**0**	**0**	**0**	**0**	**0**
6100 Paid solely by business	..	..	..	..	..	..	..	..	..	..
6200 Other	..	..	..	..	..	..	..	..	..	..

.. Not available

Note: Year ending 31st December.

The data are on a cash basis.

Figures exclude tax revenues collected by sub-national governments as the data are not available.

Headings 1110, 1210, 3000, 5111, 5123: the breakdown of taxes between the mining and non-mining sector from year 2010 is available for the first time in this edition.

Heading 2000: social security contributions are available for the first time in this edition.

Heading 5121: The road user charge fund (RUC) is funded through fuel levies, vehicle licenses and vehicle registrations fees, however it is not possible to distinguish between these revenues. As fuel levies represent around 65% of these revenues, the totality of the RUC revenues is classified under heading 5121.

Heading 5126: The foreign travel tax on air tickets until mid-2018 is part of other taxes classified in income taxes in Sierra Leone's classification. From 2018, its collection is part of the Treasury Single Account collection classified in non-tax revenues under heading "Sales of goods and services".

Source: Sierra Leone National Revenue Authority.

Table 5.31. Somalia – Details of tax revenue

Million USD

	1995	2000	2005	2010	2015	2018	2019	2020	2021	2022
Total tax revenue	**..**	**..**	**..**	**..**	**84**	**137**	**191**	**218**	**248**	**269**
1000 Taxes on income, profits and capital gains	**..**	**..**	**..**	**..**	**2**	**9**	**15**	**23**	**24**	**30**
1100 Of individuals	..	..	..	..	1	7	10	18	22	26
1110 On income and profits	..	..	..	..	1	7	10	18	22	26
On wages and salaries of public sector employees	..	..	..	..	..	..	..	..	..	..
On wages and salaries of private sector employees	..	..	..	..	..	..	..	..	..	..
1120 On capital gains	..	..	..	..	0	0	0	0	0	0
1200 Corporate	..	..	..	..	1	1	4	4	2	1
1210 On profits	..	..	..	..	1	1	4	4	2	1
Corporate profits tax	..	..	..	..	..	..	..	..	..	..
1220 On capital gains of corporates	..	..	..	..	0	0	0	0	0	0
1300 Unallocable between 1100 and 1200	..	..	..	..	0	0	1	1	1	3
Rental income tax	..	..	..	..	0	0	1	1	1	3
2000 Social security contributions	**..**	**..**	**..**	**..**	**..**	**..**	**..**	**..**	**..**	**..**
2100 Employees	..	..	..	..	..	..	..	..	..	..
2110 On a payroll basis	..	..	..	..	..	..	..	..	..	..
2120 On an income tax basis	..	..	..	..	..	..	..	..	..	..
2200 Employers	..	..	..	..	..	..	..	..	..	..
2210 On a payroll basis	..	..	..	..	..	..	..	..	..	..
2220 On an income tax basis	..	..	..	..	..	..	..	..	..	..
2300 Self-employed or non-employed	..	..	..	..	..	..	..	..	..	..
2310 On a payroll basis	..	..	..	..	..	..	..	..	..	..
2320 On an income tax basis	..	..	..	..	..	..	..	..	..	..
2400 Unallocable between 2100, 2200 and 2300	..	..	..	..	..	..	..	..	..	..
2410 On a payroll basis	..	..	..	..	..	..	..	..	..	..
2420 On an income tax basis	..	..	..	..	..	..	..	..	..	..
3000 Taxes on payroll and workforce	**..**	**..**	**..**	**..**	**0**	**0**	**0**	**0**	**0**	**0**
4000 Taxes on property	**..**	**..**	**..**	**..**	**0**	**3**	**2**	**2**	**4**	**2**
4100 Recurrent taxes on immovable property	..	..	..	..	0	0	0	0	0	0
4110 Households	..	..	..	..	..	..	..	..	..	..
4120 Others	..	..	..	..	..	..	..	..	..	..
4200 Recurrent taxes on net wealth	..	..	..	..	0	0	0	0	0	0
4210 Individual	..	..	..	..	..	..	..	..	..	..
4220 Corporate	..	..	..	..	..	..	..	..	..	..
4300 Estate, inheritance and gift taxes	..	..	..	..	0	0	0	0	0	0
4310 Estate and inheritance taxes	..	..	..	..	..	..	..	..	..	..
4320 Gift taxes	..	..	..	..	..	..	..	..	..	..
4400 Taxes on financial and capital transactions	..	..	..	..	0	3	2	2	4	2
4500 Other non-reccurrent taxes on property	..	..	..	..	0	0	0	0	0	0
4510 On net wealth	..	..	..	..	..	..	..	..	..	..
4520 Other non-recurrent taxes	..	..	..	..	..	..	..	..	..	..
4600 Other recurrent taxes on property	..	..	..	..	0	0	0	0	0	0
5000 Taxes on goods and services	**..**	**..**	**..**	**..**	**82**	**126**	**175**	**190**	**217**	**234**
5100 Taxes on production, sale, transfer, etc	..	..	..	..	79	126	167	179	206	221
5110 General taxes on goods and services	..	..	..	..	5	22	29	32	36	41
5111 Value added taxes	..	..	..	..	0	0	0	0	0	0
5112 Sales tax	..	..	..	..	3	22	29	31	36	41
Sales taxes - Hotels	..	..	..	..	2	3	1	1	1	1
Sales taxes - Telecommunications	..	..	..	..	0	6	7	2	4	3
Sales taxes - Airline tickets	..	..	..	..	1	0	1	1	1	4
Sales taxes - Imported goods	..	..	..	..	0	13	20	28	31	33
5113 Other	..	..	..	..	2	0	0	0	0	0
5120 Taxes on specific goods and services	..	..	..	..	74	104	138	148	169	180
5121 Excises	..	..	..	..	0	0	0	0	0	0
5122 Profits of fiscal monopolies	..	..	..	..	0	0	0	0	0	0
5123 Customs and import duties	..	..	..	..	74	104	136	144	166	175
Customs and other import duties	..	..	..	..	7	8	30	50	53	65
Consumption goods	..	..	..	..	15	26	32	33	34	32

Table 5.31. Somalia – Details of tax revenue (continued)

Million USD

	1995	2000	2005	2010	2015	2018	2019	2020	2021	2022
Fuel and lubricants	..	..	..	..	9	8	9	10	17	20
Building materials	..	..	..	..	3	4	3	3	3	4
Khat	..	..	..	..	11	13	17	6	12	14
Clothes and shoes	..	..	..	..	12	14	9	8	9	6
Electric and electronics	..	..	..	..	4	5	7	6	6	12
Vehicle and spare parts	..	..	..	..	4	9	8	7	9	7
Other products	..	..	..	..	9	13	15	14	15	4
Stamp duties	..	..	..	..	1	3	8	8	10	11
5124 Taxes on exports	..	..	..	..	0	0	2	4	4	5
5125 Taxes on investment goods	..	..	..	..	0	0	0	0	0	0
5126 Taxes on specific services	..	..	..	..	0	0	0	0	0	0
5127 Other taxes on internat. trade and transactions	..	..	..	..	0	0	0	0	0	0
5128 Other taxes	..	..	..	..	0	0	0	0	0	0
5130 Unallocable between 5110 and 5120	..	..	..	..	0	0	0	0	0	0
5200 Taxes on use of goods and to perform activities	..	..	..	..	3	0	8	10	11	13
5210 Recurrent taxes	..	..	..	..	3	0	8	10	11	13
5211 Paid by households: motor vehicles	..	..	..	..	3	0	2	2	2	1
5212 Paid by others: motor vehicles	..	..	..	..	0	0	0	0	0	0
5213 Paid in respect of other goods	..	..	..	..	0	0	6	9	10	12
5220 Non-recurrent taxes	..	..	..	..	0	0	0	0	0	0
5300 Unallocable between 5100 and 5200	..	..	..	..	0	0	0	0	0	0
6000 Other taxes	**..**	**..**	**..**	**..**	**0**	**0**	**0**	**3**	**3**	**2**
6100 Paid solely by business	..	..	..	..	..	..	..	..	..	..
6200 Other	..	..	..	..	..	..	..	..	..	..

.. Not available

Note: Year ending 31st December.

The data are on a cash basis.

Data exclude revenue collected on the local level as data were not available.

Data include revenues collected directly by the Federal Government of Somalia and the Federal Member States (FMS): Puntland, Jubaland, South West, Galmudug, Hirshabelle and the Benadir Regional Authority. Data from the FMS is only available from 2019 onwards.

The data are not consolidated however they do not include transfers received from the FGS and represent direct collections only.

Source: Ministry of Finance of Somalia.

Table 5.32. South Africa – Details of tax revenue

Million ZAR

	1995	2000	2005	2010	2015	2018	2019	2020	2021	2022
Total tax revenue	**121 920**	**211 561**	**418 823**	**706 530**	**1 167 531**	**1 419 087**	**1 469 099**	**1 398 144**	**1 632 697**	**1 794 153**
1000 Taxes on income, profits and capital gains	**65 565**	**119 979**	**220 197**	**368 118**	**604 881**	**732 459**	**764 053**	**710 904**	**880 709**	**964 417**
1100 Of individuals	49 520	87 105	122 279	219 886	389 883	485 458	519 034	493 137	537 404	587 741
1110 On income and profits	49 520	87 105	122 279	219 886	389 883	485 458	519 034	493 137	537 404	587 741
Employees tax	..	..	..	213 113	379 535	471 062	509 023	490 000	538 832	583 372
Employment Tax Incentive (ETI) refunds	..	..	..	0	- 3 349	- 4 275	- 4 590	- 7 081	- 6 799	- 4 814
PIT Provisional tax	..	..	..	15 719	24 200	33 426	32 138	29 149	28 291	31 195
PIT Assessment payments	..	..	..	7 425	9 970	16 230	13 158	12 831	13 810	14 978
PIT Refunds	..	..	..	- 16 372	- 20 474	- 30 986	- 30 695	- 31 762	- 36 730	- 36 989
1120 On capital gains	..	..	..	..	..	..	..	..	..	..
1200 Corporate	14 427	23 987	82 628	132 275	191 348	215 939	215 346	194 433	309 017	338 391
1210 On profits	14 427	23 987	82 628	132 275	191 348	215 939	215 346	194 433	309 017	338 391
CIT Provisional tax	..	..	..	136 615	190 437	222 178	221 026	201 664	308 812	342 017
CIT Assessment payments	..	..	..	9 051	11 119	13 714	11 953	13 751	17 678	14 574
Royalties	..	..	..	161	369	676	633	549	680	646
CIT Refunds	..	..	..	- 13 552	- 10 577	- 20 630	- 18 266	- 21 531	- 18 153	- 18 846
1220 On capital gains of corporates	..	..	..	..	..	..	..	..	..	..
1300 Unallocable between 1100 and 1200	1 618	8 887	15 290	15 957	23 649	31 062	29 673	23 334	34 288	38 285
Dividend Tax (DT) / Secondary Tax on Companies (STC)	..	..	..	15 871	23 647	30 359	29 098	22 831	33 815	37 629
Withholding tax on interest	..	..	..	0	0	703	574	504	473	656
Tax on retirement funds	..	..	..	63	0	0	0	0	- 0	0
Small Business Tax Amnesty	..	..	..	23	2	0	0	- 0	0	- 0
Other unallocable income taxes	..	..	..	0	0	0	0	0	0	0
2000 Social security contributions	**0**	**0**	**6 477**	**11 117**	**17 138**	**19 028**	**19 799**	**18 927**	**20 824**	**23 006**
2100 Employees	..	..	3 254	5 740	8 724	9 567	9 957	9 517	10 478	11 563
2110 On a payroll basis	..	..	31	363	310	107	115	107	131	121
2120 On an income tax basis	..	..	3 223	5 377	8 414	9 460	9 842	9 410	10 347	11 442
2200 Employers	..	..	3 223	5 377	8 414	9 460	9 842	9 410	10 347	11 442
2210 On a payroll basis	..	..	0	0	0	0	0	0	0	0
2220 On an income tax basis	..	..	3 223	5 377	8 414	9 460	9 842	9 410	10 347	11 442
2300 Self-employed or non-employed	..	..	0	0	0	0	0	0	0	0
2310 On a payroll basis	..	..	..	..	..	..	..	..	..	..
2320 On an income tax basis	..	..	..	..	..	..	..	..	..	..
2400 Unallocable between 2100, 2200 and 2300	..	..	0	0	0	0	0	0	0	0
2410 On a payroll basis	..	..	..	..	..	..	..	..	..	..
2420 On an income tax basis	..	..	..	..	..	..	..	..	..	..
3000 Taxes on payroll and workforce	**0**	**870**	**4 839**	**8 240**	**15 111**	**17 265**	**18 062**	**12 557**	**18 842**	**20 596**
4000 Taxes on property	**2 131**	**3 829**	**23 530**	**40 108**	**59 110**	**83 554**	**92 320**	**94 415**	**67 092**	**81 961**
4100 Recurrent taxes on immovable property	0	0	12 906	31 041	44 618	67 373	76 104	79 394	46 124	60 017
4110 Households	..	..	12 258	30 533	44 169	66 824	70 103	73 390	39 895	60 017
4120 Others	..	..	648	508	449	549	6 001	6 004	6 229	0
4200 Recurrent taxes on net wealth	0	0	0	0	0	0	0	0	0	0
4210 Individual	..	..	..	..	..	..	..	..	..	..
4220 Corporate	..	..	..	..	..	..	..	..	..	..
4300 Estate, inheritance and gift taxes	222	436	626	855	2 065	2 740	2 780	2 953	3 514	4 224
4310 Estate and inheritance taxes	164	417	598	794	1 918	1 894	2 174	2 359	2 942	3 614
4320 Gift taxes	57	19	28	61	147	846	605	594	573	610
4400 Taxes on financial and capital transactions	397	1 094	1 718	2 912	5 069	5 967	6 235	5 260	7 244	6 070
4500 Other non-reccurrent taxes on property	1 512	2 299	8 280	5 300	7 358	7 474	7 201	6 808	10 210	11 649
4510 On net wealth	0	0	0	0	0	0	0	0	0	0
4520 Other non-recurrent taxes	1 512	2 299	8 280	5 300	7 358	7 474	7 201	6 808	10 210	11 649
4600 Other recurrent taxes on property	0	0	0	0	0	0	0	0	0	0
5000 Taxes on goods and services	**52 938**	**84 462**	**162 918**	**278 924**	**471 292**	**566 791**	**574 856**	**561 340**	**645 230**	**704 172**
5100 Taxes on production, sale, transfer, etc	52 938	84 462	159 589	273 602	463 434	555 592	573 447	548 293	630 998	689 342
5110 General taxes on goods and services	31 729	52 054	109 274	170 548	277 551	324 717	329 415	333 372	374 693	413 905
5111 Value added taxes	31 729	52 054	109 274	170 552	277 530	324 696	329 397	333 375	374 684	413 895
Domestic VAT	18 954	52 547	126 492	202 483	303 210	368 766	392 919	390 367	436 980	479 218
VAT on imports	12 775	25 148	42 615	78 697	148 467	169 033	181 777	161 679	192 374	241 033
VAT refunds	0	- 25 641	- 59 833	- 110 627	- 174 147	- 213 103	- 245 298	- 218 672	- 254 670	- 306 357

Table 5.32. South Africa – Details of tax revenue (continued)

Million ZAR

	1995	2000	2005	2010	2015	2018	2019	2020	2021	2022
5112 Sales tax	0	0	0	- 5	21	20	18	- 3	9	11
5113 Other	0	0	0	0	0	0	0	0	0	0
5120 Taxes on specific goods and services	21 209	32 408	50 315	103 054	185 883	230 875	244 032	214 920	256 305	275 437
5121 Excises	15 225	24 341	35 490	76 239	137 870	172 198	183 860	165 665	198 142	199 215
Specific excise tax - Domestic	..	..	..	22 448	34 918	41 568	47 811	36 500	48 448	55 874
Ad valorem excise - Domestic	..	..	..	1 569	3 295	4 163	4 274	3 035	4 772	4 325
Fuel levy	..	..	..	32 758	56 694	74 376	78 361	76 204	86 787	79 431
Plastic bags	..	..	..	177	213	287	328	493	639	711
Electricity levy	..	..	..	5 065	8 481	8 448	8 315	7 833	7 932	7 576
Incandescent light bulb levy	..	..	..	180	63	46	34	26	25	25
CO2 tax - Motor vehicle emissions	..	..	..	205	1 429	1 376	1 355	1 248	2 037	2 597
Road Accident Fund (RAF)	..	..	..	13 837	32 778	41 189	42 658	39 756	46 775	47 936
Tyre Levy	..	..	..	0	0	744	724	568	727	740
5122 Profits of fiscal monopolies	0	0	0	0	0	0	0	0	0	0
5123 Customs and import duties	5 129	7 714	13 294	25 196	43 965	53 936	55 752	47 064	54 049	70 528
Import duties	..	..	..	..	32 130	37 649	37 595	32 890	36 836	46 666
Ad valorem import duty	..	..	..	..	8 495	10 091	10 580	8 252	9 583	15 192
Excise on imports	..	..	..	..	3 340	6 191	7 575	5 919	7 630	8 670
International Oil Pollution Levy	..	..	..	..	0	5	3	3	0	0
5124 Taxes on exports	0	0	0	61	121	62	94	70	289	1 088
Diamond export duties	..	..	..	61	121	62	94	70	108	186
Export tax on scrap metal	..	..	..	0	0	0	0	0	181	902
5125 Taxes on investment goods	0	0	0	0	0	0	0	0	0	0
5126 Taxes on specific services	0	0	1 320	2 252	3 224	3 943	3 523	1 948	2 460	3 571
5127 Other taxes on internat. trade and transactions	855	353	211	- 695	703	736	804	173	1 364	1 035
5128 Other taxes	0	0	0	0	0	0	0	0	0	0
5130 Unallocable between 5110 and 5120	0	0	0	0	0	0	0	0	0	0
5200 Taxes on use of goods and to perform activities	0	0	3 328	5 322	7 858	11 199	1 409	13 047	14 233	14 830
5210 Recurrent taxes	..	..	3 328	5 322	7 858	11 199	1 409	13 047	14 233	14 830
5211 Paid by households: motor vehicles	..	..	2 644	4 046	6 234	8 706	922	9 691	10 000	10 452
5212 Paid by others: motor vehicles	..	..	661	1 012	1 558	2 176	231	2 423	2 500	2 613
5213 Paid in respect of other goods	..	..	23	264	66	317	256	933	1 733	1 765
Universal Service Fund	..	..	0	233	6	222	193	244	258	85
Carbon Tax	..	..	0	0	0	0	0	626	1 408	1 597
Provincial liquor licences	..	..	23	31	60	95	64	63	67	83
5220 Non-recurrent taxes	..	..	0	0	0	0	0	0	0	0
5300 Unallocable between 5100 and 5200	0	0	0	0	0	0	0	0	0	0
6000 Other taxes	**1 286**	**2 420**	**863**	**23**	**- 1**	**- 11**	**10**	**1**	**- 1**	**2**
6100 Paid solely by business	0	0	0	0	0	0	0	0	0	0
6200 Other	1 286	2 420	863	23	- 1	- 11	10	1	- 1	2
Stamp duties and fees	..	..	..	9	0	0	0	1	- 0	0
Unallocated tax revenues	..	..	..	14	- 1	- 11	10	- 0	- 1	2
Memo items:	..	..	..	..	..	..	..	..	..	..
SACU expenditure	..	..	14 145	17 905	51 022	56 921	60 264	25 593	67 761	100 163

.. Not available

Note: Year ending 31st December with the exception of social security contributions and taxes at provincial and local levels which are reported on a fiscal year basis beginning 1st April, meaning that the data for 2022 represent April 2022 to March 2023.

Tax revenues on national and provincial government level in South Africa are on a cash basis, while local authorities and public entities are on an accrual basis. Data on local government revenues were not available for the years 2019/20, 2020/21, and 2021/22.

Data prior to 1995/96 were restated retrospectively to aggregate the revenues from TBVC States and Self-Governing Territories.

With the adoption of the interim Constitution in 1994, these were abolished:

-TBVC States: Transkei, Bophuthatswana, Venda and Ciskei.

-Self-Governing Territories: Gazankulu, Kangwane, Kwandebele, Kwazulu, Lebowa and Qwaqwa.

Tax revenues at the local and provincial levels are only available from 2003 (representing fiscal year 2003/04). Local tax revenues are not reported for the years 2019 onwards.

Headings 1110 and 1120: The figures include Capital Gains Tax (CGT). CGT cannot be listed separately under 1120 and 1220 because the data that South African Revenue Service (SARS) collated for CGT are for liability raised and not actual CGT collections received. The figures exclude interest and fines from 1994 onwards. Figures on ETI refunds, which started being collected in 2014, are now reported under 1110.

Heading 2000: the social security contributions in South Africa include contributions to the Unemployment Insurance Fund (UIF). Standard practice in South Africa is to classify UIF under non-tax revenue. The methodology applied in the compilation of the data was to allocate 50% of the total social security contributions (UIF) to each of employees and employers. Revenues collected under the Occupational Diseases in Mines and Works Act are reported under heading 2110, social security contributions by employees on a payroll basis. Figures for these last revenues were not available for 2021.

Heading 4120: the figures refer to penalties and collection charges on property rates.

Headings 4110 and 4120: These are local government revenues for which figures are missing for the year 2019 onwards. Recurrent taxes on immovable property were divided into collections on households (4110) and penalties and collection charges (4120). As of 2022, Penalties and Collection charges are no longer reported as a separate line item for local revenues from property rates, and therefore are not reported here.
Heading 5111: includes interests and fines.
Heading 5121: following the OECD classification, the Road Accident Fund (RAF) is classified as an excise. The national classification of South Africa classifies this revenue as a social security contribution.
Headings 5121 and 5123: The data for customs duties and excise include revenue on import duties plus specific and ad valorem excise duties that will be paid to Botswana, Eswatini, Lesotho and Namibia (BELN) through the revenue sharing agreement.
Heading 5123: SARS only started separately reporting ordinary custom duties on imported goods, specific excise duties on imported goods and ad valorem duties on imported goods from April 2012. From April 2014 onwards, the Customs Duty amounts for the specific tariff headings under chapter 27 (Mineral Fuels) were treated as fuel levies (5121 Excises). Some estimation was used for the year 2012 due to missing information. Revenues from the International Pollution Levy were reported for the first time in this edition of *Revenue Statistics in Africa*.
Headings 5127 and 6200: include negative figures due to refund accounting adjustments.
Heading 5211: an 80:20 ratio was used to split provincial recurrent motor vehicle taxes based on research about South Africa's commercial and private household motor vehicle fleet.
Heading 6200: includes stamp duties and fees plus unallocated tax revenue.
Taxes that were discontinued and introduced (causing breaks in the data) include the following:

a. Ordinary levy discontinued in March 2003 (heading 5127).
b. Demutualisation charge has been included in heading 4400. There were two collections in March 1999 and August 1999.
c. Secondary Tax on Companies (STC) in heading 1300 effective from July 1993 and changed to Dividends Tax (DT) in April 2012.
d. Small business tax amnesty (heading 1300) effective from March 2007.
e. VAT (heading 5111) effective from September 1991 at a rate of 10% and increased to 14% in 1993. Prior to that, sales tax data was restated to VAT.
f. Levy on financial services (heading 4400) effective from January 1992.
g. Skills development levy (heading 3000) effective from May 2000.
h. Excises (5121)
   - Plastic bags effective from June 2005.
   - Electricity levy effective from August 2009.
   - Incandescent light bulbs effective from March 2010.
   - CO^2 tax effective from September 2010.
i. Air departure tax (heading 5126) effective from December 2000.
j. Universal services fund (heading 5213 paid in respect of other goods) effective from March 2006.

Memo items: the Southern African Customs Union (SACU) expenditure records the difference between South Africa contributions to the SACU pool and the South Africa revenue share from the SACU pool that includes the balance of the "surplus/deficit" for that fiscal year and allocations to the SACU secretariat. The figures for 2013/14 figures differ from numbers published in South African tax statistics since some Fuel Levy imports were included in that year.
Source: Data on national government taxation from the South African Revenue Service (SARS); data on social security contributions, and taxes levied at the provincial and local level from the National Treasury of South Africa.

Table 5.33. Togo – Details of tax revenue

Million XOF

	1995	2000	2005	2010	2015	2018	2019	2020	2021	2022
Total tax revenue	**..**	**99 994**	**159 843**	**250 441**	**533 556**	**576 528**	**634 515**	**669 838**	**792 918**	**883 698**
1000 Taxes on income, profits and capital gains	**..**	**20 928**	**37 656**	**41 200**	**88 658**	**117 078**	**136 035**	**132 485**	**184 113**	**192 458**
1100 Of individuals	..	9 440	17 272	18 000	30 791	44 595	48 979	50 924	70 039	65 327
1110 On income and profits	..	9 440	17 272	18 000	30 791	44 595	48 979	50 920	70 032	64 045
Tax on the revenue of road haulers	..	452	514	393	379	368	261	0	0	0
Withholding tax on investment income	..	1 185	2 217	6 106	8 365	11 183	11 687	9 023	21 921	12 992
Income tax on individuals	..	7 804	14 540	11 500	22 046	33 043	36 890	41 776	48 077	51 028
Personal income tax (transfers to local authorities)	..	..	..	1	0	0	0	0	0	0
Property tax on undeveloped properties (TFPNB) - Central government	..	0	0	0	0	0	56	81	14	12
Property tax on undeveloped properties (TFPNB) - Local government	..	..	..	0	0	0	84	39	19	13
1120 On capital gains	..	0	0	0	0	0	0	4	8	1 283
Capital gains tax (TPV)	..	..	..	..	..	..	0	4	8	1 283
1200 Corporate	..	11 488	20 385	23 200	57 867	72 483	87 056	81 560	114 074	127 130
1210 On profits	..	11 488	20 385	23 200	57 867	72 483	87 056	81 560	114 074	127 130
Corporate tax	..	8 997	16 525	18 280	51 177	64 851	76 670	74 026	101 112	111 661
Profits from commercial and industrial companies	..	2 490	3 860	4 920	6 691	7 632	10 387	7 534	12 962	15 470
1220 On capital gains of corporates	..	0	0	0	0	0	0	0	0	0
1300 Unallocable between 1100 and 1200	..	0	0	0	0	0	0	0	0	0
2000 Social security contributions	**..**	**..**	**..**	**..**	**..**	**..**	**..**	**..**	**..**	**..**
2100 Employees	..	..	..	..	..	..	..	..	..	..
2110 On a payroll basis	..	..	..	..	..	..	..	..	..	..
2120 On an income tax basis	..	..	..	..	..	..	..	..	..	..
2200 Employers	..	..	..	..	..	..	..	..	..	..
2210 On a payroll basis	..	..	..	..	..	..	..	..	..	..
2220 On an income tax basis	..	..	..	..	..	..	..	..	..	..
2300 Self-employed or non-employed	..	..	..	..	..	..	..	..	..	..
2310 On a payroll basis	..	..	..	..	..	..	..	..	..	..
2320 On an income tax basis	..	..	..	..	..	..	..	..	..	..
2400 Unallocable between 2100, 2200 and 2300	..	..	..	..	..	..	..	..	..	..
2410 On a payroll basis	..	..	..	..	..	..	..	..	..	..
2420 On an income tax basis	..	..	..	..	..	..	..	..	..	..
3000 Taxes on payroll and workforce	**..**	**1 973**	**2 463**	**5 491**	**4 551**	**4 757**	**2 262**	**770**	**505**	**528**
Complementary tax on income	..	79	169	1 220	956	1 042	953	500	344	463
Taxes / wages	..	1 894	2 294	4 137	3 284	3 253	1 119	142	105	33
Supplementary tax on income tax (transfers to local authorities)	..	..	..	134	311	463	190	128	56	32
4000 Taxes on property	**..**	**374**	**599**	**1 898**	**4 360**	**4 819**	**5 048**	**5 462**	**4 090**	**5 629**
4100 Recurrent taxes on immovable property	..	374	599	1 898	4 360	4 819	5 048	5 190	3 936	5 584
Property tax on developed property	..	278	435	655	1 465	1 410	1 531	1 698	1 014	991
Real estate registration fees	..	96	164	335	613	334	345	1 238	1 172	2 584
Waste removal tax (transfers to local authorities)	..	..	..	129	315	407	360	84	15	14
Property tax on built properties (transfers to local authorities)	..	..	..	553	1 404	2 032	2 078	1 534	984	1 111
4110 Households	..	..	..	226	563	636	735	638	750	884
Housing tax (transfers to local authorities)	..	..	..	226	563	636	735	638	750	884
4120 Others	..	0	0	0	0	0	0	0	0	0
4200 Recurrent taxes on net wealth	..	0	0	0	0	0	0	0	0	0
4210 Individual	..	..	..	..	..	..	..	..	..	..
4220 Corporate	..	..	..	..	..	..	..	..	..	..
4300 Estate, inheritance and gift taxes	..	0	0	0	0	0	0	0	0	0
4310 Estate and inheritance taxes	..	..	..	..	..	..	..	..	..	..
4320 Gift taxes	..	..	..	..	..	..	..	..	..	..
4400 Taxes on financial and capital transactions	..	0	0	0	0	0	0	272	154	45
Land ownership tax	..	..	..	..	..	..	..	272	154	45
4500 Other non-reccurrent taxes on property	..	0	0	0	0	0	0	0	0	0
4510 On net wealth	..	..	..	..	..	..	..	..	..	..
4520 Other non-recurrent taxes	..	..	..	..	..	..	..	..	..	..

Table 5.33. Togo – Details of tax revenue (continued)

Million XOF

	1995	2000	2005	2010	2015	2018	2019	2020	2021	2022
4600 Other recurrent taxes on property	..	0	0	0	0	0	0	0	0	0
5000 Taxes on goods and services	**..**	**74 771**	**116 641**	**196 239**	**427 424**	**439 693**	**481 493**	**515 893**	**591 852**	**669 919**
5100 Taxes on production, sale, transfer, etc	..	74 662	116 483	195 813	425 367	437 006	474 721	505 853	576 414	643 170
5110 General taxes on goods and services	..	36 941	64 120	115 056	250 410	256 847	282 656	291 843	327 283	364 098
5111 Value added taxes	..	36 073	62 989	110 316	236 011	237 537	268 602	280 325	325 465	362 789
VAT revenues (customs)	..	25 101	44 182	69 840	167 228	142 211	160 514	176 623	202 194	229 283
VAT revenues (domestic)	..	10 972	18 807	40 476	68 783	95 325	108 088	103 702	123 271	133 507
5112 Sales tax	..	0	0	0	0	0	0	0	0	0
5113 Other	..	868	1 131	4 740	14 399	19 311	14 054	11 518	1 818	1 308
Unified occupation tax	..	146	155	334	507	537	593	340	272	126
Business tax	..	722	976	1 587	6 693	7 270	5 060	4 184	309	22
Unified business tax (transfers to local authorities)	..	..	..	206	507	597	810	719	774	1 127
Business tax (transfers to local authorities)	..	..	..	2 613	6 693	10 906	7 591	6 276	464	33
5120 Taxes on specific goods and services	..	37 696	52 336	80 724	174 957	180 159	192 064	214 010	249 131	279 073
5121 Excises	..	12 785	14 803	16 360	35 150	44 429	38 206	52 400	61 221	56 139
Excise fees / petroleum products	..	11 773	11 852	11 738	17 972	22 978	20 614	28 910	32 173	29 241
Other excise fees	..	1 012	2 950	4 622	8 246	11 835	16 237	18 323	23 700	21 320
Oil sector debt relief levy (PADSP)	..	0	0	0	8 932	9 616	1 356	5 167	5 349	5 578
5122 Profits of fiscal monopolies	..	0	0	0	0	0	0	0	0	0
5123 Customs and import duties	..	22 559	35 143	61 676	122 750	117 608	135 991	142 419	166 427	197 201
Customs fees	..	18 519	30 023	52 941	101 730	90 186	103 536	108 532	125 235	143 821
Statistical royalties	..	2 717	3 720	6 763	13 578	18 447	23 012	24 459	30 188	39 936
Customs stamps	..	94	138	297	424	285	290	313	387	1 076
Cards and vignettes	..	186	209	237	369	872	919	448	414	658
Infrastructure protection and maintenance tax	..	1 039	1 050	1 434	2 958	3 917	3 942	4 230	4 910	4 830
Products of customs credits	..	2	2	2	5	8	9	9	12	14
National solidarity fee	..	0	0	0	3 686	3 893	4 284	4 427	5 281	6 866
Remittances	..	1	0	0	0	0	0	0	0	0
Virtual warehouses	..	1	2	2	0	0	0	0	0	0
5124 Taxes on exports	..	302	314	1 430	2 728	2 977	3 104	2 727	4 147	6 695
Special tax on re-exports	..	302	314	1 430	2 260	2 685	3 104	2 727	4 147	6 695
Mining royalties (66.67%)	..	0	0	0	468	292	0	0	0	0
5125 Taxes on investment goods	..	0	0	0	0	0	0	0	0	0
5126 Taxes on specific services	..	2 049	2 076	1 258	14 329	15 146	14 763	16 464	17 336	19 038
Gambling tax	..	151	206	347	913	1 184	1 343	1 265	1 465	1 430
Tax / insurances agreements	..	227	378	815	2 035	2 158	2 248	2 571	2 850	2 634
Tax on Financial Transactions	..	1 671	1 491	0	11 140	11 508	10 466	12 180	12 452	14 352
Tax on games of chance (transfers to local authorities)	..	..	..	94	228	296	336	316	366	358
Entertainment tax (transfers to local authorities)	..	..	..	2	13	0	28	17	3	1
Air ticket issuance tax (TEBA)	..	0	0	0	0	0	342	115	200	263
5127 Other taxes on internat. trade and transactions	..	0	0	0	0	0	0	0	0	0
5128 Other taxes	..	0	0	0	0	0	0	0	0	0
5130 Unallocable between 5110 and 5120	..	25	28	33	0	0	0	0	0	0
Customs revenue on bonded products	..	25	28	33	..	..	..	..	..	..
5200 Taxes on use of goods and to perform activities	..	108	158	426	2 057	2 687	6 772	10 040	15 438	26 749
5210 Recurrent taxes	..	108	158	426	2 057	2 687	6 772	10 040	15 438	26 749
5211 Paid by households: motor vehicles	..	0	0	0	0	0	223	703	1 899	2 270
Motor vehicle tax (TVM)	..	..	..	..	..	..	223	703	1 899	2 270
5212 Paid by others: motor vehicles	..	2	5	0	287	312	260	74	23	6
Tax on company vehicles	..	2	5	..	287	312	260	74	23	6
5213 Paid in respect of other goods	..	106	154	426	1 770	2 375	6 290	9 263	13 516	24 472
Special tax on the manufacturing and sales of drinks	..	106	154	162	1 145	1 521	482	8	0	0
Special tax on the manufacturing and sales of drinks (transfers to local authorities)	..	..	..	264	625	855	697	13	0	0
Duty on non - salary economic activities of physical persons - Central government	..	0	0	0	0	0	1 916	7 204	5 068	13 030
Duty on non - salary economic activities of physical persons - Local governments	..	0	0	0	0	0	3 194	2 038	8 447	11 441

Table 5.33. Togo – Details of tax revenue (continued)

Million XOF

	1995	2000	2005	2010	2015	2018	2019	2020	2021	2022
5220 Non-recurrent taxes	..	0	0	0	0	0	0	0	0	0
5300 Unallocable between 5100 and 5200	..	0	0	0	0	0	0	0	0	0
6000 Other taxes	**..**	**1 949**	**2 483**	**5 612**	**8 563**	**10 180**	**9 676**	**15 228**	**12 357**	**15 164**
Stamp duties	..	1 471	1 668	3 135	3 612	3 258	3 072	2 913	3 428	3 722
Registration fees	..	478	816	2 436	4 949	6 553	6 392	11 950	8 568	11 022
Registration fee (transfers to local authorities)	..	..	..	41	2	369	213	364	361	420
6100 Paid solely by business	..	..	..	..	..	..	..	..	..	..
6200 Other	..	..	..	..	..	..	..	..	..	..
Memo items:	..	..	..	..	..	..	..	..	..	..
Support for oil policy	..	0	0	3 700	5 748	13 332	7 048	622	21 169	63 269
Excise duties and taxes on petroleum going to the Autonomous Road Maintenance Financing Company (SAFER)	..	5 519	7 624	7 339	9 495	13 820	10 999	15 234	17 206	15 712

.. Not available

Note: Year ending 31st December.

The data are on a cash basis.

Figures exclude tax revenues collected by sub-national governments as the data are not available.

The figures in headings 1110, 3000, 4100, 5113, 5126, 5213 and 6000 include revenues collected by the Togolese tax authorities on behalf of sub-national governments. This applies to the period 2008-21 and the lines concerned are highlighted with the words "Transfers to sub-national governments". These revenues are included in central government revenues following the OECD *Interpretative Guide*. Under Togo's national classification they are not included in state budget revenues.

Heading 1110: Collection of revenues from property tax on undeveloped land (*TFPNB: taxes foncières sur les propriétés non bâties*) began in 2019.

Heading 1110: Income tax on road hauliers was abolished in 2019.

Heading 1120: The collection of revenues from capital gains tax began in 2019.

Heading 2000: Data on social security contributions are not available.

Heading 4400: The collection of land conservation fees (DCPF) started in 2020.

Heading 5121: The "Oil sector debt relief levy" (*PADSP*: *Prélèvement pour apurement de la dette du secteur pétrolier*) is included in tax revenues in this edition following the OECD classification of taxes (see the *Interpretative Guide* in Annex A). Under Togo's national classification, it is included in non-tax revenues.

Heading 5126: Collection of revenues from the "Tax on the Issue of Airline Tickets" (*TEBA: Taxe à l'émission des billets d'avion*) began in 2019.

Heading 5211: Collection of revenues from the tax on motor vehicles (*TVM: Taxe sur les véhicules à moteur*) began in 2019.

Data on VAT refunds are not available because in Togo VAT credits are not refunded using conventional means of payment (bank transfer, cheque, cash, etc.). Taxpayers with a VAT credit submit a refund request to the tax authorities who issue a refund certificate. This certificate can be used by taxpayers to pay not only subsequent VAT returns but also other taxes.

Heading 5213: The collection of revenues from licence fees on economic activity of self-employed persons began in 2019.

Under Togo's national classification, fines and penalties relating to taxes, confiscations and customs sales and refunds of the community solidarity levy are included in tax revenues. These revenues are included in non-tax revenues in this edition following the OECD classification of taxes (see the *Interpretative Guide* in Annex A).

Soutien à la politique pétrolière (SPP) is a fund financed by a levy on VAT collected by customs, except for the years 2010-12 when the SPP was financed by a government grant.

Source: Togolese Revenue Office (*OTR: Office Togolais des Recettes*).

Table 5.34. Tunisia – Details of tax revenue

Million TND

	1995	2000	2005	2010	2016	2018	2019	2020	2021	2022
Total tax revenue	..	**7 196**	**10 146**	**17 143**	**26 596**	**33 824**	**39 450**	**38 829**	**42 449**	**48 111**
1000 Taxes on income, profits and capital gains	..	**1 624**	**2 927**	**5 091**	**7 384**	**8 979**	**12 486**	**12 005**	**12 521**	**14 799**
1100 Of individuals	..	1 049	1 565	2 657	5 931	6 359	8 713	8 945	9 501	10 524
1110 On income and profits	..	1 037	1 560	2 644	5 887	6 311	8 658	8 898	9 442	10 431
Salaries and wages	..	742	1 160	2 006	4 107	4 054	5 800	6 125	6 745	7 432
Fees, commissions, brokerage and rents (personal)	..	20	93	184	483	508	665	623	567	632
Interests deposits of special savings accounts	..	65	43	68	176	270	315	339	330	423
Income from securities (personal)	..	32	63	75	269	310	498	573	540	560
Advances on deals (personal)	..	27	24	50	508	720	821	716	681	649
Business profits	..	43	56	94	142	154	201	171	196	279
Non-commercial profits	..	17	24	49	79	98	123	117	107	182
Flat tax	..	14	16	25	37	48	64	47	64	74
Farm incomes	..	5	4	8	22	26	33	39	40	40
Land and other income	..	5	4	8	22	30	40	43	43	59
Other taxes on income and profits	..	66	73	78	42	93	99	105	129	102
1120 On capital gains	..	12	5	13	45	48	54	48	60	93
1200 Corporate	..	575	1 360	2 432	1 450	2 620	3 774	3 060	3 019	4 275
1210 On profits	..	575	1 359	2 424	1 442	2 613	3 763	3 037	3 003	4 261
Oil companies	..	96	459	813	346	709	959	447	638	1 221
Non-oil companies	..	359	644	864	806	1 149	1 984	1 877	1 594	2 187
Advances on deals (corporations)	..	33	97	356	46	57	48	55	41	43
Advance on imports	..	7	28	111	198	430	468	285	345	383
Income from securities (corporations)	..	58	68	113	27	226	269	298	338	384
Fees, commissions, brokerage and rents (corporations)	..	16	52	125	2	5	4	3	3	5
Royalties paid to non-residents	..	3	8	39	9	4	18	27	43	30
Other taxes on profits	..	3	3	3	9	33	12	46	1	7
1220 On capital gains of corporates	..	0	1	7	7	7	11	23	16	15
1300 Unallocable between 1100 and 1200	..	0	2	2	4	0	0	0	0	0
2000 Social security contributions	..	**1 551**	**2 307**	**4 629**	**8 415**	**9 826**	**11 172**	**11 982**	**12 598**	**13 247**
2100 Employees	..	..	..	..	..	..	..	..	..	..
2110 On a payroll basis	..	..	..	..	..	..	..	..	..	..
2120 On an income tax basis	..	..	..	..	..	..	..	..	..	..
2200 Employers	..	..	..	..	..	..	..	..	..	..
2210 On a payroll basis	..	..	..	..	..	..	..	..	..	..
2220 On an income tax basis	..	..	..	..	..	..	..	..	..	..
2300 Self-employed or non-employed	..	..	..	..	..	..	..	..	..	..
2310 On a payroll basis	..	..	..	..	..	..	..	..	..	..
2320 On an income tax basis	..	..	..	..	..	..	..	..	..	..
2400 Unallocable between 2100, 2200 and 2300	..	1 551	2 307	4 629	8 415	9 826	11 172	11 982	12 598	13 247
2410 On a payroll basis	..	..	..	..	..	..	..	..	..	..
2420 On an income tax basis	..	..	..	..	..	..	..	..	..	..
3000 Taxes on payroll and workforce	..	**107**	**114**	**199**	**345**	**405**	**457**	**445**	**488**	**551**
Fund promoting social housing	..	71	74	124	215	246	278	287	307	329
Vocational training tax	..	35	40	75	130	159	179	159	181	222
4000 Taxes on property	..	**81**	**104**	**177**	**299**	**308**	**371**	**308**	**405**	**480**
4100 Recurrent taxes on immovable property	..	7	7	10	11	13	18	14	12	12
4110 Households	..	7	7	10	11	13	18	14	12	0
4120 Others	..	0	0	0	0	0	0	0	0	0
4200 Recurrent taxes on net wealth	..	0	0	0	0	0	0	0	0	0
4210 Individual	..	..	..	..	..	..	..	..	..	..
4220 Corporate	..	..	..	..	..	..	..	..	..	..
4300 Estate, inheritance and gift taxes	..	0	0	0	0	0	0	0	0	0
4310 Estate and inheritance taxes	..	..	..	..	..	..	..	..	..	..
4320 Gift taxes	..	..	..	..	..	..	..	..	..	..
4400 Taxes on financial and capital transactions	..	74	97	168	288	295	353	294	393	469
4500 Other non-reccurrent taxes on property	..	0	0	0	0	0	0	0	0	0
4510 On net wealth	..	..	..	..	..	..	..	..	..	..
4520 Other non-recurrent taxes	..	..	..	..	..	..	..	..	..	..

Table 5.34. Tunisia – Details of tax revenue (continued)

Million TND

	1995	2000	2005	2010	2016	2018	2019	2020	2021	2022
4600 Other recurrent taxes on property	..	0	0	0	0	0	0	0	0	0
5000 Taxes on goods and services	**..**	**3 729**	**4 567**	**6 768**	**9 523**	**13 444**	**14 026**	**13 377**	**15 561**	**17 990**
5100 Taxes on production, sale, transfer, etc	..	3 665	4 458	6 612	9 300	13 222	13 803	13 179	15 327	17 732
5110 General taxes on goods and services	..	1 814	2 347	3 819	5 288	7 696	8 044	7 424	9 040	10 627
5111 Value added taxes	..	1 792	2 301	3 750	5 118	7 425	7 797	7 201	8 765	10 174
VAT revenues (gross)	..	..	2 419	4 163	5 771	7 787	8 093	7 706	9 073	10 514
VAT refunds	..	..	- 118	- 414	- 653	- 362	- 296	- 506	- 308	- 340
5112 Sales tax	..	0	0	0	0	0	0	0	0	0
5113 Other	..	21	46	69	170	271	246	223	275	453
5120 Taxes on specific goods and services	..	1 851	2 111	2 793	4 012	5 527	5 760	5 755	6 286	7 106
5121 Excises	..	1 023	1 340	1 814	2 876	3 621	3 692	3 717	4 001	4 456
Tobacco	..	371	601	799	1 248	1 490	1 633	1 757	1 717	1 915
Alcoholic drinks	..	147	146	174	336	431	408	376	476	458
Essences and oils	..	260	269	268	649	757	760	727	778	801
Cars	..	86	91	242	285	338	299	279	375	501
Excise taxes on other products	..	19	28	31	44	60	66	65	105	131
Cement	..	11	13	17	15	17	17	15	18	18
Other excise taxes	..	131	192	282	299	528	509	498	532	631
5122 Profits of fiscal monopolies	..	0	0	0	0	0	0	0	0	0
5123 Customs and import duties	..	654	524	620	742	1 235	1 335	1 303	1 494	1 827
Import customs duties excluding tobacco	..	565	424	428	429	894	948	920	1 085	1 401
Royalties on customs services	..	68	81	142	188	221	234	219	251	298
Tax on sales of imported cement	..	0	0	0	28	0	0	0	0	0
Tobacco	..	9	12	23	37	57	71	67	53	45
Other import customs duties	..	0	4	4	0	0	0	0	0	0
Import levy	..	12	3	20	45	46	51	61	66	42
Other taxes and import levies	..	1	1	3	15	17	32	36	38	41
5124 Taxes on exports	..	11	9	27	30	72	101	83	102	113
5125 Taxes on investment goods	..	0	0	0	0	0	0	0	0	0
5126 Taxes on specific services	..	162	236	330	363	599	633	652	689	710
Telecommunication tax	..	72	91	136	153	178	179	193	200	175
Tax on payments for transportation	..	55	84	105	67	141	142	133	141	144
Tax on insurance	..	33	59	86	138	197	210	220	241	258
Other taxes on specific services	..	2	2	3	5	82	102	105	107	133
5127 Other taxes on internat. trade and transactions	..	0	0	0	0	0	0	0	0	0
5128 Other taxes	..	0	1	1	0	0	0	0	0	0
5130 Unallocable between 5110 and 5120	..	0	0	0	0	0	0	0	0	0
5200 Taxes on use of goods and to perform activities	..	64	109	156	223	222	222	199	234	258
5210 Recurrent taxes	..	55	77	103	160	167	167	175	187	212
5211 Paid by households: motor vehicles	..	35	44	60	91	101	105	105	113	130
5212 Paid by others: motor vehicles	..	18	28	43	69	67	62	70	75	82
5213 Paid in respect of other goods	..	1	6	0	0	0	0	0	0	0
5220 Non-recurrent taxes	..	9	32	53	63	54	55	24	47	45
5300 Unallocable between 5100 and 5200	..	0	0	0	0	0	0	0	0	0
6000 Other taxes	**..**	**104**	**126**	**279**	**630**	**862**	**938**	**711**	**877**	**1 043**
Stamp duties	..	25	32	133	350	447	484	425	489	508
Registration fees	..	40	67	107	201	248	256	215	255	320
Duty on foreign travel	..	12	12	21	35	42	43	12	18	35
Various	..	28	15	17	43	125	156	58	116	180
6100 Paid solely by business	..	..	..	..	..	..	..	..	..	..
6200 Other	..	..	..	..	..	..	..	..	..	..

.. Not available

Note: Year ending 31st December.The data are on a cash basis.

Figures exclude tax revenues collected by sub-national governments as the data are not available.

Taxes allocated to the Special Treasury Accounts (*Fonds spéciaux du Trésor*) and to Joint funds (*Fonds de concours*) are included in the data for the period 2000-22.

Heading 1210 excludes oil company royalties. In Tunisia, they have been reported as a supplement to corporation tax since April 2012.

Social security contributions under heading 2000 are not included in tax revenues in Tunisia. Data for 2022 are estimated.

Source: Ministry of Finance, Tunisia for all tax revenue data, Ministry of Social Affairs, Tunisia for data on social security contributions.

Table 5.35. Uganda – Details of tax revenue

Million UGX

	1995	2000	2005	2010	2015	2018	2019	2020	2021	2022
Total tax revenue	**521 679**	**999 659**	**1 935 472**	**4 252 022**	**9 762 430**	**14 067 590**	**16 130 637**	**16 019 865**	**18 459 200**	**20 558 466**
1000 Taxes on income, profits and capital gains	**77 170**	**181 905**	**560 351**	**1 340 327**	**3 387 902**	**4 821 107**	**5 677 950**	**6 026 000**	**6 785 540**	**7 482 270**
1100 Of individuals	52 681	136 806	392 037	958 294	2 382 729	3 479 276	4 033 859	4 239 310	4 647 390	5 749 510
1110 On income and profits	52 681	136 806	392 037	958 294	2 382 729	3 479 276	4 033 859	4 239 310	4 647 390	5 749 510
Pay-as-you-earn (PAYE) tax	20 329	83 471	245 325	657 920	1 613 243	2 396 113	2 811 297	3 039 830	3 109 140	3 634 256
Rental income tax	0	0	0	0	27 649	88 747	115 229	103 690	117 240	156 103
Other income tax (not counting withholding tax)	9 153	11 220	13 899	19 001	42 189	60 485	66 505	56 390	115 990	613 960
Withholding tax on imports	14 256	23 349	47 399	68 581	152 787	179 643	194 169	166 410	186 040	167 781
Withholding tax on general supplies	0	0	85 414	120 061	282 825	337 521	434 281	505 100	525 280	532 460
Withholding tax on government payments	0	0	0	44 446	89 367	73 824	76 776	68 670	70 350	65 230
Withholding tax management and professional fees	0	0	0	24 886	45 447	89 563	116 368	121 390	111 610	88 250
Withholding tax on dividends	0	0	0	11 237	61 823	87 745	74 635	54 920	220 690	120 140
Withholding tax non residents	0	0	0	1 356	57 106	152 988	102 942	114 490	162 380	289 910
Withholding tax in the extractive sector	0	0	0	0	0	0	0	0	0	67 270
Other withholding tax or unclassified	8 943	18 766	0	10 806	10 293	12 646	42 657	18 420	19 670	14 150
1120 On capital gains	0	0	0	0	0	0	0	0	0	0
1200 Corporate	24 489	40 891	160 030	315 379	714 772	884 802	1 167 745	1 302 300	1 567 650	1 635 856
1210 On profits	24 489	40 891	160 030	315 379	714 772	884 802	1 167 745	1 302 300	1 567 650	1 635 856
Corporation Tax	24 489	40 891	160 030	315 379	714 772	884 802	1 167 745	1 302 300	1 567 650	1 635 856
1220 On capital gains of corporates	0	0	0	0	0	0	0	0	0	0
1300 Unallocable between 1100 and 1200	0	4 207	8 284	66 654	290 401	457 028	476 346	484 390	570 500	96 904
Tax on Bank Interest	..	4 207	8 284	66 654	290 401	457 028	476 346	484 390	570 500	96 904
2000 Social security contributions	**0**	**0**	**0**	**0**	**0**	**0**	**0**	**0**	**0**	**0**
2100 Employees	..	..	..	..	..	..	..	..	..	..
2110 On a payroll basis	..	..	..	..	..	..	..	..	..	..
2120 On an income tax basis	..	..	..	..	..	..	..	..	..	..
2200 Employers	..	..	..	..	..	..	..	..	..	..
2210 On a payroll basis	..	..	..	..	..	..	..	..	..	..
2220 On an income tax basis	..	..	..	..	..	..	..	..	..	..
2300 Self-employed or non-employed	..	..	..	..	..	..	..	..	..	..
2310 On a payroll basis	..	..	..	..	..	..	..	..	..	..
2320 On an income tax basis	..	..	..	..	..	..	..	..	..	..
2400 Unallocable between 2100, 2200 and 2300	..	..	..	..	..	..	..	..	..	..
2410 On a payroll basis	..	..	..	..	..	..	..	..	..	..
2420 On an income tax basis	..	..	..	..	..	..	..	..	..	..
3000 Taxes on payroll and workforce	**0**	**0**	**0**	**0**	**0**	**0**	**0**	**0**	**0**	**0**
4000 Taxes on property	**0**	**0**	**0**	**0**	**48 990**	**57 185**	**231 258**	**179 577**	**251 700**	**298 561**
4100 Recurrent taxes on immovable property	..	..	..	..	0	0	0	0	0	0
4110 Households	..	..	..	..	..	..	..	..	..	..
4120 Others	..	..	..	..	..	..	..	..	..	..
4200 Recurrent taxes on net wealth	..	..	..	..	0	0	0	0	0	0
4210 Individual	..	..	..	..	..	..	..	..	..	..
4220 Corporate	..	..	..	..	..	..	..	..	..	..
4300 Estate, inheritance and gift taxes	..	..	..	..	0	0	0	0	0	0
4310 Estate and inheritance taxes	..	..	..	..	..	..	..	..	..	..
4320 Gift taxes	..	..	..	..	..	..	..	..	..	..
4400 Taxes on financial and capital transactions	..	..	..	..	48 990	57 185	231 258	179 577	251 700	298 561
Tax on mobile money transfers	..	..	..	..	48 990	57 185	74 027	79 017	113 980	133 984
Levy on mobile money	..	..	..	..	..	..	..	..	..	..
4500 Other non-reccurrent taxes on property	..	..	..	..	..	..	..	..	..	..
4510 On net wealth	..	..	..	..	..	..	..	..	..	..
4520 Other non-recurrent taxes	..	..	..	..	..	..	..	..	..	..
4600 Other recurrent taxes on property	..	..	..	..	..	..	..	..	..	..
5000 Taxes on goods and services	**428 807**	**815 835**	**1 372 355**	**2 861 862**	**6 302 611**	**9 156 781**	**10 226 403**	**9 763 768**	**11 373 640**	**12 760 845**
5100 Taxes on production, sale, transfer, etc	415 342	793 285	1 308 282	2 772 331	6 153 139	8 986 282	10 054 479	9 596 388	11 174 870	12 550 568
5110 General taxes on goods and services	158 745	329 755	638 773	1 371 561	3 151 723	4 503 033	4 976 108	4 767 650	5 524 140	6 252 799
5111 Value added taxes	158 745	329 755	638 773	1 371 561	3 151 723	4 503 033	4 976 108	4 767 650	5 517 560	6 245 339
VAT on imports (government taxes)	7 771	16 628	10 444	35 775	0	0	0	0	0	0

Table 5.35. Uganda – Details of tax revenue (continued)

Million UGX

	1995	2000	2005	2010	2016	2018	2019	2020	2021	2022
VAT on imports (non-government taxes)	67 110	178 868	365 418	763 398	1 783 518	2 416 568	2 664 812	2 498 390	2 832 470	3 291 636
VAT on phone talk time	0	0	0	93 277	152 747	213 549	200 283	154 820	151 620	248 609
VAT on beer	15 771	11 586	16 771	37 034	108 831	145 809	122 117	138 820	156 340	152 909
VAT on electricity	0	0	0	74 584	112 811	170 471	170 536	170 830	175 760	195 291
VAT on sugar	0	0	0	64 276	110 801	149 558	120 790	100 870	104 330	136 512
VAT on soft drinks	9 515	5 139	12 028	15 846	32 385	42 791	76 960	81 480	66 190	88 657
VAT on cement	0	0	0	25 161	53 086	81 095	87 557	120 190	205 770	147 070
VAT on cigarettes	13 437	6 904	6 641	1 411	16 759	9 522	4 295	430	530	1 051
Other VAT	45 141	140 630	263 679	359 821	923 754	1 407 037	1 756 848	1 826 180	2 128 260	2 325 805
VAT refunds	..	- 30 000	- 36 208	- 99 023	- 142 970	- 133 368	- 228 090	- 324 360	- 303 710	- 342 200
5112 Sales tax	0	0	0	0	0	0	0	0	0	0
5113 Other	0	0	0	0	0	0	0	0	6 580	7 460
Presumptive tax on small businesses	..	..	..	..	..	..	..	..	6 580	7 460
5120 Taxes on specific goods and services	256 597	463 530	669 509	1 400 770	3 001 416	4 483 248	5 078 371	4 828 738	5 650 730	6 297 769
5121 Excises	51 966	132 953	187 615	275 929	785 599	1 064 881	1 183 226	1 126 874	1 263 240	1 429 307
Excise tax on beer	18 483	59 938	60 704	98 864	146 853	263 072	269 276	267 890	300 040	324 844
Excise tax on phone talk time	0	0	24 901	99 490	184 175	178 966	211 878	231 260	261 680	289 623
Excise tax on soft drinks	7 134	13 348	15 304	27 907	71 799	118 869	125 992	120 530	152 420	176 015
Excise tax on cigarettes	22 267	33 572	28 632	7 698	14 979	15 591	14 912	21 020	27 000	21 388
Excise tax on spirits / waragi	742	915	6 463	10 376	53 331	157 512	155 648	104 550	114 620	123 770
Excise on international calls	0	0	0	0	65 142	33 341	34 937	27 051	27 310	26 077
Excise tax on sugar	0	0	0	17 187	17 854	30 277	35 526	40 104	46 290	59 597
Excise tax on cement	1	1	1	8 228	17 773	26 741	32 089	34 514	43 720	44 020
Other excise taxes	3 339	25 180	51 610	84 179	213 693	240 512	302 968	279 955	290 160	363 971
Tax refunds due to diesel tax exemption	0	0	0	- 77 999	0	0	0	0	0	0
5122 Profits of fiscal monopolies	0	0	0	0	0	0	0	0	0	0
5123 Customs and import duties	203 052	330 339	480 361	1 122 850	2 188 774	3 333 021	3 712 469	3 509 490	4 216 680	4 614 855
Petroleum duty	119 662	197 202	309 024	716 234	1 197 749	1 811 817	2 038 658	2 012 540	2 453 380	2 686 273
Surcharge on used imports	0	0	0	38 621	95 895	209 782	230 784	206 650	265 330	257 207
Non-oil imports	6 100	5 301	3 653	21 651	0	0	0	0	0	0
Commission on imports	12 150	22 746	19 567	2	0	0	0	0	0	0
Infrastructure Levy	0	0	0	0	57 268	87 669	92 569	81 530	94 850	114 312
Other import duties	65 139	105 090	153 667	346 621	841 381	1 223 753	1 350 458	1 208 770	1 403 120	1 557 062
Fixed duty drawbacks	0	0	- 5 550	- 280	- 3 520	0	0	0	0	0
5124 Taxes on exports	0	0	1 165	122	13 186	12 442	20 604	14 940	3 000	12 410
Hides and Skins Levy / Exports Levy	..	..	1 165	122	13 186	12 442	20 604	14 940	3 000	12 410
5125 Taxes on investment goods	0	0	0	0	0	0	0	0	0	0
5126 Taxes on specific services	1 580	238	368	1 869	13 858	72 904	162 072	177 434	167 810	241 198
Casino and lottery tax	1 580	238	368	1 869	13 858	29 216	27 896	19 040	13 310	53 682
Bank charges	0	0	0	0	0	43 688	84 650	98 674	95 380	101 752
Tax on over-the-top internet services	0	0	0	0	0	0	49 525	59 720	59 120	85 764
5127 Other taxes on internat. trade and transactions	0	0	0	0	0	0	0	0	0	0
5128 Other taxes	0	0	0	0	0	0	0	0	0	0
5130 Unallocable between 5110 and 5120	0	0	0	0	0	0	0	0	0	0
5200 Taxes on use of goods and to perform activities	13 465	22 551	64 073	89 531	149 472	170 499	171 924	167 380	198 770	210 277
5210 Recurrent taxes	10 412	17 890	52 440	64 096	91 886	98 194	96 556	93 820	116 440	131 473
5211 Paid by households: motor vehicles	10 412	17 890	52 440	64 096	91 886	98 194	96 556	93 820	116 440	131 473
Fees and licences	10 085	17 890	52 440	64 096	91 886	98 194	96 556	93 820	116 440	131 473
Road user charges	327	0	0	0	0	0	0	0	0	0
5212 Paid by others: motor vehicles	0	0	0	0	0	0	0	0	0	0
5213 Paid in respect of other goods	0	0	0	0	0	0	0	0	0	0
5220 Non-recurrent taxes	3 053	4 660	11 633	25 434	57 586	72 305	75 368	73 560	82 330	78 804
Temporary Road Licences	3 053	4 660	11 633	25 434	57 586	72 305	75 368	73 560	82 330	78 804
5300 Unallocable between 5100 and 5200	0	0	0	0	0	0	0	0	0	0
6000 Other taxes	**15 702**	**1 919**	**2 766**	**49 833**	**22 927**	**32 518**	**- 4 974**	**50 520**	**48 320**	**16 790**
6100 Paid solely by business	0	0	0	0	0	0	0	0	0	0
6200 Other	15 702	1 919	2 766	49 833	22 927	32 518	- 4 974	50 520	48 320	16 790
Stamp duties and embossing fees	1 451	1 919	6 946	26 256	48 557	73 945	100 337	87 090	125 490	113 280
Coffee stabilisation tax	14 250	0	0	0	0	0	0	0	0	0

Table 5.35. Uganda – Details of tax revenue (continued)

Million UGX

	1995	2000	2005	2010	2016	2018	2019	2020	2021	2022
Government payments on behalf of private companies	0	0	0	0	0	0	0	0	0	0
Agricultural products	1	0	0	0	0	0	0	0	0	0
Un-allocated revenue	0	0	0	29 457	0	0	0	0	0	0
Tax refunds	0	0	- 4 180	- 5 880	- 25 630	- 41 428	- 105 311	- 36 570	- 77 170	- 96 490
Memo items:	..	..	..	..	..	..	..	..	..	..
Gross domestic VAT	0	164 259	299 119	671 411	1 520 175	2 234 810	2 554 450	2 608 580	2 992 940	3 295 900
VAT on imports (non-government taxes)	0	178 868	365 418	763 398	1 783 518	2 416 570	2 664 810	2 498 390	2 832 470	3 291 640
VAT on imports (government taxes)	7 771	16 628	10 444	35 775	0	0	0	0	0	0

.. Not available

Note: Data are reported on a fiscal year basis beginning 1st July. For example, the data for 2022 represent July 2021 to June 2022.

The data are on a cash basis.

Figures exclude tax revenues collected by sub-national governments as the data are not available. The National Social Security Fund is self-described as a national saving scheme, or a provident fund, which does not meet the definition of social security fund used within Revenue Statistics in Africa, and therefore its revenues are excluded from the data reported here.

Heading 1110: Withholding taxes from the extractive sector are reported separately for the year 2021/22. In previous years, withholding taxes from the extractive sector are reported as part of other forms of withholding taxes.

Heading 4000: Property tax is levied annually by local authorities. Revenue from property tax is not available.

Heading 4400: Taxes on mobile money transfers were reported under excise duties in previous editions. The Levy on Mobile Money was reported as a Tax on Specific Services in previous years. These are both reported as excise duties in Uganda budget documents.

Heading 5121: The "other excises taxes" category includes revenues from excises on bottled water and cosmetics, sweets and chocolates, furniture, cooking oil, plastics, motor vehicle lubricants, and milk. Excises on plastics and motor vehicle lubricants were reported for the first time for the year 2022.

Revenues from driver permits are considered non-tax revenue under the OECD classification, as set out in the *Interpretative Guide* in Annex A. The national classification of Uganda classifies this revenue as tax revenue.

Source: Uganda Revenue Authority.

Table 5.36. Zambia – Details of tax revenue

Million ZMK

	1995	2000	2005	2010	2015	2018	2019	2020	2021	2022
Total tax revenue	..	..	..	..	**26 203**	**44 485**	**48 719**	**52 264**	**71 436**	**79 817**
1000 Taxes on income, profits and capital gains	..	..	..	..	**12 408**	**19 863**	**23 696**	**28 748**	**41 921**	**47 233**
1100 Of individuals	..	..	..	..	7 444	10 426	11 625	14 229	14 972	18 102
1110 On income and profits	..	..	..	..	7 444	10 426	11 625	14 229	14 972	18 102
1120 On capital gains	..	..	..	..	0	0	0	0	0	0
1200 Corporate	..	..	..	..	2 876	6 177	7 916	9 530	19 506	21 050
1210 On profits	..	..	..	..	2 876	6 177	7 916	9 530	19 506	21 050
Company tax (extractive)	..	..	..	..	418	2 357	3 233	5 300	12 702	12 211
Company tax (non-extractive)	..	..	..	..	2 428	3 617	4 509	4 213	6 789	8 791
Advance income tax	..	..	..	..	29	204	174	18	15	47
1220 On capital gains of corporates	..	..	..	..	0	0	0	0	0	0
1300 Unallocable between 1100 and 1200	..	..	..	..	2 089	3 259	4 155	4 989	7 443	8 082
Withholding tax (rent, interest and royalties)	..	..	..	..	1 687	2 876	3 574	4 505	6 525	6 842
Other withholding taxes	..	..	..	..	402	384	581	484	917	1 239
2000 Social security contributions	..	..	..	..	..	..	..	..	..	..
2100 Employees	..	..	..	..	..	..	..	..	..	..
2110 On a payroll basis	..	..	..	..	..	..	..	..	..	..
2120 On an income tax basis	..	..	..	..	..	..	..	..	..	..
2200 Employers	..	..	..	..	..	..	..	..	..	..
2210 On a payroll basis	..	..	..	..	..	..	..	..	..	..
2220 On an income tax basis	..	..	..	..	..	..	..	..	..	..
2300 Self-employed or non-employed	..	..	..	..	..	..	..	..	..	..
2310 On a payroll basis	..	..	..	..	..	..	..	..	..	..
2320 On an income tax basis	..	..	..	..	..	..	..	..	..	..
2400 Unallocable between 2100, 2200 and 2300	..	..	..	..	..	..	..	..	..	..
2410 On a payroll basis	..	..	..	..	..	..	..	..	..	..
2420 On an income tax basis	..	..	..	..	..	..	..	..	..	..
3000 Taxes on payroll and workforce	..	..	..	..	**0**	**173**	**186**	**169**	**221**	**226**
4000 Taxes on property	..	..	..	..	**316**	**218**	**368**	**337**	**372**	**443**
4100 Recurrent taxes on immovable property	..	..	..	..	0	0	0	0	0	0
4110 Households	..	..	..	..	..	..	..	..	..	..
4120 Others	..	..	..	..	..	..	..	..	..	..
4200 Recurrent taxes on net wealth	..	..	..	..	0	0	0	0	0	0
4210 Individual	..	..	..	..	..	..	..	..	..	..
4220 Corporate	..	..	..	..	..	..	..	..	..	..
4300 Estate, inheritance and gift taxes	..	..	..	..	0	0	0	0	0	0
4310 Estate and inheritance taxes	..	..	..	..	..	..	..	..	..	..
4320 Gift taxes	..	..	..	..	..	..	..	..	..	..
4400 Taxes on financial and capital transactions	..	..	..	..	316	218	368	337	372	443
4500 Other non-reccurrent taxes on property	..	..	..	..	0	0	0	0	0	0
4510 On net wealth	..	..	..	..	..	..	..	..	..	..
4520 Other non-recurrent taxes	..	..	..	..	..	..	..	..	..	..
4600 Other recurrent taxes on property	..	..	..	..	0	0	0	0	0	0
5000 Taxes on goods and services	..	..	..	..	**13 478**	**24 231**	**24 470**	**23 010**	**28 923**	**31 915**
5100 Taxes on production, sale, transfer, etc	..	..	..	..	13 451	24 133	24 383	22 981	28 879	31 857
5110 General taxes on goods and services	..	..	..	..	8 271	17 471	16 791	14 682	19 147	20 815
5111 Value added taxes	..	..	..	..	8 237	17 352	16 685	14 532	18 956	20 580
VAT on domestic goods	..	..	..	..	1 533	6 497	6 050	3 423	6 541	5 890
VAT on imports	..	..	..	..	6 704	10 854	10 634	11 109	12 416	14 691
5112 Sales tax	..	..	..	..	0	0	0	0	0	0
5113 Other	..	..	..	..	34	119	107	151	191	235
5120 Taxes on specific goods and services	..	..	..	..	5 180	6 662	7 592	8 299	9 732	11 042
5121 Excises	..	..	..	..	2 629	2 872	2 914	3 766	3 213	3 911
Alcoholic beverages	..	..	..	..	653	703	936	1 009	1 357	1 487
Motor vehicles	..	..	..	..	338	333	264	276	387	684
Electricity	..	..	..	..	125	177	222	459	580	548
Excise on fuel	..	..	..	..	830	955	651	1 159	207	293
Hydro carbon oils	..	..	..	..	508	412	496	522	300	431
Cigarettes	..	..	..	..	117	60	109	113	123	177

Table 5.36. Zambia – Details of tax revenue (continued)

Million ZMK

	1995	2000	2005	2010	2015	2018	2019	2020	2021	2022
Carbon	..	..	..	..	27	39	61	68	78	95
Cement and related products	..	..	..	..	0	152	102	78	71	59
Other excises	..	..	..	..	30	42	73	83	109	138
5122 Profits of fiscal monopolies	..	..	..	..	0	0	0	0	0	0
5123 Customs and import duties	..	..	..	..	1 902	3 144	3 539	3 447	5 218	6 105
5124 Taxes on exports	..	..	..	..	28	10	324	133	99	103
5125 Taxes on investment goods	..	..	..	..	0	0	0	0	0	0
5126 Taxes on specific services	..	..	..	..	622	637	815	953	1 202	923
5127 Other taxes on internat. trade and transactions	..	..	..	..	0	0	0	0	0	0
5128 Other taxes	..	..	..	..	0	0	0	0	0	0
5130 Unallocable between 5110 and 5120	..	..	..	..	0	0	0	0	0	0
5200 Taxes on use of goods and to perform activities	..	..	..	..	27	98	87	29	43	58
5210 Recurrent taxes	..	..	..	..	27	98	87	29	43	58
5211 Paid by households: motor vehicles	..	..	..	..	26	94	81	22	36	50
5212 Paid by others: motor vehicles	..	..	..	..	0	0	0	0	0	0
5213 Paid in respect of other goods	..	..	..	..	1	4	6	7	8	8
5220 Non-recurrent taxes	..	..	..	..	0	0	0	0	0	0
5300 Unallocable between 5100 and 5200	..	..	..	..	0	0	0	0	0	0
6000 Other taxes	**..**	**..**	**..**	**..**	**0**	**0**	**0**	**0**	**0**	**0**
6100 Paid solely by business	..	..	..	..	..	..	..	..	..	..
6200 Other	..	..	..	..	..	..	..	..	..	..

.. Not available

Note: Year ending 31st December.

The data are on a cash basis.

Source : Zambia Revenue Authority.

6 Country tables, 1995-2022 – Non-tax revenues

Non-tax revenue tables, 1995-2022

In all of the following tables, ".." indicates not available or not applicable. The main series in this volume covers the years 1995 to 2022. Figures referring to 1990-94, 1996-99, 2001-04, 2006-09, 2011-14 and 2016-17 in Table 6.1 and Tables 6.4 to 6.39 have been omitted because of lack of space. Complete series are, however, available online at the OECD Data Explorer and can be accessed at https://data-explorer.oecd.org/ within the theme Taxation/Global tax revenue or by searching for African non-tax revenues. No data on non-tax revenues were available for Burkina Faso in this edition.

Table 6.1. Total non-tax revenue as percentage of GDP, 1995-2022

	1995	2000	2005	2010	2015	2018	2019	2020	2021	2022
Botswana	..	..	26.9	19.3	19.4	17.1	16.8	15.2	16.4	14.7
Cabo Verde	21.2	7.6	9.6	8.8	7.0	5.0	7.2	6.3	5.3	3.9
Cameroon	2.9	7.0	5.8	4.1	3.8	3.2	3.5	2.3	2.7	4.0
Chad	..	..	..	3.9	3.9	4.5	3.8	4.2	1.9	2.7
Congo	..	13.8	5.9	23.3	8.5	16.2	17.2	10.6	15.0	23.7
Congo, Dem. Rep.	..	..	..	6.0	4.4	2.7	2.3	2.3	4.6	3.9
Côte d'Ivoire	0.7	0.8	1.6	1.2	2.4	1.5	1.5	1.3	1.3	1.2
Egypt	..	..	6.6	8.1	6.4	4.4	4.0	4.1	4.4	4.9
Equatorial Guinea	..	..	24.4	18.8	15.0	13.6	9.3	6.3	9.8	23.1
Eswatini	10.9	12.5	15.8	8.1	14.5	11.9	13.1	14.8	10.9	9.6
Gabon	..	..	..	0.1	0.6	5.3	5.7	4.5	5.7	7.8
Ghana	..	1.6	3.0	3.7	4.9	3.3	3.2	2.8	2.7	3.3
Guinea	..	2.3	1.7	0.8	1.1	2.9	2.2	2.2	2.1	2.6
Kenya	..	..	1.7	1.2	1.5	2.1	2.1	3.8	2.3	2.0
Lesotho	..	..	26.9	33.4	29.6	25.6	26.0	34.6	31.4	22.1
Madagascar	0.0	2.8	5.4	3.0	1.5	3.0	3.4	2.9	1.0	1.6
Malawi	..	..	5.2	7.8	3.1	1.8	2.0	1.5	4.6	2.0
Mali	5.9	5.8	5.3	4.9	2.6	2.4	3.2	2.3	1.9	1.6
Mauritania	..	..	..	6.3	6.4	6.8	5.5	4.6	4.7	4.0
Mauritius[1]	3.4	2.7	2.3	3.7	2.7	4.2	2.8	3.2	2.3	3.9
Morocco	..	2.1	2.8	3.3	3.6	3.4	4.0	3.2	2.8	2.9
Mozambique	..	..	..	8.3	4.9	5.3	4.3	6.8	5.8	7.4
Namibia	..	..	..	9.4	14.0	11.8	12.7	14.6	10.4	11.0
Niger	..	4.1	6.3	4.7	5.8	7.3	7.8	8.3	8.1	5.5
Nigeria[2]	..	..	..	7.9	3.1	3.3	3.9	3.4	4.0	4.6
Rwanda	..	9.9	11.1	11.6	8.6	7.8	7.2	7.8	8.6	8.7
Senegal	..	1.6	1.8	2.6	3.5	3.4	2.8	3.4	3.4	2.4
Seychelles	..	..	..	6.2	6.5	6.1	5.4	6.9	8.1	6.3
Sierra Leone	..	..	8.2	5.7	6.3	4.7	6.4	8.6	7.6	9.2
Somalia	..	..	..	..	0.8	1.7	2.0	4.1	2.4	5.2
South Africa	0.5	0.4	0.5	0.5	0.4	0.5	0.5	0.6	0.7	0.7
Togo	..	1.3	2.0	8.1	3.0	5.6	4.9	3.9	3.0	3.6
Tunisia	..	2.3	2.5	2.7	1.9	2.9	3.1	3.0	2.8	4.3
Uganda	3.5	4.7	5.7	1.8	1.2	1.0	1.3	1.3	1.9	1.4
Zambia	..	..	..	..	2.2	1.7	1.7	2.1	3.4	2.5
Africa (35) average[3]	**..**	**..**	**..**	**..**	**5.9**	**5.8**	**5.8**	**5.9**	**5.8**	**6.2**

.. Not available

Note: The figures include sub-national government non-tax revenues for Eswatini, Kenya (2014 onwards), Mauritius, Morocco, Nigeria (2010 onwards), and Somalia (2019 onwards). Sub-national government non-tax revenues are not available in other countries. See the country tables in Chapter 6 for further information.

1. Data for Mauritius are on a July-June fiscal year basis except for the years 2010-15 when they were reported on a calendar year basis. Please see Chapter 6 for more details.
2. Non-tax revenues reported for Nigeria include revenues collected by Local Government Areas (LGAs). These revenues are reported under "Miscellaneous and unidentified revenue" although they include some tax revenues.
3. Represents an unweighted average of the 35 African countries in this publication. Data on tax revenues were available for Burkina Faso for this edition, but not non-tax revenues.

Table 6.2. Non-tax revenue of main headings as percentage of GDP, 2022

	Grants	Property income				Sales of goods and services	Fines, penalties and forfeits	Miscellaneous and unidentified revenue
		Total	Rents and royalties	Interest and dividends	Other property income			
Botswana	0.0	9.0	2.3	6.8	0.0	0.3	0.0	5.4
Cabo Verde	0.7	0.1	..	..	..	2.2	0.1	0.6
Cameroon	0.4	3.1	3.0	0.1	0.0	0.2	0.3	0.0
Chad	0.9	1.4	1.4	0.0	0.0	0.0	0.1	0.2
Congo	0.6	23.1	22.9	0.0	0.2	0.0	0.0	0.0
Congo, Dem. Rep.	1.6	1.7	1.5	0.1	0.0	0.3	0.3	0.0
Côte d'Ivoire	0.5	0.3	0.2	0.1	0.0	0.2	0.0	0.2
Egypt	0.0	1.3	0.4	0.9	0.0	2.3	0.0	1.3
Equatorial Guinea	0.0	22.7	9.6	13.0	0.1	0.3	0.0	0.0
Eswatini	0.2	1.9	0.1	1.8	0.0	0.2	0.0	7.2
Gabon	0.0	7.7	7.2	0.5	0.0	0.0	0.1	0.0
Ghana	0.2	1.8	0.7	1.1	0.0	1.3	0.0	0.0
Guinea	0.5	1.5	1.1	0.5	0.0	0.2	0.0	0.4
Kenya	0.3	0.6	0.0	0.6	0.0	0.4	0.0	0.6
Lesotho	2.9	5.5	5.0	0.5	0.0	0.0	0.0	13.7
Madagascar	1.3	0.3	0.1	0.2	0.0	0.0	0.0	0.0
Malawi	1.3	0.1	0.0	0.1	0.0	0.6	0.0	0.0
Mali	0.4	0.7	0.0	0.7	0.0	0.2	0.1	0.1
Mauritania	0.0	3.6	3.1	0.5	0.0	0.2	0.1	0.0
Mauritius	0.4	2.4	0.2	0.2	2.0	1.0	0.1	0.2
Morocco	0.0	0.9	0.3	0.6	0.0	1.1	0.2	0.7
Mozambique	4.1	1.8	1.1	0.7	0.0	1.4	0.1	0.0
Namibia	0.0	3.4	1.2	2.2	0.0	0.8	0.0	6.7
Niger	4.7	0.4	0.2	0.1	0.0	0.1	0.1	0.2
Nigeria[1]	0.5	2.9	2.9	0.0	0.0	0.0	0.0	1.1
Rwanda[2]	5.8	..	..	..	..	..	..	2.8
Senegal	0.9	0.7	0.4	0.3	..	0.1	0.0	0.7
Seychelles	1.4	2.9	0.8	2.1	0.0	1.8	0.0	0.2
Sierra Leone	6.6	0.9	0.9	0.0	0.0	1.1	0.0	0.6
Somalia	4.2	0.1	0.1	0.0	0.0	0.9	0.0	0.0
South Africa	0.0	0.5	0.4	0.1	0.0	0.1	0.1	0.0
Togo	2.5	0.6	0.1	0.6	0.0	0.2	0.0	0.2
Tunisia	1.0	2.6	2.1	0.5	0.0	0.0	0.5	0.2
Uganda	0.7	0.0	0.0	0.0	0.0	0.7	0.0	0.0
Zambia	0.4	2.1	2.1	0.0	0.0	0.0	0.0	0.0
Africa (35) average[3]	**1.3**	**3.2**	**2.2**	**1.1**	**0.1**	**0.5**	**0.1**	**1.2**

.. Not available

Note: The figures include sub-national government non-tax revenues for Eswatini, Kenya (2014 onwards), Mauritius, Morocco, Nigeria (2010 onwards), and Somalia (2019 onwards). Sub-national government non-tax revenues are not available in other countries. See the country tables in Chapter 6 for further information.

1. Non-tax revenues reported for Nigeria include revenues collected by Local Government Areas (LGAs). These revenues are reported under "Miscellaneous and unidentified revenue" although they include some tax revenues.
2. For Rwanda, "Miscellaneous and unidentified revenue" includes non-tax fines, administrative fees and revenue from public property and public assets for Rwanda. These data could not be disaggregated to allocate revenue to the relevant non-tax revenue categories.
3. Represents an unweighted average of the 35 African countries in this publication. Data on tax revenues were available for Burkina Faso for this edition, but not non-tax revenues.

Table 6.3. Non-tax revenue of main headings as percentage of total non-tax revenue, 2022

	Grants	Property income				Sales of goods and services	Fines, penalties and forfeits	Miscellaneous and unidentified revenue
		Total	Rents and royalties	Interest and dividends	Other property income			
Botswana	0.0	61.5	15.3	46.2	0.0	1.9	0.1	36.5
Cabo Verde	18.6	3.8	..	..	..	57.9	3.2	16.5
Cameroon	9.4	78.0	75.2	2.8	0.0	6.0	6.3	0.3
Chad	33.4	51.6	51.6	0.0	0.0	1.2	5.2	8.6
Congo	2.6	97.3	96.7	0.0	0.7	0.0	0.0	0.0
Congo, Dem. Rep.	40.9	42.6	39.5	3.1	0.0	8.7	7.6	0.2
Côte d'Ivoire	43.0	21.3	16.0	5.4	0.0	19.0	0.0	16.6
Egypt	0.7	25.8	7.3	18.2	0.3	46.4	0.8	26.3
Equatorial Guinea	0.0	98.5	41.6	56.3	0.6	1.4	0.0	0.1
Eswatini	2.4	20.2	1.5	18.2	0.4	2.6	0.5	74.4
Gabon	0.0	98.7	92.3	6.5	0.0	0.4	0.9	0.0
Ghana	5.6	54.4	21.5	32.9	0.0	39.1	0.0	0.9
Guinea	18.5	58.5	40.8	17.7	0.0	7.3	0.4	15.4
Kenya	16.7	29.9	0.6	28.2	1.1	20.9	0.6	32.0
Lesotho	13.2	24.8	22.5	2.3	0.0	0.2	0.0	61.8
Madagascar	80.7	16.9	6.0	10.9	0.0	1.3	0.1	1.0
Malawi	63.0	4.6	0.0	4.6	0.0	30.4	2.0	0.0
Mali	28.8	46.7	1.5	43.2	2.0	10.6	7.0	6.8
Mauritania	0.0	90.4	78.2	12.2	0.0	5.2	3.5	1.0
Mauritius	8.9	60.3	5.4	3.9	50.9	24.3	2.2	4.2
Morocco	0.0	31.8	10.1	21.7	0.0	36.6	6.0	25.6
Mozambique	54.8	24.6	15.4	9.2	0.0	19.1	1.4	0.1
Namibia	0.0	31.0	10.8	20.2	0.0	7.6	0.4	61.0
Niger	85.0	7.2	4.5	2.7	0.1	1.8	2.5	3.4
Nigeria[1]	11.8	63.6	63.6	0.0	0.0	0.0	0.0	24.7
Rwanda[2]	67.2	..	..	..	..	..	..	32.8
Senegal	37.9	30.4	16.6	13.8	..	2.9	0.0	28.9
Seychelles	21.9	46.0	12.6	33.4	0.0	29.5	0.0	2.7
Sierra Leone	72.5	9.8	9.8	0.0	0.0	11.6	0.0	6.1
Somalia	79.9	2.0	2.0	0.0	0.0	17.6	0.0	0.4
South Africa	2.0	76.4	57.9	18.5	0.0	9.1	11.0	1.5
Togo	69.5	17.9	1.8	16.1	0.0	6.6	0.2	5.8
Tunisia	22.5	61.2	48.5	12.7	0.0	0.9	10.9	4.5
Uganda	51.4	0.5	0.5	0.0	0.0	48.1	0.0	0.0
Zambia	15.8	83.5	83.5	0.0	0.0	0.1	0.6	0.0
Africa (35) average[3]	**28.0**	**43.3**	**28.8**	**14.0**	**1.8**	**14.0**	**2.2**	**14.3**

.. Not available

Note: The figures include sub-national government non-tax revenues for Eswatini, Kenya (2014 onwards), Mauritius, Morocco, Nigeria (2010 onwards), and Somalia (2019 onwards). Sub-national government non-tax revenues are not available in other countries. See the country tables in Chapter 6 for further information.

1. Non-tax revenues reported for Nigeria include revenues collected by Local Government Areas (LGAs). These revenues are reported under "Miscellaneous and unidentified revenue" although they include some tax revenues.
2. For Rwanda, "miscellaneous and unidentified revenues" includes non-tax fines, administrative fees and revenue from public property and public assets for Rwanda. These data could not be disaggregated to allocate revenue to the relevant non-tax revenue categories.
3. Represents an unweighted average of the 35 African countries in this publication. Data on tax revenues were available for Burkina Faso for this edition, but not non-tax revenues.

Table 6.4. Total non-tax revenue in millions of US dollars, 1995-2022

	1995	2000	2005	2010	2015	2018	2019	2020	2021	2022
Botswana	..	..	2 650	2 558	2 704	2 897	2 734	2 408	3 149	2 995
Cabo Verde	114	46	100	161	122	104	161	115	106	87
Cameroon	295	720	1 140	1 134	1 220	1 293	1 407	951	1 208	1 783
Chad	..	..	..	561	572	685	568	608	298	443
Congo	..	499	390	3 065	1 015	2 397	2 399	1 217	2 011	3 307
Congo, Dem. Rep.	..	..	..	1 330	1 783	1 273	1 162	1 143	2 651	2 574
Côte d'Ivoire	108	121	386	414	1 108	879	910	814	957	873
Egypt	..	..	6 196	18 520	22 574	11 609	12 794	15 564	18 697	23 167
Equatorial Guinea	..	..	1 995	3 062	1 978	1 785	1 057	626	1 199	2 713
Eswatini	208	212	508	367	581	552	573	620	529	464
Gabon	..	..	..	21	92	897	964	692	1 154	1 635
Ghana	..	178	730	1 612	2 419	2 195	2 161	1 951	2 114	2 360
Guinea	..	95	79	55	93	346	300	317	339	518
Kenya	..	..	424	514	1 037	1 819	2 008	3 815	2 464	2 248
Lesotho	..	..	466	788	651	632	604	724	761	514
Madagascar		128	315	297	173	415	485	373	142	240
Malawi	..	..	262	723	268	173	214	177	564	253
Mali	197	173	329	519	336	408	552	414	371	292
Mauritania	..	..	..	357	397	505	432	385	428	388
Mauritius[1]	140	128	161	372	323	593	406	413	269	481
Morocco	..	873	1 889	3 323	3 961	4 311	5 104	3 901	4 003	3 837
Mozambique	..	..	..	943	789	797	666	972	941	1 367
Namibia	..	..	..	1 088	1 572	1 578	1 531	1 609	1 296	1 378
Niger	..	92	275	366	560	934	1 003	1 138	1 205	854
Nigeria[2]	..	..	..	29 232	15 114	13 719	17 608	14 502	17 764	21 779
Rwanda	..	203	328	712	736	756	744	792	945	1 153
Senegal	..	96	200	412	621	784	647	826	939	659
Seychelles	..	..	..	60	93	108	100	96	120	129
Sierra Leone	..	..	133	146	268	191	259	350	316	375
Somalia	..	..	..	..	57	140	192	373	236	546
South Africa	790	596	1 399	2 211	1 406	2 093	2 034	1 868	2 970	2 676
Togo	..	27	61	384	174	391	342	287	254	294
Tunisia	..	529	831	1 257	891	1 229	1 305	1 275	1 292	1 975
Uganda	241	367	665	438	383	317	455	509	755	621
Zambia	..	..	..	..	477	442	395	388	747	738
Africa (35) average[3]	**..**	**..**	**..**	**..**	**1 901**	**1 693**	**1 836**	**1 777**	**2 091**	**2 449**

.. Not available

Note: The figures include sub-national government non-tax revenues for Eswatini, Kenya (2014 onwards), Mauritius, Morocco, Nigeria (2010 onwards), and Somalia (2019 onwards). Sub-national government non-tax revenues are not available in other countries. See the country tables in Chapter 6 for further information.

1. Data for Mauritius are on a July-June fiscal year basis except for the years 2010-15 when they were reported on a calendar year basis. Please see Chapter 5 for more details.
2. Non-tax revenues reported for Nigeria include revenues collected by Local Government Areas (LGAs). These revenues are reported under "Miscellaneous and unidentified revenue" although they include some tax revenues.
3. Represents an unweighted average of the 35 African countries in this publication. Data on tax revenues were available for Burkina Faso for this edition, but not non-tax revenues.

Table 6.5. Botswana – Details of non-tax revenue

Million BWP

	1995	2000	2005	2010	2015	2018	2019	2020	2021	2022
Total non-tax revenue	..	..	**14 034**	**17 412**	**27 953**	**29 941**	**29 844**	**27 330**	**35 982**	**37 967**
Grants	..	..	0	210	74	1	24	28	26	2
Grants	..	..	0	210	74	1	24	28	26	2
IMF Gold Sales	..	..	0	0	0	0	0	0	0	0
Property income	..	..	9 159	9 914	11 152	14 171	15 114	10 296	21 151	23 353
Rents and royalties	..	..	1 589	2 071	3 223	3 403	3 476	2 069	4 912	5 818
Mineral Royalties	..	..	1 577	2 057	3 215	3 383	3 463	2 062	4 903	5 809
Royalties and Dividends	..	..	0	0	0	0	0	0	0	0
Rent of Land	..	..	12	14	8	20	13	7	9	9
Interest and dividends	..	..	7 569	7 842	7 929	10 768	11 638	8 227	16 239	17 535
Mineral Dividends	..	..	6 573	7 054	6 766	9 905	6 547	4 196	10 473	17 105
Bank of Botswana Revenue	..	..	741	700	1 133	740	5 049	4 009	5 581	425
Profits From Public Enterprises	..	..	171	61	18	117	10	21	3	3
Interest: Parastatals (DDF)	..	..	38	20	8	1	29	0	48	0
Interest: Local Authorities	..	..	1	0	0	0	0	0	0	0
Interest: Deposits	..	..	46	8	4	5	3	0	0	1
Other interest revenue	..	..	0	0	0	0	0	0	134	0
Other property income	..	..	0	0	0	0	0	0	0	0
Sales of goods and services	..	..	908	1 047	811	930	656	478	549	710
Motor vehicle revenues	..	..	342	363	50	36	40	34	37	44
Petrol, Oil and Lubricants	..	..	54	182	231	217	111	67	25	22
Water revenues	..	..	167	42	2	2	2	3	4	4
Fees and charges	..	..	84	107	129	123	137	68	121	240
Rent of buildings and equipment	..	..	73	86	97	97	99	100	109	115
Sale of livestock	..	..	2	5	2	2	1	1	1	3
Registrations, licences and certificates	..	..	19	22	33	33	39	29	45	53
Other sales of goods and services	..	..	167	242	269	419	227	176	207	229
Fines, penalties and forfeits	..	..	36	31	93	42	60	62	100	46
Traffic fines	..	..	0	0	44	0	0	0	0	0
Court fines	..	..	19	20	38	22	23	34	29	20
Bond revenues	..	..	1	1	1	1	2	1	3	0
Income tax penalty	..	..	11	0	0	0	0	0	0	0
Other fines, penalties and forfeits	..	..	5	10	11	19	36	27	69	25
Miscellaneous and unidentified revenue	..	..	3 931	6 210	15 823	14 797	13 991	16 466	14 157	13 857
SACU revenue	..	..	3 930	6 207	15 818	14 789	13 976	16 459	14 148	13 845
Recovery of arrears of revenue	..	..	0	3	5	8	14	6	8	12
Revenue from local authorities	..	..	0	0	0	0	0	0	0	0
Reimbursement of medical claims (revenue)	..	..	1	1	1	1	1	0	1	0
Total tax and non-tax revenue	..	..	*22 071*	*31 712*	*47 285*	*53 229*	*54 201*	*49 303*	*68 236*	*73 200*

.. Not available

Note: Data are on a fiscal year basis beginning 1st April. For example, the data for 2022 represent April 2022 to March 2023.

The data are on a cash basis.

Figures exclude non-tax revenues collected by sub-national governments as the data are not available.

Source: Botswana Ministry of Finance and Economic Development, and Statistics Botswana.

Table 6.6. Cabo Verde – Details of non-tax revenues

Million CVE

	1995	2000	2005	2010	2015	2018	2019	2020	2021	2022
Total non-tax revenue	**8 744**	**5 372**	**8 902**	**13 396**	**12 116**	**10 368**	**16 034**	**11 105**	**9 885**	**9 105**
Grants	6 848	3 931	6 610	9 440	3 958	2 265	6 145	5 302	3 519	1 692
Current transfers from foreign governments	6 848	0	0	0	370	851	551	571	2 851	864
Budget aid	0	..	..	..	0	0	0	0	1 267	0
Food aid	1 064	..	..	..	0	0	0	0	0	8
Direct donations	5 161	..	..	..	353	846	548	571	1 575	820
Other current transfers	623	..	..	..	17	5	4	0	8	36
Capital transfers from foreign governments	0	3 931	6 610	9 440	3 588	1 414	5 594	4 730	669	828
Financial aid	..	0	551	3 085	1 282	1 103	2 006	2 287	0	276
Food aid	..	672	750	338	0	161	231	106	90	120
Direct donations	..	3 259	5 138	6 018	2 048	158	3 357	2 336	571	430
Other capital transfers	..	0	171	0	259	0	0	2	0	3
Property income	487	364	95	316	1 022	1 793	2 632	1 135	1 219	343
Rents and royalties	..	..	..	..	..	..	..	..	..	..
Interest and dividends	..	..	..	..	..	..	..	..	..	..
Other property income	..	..	..	..	..	..	..	..	..	..
Sales of goods and services	382	592	1 496	3 077	4 652	5 509	5 987	3 719	4 326	5 275
Fees	192	448	1 445	3 003	4 492	5 293	5 841	3 628	4 184	5 133
Sales	190	144	51	74	160	216	146	91	141	141
Fines, penalties and forfeits	64	54	169	376	404	369	433	220	187	296
Miscellaneous and unidentified revenue	963	431	532	187	2 079	431	838	730	633	1 499
Other transfers	425	413	150	41	36	24	242	192	230	359
Other unspecified revenues	538	18	382	146	2 043	407	595	538	403	1 140
Total tax and non-tax revenue	*15 034*	*16 346*	*27 731*	*39 686*	*42 807*	*50 706*	*57 481*	*44 236*	*43 012*	*52 009*

.. Not available

Note: Year ending 31st December.

The data are on a cash basis.

Figures exclude non-tax revenues collected by sub-national governments as the data are not available.

This publication does not include proceeds from the sale of non-financial assets reported in Cabo Verde's budget documents. Under Cabo Verde's national classification, proceeds from the sale of non-financial assets are included in non-tax revenues. Following the OECD classification of taxes (see the Interpretative Guide in Annex B), proceeds from the sale of assets are not classified as revenues (tax or non-tax) since the transaction does not increase the net worth.

The ECOWAS (Economic Community of West African States) community levy is not included in total non-tax or tax revenues and is presented separately under the heading "Memo item". Under Cabo Verde's national classification, it is included in tax revenues. Following the OECD classification of taxes (see the Interpretative Guide in Annex A § 4), this payment is not included in taxes.

Source: Ministry of Finance and Planning, Cabo Verde.

Table 6.7. Cameroon – Details of non-tax revenues

Million XAF

	1995	2000	2005	2010	2015	2018	2019	2020	2021	2022
Total non-tax revenue	**153 206**	**527 053**	**600 552**	**560 690**	**721 082**	**717 707**	**824 233**	**546 454**	**669 451**	**1 109 462**
Grants	0	6 900	91 404	78 805	18 089	86 700	133 300	41 700	66 200	104 200
Property income	90 400	404 500	446 825	442 296	465 541	510 077	551 526	398 084	479 105	865 344
Rents and royalties	90 400	404 500	410 657	437 650	445 587	499 042	527 789	379 185	463 353	834 359
Petroleum royalties	87 610	399 300	367 955	418 971	384 630	413 325	471 518	321 370	409 044	774 514
Pipeline right of access	0	0	14 065	9 080	36 201	29 543	35 013	36 818	31 336	36 531
Other rents and royalties	2 790	5 200	28 637	9 599	24 756	56 175	21 257	20 997	22 972	23 314
Interest and dividends	..	..	36 169	4 646	19 954	11 035	23 737	18 899	15 752	30 985
Other property income	..	..	0	0	0	0	0	0	0	0
Sales of goods and services	26 700	33 500	40 262	37 732	188 402	48 055	56 291	31 607	55 114	66 481
Fines, penalties and forfeits	0	0	444	1 857	26 849	57 334	61 259	71 960	57 906	70 131
Miscellaneous and unidentified revenue	36 106	82 153	21 616	0	22 201	15 541	21 857	3 102	11 126	3 307
Total tax and non-tax revenue	*634 589*	*1 337 553*	*1 735 808*	*2 132 385*	*3 409 008*	*3 864 201*	*4 046 395*	*3 560 542*	*4 024 767*	*4 999 048*

.. Not available

Note: Year ending 31st December.

The data are on a cash basis.

Figures exclude non-tax revenues collected by sub-national governments as the data are not available.

Property income includes taxes on property and quarrying and rents on water production following the OECD classification of taxes (see the Interpretative Guide in Annex B). Under Cameroon's national classification they are included in tax revenues.

Miscellaneous and unidentified revenues include capital transfers not included elsewhere and voluntary transfers other than grants.

Source: Ministry of Finance, Cameroon.

Table 6.8. Chad – Details of non-tax revenues

Million XAF

	1995	2000	2005	2010	2015	2018	2019	2020	2021	2022
Total non-tax revenue	**..**	**..**	**..**	**277 273**	**337 904**	**380 063**	**332 670**	**349 717**	**165 366**	**275 886**
Grants	..	..	..	68 799	221 884	199 244	106 891	248 109	16 088	92 125
Property income	..	..	..	190 753	86 094	146 899	198 643	69 282	129 983	142 427
Rents and royalties	..	..	..	190 753	86 094	146 899	198 643	69 282	129 983	142 427
Oil royalties and dividends	..	..	..	185 445	86 094	58 653	88 201	65 252	114 422	117 993
Other oil revenues	..	..	..	5 308	0	88 246	110 442	4 030	15 561	21 305
Mining royalties	..	..	..	..	..	..	..	..	..	3 129
Interest and dividends	..	..	..	0	0	0	0	0	0	0
Other property income	..	..	..	0	0	0	0	0	0	0
Sales of goods and services	..	..	..	6 539	12 230	4 594	18 172	7 565	6 946	3 352
Fines, penalties and forfeits	..	..	..	6 474	1 528	5 678	4 419	4 757	3 533	14 393
Miscellaneous and unidentified revenue	..	..	..	4 708	16 168	23 648	4 545	20 004	8 816	23 588
Total tax and non-tax revenue	*..*	*..*	*..*	*1 050 537*	*712 083*	*862 846*	*852 044*	*1 251 633*	*817 654*	*1 364 160*

.. Not available

Note: Year ending 31st December.

The data are on a cash basis.

Figures exclude tax revenues collected by sub-national governments as the data are not available.

Chad adopted a new budgetary nomenclature from 2022, so the data in this edition are presented differently.

Revenues from mining royalties are reported separately under Chad's new budgetary nomenclature.

Revenues from "Property income" for years prior to 2022 have been reclassified under "Mining royalties", since the latter represents the largest proportion of these revenues.

Revenues from tax fines, government securities and the audiovisual licence fee are included in non-tax revenues following the OECD classification of taxes (see the Interpretative Guide in Annex A). Under Chad's national classification they are included in tax revenues.

The heading "Fines, penalties and forfeits" for 2022 includes non-itemised revenues from "Miscellaneous contributions", which includes revenues from tax-base assessment penalties and tax fines, poll taxes, rental value tax, with tax-base assessment penalties and tax fines accounting for the majority of these revenues. Chad includes revenues from "Miscellaneous contributions" in income and profit tax.

Revenues from tax fines are recorded under the heading "Fines, penalties and forfeits". Revenues from government securities and audiovisual licence fees are recorded under the heading "Sales of goods and services".

Source: Ministry of Finance and Budget, Chad.

Table 6.9. Congo – Details of non-tax revenues

Million XAF

	1995	2000	2005	2010	2015	2018	2019	2020	2021	2022
Total non-tax revenue	**..**	**355 390**	**205 249**	**1 515 115**	**600 062**	**1 330 954**	**1 405 657**	**699 483**	**1 114 733**	**2 058 637**
Grants	..	5 000	47 438	1 359 181	38 145	5 925	56 860	21 366	38 100	53 900
Property income	..	350 390	157 811	154 506	554 918	1 323 391	1 348 516	677 302	1 075 381	2 004 036
Rents and royalties	..	350 390	157 811	154 453	549 122	1 310 984	1 332 828	662 876	1 060 110	1 990 555
Oil revenue	..	350 390	157 811	152 746	541 297	1 293 311	1 317 000	651 000	1 049 000	1 972 800
Oil royalty	..	..	..	0	70	77	13	8	0	0
Mining royalty	..	..	..	2	60	1	1	9	3	0
Forest royalty	..	..	..	1 705	7 696	17 594	15 814	11 859	11 107	17 755
Interest and dividends	..	..	..	0	0	0	0	0	0	0
Other property income	..	..	..	53	5 796	12 407	15 688	14 426	15 271	13 480
Sales of goods and services	..	..	..	16	30	48	207	5	150	83
Fines, penalties and forfeits	..	..	..	1 077	1 721	1 590	73	810	1 103	13
Miscellaneous and unidentified revenue	..	..	..	336	5 248	0	0	0	0	606
Total tax and non-tax revenue	..	*454 074*	*411 665*	*1 978 038*	*1 531 479*	*1 953 917*	*2 078 519*	*1 347 499*	*1 725 500*	*2 831 264*

.. Not available

Note: Year ending 31st December.

The data are on a cash basis.

Figures exclude non-tax revenues collected by sub-national governments as the data are not available.

Revenues from grants and oil revenues are derived from several public sources (TOFE 2018, Perspective de l'économie Congolaise, Lois de finances, IMF public finance statistics database, IMF Article IV country report).

Heading "Rents and royalties": As from 2017, this heading includes timber rents and diamond royalties collected by the General Directorate of Customs and Indirect Duties (Direction Générale des douanes et des droits indirects).

Source: Ministry of Economy and Finance, Republic of the Congo, IMF.

Table 6.10. Congo Dem. Rep. – Details of non-tax revenues

Million CDF

	1995	2000	2005	2010	2015	2018	2019	2020	2021	2022
Total non-tax revenue				**1 206 158**	**1 651 247**	**2 065 548**	**1 915 421**	**2 116 365**	**5 276 706**	**5 166 428**
Grants				656 421	1 108 062	851 000	638 806	930 571	2 915 000	2 115 000
Property income				397 162	328 729	796 073	841 845	828 625	1 549 404	2 202 213
Rents and royalties				357 515	290 419	734 297	765 511	775 571	1 458 910	2 039 487
Royalties on petroleum corporation				39 705	19 050	41 483	34 353	27 259	77 698	90 492
Mining rents and royalties				139 802	143 702	408 754	385 847	545 897	1 021 295	1 472 367
Annual surface / land fees (mines)				25 464	20 689	13 970	10 199	11 730	19 308	22 782
Signature bonus - Renewal (hydrocarbons)				4 566	624	736	1 041	1 652	29 869	37 224
Rents on annual exploitation and other royalties (telecommunications)				50 603	38 635	53 312	94 410	108 156	113 962	129 116
Concession, extraction and other authorisations				9 126	5 789	131 631	101 098	2 396	11 098	3 509
Forestry and wildlife permits				3 541	387	771	2 171	3 484	4 942	12 068
Distributional margin (petroleum revenues)				84 491	52 694	83 408	127 330	65 303	170 435	271 556
Surface rights on exploration permits and concession (hydrocarbons)				10	8 791	30	8 502	8 355	10 010	230
Other rents				207	58	202	558	1 338	291	142
Interest and dividends				39 301	37 159	40 811	75 305	52 225	90 403	162 038
On shore dividends (petrol revenues)				8 068	14 665	10 994	20 246	15 852	9 690	7 229
Off shore participation (petrol revenues)				25 347	15 806	24 271	41 892	19 716	52 323	80 575
Other dividends and participation				5 886	6 688	5 546	13 167	16 657	28 390	74 233
Other property income				345	1 152	20 965	1 029	829	92	688
Sales of goods and services				116 573	162 555	315 997	282 789	264 745	356 337	447 001
Print sales				1 106	690	219	75	158	453	779
Tax on numbering	..	..	..	16 464	26 110	51 014	45 573	44 887	54 984	56 697
Tax on regulations and changes to certifications / telecommunication tax	..	..	..	13 180	36 198	20 191	18 050	19 019	16 889	13 339
Passports, visa and work permits	..	..	..	20 859	31 053	45 946	42 369	27 344	54 805	61 202
Fees for provision of security by Congolese National Police	..	..	..	4 247	11 337	23 016	34 594	32 749	24 610	25 478
Inspection fees for toxic and / or narcotic products	..	..	..	647	7 328	7 736	7 075	59 715	2 537	102 408
Fees for disinfection and sanitary inspections of thrift stores				3 828	3 111	14 156	53 800	17 897	90 135	6 715
Accreditation				1 181	559	995	1 364	1 309	1 697	3 158
Other				55 059	43 646	148 256	75 130	57 626	106 189	170 736
Rents, National Social Security Institut (INSS)				0	2 524	4 468	4 759	4 040	4 040	6 490
Fines, penalties and forfeits				35 378	50 772	101 256	150 692	80 604	400 076	394 422
Fines and penalties (DGI) - excluding natural resources (from 2022)				15 455	15 160	65 525	90 865	43 701	196 201	195 047
Fines and penalties (DGI) - mining				..	..	..	..	..	..	42 431
Fines and penalties (DGI) – hydrocarbons				..	..	..	..	..	..	8 366
Fines and penalties (DGI) - forests				..	..	..	..	..	..	223
Fines and penalties (DGDA)				1 561	4 093	1 910	1 633	1 246	116 781	11 044
Fines and penalties (DGRAD)	..	..	..	18 363	31 518	33 821	58 194	35 657	87 095	137 310
Miscellaneous and unidentified revenue	..			625	1 129	1 222	1 289	11 821	55 889	7 792
Total tax and non-tax revenue	..			*2 890 521*	*5 138 807*	*7 995 292*	*8 295 943*	*8 729 842*	*15 539 402*	*21 713 622*

.. Not available

Note: Year ending 31st December.

The data are on a cash basis.

Figures exclude non-tax revenues collected by sub-national governments as the data are not available.

Data on grants for 2021 and 2022 are projections from IMF reports No. 22/210 and No. 23/434 respectively.

Revenues from the print sales are included in non-tax revenues following the OECD classification of taxes (see the Interpretative Guide in Annex B). Under The Democratic Republic of Congo's national classification revenues from print sales are included in tax revenues.

Some revenues - considered as taxes in the Democratic Republic of Congo - are considered as administrative costs and are included in non-tax revenues following the OECD classification of taxes (see the Interpretative Guide in Annex B).

Source: Ministry of Finance, Democratic Republic of Congo; IMF.

Table 6.11. Côte d'Ivoire – Details of non-tax revenues

Million CDF

	1995	2000	2005	2010	2015	2018	2019	2020	2021	2022
Total non-tax revenue	**54 156**	**86 004**	**203 671**	**205 073**	**654 836**	**488 004**	**533 356**	**467 932**	**530 266**	**543 080**
Grants	35 000	33 500	94 628	106 540	282 200	246 158	274 912	193 269	184 600	233 700
Property income	1 356	4 204	5 555	76 308	285 955	145 071	135 074	98 988	106 200	115 780
Rents and royalties	1 356	4 204	5 555	44 902	255 515	121 350	107 057	58 889	72 049	86 708
Revenues from public lands	0	0	0	283	2 111	2 160	3 578	4 104	6 280	7 048
Oil exploitation tax	0	0	0	27 275	30 851	36 888	44 522	28 012	32 286	39 020
Oil contract signing bonus	0	0	0	0	0	6 039	8 088	0	1 949	3 555
Land royalties (except ad valorem tax 2012-2021)	1 356	4 204	5 555	7 696	37 224	31 812	23 425	26 632	31 534	37 085
Other rents and royalties	0	0	0	9 647	185 329	44 451	27 444	142	0	0
Interest and dividends	0	0	0	27 981	30 440	23 721	28 017	40 099	34 151	29 072
Other property income	0	0	0	3 426	0	0	0	0	0	0
Sales of goods and services	0	0	13 200	21 700	35 414	47 111	57 937	76 599	87 681	103 358
Ivoirian television broadcast royalty (RTI)	..	..	0	4 107	6 244	8 587	10 342	9 493	11 411	12 067
Broadcasting tax	..	..	0	0	0	0	0	0	0	0
Road tolls	..	..	0	0	0	0	0	16 461	21 680	25 676
Other sales of goods and services	..	..	13 200	17 592	29 170	38 524	47 595	50 645	54 590	65 615
Fines, penalties and forfeits	0	0	0	173	0	0	0	0	0	0
Miscellaneous and unidentified revenue	17 800	48 300	90 288	353	51 267	49 664	65 433	99 076	151 785	90 242
Total tax and non-tax revenue	*978 628*	*1 255 611*	*1 610 948*	*2 240 542*	*4 069 254*	*4 682 693*	*5 061 198*	*5 202 418*	*6 072 398*	*6 315 657*

.. Not available

Note: Year ending 31st December.

The data are on a cash basis.

Figures exclude non-tax revenues collected by sub-national governments as the data are not available.

Revenues from property taxes, the ad valorem tax and operating tax are included in non-tax revenues following the OECD classification of taxes (see the Interpretative Guide in Annex B). Under Côte d'Ivoire's national classification they are included in tax revenues.

Revenues from property taxes exclude the ad-valorem tax for the period 2012 to 2022, during which it was possible to differentiate between these types of revenue.

The broadcasting taxand the Ivoirian television broadcast royalty (RTI) are included in non-tax revenues following the OECD classification of taxes (see the Interpretative Guide in Annex B). Under Côte d'Ivoire's national classification, they are included in tax revenues.

Miscellaneous and unidentified revenues include capital transfers not included elsewhere and voluntary transfers other than grants.

Source: Ministry of Economy and Finance, Côte d'Ivoire.

Table 6.12. Egypt – Details of non-tax revenues

Million EGP

	1995	2000	2005	2010	2015	2018	2019	2020	2021	2022
Total non-tax revenue	**..**	**..**	**37 270**	**102 149**	**166 134**	**205 853**	**225 222**	**250 335**	**294 307**	**382 314**
Grants	..	..	2 114	3 830	25 243	1 914	1 848	1 806	1 642	2 554
Grants from foreign governments	..	..	2 114	3 497	24 942	1 006	1 100	1 007	819	348
Grants from international organisations	..	..	0	332	302	908	747	798	824	2 205
Property income	..	..	18 672	55 533	83 283	74 150	75 222	68 950	83 213	98 723
Rents and royalties	..	..	1 114	7 216	8 252	18 262	20 964	17 488	20 414	27 889
Royalties on petroleum	..	..	0	2 750	5 964	11 610	14 148	11 178	14 680	20 714
Royalties on Suez Canal	..	..	1 068	1 354	1 945	5 163	5 157	4 600	4 500	5 750
Mining royalties	..	..	17	46	230	1 205	1 208	1 420	920	1 015
Other royalties	..	..	30	3 066	113	284	451	291	313	410
Interest and dividends	..	..	17 233	48 315	74 894	55 616	53 812	50 952	62 569	69 638
Suez Canal Authority (SCA)	..	..	9 651	12 729	19 214	23 718	30 308	18 354	28 082	27 734
Central Bank of Egypt (CBE)	..	..	4 999	205	13 417	5 233	0	0	0	0
Economic authorities	..	..	402	1 431	10 093	8 297	10 817	12 045	11 861	11 108
Public and private companies and enterprises	..	..	245	3 272	3 295	6 867	5 408	8 631	11 185	12 336
Egyptian General Petroleum Corporation (EGPC)	..	..	154	25 546	25 414	8 144	1 278	2 093	3 596	10 335
Other dividends and interests	..	..	1 782	5 130	3 460	3 358	6 001	9 830	7 846	8 124
Other property income	..	..	324	2	137	272	447	509	230	1 196
Sales of goods and services	..	..	8 979	25 661	27 583	62 243	73 342	77 956	117 721	177 351
Administrative fees	..	..	1 505	2 681	4 482	10 437	12 520	10 463	7 457	10 319
Development fees	..	..	294	841	931	403	1 991	2 352	9 929	11 178
Service fees	..	..	3 170	3 572	8 352	15 343	17 147	15 757	17 915	26 063
Capital revenues	..	..	3 986	16 962	13 610	35 803	41 252	48 099	81 363	129 602
Licences	..	..	0	1 557	128	125	276	1 136	917	0
Other sales of goods and services	..	..	24	49	80	134	156	149	141	188
Fines, penalties and forfeits	..	..	343	653	1 193	1 732	2 379	2 871	2 658	3 159
Miscellaneous and unidentified revenue	..	..	7 163	16 472	28 831	65 814	72 431	98 753	89 073	100 528
Current revenues from special accounts and funds	..	..	4 842	12 268	17 797	35 732	36 128	42 787	39 497	51 509
Voluntary transfers other than grants	..	..	1 084	684	901	2 143	2 316	2 262	5 958	7 882
Current revenues	..	..	1 114	3 312	9 827	27 576	33 685	53 405	43 258	40 747
Other revenues	..	..	123	208	306	363	303	300	360	390
Total tax and non-tax revenue	..	..	*126 239*	*299 115*	*524 792*	*929 958*	*1 075 264*	*1 085 400*	*1 234 017*	*1 495 045*

.. Not available

Note: Fiscal year ends on 30 June. For example, the data for 2022 represent July 2021 to June 2022.

The data are on a cash basis.

Figures exclude non-tax revenues collected by sub-national governments as the data are not available. These data are estimated to be insignificant.

Royalties on the Suez Canal as well as other royalties and administrative fees are reported as tax revenues in Egypt. In accordance with the OECD classification, as set out in the Interpretative Guide in Annex A, these revenues are considered non-tax revenues.

Source: Ministry of Finance.

Table 6.13. Equatorial Guinea – Details of non-tax revenues

Million XAF

	1995	2000	2005	2010	2015	2018	2019	2020	2021	2022
Total non-tax revenue	**..**	**..**	**1 051 820**	**1 515 259**	**1 169 328**	**991 642**	**619 121**	**360 207**	**664 693**	**1 692 234**
Grants	..	..	17 533	0	0	0	1 648	576	1 031	518
Property income	..	..	1 012 089	1 489 017	1 087 688	962 877	595 780	337 859	627 290	1 666 263
Rents and royalties	..	..	518 258	957 200	688 968	604 305	373 890	227 588	468 162	704 068
Petroleum royalties	..	..	462 289	951 507	680 217	590 596	355 668	211 397	454 405	690 983
Surface royalties	..	..	51 284	844	1 842	1 794	400	84	190	27
Fishing and concessional royalties	..	..	2 021	4 850	6 909	11 915	17 822	16 107	13 567	13 059
GEOGAM gas sales	..	..	2 664	0	0	0	0	0	0	0
Interest and dividends	..	..	491 560	437 662	380 575	328 453	206 847	97 177	149 761	952 525
Shareholder participation in oil revenues	..	..	476 917	257 392	237 800	134 422	108 655	63 718	113 129	147 246
Oil dividends	..	..	0	146 345	134 965	185 706	93 018	26 545	32 565	234 008
Non-oil dividends	..	..	1 622	17 314	7 538	7 794	1 454	3 762	707	118
Interest on reserve funds	..	..	12 554	6 977	43	498	3 561	2 997	3 194	3 686
Other interest (banking, deferrals)	..	..	467	9 635	52	1	0	0	0	0
INSESO: Interest and dividends	..	..	..	..	178	32	160	155	166	202
Gas monetisation	..	..	0	0	0	0	0	0	0	567 264
Other property income	..	..	2 271	94 155	18 145	30 119	15 043	13 094	9 367	9 671
Contributions of public companies and independent entities	..	..	0	1 624	4 149	26 104	15 037	13 090	9 367	9 671
Other oil - related property income	..	..	2 271	92 531	13 997	4 015	6	5	0	0
Sales of goods and services	..	..	4 912	15 935	24 901	17 470	17 345	18 095	20 236	22 869
Administrative fees and government services	..	..	4 344	13 975	19 669	14 234	13 929	13 890	15 706	18 457
Consular fees	..	..	294	1 357	973	1 694	123	106	639	846
Tolls	..	..	184	458	2 714	383	2 249	2 356	2 404	2 457
Rentals of government buildings	..	..	90	145	132	139	42	10	0	0
INSESO: Medical goods and services	..	..	..	..	1 355	875	850	1 619	1 396	1 019
INSESO: Other goods and services	..	..	..	..	59	144	151	113	90	89
INSESO: Provincial medical fees	..	..	..	..	0	0	0	0	0	0
Fines, penalties and forfeits	..	..	0	0	258	451	319	85	1 608	513
INSESO: Sanctions, arrears and penalties	..	..	..	..	258	451	319	85	71	50
Other fines and penalties, excluding INSESO	..	..	..	..	0	0	0	0	1 537	463
Miscellaneous and unidentified revenue	..	..	17 286	10 307	56 481	10 843	4 029	3 591	14 528	2 071
INSESO: Other revenues	..	..	..	..	0	256	4	0	4	1
Transfers from other institutions	..	..	17 286	10 307	56 481	10 587	4 025	3 193	8 798	500
Other revenues, excluding INSESO and transfers	..	..	0	0	0	0	0	399	5 726	1 570
Total tax and non-tax revenue	*..*	*..*	*1 407 860*	*2 127 636*	*2 105 235*	*1 471 741*	*1 270 542*	*850 596*	*1 068 748*	*2 289 405*

.. Not available

Note: Year ending 31st December.

The data are on a cash basis.

Equatorial Guinea launched a new gas monetisation project in May 2018, but the government only began collecting revenues from this project in 2022. These revenues result from a revenue sharing agreement between the government of Equatorial Guinea and the corporations developing this project.

Source: Ministry of Finance, Economy and Planning; National Institute of Social Security of Equatorial Guinea (Instituto Nacional de Seguridad Social de Guinea Ecuatorial (INSESO)).

Table 6.14. Eswatini – Details of non-tax revenues

Million SZL

	1995	2000	2005	2010	2015	2018	2019	2020	2021	2022
Total non-tax revenue	**789**	**1 549**	**3 285**	**2 679**	**7 685**	**7 466**	**8 539**	**9 904**	**8 024**	**7 836**
Grants	1	3	7	11	144	169	238	154	221	185
Property income	26	95	67	553	494	1 069	1 784	1 200	1 101	1 580
Rents and royalties	0	0	0	3	72	81	143	83	33	120
Land concession rents, postal revenue	0	0	0	0	0	0	0	0	0	0
Rents attributed to social security funds	0	0	0	3	72	81	143	83	33	120
Interest and dividends	19	91	65	548	391	919	1 546	1 006	966	1 427
Local interest collected by central government	7	21	25	538	60	28	16	20	6	9
Central bank profit	6	0	0	0	245	0	430	43	55	173
External interest and interest on capital	5	69	13	0	0	3	2	4	4	4
Dividends	1	1	27	8	11	106	207	108	146	197
Interest and dividends collected by social security funds	0	0	0	1	75	783	891	831	755	1 044
Other property income	7	4	1	1	31	69	95	110	102	33
Quitrents	0	0	0	0	0	0	0	0	0	0
Local government property income	7	4	1	1	31	69	95	110	102	33
Sales of goods and services	16	40	63	115	73	325	137	139	271	202
Sundry fees	7	13	40	38	6	246	39	67	175	99
Passports, citizenship and resident permits	3	5	5	25	25	33	40	22	33	36
Rental of government real estate	2	3	6	7	11	13	13	12	12	12
Driver's licences, motor vehicle certification	0	1	3	8	11	15	16	16	18	16
Hospital and medical services	0	5	4	6	6	8	8	6	6	7
Hire of government plants and vehicles	0	0	0	21	0	0	0	0	0	1
Aviation fees	0	12	1	0	0	0	0	0	0	0
Sale of government furniture and vehicles	0	0	0	6	7	2	2	5	11	15
Sale of agricultural products and services	1	2	1	1	2	3	3	3	3	3
Public service transport fees	1	0	1	1	1	1	1	1	1	0
Sale of government publications	0	0	0	1	1	1	1	2	2	2
Prison industry sales	0	0	0	0	0	0	0	0	0	0
Local government sales of goods and services	0	0	1	1	2	5	14	8	13	11
Fines, penalties and forfeits	2	4	11	28	33	46	49	46	39	38
Traffic fines	1	2	5	15	13	15	16	21	16	11
Judicial fines and other penalties	0	1	4	10	18	24	25	19	14	12
Interest and penalties on late tax payments	0	0	1	1	2	4	5	6	10	13
Pay-as-you-earn (PAYE) penalties	0	1	1	1	0	0	0	0	0	0
Fines, penalties and forfeits (local non-tax revenue)	0	0	0	0	0	3	2	0	0	2
Miscellaneous and unidentified revenue	744	1 407	3 138	1 972	6 942	5 856	6 332	8 365	6 390	5 831
SACU revenue	744	1 406	3 136	1 969	6 931	5 844	6 318	8 349	6 375	5 818
SACU penalties	0	0	1	2	9	9	7	10	11	5
Miscellaneous and unidentified revenue (local non-tax revenue)	0	0	0	2	3	3	7	6	4	9
Total tax and non-tax revenue	*1 534*	*2 876*	*5 692*	*7 267*	*15 592*	*18 357*	*20 432*	*21 821*	*20 808*	*22 140*

.. Not available

Note: Data are reported on a fiscal year basis beginning 1st April. For example, the data for 2022 represent April 2022 to March 2023.

The data are on a cash basis.

Revenues from motor vehicle licences, the change of ownership fees and the registration of new motor vehicles are considered as tax revenue under the OECD classification as set out in the Interpretative Guide in Annex A and are classified under heading 5211 (Recurrent taxes paid by households: motor vehicles). The national classification of Eswatini classifies these revenues as non-tax revenues.

Revenues from business and sundry licences are considered as tax revenue under the OECD classification, as set out in the Interpretative Guide in Annex A and are classified under heading 5213 (Recurrent taxes paid on use of goods and perform activities other than on motor vehicles). The national classification of Eswatini classifies these revenues as non-tax revenues.

The revenues from the registrations of specific goods (e.g. firearms) are considered as tax revenue under the OECD classification, as set out in the Interpretative Guide in Annex A and are classified under heading 5220 (Non-recurrent taxes on use of goods and perform activities). The national classification of Eswatini classifies these revenues as non-tax revenues.

The revenues from the education loans' repayments do not represent an increase of net worth resulting from a transaction and therefore are not considered as revenues under the OECD classification, as set out in the Interpretative Guide in Annex B.

Revenue from PAYE Penalties, tax interests and penalties on taxes are considered as non-tax revenue under the OECD classification, as set out in the Interpretative Guide in Annex A. The national classification of Eswatini classifies it as tax revenues.

Source: Eswatini Revenue Service; Local Government; Eswatini National Provident Fund and Public Service Pension Fund; Ministry of Economic Planning and Development; Central Government.

Table 6.15. Gabon – Details of non-tax revenues

Million XAF

	1995	2000	2005	2010	2015	2018	2019	2020	2021	2022
Total non-tax revenue	**..**	**..**	**..**	**10 231**	**54 147**	**497 870**	**564 628**	**397 568**	**639 633**	**1 017 598**
Grants	..	..	..							
Property income	..	..	..	6 717	25 905	455 275	556 692	387 314	628 252	1 004 561
Rents and royalties	..	..	..	6 527	10 438	431 784	539 900	335 343	588 874	938 878
Land royalty - mining sector	..	..	..	864	830	2 454	2 278	1 612	2 369	2 045
Mining estates - manganese	..	..	..	0	0	0	0	0	1 615	13
Other mining income	..	..	..	2	6 607	1 008	77	268	1 089	6 658
Other mining royalties	..	..	..	529	564	242	481	194	275	365
Oil royalties	..	..	..	0	0	0	0	0	0	1 271
Surface area tax (forest)	..	..	..	3 423	2 437	2 891	3 691	3 438	7 408	9 247
Forest allocation fee	..	..	..	1 409	0	1 961	2 366	1 733	0	40
Other forest royalties	..	..	..	300	0	3	0	0	0	0
Petroleum revenues from Direction Générale des Hydrocarbures	..	..	..			423 225	531 007	328 097	576 117	919 238
Interest and dividends	..	..	..	191	15 467	23 491	16 792	51 971	39 378	65 683
Income from profit-sharing	..	..	..	191	15 467	23 491	16 792	16 771	25 740	18 521
Direction Générale des Hydrocarbures oil dividends	..	..	..		0	0	0	35 200	13 638	47 162
Other property income	..	..	..	0	0	0	0	0	0	0
Sales of goods and services	..	..	..	649	4 032	24 748	2 149	3 742	6 218	3 653
Registration fees on deeds	..	..	..	357	3 014	24 693	2 107	3 674	6 066	3 632
Administrative fees and charges	..	..	..	292	1 018	55	42	68	152	22
Fines, penalties and forfeits	..	..	..	2 865	24 210	17 847	5 787	6 512	5 162	9 361
Recovery penalties	..	..	..	704	16 485	12 323	4 466	4 431	3 556	5 043
Value-added tax penalties	..	..	..	909	6 640	4 455	920	1 067	841	1 456
Other fines and penalties	..	..	..	1 252	1 084	1 068	400	1 014	766	2 862
Miscellaneous and unidentified revenue	..	..	..	0	0	0	0	0	0	22
Total tax and non-tax revenue	..	..	..	*914 078*	*1 356 351*	*1 466 979*	*1 756 326*	*1 529 184*	*1 796 747*	*2 515 533*

.. Not available

Note: Year ending 31st December.

The data are on a cash basis.

Figures exclude non-tax revenues collected by sub-national governments as the data are not available.

Non-tax revenues include revenues from fines and penalties relating to taxes (under the heading "Fines, penalties and forfeits") and certain registration fees (under the heading "Sales of goods and services"). Under Gabon's national classification they are included in tax revenues.

Non-tax revenues for years prior to 2014 do not include oil revenues from the Directorate of Hydrocarbons (Direction Générale des Hydrocarbures) because they are not available.

Proceeds from the sales of assets are not classified as revenues since the transaction does not increase the net worth, following the OECD classification of taxes (see the Interpretative Guide in Annexes A and B). Under Gabon's national classification they are included in non-tax revenues.

Source: Ministry of Economy and Participations, Gabon.

Table 6.16. Ghana – Details of non-tax revenues

Million GHS

	1995	2000	2005	2010	2015	2018	2019	2020	2021	2022
Total non-tax revenue	**..**	**97**	**661**	**2 306**	**8 978**	**10 071**	**11 272**	**10 922**	**12 259**	**19 931**
Grants	..	57	535	1 080	2 689	1 135	986	1 229	1 182	1 119
Project grants	..	24	284	591	1 744	1 121	986	1 229	1 182	1 119
Programme grants	..	34	135	288	945	14	0	0	0	0
International debt relief	..	0	116	201	0	0	0	0	0	0
Property income	..	7	18	347	3 003	5 075	5 517	4 916	5 404	10 833
Rents and royalties	..	0	0	0	908	1 969	2 328	2 476	2 638	4 277
Mineral royalties (aside from oil)	..	..	..	..	518	744	1 057	1 376	1 309	1 796
Oil revenues	..	..	..	..	384	1 213	1 252	1 092	1 323	2 456
Lodgements to MDAs and MMDAs: Surface rentals from Oil / PHF Interest	..	..	..	..	6	12	19	7	6	25
Lodgements to MDAs and MMDAs: Fees from granting of new stability agreements	..	..	..	..	0	0	0	0	0	0
Revenue from oil companies (includes corporate tax)	..	..	..	..	0	0	0	0	0	0
Interest and dividends	..	7	18	347	2 095	3 106	3 189	2 441	2 765	6 556
Lodgements to MDAs and MMDAs: Dividend, interest and profits from oil companies	..	0	0	0	995	2 531	2 691	1 696	1 817	6 082
Lodgements to MDAs and MMDAs: Dividend, interest and profits aside from oil companies	..	7	18	347	726	139	106	275	475	474
SSNIT revenue - Investment income	..	0	0	0	375	436	392	469	474	0
Other property income	..	0	0	0	0	0	0	0	0	0
Sales of goods and services	..	32	108	879	3 195	3 719	4 576	4 568	5 477	7 793
Retentions by MDAs and MMDAs	..	23	78	685	2 531	3 165	3 953	4 003	4 708	7 018
Lodgements to MDAs and MMDAs: Fees and charges	..	10	30	194	663	555	623	565	769	774
Lodgements to MDAs and MMDAs: Gas receipts	..	0	0	0	2	0	0	0	0	0
Fines, penalties and forfeits	..	0	0	0	0	0	0	0	0	0
Miscellaneous and unidentified revenue	..	0	0	0	91	142	194	209	197	187
Yield from budget capping policy	..	..	..	..	0	101	115	120	135	187
SSNIT revenue - Miscellaneous income	..	..	..	..	91	41	79	89	62	0
Total tax and non-tax revenue	..	*584*	*3 004*	*9 001*	*32 570*	*52 256*	*58 311*	*62 390*	*77 117*	*105 127*

.. Not available

Note: Year ending 31st December.

The data are on a cash basis.

Figures exclude non-tax revenues collected by sub-national governments as the data are not available.

Revenues for MDAs (Municipalities, Departments and Agencies) and MMDAs (Metropolitan, Municipal and District Assemblies) contain a mixture of revenues collected at the local level, and revenues collected at a federal level. These are reported as revenues to the central government.

Yield from budget capping policy has been added to the classification in this edition. The Earmarked Funds and Capping Realignment Bill into law in 2017.

Source: Ghana Statistical Service.

Table 6.17. Guinea – Details of non-tax revenues

Million GNF

	1995	2000	2005	2010	2015	2018	2019	2020	2021	2022
Total non-tax revenue	..	**165 427**	**286 519**	**313 794**	**699 211**	**3 115 465**	**2 754 357**	**3 029 609**	**3 313 603**	**4 505 926**
Grants	..	125 270	91 941	108 159	337 842	1 510 193	574 549	1 538 913	970 660	831 444
Restricted donations	..	123 889	27 500	102 824	249 273	1 061 327	358 321	547 360	930 169	831 444
Unrestricted donations	..	1 381	3 777	0	88 569	448 867	216 229	991 553	40 491	0
Other donations	..	0	60 664	5 334	0	0	0	0	0	0
Property income	..	18 673	110 746	137 445	163 344	1 024 036	1 041 805	1 353 083	1 977 009	2 637 273
Rents and royalties	..	14 611	101 400	54 880	130 515	922 930	977 636	1 005 291	1 588 925	1 840 229
Mining extraction tax (TME)	..	0	0	0	0	615 851	650 148	729 661	1 165 958	1 476 115
GSM cell phone radio royalties	..	0	81 366	13 118	82 800	20 000	128 750	116 543	162 592	186 351
Fishing company royalties	..	9 543	17 621	5 226	18 409	61 142	70 585	74 497	89 185	88 607
Mining royalties	..	38	441	29 697	18 380	205 686	105 683	61 025	143 043	57 246
Collected buyer's counters (diamonds)	..	455	609	2 814	3 982	5 797	3 651	4 853	7 013	6 160
Other royalties	..	4 575	1 364	4 025	6 945	14 454	18 818	18 712	21 134	25 750
Interest and dividends	..	4 062	9 346	82 565	32 829	101 106	64 169	347 792	388 084	797 044
Other property income	..	0	0	0	0	0	0	0	0	0
Sales of goods and services	..	5 142	49 013	40 493	109 183	93 113	91 246	99 927	263 529	327 784
Administrative fees and charges	..	3 699	2 394	6 149	75 275	90 274	87 488	90 375	248 523	310 747
Infrastructure leasing	..	0	40 418	33 177	31 871	0	269	0	0	0
Rental income	..	1 384	5 875	759	785	603	556	513	1 210	223
Building rental	..	59	326	410	1 252	2 236	2 933	9 038	13 796	16 814
Other administrative revenue	..	0	0	0	0	0	0	0	0	0
Fines, penalties and forfeits	..	705	5 010	7 672	26 711	26 198	45 334	37 185	29 482	16 944
Miscellaneous and unidentified revenue	..	15 637	29 809	20 025	62 131	461 925	1 001 423	500	72 922	692 480
Accidental income	..	7 993	29 734	16 422	28 000	400 250	784 281	162	57 214	661 172
Other revenue from miscellaneous products	..	7 645	76	3 603	34 131	61 675	217 142	339	15 708	31 308
Total tax and non-tax revenue	..	*692 549*	*1 663 263*	*4 246 059*	*9 275 617*	*15 912 126*	*17 834 661*	*18 803 505*	*20 988 455*	*22 841 117*

.. Not available

Note: Year ending 31st December.

The data are on a cash basis.

Figures exclude non-tax revenues collected by sub-national governments as the data are not available.

Revenues from mining taxes on extraction, fees for administrative services, auction proceeds and fines and penalties relating to taxes are included in non-tax revenues following the OECD classification of taxes (see the Interpretative Guide in Annexes A and B) respectively as "Rents and royalties", "Sales of goods and services" and "Fines, penalties and forfeits". Under Guinea's national classification they are included in tax revenues.

Source: Ministry of Budget, Guinea.

Table 6.18. Kenya – Details of non-tax revenues

Million KES

	1995	2000	2005	2010	2015	2018	2019	2020	2021	2022
Total non-tax revenue	**..**	**..**	**32 767**	**40 293**	**96 277**	**186 130**	**204 133**	**397 233**	**265 805**	**255 320**
Grants	..	..	14 905	20 710	12 020	26 484	19 692	19 820	31 816	42 568
Grants from foreign governments	..	..	14 905	9 215	2 644	2 696	2 289	4 151	2 932	7 947
Grants from International orgs	..	..	0	11 495	9 376	23 788	17 402	15 669	28 884	34 621
Property income	..	..	5 255	9 921	16 216	43 670	49 280	165 386	96 686	76 262
Rents and royalties	..	..	727	1 184	695	1 606	1 576	1 398	1 599	1 421
Rent of land	..	..	674	1 108	8	753	610	472	520	542
Kenya Airports Authority (KAA) concession fees	..	..	53	77	113	131	134	120	145	149
Base titanium royalty	..	..	0	0	338	491	520	509	536	451
Mining royalties	..	..	0	0	136	95	117	193	164	125
Royalties from Soda Ash	..	..	0	0	100	135	195	105	235	155
Interest and dividends	..	..	2 027	8 736	10 781	34 137	39 704	93 887	92 309	72 064
Profits and dividends	..	..	1 185	8 354	9 002	32 023	37 526	92 090	90 214	69 864
Interests	..	..	843	382	1 779	2 114	2 178	1 797	2 095	2 200
Other property income	..	..	2 500	0	4 740	7 927	8 000	70 101	2 777	2 777
Surplus funds from regulatory authority	..	..	2 500	..	4 740	7 927	8 000	70 101	2 777	2 777
Sales of goods and services	..	..	1 548	2 302	45 302	48 576	63 521	54 981	50 118	53 303
Work Permits	..	..	0	0	4 098	2	8 333	3 694	5 728	5 125
Road Transit Toll	..	..	293	457	562	766	840	912	1 185	1 405
Immigration Visas and other Consular Fees	..	..	0	0	2 822	8 980	5 083	6 058	1 359	3 623
Fees under Traffic Act	..	..	304	1 188	0	1 326	1 647	1 574	2 201	2 263
Land administration fees	..	..	55	0	1 826	722	959	1 095	501	897
Motor driver's licences	..	..	376	656	0	0	0	0	0	0
Passport Fees	..	..	0	0	570	1 116	2 461	1 333	1 218	1 667
Rent of Government Buildings and Housing	..	..	520	0	135	157	459	437	482	0
Other fees for administrative services	..	..	0	0	556	1 756	2 436	2 139	1 993	1 658
Hire of security service fees	..	..	0	0	372	854	566	893	740	635
Registration of organisations, professionals and agreements	..	..	0	0	296	36	121	864	7	6
Registration of births, deaths and marriages	..	..	0	0	214	370	313	211	259	118
Other non-tax revenue collected by local government	..	..	..	..	33 849	32 492	40 305	35 773	34 444	35 908
Fines, penalties and forfeits	..	..	200	229	1 459	1 124	1 567	1 283	1 271	1 422
Miscellaneous and unidentified revenue	..	..	10 859	7 131	21 281	66 276	70 072	155 762	85 914	81 765
Contribution from government employees to social and welfare schemes within government	..	..	558	341	871	203	213	193	245	154
National Social Security Fund	..	..	4 097	6 790	9 210	9 988	14 036	14 771	14 322	16 438
Other Miscellaneous	..	..	6 204	0	11 200	56 085	55 823	140 799	71 347	65 173
Total tax and non-tax revenue	..	..	*311 480*	*585 812*	*1 192 903*	*1 680 490*	*1 818 990*	*2 073 311*	*2 019 066*	*2 387 029*

.. Not available

Note: Data are reported on a fiscal year basis beginning 1st July. For example, the data for 2022 represent July 2021 to June 2022.

The data are on a cash basis.

Detailed non-tax revenue data are not readily available for 2001, 2002, 2003, 2004, 2006, 2011 and 2012. Figures exclude non-tax revenues collected by sub-national governments as the data are not available.

The national classification of Kenya classifies revenues from the airport revenue, aviation revenue, petroleum development levy, Foreign Motor Vehicles (FMV) levy, road maintenance levy, sugar levy, petroleum regulatory levy, merchant superintendent shipping levy, railway development levy, revenue stamps, Kenya Bureau of Standards (KEBS) tax and land rates as non-tax revenues. They are considered in this publication as tax revenues under the OECD classification, as set out in the Interpretative Guide in Annex A.

Source: Kenya Revenue Authority (KRA).

Table 6.19. Lesotho – Details of non-tax revenues

Million LSL

	1995	2000	2005	2010	2015	2018	2019	2020	2021	2022
Total non-tax revenue	**..**	**..**	**2 980**	**5 668**	**8 978**	**8 691**	**8 929**	**11 850**	**11 305**	**8 740**
Grants	..	..	222	1 306	966	1 373	1 256	1 049	1 757	1 155
Property income	..	..	274	1 583	1 394	1 613	1 330	1 677	1 948	2 171
Rents and royalties	..	..	270	897	993	1 294	1 154	1 559	1 869	1 969
Water royalties	..	..	236	432	740	937	793	1 074	1 303	1 423
Mining and other royalties	..	..	34	465	252	357	361	485	566	546
Interest and dividends	..	..	5	686	401	319	176	118	79	202
Mining dividends	..	..	..	126	254	319	16	118	0	0
Non - mining dividends	..	..	..	560	147	- 0	160	0	79	202
Other property income	..	..	0	0	0	0	0	0	0	0
Sales of goods and services	..	..	170	149	216	166	115	143	63	14
Fines, penalties and forfeits	..	..	7	2	4	0	1	1	0	0
Fines for traffic offences	..	..	7	2	4	0	1	1	0	0
Miscellaneous and unidentified revenue	..	..	2 306	2 628	6 398	5 538	6 226	8 981	7 537	5 400
SACU revenue	..	..	2 306	2 628	6 398	5 538	6 226	8 981	7 537	5 400
Total tax and non-tax revenue	..	..	*4 560*	*8 945*	*14 850*	*15 980*	*16 177*	*18 621*	*19 131*	*17 162*

.. Not available

Note: Data are on a fiscal year basis beginning 1st April. For example, the data for 2022 represent April 2022 to March 2023.

Data are reported on a cash basis.

Figures exclude non-tax revenues collected by sub-national governments as the data are not available.

Source: Revenue Services Lesotho for all revenues except for transfers from the SACU Common Revenue Pool. Lesotho Ministry of Finance budget reports for SACU revenues.

Table 6.20. Madagascar – Details of non-tax revenues

Million MGA

	1995	2000	2005	2010	2015	2018	2019	2020	2021	2022
Total non-tax revenue	**..**	**172 677**	**630 632**	**619 717**	**506 489**	**1 383 116**	**1 754 983**	**1 411 620**	**543 066**	**982 868**
Grants	..	153 554	547 855	351 388	423 925	1 231 133	1 586 813	1 242 700	370 900	793 497
Donations - foreign government programs	..	0	49 571	0	39 869	414 183	365 104	434 700	1 100	2 511
Donations - projects of international institutions	..	153 554	438 520	336 704	384 056	816 950	1 221 709	808 000	369 800	790 986
Heavily Indebted Pour Countries (HIPC) Initiative funds	..	0	59 764	14 684	0	0	0	0	0	0
Property income	..	17 649	26 100	266 340	59 980	109 916	119 659	131 755	150 224	166 091
Rents and royalties	..	5 649	17 092	241 311	14 064	14 663	12 931	28 131	33 847	59 342
Interest and dividends	..	12 000	9 008	25 029	45 916	95 253	106 728	103 624	116 377	106 749
Other property income	..	0	0	0	0	0	0	0	0	0
Sales of goods and services	..	1 474	5 204	1 989	6 483	22 655	27 486	16 432	6 775	12 734
Fines, penalties and forfeits	..	0	0	0	519	581	1 139	862	1 078	1 009
Miscellaneous and unidentified revenue	..	0	51 473	0	15 581	18 832	19 886	19 871	14 089	9 537
Total tax and non-tax revenue	..	*764 577*	*1 647 034*	*2 395 900*	*3 611 756*	*6 389 641*	*7 400 464*	*6 422 910*	*6 492 930*	*8 165 868*

.. Not available

Note: Year ending 31st December.

The data are on a cash basis.

Figures exclude non-tax revenues collected by sub-national governments as the data are not available.

The heading "Sales of goods and services" includes revenues from visa stamps from 2015 following the OECD classification of taxes (see the Interpretative Guide in Annexes A and B). Until 2014, these revenues were included in tax revenues because it was not possible to separate them from other revenues.

The heading "Fines, penalties and forfeits" includes revenues from tax penalties from 2015 following the OECD classification of taxes (see the Interpretative Guide in Annexes A and B). Until 2014, these revenues were included in tax revenues because it was not possible to separate them from other revenues.

Source: Ministry of Economy and Finance, Madagascar.

Table 6.21. Malawi – Details of non-tax revenues

Million MWK

	1995	2000	2005	2010	2015	2018	2019	2020	2021	2022
Total non-tax revenue	..	..	**29 851**	**105 601**	**124 112**	**126 362**	**158 345**	**131 497**	**435 826**	**220 662**
Grants	..	..	24 227	78 448	79 392	70 155	115 136	127 113	364 204	138 961
Property income	..	..	760	3 466	32 815	20 083	7 571	1 787	36 867	10 082
Rents and royalties	..	..	0	0	0	0	0	0	0	0
Interest and dividends	..	..	760	3 466	32 815	20 083	7 571	1 787	36 867	10 082
Parastatal dividends	..	..	760	3 466	32 815	20 083	7 571	1 787	36 867	10 082
Other property income	..	..	0	0	0	0	0	0	0	0
Sales of goods and services	..	..	3 108	13 724	11 397	34 639	27 064	2 349	26 181	67 103
Fertiliser sales revenue	..	..	0	736	0	0	0	0	0	0
Receipts from fertiliser option	..	..	0	0	0	0	0	0	0	0
Maize sales	..	..	468	0	0	0	0	0	0	0
Departmental receipts	..	..	2 640	12 988	11 397	34 639	27 064	2 333	23 175	61 912
Treasury funds	..	..	0	0	0	0	0	17	3 006	5 191
Fines, penalties and forfeits	..	..	15	205	509	1 485	8 574	247	8 574	4 515
Penalties	..	..	15	205	509	1 485	8 574	247	8 574	4 515
Miscellaneous and unidentified revenue	..	..	1 742	9 758	0	0	0	0	0	0
Other current transfers not elsewhere classified	..	..	1 742	9 758	..	..	..	..	..	..
Total tax and non-tax revenue	..	..	*81 034*	*258 346*	*609 438*	*1 007 257*	*1 127 275*	*1 202 414*	*1 596 308*	*1 583 144*

.. Not available

Note: Unless otherwise indicated, data are on a fiscal year basis beginning 1st July. For example, the data for 2022 represent July 1, 2021 to June 30, 2022.

Data are reported on a cash basis.

The figure for grants in 2022 is provisional and is based on Malawi budget documents that are reported on a July 2021 to March 2022, nine-month, shortened fiscal year.

Figures exclude revenues from business licenses and permits collected by city and district councils from business entities within their jurisdictions.

Source: Ministry of Finance, Economic Planning and Development of Malawi.

Table 6.22. Mali – Details of non-tax revenues

Million XOF

	1995	2000	2005	2010	2015	2018	2019	2020	2021	2022
Total non-tax revenue	**97 332**	**122 795**	**173 446**	**256 632**	**198 795**	**226 436**	**323 146**	**237 832**	**205 722**	**181 581**
Grants	86 170	102 481	138 317	190 540	112 124	136 049	208 841	133 452	75 181	52 353
Donations - Foreign governments	0	0	0	22 263	20 665	6 129	8 056	6 563	600	941
Donations - International institutions	86 170	102 481	115 684	160 368	79 066	110 927	183 184	100 243	65 792	42 156
Heavily Indebted Pour Countries (HIPC) Initiative funds	0	0	22 633	7 909	12 393	18 993	17 601	26 646	8 789	9 257
Exceptional funds: assistance funds for conversion of monetary debt	0	0	0	0	0	0	0	0	0	0
Property income	1 753	9 669	12 421	34 564	48 278	50 229	62 544	64 984	90 143	84 808
Rents and royalties	1 168	358	507	650	1 735	21 023	15 972	1 249	1 727	2 662
Ordinary concessions	143	336	257	262	1 315	20 425	15 049	618	756	1 856
Fees based on land area	7	22	241	388	262	371	465	353	516	650
Tax on extraction	1 018	0	9	0	158	107	364	219	439	141
Other rents and fees - Extra-budgetary	0	0	0	0	0	121	95	59	16	15
Interest and dividends	585	9 311	11 914	32 873	46 122	26 960	45 429	62 676	86 547	78 460
Income from securities, titles and dividends	585	9 296	11 908	30 500	41 261	7 201	24 624	35 052	64 214	54 124
Other interest and dividends (government budget)	0	15	6	0	0	15 726	17 093	23 297	19 532	22 555
Interest on bank accounts (INPS)	0	0	0	2 373	3 549	2 230	2 029	2 857	956	0
CANAM - Interest in banking investments	0	0	0	0	1 312	1 802	1 684	1 470	1 846	1 781
Other property income	0	0	0	1 041	420	2 246	1 142	1 059	1 869	3 686
Other property revenue (CMSS)	..	..	..	0	140	47	101	73	164	196
Other property revenue (INPS)	..	..	..	1 041	281	2 199	1 041	986	1 705	3 489
Sales of goods and services	4 027	3 924	7 488	13 208	22 860	21 957	26 640	20 028	18 153	19 302
Services, evacuations, imports, exports - Extra-budgetary	0	0	0	0	0	3 351	2 828	2 759	3 722	2 828
Chancery fees	834	886	1 949	2 152	4 310	4 255	9 033	2 983	3 029	2 185
Passports and identity cards, visas	288	473	1 466	2 609	2 680	3 251	5 345	1 415	1 472	1 543
Revenues from the registrees (Treasury - BN)	1 503	981	154	91	0	0	0	0	0	0
Administrative fees from vehicles	440	497	591	813	1 200	1 137	1 163	1 543	1 458	1 542
Customs sales	5	15	24	117	26	19	87	20	67	80
Rental of state buildings	27	393	36	0	0	0	0	36	14	13
Other sales of goods and services (government budget)	930	679	197	6 460	12 598	6 584	3 107	1 845	3 356	6 189
Malian social security fund (CMSS) revenue - Excl. contributions	0	0	403	699	995	779	1 225	1 629	1 288	2 208
National Institute of Social Welfare (INPS) revenue - Excl. contributions	0	0	2 668	267	1 040	1 436	2 872	6 717	3 032	1 730
Rental of state buildings - Extra-budgetary	..	..	0	0	0	517	322	429	50	398
Other sales of goods and services - Extra-budgetary	..	..	0	0	0	540	632	544	460	462
CANAM - Various products	..	..	..	..	12	89	26	107	207	123
Fines, penalties and forfeits	2 159	2 786	4 656	8 010	12 764	8 753	16 288	12 867	14 815	12 714
Penalties on direct taxes	160	352	1 154	3 939	4 753	2 983	4 481	3 473	6 458	5 611
Penalties on indirect taxes	1 130	1 528	2 602	1 418	3 101	1 800	5 197	4 024	1 355	1 818
Fines and confiscations	717	710	592	1 268	2 738	1 487	2 007	2 156	2 830	4 597
Administration of forestries, fisheries and hunting	18	98	45	153	0	0	0	0	0	0
Court fines and fees	134	98	243	249	397	296	0	329	562	567
Other penalties (government budget)	0	0	20	77	624	50	96	138	90	121
Penalties and legal costs (INPS)	0	0	0	906	1 151	2 137	4 507	2 747	3 521	0
Miscellaneous and unidentified revenue	3 223	3 935	10 564	10 309	2 769	9 448	8 834	6 501	7 430	12 403
Compensation for loss of revenue	0	0	5 260	0	0	0	0	0	0	0
Arbitrated fines	117	268	41	66	41	60	89	160	105	139
Other miscellaneous income	3 106	3 667	5 263	10 243	2 728	8 099	6 756	4 590	5 325	10 454
Other miscellaneous revenue - Extra-budgetary	..	..	..	..	..	1 289	1 988	1 743	1 981	1 796
CANAM - Product of litigation	..	..	..	..	..	0	0	8	19	14
Total tax and non-tax revenue	*221 535*	*362 157*	*650 221*	*1 004 877*	*1 406 036*	*1 537 139*	*2 156 360*	*2 124 767*	*2 381 307*	*2 269 741*

.. Not available

Note: Year ending 31st December.

The data are on a cash basis.

Figures exclude non-tax revenues collected by sub-national governments as the data are not available.

Data from CANAM are presented in the headings "Interest and dividends", "Sales of goods and services", and "Miscellaneous and unidentified revenue".

Source: Ministry of Economy and Finance and the National Treasury and Public Accounting Directorate, Mali.

Table 6.23. Mauritania – Details of non-tax revenues

Million MRU

	1995	2000	2005	2010	2015	2018	2019	2020	2021	2022
Total non-tax revenue	**..**	**..**	**..**	**9 833**	**12 868**	**18 008**	**15 862**	**13 986**	**15 597**	**14 306**
Grants	..	..	..	830	1 988	201	2 211	0	106	0
Current donations - foreign states	..	..	..	0	1 988	0	0	..	..	..
Current donations- organisations	..	..	..	830	0	201	2 211	..	106	..
Property income	..	..	..	8 172	9 551	15 189	11 789	11 972	11 877	12 933
Rents and royalties	..	..	..	6 843	8 112	13 880	10 617	10 262	9 695	11 182
Fishing agreements	..	..	..	3 945	4 068	5 859	6 665	6 971	4 755	5 448
Fishing access rights	..	..	..	208	318	1 643	869	364	770	1 079
Telecom licences and sanctions	..	..	..	3	1 906	452	347	993	1 826	1 586
Mining and exploration permits	..	..	..	1 562	635	615	902	1 389	2 010	1 948
Signature bonus - oil	..	..	..	73	0	5 141	1 637	0	0	0
Royalties and other revenues - oil	..	..	..	1 035	1 150	126	128	535	306	1 105
State royalties and concessions	..	..	..	16	35	45	69	11	27	17
Interest and dividends	..	..	..	1 329	1 439	1 308	1 171	1 710	2 182	1 750
Other property income	..	..	..	0	0	0	0	0	0	0
Sales of goods and services	..	..	..	127	486	508	458	393	547	742
Visas	..	..	..	0	150	179	178	92	154	193
Passports	..	..	..	0	102	167	93	67	144	219
Vehicle registrations and driving licenses	..	..	..	0	54	40	59	51	84	91
Administrative fees	..	..	..	106	181	98	106	100	130	208
Universities, institutes and national centers	..	..	..	21	0	24	21	84	34	32
Fines, penalties and forfeits	..	..	..	206	393	519	476	705	2 035	495
Fishing fines	..	..	..	75	57	80	139	160	156	124
Other fines	..	..	..	131	336	439	336	544	1 879	371
Miscellaneous and unidentified revenue	..	..	..	498	450	1 591	929	916	1 033	137
Total tax and non-tax revenue	..	..	..	*25 015*	*41 961*	*58 374*	*55 795*	*52 587*	*63 481*	*67 377*

.. Not available

Note: Note: Year ending 31st December.

The data are on a cash basis.

The figures do not include revenues from land registration fees which are included in tax revenues following the OECD classification of taxes (see the Interpretative Guide in Annex A) but included in non-tax revenues in Mauritania.

Source: Ministry of Finance, Mauritania.

Table 6.24. Mauritius – Details of non-tax revenues

Million MUR

	1995	2000	2005	2010	2015	2018	2019	2020	2021	2022
Total non-tax revenue	**2 467**	**3 293**	**4 590**	**11 458**	**11 320**	**20 279**	**14 070**	**15 348**	**10 894**	**20 697**
Grants	262	161	444	1 991	1 202	2 635	1 998	4 386	345	1 850
Grants from foreign governments	..	..	..	2	183	2 248	1 580	4 140	122	1 740
Grants from international organizations	..	..	..	1 989	1 019	387	418	246	223	111
Property income	1 671	2 370	2 395	5 020	3 604	5 060	4 151	5 655	5 048	12 475
Rents and royalties	0	0	0	1 284	752	1 171	1 192	982	478	1 127
Interest and dividends	0	0	0	979	873	1 051	430	784	309	808
Interest	..	..	..	392	382	271	244	232	198	183
Dividends	..	..	..	587	492	780	186	552	111	626
Other property income	1 671	2 370	2 395	2 756	1 979	2 838	2 529	3 889	4 261	10 540
Other property income - Budgetary	1 196	1 692	1 235	1 549	1 392	1 039	1 138	2 152	992	8 445
Other property income - Extra-budgetary	26	58	136	349	33	235	235	414	165	762
Other property income - Social security funds	424	544	973	777	529	1 531	1 103	1 278	3 074	1 309
Other property income - Regional government	0	0	6	11	5	12	19	13	20	14
Other property income - Local government	25	76	45	71	20	20	34	32	11	11
Sales of goods and services	442	626	1 385	2 028	3 633	4 056	4 358	3 913	3 720	5 030
Work / occupational permits	0	0	47	95	194	266	277	221	148	284
Extra-budgetary fees, charges, and non-industrial sales	140	177	397	543	1 219	1 671	1 362	1 405	1 417	1 782
Fees, charges, and non-industrial sales by social security funds	17	20	40	51	78	0	271	106	101	566
Regional government sales of goods and services	0	0	6	5	4	11	7	13	12	12
Local government sales of goods and services	22	60	96	113	353	445	619	553	583	683
Other sales of goods and services	264	370	799	1 222	1 786	1 663	1 821	1 615	1 457	1 703
Fines, penalties and forfeits	27	65	152	272	292	284	359	320	247	465
Budgetary fines, penalties and forfeits	27	65	151	269	290	238	339	302	327	439
Extra-budgetary fines, penalties and forfeits	0	0	0	0	0	34	0	0	0	0
Regional government fines, penalties and forfeits	0	0	1	3	2	5	5	5	- 80	7
Local government fines, penalties and forfeits	0	0	0	0	0	8	15	13	0	19
Miscellaneous and unidentified revenue	65	70	214	2 147	2 588	8 244	3 204	1 074	1 536	876
Budgetary miscellaneous and unidentified revenue	26	10	13	1 803	157	242	229	156	126	159
Extra-budgetary miscellaneous and unidentified revenue	36	44	185	293	1 092	3 085	1 209	524	1 158	703
Miscellaneous and unidentified revenue for social security funds	0	4	0	3	0	0	0	0	0	0
Regional government miscellaneous and unidentified revenue	0	0	0	1	0	1	0	4	4	14
Local government miscellaneous and unidentified revenue	4	13	16	47	0	3	11	18	98	1
Transfers from special funds	0	0	0	0	1 339	4 914	1 755	372	150	0
Total tax and non-tax revenue	*14 729*	*25 439*	*39 417*	*69 862*	*90 544*	*116 031*	*117 456*	*112 623*	*103 569*	*137 725*

.. Not available

Note: Data are on a fiscal year basis beginning 1st July for years prior to 2010 (for example the data for 2009 represent July 2008 to June 2009) and are on a calendar year basis from 2010-15. Mauritius went back to a July-June fiscal year in 2015. Figures for 2016 correspond to the July-June 2015/16 fiscal year, while figures for 2015 correspond to the January-December calendar year. The calendar year 2015 is not used in national budget reporting by Mauritius, which means that official figures are not available for all revenue categories for this period.

Where data was missing for 2015, quarterly revenue figures at the aggregate level were used along with fiscal year revenue data to produce estimates.

Data are reported on a cash basis.

Figures taken from the Digest of Public Finance Statistics were adjusted in order to ensure that the sum of the revenues for different levels of governments would be equal to consolidated total revenues reported for the general government of Mauritius.

For the years 1989/90-2005/06, budgetary rents and royalties, interest and dividends are all reported under the heading "Other property income - Budgetary". For the years 2006/07 onwards, budgetary rents and royalties, interest and dividends are reported under separate headings.

Grants revenue for the years from 2017/18 onwards reflects consolidated general government revenues rather than consolidated central government revenues.

Sales of goods and services corresponds to the category "122 Fees, charges and non-industrial sales" in the Digest of Public Sector Statistics for the years up to 2006/07. For subsequent years, this excludes a number of sub-categories, such as licence fees, and work permits which are classified under other revenue categories.

Revenues reported as "Transfers from special funds" in fact represent funds raised from various sources, including tax revenues, non-tax revenues, and inter-governmental transfers which are not properly classified as revenues. Special Funds are special purpose vehicles set up by way of legislation for a specific purpose, i.e. to finance a dedicated programme or projects. Funds are transferred to the Fund from the Consolidated Fund through an appropriate expenditure item in the budget. Such Funds also generate their own revenue in terms of, for example, a levy imposed on petroleum products or contributions from international institutions and friendly countries. As such, once the dedicated programme or projects are completed, the available balance in the Special Funds are transferred to the Consolidated Fund and reported as revenues in budget documents for Mauritius.

Source: Mauritius Revenue Authority for the central government budgetary tax data from 2007 to 2014. Statistics Mauritius for extra-budgetary, local government, regional government and social security revenues from 1990 to 2022, as well as for budgetary central government tax revenues up to 2006; Ministry of Finance budget estimates for detailed revenue figures for the periods July 2005-June 2008, for 2016-22, and for the figures used to estimate calendar year 2015 revenues.

Table 6.25. Morocco – Details of non-tax revenues

Million MAD

	1995	2000	2005	2010	2015	2018	2019	2020	2021	2022
Total non-tax revenue	..	**9 278**	**16 745**	**27 970**	**38 673**	**40 466**	**49 088**	**37 043**	**35 981**	**38 982**
Grants	..	2	1 163	199	0	0	0	276	0	0
Property income	..	3 125	4 878	9 786	8 934	9 836	10 401	8 687	10 411	12 396
Rents and royalties	..	1 507	2 892	3 868	5 192	4 738	4 865	2 901	4 498	3 920
Pipeline fee	..	298	1 369	1 442	1 765	1 538	1 011	455	763	7
Royalties and contributions for deep-sea fishing licences	..	94	38	329	520	235	773	93	936	412
Royalties for the occupation of public lands	..	132	214	331	281	273	260	98	182	244
Other royalties	..	7	8	63	6	6	10	4	8	10
Rents and royalties received by local authorities	..	977	1 262	1 703	2 620	2 686	2 809	2 251	2 608	3 248
Interest and dividends	..	1 618	1 986	5 918	3 742	5 098	5 537	5 786	5 912	8 475
Dividends of public monopolies	..	1 008	1 540	5 584	3 236	4 650	5 197	5 354	5 349	7 955
Interest on investments and advances	..	419	198	96	195	119	4	7	98	91
Interest and dividends received by local authorities	..	191	248	239	311	329	336	425	465	429
Other property income	..	0	0	0	0	0	0	0	0	0
Sales of goods and services	..	4 573	7 315	10 286	16 009	17 990	20 791	13 182	13 389	14 275
ID cards, passports and miscellaneous documents	..	453	511	567	498	950	1 111	746	989	1 362
Products from certain public establishments	..	1 544	3 038	2 990	5 462	4 425	7 487	4 194	5 255	5 037
Revenues from public buildings (rents, rental charges, etc.)	..	137	172	250	265	335	327	275	374	385
Other products and miscellaneous revenues	..	175	824	646	965	1 661	825	777	706	580
Sales of goods and services by local authorities	..	2 265	2 770	5 832	8 819	10 619	11 040	7 190	6 066	6 911
Fines, penalties and forfeits	..	398	851	2 802	2 994	3 963	5 872	1 496	1 946	2 340
Fines and penalties	..	17	42	21	61	66	63	45	59	66
Transactional fines	..	36	90	130	706	481	425	124	162	190
Other revenues (proceeds of forfeitures, penalties and fines other than taxes)	..	6	9	1	0	0	0	0	0	54
Surcharges and penalties	..	339	709	2 650	2 226	3 416	5 385	1 328	1 725	2 030
Miscellaneous and unidentified revenue	..	1 180	2 539	4 897	10 736	8 678	12 024	13 402	10 235	9 971
Competition fund	..	147	968	3 597	3 453	1 944	1 973	6 922	1 514	2 628
Debt spending mitigation revenues	..	801	879	480	4 386	963	3 164	1 526	1 726	384
Refunds of wages and salaries	..	55	157	99	62	957	919	829	966	951
Prescribed amounts payable out of the Consolidated Revenue Fund	..	30	224	39	97	305	866	67	102	118
Other (various reimbursements to the State)	..	7	29	6	254	11	12	11	72	5
Miscellaneous and unidentified revenue from local authorities	..	139	281	677	2 484	4 498	5 089	4 048	5 855	5 886
Total tax and non-tax revenue	..	*100 178*	*154 185*	*244 738*	*303 742*	*353 683*	*376 426*	*351 377*	*383 382*	*436 924*

.. Not available

Note: Year ending 31st December.

The data are on a cash basis.

Surcharges and penalties (Tax Department -DGI): Revenues from tax surcharges and penalties are considered as non-tax revenues following the OECD classification of taxes (see the Interpretative Guide in Annexes A and B). Under Morocco's national classification they are included in tax revenues.

Source: Ministry of Economy and Finance, Morocco.

Table 6.26. Mozambique – Details of non-tax revenues

Million MZN

	1995	2000	2005	2010	2015	2018	2019	2020	2021	2022
Total non-tax revenue	..	..	..	**32 035**	**31 566**	**48 060**	**41 656**	**67 529**	**61 581**	**87 253**
Grants	..	..	..	27 318	18 677	17 672	11 106	38 364	25 250	47 776
Property income	..	..	..	399	1 164	13 621	11 800	10 058	15 974	21 476
Rents and royalties	..	..	..	260	137	9 102	8 857	5 031	9 590	13 454
Mining production tax	..	..	..	0	0	3 077	1 946	1 252	2 374	7 274
Oil production tax	..	..	..	0	0	564	608	338	484	644
Energy Potential Exploitation Concession	..	..	..	0	0	2 395	3 019	2 566	3 714	2 932
Maritime zone	..	..	..	0	0	397	407	487	1 324	1 623
Nature Protection Zone	..	..	..	0	0	94	129	24	94	465
Royalties and surface tax	..	..	..	60	59	263	356	364	394	515
Forest Resources Exploitation Fee	..	..	..	0	0	247	160	0	323	0
Fee for the exploitation of wildlife resources	..	..	..	0	0	1	5	0	30	0
Concession to exploit other public domain assets	..	..	..	0	0	2 065	2 227	0	852	0
Income from State Assets	..	..	..	200	78	0	0	0	0	0
Interest and dividends	..	..	..	139	1 027	4 519	2 943	5 028	6 385	8 022
Dividends	..	..	..	139	1 027	4 519	2 943	5 028	6 309	7 852
Profits of State companies	..	..	..	0	0	0	0	0	76	170
Other property income	..	..	..	0	0	0	0	0	0	0
Sales of goods and services	..	..	..	453	2 052	14 981	14 855	13 089	16 000	16 644
Service fees	..	..	..	453	2 052	9 560	9 782	8 639	10 282	10 372
Education	..	..	..	0	0	2 028	1 984	0	1 904	0
Hospitals	..	..	..	0	0	990	908	0	987	0
Identification documentation, declarations and certificates	..	..	..	0	0	1 179	1 232	0	1 515	0
Technical and scientific publications and documentation	..	..	..	0	0	8	1	0	0	0
Cultural and sporting events	..	..	..	0	0	19	25	0	9	0
Supplies	..	..	..	0	0	113	133	0	153	0
Surveys and inspections of activities	..	..	..	0	0	195	41	0	18	0
Public Hearings	..	..	..	0	0	67	9	0	14	0
Real estate fees and disposals of goods	..	..	..	0	0	235	238	271	457	233
Local fees	..	..	..	0	0	0	0	0	0	1
Miscellaneous activities and sales of goods and services not identified	..	..	..	0	0	587	503	4 179	660	6 038
Fines, penalties and forfeits	..	..	..	0	0	849	1 191	554	926	1 248
Miscellaneous and unidentified revenue	..	..	..	3 864	9 673	937	2 704	5 463	3 430	109
Total non-tax revenue excluding grants	..	..	..	*4 716*	*12 888*	*30 388*	*30 550*	*29 165*	*36 331*	*39 477*

.. Not available

Note: Year ending 31st December.

The data are on a cash basis.

Figures exclude non-tax revenues collected by sub-national governments as the data are not available.

Sales of real estate, companies and other state assets as well as repayments of internal loans do not represent an increase of net worth resulting from a transaction and therefore are not considered as revenues under the OECD classification, as set out in the Interpretative Guide in Annex B. The national classification of Mozambique account them as revenue.

Revenue from the "Mining production tax", "Oil production tax", "surface tax" are considered non-tax revenue under the OECD classification, as set out in the Interpretative Guide in Annex B. The national classification of Mozambique classifies it as tax revenue.

Source: Mozambique Revenue Authority, IMF Government Finance Statistics for grants.

Table 6.27. Namibia – Details of non-tax revenues

Million NAD

	1995	2000	2005	2010	2015	2018	2019	2020	2021	2022
Total non-tax revenue	**..**	**..**	**..**	**7 948**	**20 781**	**21 336**	**22 799**	**25 728**	**19 674**	**23 265**
Grants	..	..	..	24	152	72	98	266	18	0
Property income	..	..	..	1 373	2 568	2 571	2 653	2 331	4 243	7 201
Rents and royalties	..	..	..	1 015	1 482	1 869	1 520	1 713	2 195	2 512
Diamond royalties	..	..	..	602	1 060	1 255	707	881	679	1 559
Other mineral royalties	..	..	..	280	309	347	546	619	711	599
Fishing quota levies and auction	..	..	..	133	113	267	267	213	805	354
Interest and dividends	..	..	..	358	1 086	702	1 133	618	2 048	4 689
Other property income	..	..	..	0	0	0	0	0	0	0
Sales of goods and services	..	..	..	534	628	1 228	1 027	780	97	1 777
Fines, penalties and forfeits	..	..	..	43	78	90	99	99	567	97
Miscellaneous and unidentified revenue	..	..	..	5 975	17 355	17 375	18 922	22 252	14 750	14 190
SACU Revenue Pool Share	..	..	..	5 975	17 355	17 375	18 922	22 252	14 750	14 190
Total tax and non-tax revenue	..	..	..	*23 682*	*52 754*	*56 504*	*59 046*	*58 490*	*56 538*	*64 945*

.. Not available

Note: Data are on a fiscal year basis beginning 1st April. For example, the data for 2022 represent April 2022 to March 2023.

Data are on a cash basis.

Figures exclude tax revenues collected by sub-national governments as the data are not available.

Source: Namibia Revenue Agency.

Table 6.28. Niger – Details of non-tax revenues

Million XOF

	1995	2000	2005	2010	2015	2018	2019	2020	2021	2022
Total non-tax revenue	**..**	**65 672**	**145 022**	**180 746**	**331 067**	**518 451**	**587 486**	**653 819**	**667 993**	**531 833**
Grants	..	59 240	134 000	130 144	232 611	428 900	514 000	535 990	605 144	452 280
Property income	..	4 751	5 998	28 436	40 249	47 496	30 975	33 590	29 823	38 546
Rents and royalties	..	4 673	5 156	14 977	32 963	38 235	16 258	19 506	18 147	23 729
Signature bonus	..	0	0	0	17 044	22 974	0	0	0	0
Mining royalty (RM)	..	4 519	4 732	14 381	11 323	7 214	6 877	9 801	7 707	4 416
Petroleum surface royalty	..	0	0	0	2 776	3 046	4 443	4 516	4 460	4 510
Land registration	..	50	281	429	950	2 650	1 801	3 704	3 329	3 350
Mining surface royalty	..	0	0	0	449	1 463	2 191	1 060	1 761	8 586
Retention for housing	..	6	3	25	173	139	182	43	33	11
Provisional concessions	..	0	73	86	164	288	286	69	224	1 963
Logging permits	..	65	18	42	52	191	277	203	88	490
Land demarcation	..	4	13	9	20	190	124	109	192	192
Final concessions	..	29	35	5	12	82	76	1	355	210
Interest and dividends	..	0	653	13 166	6 996	8 864	14 333	13 648	11 194	14 364
Dividends	..	..	653	12 081	2 990	5 263	10 558	9 369	7 291	8 365
Oil profits	..	..	0	0	3 577	3 430	3 651	3 553	3 523	4 837
Interest income	..	..	0	1 084	430	170	124	726	380	1 162
Other property income	..	78	189	293	290	398	384	436	481	453
Public domain occupation rights	..	78	189	293	290	398	384	436	481	453
Sales of goods and services	..	85	281	289	36 492	15 429	7 503	8 270	9 387	9 432
Cellular phone licence sales	..	0	0	0	34 000	10 000	2 000	0	89	0
Commission on transfers Central Bank (BCEAO)	..	0	0	42	1 090	3 905	3 826	5 255	5 459	5 283
Passport/interpol visa sales	..	0	0	0	469	731	1 076	913	1 011	1 196
International vaccination	..	0	0	0	239	179	154	172	29	179
Vehicle registration/transportation	..	0	0	0	143	3	51	143	442	427
Forestry revenues	..	30	110	159	127	20	13	13	0	0
Print sales DGI, DGD	..	0	0	0	104	43	13	215	22	19
Chancery duties	..	0	4	3	76	17	10	11	15	29
Real estate rental	..	9	135	63	9	29	22	447	286	192
Other sales of goods and services	..	46	32	21	235	503	337	320	715	859
Various exceptional services	..	0	0	0	0	0	0	781	1 319	1 248
Fines, penalties and forfeits	..	1 348	1 702	4 849	14 080	17 457	22 269	13 825	13 566	13 495
DGI fines and penalties	..	1 188	1 064	3 329	11 370	15 572	19 523	10 773	11 251	9 671
Police fines and costs	..	0	76	482	1 230	909	1 553	1 739	1 100	2 090
Fines and confiscations	..	159	122	214	842	561	471	628	782	602
Fines, costs and penalties - gendarmerie and police	..	0	402	769	595	266	431	491	266	525
Forestry and hunting fines and seizures	..	1	27	45	26	32	212	68	48	322
Fines and court fees	..	0	4	8	9	85	52	112	119	266
Fines and seizures for price-weight-measurement controls	..	0	6	1	8	32	26	14	0	19
Miscellaneous and unidentified revenue	..	249	3 040	17 029	7 635	9 168	12 739	62 144	10 074	18 080
Other miscellaneous receipts - National Treasury	..	0	0	16 494	4 921	8 539	12 386	61 751	9 953	17 945
Other miscellaneous revenues	..	249	250	420	779	251	188	307	65	82
WAEMU repayments and miscellaneous income ARC	..	0	2 790	114	1 935	0	0	0	0	0
Commissariat for the Organisation of the Hajj and Umrah (COHO)	..	0	0	0	0	378	166	86	55	54
Total tax and non-tax revenue	..	*177 044*	*330 024*	*546 177*	*1 035 483*	*1 315 122*	*1 373 837*	*1 427 795*	*1 532 504*	*1 453 329*

.. Not available

Note: Year ending 31st December.

The data are on a cash basis.

Figures exclude non-tax revenues collected by sub-national governments as the data are not available.

Data for the period 2000-04 should be interpreted with caution as non-tax data collected by the Direction Générale du Trésor et de la Comptabilité Publique (DGTCP) are not available for this period.

Following the OECD classification of taxes (see the Interpretative Guide in Annex B), proceeds from the sale of buildings are not considered as revenues (tax or non-tax) since the transaction does not increase the net worth. Under Niger's national classification they are included in non-tax revenues.

Source: Directorate General of Taxes, Niger.

Table 6.29. Nigeria – Details of non-tax revenues

Million NGN

	1995	2000	2005	2010	2015	2018	2019	2020	2021	2022
Total non-tax revenue	**..**	**..**	**..**	**4 393 536**	**2 921 280**	**4 199 152**	**5 722 647**	**5 209 338**	**7 085 813**	**9 232 332**
Grants	..	..	..	335	49 288	88 292	591 157	1 672 193	1 158 057	1 086 481
Property income	..	..	..	4 266 330	2 622 660	2 636 270	3 127 320	3 065 216	5 349 530	5 868 371
Rents and royalties	..	..	..	4 266 330	2 622 660	2 636 270	3 127 320	3 065 216	5 349 530	5 868 371
Revenue from oil	..	..	..	3 574 420	2 059 110	1 395 650	1 734 790	873 135	2 287 330	2 401 700
Revenue from royalties	..	..	..	691 910	563 550	1 235 200	1 387 220	1 273 232	1 787 870	2 447 201
Revenue from fees and licences	..	..	..	0	0	5 420	5 310	918 849	1 274 330	1 019 470
Interest and dividends	..	..	..	0	0	0	0	0	0	0
Other property income	..	..	..	0	0	0	0	0	0	0
Sales of goods and services	..	..	..	0	0	0	0	0	0	0
Fines, penalties and forfeits	..	..	..	0	0	0	0	0	0	0
Miscellaneous and unidentified revenue	..	..	..	126 870	249 332	1 474 590	2 004 170	471 929	578 226	2 277 480
Other non-tax revenue (federal)	..	..	..	6 440	44 530	1 123 910	1 513 430	3 999	9 490	1 699 800
Revenues collected by Local Government Areas (LGAs)	..	..	..	120 430	204 802	350 680	490 740	467 930	568 736	577 680
Total tax and non-tax revenue	*..*	*..*	*..*	*8 439 863*	*8 705 015*	*12 398 249*	*14 437 444*	*13 770 334*	*18 861 505*	*25 237 440*

.. Not available

Note: Year ending 31st December.

The data are on a cash basis.

"Revenue from oil" refers to government share of revenues from revenue sharing agreements with oil and exploration companies.

"Revenue from fees and licenses" refers to government fees collected in exchange for granting Oil Prospecting Licenses (OPL) and Oil Mining Leases (OML).

"Revenue from royalties" includes royalties charged to oil and mineral exploration companies.

Miscellaneous and unidentified revenue includes some revenues from dividends and issued profits from state-owned enterprises. Local Government Area (LGA) revenues are a mixture of tax and non-tax revenues.

Source: Federal Inland Revenue Service.

Table 6.30. Rwanda – Details of non-tax revenues

Million RWF

	1995	2000	2005	2010	2015	2018	2019	2020	2021	2022
Total non-tax revenue	**..**	**79 888**	**182 339**	**415 465**	**529 400**	**650 724**	**669 370**	**747 401**	**934 621**	**1 187 906**
Grants	..	76 710	164 477	397 352	374 600	398 686	427 498	475 830	601 296	798 120
Property income	..	..	..	..	..	..	..	..	..	..
Rents and royalties	..	..	..	..	..	..	..	..	..	..
Interest and dividends	..	..	..	..	..	..	..	..	..	..
Other property income	..	..	..	..	..	..	..	..	..	..
Sales of goods and services	..	..	..	..	..	..	..	..	..	..
Fines, penalties and forfeits	..	..	..	..	..	..	..	..	..	..
Miscellaneous and unidentified revenue	..	3 178	17 862	18 113	154 800	252 038	241 872	271 571	333 326	389 786
Total tax and non-tax revenue	*..*	*148 797*	*356 945*	*856 189*	*1 526 632*	*2 052 226*	*2 281 100*	*2 390 379*	*2 794 783*	*3 454 387*

.. Not available

Note: Year ending 31st December.

The data are on a cash basis.

Figures exclude non-tax revenues collected by sub-national governments as the data are not available.

Figures exclude fines related to tax revenues as it is not possible to split these out from tax revenues. Revenues from fines related to taxes are classified as non-tax revenues according to the OECD classification, as set out in the Interpretative Guide in Annex B. Rwanda considers these revenues as tax revenues.

Miscellaneous and unidentified revenue: this category includes non-tax fines, administrative fees and revenue from public property and public assets for Rwanda. These data could not be disaggregated to allocate revenue to the relevant non-tax revenue categories.

Source: Rwanda Revenue Authority.

Table 6.31. Senegal – Details of non-tax revenues

Million XOF

	1995	2000	2005	2010	2015	2018	2019	2020	2021	2022
Total non-tax revenue	..	**68 000**	**105 200**	**203 550**	**366 943**	**435 068**	**378 817**	**474 534**	**520 314**	**410 208**
Grants	..	64 000	75 600	161 850	232 034	256 444	224 326	324 523	150 509	155 316
Property income	..	0	26 500	39 600	84 990	76 831	100 798	108 435	222 131	124 579
Rents and royalties	..	..	14 600	20 300	35 790	43 880	64 854	61 187	87 085	68 057
Interest and dividends	..	..	11 900	19 300	49 200	32 952	35 944	47 248	133 046	56 522
Other property income	..	..	0	0	0	0	0	0	2 000	..
Sales of goods and services	..	0	0	0	0	10 310	10 997	11 135	110 760	11 731
Fines, penalties and forfeits	..	0	0	0	28 220	45	0	0	2 915	0
Miscellaneous and unidentified revenue	..	4 000	3 100	2 100	21 700	91 438	42 697	30 442	34 000	118 582
Recettes exceptionnelles (Swapp et Sonatel)	..	0	0	0	0	..	..	..	34 000	118 582
Divers reversements	..	4 000	3 100	2 100	21 700	..	..	..	0	0
Total tax and non-tax revenue	..	*627 295*	*992 448*	*1 471 349*	*2 090 075*	*2 654 884*	*2 944 985*	*3 086 526*	*3 384 744*	*3 826 723*

.. Not available

Note: Year ending 31st December.

The data are on a cash basis.

Figures exclude tax revenues collected by sub-national governments as the data are not available.

Revenues from fines and penalties on taxes are considered as non-tax revenues following the OECD classification of taxes (see the Interpretative Guide in Annexes A and B). However, it has not been possible to separate the payment of fines and penalties from the revenues corresponding to the taxes to which these fines and penalties relate and they are therefore excluded from this heading. Under Senegal's national classification they are included in tax revenues. The amounts for 2017 to 2022 relate solely to recoveries by the Directorate General of Taxes and Domains (DGID).

Source: Ministry of Economy, Finance and Planning, Senegal.

Table 6.32. Seychelles – Details of non-tax revenues

Million XOF

	1995	2000	2005	2010	2015	2018	2019	2020	2021	2022
Total non-tax revenue	**..**	**..**	**..**	**725**	**1 237**	**1 511**	**1 408**	**1 684**	**2 031**	**1 838**
Grants	..	..	..	101	144	281	94	438	685	403
Grants (main budget)	..	..	..	101	144	281	94	438	685	403
Property income	..	..	..	357	519	731	798	766	720	845
Rents and royalties	..	..	..	115	215	267	252	313	285	231
Fishing licence fees	..	..	..	93	0	0	0	98	111	0
Annual EU fishing licence fees to access Seychelles EEZ	..	..	..	0	43	42	1	23	33	31
EU fishing licence: vessel fee	..	..	..	0	37	35	79	3	3	4
Non EU fishing licence fees	..	..	..	0	60	72	1	74	43	98
Local fishing licence fees	..	..	..	0	1	2	54	1	1	0
Seychelles Pension Fund (SPF) - Rental income	..	..	..	22	74	115	118	114	94	98
Interest and dividends	..	..	..	241	304	465	546	436	435	614
Income from interest and dividends (main budget)	..	..	..	206	228	377	442	338	336	472
Financial Services Authority (FSA) rental income (dividends)	..	..	..	0	11	29	33	30	30	48
Seychelles Pension Fund (SPF) - Interest income	..	..	..	22	51	44	51	45	47	39
Seychelles Pension Fund (SPF) - Investment / dividend income	..	..	..	12	14	14	21	22	21	55
Other property income	..	..	..	0	0	0	0	18	0	0
Seychelles Pension Fund (SPF) - Profit on sale of investments	..	..	..	..	0	0	..	..	0	0
Sales of goods and services	..	..	..	191	462	466	465	432	560	542
Fees and charges (main budget)	..	..	..	191	322	336	340	262	366	392
Financial Services Authority (FSA) - fees	..	..	..	0	140	129	124	170	194	149
Seychelles Pension Fund (SPF) - Surcharges	..	..	..	0	0	1	1	1	0	0
Fines, penalties and forfeits	..	..	..	0	0	0	0	0	0	0
Miscellaneous and unidentified revenue	..	..	..	77	111	33	50	48	67	49
Other nontax (no SSF)	..	..	..	77	110	33	50	48	66	48
Seychelles Pension Fund (SPF) - Other income	..	..	..	0	2	0	0	0	1	1
Total tax and non-tax revenue	..	..	..	*4 321*	*6 711*	*8 988*	*9 025*	*8 456*	*9 184*	*9 838*

.. Not available

Note: Year ending 31st December.

The data are on a cash basis.

Figures exclude non-tax revenues collected by sub-national governments as the data are not available.

In addition to the revenues labelled "SPF" under "Rents and royalties" and "Interest and dividends", some, generally negligible, SPF revenues are counted under "Other property income", "Sales of goods and services", and "Miscellaneous and unidentified revenue". SPF revenues are not reported as government revenues in Seychelles government documents.

"Rents and royalties" includes fishing licences fees considered as non-tax revenues in accordance with the OECD classification, as set out in the Interpretative Guide in Annex B. The Seychelles classifies these revenues as tax revenues.

"Interest and dividends" includes revenues from the Financial Services Authority (FSA). FSA revenues are not reported as government revenues in Seychelles government documents.

As of 2022, revenues from fishing licence fees are reported under "non-EU fishing licence fees".

Source: Seychelles Revenue Commission; Seychelles Ministry of Finance, Economic Planning and Trade; Financial Services Authority Seychelles Annual Reports; and Seychelles Pension Fund Annual Reports.

Table 6.33. Sierra Leone – Details of non-tax revenues

Million SLL

	1995	2000	2005	2010	2015	2018	2019	2020	2021	2022
Total non-tax revenue	**..**	**..**	**393 496**	**581 304**	**1 359 374**	**1 516 270**	**2 338 842**	**3 444 342**	**3 376 594**	**5 268 051**
Grants	..	..	351 870	497 848	1 164 553	632 856	1 248 642	2 320 695	1 652 865	3 820 728
Programme funding	..	..	250 568	265 435	656 091	238 856	751 432	1 723 912	1 084 831	2 341 819
Elections Basket Fund	..	..	0	0	0	8 000	0	0	0	0
Project funding	..	..	101 302	232 413	508 462	386 000	497 210	596 783	568 034	1 478 909
Property income	..	..	15 869	34 475	126 649	317 691	341 425	354 134	603 804	515 054
Rents and royalties	..	..	15 869	34 475	126 649	317 691	341 425	354 134	603 804	515 054
Royalty on rutile	..	..	318	883	7 836	54 374	70 076	80 193	52 727	7 657
Royalty on bauxite and zircon	..	..	1 683	4 098	6 476	15 664	10 805	13 242	17 124	0
Royalty on diamonds and gold	..	..	0	6 360	28 485	71 619	77 638	89 876	71 916	167 883
Royalty on iron ore	..	..	0	0	6 119	3 468	3 453	0	221 971	86 089
Other mining licences and royalties	..	..	8 243	12 848	37 613	77 648	71 437	74 612	159 011	162 663
Royalty of fisheries	..	..	5 625	10 285	40 121	94 919	108 016	96 212	81 056	100 762
Interest and dividends	..	..	0	0	0	0	0	0	0	0
Other property income	..	..	0	0	0	0	0	0	0	0
Sales of goods and services	..	..	0	0	0	227 005	354 581	353 517	445 528	613 272
Treasury Single Account	..	..	..	..	..	227 005	354 581	353 517	445 528	613 272
Fines, penalties and forfeits	..	..	0	0	0	0	0	0	0	0
Miscellaneous and unidentified revenue	..	..	25 756	48 981	68 172	338 718	394 194	415 997	674 397	318 997
Parastatals and other MDAs	..	..	7 348	2 313	17 809	0	87 801	78 636	110 159	260 167
Other revenues	..	..	18 409	46 668	50 363	338 718	306 393	337 361	564 238	58 830
Total tax and non-tax revenue	..	..	*767 852*	*1 510 810*	*3 494 635*	*5 554 108*	*7 213 000*	*8 434 903*	*9 272 073*	*11 837 436*

.. Not available

Note: Year ending 31st December.

The data are reported on a cash basis.

Other revenues in heading “Miscellaneous and unidentified revenue” includes freight levy until 2017. The freight levy is part of the Treasury Single Account collection from 2018.

“Sales of goods and services” includes revenues by key government agencies from various sources largely relating to regulatory fees, that are centralised into the Treasury Single Account.

Source: Sierra Leone National Revenue Authority.

Table 6.34. Somalia – Details of non-tax revenues

Million USD

	1995	2000	2005	2010	2015	2018	2019	2020	2021	2022
Total non-tax revenue	**..**	**..**	**..**	**..**	**57**	**140**	**192**	**373**	**236**	**546**
Grants	..	..	..	..	27	96	108	286	147	436
Property income	..	..	..	..	0	0	10	4	4	11
Rents and royalties	..	..	..	..	0	0	10	4	4	11
Fisheries license fees	..	..	..	..	0	0	1	2	3	0
Signature bonus for petroleum companies	..	..	..	..	0	0	0	0	0	7
Telecommunication spectrum fees	..	..	..	..	0	0	9	2	1	4
Interest and dividends	..	..	..	..	0	0	0	0	0	0
Other property income	..	..	..	..	0	0	0	0	0	0
Sales of goods and services	..	..	..	..	30	44	68	71	82	96
Licences and fees	..	..	..	..	7	12	21	18	21	28
Harbour fees - Albayrak	..	..	..	..	23	29	27	31	26	29
Overflight fees (IATA)	..	..	..	..	0	0	12	16	11	15
Administrative charges and other	..	..	..	..	1	4	7	6	25	24
Fines, penalties and forfeits	..	..	..	..	0	0	0	0	0	0
Miscellaneous and unidentified revenue					0	0	6	12	2	2
Total tax and non-tax revenue	..	..	..	..	*141*	*277*	*383*	*591*	*483*	*815*

.. Not available

Note: Year ending 31st December.

The data are on a cash basis.

Data exclude revenue collected on the local level as data are not available.

Data include revenues collected directly by the Federal Government of Somalia and the Federal Member States (FMS) (Puntland, Jubaland, South West, Galmudug, Hirshabelle and the Benadir Regional Authority). Data from the FMS is only available from 2019 onwards.

The data are not consolidated however they do not include transfers received from the FGS and represent direct collections only.

Source: Ministry of Finance of Somalia.

Table 6.35. South Africa – Details of non-tax revenues

Million ZAR

	1995	2000	2005	2010	2015	2018	2019	2020	2021	2022
Total non-tax revenue	**2 864**	**4 135**	**8 899**	**16 192**	**17 934**	**27 705**	**29 388**	**30 754**	**43 904**	**43 786**
Grants	135	637	1 118	1 012	1 467	1 276	1 155	1 545	1 505	871
Property income	1 881	1 378	5 208	8 170	10 113	16 845	20 986	20 928	33 879	33 442
Rents and royalties	217	0	271	4 448	3 772	9 049	11 831	14 133	28 355	25 355
Interest and dividends	1 664	1 378	4 937	3 721	6 341	7 797	9 154	6 795	5 524	8 087
Interest	954	714	2 570	2 524	4 487	6 834	8 276	6 502	5 524	7 889
Dividends	710	664	2 366	1 197	1 853	963	878	293	0	198
Other property income	0	0	0	0	0	0	0	0	0	0
Sales of goods and services	600	2 006	2 243	2 335	2 159	2 321	2 715	1 611	2 822	4 004
Fines, penalties and forfeits	124	114	280	4 425	3 665	6 877	4 144	6 248	5 333	4 829
Interest on overdue tax: Individuals	..	..	..	1 225	993	1 991	1 563	1 446	1 601	1 544
Interest on overdue tax: Companies	..	..	..	1 744	1 707	3 135	2 214	3 709	2 912	2 251
PIT Administrative penalties	..	..	..	0	0	0	0	483	295	354
CIT Administrative penalties	..	..	..	0	0	0	0	46	97	136
Other fines, penalties and forfeits	124	114	280	1 457	965	1 752	367	563	428	544
Miscellaneous and unidentified revenue	123	0	50	251	531	386	388	423	364	640
Total tax and non-tax revenue	*124 784*	*215 696*	*427 722*	*722 722*	*1 185 465*	*1 446 792*	*1 498 488*	*1 428 898*	*1 676 600*	*1 837 939*

.. Not available

Note: Data are reported on a fiscal year basis beginning 1st April. For example, the data for 2022 represent April 2022 to March 2023.

Data are reported on a cash basis.

Figures exclude non-tax revenues collected by sub-national governments as the data are not available.

The grants data represent total grants and donations received mainly from foreign governments and multilateral institutions. Moreover, this flow does not go through the Government Revenue fund, it is earmarked for specific projects implemented across government (by line departments).

Source: National Treasury of South Africa. Data for grants are from the financial statements of the Reconstruction and Development Fund Programme (RDP) Fund administered by the office of Accountant General.

Table 6.36. Togo – Details of non-tax revenues

Million XOF

	1995	2000	2005	2010	2015	2018	2019	2020	2021	2022
Total non-tax revenue	..	**18 987**	**31 939**	**189 745**	**102 957**	**216 888**	**200 351**	**165 057**	**140 867**	**183 268**
Grants	..	4 292	13 110	80 357	57 238	105 895	122 423	99 203	83 973	127 406
Project grants	..	4 292	13 110	62 257	47 539	72 712	60 355	62 008	82 973	97 444
Programme grants	..	0	0	18 100	9 699	33 183	62 068	37 195	1 000	29 961
Property income	..	10 040	11 942	92 473	25 555	41 010	37 962	32 940	30 097	32 765
Rents and royalties	..	5 548	3 221	42 400	3 837	3 426	6 843	7 016	5 292	3 240
Mining royalties	..	0	0	0	1 270	2 322	1 777	1 872	1 660	2 237
Royalties of the reconstruction of the International Gnassingbé Eyadéma Airport (AIGE)	..	5 548	3 221	0	2 240	665	3 543	4 714	2 755	0
Royalties from Contour Global	..	0	0	0	0	332	330	431	320	227
Other state revenues	..	0	0	42 400	327	106	1 194	0	556	776
Interest and dividends	..	4 492	8 721	50 073	21 718	37 584	31 119	25 924	24 805	29 524
Dividends	..	2 416	2 696	6 745	16 179	31 592	25 366	18 975	14 803	15 502
Investment interest rates	..	771	1 838	985	4 307	1	5	89	585	2 742
Miscellaneous products (commissions, transfers to the Central Bank of West African States)	..	0	0	0	201	5 234	5 181	6 152	8 599	10 858
Other financial products	..	1 304	4 187	42 344	1 032	758	567	708	819	422
Other property income	..	0	0	0	0	0	0	0	0	0
Sales of goods and services	..	1 365	850	140	7 692	57 099	25 308	24 926	13 478	12 115
Building rentals	..	0	0	0	201	386	228	253	59	46
Telephone bills	..	0	0	0	2 000	50 440	15 500	15 500	0	0
Service fees	..	1 365	850	140	4 752	6 064	9 349	9 174	13 419	11 523
Consulting fees	..	0	0	0	739	210	230	0	0	545
Fines, penalties and forfeits	..	1 222	633	495	1 359	1 148	1 679	636	3 214	390
Fines and penalties (on tax revenues)	..	955	495	262	989	821	1 132	320	3 027	175
Fines and penalties (on customs revenues)	..	267	138	232	369	326	547	316	187	215
Miscellaneous and unidentified revenue	..	2 069	5 403	16 280	11 114	11 737	12 978	7 351	10 105	10 592
Confiscations and sales at customs	..	0	0	0	954	9 616	6 488	2 013	1 033	1 666
Tax collection order (previous administration)	..	0	0	0	6	43	0	0	75	322
Tax collection order (current administrations)	..	0	0	0	95	175	27	321	0	56
Miscellaneous royalties	..	785	1 216	0	9 754	1 114	6 368	2 941	8 996	7 213
Other non-tax revenues	..	1 284	4 187	16 280	305	789	96	2 076	1	1 335
Total tax and non-tax revenue	..	*118 981*	*191 782*	*440 185*	*636 513*	*793 416*	*834 865*	*834 894*	*933 784*	*1 066 965*

.. Not available

Note: Year ending 31st December.

The data are on a cash basis.

Non-tax revenues include revenues from other ministries and directorates other than the Ministry of Economy and Finance.

Figures exclude other revenues collected by sub-national governments on their own account, as the data are not available. Under Togo's national classification, the PADSP (Prélèvement pour l'apurement de la dette du secteur pétrolier, or "Oil sector debt relief levy") is included in non-tax revenues. It is included in tax revenues in this edition following the OECD classification of taxes (see the Interpretative Guide in Annex A).

Fines and penalties on taxes and customs duties are included in non-tax revenues in this edition following the OECD classification of taxes (see the Interpretative Guide in Annex B). Under Togo's national classification they are included in tax revenues and customs revenues, respectively.

Confiscations and customs sales include repayments of the community solidarity levy, which are included in non-tax revenues in this edition following the OECD classification of taxes (see the Interpretative Guide in Annex B. Under Togo's national classification they are included in customs tax revenues. Before 2014, these revenues were reported in the heading "Fines and penalties (customs revenues)".

Source: Togolese Revenue Office.

Table 6.37. Tunisia – Details of non-tax revenues

Million TND

	1995	2000	2005	2010	2015	2018	2019	2020	2021	2022
Total non-tax revenue	**..**	**725**	**1 078**	**1 799**	**1 539**	**3 254**	**3 828**	**3 584**	**3 609**	**6 130**
Grants	..	7	70	54	130	236	249	779	44	1 378
Property income	..	525	703	1 299	915	2 105	2 237	1 762	2 374	3 749
Rents and royalties	..	185	295	435	388	1 353	1 043	698	1 364	2 972
Royalties on oil and gas	..	177	284	415	366	1 324	1 017	675	1 337	2 945
Rents	..	8	11	19	23	29	26	23	27	28
Interest and dividends	..	341	408	864	527	752	1 194	1 065	1 009	777
Interest	..	56	87	56	8	72	72	64	91	80
Transfers from public companies and central bank profits	..	274	311	796	447	631	1 068	933	807	625
Returned credit	..	3	3	2	4	4	3	3	3	4
Other interest and dividends not elsewhere classified	..	9	8	10	68	44	50	65	108	68
Other property income	..	0	0	0	0	0	0	0	0	0
Sales of goods and services	..	22	38	40	32	72	53	34	44	58
Sales of diverse products	..	21	37	38	30	70	50	31	42	54
Administrative fees and credit rebates	..	1	1	2	2	2	2	3	2	4
Fines, penalties and forfeits	..	87	127	186	273	532	998	473	707	669
Miscellaneous and unidentified revenue	..	85	139	220	190	309	292	537	440	277
Total tax and non-tax revenue	..	*7 922*	*11 223*	*18 942*	*28 135*	*37 078*	*43 278*	*42 413*	*46 058*	*54 241*

.. Not available

Note: Year ending 31st December.

The data are on a cash basis.

Figures exclude non-tax revenues collected by sub-national governments as the data are not available.

Grants: Grants earmarked for the Special Treasury Accounts (Fonds spéciaux du Trésor) and the Joint funds (Fonds de concours) are included in the figures for grants from foreign governments and institutions.

Miscellaneous and unidentified revenue: this category includes, among other things, accidental revenues from various sources and non-tax revenues from the Special Treasury Accounts and Joint funds (excluding earmarked).

Source: Ministry of Finance, Tunisia.

Table 6.38. Uganda – Details of non-tax revenues

Million UGX

	1995	2000	2005	2010	2015	2018	2019	2020	2021	2022
Total non-tax revenue	**234 550**	**568 523**	**1 194 038**	**921 459**	**1 109 070**	**1 161 102**	**1 688 568**	**1 888 149**	**2 757 554**	**2 261 507**
Grants	234 000	566 605	1 177 119	863 608	930 810	774 198	1 201 553	1 156 386	1 953 774	1 161 964
Budget support	89 300	255 205	817 409	467 338	258 152	154 513	594 860	455 205	628 576	108 312
Project grants	144 700	311 400	359 710	396 270	672 658	619 684	606 693	701 181	1 325 198	1 053 653
Property income	0	0	2 355	4 061	8 684	17 766	16 893	13 340	12 870	11 260
Rents and royalties	..	..	2 355	4 061	8 684	17 766	16 893	13 340	12 870	11 260
Mining royalties	..	..	2 355	4 061	8 684	17 766	16 893	13 340	12 870	11 260
Interest and dividends	..	..	0	0	0	0	0	0	0	0
Other property income	..	..	0	0	0	0	0	0	0	0
Sales of goods and services	550	1 919	14 564	53 790	169 575	369 138	470 122	718 423	790 910	1 088 282
Driver's permits	550	1 919	3 877	12 373	15 921	37 335	39 425	39 110	48 540	70 053
Migration Fees	..	..	3 822	23 317	90 913	140 196	139 778	122 840	154 010	189 870
Passport fees	..	..	2 523	4 614	12 800	25 950	37 338	40 140	53 780	116 150
Uganda Registration Services Bureau	..	..	0	0	23 470	21 461	56 259	37 490	40 590	57 050
Other administrative fees	..	..	4 342	13 486	26 472	144 196	197 322	478 843	493 990	655 159
Fines, penalties and forfeits	0	0	0	0	0	0	0	0	0	0
Miscellaneous and unidentified revenue	0	0	0	0	0	0	0	0	0	0
Total tax and non-tax revenue	*756 229*	*1 568 183*	*3 129 509*	*5 173 480*	*10 871 500*	*15 228 692*	*17 819 204*	*17 908 014*	*21 216 754*	*22 819 973*

.. Not available

Note: Data are reported on a fiscal year basis beginning 1st July. For example, the data for 2022 represent July 2021 to June 2022.

The data are on a cash basis.

Figures exclude non-tax revenues collected by sub-national governments as the data are not available.

Due to a government directive, non-tax revenues collected by government departments had to be reported to the URA starting in 2019/20. For previous years, figures for such revenues are not available. These departmental revenues were reported as "non-tax revenues collected by departments other than URA" in previous editions. In this edition, these revenues are included among other non-tax revenues and are no longer reported as a separate category.

Revenue from driver's permits are considered as non-tax revenue according the OECD classification described in the OECD Interpretative Guide. The national classification of Uganda classifies it as tax revenues.

Source: Uganda Revenue Authority.

Table 6.39. Zambia – Details of non-tax revenues

Million ZMK

	1995	2000	2005	2010	2015	2018	2019	2020	2021	2022
Total non-tax revenue	**..**	**..**	**..**	**..**	**4 121**	**4 622**	**5 088**	**7 116**	**14 960**	**12 510**
Grants	..	..	..	..	369	647	839	1 715	2 481	1 981
Property income	..	..	..	..	3 749	3 937	4 185	5 348	12 417	10 445
Rents and royalties	..	..	..	..	3 749	3 937	4 185	5 348	12 417	10 445
Interest and dividends	..	..	..	..	0	0	0	0	0	0
Other property income	..	..	..	..	0	0	0	0	0	0
Sales of goods and services	..	..	..	..	0	11	11	10	7	8
Fines, penalties and forfeits	..	..	..	..	2	27	53	43	55	76
Miscellaneous and unidentified revenue	..	..	..	..	0	0	0	0	0	0
Total tax and non-tax revenue	..	..	..	..	*30 323*	*49 106*	*53 808*	*59 380*	*86 396*	*92 327*

.. Not available

Note: Year ending 31st December.

The data are on a cash basis.

Source: Zambia Revenue Authority. Grant revenue data are taken from IMF Article IV reports.

Annex A. The OECD classification of taxes and interpretative guide

Table of Contents

A.1 The OECD Classification of Taxes

1000. Taxes on income, profits and capital gains			
	1100. Taxes on income, profits and capital gains of individuals		
		1110. On income and profits	
		1120. On capital gains	
	1200. Corporate taxes on income, profits and capital gains		
		1210. On income and profits	
		1220. On capital gains	
	1300. Unallocable as between 1100 and 1200		
2000. Social security contributions			
	2100. Employees		
		2110. On a payroll basis	
		2120. On an income tax basis	
	2200. Employers		
		2210. On a payroll basis	
		2220. On an income tax basis	
	2300. Self-employed or non-employed		
		2310. On a payroll basis	
		2320. On an income tax basis	
	2400 Unallocable as between 2100, 2200 and 2300		
		2410. On a payroll basis	
		2420. On an income tax basis	
3000. Taxes on payroll and workforce			
4000. Taxes on property			
	4100. Recurrent taxes on immovable property		
		4110. Households	
		4120. Other	
	4200 Recurrent taxes on net wealth		
		4210. Individual	
		4220. Corporate	
	4300. Estate, inheritance and gift taxes		
		4310. Estate and inheritance taxes	
		4320. Gift taxes	
	4400. Taxes on financial and capital transactions		
	4500. Other non-recurrent taxes on property		
		4510. On net wealth	
		4520. Other non-recurrent taxes	
	4600. Other recurrent taxes on property		
5000. Taxes on goods and services			
	5100. Taxes on production, sale, transfer, leasing and delivery of goods and rendering of services		
		5110. General taxes	
			5111. Value added taxes
			5112. Sales taxes
			5113. Turnover and other general taxes on goods and services
		5120. Taxes on specific goods and services	
			5121. Excises
			5122. Profits of fiscal monopolies
			5123. Customs and import duties
			5124. Taxes on exports
			5125. Taxes on investment goods
			5126. Taxes on specific services
			5127. Other taxes on international trade and transactions

			5128. Other taxes on specific goods and services
		5130. Unallocable as between 5110 and 5120	
	5200. Taxes on use of goods, or on permission to use goods or perform activities		
		5210. Recurrent taxes	
			5211. Paid by households in respect of motor vehicles
			5212. Paid by others in respect of motor vehicles
			5213. Other recurrent taxes
		5220. Non-recurrent taxes	
	5300. Unallocable as between 5100 and 5200		
6000. Other taxes			
	6100. Paid solely by business		
	6200. Paid by other than business or unidentifiable		

A.2 Coverage

General criteria

1. In the OECD classification, the term "taxes" is confined to compulsory unrequited payments to the general government or to a supranational authority. Taxes are unrequited in the sense that benefits provided by government to taxpayers are not normally in proportion to their payments.

2. The term "tax" does not include fines, penalties and compulsory loans paid to government. Borderline cases between tax and non-tax revenues in relation to certain fees and charges are discussed in §12–15.

3. General government consists of the central administration, agencies whose operations are under its effective control, state and local governments and their administrations, certain social security schemes and autonomous governmental entities, excluding public enterprises. This definition of government follows that of the 2008 *System of National Accounts* (SNA).[1] In that publication, the general government sector and its sub-sectors are defined in Chapter 4, paragraphs 4.117 to 4.165.

4. Extra-budgetary units are part of the general government system. These are general government entities with individual budgets that are not fully covered by the main or general budget. These entities operate under the authority or control of a central, state, or local government. Extra-budgetary entities may have their own revenue sources, which may be supplemented by grants (transfers) from the general budget or from other sources. Even though their budgets may be subject to approval by the legislature, similar to that of budgetary accounts, they have discretion over the volume and composition of their spending. Such entities may be established to carry out specific government functions, such as road construction, or the nonmarket production of health or education services. Budgetary arrangements vary widely across countries, and various terms are used to describe these entities, but they are often referred to as "extra-budgetary funds" or "decentralised agencies."

5. Compulsory, unrequited payments collected by national governments and paid to supranational authorities are also included as taxes under the definition in paragraph 1. Taxes that are collected by national governments and paid to a supranational authority are included as tax revenues at the level of the supranational authority in the SNA2008 (paragraphs 22.60-61, 22.88 and 22.99 refer) and the ESA2010 (paragraph 20.165 refers). In Revenue Statistics, these taxes include customs duties, contributions to the EU Single Resolution Fund, and any other taxes collected by EU member states on behalf of the European Union. They are included in the tax revenue amounts in the country tables (Chapter 5) of the country in which they are collected and are attributed to the supranational level of government (see §102).

6. In countries where the church forms part of general government, church taxes are included, provided they meet the criteria set out in §1 above. As the data refer to receipts of general government

and to supranational authorities, levies paid to non-government bodies, welfare agencies or social insurance schemes outside general government, trade unions or trade associations, even where such levies are compulsory, are excluded. Compulsory payments to general government earmarked for such bodies are, however, included, provided that the government is not simply acting in an agency capacity.[2] Profits from fiscal monopolies are distinguished from those of other public enterprises and are treated as taxes because they reflect the exercise of the taxing power of the state by the use of monopoly powers (see §66–68), as are profits received by the government from the purchase and sale of foreign exchange at different rates (see §76).

7. Taxes paid by governments (e.g., social security contributions and payroll taxes paid by governments in their capacity as an employer, consumption taxes on their purchases or taxes on their property) are not excluded from the data provided. However, where it is possible to identify the amounts of revenue involved,[3] they are shown in Table 4.2 of this Report.

8. The relationship between this classification and that of the System of National Accounts (SNA) is set out in Sections A.9 and A.11 below. Because of the differences between the two classifications, the data shown in national accounts are sometimes calculated or classified differently from the practice set out in this guide. These and other differences are mentioned where appropriate (e.g., in §31 below) but it is not possible to refer to all of them. There may also be some differences between this classification and that employed domestically by certain national administrations (e.g., see §13 below), so that OECD and national statistics data may not always be consistent: any such differences, however, are likely to be very slight in terms of amounts of revenues involved.

Social security contributions

9. Compulsory social security contributions, as defined in §40, and paid to general government, are treated here as tax revenues. They may, however, differ from other taxes in that the receipt of social security benefits depends, in most countries, upon appropriate contributions having been made, although the size of the benefits is not necessarily related to the amount of the contributions. Better comparability between countries is obtained by treating social security contributions as taxes, but they are listed under a separate heading so that they can be distinguished in any analysis.

10. The strict dividing line between tax revenues (compulsory unrequited payments to general government or a supranational authority) and non-tax compulsory payments (NTCPs) (payments that are either requited or made to other institutions) is clearly defined. However, within the range of different compulsory payments to governments existing across countries, it is not always straightforward in practice to decide whether specific payments are either taxes or NTCPs. For example, compulsory pension savings that are controlled by general government and that accumulate on an individual account earning a market return or a rate that compensates for inflation would at first sight be categorised as NTCPs as opposed to taxes. However, even these payments might still be 'unrequited' and therefore classify as taxes instead of NTCPs (for example if these pension savings are not paid out when the taxpayer dies before reaching the pension age and the funds are then used to provide a minimum pension to all taxpayers that are insured). These issues result in the social security revenue figures reported for most countries being based on the premise that all types of compulsory payments to general government are judged to some extent to have a re-distributional element. It should be noted that this conclusion is based on a typically broad interpretation of the term 'unrequited' in the tax definition.

11. Social security contributions which are either voluntary or not payable to general government (see §1) are not treated as taxes, though in some countries, as indicated in the country footnotes, there are difficulties in completely eliminating voluntary contributions and certain compulsory payments to the private sector from the revenue figures. Imputed social security contributions are also not treated as taxes.

Fees, user charges and licence fees

12. Apart from vehicle licence fees, which are universally regarded as taxes, it is not easy to distinguish between those fees and user charges which are to be treated as taxes and those which are not, since, whilst a fee or charge is levied in connection with a specific service or activity, the strength of the link between the fee and the service provided may vary considerably, as may the relation between the amount of the fee and the cost of providing the service. Where the recipient of a service pays a fee clearly related to the cost of providing the service, the levy may be regarded as requited and under the definition of §1 would not be considered as a tax. In the following cases, however, a levy could be considered as 'unrequited':

- *a)* where the charge greatly exceeds the cost of providing the service;
- *b)* where the payer of the levy is not the receiver of the benefit (e.g., a fee collected from slaughterhouses to finance a service which is provided to farmers);
- *c)* where government is not providing a specific service in return for the levy which it receives even though a licence may be issued to the payer (e.g., where the government grants a hunting, fishing or shooting licence which is not accompanied by the right to use a specific area of government land);
- *d)* where benefits are received only by those paying the levy but the benefits received by each individual are not necessarily in proportion to his payments (e.g., a milk marketing levy paid by dairy farmers and used to promote the consumption of milk).
- *e)* where the payer of the levy cannot opt out from making payments (e.g. public broadcast fees where the payer is obliged to pay the levy although not consuming public broadcast service).

13. In marginal cases, however, the application of the criteria set out in §1 can be particularly difficult. The solution adopted — given the desirability of international uniformity and the relatively small amounts of revenue usually involved — is to follow the predominant practice among tax administrations rather than to allow each country to adopt its own view as to whether such levies are regarded as taxes or as non-tax revenue.[4]

14. A list of the main fees and charges in question and their normal[5] treatment in this publication is as follows:

Non-tax revenues:	**Court fees; driving licence fees; harbour fees; passport fees**
Taxes within heading 5200	Permission to perform such activities as distributing films; hunting, fishing and shooting; providing entertainment or gambling facilities; selling alcohol or tobacco; permission to own dogs or to use or own motor vehicles or guns; severance taxes

15. In practice, it may not always be possible to isolate tax receipts from non-tax revenue receipts when they are recorded together. If it is estimated that the bulk of the receipts derive from non-tax revenues, the whole amount involved is treated as a non-tax revenue; otherwise, such government receipts are included and classified according to the rules provided in §33 below.

Royalties

16. The ownership of subsoil assets in the form of deposits of minerals or fossil fuels (coal, oil, or natural gas) depends upon the way in which property rights are defined by law and also on international agreements in the case of deposits below international waters. In some cases, either the ground below which the mineral deposits are located, the deposits themselves or both may belong to a local or central government unit.

17. In such cases, these general government units may grant leases to other institutional units that permit them to extract these deposits over a specified period of time in return for a payment or series of

payments. These payments are often described as 'royalties' but they are essentially rent that accrues to owners of natural resources in return for putting these assets at the disposal of other units for specified periods of time. The rent may take the form of periodic payments of fixed amounts, irrespective of the rate of extraction, or, more commonly, they may be a function of the quantity, volume, or value of the asset extracted. Enterprises engaged in exploration on government land may make payments to general government units in exchange for the right to undertake test drilling or otherwise investigate the existence and location of subsoil assets. Such payments are also recorded as rents even though no extraction may take place. These payments are therefore classified as non-tax revenues.

18. The same principles apply when other institutional units are granted leases that permit them to fell timber in natural forests on land owned by general government units. These payments are also classified as non-tax revenues.

19. These rents or royalties paid to general government should not be confused with taxes on income and profits, severance taxes, business licenses, or other taxes. If the payments are levied on the profits from the extraction activity, then they should be classified as taxes on incomes, profits and gains (1000). In addition, any severance payments that are imposed on the extraction of minerals and fossil fuels from reserves owned privately or by another government should be classified as taxes. Payments related to the gross value of production should be classified as other taxes on goods and services (5128). Payments for a license or permit to conduct extraction operations should be classified as taxes on use of goods and on permission to use goods or perform activities (5213).

Fines and penalties

20. In principle, fines and penalties charged on overdue taxes or penalties imposed for the attempted evasion of taxes should not be recorded as tax revenues. However, it may not be possible to separate payments of fines or other penalties from the revenues from the taxes to which they relate. In this case, the fines and penalties relating to a particular tax are recorded together with the revenues from that tax and fines and penalties paid with revenue from unidentifiable taxes are classified as other taxes in Category 6000. Fines not relating to tax offences (e.g., for parking offences), or not identifiable as relating to tax offences, are also not treated as tax revenues.

A.3 Basis of reporting

Accrual or cash reporting

21. The data reported in the *Revenue Statistics* publications for recent years are predominantly recorded on an accrual basis for OECD countries, i.e. recorded at the time that the tax liability was created. Further information is provided in the footnotes to the country table in Chapter 5 of the Report.

22. However, data for earlier years and for non-OECD countries are still predominantly recorded on a cash basis, i.e. at the time at which the payment was received by government. Thus, for example, taxes withheld by employers in one year but paid to the government in the following year and taxes due in one year but actually paid in the following year are both included in the receipts of the second year. Corrective transactions, such as refunds, repayments and drawbacks, are deducted from gross revenues of the period in which they are made.

23. Data on tax revenues are recorded without offsets for the administrative expenses connected with tax collection. Similarly, where the proceeds of tax are used to subsidise particular members of the community, the subsidy is not deducted from the yield of the tax, though the tax may be shown net of subsidies in the national records of some countries.

24. As regards fiscal monopolies (heading 5122), only the amount actually transferred to the government is included in government revenues. However, if any expenditures of fiscal monopolies are considered to be government expenditures (e.g., social expenditures undertaken by fiscal monopolies at the direction of the government) they are added back for the purpose of arriving at tax revenue figures (see §66 below).

The distinction between tax and expenditure provisions

25. Because this publication is concerned only with the revenue side of government operations, no account being taken of the expenditure side, a distinction has to be made between tax and expenditure provisions. Normally there is no difficulty in making this distinction as expenditures are made outside the tax system and the tax accounts and under legislation separate from the tax legislation. In borderline cases, cash flow is used to distinguish between tax provisions and expenditure provisions. Insofar as a provision affects the flow of tax payments from the taxpayer to the government, it is regarded as a tax provision and is taken into account in the data shown in this publication. A provision which does not affect this flow is seen as an expenditure provision and is disregarded in the data recorded in this publication. A more detailed explanation of this distinction can be found in the special feature, 'Current issues in reporting tax revenues', in the 2001 edition of *Revenue Statistics.*

26. Tax allowances, exemptions and deductions against the tax base clearly affect the amount of tax paid to the government and are therefore considered as tax provisions. At the other extreme, those subsidies which cannot be offset against tax liability and which are clearly not connected with the assessment process, do not reduce tax revenues as recorded in this publication. Tax credits are amounts deductible from tax payable (as distinct from deductions from the tax base). Two types of tax credits are distinguished, those (referred to here as wastable tax credits) which are limited to the amount of the tax liability and therefore cannot give rise to a payment by the authorities to the taxpayer, and those (referred to as non-wastable tax credits) which are not so limited, so that the excess of the credit over the tax liability can be paid to the taxpayer.[6] A wastable tax credit, like a tax allowance, clearly affects the amount of tax paid to the government, and is therefore considered as a tax provision. The practice followed for non-wastable tax credits[7] is to distinguish between the 'tax expenditure component',[8] which is that portion of the credit that is used to reduce or eliminate a taxpayer's liability, and the 'transfer component', which is the portion that exceeds the taxpayer's liability and is paid to that taxpayer. Reported tax revenues should be reduced by the amount of the tax expenditure component but not by the amount of the transfer component. In addition, the amounts of the tax expenditure and transfer components should be reported as memorandum items in the country tables. Countries that are unable to distinguish between the tax expenditure and transfer components should indicate whether or not the tax revenues have been reduced by the total of these components, and provide any available estimates of the amounts of the two components. Further information is given in Chapter 1 of the Report, which illustrates the effect of alternative treatments of non-wastable tax credits on tax to GDP.

Calendar and fiscal years

27. National authorities whose fiscal years do not correspond to the calendar year show data, where possible, on a calendar year basis to permit maximum comparability with the data of other countries. There remain a few countries where data refer to fiscal years. For these the GDP data used in the comparative tables also correspond to the fiscal years.

A.4 General classification criteria

The main classification criteria

28. The classification of receipts among the main headings (1000, 2000, 3000, 4000, 5000 and 6000) is generally governed by the base on which the tax is levied: 1000 income, profits and capital gains; 2000 and 3000 earnings, payroll or number of employees; 4000 property; 5000 goods and services; 6000 multiple bases, other bases or unidentifiable bases. Where a tax is calculated on more than one base, the receipts are, where possible, split among the various headings (see §33 and §84). The headings 4000 and 5000 cover not only taxes where the tax base is the property, goods or services themselves but also certain related taxes. Thus, taxes on the transfer of property are included in 4400[9] and taxes on the use of goods or on permission to perform activities in 5200. In headings 4000 and 5000 a distinction is made in certain sub-headings between recurrent and non-recurrent taxes: recurrent taxes are defined as those levied at regular intervals (usually annually) and non-recurrent taxes are levied once and for all (see also §48 to §51, §54, §55 and §81 for particular applications of this distinction).

29. Earmarking of a tax for specific purposes does not affect the classification of tax receipts. However, as explained in §40 on the classification of social security contributions, the conferment of an entitlement to social benefits is crucial to the definition of the 2000 main heading.

30. The way that a tax is levied or collected (e.g., by use of stamps) does not affect classification.

Classification of taxpayers

31. In certain sub-headings, distinctions are made between different categories of taxpayers. These distinctions vary from tax to tax:

a) Between individuals and corporations in relation to income and net wealth taxes

The basic distinction is that corporation income taxes, as distinct from individual income taxes, are levied on the corporation as an entity, not on the individuals who own it, and without regard to the personal circumstances of these individuals. The same distinction applies to net wealth taxes on corporations and those on individuals. Taxes paid on the profits of partnerships and the income of institutions, such as life insurance or pension funds, are classified according to the same rule. They are classified as corporate taxes (1200) if they are charged on the partnership or institution as an entity without regard to the personal circumstances of the owners. Otherwise, they are treated as individual taxes (1100). Usually, there is different legislation for the corporation taxes and for the individual taxes.[10] The distinction made here between individuals and corporations does not follow the sector classification between households, enterprises, and so on of the System of National Accounts for income and outlay accounts. The SNA classification requires certain unincorporated businesses[11] to be excluded from the household sector and included with non-financial enterprises and financial institutions. The tax on the profits of these businesses, however, cannot always be separated from the tax on the other income of their owners, or can be separated only on an arbitrary basis. No attempt at this separation is made here and the whole of the individual income tax is shown together without regard to the nature of the income chargeable.

b) Between households and others in relation to taxes on immovable property

Here the distinction is that adopted by the SNA for the production and consumption expenditure accounts. The distinction is between households as consumers (i.e. excluding non-incorporated business) on the one hand and producers on the other hand. However, taxes on dwellings occupied by households, whether paid by owner-occupiers, tenants or landlords, are classified under households. This follows the common distinction made between taxes on domestic property versus taxes on business property. Some countries are not, however, in a position to make this distinction.

c) Between households and others in relation to motor vehicle licences

Here the distinction is between households as consumers on the one hand and producers on the other, as in the production and consumption expenditure accounts of the SNA.

d) Between business and others in relation to the residual taxes (6000)

The distinction is the same as in c) above between producers on the one hand and households as consumers on the other hand. Taxes which are included under the heading 6000 because they involve more than one tax base or because the tax base does not fall within any of the previous categories but which are identifiable as levyable only on producers and not on households are included under 'business'. The rest of the taxes which are included under the heading 6000 are shown as 'other' or non-identified.

Surcharges

32. Receipts from surcharges in respect of particular taxes are usually classified with the receipts from the relevant tax whether or not the surcharge is temporary. If, however, the surcharge has a characteristic which would render it classifiable in a different heading of the OECD list, receipts from the surcharge are classified under that heading separately from the relevant tax.

Unidentifiable tax receipts and residual sub-headings

33. A number of cases arise where taxes cannot be identified as belonging entirely to a heading or sub-heading of the OECD classification and the following practices are applied in such cases:

a) The heading is known, but it is not known how receipts should be allocated between sub-headings: receipts are classified in the appropriate residual sub-heading (1300, 2400, 4520, 4600, 5128, 5130, 5300 or 6200).

b) It is known that the bulk of receipts from a group of taxes (usually local taxes) is derived from taxes within a particular heading or sub-heading, but some of the taxes in the group whose amount cannot be precisely ascertained may be classifiable in other headings or sub-headings: receipts are shown in the heading or sub-heading under which most of the receipts fall.

c) Neither the heading nor sub-heading of a tax (usually local) can be identified: the tax is classified in 6200 unless it is known that it is a tax on business in which case it is classified in 6100.

A.5 Commentaries on items of the list

1000 — Taxes on income, profits and capital gains

34. This heading covers taxes levied on the net income or profits (i.e. gross income minus allowable tax reliefs) of individuals and enterprises. Also covered are taxes levied on the capital gains of individuals and enterprises, and gains from gambling.

35. Included in the heading are:

a) taxes levied predominantly on income or profits, though partially on other bases. Taxes on various bases which are not predominantly income or profits are classified according to the principles laid down in §33 and §84;

b) taxes on property, which are levied on a presumed or estimated income as part of an income tax (see also §48(a), (c) and (d));

c) compulsory payments to social security fund contributions that are levied on income but do not confer an entitlement to social benefits. When such contributions do confer an entitlement to social benefits, they are included in heading 2000 (see §40);

d) receipts from integrated scheduler income tax systems are classified as a whole in this heading, even though certain of the scheduler taxes may be based upon gross income and may not take into account the personal circumstances of the taxpayer.

36. The main subdivision of this heading is between levies on individuals (1100) and those on corporate enterprises (1200). Under each subdivision a distinction is made between taxes on income and profits (1110 and 1210), and taxes on capital gains (1120 and 1220). If certain receipts cannot be identified as appropriate to either 1100 or 1200, or if in practice this distinction cannot be made (e.g., because there are no reliable data on the recipients of payments from which withholding taxes are deducted) they are classified in 1300 as not-allocable.

Treatment of credits under imputation systems

37. Under imputation systems of corporate income tax, a company's shareholders are wholly or partly relieved of their liability to income tax on dividends paid by the company out of income or profits liable to corporate income tax. In countries with such systems,[12] part of the tax on the company's profits is available to provide relief against the shareholders' own tax liability. The relief to the shareholder takes the form of a tax credit, the amount of which may be less than, equal to, or more than the shareholder's overall tax liability. If the tax credit exceeds this tax liability the excess may be payable to the shareholder. As this type of tax credit is an integral part of the imputation system of corporate income tax, any payment to the shareholders is treated as a repayment of tax and not as expenditure (compare the treatment of other tax credits described in §26).

38. As the tax credit under imputation systems (even when exceeding tax liability) is to be regarded as a tax provision, the question arises whether it should be deducted from individual income tax receipts (1110) or corporate income tax receipts (1210). In this Report, the full amount of corporate income tax paid is shown under 1210 and no imputed tax is included under 1110. Thus, the full amount of the credit reduces the amount of 1110 whether the credit results in a reduction of personal income tax liability or whether an actual refund is made because the credit exceeds the income tax liability. (Where, however, such tax credits are deducted from corporation tax in respect of dividends paid to corporations the amounts are deducted from the receipts of 1210).

1120 and 1220 — Taxes on capital gains

39. These sub-headings comprise taxes imposed on capital gains, 1120 covering those levied on the gains of individuals and 1220 those levied on the gains of corporate enterprises, where receipts from such taxes can be separately identified. In many countries, this is not the case and the receipts from such taxes are then classified with those from the income tax. Heading 1120 also includes taxes on gains from gambling.

2000 — Social security contributions

40. Classified here are all compulsory payments to general government that confer an entitlement to receive a (contingent) future social benefit. Such payments are usually earmarked to finance social benefits and are often paid to institutions of general government that provide such benefits. However, such earmarking is not part of the definition of social security contributions and is not required for a tax to be classified here. However, conferment of an entitlement is required for a tax to be classified under this heading. So, levies on income or payroll that are earmarked for social security funds but do not confer an entitlement to benefit are excluded from this heading and shown under personal income taxes (1100) or

taxes on payroll and workforce (3000). Taxes on other bases, such as goods and services, which are earmarked for social security benefits are not shown here but are classified according to their respective bases because they generally confer no entitlement to social security benefits.

41. Contributions for the following types of social security benefits would, *inter alia*, be included: unemployment insurance benefits and supplements, accident, injury and sickness benefits, old-age, disability and survivors' pensions, family allowances, reimbursements for medical and hospital expenses or provision of hospital or medical services. Contributions may be levied on both employees and employers.

42. Contributions may be based on earnings or payroll ('on a payroll basis') or on net income after deductions and exemptions for personal circumstances ('on an income tax basis'), and the revenues from the two bases should be separately identified if possible. However, where contributions to a general social security scheme are on a payroll basis, but the contributions of particular groups (such as the self-employed) cannot be assessed on this basis and net income is used as a proxy for gross earnings, the receipts may still be classified as being on a payroll basis. In principle, this heading excludes voluntary contributions paid to social security schemes. When separately identifiable these are shown in the memorandum item on the financing of social security benefits. In practice, however, they cannot always be separately identified from compulsory contributions, in which case they are included in this heading.

43. Contributions to social insurance schemes which are not institutions of general government and to other types of insurance schemes, provident funds, pension funds, friendly societies or other saving schemes are not considered as social security contributions. Provident funds are arrangements under which the contributions of each employee and of the corresponding employer on his/her behalf are kept in a separate account earning interest and withdrawable under specific circumstances. Pension funds are separately organised schemes negotiated between employees and employers and carry provisions for different contributions and benefits, sometimes more directly tied to salary levels and length of service than under social security schemes. When contributions to these schemes are compulsory or quasi-compulsory (e.g., by virtue of agreement with professional and union organisations) they are shown in the memorandum item (refer to Table 5.39 of the Report).

44. Contributions by government employees and by governments in respect of their employees, to social security schemes classified within general government are included in this heading. Contributions to separate schemes for government employees, which can be regarded as replacing general social security schemes, are also regarded as taxes.[13] Where, however, a separate scheme is not seen as replacing a general scheme and has been negotiated between the government, in its role as an employer, and its employees, it is not regarded as social security and contributions to it are not regarded as taxes, even though the scheme may have been established by legislation.

45. This heading excludes 'imputed' contributions, which correspond to social benefits paid directly by employers to their employees or former employees or to their representatives (e.g., when employers are legally obliged to pay sickness benefits for a certain period).

46. Contributions are divided into those of employees (2100), employers (2200), and self-employed or non-employed (2300), and then further sub-divided according to the basis on which they are levied. Employees are defined for this purpose as all persons engaged in activities of business units, government bodies, private non-profit institutions, or other paid employment, except the proprietors and their unpaid family members in the case of unincorporated businesses. Members of the armed forces are included, irrespective of the duration and type of their service, if they contribute to social security schemes. The contributions of employers are defined as their payments on account of their employees to social security schemes. Where employees or employers are required to continue the payment of social security contributions when the employee becomes unemployed these contributions, data permitting, are shown in 2100 and 2200 respectively. Accordingly, the sub-heading 2300 is confined to contributions paid by the self-employed and by those outside of the labour force (e.g., disabled or retired individuals).

3000 — Taxes on payroll and workforce

47. These consist of taxes payable by enterprises assessed either as a proportion of the wages or salaries paid or as a fixed amount per person employed. They do not include compulsory social security contributions paid by employers or any taxes paid by employees themselves out of their wages or salaries

4000 — Taxes on property

48. This heading covers recurrent and non-recurrent taxes on the use, ownership or transfer of property. These include taxes on immovable property or net wealth, taxes on the change of ownership of property through inheritance or gift and taxes on financial and capital transactions. The following kinds of tax are excluded from this heading:

a) taxes on capital gains resulting from the sale of a property (1120 or 1220);

b) taxes on the use of goods or on permission to use goods or perform activities (5200); see §78;

c) taxes on immovable property levied on the basis of a presumed net income which take into account the personal circumstances of the taxpayer. They are classified as income taxes along with taxes on income and capital gains derived from property (1100);

d) taxes on the use of property for residence, where the tax is payable by either proprietor or tenant and the amount payable is a function of the user's personal circumstances (pay, dependants, and so on). They are classified as taxes on income (1100);

e) taxes on building in excess of permitted maximum density, taxes on the enlargement, construction or alteration of certain buildings beyond a permitted value and taxes on building construction. They are classified as taxes on permission to perform activities (5200);

f) taxes on the use of one's own property for special trading purposes like selling alcohol, tobacco, meat or for exploitation of land resources (e.g., United States severance taxes). They are classified as taxes on permission to perform activities (5200).

4100 — Recurrent taxes on immovable property

49. This sub-heading covers taxes levied regularly in respect of the use or ownership of immovable property.

- these taxes are levied on land and buildings;
- they can be in the form of a percentage of an assessed property value based on a national rental income, sales price, or capitalised yield; or in terms of other characteristics of real property, (for example size or location) from which a presumed rent or capital value can be derived.
- such taxes can be levied on proprietors, tenants, or both. They can also be paid by one level of government to another level of government in respect of property under the jurisdiction of the latter.
- debts are not taken into account in the assessment of these taxes, and they differ from taxes on net wealth in this respect.

50. Taxes on immovable property are further sub-divided into those paid by households (4110) and those paid by other entities (4120), according to the criteria set out in §31(*b*) above.

4200 — Recurrent taxes on net wealth

51. This sub-heading covers taxes levied regularly (in most cases annually) on net wealth, i.e. taxes on a wide range of movable and immovable property, net of debt. It is sub-divided into taxes paid by individuals (4210) and taxes paid by corporate enterprises (4220) according to the criteria set out in §31(*a*)

above. If separate figures exist for receipts paid by institutions, the tax payments involved are added to those paid by corporations.

4300 — Estate, inheritance and gift taxes

52. This sub-heading is divided into taxes on estates and inheritances (4310) and taxes on gifts (4320).[14] Estate taxes are charged on the amount of the total estate whereas inheritance taxes are charged on the shares of the individual recipients; in addition the latter may take into account the relationship of the individual recipients to the deceased.

4400 — Taxes on financial and capital transactions

53. This sub-heading comprises, *inter alia*, taxes on the issue, transfer, purchase and sale of non-financial and financial assets (including foreign exchange or securities), taxes on cheques and other forms of payment, and taxes levied on specific legal transactions such as validation of contracts and the sale of immovable property. The heading does not include:

- *a)* taxes on the use of goods or property or permission to perform certain activities (5200);
- *b)* fees paid to cover court charges, charges for birth, marriage or death certificates, which are normally regarded as non-tax revenues (see §12);
- *c)* taxes on capital gains (1000);
- *d)* recurrent taxes on immovable property (4100);
- *e)* recurrent taxes on net wealth (4200);
- *f)* once-and-for-all levies on property or wealth (4500);
- *g)* stamp taxes not related to financial and capital transactions
    - i. Stamp taxes on the sale of specific products, such as alcoholic beverages or tobacco (5121);
    - ii. Stamp taxes restricted by law to imported products (5123) or to exported products (5124); or
    - iii. Stamp taxes not falling exclusively on a single category of transaction (6000).

4500 — Other non-recurrent taxes on property

54. This sub-heading covers once-and-for-all, as distinct from recurrent, levies on property. It is divided into taxes on net wealth (4510) and other non-recurrent taxes on property (4520). Heading 4510 would include taxes levied to meet emergency expenditures, or for redistribution purposes. Heading 4520 would cover taxes levied to take account of increases in land value due to permission given to develop or provision of additional local facilities by general government, any taxes on the revaluation of capital and once-and-for-all taxes on particular items of property.

4600 — Other recurrent taxes on property

55. These rarely exist in OECD member countries, but the heading would include taxes on goods such as cattle, jewellery, windows, and other external signs of wealth.

5000 — Taxes on goods and services

56. All taxes and duties levied on the production, extraction, sale, transfer, leasing or delivery of goods, and the rendering of services (5100), or in respect of the use of goods or permission to use goods or to perform activities (5200) are included here. The heading thus covers:

a) multi-stage cumulative taxes;

b) general sales taxes — whether levied at manufacture/production, wholesale or retail level;

c) value-added taxes;

d) excises;

e) taxes levied on the import and export of goods;

f) taxes levied in respect of the use of goods and taxes on permission to use goods, or perform certain activities;

g) taxes on the extraction, processing or production of minerals and other products.

57. Borderline cases between this heading and heading 4000 (taxes on property) and 6100 (other taxes on business) are referred to in §48, §53 and §80. Residual sub-headings (5300) and (5130) cover tax receipts which cannot be allocated between 5100 and 5200 and between 5110 and 5120, respectively; see §33.

5100 — Taxes on the production, sale, transfer, leasing and delivery of goods and rendering of services

58. This sub-heading consists of all taxes, levied on transactions in goods and services on the basis of their intrinsic characteristics (e.g., value, weight of tobacco, strength of alcohol, and so on) as distinct from taxes imposed on the use of goods, or permission to use goods or perform activities, which fall under 5200.

5110 — General taxes on goods and services

59. This sub-heading includes all taxes, other than import and export duties (5123 and 5124), levied on the production, leasing, transfer, delivery or sales of a wide range of goods and/or the rendering of a wide range of services, irrespective of whether they are domestically produced or imported and irrespective of the stage of production or distribution at which they are levied. It thus covers value-added taxes, sales taxes and multi-stage cumulative taxes. Receipts from border adjustments in respect of such taxes when goods are imported are added to gross receipts for this category, and repayments of such taxes when goods are exported are deducted. These taxes are subdivided into 5111 value-added taxes, 5112 sales taxes, 5113 turnover and other general taxes on goods and services.

60. Borderline cases arise between this heading and taxes on specific goods (5120) when taxes are levied on a large number of goods, for example, the United Kingdom purchase tax (repealed in 1973) and the Japanese commodity tax (repealed in 1988). In conformity with national views, the former United Kingdom purchase tax is classified as a general tax (5112) and the former Japanese commodity tax as excises (5121).

5111 — Value-added taxes

61. All general consumption taxes charged on value-added are classified in this sub-heading, irrespective of the method of deduction and the stages at which the taxes are levied. In practice, all OECD countries with value-added taxes normally allow immediate deduction of taxes on purchases by all but the final consumer and impose tax at all stages. In some countries the heading may include certain taxes, such as those on financial and insurance activities, either because receipts from them cannot be identified separately from those from the value-added tax, or because they are regarded as an integral part of the value-added tax, even though similar taxes in other countries might be classified elsewhere (e.g., 5126 as taxes on services or 4400 as taxes on financial and capital transactions).

5112 — Sales taxes

62. All general taxes levied at one stage only, whether at manufacturing or production, wholesale or retail stage are classified here.

5113 — Turnover and other general taxes on goods and services

63. These are multi-stage cumulative taxes and taxes where elements of consumption taxes are combined with multistage taxes. These taxes are levied each time a transaction takes place without deduction for taxes paid on inputs. Multi-stage taxes can be combined with elements of value-added or sales taxes.

5120 — Taxes on specific goods and services

64. Excises, profits generated and transferred from fiscal monopolies, and customs and imports duties as well as taxes on exports, foreign exchange transactions, investment goods and betting stakes and special taxes on services, which do not form part of a general tax of 5110, are included in this category.

5121 — Excises

65. Excises are taxes levied as a product specific unit tax on a predefined limited range of goods. Excises are usually levied at differentiated rates on nonessential or luxury goods, alcoholic beverages, tobacco, and energy. Excises may be imposed at any stage of production or distribution and are usually assessed as a specific charge per unit based on characteristics by reference to the value, weight, strength, or quantity of the product. Included are special taxes on individual products such as sugar, sugar beets, matches, and chocolates; taxes levied at varying rates on a certain range of goods; and taxes levied on tobacco goods, alcoholic drinks, motor fuels, and hydrocarbon oils. If a tax collected principally on imported goods also applies, or would apply, under the same law to comparable domestically produced goods, then the revenue from this tax is classified as arising from excises rather than from import duties. This principle applies even if there is no comparable domestic production or no possibility of such production. Taxes on the use of utilities such as water, electricity, gas, and energy are regarded as excises rather than taxes on specific services (5126). Excises exclude those taxes that are levied as general taxes on goods and services (5110); profits of fiscal monopolies (5122); customs and other import duties (5123); or taxes on exports (5124).

5122 — Profits of fiscal monopolies

66. This sub-heading covers that part of the profits of fiscal monopolies which is transferred to general government or which is used to finance any expenditures considered to be government expenditures (see §24). Amounts are shown when they are transferred to general government or used to make expenditures considered to be government expenditures.

67. Fiscal monopolies reflect the exercise of the taxing power of government by the use of monopoly powers. Fiscal monopolies are non-financial public enterprises exercising a monopoly in most cases over the production or distribution of tobacco, alcoholic beverages, salt, matches, playing cards and petroleum or agricultural products (i.e. on the kind of products which are likely to be, alternatively or additionally, subject to the excises of 5121), to raise the government revenues which in other countries are gathered through taxes on dealings in such commodities by private business units. The government monopoly may be at the production stage or, as in the case of government-owned and controlled liquor stores, at the distribution stage.

68. Fiscal monopolies are distinguished from public utilities such as rail transport, electricity, post offices, and other communications, which may enjoy a monopoly or quasi-monopoly position but where the primary purpose is normally to provide basic services rather than to raise revenue for government. Transfers from such other public enterprises to the government are considered as non-tax revenues. The traditional concept of fiscal monopoly is not generally extended to include state lotteries, the profits of which are usually accordingly regarded as non-tax revenues. However, they can be included as tax revenues if the prime reason for their operation is to raise revenues to finance government expenditure. Fiscal monopoly profits are distinguished from export and import monopoly profits (5127) transferred from marketing boards or other enterprises dealing with international trade.

5123 — Customs and other import duties

69. Taxes, stamp duties and surcharges restricted by law to imported products are included here. Also included are levies on imported agricultural products which are imposed in member countries of the European Union and amounts paid by certain of these countries under the Monetary Compensation Accounts (MCA) system.[15] Customs duties collected by European Union member states on behalf of the European Union are reported under this heading at the supranational level of government in the country tables (in Chapter 5 of the Report). Excluded here are taxes collected on imports as part of a general tax on goods and services, or an excise applicable to both imported and domestically produced goods.

5124 — Taxes on exports

70. In the 1970s, export duties were levied in Australia, Canada and Portugal as a regular measure and they have been used in Finland for counter-cyclical purposes. Some member countries of the European Union pay, as part of the MCA system, a levy on exports (see note 16 to §69). Where these amounts are identifiable, they are shown in this heading. This heading does not include repayments of general consumption taxes or excises or customs duties on exported goods, which should be deducted from the gross receipts under 5110, 5121 or 5123, as appropriate.

5125 — Taxes on investment goods

71. This sub-heading covers taxes on investment goods, such as machinery. These taxes may be imposed for a number of years or temporarily for counter-cyclical purposes. Taxes on industrial inputs which are also levied on consumers [e.g., the Swedish energy tax which is classified under (5121)] are not included here.

5126 — Taxes on specific services

72. All taxes assessed on the payment for specific services, such as taxes on insurance premiums, banking services, gambling and betting stakes (e.g., from horse races, football pools, lottery tickets), transport, entertainment, restaurant and advertising charges, fall into this category. Taxes on entry to casinos, races, other similar events or venues as well as stamp taxes on specific services are also classified under this heading. Taxes levied on the gross income of companies providing a specific service (e.g. transportation [including airport and other passenger taxes] insurance, banking, entertainment, restaurants, and advertising) are also classified under this heading.

73. Tax revenues from bank levies and payments to deposit insurance and financial stability schemes are also included here:

- Compulsory payments of stability fees, bank levies and deposit insurance should generally be treated as tax revenues where the payments are made to general government or supranational authorities and are allocated to the governments' consolidated or general funds so that the government is free to make immediate use of the money for the purposes that it chooses. This principle would apply regardless of whether the government is promising to make payments to guarantee the banks' customer deposits in some future contingency.

- If the compulsory payments are made to general government and placed in funds that are earmarked to be entirely channelled back to the sector of the economy that comprises the companies that are subject to the payment, they would still generally be treated as tax revenues on the grounds that the funds would be available for the government and would reduce its budget deficit, the fee is unrequited for an individual entity and the amounts raised could be unrelated to any eventual pay out to depositors or expenditure on wider support for the financial sector.
- Payments to made to the smaller long-standing schemes for insuring 'retail' deposits, where the payment levels are consistent with the costs of insurance should be classified as fee for service.
- Any payments which involve governments realising the assets of a failed institution or receiving a priority claim on its assets in liquidation in order to fund payments of compensation to customers for their lost deposits would be treated as a fee for a service as opposed to tax revenues.
- Compulsory payments that are made to funds operated outside the government sector and non-state institutions backed by the deposit takers and all payments to voluntary schemes should not be treated as tax revenues.
- Contributions made to the EU Single Resolution Fund are also included here and recorded under the supranational level of government in the country tables.

74. Excluded from this sub-heading are:

a) taxes on services forming part of a general tax on goods and services (5110);

b) taxes on electricity, gas and energy (5121 as excises);

c) taxes on individual gains from gambling (1120 as taxes on capital gains of individuals and non-corporate enterprises) and lump-sum taxes on the transfer of private lotteries or on the permission to set up lotteries (5200);[16]

d) taxes on cheques and on the issue, transfer or redemption of securities (4400 as taxes on financial and capital transactions);

e) general taxes on turnover (5113).

5127 — Other taxes on international trade and transactions

75. This sub-heading covers revenue received by the government from the purchase and sale of foreign exchange at different rates. When the government exercises monopoly powers to extract a margin between the purchase and sales price of foreign exchange, other than to cover administrative costs, the revenue derived constitutes a compulsory levy exacted in indeterminate proportions from both purchaser and seller of foreign exchange. It is the common equivalent of an import duty and export duty levied in a single exchange rate system or of a tax on the sale or purchase of foreign exchange. Like the profits of fiscal monopolies and import or export monopolies transferred to government, it represents the exercise of monopoly powers for tax purposes and is included in tax revenues.

76. The sub-heading covers also the profits of export or import monopolies, which do not however exist in OECD countries, taxes on purchase or sale of foreign exchange, and any other taxes levied specifically on international trade or transactions.

5128 — Other taxes on specific goods and services

77. This item includes taxes on the extraction of minerals, fossil fuels and other exhaustible resources from deposits owned privately or by another government together with any other unallocable receipts from taxes on specific goods and services. Taxes on the extraction of exhaustible resources are usually a fixed amount per unit of quality or weight, but can be a percentage of value. The taxes are recorded when the

resources are extracted. Payments from the extraction of exhaustible resources from deposits owned by the government unit receiving the payment are classified as rent.

5200 — Taxes on use of goods or on permission to use goods or perform activities

78. This sub-heading covers taxes which are levied in respect of the use of goods as distinct from taxes on the goods themselves. Unlike the latter taxes – reported under 5100 –, they are not assessed on the value of the goods but usually as fixed amounts. Taxes on permission to use goods or to perform activities are also included here, as are pollution taxes not based upon the value of particular goods. It is sometimes difficult to distinguish between compulsory user charges and licence fees which are regarded as taxes and those which are excluded as non-tax revenues. The criteria which are employed are noted in §12–13.

79. Although the sub-heading refers to the 'use' of goods, registration of ownership rather than use may be what generates liability to tax, so that the taxes of this heading may apply to the ownership of animals or goods rather than their use (e.g., race horses, dogs and motor vehicles) and may apply even to unusable goods (e.g., unusable motor vehicles or guns).

80. Borderline cases arise with:

a) taxes on the permission to perform business activities which are levied on a combined income, payroll or turnover base and, accordingly, are classified following the rules in §84;

b) taxes on the ownership or use of property of headings 4100, 4200 and 4600. The heading 4100 is confined to taxes on the ownership or tenancy of immovable property and – unlike the taxes of 5200 – they are related to the value of the property. The net wealth taxes and taxes on chattels of 4200 and 4600 respectively are confined to the ownership rather than the use of assets, apply to groups of assets rather than particular goods and again are related to the value of the assets,

5210 — Recurrent taxes on use of goods and on permission to use goods or perform activities

81. The principal characteristic of taxes classified here is that they are levied at regular intervals and that they are usually fixed amounts. The most important item in terms of revenue receipts is vehicle licence taxes. This sub-heading also covers taxes on permission to hunt, shoot, fish or to sell certain products and taxes on the ownership of dogs , broadcast licence fees and taxes on the performance of certain services, provided that they meet the criteria set out in §12–13. The sub-divisions of 5210 are:

- user taxes on motor vehicles paid by households (5211);
- taxes on motor vehicles paid by others (5212); and
- other recurrent taxes (5213). This sub-heading covers business and professional licences paid by enterprises in order to obtain a licence to carry on a particular kind of business or profession when the levies are on a recurring basis. Licences such as taxi and casino licences are included. Dog licences and recurrent general licences for hunting, shooting and fishing where the right to carry out these activities is not granted as part of a normal commercial transaction are also included under this heading. Broadcast licence fees are included when the payer of the levy cannot opt out from making payments for public broadcast if one does not wish to watch or listen to public broadcast services (e.g. by declaring that one does not consume public broadcast services). Specific exemptions (for example, for elderly people) do not change the compulsory nature of the payment.

82. Excluded from sub-heading 5213 are:

a) licences where the right to carry out such activities is granted as part of a normal commercial transaction (e.g., the granting of the licence is accompanied by the right to use a specific area which is owned by government);

b) payments relating to the checks carried out by the government on the suitability and or safety of the business premises or equipment, or on the quality or standard of goods or services produced as a condition for granting such a licence. These payments are not unrequited and should be treated as payments for services rendered, unless the amounts charged for the licences are out of all proportion to the costs of the checks carried out by governments.

c) broadcast licence fees if users can opt out from paying broadcast licence fees in the case that they do not wish to consume these services while not affecting the ability to consume private broadcast services.

5220 — Non-recurrent taxes on use of goods and on permission to use goods or perform activities

83. This section covers non-recurrent taxes levied on the use of goods or on permission to use goods or perform activities and taxes levied each time goods are used. It includes taxes levied on the emission or discharge into the environment of noxious gases, liquids or other harmful substances.

- Payments for tradable emission permits issued by governments under cap and trade schemes should be recorded here at the time the emissions occur. No revenue should be recorded for permits that governments issue free of charge. The accrual basis of recording means that there can be a timing difference between the cash being received by government for the permits and the time the emission occurs. In the national accounts, this timing gives rise to a financial liability for government during the period.
- Payments made for the collection and disposal of waste or noxious substances by public authorities should be excluded as they constitute a sale of services to enterprises.

84. Other taxes falling under heading 5200 that are not levied recurrently are also included here. Thus, once-and-for-all payments for permission to sell liquor or tobacco or to set up betting shops are included provided they meet the criteria set out in §12–13.

6000 — Other taxes

85. Taxes levied on a base, or bases, other than those described under headings 1000, 3000, 4000 and 5000, or on bases of which cannot be considered to be related to any one of these headings, are included here. Where taxes are levied on a multiple base and it is possible to estimate the receipts related to each base the separate amounts are included under the appropriate headings. If separate amounts cannot be estimated and it is known that most of the receipts are derived from one base, the whole of the receipts are classified according to that base. Otherwise, they are classified here. Other revenues included here are presumptive taxes not included elsewhere in the classification system, taxes on individuals in the form of a poll tax or capitation tax, stamp taxes not related to financial and capital transactions nor falling exclusively on a single category of transaction, expenditure taxes where personal deductions or exemptions are applied and unidentifiable tax receipts. A subdivision is made between taxes levied wholly or predominantly on business (6100) and those levied on others (6200).

A.6 Conciliation with National Accounts

86. This section of the tables provides a re-conciliation between the OECD calculation of total tax revenues and the total of all taxes and social contributions paid to general government as recorded in the country's National Accounts. Where the country is a member of the European Union (EU), the comparison

is between the OECD calculation of total tax revenues and the sum of tax revenues and social contributions recorded in the combination of the general government and the institutions of the EU sectors of the National Accounts.

A.7 Memorandum item on the financing of social security benefits

87. In view of the varying relationship between taxation and social security contributions and the cases referred to in §40 to §46, a memorandum item collects together all payments earmarked for social security-type benefits, other than voluntary payments to the private sector. Data are presented as follows (refer Table 5.39 of the Report):

a) Taxes of 2000 series.

b) Taxes earmarked for social security benefits.

c) Voluntary contributions to the government.

d) Compulsory contributions to the private sector.

Guidance on the breakdown of (a) to (d) above is provided in §40 to §46.

A.8 Memorandum item on identifiable taxes paid by government

88. Identifiable taxes actually paid by government are presented in a memorandum item classified by the main headings of the OECD classification of taxes. In the vast majority of countries, only social security contributions and payroll taxes paid by government can be identified. These are, however, usually the most important taxes paid by governments (refer to Table 5.40 of the Report).

A.9 Relation of OECD classification of taxes to national accounting systems

89. A system of national accounts (SNA) seeks to provide a coherent framework for recording and presenting the main flows relating respectively to production, consumption, accumulation and external transactions of a given economic area, usually a country or a major region within a country. Government revenues are an important part of the transactions recorded in SNA. The final version of the 2008 SNA was jointly published by five international organisations: the United Nations, the International Monetary Fund, the European Union, the Organisation for Economic Co-operation and Development, and the World Bank in August 2009. The *System* is a comprehensive, consistent and flexible set of macroeconomic accounts. It is designed for use in countries with market economies, whatever their stage of economic development, and also in countries in transition to market economies. The important parts of the SNA's conceptual framework and its definitions of the various sectors of the economy have been reflected in the OECD's classification of taxes.

90. There are, however, some differences between the OECD classification of taxes and SNA concepts that are listed below. They arise because the aim of the former is to provide the maximum disaggregation of statistical data on what are generally regarded as taxes by tax administrations.

a) OECD includes compulsory social security contributions paid to general government in total tax revenues. Imputed and voluntary contributions plus those paid to private funds are not treated as taxes (§9 and §11 above);

b) there are different points of view on whether or not some levies and fees are classified as taxes (§12 and §13 above);

c) OECD excludes imputed taxes or subsidies resulting from the operation of official multiple exchange rates or from the central bank paying a rate of interest on required reserves that is different from other market rates;

d) there are differences in the treatment of non-wastable tax credits

91. As noted in §1 and §2, headings 1000 to 6000 of the OECD list of taxes cover all unrequited payments to general government or to a supranational authority, other than compulsory loans and fines. Such unrequited payments including fines, but excluding compulsory loans can be obtained from adding together the following figures in the 2008 SNA

- value-added type taxes (D.211);
- taxes and duties on imports, excluding VAT (D.212);
- export taxes (D.213);
- taxes on products, excluding VAT, import and export taxes (D.214);
- other taxes on production (D.29);
- taxes on income (D.51);
- other current taxes (D.59);
- actual social contributions (D.611 and D613), excluding voluntary contributions and payments to employment-related schemes that are not social security schemes
- capital taxes (D.91).

A.10 The OECD classification of taxes and the International Monetary Fund (GFS) system

92. The coverage and valuation of tax revenues in the GFS system and the 2008 SNA are very similar. Therefore, the differences between the OECD classification and that of the 2008 SNA (see §90 above) also apply to the GFS. In addition, the International Monetary Fund subdivides the OECD 5000 heading into section IV (Domestic Taxes on Goods and Services) and section V (Taxes on International Trade and Transactions). This reflects the fact that while the latter usually yield insignificant amounts of revenue in OECD countries, this is not the case in many non-OECD countries.

A.11 Comparison of the OECD classification of taxes with other international classifications

93. The table below describes an item by item comparison of the OECD classification of taxes and the classifications used in the following:

a) System of National Accounts (2008 SNA);

b) European System of Accounts (2010 ESA);

c) IMF Government Finance Statistics Manual (GFSM2014).

94. These comparisons represent those that would be expected to apply in the majority of cases. However in practice some flexibility should be used in their application. This is because in particular cases, countries can adopt varying approaches to the classification of revenues in National Accounts.

OECD Classification					2008 SNA	2010 ESA	GFSM2014
1000				Taxes on income, profits and capital gains			
	1100			Individuals			
		1110		Income and profits	D51-8.61a	D51A	1111
		1120		Capital gains	D51-8.61c, d	D51C, D	1111
	1200			Corporations			
		1210		Income and profits	D51-8.61b	D51B	1112
		1220		Capital gains	D51-8.61c	D51C	1112
	1300			Unallocable as between 1100 and 1200			1113
2000				Social security contributions			
	2100			Employees	D613-8.85	D613	1211
	2200			Employers	D611-8.83	D611	1212
	2300			Self-employed, non-employed	D613-8.85	D613	1213
	2400			Unallocable as between 2100, 2200 and 2300			1214
3000				Taxes on payroll and workforce	D29-7.97a	D29C	112
4000				Taxes on property			
	4100			Recurrent taxes on immovable property			
		4110		Households	D59-8.63a	D59A	1131
		4120		Other	D29-7.97b	D29A	1131
	4200			Recurrent net wealth taxes			
		4210		Individual	D59-8.63b	D59A	1132
		4220		Corporations	D59-8.63b	D59A	1132
	4300			Estate, inheritance and gift taxes			
		4310		Estate and inheritance taxes	D91-10.207b	D91A	1133
		4320		Gift taxes	D91-10.207b	D91A	1133
	4400			Taxes on financial and capital transactions	D59-7.96d; D29-7.97e	D214B, C	114114; 1161
	4500			Other non-recurrent taxes on property	D91-10.207a	D91B	1135
	4600			Other recurrent taxes on property	D59-8.63c	D59A	1136
5000				Taxes on goods and services			
	5100			Taxes on production, sale and transfer of goods and services			
		5110		General taxes on goods and services			
			5111	Value-added taxes	D211-7.89	D211; D29G	11411
			5112	Sales taxes	D2122-7.94a; D214-7.96a	D21224; D214I	11412
			5113	Turnover and other general taxes on goods and services	D214-7.96a	D214I	11413
		5120		Taxes on specific goods and services			
			5121	Excises	D2122-7.94b; D214-7.96b	D21223; D214A, B, D	1142
			5122	Profits of fiscal monopolies	D214-7.96e	D214J	1143
			5123	Customs and other import duties	D2121-7.93	D2121; D21221, 2	1151
			5124	On exports	D213-7.95a	D214K	1152-4
			5125	On investment goods			
			5126	On specific services	D2122-7.94c; D214-7.96c	D21225; D214E, F, G, H; D29F	1144; 1156
			5127	Other taxes on international trade and transactions	D2122-7.94d D29-7.95b D29-7.97g D59-8.64d	D21226; D29D; D59E	1153; 1155-6
			5128	Other taxes on specific goods and services			1146
		5130		Unallocable between 5110 and 5120			
	5200			Taxes on use of goods and on permission to use goods or perform activities			
		5210		Recurrent taxes on use of goods and on permission to use goods or perform activities			

			5211	Motor vehicle taxes households	D59-8.64c	D59D	11451
			5212	Motor vehicles taxes others	D29-7.97d	D214D; D29B	11451
			5213	Other recurrent taxes on use of goods and on permission to use goods or perform activities	D29-7.97c, d, f D59-8.64c	D29B, E, F; D59D	11452
		5220		Non-recurrent taxes on permission to use goods or perform activities			11452
	5300			Unallocable as between 5100 and 5200			
6000				Other taxes			
	6100			Payable solely by business			1161
	6200			Payable by other than business, or unidentifiable	D59-8.64a, b	D59B, C	1162

A.12 Attribution of tax revenues by sub-sectors of general government

95. The OECD classification requires a breakdown of tax revenues by sub-sectors of government. The definition of each sub-sector and the criteria to be used to attribute tax revenues between these sub-sectors are set out below. They follow the guidance of the 2008 SNA and GFSM 2014.

Sub-sectors of general government to be identified

a) Central government

96. The central government sub-sector includes all governmental departments, offices, establishments and other bodies which are agencies or instruments of the central authority whose competence extends over the whole territory, with the exception of the administration of social security funds. Central government therefore has the authority to impose taxes on all resident and non-resident units engaged in economic activities within the country.

b) State, provincial or regional government

97. This sub-sector consists of intermediate units of government exercising a competence at a level below that of central government. It includes all such units operating independently of central government in a part of a country's territory encompassing a number of smaller localities, with the exception of the administration of social security funds. In unitary countries, regional governments may be considered to have a separate existence where they have substantial autonomy to raise a significant proportion of their revenues from sources within their control and their officers are independent of external administrative control in the actual operation of the unit's activities.

98. At present, federal countries comprise the majority of cases where revenues attributed to intermediate units of government are identified separately. Colombia and Spain are the only two unitary countries in this position. In the remaining unitary countries, regional revenues are included with those of local governments.

c) Local government

99. This sub-sector includes all other units of government exercising an independent competence in part of the territory of a country, with the exception of the administration of social security funds. It encompasses various urban and/or rural jurisdictions (e.g., local authorities, municipalities, cities, boroughs, districts).

d) Social security funds

100. Social security funds form a separate sub-sector of general government. The social security sub-sector is defined in the 2008 SNA by the following extracts from paragraphs 4.124 to 4.126 and 4.147:

"Social security schemes are social insurance schemes covering the community as a whole or large section of the community that are imposed and controlled by government units. The schemes cover a wide variety of programmes, providing benefits in cash or in kind for old age, invalidity or death, survivors, sickness and maternity, work injury, unemployment, family allowance, health care, etc. There is not necessarily a direct link between the amount of the contribution paid by an individual and the benefits he or she may receive." (Paragraph 4.124).

"When social security schemes are separately organised from the other activities of government units and hold their assets and liabilities separately from the latter and engage in financial transactions on their own account they qualify as institutional units that are described as social security funds." (Paragraph 4.125).

"The amounts raised, and paid out, in social security contributions and benefits may be deliberately varied in order to achieve objectives of government policy that have no direct connection with the concept of social security as a scheme to provide social benefits to members of the community. They may be raised or lowered in order to influence the level of aggregate demand in the economy, for example. Nevertheless, so long as they remain separately constituted funds, they must be treated as separate institutional units in the SNA. (Paragraph 4.126).

"The social security funds sub-sector (of general government) consists of the social security funds operating at all levels of government. Such funds are social insurance schemes covering the community as a whole or large section of the community that are imposed by government units." (Paragraph 4.147).

101. This definition of social security funds is followed in the OECD classification with the two following exceptions which are excluded

- Schemes imposed by government and operated by bodies outside the general government sector, as defined in §3 of this manual; and
- Schemes to which all contributions are voluntary.

Supranational Authorities

102. This sub-sector covers the revenue-raising operations of supra-national authorities within a country. In practice, the only relevant supranational authority in the OECD area is that of the institutions of the European Union (EU). Tax revenues collected by member countries and paid to the EU are included in the *Revenue Statistics* at the supranational level of government. Income taxes and social security contributions collected by European Institutions and paid by European civil servants who are resident of EU member countries should not be included.

Criteria to be used for the attribution of tax revenues

103. When a government collects taxes and pays them over in whole or in part to other governments, it is necessary to determine whether the revenues should be considered to be those of the collecting government which it distributes to others as grants, or those of the beneficiary governments which the collecting government receives and passes on only as their agent. The criteria to be used in the attribution of revenues are set out in §104 to §107 which replicate paragraphs 3.70 to 3.73 from the 2008 SNA.

104. In general, a tax is attributed to the government unit that

a) exercises the authority to impose the tax (either as a principal or through the delegated authority of the principal),

b) has final discretion to set and vary the rate of the tax

105. Where an amount is collected by one government for and on behalf of another government, and the latter government has the authority to impose the tax, and set and vary its rate, then the former is acting as an agent for the latter and the tax is reassigned. Any amount retained by the collecting

government as a collection charge should be treated as a payment for a service. Any other amount retained by the collecting government, such as under a tax-sharing arrangement, should be treated as a current grant. If the collecting government was delegated the authority to set and vary the rate, then the amount collected should be treated as tax revenue of this government.

106. Where different governments jointly and equally set the rate of a tax and jointly and equally decide on the distribution of the proceeds, with no individual government having ultimate overriding authority, then the tax revenues are attributed to each government according to its respective share of the proceeds. If an arrangement allows one government unit to exercise ultimate overriding authority, then all of the tax revenue is attributed to that unit.

107. There may also be the circumstance where a tax is imposed under the constitutional or other authority of one government, but other governments individually set the tax rate in their jurisdictions. The proceeds of the tax generated in each respective government's jurisdiction are attributed as tax revenues of that government.

108. The levies paid by the member states of the EU take the form specific levies which include

a) custom duties and levies on agricultural goods (5123);

b) gross monetary compensation accounts (5123 if relating to imports and 5124 if relating to exports);

c) contributions to the Single Resolution Fund (5126); and

d) Steel, coal, sugar and milk levies (5128).

109. The custom duties collected by member states on behalf of the EU are recorded

- on a gross of collection fee basis;
- using figures adjusted so that duties are shown on a 'final destination' as opposed to a 'country of first entry' basis where such adjustments can be made. These adjustments concern in particular duties collected at important (sea) ports. Although the EU duties are collected by the authorities of the country of first entry, when possible these duties should be excluded from the revenue of the collecting country and be included in the revenue of the country of final destination

110. These are the specific EU levies that most clearly conform to the attribution criterion described in §102 above. Consequently, these amounts are footnoted as a memorandum item to the EU member state country tables (in Chapter 5) and are shown as supranational revenues against each of the tax headings identified in §108.

Notes

[1] All references to SNA are to the 2008 edition.

[2] See section A.12 of this guide for a discussion of the concept of agency capacity.

[3] It is usually possible to identify amounts of social security contributions and payroll taxes, but not other taxes paid by government.

[4] If, however, a levy which is considered as non-tax revenue by most countries is regarded as a tax — or raises substantial revenue — in one or more countries, the amounts collected are footnoted at the end of the relevant country tables, even though the amounts are not included in total tax revenues.

[5] Names, however, can frequently be misleading. For example, though a passport fee would normally be considered a non-tax revenue, if a supplementary levy on passports (as is the case in Portugal) were imposed in order to raise substantial amounts of revenue relative to the cost of providing the passport, the levy would be regarded as a tax under 5200.

[6] Sometimes the terms 'non-refundable' and 'refundable' are used, but it may be considered illogical to talk of 'refundable' when nothing has been paid.

[7] A different treatment, however, is accorded to non-wastable tax credits under imputation systems of corporate income tax (§37–39).

[8] This is not strictly a true tax expenditure in the formal sense. Such tax expenditures require identification of a benchmark tax system for each country or, preferably, a common international benchmark. In practice it has not been possible to reach agreement on a common international benchmark.

[9] Unless based on the profit made on a sale, in which case they would be classified as capital gains taxes under 1120 or 1220.

[10] In some countries the same legislation applies to both individual and corporate enterprises for particular taxes on income. However, the receipts from such taxes are usually allocable between individuals and enterprises and can therefore be shown in the appropriate sub-heading.

[11] For example, "... sufficiently self-contained and independent that they behave in the same way as corporations... (including) keeping a complete set of accounts" (2008 SNA, section 4.44).

[12] In Canada — a country also referred to as having an imputation system — the (wastable) tax credit for the shareholder is in respect of domestic corporation tax deemed to have been paid whether or not a corporation tax liability has arisen. As there is no integral connection between the corporation tax liability and the credit given against income tax under such systems, these credits for dividends are treated, along with other tax credits, on the lines described in §26.

[13] This may also apply where a scheme for government employees existed prior to the introduction of a general social security scheme.

[14] In the 2008 SNA, these are regarded as capital transfers and not as taxes (see section A.8).

[15] This is the system by which the European Union adjusts for differences between the exchange rates used to determine prices under the Common Market Agricultural Policy and actual exchange rates. Payments under the system may relate to imports or exports and where these amounts are separately identifiable they are shown under the appropriate heading (5123 or 5124). In this Report, these amounts are shown gross (i.e. without deducting any subsidies paid out under the MCA system).

[16] Transfers of profits of State lotteries are regarded as non-tax revenues (see also §68).

Annex B. Interpretative guide to non-tax revenue

Table of contents

1. Coverage

The definition of non-tax revenues and the main subcategories identified in this publication generally correspond to the concepts laid out in the 2014 IMF Government Finance Statistics Manual (GFSM). Non-tax revenues refer to increases in government net worth resulting from transactions other than tax revenues. They exclude funds arising from the repayment of previous lending by governments or from borrowing, or proceeds derived from sales of fixed capital assets, stocks, land and intangible assets or private gifts.

Non-tax revenues are made up of the following elements.

2. Grants

The GFSM 2014 states "Grants are transfers receivable by government units from non-resident government units or international organisations without the receipt of any goods, services, or assets in return. Grants are normally receivable in cash, but may also take the form of the receipt of goods or services (in kind)". These transfers are un-refundable and unrequited. Grants encompass reparations and gifts given for particular projects or programmes. The term "grants" is not used to refer to transfers to or from non-governmental units and excludes inter-governmental transfers. The remission of funds collected by one government for another in an agency capacity should not be shown as receipt of a grant by the beneficiary government but as its direct receipt of revenue.

3. Property income

This category includes income to government arising from their ownership of property, enterprises, financial assets, or intangible assets when government units place them at the disposal of other units. Sales of non-financial assets such as the sales of lands are not recorded as revenue because disposal of such an asset does not increase the net worth. Similarly, repayments on loans and loan disbursements are not revenue. Property income may take the form of dividends, interest, land rents, royalties, or withdrawals from entrepreneurial income. The main components are:

- Interest and dividends: Interest is the revenue earned by the government unit from a financial asset by putting it at the disposal of another institutional unit. Dividends are the revenue earned by placing equity funds at the disposal of a corporation (resident or non-resident corporation). This category also consists of profits of state-owned enterprises except those classified as fiscal monopolies (see §62-§64 of the OECD Interpretative Guide to tax revenue in Annex A), export and import monopoly profits (see §70-§71 of the same document) or those providing public utilities such as rail transport, electricity, post offices and other communications. In this category are included revenue from public financial institutions such as the central banks' profits, profits transferred or distributed from the operation of monetary authority functions outside the central bank and the profits of state lotteries transferred to the government. Transfers from public utilities enterprises are recorded as non-tax revenue under "sales of goods and services" whereas profits for fiscal, export or import monopolies are classified as tax revenue.
- Rents or royalties: Rent is the revenue generated from natural resources, such as land, mining, or oil resources, when a government unit places these at the disposal of private or foreign entities. The rents received relate to a resource lease-giving agreement for the exploitation and extraction of a natural resource by the lessee in return for a payment. Payments for exploration rights are also treated as rent. Rents should not be confused with other payments a government may receive related to the exploitation of subsoil and similar assets, such as severance taxes, business licenses, or other taxes (e.g. value added taxes, excises, taxes on exports, etc.). They should also

not be taken to mean incomes from the rental of buildings and equipment, which are treated as sales of goods and services. Revenues from rents and royalties are in some cases difficult to establish and depend on the agreement between the government unit and the lessee. For example rents, royalties and taxes such as corporate income taxes and VAT are sometimes encompassed in a single payment to the general government. In such cases the revenue should be classified under the category to which the majority of revenue belongs (see §71 of Annex A for further explanation.)

- Other property income: This includes revenue earned by a government unit placing funds at a disposal of quasi-corporations.[1] Conceptually this source of revenue is equivalent to that of dividends from a corporation but by definition, quasi-corporations cannot distribute income in the form of dividends. This category of "other property income" also includes retained or reinvested earnings, i.e. the percentage of distributable revenue not paid out as dividends, but retained by the corporation or quasi-corporation on foreign investment; property income from investment income disbursements and unidentified property income.

4. Sales of goods and services

Revenue under the category "sales of goods and services" is generally reported on a gross basis, without deduction of costs. Since these costs can represent a significant proportion of revenues, they cannot be regarded in total as funds available for governments to finance their general activities. This contrasts with tax revenues, where the collection costs are usually a small proportion of revenue. This difference implies that it may not be meaningful to sum tax and non-tax revenues as part of a calculation of generally available funds.

The proceeds of sales of nonfinancial assets such as the sale of buildings or lands are not classified as revenues since their disposal does not increase the net worth.

Sales of goods and services consist of:

- Sales by market establishments.[2]
- Administrative fees for services (i.e. fees for drivers' licences, passports, visas, court fees, harbour fees, fees for birth, marriage or death certificates, patent registrations, radio and television licenses when public authorities provide general broadcasting services).
- Administrative fees that are sales of services associated with a regulatory function of government (such as fees for the inspection of premises before delivering a business licence) and considered to be proportional to the cost of producing the service are included in this category. If the fee in return for the service provided by the government unit is disproportionate, then the fee will be classified as a tax. Specific examples of fees that are considered taxes include fees for permission to perform activities such as hunting, fishing and shooting; and fees for business registration where this is a legal requirement for the business to operate.
- Sales by nonmarket establishments such as fees at government hospitals, tuition fees at government schools and admission fees to museums and parks.
- Leasing of buildings and equipment.

5. Fines, penalties and forfeits

The GFSM 2014 states "Fines and penalties are compulsory transfers imposed by courts of law or bodies for violations of laws or administrative rules. Out-of-court agreements are also included (...). Forfeits are amounts deposited with a general government unit pending a legal or administrative proceeding, and that will be transferred to the unit upon resolution". For example traffic fines are included here. Fines and penalties charged on overdue taxes or penalties imposed for the evasion of taxes should be recorded in this category and not as taxes. However if it is not possible to separate the amounts paid in taxes and fines, the whole amount should be classified under the tax to which the fine relates (see §14 of Annex A for further explanation).

6. Other social contributions

This category includes the actual and imputed contributions to social insurance schemes operated by governments as employers on behalf of their employees that do not create a future defined liability. This category also includes the sum of the total voluntary contributions.[3] Excluded from this category are any contributions to funds in which the contributions of each participant and of his employer on his behalf are kept in a separate account earning interest and withdrawable under specified circumstances or any contributions to a pension fund autonomous to the general government. This category is not included in this publication.

7. Miscellaneous and unidentified revenue

This category consists of unidentified non-tax revenues or those that do not fit into any of the other categories listed above. It includes revenue such as gifts and transfers from individuals, private non-profit institutions, nongovernmental foundations, corporations, or sources other than governments and international organisations. Major non-recurrent payments receivable in compensation for extensive damages or serious injuries not covered by insurance policies are also included, such as payments of compensation for damages caused by major explosions; oil spillages; or payments receivable for damage to property other than payments from an insurance settlement.

Notes

[1] Quasi-corporations are unincorporated enterprises that exercise some functions of corporations, but have not been granted separate legal personality by statute.

[2] A market establishment is an establishment that charges economically significant prices.

[3] The IMF includes these contributions as part of their total of social security contributions.

www.ingramcontent.com/pod-product-compliance
Ingram Content Group UK Ltd.
Pitfield, Milton Keynes, MK11 3LW, UK
UKHW051459290926
15471UKWH00008B/1290